Preaching the Lectionary

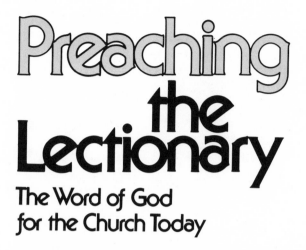

Preaching the Lectionary

The Word of God
for the Church Today

Reginald H. Fuller

Revised Edition

THE LITURGICAL PRESS
Collegeville, Minnesota
1984

Cover design by Don Bruno.

This revised edition of *Preaching the New Lectionary* (1974) comprises articles originally published in *Worship* magazine (February 1971 through February 1974; October 1974; May 1981; January 1982). The material has been substantially reedited and rearranged, and commentary on Scripture readings not previously covered has been incorporated.

Printed in the United States of America.

Library of Congress Cataloging in Publication Data
Fuller, Reginald Horace.
   Preaching the lectionary.

   Rev. ed. of: Preaching the new lectionary.
   Includes bibliographical references and index.
   1. Bible—Liturgical lessons, English. 2. Bible—
Homiletical use. I. Fuller, Reginald Horace. Preaching
the new lectionary. II. Title.
BS391.2.F8 1984   220.6   84-19361
ISBN 0-8146-1351-9 (pbk.)

In Memoriam

Edward Leith Merrow
Priest, Counselor, and Friend ✠ Easter Day 1974

Contents

viii   *Contents*

Foreword

Reading the Bible in corporate worship is the most universal and probably the least contested of Christian liturgical customs. What is read is germinal to the themes that are amplified by other liturgical segments. Ideally, the readings also provide the preacher with his or her *raison d'être*. Since they form the verbal heart of the liturgy, selection of the readings is the crucial choice that determines many subsequent choices liturgy planners must make.

The determination of such fundamental elements must not be left to whim or to the preferences of local planners. The purpose of a Lectionary is to unfold the full sweep of God's revelation, not avoiding the hard words. If properly designed, a Lectionary keeps the Church from the ever present danger of domesticating the Scriptures—muting the trumpet of their prophecy or dulling the edge of their judgment. The Scriptures are, of course, the Church's book, and they cannot be understood properly apart from the tradition and the worshiping community. But the Church must continue to allow itself to be addressed by the Scriptures, by the whole design of God. The Lectionary and the calendar together constitute the time-tested antidote for subjectivism in the liturgical reading of the Bible and the subsequent preaching of the word.

The *Ordo Lectionum Missae* (1969) was prepared in response to such statements in the Constitution on the Sacred Liturgy of Vatican II as: "The treasures of the Bible are to be opened up more lavishly, so that richer fare may be provided for the faithful at the table of God's Word" (no. 51), and ". . . the ministry of preaching is to be fulfilled with exactitude and fidelity. The sermon, moreover, should draw its content mainly from scriptural and liturgical sources" (no. 35); and in the Dogmatic Constitution on Divine Revelation: ". . . all the preaching of the Church must be nourished and ruled by sacred Scripture. For in the sacred books, the Father who is in heaven meets his children with great love and speaks with them" (no. 21).

Adoption of a three-year cycle has made the Lectionary more comprehensive in its coverage of the biblical writings. It has also allowed for the inclusion of major books that the former Lectionary had rather neglected, such as the Gospel of Mark. The provision of a complete set of readings from the Hebrew Scriptures maintains a proper balance between the Testaments.

Preparation of the new Lectionary provided an occasion for Scripture scholars to work closely with liturgists so that the best achievements of intensive biblical scholarship in recent decades could make its proper contribution. Giving the synoptic evangelists their own integrity by assigning to each of them a year within the cycle is one obvious example. Less obvious are the scholarly principles according to which the reading from the Old Testament was coordinated with the gospel reading. An early liturgical usage common to the Churches of both East and West accounts for the reserving of Lent and Easter, in large measure, for the Fourth Gospel, which is also used to supplement the brevity of Mark's Gospel.

Publication of this Lectionary has had a far-reaching ecumenical impact, especially in North America. Both because of the sweep of its concept and the thoroughness of its scholarship, it commended itself to other Churches. The Presbyterian *Worshipbook* (1970) and the *Book of Common Prayer* (1979) of the Episcopal Church both contain Lectionaries based upon it. The *Lutheran Book of Worship* (1978) follows a similar course. The United Church of Christ and the Christian Church (Disciples of Christ) have adopted the Presbyterian revision, and the Commission on Worship of the Consultation on Church Union prepared a revision to which the Methodist Church is committed. The North American Commission on Calendar and Lectionary has recently produced for trial use a consensus Lectionary based on six variations of the three-year Lectionary (1983).

This common approach was achieved neither because of official pressure nor as the result of interconfessional dialogues, but simply because liturgical and scriptural leaders in the Churches had become convinced of the value of such a sign. It is interesting to speculate on the impact of this consensus upon Christian unity. Clergy of various backgrounds are gathering for common Bible study in anticipation of the Sunday sermon. Study groups of lay persons could be organized along similar inter-Church lines. Such ecumenical groups could provide a diversity of insight into the texts and create a beneficial climate of expectancy for the Liturgy of the Word the following Sunday.

If the new Lectionaries are to achieve their full potential in parish use, however, the Sunday pericopes will require considerable study, especially on the part of preachers. Limitations upon available time and lack of exegetical expertise make aids for such study indispensable. The series of articles projected by the editors of *Worship*, beginning in 1971, was the first to meet this need. In Professor Reginald H. Fuller they had an author who not only has impeccable credentials as a biblical scholar but is sensitive to the spirit of worship and the needs of the people. His contributions have been pastoral as well as scholarly. His articles have been helpful not only to countless preachers, but even to those who undertook revisions of the Roman Lectionary.

Common use of the treasures of the Bible has long been cherished as a sign of fundamental unity across denominational boundaries. Formerly that commonality was ensured through the use of the so-called historic pericopes. The appearance of the *Ordo Lectionum Missae* broke that common bond, but a new consensus has almost spontaneously arisen on its foundations. The Churches were ripe for such a change.

I have always been thrilled by those marvelous lines from *Grosser Gott,* "And from morn to set of sun / Through the Church the song goes on." Similarly, it is thrilling to contemplate the sign of Christian unity as the Churches of our Lord order their worship according to the same portions of Scripture and base their proclamation of God's good news on the same blessed words. The thrill is intensified as one remembers the testimony of the Prophet: ". . . so shall my word be that goes forth from my mouth; it shall return to me empty, but it shall accomplish that which I purpose, and prosper in the thing for which I sent it" (Isa 55:11).

EUGENE L. BRAND

Secretary for Ecumenical Relationships and Worship
Lutheran World Federation

Preface to the Second Edition

In the Foreword to the first edition, attention was called to the "rather odd order" in which the material was presented, starting with Lent of series C and concluding with the post-Epiphany season of series C. Also, the homiletical suggestions, where provided, were, until the fourth Sunday of the year in series A, mixed up with the exegetical comments. This was due to the way in which the series evolved as originally published in *Worship*. These anomalies, as well as a few obviously out-of-date allusions, have been removed from this revised edition. In addition, commentaries on the readings for weddings and funerals, which were published in *Worship* in May 1981 and January 1982, have been included.

The first edition enjoyed a surprising and gratifying success, and it is hoped that the rearrangement of the material and the provision of a complete series of homiletical suggestions will render this book still useful to preachers and homilists, primarily in the Roman Catholic Church, but also to members of other traditions.

REGINALD H. FULLER

Roman Table of Sundays and Holy Days: 1984–2000

Year	Sunday Cycle	Baptism of Our Lord	Sundays after Epiphany	Lent 1	Easter	Pentecost	Trinity Sunday	Corpus Christi	The Sunday of the Year after Corpus Christi is Sunday . . .	Advent 1
1984	A	Monday, Jan. 9[1]	8	Mar. 11	Apr. 22	June 10	June 17	June 24	13	Dec. 2
1985	B	Jan. 13	6	Feb. 24	Apr. 7	May 26	June 2	June 9	11	Dec. 1
1986	C[2]	Jan. 12	5	Feb. 16	Mar. 30	May 18	May 25	June 1	10	Nov. 30
1987	A	Jan. 11	8	Mar. 8	Apr. 19	June 7	June 14	June 21	13	Nov. 29
1988	B	Jan. 10	6	Feb. 21	Apr. 3	May 22	May 29	June 5	11	Nov. 27
1989	C	Monday, Jan. 9	4	Feb. 12	Mar. 26	May 14	May 21	May 28	9	Dec. 3
1990	A	Monday, Jan. 8	7	Mar. 4	Apr. 15	June 3	June 10	June 17	12	Dec. 2
1991	B	Jan. 13	5	Feb. 17	Mar. 31	May 19	May 26	June 2	10	Dec. 1
1992	C	Jan. 12	8	Mar. 8	Apr. 19	June 7	June 14	June 21	13	Nov. 29
1993	A	Jan. 10	7	Feb. 28	Apr. 11	May 30	June 6	June 13	12	Nov. 28
1994	B	Monday, Jan. 10	5	Feb. 20	Apr. 3	May 22	May 29	June 5	11	Nov. 27
1995	C	Monday, Jan. 9	7	Mar. 5	Apr. 16	June 4	June 11	June 18	12	Dec. 3
1996	A	Monday, Jan. 8	6	Feb. 25	Apr. 7	May 26	June 2	June 9	11	Dec. 1
1997	B	Jan. 12	5	Feb. 16	Mar. 30	May 18	May 25	June 1	10	Nov. 30
1998	C	Jan. 11	7	Mar. 1	Apr. 12	May 31	June 7	June 14	12	Nov. 29
1999	A	Jan. 10	6	Feb. 21	Apr. 4	May 23	May 30	June 6	11	Nov. 28
2000	B	Jan. 9	6	Feb. 20	Apr. 2	May 21	May 28	June 4	10	Dec. 3

The above Table of Sundays and Holy Days is an adaptation of the Roman calendar observed by Roman Catholics in countries where Epiphany and Corpus Christi are celebrated on Sunday.

[1] When Epiphany is transferred to a Sunday which falls on 7 or 8 January, the Baptism of the Lord is transferred to the Monday immediately following. Only one reading before the gospel is used.

[2] Year C is the year whose number is evenly divisible by three.

Preparing the Homily

Introductory Considerations

Since the Second Vatican Council, it has become increasingly accepted that the ministry of the word is an essential part of the liturgy. It is my understanding—and my observation of current practice bears this out— that in the Roman Catholic communion a homily is expected at every celebration of the liturgy. The same is undoubtedly true, and probably always has been, among Lutherans, though for them this would normally mean only on Sundays. I must confess to a sense of shame when I attend Holy Communion in my own Anglican tradition and observe that Anglican priests of all complexions, evangelical as well as High Church, are content to celebrate the Eucharist without preaching. They ought to have a strong sense of guilt at their dereliction of duty.

This requirement, or at least this desirability, that there should be proclamation of the word undoubtedly makes many demands upon the preacher, and very little help has been given in the procedure to be followed in the preparation of a homily. It was to fill this gap that, as an emergency measure, I undertook to write the commentaries that appeared in *Worship* over a space of three years and have since been reissued in book form. In what follows I shall try to analyze the procedures that I followed. Here I must confess that I did not start out with any clear-cut methods or prior understanding. True, I had certain ideas about the function of liturgical preaching, for I had written on the subject some fifteen years previously.[1] I had a general idea, gathered from my German Lutheran contacts, that there were basically three stages of sermon preparation, the third being the actual composition of the sermon.

First, it should begin with exegesis. Exegesis, as I understand it, poses the question: What did the text *mean* in its original situation? The disciples of Bultmann, following Karl Barth, insist that exegesis itself already poses the question: What does the text mean today? and that until one has heard it speak to the contemporary situation, one has not heard the text. But I agree with such different scholars as Dean Krister Stendahl[2] and Bishop

---

[1] *What Is Liturgical Preaching?* Studies in Ministry and Worship (London: SCM Press, 1957).

[2] K. Stendahl, s.v. "Exegesis" in *Interpreter's Dictionary of the Bible.*

Stephen Neill[3] in assigning this concern to a later stage—the stage of exposition. Users of the *Interpreter's Bible* will remember the two divisions exegesis and exposition. I follow the arrangements of this commentary and distinguish between exegesis, which asks: What did the text mean? and exposition, which asks: What does it mean today?

The homilist who understands his/her own task in these terms will be concerned with two poles: the word of God as it is attested in Scripture, and the concrete situation in which the congregation finds itself today. The homilist's task is to take what Scripture said and make it say the same thing, but in such a way that it can address the congregation today.

The first part of the homilist's task is, in theory, always the same. What Scripture *said* remains said in that situation for all time. What Scripture *says* is in principle variable, because the new situation always slants, though it does not determine, what was once said. Here we stumble upon Bultmann's hermeneutical principle of the *Fragestellung*, the question we bring to the text. Our questions to some extent condition what Scripture says to us. Of course, we should try to be as objective as possible in exegesis, recognizing that complete objectivity is never wholly possible. But at any rate we should not make a virtue of our lack of objectivity, as the Bultmannians seem to do.

The second part of the homilist's task is that for which he or she is uniquely and properly equipped—an intimate knowledge of the congregation, of their concerns, their joys, sorrows, temptations, and sins. Parish calls, counseling sessions, and the hearing of confessions should equip the preacher for this. It is not here but in the preliminary work of exegesis that the pastor and homilist is likely to find real difficulty. Exegesis demands certain academically acquired skills, and the homilist may well fight shy of this. The commentaries in this book were designed to help particularly at this point. They were motivated by the conviction that I had developed in Germany when I studied at Tübingen in 1938–39, that a true proclamation of the word of God depends upon a correct exegesis of the text. I will now try to lay bare some of the presuppositions of my method and the procedures that in large part developed as I went along month by month producing the commentaries.

Exegesis—Some General Considerations

To do exegesis, every method of biblical criticism must be brought into play where appropriate, for the first task of exegesis is to reconstruct the

[3] S. C. Neill, *The Interpretation of the New Testament* (London: Oxford University Press, 1964) 87.

situation for which the text was originally written. Especially important here is the question of the audience or addressee(s). As Willi Marxsen has observed, this is really more important than the question—so beloved of students who have just made their acquaintance with biblical criticism— of authorship.[4] Yet authorship is also important, precisely in this connection. It makes a difference to the situation envisaged whether one thinks, for example, that the letter to the Colossians was written by Paul or by an unknown Paulinist in the subapostolic age.

Here it is important not to be afraid of critical positions. It is useful, for instance, to divide the Pauline letters into the homologoumena (those letters about whose Pauline authorship there is no reasonable doubt) and the antilegomena (those about whose Pauline authorship there are varying degrees of doubt). The antilegomena, if post-Pauline, are to be understood as witnesses to early Catholicism—that is, to the institutional consolidation of Christianity after the deaths of the original witnesses and the nonarrival of the parousia.

We need not, of course, dismiss early Catholicism as an aberration or degeneration, like Käsemann, who discovered or rediscovered its importance. We may regard it, as I do personally, as a natural, inevitable, and justifiable development. But we cannot ignore it in our exegesis; otherwise we will make the antilegomena more Pauline than they actually are. Texts that witness to the institutionalization of the Church in this way should not be harmonized with the genuine Paul or explained away but should be allowed first to speak in their own right. But neither should their difference from the authentic Paul be so exaggerated that the texts concerned are dismissed as valueless for preaching. It has been said, for instance, that in Tübingen today the view is held that one cannot preach from a text in Acts because Acts is early Catholic and un-Pauline, and therefore is not gospel!

Turning to the Gospels, the modern view, a view that has become widely accepted since the fifties, is that these documents consist of three strata. On the top level we have the theology of the evangelist, which is commonly known as the evangelist's redaction. Below this lies the tradition, the Jesus material as it was constantly put to use in the oral period between A.D. 30 and 65/70. At the bottom is the stratum of the authentic Jesus material—authentic sayings and parables spoken by him, authentic memories of his career from his baptism to his crucifixion. As has frequently been observed, Catholics especially should feel no discomfort at

---

[4] W. Marxsen, *Introduction to the New Testament*, trans. G. Buswell (Philadelphia: Fortress Press, 1968) 10.

this modern understanding of the Gospels as largely the product of the Church, for their high doctrine of the Church should help them to accept this view.

The arrangement of a three-year cycle of readings from Matthew, Mark-John, and Luke successively has made the topmost level of the Gospel tradition—the respective evangelist's redaction—particularly important to the homilist. I once heard a parish priest complain that the same incident came up more than once in three years in the different evangelists. He suggested, therefore, that the Lectionary needed revision. But the fact of the duplication of a pericope directs the homilist to what is distinctive in that particular evangelist.

Above all, the homilist must avoid the temptation of harmonizing. A conspicuous instance of this occurred when the Marcan form of the temptation narrative was read for the first time on the first Sunday of Lent. I heard a homilist start by saying that Mark had obviously abbreviated the story, and proceed to preach about the three temptations as recorded in Q (Matthew and Luke), which he treated on a purely historical level! He thus missed the challenge of facing up to the temptation as presented by the Marcan redaction. *Why*, if he knew the Q tradition, did Mark omit the three temptations? Where did his real interest lie? Those are the questions the homilist should have asked.

A study of the Lectionary shows that most of these duplications occur on the major feasts and holy days of the year. Not only the temptation story but particularly the passion account is taken each year from a different Gospel on Passion (Palm) Sunday. The homilist should concentrate upon what is distinctive in the particular evangelist's presentation.

It is clearly important to acquaint oneself with the methods and principles of redaction criticism. The redaction is discernible in such factors as the arrangement and order of individual pericopes in any given Gospel, in touches that the evangelist has clearly added with his own hand. Where we possess the evangelist's source, this is relatively easy, for we need only compare the evangelist with that source. Thus, if we accept the two-document hypothesis (the priority of Mark and the common source of Matthew and Luke, commonly called Q), we can see where Matthew and Luke have altered Mark and where Matthew and Luke diverge in their presentation of the Q material. In the latter case, of course, it is more difficult to decide which of the two reproduces the original and which has made the alteration, but a knowledge of the stylistic peculiarities and theological interests of the two evangelists helps us to answer this question.

Where we do not possess the source of the evangelist's material, namely, in the case of Mark and in the case of the special material of Matthew and Luke, source criticism is of no use. Here only form and tradition criticism can help. Thus we can distinguish between the pure form of a pericope and the disturbance of this form by later comment or application. Even here we cannot be sure whether the accretion is due to the evangelist himself or had already taken place earlier in the tradition. But as we become more familiar with the style and concerns of any given evangelist, we learn to discern the sort of thing which that evangelist is likely to have added himself. The third type of material that allows us to pinpoint the evangelist's redaction is that composed as fresh material. A good example of this is the Marcan summaries, such as Mark 6:53-56.

This distinction between the three different levels of the tradition can be very helpful for the preacher, for it offers three possibilities of treating a particular pericope. A good instance of this is the parable of the sower. At the Jesus level, this consists of the pure parable itself (Mark 4:3-8). At a later stage in the tradition, the Hellenistic missionary Church added the allegorical interpretation (Mark 4:14-20). Finally, the evangelist Mark added from another tradition the passage on the interpretation of parables (Mark 4:10-13). The homilist will have to decide which of these three levels speaks most directly to the situation of the congregation and treat the parable at that level. It would be a mistake to reject the later levels of the tradition as valueless because they do not go back to the historical Jesus. The later levels represent successive expositions of the Jesus tradition in a new situation. Tradition is a living and growing thing. In fact, the homiletical use of a text is itself part of the history of its tradition.

Many of the Sunday pericopes consist of miracle stories. Here again there are, at least in principle, three levels of tradition. First, there is the miracle as it actually occurred in our Lord's ministry. Authentic sayings of Jesus show that for him exorcisms and healings were signs of the inbreaking of the eschatological reign or kingdom of God.[5] Next comes the shaping of these miracle stories in the post-Easter community. Usually this is in the interests of a particular Christology. Thus they may present Jesus as the eschatological prophet[6] or the divine man.[7]

[5] Matt 12:26 (Q) par.; Matt 11:4b-6 (Q) par. On the question of the historicity of Jesus' miracles, see R. H. Fuller, *Interpreting the Miracles* (London: SCM Press, 1963) 18-45.

[6] See F. Hahn, *The Titles of Jesus in Christology* (London: Lutterworth Press, 1969) 352-388; R. H. Fuller, *The Foundations of New Testament Christology* (London: Lutterworth Press, 1965) 167-173; R. E. Brown, "Jesus and Elisha," *Perspective* 12 (1971) 85-104.

[7] H. D. Betz, "Jesus as Divine Man," *Jesus and the Historian*, ed. F. J. Trotter (E. C. Colwell Festschrift; Philadelphia: Westminster Press, 1968) 114-133; J. M. Robinson and H. Koester, *Trajectories Through Early Christianity* (Philadelphia: Fortress Press, 1971) 216-219.

A good example of this is the feeding of the multitude that occurs several times in the Gospels and is read more than once in the three-year cycle. Personally, I do not doubt that Jesus celebrated an eschatological meal with his disciples in a tense atmosphere of crisis at the turning point of his ministry. But later, in the post-Easter community, this authentic memory was taken up and shaped by two different interests. The eschatological meal became a model for the Church's Eucharistic meal, while the interest in Jesus as an eschatological prophet led to the development of an emphasis on the miraculous multiplication of the loaves, a greater feat than that of Elisha (2 Kgs 4:42-44).

Finally, there is the evangelist's redaction of the miracle tradition. Mark clearly wished to reduce the emphasis on the miraculous. The reason for this was that the Christians in his Church were being tempted by false teachers (Mark 13:6, 22) to think of Jesus as a divine man who displayed his divine powers solely through his miracles. Mark did not altogether reject the picture of Jesus as a miracle-worker, for he accepted and preserved a relatively large number of such stories. But he toned them down by the device known as the "messianic secret." Demons that confessed Jesus as the Son of God (apparently a title that the false teachers used in association with their Christology) were silenced. People who were healed were likewise silenced. And above all, the disciples were silenced after the transfiguration—until after the resurrection!

Mark's point seems to be that Jesus can only be rightly confessed as Son of God in the light of his crucifixion and resurrection. We must recognize that we are dealing here, not with history as such, but with Mark's interpretation of history. The "divine man" Christology was allowed into the canon of Scripture only after it had received this Marcan correction. This would seem to forbid the homilist from exploiting the miracles of Jesus for their own sake. They can be safely treated only as prefigurations (to use Austin Farrer's word) of the supreme messianic miracle, which is the death and resurrection of Jesus. Thus, redaction criticism helps the homilist to use the miracle stories as a real proclamation of the gospel.

We see something similar happening in the great Johannine signs that occur in the Lenten series of readings. Here the "divine man" tradition is corrected, but in a different way. The miracle stories are frequently used as a launching point for typically Johannine dialogues and discourses. The best examples are the miracles of the feeding of the multitude, the blind man of Siloam, and the raising of Lazarus in chapters 6, 9, and 11 respectively. The feeding of the multitude is explained in the ensuing discourse as a sign that Jesus is the bread that came down from heaven and gives life to the world. The healing of the blind man is a sign that he is the light of the world, and the raising of Lazarus a sign that he is the resurrection and the life. Here again the homilist would not want to treat the miracle stories as they are found in the pre-Johannine tradition—simply as signs that Jesus is a great wonder-worker, perhaps the greatest of wonder-workers. Rather, to preach the gospel, the homilist will use the miracle stories as signs of what the Johannine discourse reveals Jesus to be.

The passion narratives, which are read in Holy Week, benefit the homilist if critically treated. Quite early on, the form critics saw that these narratives differ from the rest of the Gospel material in that they are more or less continuous, not a string of pericopes. Basic to them is genuine historical reminiscence of the end of Jesus—his arrest; the preliminary investigation before the Sanhedrin; the trial proper before Pilate, which established that Jesus could without too much difficulty be disposed of as a messianic pretender; and finally his actual crucifixion and death. These bare facts, however, do not themselves contain the gospel. The gospel comes from the way these bare facts were interpreted by the post-Easter Church. We know from 1 Cor 15 that from the very early days the death of Jesus received a threefold interpretation.

First, Jesus' death took place *in fulfillment of the Scriptures.* The cross was a scandal not only for the Jews but even for the believers themselves. They had to come to terms with it in their own minds, and the only way they could do so was to discover predictions of the passion in the Scriptures—what we now call the Old Testament. This led them first to those psalms that speak about the righteous sufferer and his vindication, notably Ps 118:22, which speaks of the rejected stone that became the chief cornerstone. Then there were the great passion psalms—Psalms 22 and 69. Details from these psalms have undoubtedly colored the passion narratives, and it is always a moot point whether the facts led to the prophecies or the prophecies suggested the facts. Probably it was a bit of both. The basic facts of the passion (like Judas' betrayal of Jesus, Simon's denial, and the disciples' forsaking Jesus) were so scandalous that they drove the early Christians to the Scriptures, whereas peripheral details, like the casting of lots for Jesus' garments, could well have been added to fulfill the prophecy of Psalm 22.

Second, the early community asserted that Jesus died *for our sins.* This atonement theology probably entered at a slightly later stage, perhaps after the community had hit upon Isa 53, and possibly in connection with its Passover celebration. Anyhow, it is clear that this motif has had little effect on the passion narrative itself, only upon the institution at the Lord's Supper, which was probably a separate pericope on its own (see 1 Cor 11:23-25).

The third motif was that Jesus died *as Messiah*. This is strongly attested by the title on the cross, whose historicity is beyond all doubt, though in the intention of those who perpetrated it the title meant a political pretender. But this motif has colored the Marcan form of the trial scene before the Sanhedrin (note its absence in John's Gospel), while the king motif is particularly stressed in the trial before Pilate.

Then comes each evangelist's own treatment of the passion. Mark was probably the first to combine the passion narrative with pericopes about the words and deeds of the earthly Jesus. This, too, was part of his attempt to tone down the "divine man" motif. Mark emphasizes the *theologia crucis* in his own distinctive way, which is different from that of Paul. Jesus is forsaken by all, finally even by God, for he dies with the words "My God, my God, why hast thou forsaken me?" on his lips. This must not be harmonized with the words from the cross in the other Gospels.

Matthew basically followed Mark but played down Jesus' isolation, stressing the paradox of his royalty in the midst of humiliation and the motif of Scripture fulfillment. Luke probably had an independent passion narrative that he touched up with additions from Mark. It has been said that Luke transposed the passion story from the key of tragedy to the key of pathos. John, lastly, emphasizes the majesty of Jesus in his suffering. Jesus remains master of the situation throughout. The passion is the manifestation of his glory. He dies with the triumphant cry *Tetelestai*, which the Revised Standard Version, following the King James Version, weakly renders: "It is finished." The Vulgate was better: *Consummatum est.*

In the Easter season the preacher has to handle, among other things, the resurrection narratives. We have to remember that the New Testament nowhere narrates the resurrection as such. The event in which God raised Jesus from the dead is shrouded in the mystery proper to an eschatological event, occurring at the precise point where observable history comes to an end. The two this-worldly events that *are* narrated are the discovery of the empty tomb and the appearances of the risen Lord to his disciples. Here the basic facts belong to the earliest tradition (1 Cor 15:3-8), but the *stories* of the empty tomb and the appearances are the product of later development. Surprisingly, it was the pericope of the empty tomb that first took shape (Mark 16:1-8). It was used as the vehicle for the Easter proclamation. This is uttered by an angel—*angelus interpres*, a frequent scriptural device: "He is not here, he is risen."

As 1 Cor 15:3-8 indicates, the appearances were first listed, not narrated. The appearance stories apparently had not yet taken shape by the time Mark's Gospel was written, unless we are to suppose that episodes like the walking on the water and the transfiguration are post-resurrection stories retrojected into the earthly ministry. The appearance stories as found in the later Gospels are used as vehicles for the Church's post-Easter theology, which springs from its faith in the resurrection.

The Easter event is the foundation of the Church as the eschatological community and the inauguration of the Church's mission. The kerygma and the two sacraments of baptism and the Eucharist are grounded importantly upon the Easter event, but even they have some roots in the historical Jesus. The apostolate is similarly grounded. The emphasis on the material reality of the Lord's risen body in Luke 24 and John 20, which is at variance with the more "spiritual" presentation of the earlier appearance story (Matt 28; John 21), guards against the interpretation of the encounters as purely subjective experiences rather than as revelatory disclosures of eschatological reality.

The Church Year

The context in which the homilist operates is that of the Church year. This provides a kind of hermeneutical framework in which the liturgical use of Scripture is set. It is therefore important for the homilist to understand something of the rationale of the Church year.

The Church year is centered upon the reality of salvation history, focused in the Christ-event. In the earliest Church there were two main celebrations: the Lord's Day, or Sunday, and the period of the *Pentecostē*. The first weekly observance of the Lord's Day was not so much a historical commemoration of the resurrection as the fulfillment of the Sabbath, the proleptic participation in the rest that remains for the people of God (see Heb 4:9; *Epistle of Barnabas* 15.8). The second celebration was the *Pentecostē*, the period of fifty days that began with the (Christianized) Passover and concluded with the day of Pentecost.

It could be argued that we ought to have returned to this simple calendar, with its exclusively eschatological emphasis. But for pedagogic and other reasons, it was deemed advisable to retain the articulated Church year as it developed in the main after the Age of Constantine. All the same, it is important that we learn to understand the articulated Church year in the light of the simpler eschatological scheme—an understanding as important for the preacher as for all participants in the liturgy. The articulated Church year breaks down the total complex of the Christ-event into its constitutive parts, yet it does so not merely for historical commemoration but to expound a particular aspect of the total eschatological event. Each separate "mystery," to use the language current in Roman Catholic theology, must always be seen as part of the total mystery of the Christ-event.

The Church year starts with the first Sunday of Advent, whose theme is the culmination of the future eschatology taken over from the end of the previous year. Thus, one year dovetails into another. It is this prominence of future eschatology that has led in part to the dropping of the old pericope for the day, namely, the entry into Jerusalem, which however is still retained as an option by the Lutherans. Today's theme is not the first coming of Christ in humility but his coming again in glory. It is only on the second Sunday of Advent that the thought of the first coming begins to take over in preparation for the celebration of Christ's birth.

On the second and third Sundays of Advent the figure of John the Baptist moves to the center of the stage. This is significant. At first sight John the Baptist would seem to postdate the coming of Christ, if by that coming we have in mind his birth at Bethlehem. But the appearance of the Baptist at this point calls our attention to the fact that when we speak of the first coming of Christ, we are referring not merely to Bethlehem but to his first coming in its totality, which includes the whole ministry capped by death. It is for this total coming that John serves as the forerunner.

On the fourth Sunday of Advent the Blessed Virgin Mary takes over the stage, thus serving as the immediate preparation for the birth of Christ.

Although Christ's first coming in humility is the primary focus during the second, third, and fourth weeks of Advent, the theme of the second coming is not dropped altogether. The two comings must always be considered together. The first is an anticipation of the second, and the second is the completion and fulfillment of the first. Thus, the theme of the second coming is carried through to Christmas itself, especially in the propers for the midnight Mass. The word *epiphania* is used in the Christmas readings from Titus to signify *both* comings.

When they come to deal with the incarnation itself, the propers of the Christmas Masses are clear about the place of the nativity story in the mystery of Christ. The birth is emphatically only *Vorgeschichte*, a prelude to the Christ-event proper, which really begins with the baptism of Jesus and continues through his crucifixion and subsequent vindication. In this prelude God is inserting into human history the One through whom the act of redemption will be wrought. This is the biblical way of looking at the birth stories. They are not concerned with the combination of humanity and divinity in a single person, as though humanity and divinity were abstract qualities. Thus, the affirmation of the Johannine prologue that the Word became flesh is not merely an interpretation of Christmas but declares the inauguration of a history in which the Word will be dynamically enfleshed in the career of Jesus from Jordan to Calvary. For the flesh of Jesus, in Hoskyns' words, is his whole observable history, not abstract humanity.

Although the arrangements of the revised Roman calendar at Epiphany did not go as far in the right direction as they might have, the tendency of the reform is clearly to play down the story of the Magi and to upgrade the baptism of Jesus, which was the original emphasis of this festival and which, though obscured in the West, has always remained preeminent in the East. It is in the baptism that the process of the revelation of God in the human history of Jesus properly begins; the baptism is therefore, rightly understood, the first of the epiphanies. The visit of the Magi, like the rest of the infancy stories, is only a prefigurement of the revelatory event proper.

Even though the Roman calendar has introduced the rather colorless designation of Sundays "in ordinary time" for the period between Epiphany and Lent, the propers themselves, notably the gospels and the accompanying Old Testament readings, maintain the Epiphany themes. In the stories of the early ministry, Jesus is manifested as the Messiah in word and deed. In the Episcopal and Lutheran adaptations of the Roman calendar, these epiphanies are fittingly climaxed on the last Sunday before Ash Wednesday in the reading of the transfiguration story, which the Roman Lectionary, following its ancient but purely adventitious tradition, designates for the second Sunday of Lent.

In recent times Lent has come to be thought of almost exclusively as a season of personal penitence (the Lutheran tradition has been an exception; as a glance at the Lutheran hymnals will show, even the earlier part of Lent is devoted to the passion). It is not surprising that voices continue to be raised in favor of a shorter Lent. Of course, there is a place for personal penitence, but to keep it up for forty days and forty nights tends to pall.

Wisely, the revised calendar makes a shift in emphasis that people have not yet understood. Ash Wednesday becomes the great day of penitence in the Church, a sort of Christian Yom Kippur. The readings of the Sundays in Lent now focus upon the baptismal mystery, a theme that is now reinforced by the rites of the catechumenate. Together, catechumens and faithful prepare to participate, or to renew their participation, in the baptismal mystery at the paschal feast. Thus, the emphasis of the readings is the new life to which the baptized are called and its ethical demands.

Of course, this still involves the note of penitence, but it is penitence placed in a proper evangelical perspective rather than a pious work. The second readings are drawn largely from the Pauline exhortations, or parenesis, which are based upon Hellenistic catechetical formulas, while the gospels in year A (which form the best series and are recommended for invariable use when the rites of the catechumenate are celebrated) comprise the great Johannine signs, long viewed as symbols of the Christian experience of baptism.

Holy Week speaks for itself. On Passion Sunday the theme of the triumphal entry (except in the Presbyterian/United Church of Christ adaptation of the calendar) is clearly relegated to the subordinate position it has always really had. The homily should be based upon the passion, and if it deals with the entry into Jerusalem at all, it should treat it only as the curtain-raiser to the passion.

The ancient unitary paschal feast has been split up into a group of three celebrations—Holy Thursday, Good Friday, and the Easter Vigil. Each of these three days has its own distinctive color, expressed by the different ways in which the Eucharist is celebrated on it. Holy Thursday is a brief outburst of joy. When the service concludes with the stripping of the altar and the darkening of the church, the brevity of this outburst is dramatically emphasized. The Good Friday communion—whether it be from the reserved Sacrament, as in the Roman and Episcopal provisions, or whether the Eucharist itself is celebrated, as in the Lutheran tradition and in an increasing number of Anglican churches—is celebrated in the bare church in an atmosphere of extreme austerity. At the Easter Vigil, the great point about the Eucharist is that it marks a transition from darkness to light, from sorrow to joy, from bondage to freedom, from death to life.

It is a pity that in modern parish life the fifty days of Easter count for so little compared with the forty days of Lent. The rites of the catechumenate provide some hope that a more constructive use may be made of this period. It is a time when the Church should be especially conscious of both the presence of the risen Lord in its midst and the presence of the newly baptized. The liturgical gospels reflect these two themes. We first read the appearance stories and later the farewell discourses of the Fourth Gospel. The newly baptized are, with the rest of the faithful, now enjoying the foretaste of eternal life in the Spirit-filled community.

Ascension Day emphasizes one aspect of the Easter season. This season is the celebration not only of the victory of Christ over death but preeminently of his exaltation as Lord, or *Kyrios,* of the Church and the world. Ascension Day does not inaugurate a new period but is merely an incident within the fifty days of Easter. Finally, although Pentecost celebrates the gift of the Spirit, it too merely highlights a theme that is present to some extent throughout the great fifty days. Note, for instance, the use of John 20:19-23 as the gospel on Pentecost. This has caused some perplexity. Why read on Pentecost what happened on Easter Sunday? Such objections indicate a naive historical way of thinking. The gift of the Spirit is the outcome of the total Easter event. Probably the risen Lord conveyed his Spirit in every one of his appearances, and it was not confined to a single day in the way the Lucan schematization suggests.

If Pentecost marks a single event at all, that event is the inauguration of the kerygma. And in the Church year it also marks the conclusion of the Easter season. The post-Pentecost season begins at once, and the Pentecost observance is, very rightly, no longer extended into an octave, which unduly prolonged the fifty days and obscured their unique significance.

The post-Pentecost season is bounded at each end by a solemnity—the feast of the Holy Trinity at one end and the feast of Christ the King at the other.[8] In the post-Pentecost season the systematic reading of Scripture, begun in the post-Epiphany season, is resumed. After the excitement of Christmas-Epiphany and Lent-Holy Week-Easter, it is sound to relax somewhat. Now Scripture is read in course, and the reading of it is less colored by the season of the year. Here is the chance for broad themes of theology and ethics to be broached. It is important, however, to note that at the tail end of the Sundays of the year, or the post-Pentecost period, a futurist-eschatological note comes in.[9] So we end where we began—with the theology of Christian hope.

From Exegesis to Preaching

In the first part of this introduction we offered some general considerations about exegesis, laying considerable stress on the value for the preacher or homilist of the critical approach to the Bible. We will now briefly summarize the main steps in exegesis and then consider how one might move from exegesis to sermon composition.

[8] The Lutheran provisions call particular attention to the two boundaries of the post-Pentecost season by prescribing white as the liturgical color for each occasion. They do the same thing for the two Sundays which, in their reckoning (as in the Episcopal provisions), bound the Epiphany season, that is, the Baptism of the Lord and the Transfiguration.

[9] It is much to be desired that the last Sundays in ordinary time always feature the theme of future eschatology, regardless of how many Sundays there are after Pentecost in any given year. In effect, this would mean prescribing a third last, second last, and last Sunday before Advent, as the American Book of Common Prayer Office Lectionary and the German Lutherans do.

Ideally, exegesis should start with a translation of the passage from the Greek (or Hebrew, in the case of the Old Testament). Very few, however, will be able to attempt this, so we must be realistic and suggest that where this is not possible, the best alternative would be to compare at least two different modern translations.[10] Any marked variations will call attention to a disputed point of exegesis and send the homilist to commentaries for closer investigation. In the light of findings there, the homilist must weigh the pros and cons and decide which interpretations to accept.

Second, the homilist should then look in the margins of the various versions to see if there are any disputed readings (text criticism). These too can be checked in commentaries, so that a decision can be reached as to which text to accept.

Third, the homilist should turn to points of literary criticism. What is the literary genre of this passage (e.g., miracle story, parable, sayings collection)? Having ascertained this, the homilist should look for signs of redaction that are visible, for example through the disturbance of the original genre by additional material or through changes made in a known source. What light is thrown on the evangelist's understanding of the passage by the place in which he locates it? In other words, the homilist must study the context of the passage. Introductory questions are also relevant here (date, authorship, addressees), for they determine the situation to which the text was addressed.

Fourth, the homilist should look for any significant theological words in the passage and make a study of those words with the help of a concordance or theological dictionary. The context of other passages should be considered; words should not be looked at simply in isolation.[11]

Fifth and last, in the light of the information gathered, the homilist should write out a paraphrase of the passage, stating in his or her own words what the biblical writer was saying to those addressed.

The next stage forms a bridge between the exegesis and the sermon. It is what the Germans call the *Predigtmeditation,* or sermon meditation. The preacher has to be concerned with two poles—the original message

---

[10] The English Revised Version and the American Standard Version still enjoy the advantage of being the most literal translations and therefore particularly helpful to those who know little or no Greek or Hebrew. Of the most recent translations, the Revised Standard Version is the most literal, but it occasionally substitutes a completely different idiom for the original and makes it more difficult for the student or homilist to appreciate the force of the Hebrew or Greek text.

[11] See J. Barr's provocative critique of the Kittel *Wörterbuch* method in his *Semantics of Biblical Language* (Oxford: Oxford University Press, 1961).

of the pericope, as distilled from the exegesis, and the current situation of the audience or congregation when gathered for the liturgy. Here the homilist will have to draw upon personal knowledge of their concerns as disclosed through parish visits, counseling, and the confessional, or through the media or current literature. Then it must be decided how the text speaks in judgment and mercy, in wrath and grace, to this situation. The homilist must ask: What is the law and what is the gospel contained in the text? Finally, the homilist should envisage the result sought for from the hearers: repentance, renewed faith, some act of devotion, or some concrete act of obedience.

These are the considerations that I had in view and developed as I wrote my commentaries on the readings, and it is my hope that these observations may be of help to the homilist as he or she continues the responsible task of declaring the word of God to the people of God.

Series A

ADVENT SEASON

There is some uncertainty as to what the dominant theme of Advent should be. Is it focused upon the traditional "last things"—the end of the world, the general resurrection, the last judgment, and the new heaven and new earth? Or is it a period of preparation for the feast of the incarnation? Does it place us back in the period of salvation history prior to the coming of the Messiah?

The new Lectionary has tidied up this confusion by developing the future-eschatological themes on the last Sundays *per annum* of the old year, and by bringing these themes to a climax on the first Sunday of Advent. Then, from the second Sunday of Advent on, it introduces other themes in preparation for the incarnation. Thus, the successive Church years dovetail into one another.

FIRST SUNDAY OF ADVENT

Reading I: Isaiah 2:1-5
This is a vision of the pilgrimage of all the nations to Zion to be taught the ways of Yahweh. Yahweh will arbitrate international disputes, and a universal peace will follow. The prophecy is reproduced almost verbatim in Mic 4. It is uncertain whether Micah lifted it from Isaiah or Isaiah from Micah, or whether both derived it from a common source. Scholars seem to favor the third possibility. It certainly looks like an ancient liturgical fragment.

It is important to notice two things about this vision. It is speaking about what will happen at the end of history—in other words, it is eschatological. It is not envisaged as a possibility within history. Holy Scripture does not permit us to indulge in the illusion that a time will come within history when there will be no more wars. This does not, of course, mean that we should not work to eliminate the causes of war or to avert or bring to an end particular wars. It only means that we should not cherish

1

extravagant hopes that are doomed to inevitable disappointment. The final abolition of war will be possible only when God's purpose has triumphed in the consummation of history.

The second point to notice about the vision is that it is only when the nations have been taught God's ways and walk in his paths that they will beat their swords into plowshares and live at peace with one another. "It is a beautiful vision; but, be it noted, peace rests in no human program, but in obedience to the divine law" (J. Bright in *Peake's Commentary on the Bible*).

Responsorial Psalm: 122:1-9

The responsorial psalm takes up certain points from the first reading— the pilgrimage to Zion and the ensuing peace. This psalm was sung by the pilgrims as they went up to Jerusalem for the festivals. The first part expresses the pilgrims' excitement as they arrive within the sacred precincts. They exult in the unity that Jerusalem symbolizes as the festal crowds, representing all the tribes, flow together to the temple of Yahweh.

In some strands of postexilic Judaism, it became part of the eschatological hope to envisage a day when the nations would flow together to Jerusalem (e.g., Isa 25:6). The New Testament sees this hope partially fulfilled in the admission of the Gentiles into the Church, and completely realized in the final coming of Christ. See especially Rom 9–11, where the Apostle Paul develops the thought that in bringing the collection from the Gentile churches to Jerusalem, he is symbolizing the partial fulfillment of this hope, and propounds the conviction that his mission will contribute decisively to the final fulfillment, when the fullness of the Gentiles will be gathered in and all Israel will be saved (Rom 11:25-26).

Reading II: Romans 13:11-14

This is the traditional reading for the first Sunday of Advent. It is full of great New Testament eschatological words: *night/day, darkness/light, sleep/wake, hour* and *full time.* This language presupposes the early Christian scheme of the two ages—this present evil age and the new age soon to dawn. It interprets Christian existence as a life of tension. It is lived within this present old age but is already determined by the new age that is soon to come. Christians stand in the dark with their faces lit by the coming dawn. They can therefore already cast off the works of darkness and put on the armor of light. They can live "as in the day," although actually they are still in the night.

Note that it is not by their own unaided effort that the believers are to conduct themselves becomingly as in the day, but rather by "putting on the Lord Jesus." In Gal 3:27 the same phrase is associated with baptism: "As many of you as were baptized into Christ have *put on* Christ." Hence, in our present passage Paul is exhorting Christians to live out the implications of their baptism, in the power that their baptismal status gives.

One final problem. Paul tells his readers that our "salvation" is nearer than when we first believed, that is, nearer than it was when we first became Christians. By "salvation" Paul is not thinking of salvation in an individualistic, pietistic sense, as though we were now nearer to our death and therefore to heaven. He means the great day of salvation, the consummation at the end of history. Like all the early Christians, the Apostle believed that this end was to come very shortly—so soon, in fact, that it was now appreciably nearer than when the Romans first became Christians. Paul was clearly mistaken as to the date, for we are still here today and the consummation has not come yet. Perhaps an answer can be sought along these lines: the Christian always has to live as though the final consummation were just around the corner, in the certainty of it, a certainty so strong that already the light of the new age is casting its ray upon the Christian's present existence.

Gospel: Matthew 24:37-44

This passage is from Matthew's version of the so-called synoptic apocalypse (Matt 24; Mark 13; Luke 21). Like other contemporary Jewish apocalypses, the synoptic apocalypse relates a series of catastrophes identifiable with historical events that preceded the Jewish revolt of A.D. 66–70. These events are to usher in the final consummation—the return of the Son of man, the last judgment, and the new heaven and the new earth.

Such an apocalyptic scheme creates an overall impression that conflicts with the general tenor of Jesus' teaching elsewhere, including this present passage, which Matthew has inserted from his sayings source into the synoptic apocalypse. Here, in sayings that have the freshness of authentic Jesus material, the end is depicted, not as something that is preceded by a carefully planned apocalyptic timetable, but as something that is to come suddenly, like the flood in Noah's day: "they did not know until the flood came. . . . Watch, therefore, for you do not know on what day your Lord is coming. . . . for the Son of man is coming at an hour you do not expect."

This coming of the Son of man will be accompanied by the ultimate separation of the saved and the lost. Two men will be in the field; one will be taken and the other left. Two women will be grinding at the mill; one will be taken and the other left. One will be saved, the other rejected. Therefore, watch as a householder must watch for the thief. There can be no doubt that sayings like this, rather than the synoptic apocalypse as a whole, correctly reproduce the eschatological message of Jesus.

But this brings us face to face with the same problem as in the Pauline passage, though here it is Jesus rather than the early Church that was apparently mistaken about the date of the end. It did not come soon. Once again, we can take the apocalyptic perspective as an expression of the eternal consequences of the choice with which Jesus confronts his hearers. They must certainly react as though the end were just around the corner. Joachim Jeremias has made a further bold and exciting suggestion: Jesus does not regard the will of God as fixed and immutable. God can shorten the days for the sake of the elect (Luke 18:7-8), and he can also lengthen the period of grace (Luke 13:6-9) as a free act of mercy.

The Homily

If the homilist chooses to preach on the Old Testament reading with its vision of universal peace, he/she will have to be careful to avoid the suggestion that this is a humanly realizable ideal. Rather, it is a picture of the kind of world God will establish when history comes to an end. This does not mean, however, that the vision is irrelevant to human political endeavor. All human activity is open to the "pull of the future," and it is the human task to erect "advance signs" of the final realization (J. Moltmann).

The second reading suggests several possibilities. The homilist may characterize Christian existence as an "advent situation"—the Christian lives in the present age but is decisively conditioned by the age to come. Then, too, the homilist might exhort the congregation to live out the implications of their baptism, through which they were translated into the advent situation, or wrestle with the problem of the non-fulfillment of the imminent-end expectation of the earliest Church and how that expectation can become an existential reality for the contemporary believer.

The gospel appears to present the homilist with two different possibilities: either to exhort the hearers to eschatological alertness (Watch, for at any moment you may have to make an eternal choice) or to wrestle with Jesus' as well as the early Church's expectation of the end and try to make sense of it for present Christian existence. The eternal import of the choice Jesus presses upon us means, to say the least, that we must live alertly, "as though" the end were coming at any moment. Or, taking up the suggestion of Joachim Jeremias, the homilist can lead the hearers to see how it is through the grace and mercy of God that the end did not come when Jesus said it would, but that God has given us more time to prepare for the great day.

SECOND SUNDAY OF ADVENT

Reading I: Isaiah 11:1-10

As we indicated above, the second Sunday of Advent marks the shift from future eschatology to preparation for the incarnation. This shift appears in all the readings of this Sunday, though, as we shall see, the second readings of the second and third Sundays of Advent contain echoes of the earlier theme.

In today's Old Testament reading we have one of the great messianic prophecies of Isaiah. It pictures the ideal king from the family of David. He is to be endowed with the spirit of Yahweh and with charismatic gifts. Note the three pairs: "wisdom and understanding" are powers of intellect; "counsel and might" denote practical ability; "knowledge and fear of the Lord" are gifts of piety. The benefits of the king's reign are described in idyllic terms.

This picture is much older than the messianic hope proper. It probably expresses what each succeeding generation hoped for from its Davidic king. Yet the ideal was never realized, and the poem was shelved for messianic fulfillment. Christian faith naturally found its fulfillment in the coming of Jesus, and that is the sense in which we read it in the liturgy today.

Responsorial Psalm: 72:1-2, 7-8, 12-13, 17

This psalm is remarkably similar to the prophecy we just read and suits it admirably as a responsorial reading. It is a prayer that the monarch (presumably, again, a king of David's line, for much of the prosperity of his kingdom recalls the reign of Solomon) may have used in prosperity and peace. Again, like the Isaian prophecy, this psalm was later interpreted messianically both in Judaism and in Christianity.

Reading II: Romans 15:4-9

This is the traditional epistle for this Sunday, and because Cranmer constructed a new collect on the basis of this reading, Anglicans have long called this Sunday "Bible Sunday." Unfortunately, this had the effect of distracting attention from the main Advent theme of this passage.

Two things are to be noted. First, the "scriptures" and "whatever was written in former days" refer to what we now call the Old Testament. There was as yet no New Testament in the early Church, of course; in fact, when Paul wrote his letter to the Romans, he was actually taking a hand in producing what would later become the New Testament.

On these Advent Sundays there is, as we have seen, a particular emphasis on the Old Testament as the book of promise. This theme is taken up in our present passage, with its reference to hope. Paul prays that by the encouragement of the scriptures we might have hope. The Old Testament is precisely the book of hope and promise. It is an incomplete book, pointing forward to an event that had not yet taken place, namely, the final act of God. Jew and Christian ought to be able to agree about this. But then comes the point of divergence. Christians believe that the event toward which the Old Testament points has, in principle at least, already occurred with the coming of Jesus Christ. Jews, of course, believe that the event has not yet taken place.

The Christian belief that the promises of the Old Testament have already been fulfilled in principle does not mean that there is no further room for hope. Paul says that the Old Testament scriptures were written in order that *Christians* may still have hope. The current theology of hope (J. Moltmann and J. Metz) stresses that the acts of God are always such that they contain within them the hope for more.

This pattern reproduces itself again and again throughout salvation history. When the Christian belief that God has fulfilled his promise in the sending of his Son Jesus Christ is kindled, it at once also raises the hope of the second coming. So Christian existence, like that under the Old Testament, remains an existence geared to the future. That is why the Old Testament has not become irrelevant now that the event to which it points has taken place. We still read the Old Testament to orient ourselves in hope to the future, to the final event toward which the Old Testament points—the consummation of the kingdom of God.

Gospel: Matthew 3:1-12

If the readings of this season are preparatory to the incarnation, it seems a little odd that John the Baptist should figure so prominently on these Sundays. Unlike the Old Testament prophets or the annunciation story that we shall read on the last Sunday of Advent, the Baptist does not point toward the nativity of Jesus, but rather to his ministry, life, and death: "He who is coming after me is mightier than I . . . he will baptize you with the Holy Spirit and with fire"; "Behold, the Lamb of God, who takes away the sin of the world."

When New Testament scholars speak about the incarnation, however, they tend to think of it in somewhat wider terms than popular piety or even dogmatic theology does. The incarnation, from the biblical perspective, is the whole "Christ-event," the total coming of the Son of God in the flesh, which includes not only his nativity but also his whole ministry, his death, resurrection, and ascension. In fact, most of the New Testament, aside from the infancy narratives of Matthew and Luke, can proclaim the Christ-event without speaking of the nativity at all. So when the Advent season prepares for the "advent" of Christ, this is not just his nativity but rather his total coming. The nativity is merely one way of speaking of the advent of Christ, and not the central one at that. Hence, it is wholly appropriate that John the Baptist should figure prominently in the Advent season as a herald of the Messiah's coming.

The Homily

Hope is one of the great themes of Advent. Today's reading from the letter to the Romans highlights the place of hope in the Christian life, while the Old Testament reading from Isaiah fills that hope with concrete content and places it in a historical and social context. In preparing to address this theme, the homilist would do well to read something of the works of Jürgen Moltmann and Johannes Metz.

Alternatively, the preacher might choose to focus upon the figure of John the Baptist (and perhaps devote two Sunday homilies to him—this one and the next). John the Baptist was essentially one who pointed away from himself to the One who was to come. In the same way, every preacher and every sermon points away from the preacher and away from the sermon to the Coming One, and nowhere is this more necessary than in the Advent season, during which we prepare to celebrate the coming of the Messiah into our world and to accept him as he seeks to come into our lives.

THIRD SUNDAY OF ADVENT

Reading I: Isaiah 35:1-6a, 10

Although this chapter comes from the earlier part of Isaiah (Isa 1–39), its theme and mood are far more reminiscent of the unknown prophet of the Exile whom we call Second (Deutero-) Isaiah. Like Second Isaiah, the writer of this chapter speaks of the return from Babylonian exile in terms of the Exodus: in the return to Jerusalem the miracles of the first Exodus will be repeated (see Isa 40), the wilderness will rejoice and blossom as it did in the Exodus, and the ransomed of the Lord will return and come to Zion. There will also be accompanying miracles: the eyes of the blind will be opened, the ears of the deaf will be unstopped, the lame will walk, and the tongues of the dumb will sing.

This passage is very important for the New Testament. Jesus' healing miracles, for instance, are recounted in language derived from this passage. Thus, the story of the deaf-mute in Mark 7 actually uses the unusual word *mogilalos* ("dumb") which the Septuagint (Greek Old Testament) uses in this passage. Again, in the answer to John in prison (see today's gospel), there are further echoes of this passage.

The New Testament took up such prophecies as Isa 35 and found their fulfillment in the Christ-event. It is in the coming of Christ that the wilderness blossoms as the crocus; it is in him that the *glory* of the Lord is made manifest (cf. Isa 35:2 and 40:5 with John 1:14); it is in Christ that God comes to save his people; and it is in Christ that the exiles return to Zion with great joy.

There is nothing unusual in this shift of application. It is a procedure that took place constantly throughout the Old Testament and Judaism, and it is simply continued in the New Testament. Each successive event in salvation history discloses a new meaning in previous prophecies. In this way the word of the Lord, once uttered, continues to be an effective force in salvation history.

Responsorial Psalm: 146:6c-10

This is the first of the final group of Hallel (Hallelujah) psalms in the psalter. It is a psalm of praise for Yahweh's mighty acts of salvation, and it takes up some of the themes we have already found in today's Old Testament reading. The Lord opens the eyes of the blind. "The way of the wicked he brings to ruin" in the psalm recalls the verse "your God will come with vengeance" in the reading.

Once again, Christian faith can see the fulfillment of all these blessings in the coming of Christ. It is he who executes justice for the oppressed, who feeds the hungry (Mark 6:37-44 and parallels), who upholds the widow (Mark 12:41-44). And above all, it is in him that the reign of God is established to all generations.

Reading II: James 5:7-10

Among the readings appointed for this Sunday, this is the only one that does not take up the theme of the healing miracles that accompany the advent of the Messiah. And when it speaks of the "coming" of the Lord, it means, not his first advent, but the last judgment: "The Judge is standing at the doors." This is not an oversight on the part of those who drew up the Lectionary. Here we have a lingering echo of the futurist eschatology that was dominant on the last Sundays of the old Church year and continued through the first Sunday of Advent. Even when we concentrate on the first coming, we must not lose sight of the second. Even as we rejoice with exuberant joy at the first coming, we must also listen to the warning of the impending judgment and to the challenge to be patient. The use of the farmer as an example of patience seems to be suggested by our Lord's parable of the seed growing secretly in Mark 4:26-29, where it was applied to the coming of the kingdom.

A second illustration of patience, and of suffering as well, is taken from the Old Testament prophets. This, too, is especially apt for the Advent season. The Old Testament prophets believed that the word they uttered would be fulfilled very shortly, but they had to learn that God fulfills his word in his own good time, even the word that he had promised through the prophet to fulfill very soon. Does God therefore deceive the prophets? Not if Jesus is right in maintaining that God can rescind his holy will as a free act of mercy (see gospel, first Sunday of Advent). When that happens, the lesson of patience is especially pertinent.

Gospel: Matthew 11:2-11

The casual reader of the Gospels is often puzzled by this story. How is it that John came to wonder whether Jesus was the Coming One? After all, had not John already greeted Jesus as the Coming One (Matt 3:14)? Was he perhaps having second thoughts now? Had Jesus turned out to be a different kind of Messiah from the one John had expected—one meek and lowly of heart rather than one who purged the threshing floor with the winnowing fan of judgment?

These are interesting questions, but they are irrelevant to a proper understanding of our text. The real question is the one addressed to us: Can *we* believe that he is the Coming One or must *we* look for another?

In answer to John's question—which is our question, too—Jesus does not give a straight yes or no but points to what is happening in his ministry: the blind see, the lame walk, etc. Note the oblique way in which Jesus speaks of his mighty works. He does not say that *he* is healing the blind. The blind are given their sight by God! Thus Jesus indirectly affirms that his miracles are works of God wrought through him. But he never says so directly. The hearer has to work this out for himself or herself and to make a decision of faith.

Traditional apologetics used to cite the miracles of Jesus as "proofs" of his "divinity." This is not the way the Bible uses them. They are not proofs but signs—signs for those who have eyes to see and ears to hear. And they are not signs of Jesus' divinity (a Greek rather than a biblical term) but signs that God is present and at work in Jesus. Note that Jesus' answer echoes the language of Isa 35 and other prophecies (Isa 29 and 61). So the reader is confronted with a decision: Either these works are signs of the eschatological presence of God in Jesus or they are ultimately trivial episodes with no claim to our faith. But: "Blessed is the one who takes no offense [i.e., does not stumble] at me," that is to say, the person who sees that God is eschatologically active in Jesus' word and work is already a partaker in the blessings of the messianic age.

The second part of the gospel reading deals with the place of John the Baptist in salvation history. He is the messenger who prepares the way of the Messiah; he is the expected Elijah returned to herald the end. Yet the one who is least in the kingdom of heaven is greater than he, for John stands at the threshold of the new age. He is the last of the prophets and, like them, still points forward to the kingdom of heaven and the coming of the Messiah. He still stands on the Old Testament side of the great divide between the two ages. He is the "sentinel at the frontier between the aeons" (Bornkamm).

The Homily

Unless the homilist decided last Sunday to preach on John the Baptist both last Sunday and this Sunday, the more obvious choice is to expound the Old Testament reading, responsorial psalm, and gospel as a promise and fulfillment of the first advent of the Messiah, with emphasis either on the accompanying signs or on the work of John the Baptist (the latter is the primary theme of the Sunday).

If the second reading is chosen as the basis for the homily, the second coming of the Messiah and the consequent need for patience would be highlighted. Here it is important to see that the letter of James does not stand alone but is part of the New Testament canon. Its one-sidedness (all the New Testament writings are in some way one-sided) needs to be balanced by the witness of the other books in the New Testament canon. So today the one-sided concentration of the passage from James on the second coming needs to be balanced by the emphasis on the first coming in the other readings. The Christ who is to come again is the same Christ who has already come in the incarnation. His work will then be the consummated work initiated at his first coming. Only in this way can we give an authentically Christian exposition of James.

If this is to be the second of two homilies on John the Baptist, we note that this week an element of uncertainty creeps into the Baptist's mind: Is Jesus really the Coming One? That is a question that is put to us today. Compared with human hope, is what the gospel has brought to the world really the fulfillment of our hopes? There is no *proof* that Jesus of Nazareth is indeed the Coming One. All we have to go on is his activity—the blind see, the lame walk, etc., but above all, the poor have the good news preached to them. For there, in the preaching of the gospel, is the real miracle. But that calls for a decision: Either Jesus is the Coming One or he is not. So, "Blessed is the one who takes no offense at me."

FOURTH SUNDAY OF ADVENT

The rhythm of Advent differs from that of Lent. Lent descends from Ash Wednesday through the penitential season to the abyss of Passion Week and Good Friday—and then Easter bursts suddenly upon us. Advent, on the other hand, rises in a steady crescendo toward the full light of Christmas. This rhythm is aptly symbolized by the German custom of the Advent wreath, which is popular in this country also. The crescendo of Advent is reflected in the liturgical readings, which, beginning with the prophecies of Isaiah and John the Baptist, find their culmination on the fourth Sunday of Advent in a series of readings that focus on the Blessed Virgin and the annunciation of Jesus' birth.

Reading I: Isaiah 7:10-14

This text may be interpreted at two quite different levels, though, as we shall see, there is a real connection and continuity between the two.

First, there is the meaning of the text in its original historical situation. This situation is described in 2 Kgs 16:5-9. Syria has entered into an alliance with the northern kingdom of Israel against the southern kingdom of Judah, of which Ahaz is king. Together they have laid siege to Jerusalem. Isaiah offers Ahaz a sign that everything will eventually turn out successfully, but Ahaz piously refuses such a sign, doubtless because he wants to have no truck with Isaiah's advice. But Isaiah goes on and gives the sign anyway: "A young woman shall conceive and bear a son, and shall call his name Emmanuel." It is probable that the young woman in question is the wife of the king, and the son to be born, Hezekiah. The sign, then, will concern the continuation of the Davidic dynasty, a sign that God is with his people. This is the first level of meaning.

At the second level, the text is taken up by the evangelist Matthew and applied to the birth of Jesus. The Lucan infancy narrative also echoes it (see Luke 1:31), thus indicating that this application represents a tradition earlier than the two evangelists. In the Septuagint translation used by the evangelists, "young woman" is rendered *parthenos* ("virgin"). In a sense, the resultant application of Isa 7:14 is far removed from what the prophet originally intended—he was thinking only of the immediate political situation and of the certainty that God would shortly intervene on the side of Judah. But in linking this assurance with the continuance of the Davidic line, Isaiah had expressed a hope that continued in Israel and that, for the Christian Church, found its final fulfillment in the birth of Christ from the Virgin Mary. He is the true Emmanuel, God-with-us.

Responsorial Psalm: 24:1-6

In the Anglican liturgical tradition, this psalm is associated with Ascension Day, for which it is one of the proper psalms for the second Evensong of that feast. It is equally suitable, however, for Advent, for it is one of the psalms composed for the processional entry of the king into the temple. In Christian usage, it can be applied either to the ascension, Christ's entry into heaven, or to the incarnation, his entry into the tabernacle of the flesh.

Reading II: Romans 1:1-7

This is the opening greeting of Paul to the Romans. Nearly all his letters were written to churches he himself had founded, but Romans was an exception. It was written to a church founded by others to prepare the way for a future visit by Paul (Rom 15:22). Part of its purpose was to acquaint the Christians in Rome with the Pauline version of the gospel.

Paul begins by sketching the gospel in a traditional form, in which we find a whole series of expressions not otherwise used in his letters:

> descended from David
> according to the flesh
> designated (enthroned) Son of God in power
> according to the Spirit of holiness.

Paul can safely assume that the Romans had heard of this or similar creedal statements and that they will see at once that he preaches the same faith they have received from others before him. Later on, Paul will give another formulation of the gospel: "For I am not ashamed of the gospel: it is the power of God for salvation to every one who has faith" (1:16). This is not a different gospel but the same gospel stated in Paul's own language.

Jesus himself had not called particular attention to his Davidic descent. That would have suggested to his contemporaries a political conception of messiahship from which he was at pains to dissociate himself. But the post-Easter community found it necessary in preaching to Israel to stress Jesus' Davidic descent as a vital qualification for messiahship. Thus, it passed into the general stock of Christological concepts. Here it is used to stress the earthly side of Jesus' history ("descended from David according to the flesh") as contrasted with his exalted status after the resurrection ("enthroned as Son of God . . . by his resurrection from the dead"). Thus, the Davidic descent of Jesus stresses, not his exalted majesty, but his terrestrial lowliness.

Gospel: Matthew 1:18-24

In the New Testament, the supernatural conception of Jesus figures only in the two annunciation stories in Matthew and Luke. Apart from these two stories (with the possible exception of an editorial adjustment at the end of the Matthean genealogy, Matt 1:16, though the text here is uncertain), Jesus is represented as the son of Mary and Joseph, which is what he legally was.

It is remarkable that both Matthew and Luke, whose infancy stories are in most aspects poles apart from one another, agree that Jesus was conceived by the power of the Holy Spirit, his mother remaining a virgin. Clearly the tradition is much earlier than either Matthew or Luke. But as to its ultimate origin, the historian can only conjecture.

The real question is what the evangelists intended to convey in this story. These stories are an affirmation of faith in the transcendental origin of Jesus' history. He is not a product of human evolution, the highest achievement of humanity, but the intervention of the transcendent God in human history from outside. "The incarnation is like a dagger thrust into the weft of human history" (Hoskyns). To affirm the virgin birth is not merely to affirm a theological miracle (though that, no doubt, is presupposed by the evangelists), but to affirm the faith that the evangelists were affirming in narrating the annunciations.

The Homily

Taken together, the three readings appointed for this day set forth the two perspectives on the life of Jesus. From one perspective, he is a product of human history, born of a woman, descended from David—in short, all that the Bible means when it speaks of "flesh." On the other hand, he is Emmanuel, God-with-us, the Son of God, conceived of the Holy Spirit—in fact, all that the Bible means when it speaks of "spirit." These two perspectives are what was called, in terms of later dogmatics, the doctrine of the two natures—humanity and deity. The homilist has the opportunity to prepare the hearers to enter into the mystery of this doctrine, to help them find the deity *in* the humanity, not deity and humanity as two separate entities existing side by side.

CHRISTMAS SEASON

CHRISTMAS

The feast of the nativity of our Lord has become one of the chief feasts of the Church year, second only to Easter, and like it the center of a cycle of other feasts dependent upon it. This was not always so. Christmas Day is a comparatively latecomer to the calendar, first testified to at Rome in the year 336. Unlike Easter, it was not taken over from the Jewish calendar, nor was it determined by an exact knowledge of the date of Christ's birth, for which the New Testament gives no precise information.

Nor does it appear that, as in the case of the "historical" feasts that later grew up around Easter, such as Palm Sunday, Maundy Thursday, etc., the celebration of Christmas was due to the exploitation of the local possibilities at Bethlehem, despite the fact that the building of the Church of the Nativity almost coincides with the earliest evidence of the feast (330). Rather, it appears to have been determined by the widespread pagan festivals of the winter solstice, celebrating the beginning of the return of light after the shortest day.

Thus, in origin the feast of Christmas does not have an exclusively historical motivation. It is not *merely* a commemoration of Christ's birth, but the celebration of the dawn of the light of God's eschatological self-disclosure, the coming of God's kingdom. Thus, Advent has been a fitting preparation for the celebration of the nativity.

It is interesting to recall that during the Cromwellian period in England (1649–60), efforts were made to abolish Christmas on the grounds that it had no sanction in Scripture. This proved to be one of the most unpopular measures taken at the time, and in the end did more than anything else to alienate the majority of the English people from the Puritan experiment. Actually they opposed it because of the pagan customs that had gathered around the feast.

In view of the social accretions and commercial exploitation of Christmas today—more so than in the seventeenth century—perhaps the Puritans had more justification for their case than we would like to admit. Yet, *abusus non tollit usum,* and our aim must be to work for a proper

14

understanding of Christmas among our people. This can best be done by deemphasizing its historical aspect and putting stress upon its theological (or eschatological) aspect. For that we have been prepared by the Advent readings, which serve to set the feast in its proper theological and eschatological perspective. Such an emphasis will be our endeavor as we meditate and comment upon the readings that follow.

MASS AT MIDNIGHT

Reading I: Isaiah 9:2-7
This is the most famous of all the messianic prophecies of Isaiah. Its original meaning was very different from the associations that have grown up around it in Christian use during this season. It may have been composed originally as a liturgical anthem to be sung on the occasion of the coronation of the Davidic kings of Judah. Every time a new descendant of David ascended the throne, it was hoped (note the irrepressible hope of Old Testament religion!) that *this* king would in fact prove to be the ideal king.

The joy of the occasion is expressed by two comparisons: the joy of harvest and the joy of victory on the battlefield (v. 3). The new reign ushers in freedom from want and freedom from oppression (for the allusion to Midian, see Judg 6-8) and peace (the burning of the bloody debris of the battlefield). The "birth" of the child (v. 6) was actually the enthronement of the king, which in the royal theology was conceived as God's adoption of the king as his son (see Ps 2:7). The king is hailed by a series of royal titles. This is one of the few places (cf. Ps 45:7) where the king is actually called "God." Usually it was anathema for Israelite religion, even in the royal theology, to go as far as that, though it was common enough in the surrounding nations. Probably we should understand the king's divinity in a modified sense: he is the embodiment of God's own kingship, God's representative on earth.

Christian faith reinterprets this passage. The joy is the joy of Christ's advent, which ushers in deliverance for the oppressed (Luke 4:8) and peace between God and humankind (John 14:27). The words "to us a child is born" now suggest the birth at Bethlehem rather than the enthronement of a king. This reminds us that the birth of Jesus is only the beginning of the Christ-event, that the nativity really stands for the total advent of Christ, the whole saving act of God in him. Finally, it seems more appropriate to hail Jesus rather than the king of Judah as "God." Yet, even here we must be careful. The New Testament never does so without qualification. Jesus is not *Deus in se* (such a notion would compromise the unity of God), but *Deus pro nobis*—God turned to us in grace and salvation.

Responsorial Psalm: 96:1-3, 11-13

This is probably the most magnificent of all the enthronement psalms that celebrate the kingship of Yahweh. Much of its content also appears in another place in the Old Testament, namely, 1 Chr 16, a cento of psalms put together by the Chronicler to mark the bringing of the ark into the temple by David.

The theme of a "new song" can be traced all through the Bible. The old song was sung by Moses and Israel at the Red Sea (Exod 15). One might say that the whole liturgy of the old Israel was a continuation of this old song. But it lost its zest with the passage of time and especially in the Exile: "How shall we sing the Lord's song in a strange land?" So Second Isaiah looks for a new song to be sung after the return (Isa 51:11).

This hope for a new song was disappointed at that time, and the new song became part of Israel's eschatological expectation. In the Book of Revelation, the new song's promise is fulfilled at last in the celebration of the victory of the Lamb. Christmas marks the first step toward that victory, so the Church can already here and now take up the new song (as it always does in its liturgy). In the birth at Bethlehem, Yahweh truly comes to judge and save the world.

Reading II: Titus 2:11-14

This passage speaks of the two comings of Christ: (1) "the grace of God has appeared," that is, in the Christ-event (and Bethlehem marks the inception of its appearance); (2) "awaiting our blessed hope, the appearing of the glory . . . ." The second coming, which had been the dominant theme at the beginning of Advent but had receded into the background as the season progressed and the expectation of the birth of Christ took over, is not completely forgotten now that Christmas has come. For it is only in the light of the second coming that we can celebrate the first coming. People who forget this sentimentalize Christmas into a "Baby Jesus" cult.

In the nativity Christ comes first in great humility in anticipation of his coming again in majesty and great glory. It is especially fitting that this note should be struck at the midnight Mass of Christmas, for much of our traditional imagery speaks of the Lord's second coming as taking place at midnight. This imagery goes back to the parable of the ten virgins: "At midnight there was a cry, 'Behold, the bridegroom!'" (Matt 25:6).

Gospel: Luke 2:1-14

The infancy narratives in Matthew and Luke pose very difficult problems for those who would use them to reconstruct actual history. The two narratives agree on the following points: the names of Mary and Joseph as the parents of Jesus; his supernatural conception and Bethlehem as the place of his birth; and the dating of his birth in the reign of King Herod. Clearly these items go back to earlier tradition, prior to the evangelists.

Is the location of Jesus' birth at Bethlehem simply an expression of faith in his Davidic messiahship (see Mic 5)? Probably this question will never be answered. Then there is the unsolved problem of the census. Luke dates it during the period when Quirinius was legate of Syria. This we know from Josephus to have been from A.D. 6 to 9, a dating that appears to be confirmed by the fact that Josephus places the first census in Judea (see Acts 5:37) at about A.D. 6. This was immediately after Judea came under Roman rule—a more plausible reason for a Roman census than at the time when Judea was still a quasi-independent kingdom. But this dating for the census clashes with Luke's other statement, supported by Matthew, that Jesus was born in the reign of Herod, that is, not later than 4 B.C.

Many attempts have been made to vindicate Luke's account of the nativity census. For instance, it has been suggested, on the basis of remarks by Josephus, that Quirinius had already been in Syria as early as 10-7 B.C. with a legatine commission. But the neatest solution, proposed not long ago, is a different though perfectly plausible translation of Luke 2:2: "This census took place before the one that was made when Quirinius was legate of Syria." Another problem is that we have no evidence for people returning for a census from their normal domiciles to their ancestral homes.

These historical problems should warn us that, in the words of the *Jerome Biblical Commentary*, "the details of the narrative are symbolic and biblical; they communicate the mystery of redemption, not a diary of early events" (2:121). That is certainly how the narrative should be heard at the first Mass of Christmas.

We should probably not romanticize the shepherds. They had a bad reputation as thieves, and in any case they were poor. In fact, as Joachim Jeremias has shown, they were classed with tax collectors and prostitutes as members of despised trades. This fits in perfectly with the emphasis of Luke's Gospel.

The angelic announcement is the biblical way of bringing out the meaning of an event in salvation history (see the annunciation stories). This is the birth of One who is to be the Savior, the Christ (Messiah), and Lord. In the second proclamation, made by the "multitude of the heavenly host," not his titles but the effects of the Christ-event are announced: glory to God and peace (with the full meaning of *shalom*) among people.

The words "with whom he is pleased" vary in the Greek texts. The King James Version favored a text that gave the sense "good will [i.e., God's good will or favor] toward men." The Vulgate preferred a reading that yielded, literally, the sense "to men of good will." This is probably the right text, but the literal meaning is badly misleading. "Men of good will" is a Semitic idiom that means people who are the objects of *God's* favor. So actually the Vulgate reading comes to very much the same thing as the King James translation. This is a warning against much of the loose talk about people "of good will" that goes on at Christmas time, especially in the secular world.

The Homily

The homilist may speak of Christ as our peace and link this thought with the song of the angels, or of the paradox of Christ's lowly birth and his universal reign. Bethlehem is part of the paradox of Calvary.

The numerous historical problems that the story of the nativity presents should prevent the homilist from taking it in a naive, historical way as a "diary of early events." Two lines are suggested: Explain how shepherds were members of a despised trade and show how the incarnation is meant especially for the poor, the despised, and the oppressed; or take up the angelic pronouncements as a proclamation of the meaning of the nativity, that is, with the birth of Jesus divine salvation has entered the world.

MASS AT DAWN

Reading I: Isaiah 62:11-12

This passage is from what is now commonly called Third (or Trito-) Isaiah (Isa 56–66). These chapters take up the themes of Isa 40–55, which announced the impending return of the exiles from Babylon to their homeland (Isa 40), but they reapply these themes to a new situation. It is no longer the exiles returning to their homeland but the pilgrims going up to the temple at Jerusalem for the feast (Tabernacles?). When read at the second Mass of Christmas, these themes are reapplied to the birth of Christ. The passage now speaks of the joy of the new Israel at the advent of its salvation.

Responsorial Psalm: 97:1, 6, 11-12

Like the other enthronement psalms, Psalm 97 is appropriate for any Christian festival. A different selection of verses from this psalm is used during

the Easter season in series C. The present selection includes verses 11-12,
with reference to the dawning of the light, imagery that has passed into
the lore of the season and is expressed in so many Christmas carols.

Reading II: Titus 3:4-7

This passage is very similar to the second reading at the midnight Mass
(Titus 2:11-14). Both passages speak of the "appearance" of divine salvation and can therefore be related fittingly to the nativity. But there is a
difference, too. The earlier passage went on to speak of the second coming and made it the basis of an ethical exhortation. This passage takes
a different direction. The appearance of "God our Savior" in the Christ-
event leads to our regeneration and renewal, our rebirth as children of
God (see Gal 4:5-7). Christ is Son of God by right; created human beings
forfeited divine filiation by the fall. But Christ has appeared to give us
rebirth as children of God.

This thought is succinctly expressed in the collect that Cranmer composed in 1549 for the second Mass of Christmas: "Almighty God, who
hast given us thy only-begotten Son to take our nature upon him . . . .
Grant that we, being regenerate and made thy children by adoption and
grace, may daily be renewed by thy Holy Spirit. . . ." And the Anglican
poet Christopher Wordsworth, taking up the great patristic paradoxes on
the incarnation, expressed it thus:

> God comes down that man may rise,
> Lifted by him to the skies;
> Christ is Son of Man that we
> Sons of God in him may be.

Gospel: Luke 2:15-20

This reading completes the narrative begun in the gospel for the midnight
Mass—the pilgrimage of the shepherds to Bethlehem and their visit to
Mary, Joseph, and the babe in the manger. The angelic message had told
them that the things they would see would be a "sign" (Luke 2:12). What
they see has a meaning beyond what is visible to the eye, which can only
see a baby, its mother, and her husband—a common enough sight. But
this sight is a "thing that has happened." The word translated "thing" can
also mean "word," that is, a significant, meaningful communication. So
the sight of the child is a sign communicating to the shepherds the
significance of what the angelic message had proclaimed: God's salvation
has come to earth. The shepherds do not see the salvation itself but only
its outward sign—the birth of the child, wrapped in swaddling cloths.

The Homily

If the reading from Isaiah is chosen to be expounded, the homilist might fix upon the pregnant phrase "sought out." The incarnation is God's search for man (Karl Barth), the answer to all religion, which is the search of human beings for God. The Church is the result of this search, not an institution founded by human beings for the cultivation of religion.

Should the homilist choose to base the sermon on the second reading, he/she could speak of the contrast between Christ's divine sonship, which is his by right and nature, and our filiation, which comes only by adoption and grace. There is far too much talk nowadays about all persons being children of God. In the biblical perspective, they are only potentially such until they are incorporated into Christ.

The gospel is another protest against the sentimentalizing of Christmas. We are not just celebrating the birthday of "Baby Jesus," but rather the dawn of messianic salvation, of God's peace and favor toward humankind. The homilist can use this gospel to explain the true Christian meaning of Christmas. Only in this way can "Christ be put back into Christmas."

MASS DURING THE DAY

Reading I: Isaiah 52:7-10

This magnificent passage from Second Isaiah is rather similar to the Old Testament reading for the second Mass (Isa 62:11-12), and even closer to the enthronement psalms that form the responsorial reading for all three Masses of Christmas. The prophet announces the return of Yahweh to Zion in words identical with those that scholars think were used at the new-year enthronement festival: "Your God reigns." This proclamation is described as bringing "good tidings." The Hebrew word for "good tidings" lies at the root of the New Testament Greek term *euangelion*, or "gospel." Paul took up this very text and applied it to his own apostolic work of preaching the gospel in Rom 10:15, and it probably influenced Jesus' own formulation of his message of the kingdom or reign of God.

The use of this passage in the liturgy today suggests yet another application. It can be referred to the angelic proclamation at the nativity. This is indeed a proclamation of good tidings, a publication of salvation, an announcement of the beginning of the dawn of God's reign. It is in the incarnation that the Church sees the return of Yahweh to Zion and to Jerusalem to comfort his people (Isa 40:1). Here the Lord bares his arm and the people see his salvation.

Responsorial Psalm: 98:1-6

Selections from this psalm also appear on the twenty-eighth and thirty-third Sundays of the year in series C. This selection is also very similar to the psalms used in the first and second Masses of this day and to the first reading of this Mass. Its applicability to Christmas is obvious.

218
390

Reading II: Hebrews 1:1-6

The letter to the Hebrews is unique among the letters of the New Testament. Although it clearly ends like a letter (Heb 13:22-25), it does not begin like one. The author does not start with his own name nor greet the people, as was customary. There is no statement of the author's name nor of those to whom he is writing. Instead, he plunges immediately into his theological exposition: "In many and various ways God spoke . . . ."

Actually, Hebrews looks like a series of liturgical sermons on a collection of Old Testament texts. In fact, the author himself or the editor calls the work a "word of exhortation" (Heb 13:22) . The first of these sermons, whose exordium we have here, uses a series of texts to establish Christ's superiority over the angels. It is probable that the readers, presumably Jewish Christians with syncretistic leanings, wanted to rank Christ among a whole hierarchy of angelic mediators (see the later Gnostic aeons; also Col 2:18) and thus deny the uniqueness and finality of the revelation he brought.

The author prefaces his texts with what looks like an early Christian hymn to Christ, similar in theme to the Johannine prologue, which follows as the gospel for this Mass. The hymn in Hebrews seems to be based on an earlier Jewish hymn to Wisdom. Wisdom existed with God from all eternity and was the agent of creation and preservation. She manifests herself on earth and then returns to heaven. In its Christian adaptation, the hymn identifies Christ with Wisdom as the agent of creation and preservation. He appears on earth. Note that the whole Christ-event is covered by the words "when he had made purification for sins." There is no explicit mention of his incarnation or earthly life as in most of the other hymns, although the author himself does add an allusion to his entry into the world in verse 6. After his sojourn on earth, Christ returns to heaven and is exalted to the right hand of the Majesty on high, triumphant over the angels, who are here conceived, as so often in early Christian mythology, as hostile powers.

A further point to be noted about this hymn is that it sets Christ's revelation of God in Israel's salvation history. The same God who has now spoken "in the last days" (that is, eschatologically) in his Son had spoken previously "in many and various ways." In the Greek, the word for "many" brings out the fragmentary, partial character of the previous revelations.

This is a very important passage, for it relates the final revelation of God in Christ to the Jewish religion, and by analogy to other religions, too. All religions contain fragmentary and partial disclosures of God, and each religion has its own distinctive insight. But what was fragmentary and partial is now finally and fully disclosed in Christ. Here we have the biblical approach to the question of the non-Christian religions, which has exercised Christian thought so much since Vatican II: the claim that the final revelation is given in Jesus Christ. Of course, our apprehensions of it are never final. The finality of the revelation must not be confused with any particular Christian theology or expression of the Christian religion, for all these are still fragmentary in character. Our claim is for Christ, not for our understanding of him. This is not a piece of religious imperialism or triumphalism. It follows directly from the eschatological character of Christ's revelation: God has spoken "in these last days," not merely through the prophets but through his Son, the unique and final embodiment of his total self-disclosure.

Gospel: John 1:1-18 (long form); 1:1-5, 9-14 (short form)

It is fairly certain that the evangelist John did not himself compose the hymn to the Logos, but that it existed prior to his use of it. Yet, its origin is much in dispute. Some think that it came from Gnostic sources; some regard it as a Hellenistic-Jewish hymn to Wisdom. It has even been suggested that it was a hymn to John the Baptist, celebrated in the "baptist" circles as the bearer of the final revelation of God. It would then have been adapted by the evangelist for Christian use by adding a series of "footnotes" to the hymn: "He [the Baptist] was not the light," etc. It is interesting that the short form of the gospel drops precisely these parenthetical notes.

Whatever its origin, the Johannine prologue sketches in the eternal background of what happened in the ministry, life, and death of Jesus. This whole ministry was the revelation of the Word-made-flesh, the embodiment in a human life of the totality of God's self-communication to human beings. This self-communication did not begin with the Christ-event; it began with creation (see Heb 1:1-4). God created the universe in order to communicate himself to it in love. He communicated himself to men and women throughout history. This he did especially, though not exclusively, in Israel's salvation history recorded in the Old Testament. As the prologue puts it: "the life was the light of men. . . . The true light that enlightens every man was coming into the world." The reception of this revelation (here the evangelist has in mind the consequence of the incarnation) gives men and women the power to become children of God.

It is often debated just where John moves from the preexistent Christ to the incarnate Christ. Clearly he has done so by verse 14. Yet, the parentheses about the Baptist have the effect of changing the earlier statements about the Logos into statements about the Word-made-flesh. Thus, the whole Johannine prologue is a commentary on the rest of John's Gospel. The entire life of Christ is the story of the Word-made-flesh.

The Homily

The prologue to the letter to the Hebrews provides the preacher with a magnificent opportunity to expound the fragmentary and partial character of God's self-disclosure in the other religions and the finality of his revelation in Christ.

The angel at the nativity, Paul in his apostleship, and the Church today all make the same proclamation: "Your God reigns"—through the sending of Jesus Christ into the world. The incarnation as the good news of God's reign—this should be the theme if the homilist chooses to preach on the Old Testament reading.

But perhaps the most obvious course for the homilist to take would be to combine Heb 1:1-3 and John 1:1-14. Both speak of the Christ-event as the culmination of God's revelation or self-communication to the world in creation, to humankind in general (John 1), and to Israel in particular (Heb 1).

Sunday in the Octave of Christmas

HOLY FAMILY

The popular devotions that had gathered, in the Latin rite, around the Sunday in the octave of Epiphany as a result of its old gospel, Luke 2:42-52, have now been officially recognized and transferred to this Sunday. (Incidentally, the Episcopal Church has not gone along with this but observes the octave of Christmas as a continuation of the celebration of the nativity, with special emphasis on its theological aspects. The readings are Isa 60:13-21; Gal 4:4-7; and John 1:1-18.)

Reading I: Sirach 3:2-6, 12-14

This passage is obviously a commentary on the fifth (fourth) commandment: Honor thy father and thy mother. It adds the point that obedience to this commandment atones for sins (vv. 3, 14), an ideal typical of later Judaism. This latter point should not be taken with full theological seriousness. The central message of the New Testament is, of course, that atonement for sins is through Christ alone. The point should be taken merely as an incentive or inducement to obey this commandment, for in a loose, non-theological sense it may well be said that love of one's parents makes up for many sins.

Responsorial Psalm: 128:1-5

This wisdom psalm, with its introductory beatitude ("Blessed is every one who fears the Lord") presents the fear of the Lord as the basis of family, social, and economic prosperity. On a superficial level, it seems to express a naive, Deuteronomic confidence that obedience to the law will be an insurance against disaster, and a conviction that disaster can always be explained as punishment for disobedience, views seriously questioned already in the Book of Job. Yet, there is something to it. Where there is a wholesome respect for God and his will, human relationships do stand a better chance of being well ordered and harmonious. Those who fear the Lord are not tempted to put themselves in the place of God, to boast in their personal achievements. Such persons are therefore freed to love their neighbor and make it easier for the neighbor to love in return.

Reading II: Colossians 3:12-21

This is part of the "parenesis," or ethical section, of the letter to the Colossians. Such exhortations follow a regular pattern that is widely believed to reproduce the structure of a primitive Christian catechism.

The passage begins with a list of virtues, introduced by the imperative "Put on." This language reflects the vesting of the candidate as he or she came up out of the baptismal font. This imperative may be preceded by another, namely, "Put off," followed by a list of vices. This recalls the stripping of the candidate prior to baptism.

Following these general exhortations, there is often, especially in the later New Testament letters, a "Haustafel," or household code, listing the various members of family and society and their respective duties.

Such codes were apparently derived from Stoic teaching via Hellenistic Judaism, whence they passed into Greek-speaking Christianity. That is why they reflect the subordinationist ethic of contemporary society ("Wives, be subject"—not an idea that is likely to appeal to feminists!). But this subjectionist element, derived as it is from Stoicism, is not the distinctively Christian element in the code. That is found in the words "in the Lord"; in the injunction to husbands to *love* their wives; in the earlier definition of love as forgiveness; and in specifying the motivation for forgiveness as Christ's forgiveness of sinners. Here we should be able to find the raw materials for the formulation of a Christian ethic for a society that is not organized on a hierarchical, subordinationist pattern.

Gospel: Matthew 2:13-15, 19-23

Only by a questionable extrapolation from the text, involving an illegitimate historicization, would it be possible to relate this gospel to the theme of the Holy Family. Matthew's concern is rather to present Jesus as recapitulating in his life the history of Israel. The quotation from Hosea, "Out of Egypt have I called my son," originally applied to the calling of Israel in the Exodus. For Matthew, Jesus is the second Moses and the true Israel—ideas that he expresses by means of a midrashic narrative based on the text from Hosea.

Matthew next has to bring Jesus from Bethlehem to Nazareth. This is achieved differently by Luke, who represents the Holy Family as permanently domiciled in Nazareth and as only visitors to Bethlehem for the census. Matthew does it by means of an otherwise unknown text, said to be from Scripture. It is commonly thought that whatever its immediate origin (some lost apocryphal work?), it is ultimately based on Isa 11:1, where the Davidic Messiah is described as "a shoot [Hebrew: *neser*, suggesting "Nazarene" and "Nazareth"] from the stump of Jesse." Once again Matthew sees the movements of the Holy Family as the fulfillment of Scripture.

The Homily

There is, of course, no question that the place of the family in Christian life needs emphasis now more than ever before, since the stability and integrity of family life are threatened on every side. Equally it is true that the life of the Holy Family provides the model for all Christian family life. Yet, a word of warning against sentimentalizing the occasion: it will best be avoided if the homily sticks closely to the Scripture readings of the day.

Sirach, of course, takes for granted the simple subordinationist ethic of the Hellenistic world. In our day the nuclear family and the consequent segregation of the sexes raise quite serious hermeneutical problems (a former seminarian of mine observed that no grandparents resided in his suburban parish). How does one make the simple ethic of biblical times relevant to contemporary society? What does the commandment say to a society that banishes its parents to an old people's home hundreds of miles away or leaves them to the care of social workers and the welfare state? How can we restore the personal relationships that were the strength of the old four-generation family in a society so structured that it is impossible to return to the models of the past? The homilist can hardly be expected to offer answers to these problems, but the text does at least suggest that people ought to be made aware of the questions.

In the reading from Colossians, as in the first reading, the homilist is faced with a delicate hermeneutical problem that cannot be avoided if the text is to speak relevantly to the contemporary believer. We must distinguish between the essence of the Christian ethic and the temporal garb in which it is clothed.

Because of the historical problems involved in the gospel reading, and because of its theology (fulfillment of Scripture, Christ as the new Israel), and also because it is difficult to relate it to the day's theme, we suggest that the homilist avoid it and instead preach on either the Old Testament reading from Sirach or the New Testament selection from Colossians.

January 1
SOLEMNITY OF MARY, MOTHER OF GOD

The title of this feast is apparently suggested by two sentences from the day's readings. One is from the second reading: "God sent forth his Son, born of woman." The other is from the gospel: "Mary kept all these things, pondering them in her heart." Only the former sentence has relevance to the *Theotokos*, for it speaks of Mary's *giving birth* to the Son of God. The latter sentence treats Mary rather as the paradigm of faith, and therefore of the Christian believer and the true Israel. The calendar of the Episcopal Church uses the same gospel, which is traditional for this day, but has a different title for the feast: The Holy Name of Our Lord Jesus Christ. This takes its cue from the last verse of the gospel, as did the old title, the Circumcision. Whatever the precise title of the day, its major concern is still the birth of Christ as the beginning of the saving act of God.

Reading I: Numbers 6:22-27
This reading comprises the Aaronic blessing, which, like the *tersanctus* of Isa 6 with its threefold form, is a remarkable anticipation of the Trinitarian faith of the Church. Special attention is directed, in the caption to the reading, to the last verse: "So shall they put my name upon the people of Israel, and I will bless them," which suggests an emphasis on the holy name.

People often ask glibly, "What's in a name?" In biblical thought the answer is "Everything!" The name stands for the whole person, his/her character and power of personality. The name of God is the Being of God himself, all that he has manifested himself to be in his revelation in salvation history, culminating in the Christ-event. To "bless" means to invoke upon the faithful all that God is and all that he has done for his people. The name of Jesus is the name of the triune God made manifest and present in saving power. This is surely an appropriate blessing for the new civil year.

Responsorial Psalm: 67:1-2, 4-5, 7

This psalm is also used on the sixth Sunday of Easter in series C. As the response shows, the emphasis is on prayer for God's blessing, which fits in perfectly with the first reading. 434

Reading II: Galatians 4:4-7

This is the traditional lesson for the first Sunday after Christmas, where it has been retained in the Episcopal Lectionary. According to recent scholarly investigation, this passage is a pre-Pauline creedal formula that Paul has expanded. The words "born under the law, to redeem those who were under the law" suggests the particular preoccupations of the Apostle, and therefore were probably insertions by him. This leaves us with the formula:

> God sent forth his Son
> (born of woman)
> that we might receive adoption as sons.

One can see from this that the purpose clause follows immediately upon the sending clause: the Son was sent that we might become sons and daughters. This purpose clause is very important, for it indicates that the nativity is not just a beautiful story devoid of connection with our own existence. People today ask, "What has the birth of Christ got to do with me?" The answer is that on it depends my whole status before God as his adopted child. He became human through a human birth precisely in order that we might be elevated to the status of children of God. For further comment on this profound theological theme, see the second reading of the Mass at Dawn on Christmas.

But we cannot dismiss Paul's addition about the law as having no relevance. It points toward the event mentioned at the end of the gospel— Jesus' circumcision. In this he is shown to be "born under the law." In his incarnation and earthly life, he places himself under human limitations and enters into human culture, including all the restrictions of human freedom that characterize human life. For Paul, the law was precisely such a restriction. It told people what to do but left them powerless to do it. Only by complete submission to human bondage could the Son of God liberate people from it, for only he remained truly free, and only he is therefore able, in Van Buren's suggestive metaphor, to pass on the contagion of that freedom to others.

Gospel: Luke 2:16-21

This gospel is almost identical with that of the second Mass of Christmas.   19
The only differences are that it starts at verse 16 instead of verse 15, and that it goes on to include verse 21, the circumcision and naming of Jesus. This is clearly meant to be the climactic verse of today's reading.

The Homily

There is much concern today about freedom, both individual and social. It is therefore most important that the Christian understanding of freedom be made clear. It is that Christ liberated men and women from the powers that hold human life in thrall, thus opening up for them freedom to love God and neighbor. The reading from Galatians offers the homilist an opportunity to expound the nature of true human freedom that God gives through Christ. This would be an appropriate theme for New Year's Day, as we are conscious that we move from the past into the future.

Should the homilist choose to preach on the gospel reading, particular attention should be drawn to verse 21. The homilist can either speak of the circumcision and link it up with Paul's "born under the law," along the lines suggested in our comments on the second reading, or link up the name of Jesus with the reflections about the "name" in the first reading.

[*In countries where the feast of the Epiphany is transferred to the Sunday day between January 2 and January 8, inclusive, the* SECOND SUNDAY AFTER CHRISTMAS *is omitted.*]

January 6
or the Sunday occurring between January 2 and 8, inclusive

EPIPHANY

The feast of Epiphany originated in the East, where it was primarily a commemoration of the Lord's baptism. This was the first of his "epiphanies," or manifestations. Further epiphanies, such as the miracle at Cana, came later. When this festival spread to the West, it assimilated

some of the associations of the Western Christmas and became primarily
a commemoration of the visit of the Magi.

This interpretation of Epiphany, however, remained peculiar to the
West. In turn, the visit of the Magi came to be regarded as a manifestation to the Gentiles, as in the collect of the Roman Missal and the Book
of Common Prayer: "Deus, qui hodierna die Unigenitum tuum *gentibus*
stella duce revelasti . . .," and in the choice of the epistle for the day from
the letter to the Ephesians. Later still, especially in Lutheranism, Epiphany
became the day to emphasize the Church's missionary work. The current
Lectionary shows an attempt to restore the primary emphasis to the revelation of God in Christ and to relate all those secondary features to this
primary theme.

Reading I: Isaiah 60:1-6

In its original context, the first part of this reading hailed the fulfillment
of Isa 40ff—the return of the exiles to Jerusalem. The light has now come
and the glory of the Lord has been revealed. The second part predicts the
eschatological pilgrimage of the Gentiles to Jerusalem that will follow upon
the rebuilding of the city.

This reading is doubly suited to Epiphany when given a Christian interpretation. First, the incarnation replaces the return from Babylon as
God's great act of salvation. In the revelation of God in Christ, the light
has indeed shone in the darkness, and the glory of the Lord has risen upon
the world. And as the Gentiles respond to that revelation, a response symbolically prefigured in the journey of the Magi, the eschatological
pilgrimage of the Gentiles to Zion is fulfilled.

This Old Testament passage has clearly colored the narrative of the
Magi in Matt 2 (gold and frankincense!). It also continued to influence
the development of popular legend by adding details from the Old Testament ignored by Matthew (kings and camels, for example).

Responsorial Psalm: 72:1-2, 7-8, 10-13

This psalm was probably composed as a coronation hymn for a Davidic
king. Expressive of the genius of Hebrew monarchy at its best, and in
marked contrast to the brutal tyrannies of many Oriental potentates, the
hymn depicts the king as the source of justice and compassion for the poor.
In all fairness, however, it should be noted that a similar portrait of monarchy characterizes the Code of Hammurabi.

The exaggerated language of the third stanza, with its picture of kings
coming from afar—in fact, *all* kings and nations coming to do homage
to the Davidic king of Judah—is simply a poetic expression of Judah's hope

that under the new king it will become the top nation as it was in the reign of David.

Reading II: Ephesians 3:2-3a, 5-6

The choice of this reading is intriguing (the old Roman Missal had Isa 60:1-6), for it is the same passage that Cranmer appointed for Epiphany in the Book of Common Prayer, though in longer form (vv. 1-12). The reading combines the same two themes found in the first reading: the revelation or epiphany of God in Christ ("the mystery . . . made known to me by revelation") and the participation of the Gentiles in the messianic salvation ("how the Gentiles are fellow heirs, members of the same body, and partakers of the promise").

The letter to the Ephesians was written, whether by Paul himself or by one of his closest disciples and successors, at a time when the Apostle's work was complete and the unity of Jews and Gentiles in the Church, for which he had striven throughout his apostolic career, was an accomplished fact. Matthew, too, was a beneficiary of this achievement (even if his view of the law is very different), and it is precisely because of Paul's success that this evangelist can use the story of the Magi to symbolize the universality of the gospel.

Gospel: Matthew 2:1-12

Many different elements have gone into the shaping of this familiar story.

1) There is the primitive Christian kerygma of Jesus' birth from Davidic descent, which would qualify him in Jewish eyes for messiahship. This kerygma is further expressed in the tradition that Jesus was born in Bethlehem, the city of David (a tradition about which, as we have already noted, Matthew and Luke agree).

2) There is the tradition, also common to Matthew and Luke, that Jesus' birth took place near the end of the reign of Herod the Great.

3) There is a folk memory of Herod's character and of his psychopathic fear of usurpation during the closing years of his reign.

4) There is the widespread Hellenistic belief in the East as the source of wisdom.

5) There is the motif of the star as symbol of the Messiah. It is surprising in this connection that Matthew makes no use of Num 24:17. This text played a prominent role at Qumran, and it must have shaped the Magi story before it reached Matthew.

6) The same failure to cite obvious Old Testament texts applies to the mention of the presentation of gold, frankincense, and myrrh, which, as we have seen, is based on our first reading and the responsorial psalm.

Again, we must suppose that these Old Testament passages influenced the formation of the story, and that Matthew for some reason did not see fit to quote the passages in question. Only the formula quotation from Micah can be attributed to the evangelist with any degree of certainty, although it is unusual for such quotations to be placed on the lips of the *dramatis personae*. The thought that the Magi were Gentiles, underscored at least as early as the Gregorian Sacramentary (see the collect of the day in the Roman Missal, quoted above), is not at all emphasized in the narrative itself, though it is certainly present in the Old Testament scriptures that lie behind it.

The Homily
Christian faith sees the picture of Psalm 72 fulfilled in Christ and the universality of his gospel. Again, this fulfillment is symbolically expressed in the visit of the Magi, who "bring gifts" and "fall down before him." The psalm complements the Old Testament reading, adding what was missing there, namely, the messianic King. The homilist will therefore find it appropriate to enlarge the imagery of the Old Testament reading by bringing in the figure of the king from the psalm.

In preaching on the gospel, it would seem to be faithful to the evangelist's intention if the homilist avoided putting too much stress on the Gentile origin of the Magi. The point of the story as read today seems to be that by a series of signs (the star, fear of Herod, the quest of discovery, and adoration of the Christ Child by the Magi), that Child is manifested as the epiphany or revelation of God in the world.

Sunday after January 6
(transferred to Monday when it coincides with Epiphany)
BAPTISM OF THE LORD

In the Eastern Church, the primary emphasis of Epiphany was theological rather than historical: the epiphany of God in the humanity of the incarnate One. Indeed, the whole life of Christ was a series of epiphanies, of which his baptism was the first and most important. The original prominence of the baptismal epiphany was never completely forgotten in the West, but it was relegated to a corner in the liturgy—in the Roman Missal, to the gospel for the octave; in the Book of Common Prayer of 1928, to an office lesson. The revisers of the calendar could hardly have been expected to restore the baptism to its Eastern prominence by putting it on the actual day of Epiphany. The story of the Magi is too popular in

Western Christian lore for that. In the present calendar, the baptism is celebrated on the Sunday after January 6 if this Sunday does not coincide with Epiphany; if it does coincide, the baptism is transferred to the Monday after Epiphany. Thus, the feast has regained some prominence, and for this we may be glad. It helps to reinforce the theological, as opposed to the historical, emphasis of our Western Christmas cycle of feasts.

Reading I: Isaiah 42:1-4, 6-7

This passage, the first of the servant songs in Second Isaiah, has deeply impregnated the Gospel narratives of our Lord's baptism. The heavenly voice at the baptism ("This is my beloved Son, with whom I am well pleased") is, in part at least, an echo of the words "in whom my soul delights" (Isa 42:1). The word for "beloved" may be an alternative rendering of "chosen," and it is held by some that the word "son" is based on an ambiguous rendering of the original Aramaic word for "servant."

Note that Matt 12:18 has a formula quotation of Isa 42:1-4 as an explanation of Jesus' command to the healed not to make him known, the emphasis here being on verses 2-3 in the Isaian prophecy.

The original identity of the servant is a much controverted question. Some think that he represents the whole nation of Israel; others, a faithful remnant; and still others, an individual figure—the prophet himself, or some prophet or king of the past, or perhaps a messianic figure of the future. What the original meaning was need not concern us here. In the liturgy today, as in the evangelists, the servant is identified with Jesus, who is manifested as such in his baptism.

The latter part of the song speaks of the work of the servant: to establish peace on earth, to be a covenant to Israel and a revelation to the nations, to open the eyes of the blind, and to proclaim the liberation of captives. This forms a suitable introduction to the stories from the earthly ministry of Jesus that will be read between now and the beginning of Lent. Jesus' words and deeds are an epiphany of the servant of the Lord.

Responsorial Psalm: 29:1-4, 9b-10

In some ways this psalm is like the other enthronement psalms we have encountered, for it celebrates the kingship of Yahweh ("the Lord sits enthroned as king for ever"). But there are differences. The second stanza suggests that the psalm had its origin in a pagan hymn to Baal-hadad, the storm god of Canaan. Its meter also recalls Canaanite poetry as known from Ugaritic texts. But if that was its origin, the hymn has been thoroughly baptized: the storm has become an epiphany of Yahweh, the Creator-God.

In its present liturgical context, however, the hymn acquires yet another meaning. "The voice of the Lord upon the waters" suggests a voice from heaven at the baptism of Jesus. So the psalm becomes a celebration of the epiphany of God that takes place at the baptism of Jesus.

Reading II: Acts 10:34-38

This passage comes from one of the kerygmatic speeches of Acts, that is, formulations of the kerygma, or preaching of the early Church. It is remarkable as the only reference to Jesus' baptism outside the Gospels. Like Mark and John, it presents that event as the beginning of Jesus' story. In his baptism he is anointed with the Holy Spirit and so equipped for his ministry of healing and exorcism. Note how the history of Jesus is told as a series of acts of God. It is *God* who preaches the good news of peace in Jesus Christ, *God* who anoints him, and *God* who is with him in the performance of his miracles.

It is often held that there is a radical difference between the message of Jesus and the proclamation of the early Church. Jesus preached the kingdom, but the Church preached Jesus! There is certainly a formal difference here but not a material one. In proclaiming the kingdom, in performing exorcisms and healings, Jesus was witnessing to the presence of God acting eschatologically in his own words and works. And in proclaiming Jesus, the Church, as we can see from the present reading, was proclaiming that God had been present in Jesus' word and work. The Church proclaimed Jesus precisely as the act of God, the epiphany of his saving presence. This epiphany is activated at the baptism.

Gospel: Matthew 3:13-17

Matthew's account of the baptism differs from that of Mark, which Matthew probably used as his basic source, in two points. First, there is the little dialogue between Jesus and John. Matthew inserted this because in some way he felt that Jesus' baptism at the hands of John created difficulties. It is often thought that Matthew's problem was the sinlessness of Jesus—how could the sinless One submit to a baptism of repentance for the remission of sin? But there is not a trace of concern about Jesus' sinlessness in the narrative. All the stress is on the *persons* of John and Jesus: "*I* need to be baptized by *you*, and do *you* come to *me*?"

As we saw in our discussion of the Johannine prologue (Christmas, Mass During the Day), there was a "baptist" sect which held that John was the bearer of God's final revelation, in competition with the Christian Church. This made the story of Jesus' baptism (whose historicity, for that very reason, is beyond all reasonable doubt) embarrassing for Christians. It would seem that by submitting to John's baptism, Jesus tacitly admitted John's superiority to himself, and therefore sided with the "baptists" against the Christians. Matthew explains Jesus' submission to John's baptism by inserting this little dialogue, in which Jesus gives the reason: "thus it is fitting for us to fulfill all *righteousness*." This word recalls that of Isa 42:6 in the first reading: "I have called you in righteousness," that is, in order to fulfill my purpose in salvation history. Thus, Jesus' reply to John underlines the servant Christology of the baptism narrative. Jesus' submission to John's baptism was part of God's plan, so that Jesus would be manifested as the servant of Yahweh, now about to embark upon his mission.

Matthew's second change is in the wording of the voice from heaven. Mark has: "Thou art my beloved Son," thus making it a direct address to Jesus only. This suggests that originally the baptism was pictured as a personal experience of Jesus—his call from God to begin his mission. Mark may already have intended this, for by including it in his Gospel he wants to explain to the reader who Jesus is, not as part of Jesus' biography. But Matthew wants to make it quite clear that the baptism is rather an epiphany declaring to the Church the true identity of Jesus: he is the servant of Yahweh, fulfilling in his person the mission of the servant as depicted in Second Isaiah.

The Homily

Probably the homilist would be best advised not to treat the Old Testament reading separately but to take it together with the baptism story, with which it is so closely associated.

Should the homilist choose to comment on the responsorial psalm, it is its Christian reinterpretation that should be brought out. The homilist would not, of course, suggest that this was the original meaning but would bring out the new meaning that Scripture acquires in the light of the Christ-event.

The reading from Acts would enable the homilist to explain epiphany as saving presence, a saving presence that is shown forth in Christ from his baptism and through his proclamation and works, which will engage our attention in the liturgy during the coming weeks.

Since, however, the homilist's main task is to proclaim Jesus as servant, the Old Testament reading from the first servant song, Matthew's treatment of the baptism as brought out in the dialogue between Jesus and John, and the change Matthew made in the voice from heaven could provide the homily for today.

LENTEN SEASON

ASH WEDNESDAY

The liturgical changes of recent years emphasize that Ash Wednesday is not just the first of the forty days of Lent but is a special day of its own. Along with Good Friday, it is one of the two days on which both the Roman Catholic and the Episcopal Churches prescribe a full fast. Fasting has a number of purposes; in the Bible its chief purpose is to reinforce prayer, especially penitential prayer. Ash Wednesday is the Christian Yom Kippur.

Reading I: Joel 2:12-18

It is not known who Joel was or exactly when he lived and prophesied. He seems to have been a spokesman for Yahweh connected in some way with the temple—a priest, perhaps, or some kind of public relations officer.

The prophecies in chapters 1 and 2 were occasioned by a plague of locusts, which was too frequent an occurrence to enable us to date the work precisely; probably it was produced in the early part of the fourth century B.C., at a time when prophecy was beginning to merge into apocalyptic. This is shown by the way Joel takes the plague of locusts as a symbol of the end of history, the day of the Lord. He therefore issues a call for repentance. ("Turn," *shûbh,* means a complete conversion of heart, not just an outpouring of remorse, though the prophet does not deny the place for ritual expression of repentance. Ritualization is important, but it must be accompanied by a change of heart. If the people respond in that way, there is at least a chance that Yahweh will be gracious, though they must not presume on his graciousness.)

Responsorial Psalm: 51:1-4b, 10-11, 12, 15

This is the penitential psalm *par excellence,* the fourth of the seven traditional penitential psalms. The King James Version informs us that it was recited by David after his adultery with Bathsheba, a view that hardly commends itself to modern scholars. (A movie many years ago had David recite Psalm 23 on that occasion, a far less appropriate choice and typically Hollywood!)

The psalm is to be classified as an individual lament expressing penitence for some unspecified grievous sin. As such, nothing could be more appropriate for Ash Wednesday. The four stanzas are structured as follows: (1) an appeal to God's covenant faithfulness; (2) the penitent's acknowledgment of sin, that is, as an offense against God and not merely against others; (3) a prayer for future renewal (Ps 51:11 and Isa 63:10-11 are the only two places in the Old Testament where the term "holy Spirit" is found; the term must not be given its fully developed Christian sense of the third Person of the Blessed Trinity, although Christian devotion can legitimately read it in that sense; rather, it means God's action in the human person); (4) this renewal, finally, will lead the forgiven penitent to praise God. Thus, the psalm looks beyond Ash Wednesday and Lent to the joy of Easter.

Reading II: 2 Corinthians 5:20–6:2

Salvation history is inaugurated in the event in which "for our sake [God] made him to be sin who knew no sin." What does this mean? It can best be understood from the word at the cross: "My God, my God, why hast thou forsaken me?" Here Christ enters into the direct results of sin— alienation from God—so that we who are sinners and therefore alienated from God "might become the righteousness of God," that is, reconciled to him. He crosses over to where we are to bring us to where he is.

Paul's appeal for reconciliation was prompted by the Corinthians' turning against him, and against the gospel preached by him, to false apostles preaching a different gospel. Paul is trying to swing the Corinthians around to his side again. It is, therefore, an appeal to be reconciled not only personally to Paul but also to the gospel, and therefore to God himself. Otherwise they will have accepted the grace of God in vain.

Picking up the language of Isa 49:8 (just as Jesus' inaugural address in the synagogue at Nazareth had picked up the language of Isa 61:1), Paul identifies the "now" of the text with his present moment of writing. The "now" is the moment when the gospel is proclaimed, a "now" that at once makes present the Christ-event, bringing it out of its past, and that confronts the Corinthians with a decision that determines their eschatological future. Past and future are brought together in the "now" of proclamation.

Gospel: Matthew 6:1-6, 16-18

In this section of the Sermon on the Mount, the duties of piety (literally "righteousness") are set out in triadic form: almsgiving, prayer, and fasting. Such threefold tabulations of devotional practice were common in

Pharisaic and rabbinic teaching, and probably passed from that source into early Christian catechesis.

It is unlikely that Jesus himself was responsible for the triadic formulation. He certainly taught his disciples to pray. He certainly approved of almsgiving, as the story of the widow's mite shows. But his attitude toward fasting was somewhat ambivalent. On the one hand, he fasted himself (the temptations), and on the other hand, during his ministry he and his disciples apparently abandoned fasting as incompatible with the joy signalized by the advent of the kingdom of God (Mark 2:18-19 parr.).

Fasting was resumed by the post-Easter community, however, after the bridegroom was taken away (Mark 2:20). We know that the early Church observed a pre-paschal fast of twenty-four to thirty-six hours (which later was extended and eventually developed into the six-week Lenten fast) and also a weekly fast on Wednesdays and Fridays (as we know from the *Didache*).

The emphasis on motive—not to secure merit but as an expression of heartfelt devotion—is true to Jesus and is in the prophetic spirit (see the first reading). So we can think of Matthew's Church formulating the sayings of Jesus along rabbinic lines, in the triadic form.

The Homily

Lent is the season when we take our devotional duties more seriously. These may include, on the first day of Lent, special public acts of penitence, analogous to the procession between the vestibule and the altar mentioned by Joel. Then all through Lent we are summoned to practice almsgiving, prayer, and fasting. The homilist might suggest what concrete forms these acts of devotion should take and urge that they be not merely outward acts of piety but genuine expressions of a penitent heart. Penitence means turning right around—in other words, conversion. *Now* is the time for this, for "now is the day of salvation" (second reading).

FIRST SUNDAY OF LENT

The purpose of the Lenten readings is to prepare the people of God for participation in the paschal feast. The Old Testament readings focus upon salvation history as the presupposition of, preparation for, and in some respects a prefiguring of, the redemptive act of God in Christ. The second readings set forth our participation in the death and resurrection of Christ through baptism and in the Christian life. The gospel readings of series A, after the accounts of the temptation and the transfiguration, which are traditional on the first two Sundays, take up the great Johannine signs, which are prefigurements both of the saving events of Christ's death and resurrection and of our participation in those saving events through baptism.

Reading I: Genesis 2:7-9; 3:1-7

If we are to understand the saving significance of Christ's death and resurrection, the most important presupposition is that human beings are God's creation and yet are fallen creatures. Something has gone wrong. Humanity is not what God intended it to be.

These two great theological truths—creation and the fall—are expressed in Gen 2 and 3 in the terms of the then current mythology: the story of Adam and Eve in the garden of Eden and their eating the forbidden fruit at the serpent's behest. There is another equally mythological but less primitive account of the creation in chapter 1. This account states in more theological terms that God created man and woman in his own image and likeness. They are the culmination of creation. Chapter 2 depicts man and woman more at the center of creation: God makes man and woman, puts them in the garden, and then surrounds them with all the things they need. In either case, the theological meaning is the same: human beings occupy a distinctive place in God's creation.

The Hebrew word for "man" is *adam.* Even if the author intended this as a proper name for an individual first man, "Adam" stands for Everyman. Today, of course, it is difficult to take Adam as an actual historical individual; it is easier to understand him as the personification of Everyman. Adam's story is the story of us all.

Nor should we press the role of Eve too much, as has often been done in the past (see, for example, 1 Tim 2:13-14) and make woman more responsible than man for the entry of sin into the world. After all, Paul in Rom 5 says nothing about Eve and blames it all on Adam. Man and woman are jointly responsible for their fallen condition, even if here, as in everything else, each has a distinctive part to play.

The ancient story in Genesis shows profound theological insight. Its basic message is that human beings cannot blame God or an evil fate for their plight—they are directly responsible for it themselves. Man and woman made wrong choices, which conflict with their destiny as God created them. These choices cumulatively weigh against their chance to make right choices, but that does not deprive them of their responsibility.

Responsorial Psalm: 51:1-4, 10-12, 15

This psalm is also used on the twenty-fourth Sunday of the year in series *504* C. There we suggest that, since it is read as a response to the reading from Exod 32 (Moses as mediator), it should be interpreted Christologically. It expresses the truth that Christ is the Mediator who, though sinless, bears the sins of the world.

On this Sunday, however, we suggest a different interpretation. Here man and woman take upon themselves the responsibility for their own sinful condition as a result of the fall. The Genesis story is not about a specific sin or sins, but about the underlying sinfulness of human beings, their basic primary choice, of which specific sins are the fruit.

Psalm 51 is the classic treatment of repentance. It passes beyond mere shame at the consequences of sin (attrition) to an acknowledgment of guilt before God (contrition): "Against thee, thee only, have I sinned." It sees forgiveness not only as the removal of guilt but as the restoration of the right relationship to God: "Cast me not away from thy presence . . . . Restore to me the joy of thy salvation . . . . Put a new and right spirit within me." For a classical treatment of repentance in the New Testament, see 2 Cor 7:9-11.

Reading II: Romans 5:12-19 (long form); 5:12, 17-19 (short form)

As on other occasions, the shorter version is very instructive for understanding the full text. First, it simplifies Paul's argument by removing the curious digression about the period between Adam and Moses, when people did not live under the law and therefore could not be held accountable. This is hardly a burning issue for us today. Furthermore, it interrupts the flow of the argument and even the grammatical structure of the opening sentence. The opening "as" needs a "so" clause to complement it, but instead we have "and so," which denotes the result of the opening clause.

The shortened form neatly drops the "and" before the "so," thus enabling Paul to complete his analogy. The sin of Adam and his consequent death are analogous to the sin of all human beings and the consequent spread of death to all. But is that the analogy Paul intended to draw?

Was it not rather an analogy between Adam and Christ? Paul's parenthesis makes him lose the thread of his argument, but the concluding clause
of the paragraph, "Adam . . . was a type of the one who was to come,"
and the two "as" clauses in the concluding paragraph suggest that this
was his original intention. As Adam began a history of fallen humankind
characterized by sin and death, so Christ began a new history of
humankind characterized by acquittal, life, and righteousness.

Yet, this is not an analogy in which both sides are of equal weight,
and so the middle paragraph is inserted: "If Adam . . . , how much more
(Christ)." Christ's achievement is far greater than Adam's, for Adam only
introduced sin and death, whereas Christ introduced acquittal, life, and
righteousness. Death was negative, life is positive. Death's dominion
enslaves, Christ's dominion sets free.

Note how fittingly this reading from Romans complements the reading
from Genesis. It takes up Adam's fall and balances it with restoration in
Christ.

Gospel: Matthew 4:1-11

Series A preserves the traditional reading of the Matthean temptation account; series C substitutes the account given in Luke's Gospel. The two
versions are practically identical in wording, and the commonly held view
today is that both evangelists took the story from the lost common source
known as Q.

There is only one major difference between the two versions, namely,
the order of the temptations. Matthew has bread-temple-mountain, and
Luke has bread-mountain-temple. Since Matthew is more given to the rearrangement of his sources than Luke, it seems more likely that it was Matthew who altered Q. Why did he do so? Probably because he wanted to
bring together the two questions relating to Jesus as Son of God. This emphasizes that, for Matthew, Jesus' temptations are messianic in character.
The order of Q-Luke, on the other hand, emphasizes that Jesus is the new
Adam, the antitype of the first Adam, who fell when tempted in paradise
(A. Feuillet). Despite the fact that we read the Matthean version of the
temptations today, by reading it with Rom 5 and Gen 2–3 we are almost
bound to take them in the Q-Lucan sense, that is, as the temptations of
the new Adam.

The Homily

Despite the complications of Rom 5, even in the shorter version (obtained,
as we saw, by only slightly reinterpreting Paul's argument), the homilist
has a magnificent opportunity to relate the Genesis story to the gospel

406

by means of the analogy in Romans between Adam and Christ, fall and obedience, death and life, fallen humanity and redeemed humanity. The theme will be that of Newman's hymn:

> O loving wisdom of our God!
> When all was sin and shame,
> A second Adam to the fight
> And to the rescue came.

> O wisest love! that flesh and blood,
> Which did in Adam fail,
> Should strive afresh against the foe
> Should strive and should prevail.

Perhaps at the moment it is easier for us to believe in Gen 3 than in Rom 5, to accept our fallenness rather than our redemption through Christ. The effects of the fall are so obvious all around us—war, racism, injustice, drugs, pollution, crime, and so on. That Christ's coming has really made any difference is hard to see. The Church? Even the Church is mixed up with the fallenness of humankind. The influence of Christianity on civilization? A very ambiguous influence at best. The lives of the saints? Yes, there is something there; yet, the real life of the saints, like our own, is, in the last resort, hidden with Christ in God and discernible as grace rather than as achievement only to the eye of faith.

It seems that here, as in other matters, we have to walk by faith and not by sight. Is faith, then, a cop-out? To the non-believer it must inevitably seem so. To the believer, however, it is the only clue for a sane understanding of the human condition in this world, capable of explaining both the dark side of human existence as the effect of the fall and the brighter side as the effect of the coming and the achievement of the second Adam.

SECOND SUNDAY OF LENT

Reading I: Genesis 12:1-4a

Since the rise of modern biblical criticism, the question has often been asked: Did Jesus intend to found a Church? If by that we mean: Did Jesus foresee and intend that the outcome of his work should be an ecclesiastical organization such as emerged in the second, the fourth, the thirteenth, or the sixteenth century, the answer is pretty certainly no. But if by "Church" we mean, as biblically we should, the people of God, then the answer is that the question is wrongly put. For the people of God was founded with the call of Abraham (as the caption to this reading puts it, he is the "father of God's people"; see Rom 5:16-18). This makes it clear that he is the father of Christian believers no less than of his physical descendants.

Some years ago, there was a revival of biblical theology centered on the notion of the "God who acts." During that period the Bible came to be known as the "Book of the Acts of God." Theologians were constantly speaking of the mighty acts of God in history.

But then the question was raised: How can we today really conceive a God who acts in history? How can the nexus of cause and effect be broken by God, which this notion seems to imply? Part of the answer is suggested by this reading. God acts by calling key individuals like Abraham, and it is by these human responses that a channel for the execution of God's will is carved out in the world. It is because Abraham left his country that God was able to create of him a great nation, a blessing to all the nations of the world. Christian faith since the time of Paul has seen that promise fulfilled not only in Israel's salvation history as recorded in the Old Testament, but still more in the coming of Christ and in the history of the Christian Church. This whole history can be understood as a response to the call of God, a call going out to a whole series of key persons, beginning with Abraham and culminating with Jesus Christ and his apostles. That is why Paul can use Abraham as the paradigm of faith, even of Christian faith. Faith is obedient response to the call of God, and therefore it opens up channels for the redemptive action of God in history and in the world.

Responsorial Psalm: 33:4-5, 18-20, 22

This psalm is fully consonant with our interpretation of the call of Abraham. God works in history through his word (first stanza). It is human response in faith, hope, and obedience that paves the way for the effective working of God in history (second and third stanzas).

Reading II: 2 Timothy 1:8b-10

It is somewhat surprising to find a reading from the second letter to Timothy interrupting a series of readings from Romans. The reading about Abraham in Genesis might have suggested an excerpt from Rom 4, and we hope that this possibility will be considered when the Lectionary is reviewed.

Yet, the passage from 2 Tim is not inappropriate. It picks up the theme of calling from Gen 12 and speaks of the call to be a Christian. It emphasizes that this call is based, not on our own merits, but on God's purpose set long ago—when he called, for example, Abraham. This long-established purpose has now been manifested in Jesus Christ, who has brought life and immortality to light. This last point, then, serves to introduce the theme of the transfiguration, in which Jesus is manifested as the Savior who brings life and immortality to light.

Gospel: Matthew 17:1-9

The transfiguration looks forward to the passion and the subsequent glorification of Jesus in his resurrection. Luke's version, read on the second Sunday of Lent in series C and commented upon there, brings out more clearly the episode's connection with the passion: Moses and Elijah talk with Jesus about his "departure [Greek: *exodos*] which he was to accomplish at Jerusalem."

Matthew follows Mark quite closely, except for the addition of verses 6 and 7, the disciples' "fear" (so the Greek) and Jesus' attempt to quiet their fear by his reassuring touch and the words "Rise, and have no fear." In the Bible, fear is always the human reaction to a theophany (see, for example, Rev 1:17). It is overcome, not by saying that confrontation with the presence of God is a casual, everyday experience which there is no reason to fear, but only by the encouraging word of Christ (see Matt 14:27; 28:5, 10).

The Homily

A theme common to the first two readings is God's call to participate in salvation history (Abraham, Christians). There have been times when the idea of vocation or calling was too narrowly restricted to the priesthood or religious life. It would, of course, be unbiblical to deny that there are special forms of vocations that involve a special task in salvation history. Thus, God called Abraham; the earthly Jesus called the Twelve; and the risen Christ called the apostles, including Paul. But this special call rests upon the general call, which is basic and common to all Christians, to participate in God's salvation. Jesus, in Mark's Gospel, chooses the Twelve from a larger number of disciples who had already been called. The homily could clarify the difference between the general and special calls.

Should the homilist wish to preach on the transfiguration story, it would be natural this year to stress that element which, as we have seen, is of special concern to Matthew—the fear of the three disciples and Jesus' word of reassurance. One of the less fortunate effects of liturgical renewal has been a loss of wholesome awe in the presence of the holy realities of the liturgy. In an Anglican context, Archbishop Michael Ramsey has written: "The awe in the individual's approach to Holy Communion which characterized both the Tractarians and the Evangelicals of old stands in contrast with the ease with which our congregations come tripping to the altar week by week."

I suspect that, *mutatis mutandis,* the same warning would be relevant in the Roman communion since Vatican II. Lent—and particularly this second Sunday of Lent, when Matthew's account of the transfiguration is read—would be a suitable time to emphasize this now frequently forgotten theme: the *mysterium* of the liturgy is *tremendum* as well as *fascinans.*

THIRD SUNDAY OF LENT

Reading I: Exodus 17:3-7

This passage has clearly been chosen to fit with the gospel, in which Jesus promises the woman of Samaria that he will give her the water of life. In the dry climate of Palestine, water is an obvious symbol of salvation, and the allusion to the sacraments is not far below the surface in the Johannine discourse recounted in the gospel. In 1 Cor 10, Paul uses the episode of the rock from Exod 17, etc., as a type of the Christian sacraments (specifically there with reference to the Eucharistic cup).

But a different emphasis in this first reading is suggested by the responsorial psalm. This psalm picks up the theme of the Israelites' hardening of their hearts during their wanderings through the wilderness: "Harden not your hearts, as at Meribah, as on the day at Massah in the wilderness," which recalls Exod 17:7: "[Moses] called the name of the place Massah and Meribah, because of the fault-finding of the children of Israel."

It is worth noting that the letter to the Hebrews (3:7–4:11) takes up the theme of Psalm 95 and uses it as the basis for an exhortation to the Jewish Christians at Rome (?). They had been Christians for more than a generation. The first flush of their enthusiasm had worn off, and they were finding life wearisome. The author of the letter compares their situation to that of the children of Israel in the wilderness, who were also finding the going tough and were getting tired.

Responsorial Psalm: 95:1-2, 6-9

This psalm is also used on the eighteenth Sunday of the year in series C.   492
The emphasis today rests clearly on the third stanza (see the commentary on Reading I above).

Reading II: Romans 5:1-2, 5-8

In Rom 3:21 through chapter 4, Paul explains the act of God in Christ in terms of justification. He now sums up his argument ("Since we are justified") and unfolds its consequences: we have peace with God, we have access to grace, and we have a joyful hope of sharing the glory of God. The ground of all this is that the Holy Spirit has been given to us. Justification and the gift of the indwelling Spirit are really one and the same thing. When a person receives the gift of the indwelling Spirit, he/she is justified. When a person is justified, he/she receives the gift of the indwelling Spirit.

In a course of lectures on justification delivered in his Anglican days and reissued many years later after he had become a Roman Catholic, John Henry Newman sought to find a *via media* between the Reformation and the Council of Trent on the doctrine of justification, a way that would do justice to the legitimate concerns of both sides and yet transcend the antithesis. The interesting thing for us is that he sought it precisely in this understanding of justification as the gift of the indwelling Spirit. On the one hand, this avoided the notion suggested by much Reformation theology that justification is no more than the external imputation of righteousness, leaving a person just as much a sinner as before, and, on the other hand, the Tridentine suggestion that justification means what it means etymologically, namely, to *make* just, implying that the justified person has already become righteous in a moral sense. The Reformers were right in protesting that the justified person is still a sinner, and the Tridentine doctrine was right in asserting that justification makes a real difference. The way out of this dilemma is suggested by Rom 5:2: Justification is the gift of the indwelling Spirit, which initiates a transformation into the risen state.

Justification and the gift of the Spirit are the outcome of God's love. That love is not an abstract idea but something that happened—on the cross. The love of God in Christ on the cross was pure love, love not caused by the attractiveness of its object: while we were yet sinners and while we were yet helpless, Christ died for us. Through the cross God accepts sinners, and his acceptance of them is manifested by sending his Spirit to dwell in them and gradually transform them, so that eventually they will become in reality what they are in theory, namely, righteous.

Gospel: John 4:5-42 (long form); 4:5-15, 19b-26, 39a, 40-42 (short form)

A multiplicity of themes jostle one another in this dialogue between Jesus and the Samaritan woman. Among them are: (1) Jesus' request for water, leading to the declaration that he is the giver of life; (2) Jesus' suggestion that the woman call her husband, leading to an exposure of her matrimonial past (which some take as an allegorical reference to the Samaritan Bible, which has only the first five books of the Old Testament); (3) the woman's shift of the conversation to the basic dispute between the Jews and the Samaritans—the proper place to worship Yahweh—leading to Jesus' pronouncement that the old Jewish-Samaritan debate is about to be transcended by worship in spirit and truth; (4) the woman's assurance that the dispute will be cleared up in the messianic age, leading to Jesus' declaration that he *is* the Messiah; (5) the woman's departure to fetch her friends to see Jesus, interrupted by the sixth theme and resumed later in the conversion of many Samaritans; and finally, sandwiched between the two parts of the fifth theme, (6) the disciples' return to Jesus and their perplexity over his refusal to eat, leading to the declaration that his food is to do his Father's will, followed by sayings about the harvest, the latter preparing the way for the Samaritan conversions. The short form of the gospel simplifies the discourse by omitting (2) and (6).

There are many reasons why modern scholars do not regard the Johannine discourses and dialogues as transcripts of what the earthly Jesus actually said. There may be an original nucleus to this story, in which Jesus encountered a Samaritan woman and asked her for some water to drink, leading to some pronouncement by Jesus about the imminence of the kingdom of God. But the original point has been lost, and the story as it now stands has been expanded to cover various topics of interest in John's Church, topics that came up largely as a result of the Samaritan mission, but also topics that express the evangelist's interpretation of Jesus as the bringer of the final revelation of God. In this interpretation the evangelist appropriates a Gnostic (?) style and Gnostic categories.

On the whole, we must take the dialogue as a Christian meditation on the meaning of Jesus for faith: he is the bringer of salvation; he exposes human sin; he inaugurates the true worship of God, which transcends all human approaches to God and is a worship in spirit and truth, a worship based upon the gospel. It is because Jesus is the bringer of the final revelation of God that he draws all to himself as Savior of the world.

The Homily

This Sunday provides an embarrassment of riches, and the homilist must obviously be selective. For Lent and for the current situation of the Church, perhaps an attack on the problem of acedia (a "couldn't-care-less" attitude), starting from a consideration of the "murmuring" of the Israelites in the wilderness, would be most appropriate. In the unlikely event that it is accessible, we would recommend that the homilist obtain a copy of "An Introductory Essay Concerning Accidy" in *The Spirit of Discipline* by Francis Paget (published in 1902 by Longmans, Green and Co., London). This is a notable treatment of this subject and an Anglican classic of spirituality.

Of course, there are other possibilities for the homily, and at another season of the year one would be drawn to the concept of worship in spirit and truth. This is often thought, at least in Protestantism, to refer to inner sincerity and fellowship of the heart, and is sometimes contrasted with formal prayer "out of a book." But worship "in spirit" means worship prompted by the Holy Spirit, and worship "in truth" means worship based on the revelation of God in Jesus Christ, who is the truth. Bultmann's comment is apt: "The cultic worship of God is contrasted, not with a spiritual, inward form of worship, but with the eschatological worship."

A third possibility, which, however, broaches the theme traditionally associated with the fourth Sunday of Lent, would be to combine the theme of the water from the rock in the first reading with the promise of Christ to give the water of life in the gospel. Again, Bultmann is helpful: "The revelation brought by Jesus gives life and thus stills the desire which no earthly water can satisfy."

FOURTH SUNDAY OF LENT

Reading I: 1 Samuel 16:1b, 6-7, 10-13a

This Old Testament reading for today is somewhat of a puzzle, and just what the revisers of the Lectionary had in mind in placing it with the other two readings, which have the theme of Christ as the light, is not clear. Could it be that the anointing of David as king (=shepherd in the responsorial psalm) is a type of Christ's baptism, which is his call to take up his mission as light of the world, and of the baptism of the believer, who there receives the illumination of the Spirit?

Responsorial Psalm: 23:1-6

It is not clear whether this psalm was chosen to go with the first reading or whether it was first suggested by the traditional, though originally fortuitous, association of this Sunday with the idea of refreshment. In Christian usage, "Lord" can of course be interpreted to mean Christ. The third stanza, which speaks of the Lord's anointing the psalmist's head with oil, suggests some link with the anointing of David in the first reading, but the typology is too complicated to develop profitably in a homily. Those responsible should either explain their intentions or revise their choice.

Reading II: Ephesians 5:8-14

This reading overlaps with the old epistle of the Roman Missal for the third Sunday of Lent. In the Book of Common Prayer, that epistle was lengthened to run through verse 14, as here. It seems to have had a fortuitous connection with the station Mass at St. Lawrence celebrated on that day at Rome. But its baptismal associations (a catechesis based on the contrasts *once/now*, *darkness/light* and the concluding quotation from an early baptismal hymn) have always made this passage highly suitable for Lent. Now it becomes even more appropriate as a complement to the gospel, with its message of Jesus as the light of the world.

Gospel: John 9:1-41 (long form); 9:1, 6-9, 13-17, 34-38 (short form)

The most likely explanation of the seven miracles (signs) in the Fourth Gospel is that they existed together in a "Book of Signs" and that the evangelist used them as the basis for his discourses or dialogues.

The original story in today's gospel must have simply told how a man was born blind and was healed by Jesus. This was later expanded by a trial scene, in which the man was charged with having become an adherent of Jesus. This stage of development reflects the expulsion of Jewish converts to Christianity from the synagogue. The evangelist then added the Christological elements, such as verses 4-5, which declare Jesus to be the light of the world, and the discussion about his origins (vv. 29-34).[1]

Thus, the healing of the blind man is, for the evangelist, a Christological sign—it shows that Christ is the light that has come into the darkness of the world. In other words, he is the revelation of God. It is easy to see how the healing of a blind man would lend itself to such Christological treatment. Moreover, the mode of healing—washing in the pool of Siloam—suggests a further connection with baptism, which in the early Church was known as "illumination" (*phōtismos*).

The short form of the gospel reduces the story more or less to its original narrative form, omitting most of the features derived from the Church-synagogue relations and the evangelist's Christological insertions. Inadvertently, however, this has the effect of removing what was, for the evangelist, the main point of the story (Jesus as the light of the world) and its connection with the second reading ("Christ shall give you light"). Fortunately, the versicle before the gospel preserves the theme of light. It is thus imperative that verse 5 be restored to the short form.

The Homily

The clearest choice for the homilist is to take the second reading and the gospel together, proclaiming Christ as the light that has illuminated us in baptism by bringing us to the revelation of God. Naturally, reference

---

[1] Bultmann's commentary, which is notorious for its wholesale rearrangement of the text, would include within this discourse passages in other chapters that deal with Jesus as the light of the world (8:12; 8:21-29; 10:21; 12:34-36; 12:44-50).

would be made to Lent as the season in which our baptism is renewed and in which we prepare to renew our baptismal vows at the Easter Vigil. Mention would also be made of the ethical obligations that this involves (see Eph 5:11-12). The homilist might bring in David's anointing as a type of the Christian's illumination in baptism, with a further allusion to the third stanza of the responsorial psalm.

FIFTH SUNDAY OF LENT

Reading I: Ezekiel 37:12-14

The three readings of this Sunday fit together beautifully, for all concern the resurrection to newness of life. The passage from Ezekiel concludes and interprets the vision of the valley of dry bones (obviously a battlefield) that are gradually restored to life. The interpretation identifies the bones with Israel in exile, and the resurrection of the bones with Israel's restoration to its homeland after the Babylonian Exile.

However, it is interesting to note how the text shifts from the dry bones to graves: "I will open your *graves*, and raise you from your *graves*." This shift suggests that already by Ezekiel's time (see Isa 26:19) the expectation of a general resurrection at the last day was beginning to emerge, an expectation that was to be developed in later apocalyptic literature. But that is not the point here. Rather, the language of this future hope is transferred to Israel's return from exile. It will be like resurrection from the grave. In this figurative resurrection God will bring his people to newness of life and put his Spirit within them. This two-level theme—the restoration of God's people and the eschatological resurrection of the dead—thus start hand in hand as they will continue through apocalyptic literature to the New Testament.

Responsorial Psalm: 130:1-8

The juxtaposition of two passages of Scripture often brings out new meanings in them. This is what happens here. Usually one thinks of the *De profundis* as a penitential psalm, but when it is placed side by side with Ezekiel's vision, it acquires a new emphasis: it is both the cry of the individual in the depths of sin and death and also the cry of the people of God (note the shift at the end of the third through the fourth stanza from the individual to the community) for restoration from exile in the land of darkness and the shadow of death.

This hoped-for corporate redemption occurred in Israel's restoration from exile. It is still the hope of the Christian community in which the

Spirit dwells, and it is to be finally fulfilled in the general resurrection from the dead.

Reading II: Romans 8:8-11

The same two-level use of language is continued in this reading. The first level, that of resurrection from the dead, is now applied to Christ. God raised Jesus from the dead by his Spirit (see Rom 1:4). Now Christians, through their baptism, have received the indwelling of the Spirit which raised Jesus from the dead: "your spirits are alive because of righteousness." This is the second level—the restoration of the people of God to newness of life (note the words "because of righteousness"; as we saw on the third Sunday of Lent, the new life created by the indwelling Spirit is the effect of justification). Finally, the first level of resurrection is still expected for Christians, too: "he who raised Christ Jesus from the dead will give life to your mortal bodies." The risen life of the Church in the Spirit is an anticipation of the general resurrection at the last day.

The biblical hope is not a belief in the intrinsic immortality of the person, as though there were some part of us, such as the soul or the spirit, that is in and by itself immortal. The whole person—body, soul, and spirit—is subject to decay and death. But Christ has broken this subjection; he has burst the bonds of decay and death by his resurrection from the dead, in which he was raised to a totally transformed existence.

Through baptism believers have received the indwelling Spirit, as a result of which resurrection and renewal of the whole person, body and soul, has been initiated. True, even the bodies of Christians are still subject to sickness, decay, and death. But the indwelling Spirit is a sign in our mortal bodies that betokens the beginning of a new life that cannot be destroyed by death. This, as Oscar Cullmann has suggested, is manifested in two ways: in the daily renewal of our inward self (2 Cor 4:16; cf. Eph 3:16) and in the occurrence of miracles of healing in the bodies of Christians. The present indwelling of the Spirit is an anticipation of the complete renewal of life that will come at the general resurrection.

Gospel: John 11:1-45 (long form); 11:3-7, 17, 20-27, 33b-45 (short form)

Here again the evangelist has combined a narrative from his source, which consisted of seven miracle stories, with a body of discourse material. In the original source, the raising of Lazarus would have been a straightforward story of a resuscitation. Similar stories are the raising of Jairus' daughter and of the son of the widow of Naim. But note the progression of the miraculous: Jairus' daughter had just died; the widow's son was being carried to the grave, so he must have died earlier that day, for Jewish law required interment within twenty-four hours; but Lazarus had been dead for four days already.

The evangelist has placed the raising of Lazarus at a crucial point in Jesus' career. It occasions his final journey to Judea and Jerusalem, and the sensation created by Lazarus' resuscitation sets in motion the events that will lead to the crucifixion. Contrast this with the synoptic accounts, where the cleansing of the temple leads to the Sanhedrin's decision to get rid of Jesus. One should not try to harmonize the accounts. The synoptic accounts look closer to history, and in John's source the cleansing of the temple, now transferred for programmatic reasons to chapter 2, was probably in a similar position.

The evangelist has also placed the story of Lazarus here for theological reasons. Jesus goes to his death as the one who is the resurrection and the life and who will die to inaugurate the resurrection of all. The theological interpretation is brought out by the dialogue and discourse material with which the evangelist farced the story itself. Therefore, the high point of this gospel is the great pronouncement of verses 25-26: "I am the resurrection and the life; he who believes in me, though he die, yet shall he live, and whoever lives and believes in me shall never die." This serves the same function as "I am the light of the world" in the healing of the blind man in chapter 9.

The short form of the gospel prunes away some of the dialogue material, the preliminary discussion between Jesus and his disciples (vv. 8-16), and some of the narrative detail (vv. 18-19, 28-32a), and in so doing throws the central pronouncement into sharper relief.

The Homily

Once again, the homilist's choices are clear. All three readings revolve around the theme of death-resurrection—Christ going to his death and beyond it to resurrection, and our death and resurrection in him. If the homily is based primarily on the first reading, it will emphasize God's power to renew constantly his Church within history. If the preacher opts for the gospel, it may be combined with the second reading to draw out the present reality of the resurrection of life in the believer through the indwelling Spirit, a present reality, however, that does not exclude but anticipates the final resurrection of the whole person at the final consummation.

PASSION SUNDAY (PALM SUNDAY)

The Procession with Palms: Matthew 21:1-11

The triumphal entry of Jesus into Jerusalem is a subsidiary motif in to-day's liturgy, and if the homilist deals with it at all, it should be treated as a curtain-raiser to the passion story. For the passion has always been, in fact if not in popular estimation, the major theme of this day.

In series A we read Matthew's version of the entry into Jerusalem. It has three special features. First, unlike Mark and Luke, though like John, it explicitly cites the prophecy of Zechariah (v. 5). Such fulfillment quotations are characteristic of Matthew. Sometimes the citations are applied rather mechanically, as in the present case. Matthew seems to imply that Jesus was seated upon *both* the ass and the foal (v. 7)! The word "thereon" obscures this; the Greek means "on them." Actually, in Zechariah "ass" and "colt, the foal of an ass" are synonymous parallelism, saying the same thing twice but in different words, which is a characteristic of Hebrew poetry. Behind Matthew's fulfillment quotations, some of them almost trivial, rests the genuine insight of Christian faith that the events of Jesus' earthly life were the execution of God's saving purpose, fulfilling the promises contained in the Old Testament history of his mighty acts toward Israel.

The second notable feature about Matthew's version of the entry into Jerusalem is his change in the cry of the crowd. Mark wrote, "Blessed is the kingdom of our father David that is coming." Matthew has made it Christological: "Hosanna to the *Son of David*. Blessed is *he who comes* in the name of the Lord" (v. 9). This reflects the way the tradition developed: Jesus preached the kingdom of God, and the early Church preached Jesus as the Christ. Yet the one really implies the other. Jesus did not announce the coming of the kingdom as an abstract idea detached from his own person or as something purely future, even if imminent. Rather, he announced it as the inbreaking of the saving power of God in his own presence, his own words and works. The *Hosanna* and the *Benedictus*, placed in this position in Matthew's narrative and read on this Sunday, tell us that the event of the cross is the culmination of the inbreaking of the saving act of God in Jesus Christ. The cross is not a meaningless or tragic episode attached to the end of an otherwise glorious life; it is the culmination of the movement of God toward humankind, which is the whole history of Jesus.

The third feature is the response of the crowd after Jesus had entered the city: "This is the prophet Jesus from Nazareth of Galilee." To call Jesus a prophet may seem to us a minimizing Christology, but to the earliest

Church this was not so. Jesus was not merely one of the long line of Old Testament prophets. Nor does it mean that he came as a social reformer. He was the last emissary from God, bringing with him God's final and decisive word to his people.

Some modern New Testament scholars think that the entry story would have been more appropriate for the feast of Tabernacles (see John 7:2). Indeed, historically speaking, it may well have occurred on that occasion. Jesus visited Jerusalem to lay down his last challenge to his people at the heart of their religious center. By bringing the entry into close relation to the passion, however, Mark and the evangelists who follow him make it clear what the meaning of the cross is: God's final coming in judgment and salvation.

Reading I: Isaiah 50:4-7

This is the third servant song of Second Isaiah. The situation presupposed is that Israel in exile is rejecting the prophet's message. The people are "weary" (of his constant predictions of deliverance despite the continuation of the exile?). But the prophet is undeterred. God has given him the word and he must deliver it, even at the cost of personal suffering. And he is confident that God will eventually prove him right.

In exactly the same way, Jesus' passion was the outcome of his obedient delivery of the message of the kingdom despite his people's rejection, and his constant reliance that God would prove him right. The passion and death of Christ are not isolated events but of a piece with his whole ministry. The early Church was right in seeing that the servant songs came to rest in the passion and death of its Lord.

Responsorial Psalm: 22:7-8, 16-17a, 18-19, 22-23ab

Psalm 22 is the passion psalm *par excellence*. It was probably the first Old Testament passage to be adopted in the "passion apologetic" (the term of B. Lindars) of the early community. After Easter the early Christians had to reconcile, both for their own faith and for their hoped-for converts from Judaism, their conviction that Jesus was indeed the expected deliverer with the scandalous events of his passion. They found their earliest answer in Psalm 22.

This psalm can serve thus because it describes the sufferings of the righteous in language that astoundingly anticipates the events of the passion, not so much through mechanical prediction as through the psalmist's profound insight into the nature of innocent suffering. But more, it goes on to speak of the vindication of the righteous one (note vv. 22-23ab, the fourth stanza in the arrangement of the psalm as used in today's liturgy).[1]

Reading II: Philippians 2:6-11
Modern New Testament scholars are widely agreed that this is a hymn composed prior to Paul's time. It is often called *Carmen Christi*, from Pliny's description of Christian worship. There is much dispute about its proper division into stanzas, but the following reconstruction has much to commend it.

I

Christ Jesus, though he was in the form of God,
did not count equality with God a thing to be grasped,
but emptied himself,
taking the form of a servant,

II

being born in the likeness of men,
and being found in human form he humbled himself
and became obedient unto death
[even death on a cross: *added by Paul*].

III

Therefore God has highly exalted him
and bestowed on him the name
which is above every name,

IV

that at the name of Jesus
every knee should bow [in heaven and on earth
and under the earth: *may be a later,*
though pre-Pauline, addition]
and every tongue confess that Jesus Christ is Lord,
[to the glory of God the Father: *perhaps*
added by Paul].

The first stanza will refer to the pre-incarnate existence of the Christ: he was of equal status with the Father (see the Old Testament speculations about the divine wisdom). This status he voluntarily surrendered

---

[1]   Psalm 22 has especially colored the way Mark and Matthew tell the passion story (less so Luke). The question inevitably arises whether some of the details of the narration have been taken from the psalm rather than from historical memory. This may have happened in some of the peripheral details, for example the division of the garments, but the main facts of the passion stand because of their scandalous nature. It was this scandalous nature that sent the early Christians to their Old Testaments, not their reading of the Old Testament that led them to gratuitously invent fresh scandalous events.

and became subject to human bondage to the powers of evil ("the form of a servant": some refer this to the suffering servant, but at this point the hymn refers to what is common between Christ and all human beings, not to what distinguishes him from them). The last line of the second stanza refers to what is unique: he "became obedient unto death" (Paul emphasizes that that was the scandal—the death on the cross).

The third stanza marks the turning point of the Redeemer's way—his exaltation—while the last stanza speaks of his ultimate triumph over the whole created universe.

The *Carmen Christi* sets the death of Christ in its total context. It is at once the nadir of the divine condescension begun in the incarnation and the ground of Christ's exaltation and final triumph.

Gospel: Matthew 26:14-27:66 (long form); 27:11-54 (short form)

In each year's commentary we seek to bring out the overall characteristics of the passion accounts in the Gospels. Matthew's account brings out the royalty of Christ, but it is a paradoxical royalty, manifesting itself precisely in humiliation. The royal note is struck by the triumphal entry and is strongly underlined in the trial scene between Pilate and Jesus (27:11-26), in the scene of the mocking by the Roman soldiers (27:27-31), in the title on the cross (27:37), and in the mockery by the bystanders (27:42).

On the other hand, the humiliation of Jesus is most emphasized by the cry from the cross: "My God, my God, why hast thou forsaken me?" (27:46). Of all the words attributed to Jesus on the cross in all four Gospels, this has the highest claim to authenticity. It is preserved in the oldest tradition (Mark-Matt). It was offensive to the later evangelists, who substituted more harmless words for it (Luke-John). It lent itself to later heretical rewriting (Gospel of Peter, which has "My power, my power . . .," expressive of that writing's Docetic Christology, according to which the Christ [or divinity] left the man Jesus before his death). Mark's Gospel gives the cry in Aramaic.

The cry certainly expresses the meaning of the cross more profoundly than anything else in the passion narrative. Unlike the other Old Testament citations, which were designed to relieve the events of the passion of their scandalous character, the cry from the cross actually enhances the scandal. It states what Paul in a more theological vein expressed when he said that "he [God] made him [Christ] to be sin who knew no sin, so that in him we might become the righteousness of God" (2 Cor 5:21).

When Jesus ate with the riff-raff, he crossed over from God's side and put himself on the side of sinners in order that he might seek and save them. On the cross he carries this action to its lowest point. The human being as a sinner is under what the Bible calls the "wrath" of God, that is to say, alienation from God, the sense of God's absence that springs not only from finitude but from willful rebellion. The word from the cross gives Jesus' death its theological meaning. His death is not just the ordinary dying of any person, a biological event—it is Jesus, not against God but for God, enduring the most bitter consequences of sin. Only by this identification does Jesus liberate from sin and death, both understood, as here, in their theological sense. The cry is not only *one* of the words from the cross—it is *the* word of the cross, the interpretive word that gives the cross its whole meaning as redemptive event.

Other peculiar features of Matthew's passion account are of less moment. They include Jesus' words to Peter at the arrest (26:52-53); the suicide of Judas (27:24-25); a slight but very moving expansion of the crowd's mockery (27:43; Bach's treatment of the phrase "for he said he was the Son of God" is one of the most impressive parts of the *Matthäuspassion*); the opening of the graves of the saints at the death of Jesus and their appearance after the resurrection, an event that is made to serve as one of the contributory factors in the centurion's confession (27:54). Some of these additions are pious and devotional, some legendary and symbolic, some apologetic. Otherwise, Matthew follows his Marcan source very closely.

The Homily

We would suggest three different possibilities for the homilist today. First, he or she may decide to give a course of homilies during Holy Week on the servant songs of Deutero-Isaiah (the first song, Isa 42:1-7, is appointed for Monday of this week; the second song, Isa 49:1-6, for Tuesday; the third song, Isa 50:4-9a, today's first reading, is repeated on Wednesday; the fourth song, Isa 52:13–53:12, is used on Good Friday). The homilist may show how the prophet of the Exile meditated on the place of suffering in God's plan of salvation, how his insights found their fulfillment in the sufferings of Christ, and how Christ's sufferings give meaning to all human suffering, especially that of his people.

The second possibility would be to base the homily on the *Carmen Christi*. Here the cross is viewed as the culmination of the path of humiliation that began with the incarnation of the Son of God and continued throughout his whole life of obedience. The hymn forms the theological basis of the exhortation to humility that Paul delivers to his congregation, keeping his eye on their particular problems. The homilist can do the same, keeping an eye on the particular problems of his/her own congregation.

The third possibility for the homilist would be to bring out the unique features of Matthew's passion narrative as described above. To get at the heart of the message of the cross this day, the cry from the cross (27:46) would be the text to choose.

EASTER TRIDUUM

HOLY THURSDAY

Mass of the Lord's Supper

A rubric in the Roman Missal notes that three principal mysteries are commemorated in this Mass and should be explained in the homily: the institution of the Eucharist; the institution of the priesthood; and Christ's commandment of brotherly love. The first is covered by the first and second readings; the second, by the gospel; the third is implicit in all three readings. The readings are the same every year.

Reading I: Exodus 12:1-8, 11-14

Although it is much disputed whether the Last Supper was a Passover (so the synoptic Gospels) or a meal preceding the Passover by twenty-four hours (so John), two things are certain: the original meal of Jesus and his disciples was undoubtedly surrounded by Passover associations, and the accounts of the institution have been impregnated with paschal theology, both in Paul (see the second reading) and in the Synoptists. Preeminently, too, the Israelite Passover provided the background for the annual Christian feast, and therefore most especially for the Easter Eucharist at the conclusion of the vigil. It is therefore doubly fitting that the triduum should begin with this reading.

Three points may be made here. (1) The Passover is an (annual) memorial of the great redemptive act of God that constituted his first people. "Memorial" means more than mentally recalling. The devout Jew believed that at the celebration of Passover he/she was actually coming out of Egypt with his/her ancestors. The same realism colors the Christian Eucharist and preeminently the triduum.

2) The shedding of the blood of the lamb provided an obvious type for the death of the Lamb of God, who takes away the sin of the world. For the Christian dispensation, the bloodshedding is more than a ritual or cultic act—it is a moral act (Heb 10:5-9) that becomes an event of salvation history. It is the making present of this event that is one of the main meanings of the Eucharist.

3) The Passover was eaten in great haste and expectation. In the course of centuries, this sense of urgency was transformed into an expectation of the Messiah, who was to come that night. The early Christians likewise began their Passover celebration looking for the coming of Christ, and even when the second coming did not occur, they believed that he came in the Easter Eucharist in anticipation of his final coming (*Marana tha!*).

Responsorial Psalm: 116:12-13, 15, 16bc, 17-18

This psalm underlines two aspects of the Eucharist: the sacrifice of thanksgiving and the communion among believers, a sharing of the cup. Some traditions have overemphasized the one to the exclusion of the other. The Eucharist is both together.

Reading II: 1 Corinthians 11:23-26

This is one of the earliest fragments of Christian tradition preserved in the New Testament (see also 1 Cor 15:3-7). Paul says that he "received" it before he "delivered" it to the Corinthians about A.D. 50, and the words for "receive" and "deliver" represent words for the handing on of tradition as in rabbinic practice. So we are dealing here, not with a vision "received from the Lord," but with a tradition handed down through human witnesses, though always under the supervision of the exalted Christ.

This is not a complete description of the Last Supper but a liturgically stylized account, selecting and interpreting those features of the meal that were of importance for the Christian Eucharist. Its mention of the supper between the bread and the cup indicates its primitive character. Only Paul and the long text of Luke mention the command to repeat it in memory of Christ, but the other accounts presume this by their very existence, for they were recorded precisely because the Church was "doing this" as a memorial of the Lord.

Paul also preserves what is more prominent in the synoptic accounts— the anticipation of the second coming. In Paul, as in the Synoptists, the Eucharist looks both backward and forward—backward to the redemptive event of the cross here made present, and forward to the second coming here anticipated.

Gospel: John 13:1-15

The theme of brotherly love is introduced at the footwashing, as the Lord says: "I have given you an example, that you also should do as I have done to you" (13:15). This example is further defined later in the discourse, after the supper: "I give you a new commandment: Love one another as

I have loved you" (13:34, the versicle before the gospel; the Latin *mandatum* gave this day its traditional English name of Maundy Thursday).

Modern exegetes find two themes in the footwashing, the first symbolic, the second exemplary. The symbolic meaning asserts that Jesus lays aside his garments as a parable of humiliation. He stooped, first to become incarnate, then to die in order to cleanse humankind of sin; finally he returns in glory to the Father. The whole incident is an acted parable of the *Carmen Christi* (see the second reading of Passion Sunday). The symbolic meaning is expressed in verse 3: "Jesus, knowing that the Father had given all things into his hands, and that he had come from God and was going to God . . . ." The exemplary meaning is expressed in verse 15: "For I have given you an example, that you should do as I have done to you."

The Homily

The themes for the homily are spelled out in the rubric given in the Roman Missal: the institution of the Eucharist, the institution of the priesthood, and the commandment of mutual love among Christians.

The combination of the reading from Exodus and the Pauline form of the institution of the Eucharist suggests that the homilist should concentrate on the memorial aspect of the Eucharist. A careful distinction should be drawn between the Reformation/modern idea of remembering, that is, merely recalling in our minds; the medieval notion that Christ's sacrifice is somehow repeated in the Mass—a notion that the Reformers rejected as unbiblical; and the Hebraic-biblical notion of anamnesis, which means recalling a past event before God in such a way that it becomes dynamically operative in its effects, or to quote the Anglican-Roman Catholic International Commission, "the once-for-all event of salvation becomes effective in the present through the action of the Holy Spirit" (*The Final Report*, p. 19).

If the homilist chooses to speak on the mutual love of Christians, the gospel reading will help to see that this love is grounded in the condescending love of God enacted in Jesus Christ. It is not just a matter of copying an external example. Neither meaning of the footwashing—the symbolic or the exemplary—must be treated in isolation from the other; the exemplary meaning is enclosed within the symbolic. The redemptive act of God alone makes possible the following of Christ's example, and unless we follow that example and reproduce in our own human existence the pattern of his, the redemptive act becomes an abstract myth divorced from our own existence.

The third suggested theme, the institution of the priesthood, requires very careful handling. It would be easy to move straight from the command "Do this in remembrance of me" to the institution of the Christian priesthood. But this would be an oversimplification for two reasons. First, Vatican II, especially in the Decree on the Ministry and Life of Priests, set the Eucharistic presidency in the wider context of a total pastoral ministry of word and sacrament. Second, there is no explicit evidence in the New Testament as to who presided at the Eucharist (see Raymond Brown, *Priest and Bishop: Biblical Reflections* [New York: Paulist Press, 1970]). Only in the second century does it become clear that it is the bishop who presides with his presbyters; only later still does the presbyter become the normal Eucharistic president; and finally, even later (Cyprian) is the title *sacerdos* accorded to the presider at the Eucharist.

Therefore, the command "Do this" (plural) is addressed to the Christian Church as a whole. The Eucharist is an action of the whole Church and the preeminent expression of its priestly character (see 1 Pet 2:1-10; Rev 1:6; and perhaps Heb 13:15). Thus, whoever presides at the Eucharist and recites the great thanksgiving is the mouthpiece of the Church's priesthood. At the same time, by showing forth Christ as both victim and priest in the great Eucharistic action, the president of the assembly exhibits the priesthood of Christ to the Church.

GOOD FRIDAY

The readings for this day are the same every year. The reader will find some additional comments under series B and C. *251* *420*

Reading I: Isaiah 52:13-53:12

The fourth servant song contributed three essential points to the early Church's understanding of Jesus' crucifixion: Christ's suffering was innocent, vicarious, and redemptive; it avails for all persons; and the righteous sufferer will be finally vindicated.

New Testament scholars are divided on whether Jesus himself made use of this chapter for the understanding of his mission, because sayings in which references to Isaiah occur (the ransom saying in Mark 10:45 and the words "for many" in Mark 14:24, the institution narrative) are probably later additions. Moreover, while some of the passion predictions may echo the language of Isa 53 (see especially Mark 9:12), they may well be, in their present form, *vaticinia ex eventu.*

It is important that we see the cross, not as the mechanical fulfillment of a preconceived dogmatic scheme, but as the culmination of the intensely personal mission of Jesus as a whole. He identified himself completely with sinners during his ministry, and in so doing he broke through the barrier of sin set up between God and humanity. He stood for God on the side of sinners.

Because the early Church saw the cross in the light of Jesus' whole ministry, it found in Isa 53 an almost perfect prophecy of the passion and used it as a quarry for its own theological statements about the passion. But these statements are not abstract theologoumena; they are an attempt to capture in words, and to pass on to those who did not have the direct experience of the crucifixion, the meaning of a real flesh-and-blood history as the action of God *pro nobis*—for us and for our salvation.

Responsorial Psalm: 31:1, 5, 11-12, 14-16, 24

Verse 5 of this Compline psalm provided for Luke the crucified One's last word, which he substituted for the word from Ps 22:1 in Mark-Matthew. This word, "Into thy hand I commit my spirit," lacks the profound theological depth of that other saying; yet it has a point to make. As well as being God's act of salvation for human beings, the cross is also the human offering of perfect obedience to God. This thought can be linked with the high priesthood of Christ, which the second reading will bring before us.

Reading II: Hebrews 4:14-16; 5:7-9

This is the third enunciation of the theme of Hebrews—the priesthood of Christ. His high priesthood is characterized in three ways: sympathy for human weakness as the result of his own earthly experiences; the answer to his prayer for deliverance; and his learning of obedience.

As we said above in commenting on the responsorial psalm, the cross, as well as being God's act of salvation in identifying perfectly with sinners, is also a human offering of perfect obedience to God's will. This, in fact, is the quintessential expression of Christ's high priesthood in Hebrews (see the citation of Ps 40:6-8 in Heb 10:5-10). The real sacrifice that God demands of human creatures is the perfect offering of themselves in obedience. Because of sin, they were unable to offer this sacrifice. The Levitical sacrifices of the old covenant could not take away sin, for they were not that perfect sacrifice but a permanent witness to their inadequacy, as the writers of Psalms 40 and 51 knew. They were destined to last until God provided this perfect sacrifice, which he did in sending his Son.

Thus, through Christ, God does for us what we cannot do, namely, offer the perfect sacrifice required by him. This does not mean that we are let off scot-free and have nothing to do for our part; rather, it means that we are caught up into Christ's self-sacrifice and are enabled in him to offer ourselves, our souls, and our bodies in union with his sacrifice, so that the imperfection of our sacrifice is transformed by the perfection of his sacrifice.

Gospel: John 18:1–19:42

As we have seen, each evangelist has his own particular perspective on the passion, and John's perspective is that the kingship of Jesus constantly shines through his humiliation. All the way through, Jesus is in command of the situation. He sets his passion in motion by voluntarily coming forward for his arrest. The temple police, awed by his personality, fall back. Peter would stop the arrest, but Jesus intervenes.

On the cross, Jesus makes his last will, bequeathing his mother to the disciple and the disciple to his mother (John may regard Mary as a symbol of the Church). Finally, it is Jesus who decides on the moment of his death—he gives up his spirit. The passion narrative is a commentary on the saying: "I lay down my life, that I may take it again. No one takes it from me, but I lay it down of my own accord" (John 10:17-18).

Although the evangelist has packed most of his theology of the cross into his discourses, especially in the farewell address, at least two points of interpretation are brought out in the narrative. First, Pilate (like Caiaphas earlier, on the atoning death) bears unwitting testimony to Christ's kingship when he brings Jesus before the people and when he refuses to alter the inscription on the cross. The second point is that the Baptist had proclaimed Jesus as the true paschal Lamb of God who takes away the world's sin, and now Christ dies as such at the moment when the Passover lambs are being slaughtered. Then at his death he announces the completion of his sacrifice: "It is accomplished" (John 19:30; the RSV translation, "It is finished," is weak; the Vulgate's *Consummatum est* gets the point).

The Homily

We have stressed in our comments the two-way significance of the cross: God to us, we to God. This corresponds to the traditional dogmatic formula of the twofold office of Christ (*duplex munus*) as king and priest, which in turn corresponds to the yet older dogmatic formula of the two natures, divine and human.

As king, Christ comes from God's side and exercises his saving power among sinful men and women, identifying himself completely with them, standing where they are, and bringing the saving compassion of God to them. The crucifixion, historically speaking, is the outcome precisely of this earlier activity of Jesus among people—his preaching of the kingdom, his teaching in parables, his eating with outcasts, and his calling of people to follow him. "For this I was born, and for this I have come into the world, to bear witness to the truth" (John 18:37). The cross is therefore the nadir of Jesus' kingly service of God toward us.

Christ is also the priest. At the moment of his baptism, Jesus says yes to the call of God, and at each moment of his ministry he offers himself to the Father in perfect obedience, so that the Father's words become his words, and the Father's works his own works. His cross is not a meaningless, tragic end to a life that had quite different meaning (like, say, the death of Camus), but the culmination of a whole real life of moment-by-moment surrender to the will of God.

The homilist might bring out these two aspects of the cross—Christ as king and Christ as priest. The reading from Hebrews and the passage about Christ's kingship in John's passion account will be helpful for this.

EASTER VIGIL

This is the archetypal liturgy of the whole Church year. It consists of four parts: (1) the service of light with the Easter proclamation; (2) the liturgy of the word; (3) the liturgy of baptism; (4) the liturgy of the Eucharist.

The origins of the light service are probably pagan, and their Christian meaning is uncertain though strangely moving. It is perhaps well, therefore, that it is recommended that this ceremony be performed outside the church, and suggested that other ceremonies more adapted to the culture of a particular region may be substituted. (Some Anglicans carry out the ceremony of the new fire *after* the prophecies, so that its kindling marks the *transitus* of the Messiah.)

The Easter proclamation focuses upon the three main themes of the vigil service: the deliverance of Israel in the Exodus ("This is the night when you first saved *our* fathers"); the baptismal deliverance of the new Israel ("This is the night when Christians everywhere . . . are restored to grace"); the resurrection of Christ ("This is the night when Jesus Christ broke the chains . . . .").

Seven readings from the Old Testament and two from the New Testament are assigned to the Easter Vigil. Some may be omitted if circumstances warrant it; however, it is recommended that three selections from the Old Testament be read before the epistle and gospel. The third reading from Exodus about the escape through the Red Sea should always be used, the rubrics advise.

Reading I: Genesis 1:1–2:2 (long form); 1:1, 26-31a (short form)

It is appropriate to read the story of the first creation on the night that celebrates the inauguration of the new creation. The Genesis story is not to be read as historical narration. Its importance is proclamatory: God is the source of the whole creative process; it depends at each moment on him. Human beings comprise the one species selected by God to bear his image, to have an I-thou relationship with the source of all being. The reading of this story further points toward the new creation and restoration of the divine image, which had been defaced by sin.

Responsorial Psalm: 104:1-2a, 5-6, 10, 12-14, 24, 35c;
    or 33:4-7, 12-13, 20, 22

Psalm 104 is a hymn of praise to God for his works in creation. The dominant theology of the Spirit in the wisdom literature ("the Spirit of God fills the world") stresses the work of the Spirit in the created order. By contrast, the New Testament concentrates almost exclusively on the eschatological work of the Spirit. The pneumatology of the New Testament is conditioned by its Christology. When the psalmist speaks of the "renewal" of creation through the Spirit, he is probably thinking of no more than the renewal of nature at springtime. But in Christian use it can be reinterpreted to mean the eschatological renewal of creation, a renewal of which the Church is the first fruits.

Psalm 33 is in part a hymn praising God for his creative activity, a theme that is highlighted in the second stanza of the present selection. When this stanza speaks of God's creating the universe by his word, it is thinking of the Genesis story that has just been read: God created the world by saying, "Let there be light," etc. In later development the word of God was hypostatized (Wisdom of Solomon, Philo), and finally in the Fourth Gospel it was identified with the Logos, which thus eventually became the second Person of the Blessed Trinity.

Reading II: Genesis 22:1-18 (long form); 22:1-2, 9a, 10-13, 15-18 (short form)

Special interest attaches to this reading because already in Jewish tradition the "binding" of Isaac was associated with the Passover. The story was expanded to bring out, among other things, the following points: Isaac freely consented to die as a sacrifice, and his sacrifice was victorious, available for the sanctification of humankind. The Isaac story was therefore ready for the early Christians to use as a type of Christ's sacrifice, which is exactly what Paul does in Rom 8:32. There are even suggestions in Judaism that Isaac's reprieve was a kind of death and resurrection, thus making it eminently fitting for use at the Easter Vigil.

Responsorial Psalm: 16:5, 8-11

This psalm is used on the thirty-third Sunday of the year in series B, where   368
it is a direct response to the proclamation of Christ's resurrection. Here
it is a response to the binding of Isaac, in which the Church Fathers saw
a type of Christ's resurrection.

Reading III: Exodus 14:15–15:1

This is the most important reading in the whole series, an importance
underlined by the requirement that this passage must invariably be used.
It appears that its use on this occasion goes back to the earliest days of
Christianity and was probably taken over from the Jewish paschal liturgy.
The crossing of the Red Sea is the supreme type of Christ's death and resurrection, and of the Christian's dying and rising again with him in baptism
(see 1 Cor 10:1-11).

Responsorial Psalm: Exodus 15:1-6, 17-18

This, the Song of Moses, is the most famous of the Old Testament psalms
outside the psalter. Opinions have varied as to its antiquity. Earlier critics
supposed it to be a much later composition because of its apparent
references to later history; but recently it has been thought to have
originated not long after the settlement of Canaan (the Song of Miriam,
in verse 21, is thought to be actually contemporary with the Exodus).
Perhaps the solution is that there was a primitive nucleus to which stanzas were added later as history unfolded. We can well imagine its being
used liturgically in the ancient Passover celebration. All through, it
presumes the Canaanite idea of warfare as a sacred function.

Reading IV: Isaiah 54:5-14

The historical situation in which Second Isaiah delivered his prophecies
was Israel's impending return from exile in Babylon. Much of the language
used to describe this return was drawn from the language used to narrate
the earlier event of the Exodus (see especially Isa 40:1-5). Since the Exodus
came to be regarded as a type for, and a quarry of language for the description of, the Christ-event, it is natural that the language of the return from
exile should be similarly used. Christ's death and resurrection are the
Church's return from Babylonian captivity as well as her exodus from
Egyptian bondage.

   In this passage the image of Yahweh's marriage with Israel is picked
up from the Book of Exodus and reapplied to the Exile. In the Exodus,
God had first taken Israel as a young bride; in the Exile, he had cast her
off like a "wife of youth." But this was only for a brief moment. Now,

in his great compassion, Yahweh is taking her back. (Note the frequency of the word "compassion," a key word in the Gospel record of Jesus' deeds.)

Another image appropriated in this passage is that of the flood. The Exile is like the flood, with Israel as a storm-tossed ark. Again, the flood and its abatement provide an image for speaking about the Christ-event (see 1 Pet 3:20-21).

A third picture is that of the restoration of the city of Jerusalem, rebuilt with precious jewels. This imagery is also taken up in the New Testament and applied to the consummated kingdom, and therefore already mirrored in the life of the earthly Church.

Responsorial Psalm: 30:1, 3-5, 10-11a, 12b

In origin, this psalm is the thanksgiving of an individual for deliverance from death (see first stanza and refrain). Already in Israel, when it was taken up into the hymnbook of the temple, this psalm would have acquired a more corporate meaning, and in Christian usage it celebrates the paschal *transitus* from sorrow to joy: "Weeping may tarry for the night, but joy comes with the morning" (second stanza), and "Thou hast turned for me my mourning into dancing" (third stanza).

Reading V: Isaiah 55:1-11

This reading is an invitation to the eschatological banquet anticipated in the paschal Eucharist: "Come, buy and eat! Come, buy wine and milk" (v. 1). It is the feast of the new covenant (v. 3) with the messianic king ("my steadfast, sure love for David," v. 3). In this banquet the presence of Yahweh is near (v. 6) and available for participation—but on one condition: penitence and the reception of pardon for sin (vv. 6-7).

For this moment all of our Lenten devotions, our going to confession and receiving absolution, have been preparatory; all these exercises are gathered up into this reading. God's ways transcend all our ways (v. 8). He calls into existence things that do not exist, and he gives life to the dead (Rom 4:17). He has raised Jesus from the dead and has raised us from the death of sin to the life of righteousness (see the epistle). In the mission of Christ, God's word did not return to him empty but truly accomplished that which he had purposed in sending it (v. 11).

Responsorial Psalm: Isaiah 12:2-3, 4b-6

Although this passage (the first song of Isaiah, *Ecce, Deus*) occurs in Proto-Isaiah, its spirit is more akin to Deutero-Isaiah. It celebrates the return from exile as a second Exodus and is a new song, patterned on the original song of Moses, as the close verbal parallelism between the third stanza and Exod 15:1 shows. As in the fifth reading, we have here the same four-fold pattern: exodus/return from exile/Christ's death and resurrection/the foundation of the Church and our initiation into it through baptism and the Eucharist.

Reading VI: Baruch 3:9-15, 32–4:4

This passage is typical of the way in which the later Jewish wisdom literature adapted the earlier prophetic teaching about salvation history. The old language of salvation history survives: "Why is it, O Israel, why is it that you are in the land of your enemies?"—language that is reminiscent of the Exile and of the hymns of Deutero-Isaiah. But the exile is no longer located in a geographical Babylon; it has become exile from the true knowledge of heavenly wisdom. Wisdom is here equated with the Torah, or Jewish law, and at the same time hypostatized or personified. The phrase "she appeared upon earth and lived among men" (Bar 3:37) is especially interesting for the student of the New Testament, for it shows how the wisdom speculations of pre-Christian Judaism provided the language and thought-patterns in which the New Testament formulated its faith in the incarnation (see John 1:14).

The inclusion of such wisdom literature among the readings for the Easter Vigil is a salutary reminder that the images of Egyptian bondage and Babylonian exile are now to be taken figuratively. They are descriptions especially applicable to modern men and women, for they speak of alienation from God, a sense of God's absence. This was one of the elements of truth behind the "death of God" theology that was in vogue some years ago.

Responsorial Psalm: 19:7-10

Psalm 19 falls into two distinct halves, perhaps indicating the combination of two different psalms. The first half is a nature psalm and praises God for his gift of sunlight. The second half, beginning with verse 7, praises God for the gift of the light of his law. Today's selection is taken from the second half and follows appropriately upon the reading from Baruch, since wisdom and law (Torah) are closely akin, if not identical.

The refrain highlights the truth that the Lord has the words of everlasting life. The word of God is his self-communication. This self-communication was present in creation, in Israel's Torah, but above all in the life, death, and resurrection of Jesus Christ, the Word-made-flesh, as the Johannine prologue puts it, thereby meaning the whole history of Jesus. The words of everlasting life are therefore spoken supremely in the death and resurrection of Christ. This is God's final word to humankind, his final act of self-communication, which is the source of "everlasting life," authentic existence.

Reading VII: Ezekiel 36:16-17a, 18-28

This is another passage that speaks of the return from exile in Babylon (and other countries—see Ezek 36:24). Ezekiel, like the earlier prophets, understands the Exile as punishment for Israel's sin (v. 19). The return, therefore, must be accompanied by an act of purification: "I will sprinkle clean water upon you . . ." (v. 25), the gift of a new heart (that is, one that is sensitive to the demands of God's law), and a new spirit. Christian faith sees all these purposes fulfilled, not in the return, but in the death and resurrection of Christ, whose benefits are made available by baptism with its accompanying ceremonies (the sprinkling of water and the gift of the Spirit).

In the old, atomized understanding of the Church year, it was customary to think of Pentecost as the birthday of the Church. Our renewed understanding of the unitary character of the Christ-event, celebrated in this Easter Vigil, should remove any sense of incongruity in celebrating the birth of the Church this night.

Responsorial Psalm: 42:2, 4bc; 43:3, 4 or 51:10-13, 16-17

The use of this psalm (Psalms 42 and 43 are really one psalm) at the Easter Vigil is a very ancient tradition. It was originally an individual lament. The psalmist is staying by the springs of the Jordan at the foot of Mount Hermon, lamenting his absence from Jerusalem and from the worship at the temple. Taken in its liturgical context here (recall the former use of Psalm 43 in the priest's preparation before Mass), the psalm expresses the worshiper's sense of God's absence and his/her longing to participate in the liturgy and to be restored to the presence of God.

Psalm 51 may serve as the responsorial psalm when baptism is celebrated at the Easter Vigil. A different selection of verses from this psalm was used on the first Sunday of Lent this year. The first stanza picks up the reference to the "new heart" of Ezek 36:26. The psalm forms a fitting conclusion to our Lenten devotions. Participation in the Eucharist is the supreme moment when we partake in the forgiveness of sins that has been made available by the Christ-event.

Epistle: Romans 6:3-11

This epistle marks the decisive turning point in the vigil service. Here we move from the Old Testament to the New, from type and prophecy to fulfillment (hence the rubric that the altar candles be lit at this point). The basic significance of the vigil service lies in the experience of this turning point. This is the *transitus*, the passing from darkness to light, from death to life, from bondage to freedom, from the old age to the age to come.

This transition, accomplished in our baptism, is possible for us because Christ made it first. But it has to be renewed constantly. Note that the verbs that speak of our dying with Christ are in the past tense (that was accomplished once for all in baptism), while the verbs that speak of our resurrection are hypothetical and future, and depend upon our moral obedience. Our dying to sin with Christ has to be renewed constantly by a daily decision (see 1 Cor 15:31a).

Responsorial Psalm: 118:1-2, 15-16a, 17, 22-23

Selections from this psalm are frequently used in the Easter season. With its reference to the rejection of the stone and its subsequent elevation to be the chief cornerstone, this was perhaps the earliest Old Testament passage that the primitive community applied to the death and resurrection of Christ. It was the basic Old Testament passage for the "no-yes" interpretation of the death and resurrection: the death of Jesus as Israel's (and all humanity's) "no" to Jesus, and the resurrection as God's vindication of him, his "yes" to all that Jesus had said and done and suffered during his earthly life.

Gospel: Matthew 28:1-10

The story of the empty tomb in Matthew's Gospel is best explained as an editing of the more primitive Marcan account by the addition of other oral traditions. The first addition features the earthquake and an elaborate description of the angel (Mark had simply "young man"), the rolling away of the stone, and the angel sitting upon it. This is the nearest thing we have to an actual description of the resurrection in the New Testament. In the apocryphal Gospel of Peter, the angel actually rolls away the stone to let the risen One come out of the tomb. These additions comport awkwardly with the visit of the women, for we are not told whether the women actually saw this happen or whether they arrived after it had happened. If, as we suppose, Matthew has selected features from a popular legend (evidenced more fully in the Gospel of Peter) and combined them with his Marcan material, the effect in his version is that the angel has become no longer the agent of the miracle of the rolling away of the stone but, as in Mark, simply an interpreting angel (*angelus interpres*) for the benefit of the women.

In the episode of the women at the tomb, the following differences from Mark's account are noted: (1) only two women appear: Salome is omitted, apparently to remove the discrepancy between the two Marcan lists of the names of the women—that at the burial and that at the visit to the tomb; (2) the motive of the women's visit to the tomb: in Mark it was to see to the burial rites left unfinished on the eve of the sabbath, while in Matthew it is merely to see the sepulchre; (3) in the angel's (Mark: young man's) instruction to the women, telling them to report to the disciples, the name of Peter is dropped, presumably because Matthew goes on to narrate (28:16-20) a single appearance to all the disciples, without a special one to Peter; (4) Mark's concluding statement about the subsequent silence of the women is omitted as ill comporting with their subsequent conduct.

The third episode in the pericope is the appearance of the risen One to the women. We have no certain clue as to whether this is an earlier tradition or a redactional composition of Matthew. Traditional piety and contemporary Christian feminists agree in wanting it to be genuinely historical, while critics object that its absence from the most primitive lists of appearances in 1 Cor 15:3-8 tells decisively against its primitive character. These critics conclude that it is a product of the tendency to coalesce the originally distinct traditions of the empty tomb and the appearances. For such critics this would be the earliest example of the trend, manifest later in Luke and in John 20, to relocate the appearances in Jerusalem instead of Galilee. It is also an example of the tendency to materialize the appearances.

The Homily
Since series B and C have a different gospel, we will confine our homiletical hints for this year to the gospel reading from Matthew. Mark had left it unclear whether the women delivered the angel's message, but Matthew makes it doubly clear that they did. After hearing the angel, the women departed—not with fear, as in Mark, but with great joy—and ran to tell the disciples. Jesus intercepted them on the way and reinforced the angel's instructions. So the women became the first messengers of the resurrection. All this, of course, is Matthean redaction, and it is uncertain how much of it is historical, especially the appearance of Jesus to the women.

One thing, however, seems to have a firm root in history. This is that the testimony to the empty tomb rests solely upon the eyewitness of women. It was they who reported this to the male disciples. Thus, women had a primary and essential role to play in the witness to the resurrection. Mary Magdalene has for this reason been called "the apostle to the apostles." The homilist might well choose to uphold the importance of the role of these women in the establishment of the Easter faith (see Raymond E. Brown, *The Community of the Beloved Disciple* [New York: Paulist Press, 1979] 189-90).

EASTER SEASON

EASTER SUNDAY

The Easter Sunday Mass is not itself the paschal liturgy. That took place at the culmination of the Easter Vigil. Rather, this is the first of a series of Masses that belong to the great fifty days. In them we reflect upon the post-Easter revelations of the risen Christ and the fruits of our redemption in him. The readings are the same every year.

Reading I: Acts 10:34a, 37-43

New Testament scholars regard the "kerygmatic" speeches of the Acts of the Apostles, not as records of what was actually said by Peter or others on a particular occasion, but as samples of the "kerygma," or basic message of the earliest Jerusalem church. While Luke undoubtedly had a hand in giving them their present shape, they enshrine very early Christological patterns. This sermon, for example, contains the following points:

1) The earthly ministry of Jesus, culminating in his death, met with Israel's rejection of the proffered salvation. The word "tree" calls attention to the scandalous nature of Christ's death: "Cursed is he who hangs on a tree" (Deut 21:23; see Gal 3:13).

2) Christ's resurrection was God's vindication of Jesus and all that he had stood for, in face of his contemporaries' rejection of it. This "no-yes" interpretation of Golgotha and Easter is characteristic of the earliest period.

3) The apostles witness the events from the beginning of the earthly ministry through the post-resurrection appearances.

Note, too, the suggestion, present elsewhere, that the context of the resurrection appearances was, at least sometimes, a meal. The roots of the Christian Eucharist lie not only in the Last Supper but in the meals that the risen Lord celebrated with his disciples after his resurrection.

Responsorial Psalm: 118:1-2, 15-16a, 17, 22-23

Psalm 118, with its reference to the stone rejected and made the headstone of the corner, was perhaps the earliest psalm that the primitive community applied to the death and resurrection of Christ. It was the basic Old Testament text for the "no-yes" interpretation of the earliest kerygma.

Reading II (first alternate): Colossians 3:1-4

"If you have been raised with Christ" is a common turn of phrase. It means "If (and of course you are)." Colossians is more positive than Rom 6 (see the Easter Vigil service) that baptism includes *both* the dying *and* the rising with Christ. But it still maintains two reservations: the resurrection with Christ has to be implemented by constant moral effort; it is a hidden reality that is not finally revealed until Christ's second coming.

69

Reading II (second alternate): 1 Corinthians 5:6b-8

As the Jewish housewife spring-cleaned before Passover to make sure that there was not a crumb of leavened bread left in the house, so Paul, in figurative language, urges the Christians of Corinth to purge the leaven of malice and evil so that they may celebrate the festival of Christ's sacrifice as the true paschal Lamb with the unleavened bread of sincerity and truth. This is the earliest reference we have to the Christian reinterpretation of the Passover. It may even indicate that 1 Corinthians was written with the feast in view.

Gospel: John 20:1-9

This text is a combination of two different traditions. The one is the well-attested and reliable tradition that Mary Magdalene (other names are added in various forms of the tradition, but there is no consistency here) visited the grave of Jesus on Easter morning, found it empty, and reported the fact to the disciples. The other, less attested tradition is of Peter's visit to the grave (see Luke 24:12). (In the earliest and strongly attested tradition, Peter was the recipient of the first *appearance.*) To the less attested tradition John has added the race between Peter and the "other disciple," probably with a symbolic significance. The "other disciple" comes to faith in the resurrection through the mere sight of the empty tomb. In the earlier tradition, however, the disciples come to faith in the resurrection through seeing the risen Lord.

The Homily

Since 1972 there has been much discussion among German Catholic theologians on the question, How does one come to resurrection faith? The debate has centered on whether it was through the Easter appearances, through the empty tomb, or through the prior teaching of the earthly Jesus that the original disciples came to that faith. In today's gospel we have the only example in the New Testament of one who came to Easter faith through the sight of the empty tomb. It might be a suitable theme for the homilist to wrestle with: How do *we* come to Easter faith today?

SECOND SUNDAY OF EASTER

Reading I: Acts 2:42-47

Readings from the Acts of the Apostles take the place of readings from the Old Testament during the Easter season in series A, B, and C. Such readings are appropriate because they show the continuing work of the risen Christ in his Church. Luke, by defining his first volume as a record of all that Jesus *began* to do and to teach (Acts 1:1), implies that his second volume covers what Jesus *continued* to do and teach.

Verse 42 is a succinct characterization of the life of the apostolic Church. Here we see the necessary signs of the presence of the Church. Where these signs are, there the Church is.

1) *The Apostles' Teaching.* The sharp distinction between *didachē* (teaching) and *kerygma* (preaching) was probably overdrawn. Certainly the gospel has to be proclaimed in a different way to outsiders (see the kerygmatic speeches of Acts) from the way it is proclaimed in the ongoing life of the Church. But the teaching here must include the continued preaching of the gospel to the already existing Church, a function that is necessary to keep the Church in being as a Church. In the interest of such teaching, the sayings of Jesus and incidents from his life would have to be remembered and be given shape, and so the gospel tradition would gradually have evolved.

2) *Fellowship.* The Greek word used in verse 42 is *koinōnia,* which means common life, a shared life. In the Christian community this is based on the sharing of the risen Christ's life with his people—what Paul in 2 Cor 13:14 calls the *koinōnia* of the Spirit, and what the Johannine writer means when he speaks of his readers as having fellowship "with us," that is, with those who have seen the risen Christ.

But this vertical dimension of *koinōnia* produces a horizontal dimension. The early Christians, we are told, "had all things in common," the so-called early Christian communism described in the ensuing verses. Of course, such communism was not based on any economic doctrine but was a spontaneous expression of Christian *agapē,* necessitated in any case by the removal of the Galilean fisherfolk to the capital. Nor can it have been so general as Luke suggests in his idealized picture ("*all* who believed"), for when he speaks of Barnabas in 4:36-37, he seems to imply that there was something exceptional in what he did. This shows that the so-called communism was not meant as law for the Church for all time. In Paul's churches it took the form of the collection for the Jerusalem church. Nonetheless, there must be some concrete expression of the horizontal dimension of *koinōnia* as an essential mark of the Church.

3) *The Breaking of the Bread.* Scholars have debated whether this is a reference to the Eucharist or not. If we mean the Eucharist as it later developed (by the time of Paul, for example, when the backward- and forward-looking elements combined), it would be an anachronism to call it such. But verse 46 expands on the brief summary of verse 42 to show that this daily meal had a distinctly sacral character. There we read that they took their food "with glad and generous hearts." The Greek word (*agalliasis*) represented by the English adjective "glad" is a noun meaning exuberant joy at the coming of the Messiah (so Bultmann). This shows that the daily meal was an anticipation of the messianic banquet, a partial fulfillment of the Lord's promise at the Last Supper that he would eat and drink with his disciples in the consummated kingdom of God.

4) *The Prayers.* This rather unspecific term probably refers to participation in the hours of prayer of Jewish devotion. It is curious to find the earliest Christians participating in the prayers of the Jewish temple. Stephen would later have something to say about that, and then the breach between Christianity and Judaism would be widened. The observance of daily hours of prayer, originally a devout practice of individuals, was eventually developed into the monastic office. A private prayer-life is clearly one of the marks of the Christian community.

One more comment. This summary does not mention baptism as one of the signs of the Church's presence. There is an oblique reference to it in the final sentence of our reading: "And the Lord added to their number day by day those who were being saved." Baptism was the means by which this "addition" was effected. The phraseology tells us much about early Christian thinking on baptism. Baptism is an act through which God works, bringing the convert into an already existing community of those who are on the way to final salvation. One does not become a member of the Church as a result of individual decisions to get together after an individual experience of salvation.

Responsorial Psalm: 118:2-4, 13-15ab, 22-24
This is a slightly different selection of verses from the same psalm that was used on Easter Sunday. We refer the reader to our comments there.   72

Reading II: 1 Peter 1:3-9
It is widely believed among contemporary New Testament scholars that 1 Peter is based on an Easter baptismal homily. Some even think that it is a baptismal liturgy, but that is probably going a little too far. Through their baptismal identification with Christ's death and resurrection, Christians have experienced a new birth. But the author warns his readers that

this new life is not yet completely realized. They are being guarded for a salvation to be revealed in the last time, and meanwhile they may have to face various trials and have their faith tested in the fire of persecution.

Speaking with apostolic authority, that is, as one whose faith is grounded on his having "seen" the risen Lord, the author distinguishes himself from his hearers, who depend for their faith on the eyewitness of others because they have "not seen." This adumbrates a theme that is to be developed in the story of Thomas in the gospel that follows.

Gospel: John 20:19-31

This is the traditional gospel of Low Sunday. The author is here wrestling with what became a real problem in the post-apostolic Church: How could one believe in the risen Lord without the benefit of a resurrection appearance? The answer is that even seeing, as in the case of Thomas, is no guarantee of faith. For Thomas, faith came by hearing the word of the risen One addressing him personally. For those who come after, faith comes through hearing the word of God, through hearing the risen One speak through his apostolic messengers.

The Homily

Two themes can be suggested for the homily today. One is the essential marks of the life of a Christian community: the apostles' teaching, the sacraments, prayer, and a common life. These marks must be applied quite concretely to the life of the local congregation.

The other theme is that of seeing/not seeing and believing. This should be related existentially to the doubts of the modern Christian. Perhaps we tend to regard having doubts as something to be ashamed of, so it would be a good thing to bring it all out into the open and to deal pastorally with the problem of doubt.

THIRD SUNDAY OF EASTER

Reading I: Acts 2:14, 22-28

This passage is part of the first kerygmatic speech in Acts, put into the mouth of Peter on the day of Pentecost. It prefaces the central events of the death and resurrection of Jesus with a brief summary of his earthly ministry and concludes with a proof text for the resurrection. As the caption to the reading suggests, it is on this proof text that the emphasis should lie. It was not possible for Christ to be held by the powers of death. Why not? Did his divinity give him an unfair advantage over us? That is to ask the question the wrong way around. The divinity of Christ is rather a confession of faith that we make after being confronted with the story of his fate.

Christ could not be held by the power of death because in his cross he had overcome it. Death, understood at the theological rather than the biological level, means a person's ultimate separation from God as the result of rebellion and consequent alienation. Jesus had faced final separation from God in full obedience to his will right up to the end, and thereby he overcame separation from God. He could not be held by the pangs of death because he was what he was—but what he was did not involve some abstract quality of divinity that gave him unfair advantages over us, but his complete obedience to the will of God, which none of us has ever achieved. The resurrection did not snatch victory from the jaws of defeat or reverse the tragedy of the cross like a *deus ex machina.* The resurrection made manifest what was true of the cross itself—that it was in fact the victory over human alienation and separation from God, over all that the New Testament means when it speaks of sin, the wrath of God, and death.

Responsorial Psalm: 16:1-2a, 5, 7-11

Quite fittingly, the responsorial psalm is the psalm from which the proof text in Peter's sermon in the first reading was taken. Originally this psalm probably contained no hope of life after death, but was a thanksgiving for delivery from a plight near death. But as it passed into Christian usage, it acquired a much deeper meaning in the light of Christ's death and resurrection. It is not really a *proof* text, for it does not prove the resurrection of Christ, but it does show that the God of the Old Testament is the same God who is finally revealed in the resurrection of Jesus Christ, a God who rescues people from the power of death and opens up the path of life.

Reading II: 1 Peter 1:17-21

In this passage the paschal-baptismal associations of 1 Peter again come out clearly. In the Christ-event we were "ransomed by the blood of the Lamb." This primitive Christian language interprets the death of Christ in terms of the Passover. The Passover lamb was not originally interpreted as a ransom for sin or a means of expiation, but it did acquire that meaning in later Judaism. It was this later interpretation of the Passover that gave the early Christians some of the language with which to speak of the significance of the death of Christ. The language may be crude and cultic, but "ransom" does speak of the liberation that Christian experience has always known to be the consequence of Christ's death (though we must not press it and ask to whom the ransom was paid; it must be left at the level of poetry and liturgy). Again, "blood" speaks of the event of the cross, of Jesus' total surrender of his will and life to the Father that was the means of that liberation.

Two consequences of this faith are spelled out for present behavior. At the beginning of the passage, the readers are told, ". . . conduct yourselves with fear throughout the time of your exile." By shifting the metaphor from redemption from Egyptian bondage to a present existence in Babylonian exile, the writer damps down overenthusiastic claims about the consequences of our participation in Christ's resurrection and insists on the "not yet" aspect of it. We do belong to heaven, but we still have to live on earth meanwhile. Therefore "fear"—circumspection—must characterize the Christian life.

But there is a positive side of this "not-yet-ness," too, which is picked up in the final verse of our reading: it is an existence characterized by confidence and hope—not hope that everything will turn out all right (the readers were due for the fiery trial of persecution anyhow), but the hope of final participation in the glory of Christ.

Gospel: Luke 24:13-35

This is the most beautiful of all the appearance stories, and it seems almost blasphemy for the critical scholar to lay hands upon it. Nevertheless, modern New Testament study shows that this story grew up through the years from an original nucleus and became the repository for theological ideas at various stages of development. Finally, Luke, with consummate literary skill, made it into a vivid narrative.

In its present form, the story reflects the pattern of early Christian worship. The self-manifestation of the risen One takes place through the two events of the exposition of the Scriptures and the breaking of the bread. These two events take place in every liturgy; word and sacrament are integral parts of a single coming of Christ to his own.

Over thirty years ago, Karl Barth wrote in his Gifford Lectures the following words: "What we know today as the church service in Roman Catholicism *and* in Protestantism is a torso. The Roman Catholic Church has a sacramental service without preaching. But I wish to speak at the moment not for or against her, but about our own Protestant Church. We have a service with a sermon but without sacraments. Both types of service are impossible." Barth would have to revise his words about Roman Catholicism today, but I wonder parenthetically whether Protestants have paid sufficient heed to his words!

The Homily

There can be no question that today the liturgical preacher will want to expound the Emmaus story as a pattern of what happens in the liturgy. People are often puzzled by the various modes of Christ's presence. In what way is he present in his word, and is he present in a different way in his sacrament? Here is a chance to explain how both word and sacrament are integral parts of a single coming of the risen Christ to his people and to every Christian assembly.

FOURTH SUNDAY OF EASTER

Reading I: Acts 2:14a, 36-41

This reading gives the tail end of Peter's kerygmatic sermon at Pentecost (a substantial part of which was read last Sunday) and goes on to indicate the response of his hearers. The conclusion of the sermon sums up the whole kerygma in a single Christological formula: "God has made him both Lord and Christ, this Jesus whom you crucified." Such a statement puzzles those who approach the New Testament with the presuppositions of later dogmatics. It looks like "adoptionism"—the view that Jesus was a man who was made divine at his resurrection, the later heresy that a colleague of mine once wittily defined as the theory that Jesus was a man but graduated in divinity with honors. This, however, is to read back the later ontological Christology of the patristic Church into the Hebraic parts of the New Testament. Hebrew thought viewed matters in functional rather than ontological categories (see Gregory Dix's book *Jew and Greek*). "Lord" and "Christ" are functional terms, meaning that from the resurrection onward, the risen and exalted One exercised the functions of Messiah and Kyrios. Henceforth he rules over his people, forgives them, nourishes them with his word and sacraments, and commands their obedience. All that God does toward his people is done through Christ. All God's acts bring along with them, as it were, the salvation that Jesus wrought in his earthly history. It is as important to say that *Jesus* is Lord and Christ as it is to say that Jesus is *Lord and Christ*.

The response that preaching evokes is, "What shall we do?" The answer is, "Repent and be baptized." Repentance in this context does not merely mean sorrow for past individual sins but a radical reassessment of Jesus and his significance. By crucifying him, Jesus' contemporaries rejected him. For them, he was not the emissary of God, the bringer of salvation, but either an impostor or a deluded fanatic. Now they must reassess him: he *is* the emissary of God and the bringer of salvation. Baptism is the event in and through which converts are brought into the sphere of his salvation. They receive forgiveness of sins, which again has a far richer meaning than the remission of individual peccadilloes—it means God's eschatological salvation in its wholeness. And they receive the gift of the Holy Spirit, for baptism "adds" them to the Spirit-bearing community (see the first reading for the second Sunday of Easter).

74

Responsorial Psalm: 23:1-6

The theme of Christ as Good Shepherd, which used to belong to the second Sunday after Easter, has been transferred to this Sunday. This, the most familiar of psalms, introduces the shepherd passages in the second reading and the gospel.

In the original psalm, it was Yahweh who was the Shepherd. When the Greek-speaking Christians adopted the title *Kyrios* for the exalted Christ, as a translation of the Aramaic *mari* (cf. *Marana tha*), the consequence was that many of the passages in the Greek New Testament that spoke about Yahweh-Kyrios were transferred to Christ-Kyrios. This did not involve any compromise of Old Testament Jewish monotheism. It meant that henceforth the exalted Christ is that aspect of the being of God that is turned toward us in saving action. Ultimately, of course, this would lead to the formation of the doctrine of the Trinity. Meanwhile, even the earliest Church believed that God acts in us through the exalted Christ. Through him God exercises his Lordship, which includes his work as Shepherd, the one who nourishes and defends his people.

Reading II: 1 Peter 2:20b-25

This is the traditional epistle for Good Shepherd Sunday. We recall that the materials used in this letter were taken from a baptismal homily. The author is exhorting his readers to be patient. He holds up Christ in his passion as an example, quoting an early hymn that draws upon the suffering servant song in Isa 53.

But, as so often happened when things were quoted, the author continues to quote when he gets beyond the point he wishes to make, and speaks of Christ's passion not merely as an example of patience but as redemptive: "He himself bore our sins in his body on the tree." "Tree" was an early Christian designation for the cross, recalling with defiant apologetic the Deuteronomic curse on all who hanged upon a tree. Christ's wounds bring healing, and by his redemptive death we are enabled to die to sin and live to righteousness.

At this point the writer turns from the hymn to his readers. He recalls their conversion and tells them that, having strayed, they have now returned to the Shepherd and Guardian (the Greek word is *episkopos*, "bishop") of their souls. This last phrase throws an interesting sidelight on the development of the Church's ministry by the time 1 Peter was written. While formally it was the ministerial designations (shepherd-pastor and bishop) that provided Christological titles, it was really the other way around. The Church's ministers are bishops and shepherds because it is through them that the risen Christ exercises his shepherding and overseeing.

Gospel: John 10:1-10

There is a long and complicated history behind the discourse of the Good Shepherd. It begins with a fusion of two parables (vv. 1-3a and 3b-5). In the first parable the picture is of a sheepfold into which two parties seek to enter—a prowler and the shepherd himself. The second parable concerns the relationship between the sheep and the shepherd on the one hand, and the stranger on the other.

The combined parables are followed by an allegorical interpretation in which the Johannine Christ successively identifies himself with the gate and the shepherd. Today New Testament scholars would regard the two parables as originally separate and possibly authentic parables of Jesus. The fusion must have happened in oral transmission, while the allegorical interpretation would be the work of the evangelist himself.

The first parable is a challenge to Israel's religious authorities. Will they accept Jesus' message? This challenge must belong to the final part of Jesus' ministry in Jerusalem. In the second parable, the situation is earlier in Jesus' ministry. He can offer no external credentials for his authority, but there are those who respond in faith to his message because they hear in it the authentic voice of God.

In the last analysis, both identifications of Jesus—gate and shepherd—make the same point. The risen Christ is the One who nourishes his people in his word and sacraments, giving them life and enabling them to have it abundantly.

The Homily

The theme of Christ the Shepherd binds the psalm, the second reading, and the gospel together. As Shepherd, Christ feeds his Church through the apostolic ministry. This should be the subject for today's homily. In expounding it, the homilist may also draw upon the first reading, which speaks about baptism. The ostensibly adoptionist Christology of that reading can be used to draw out the fact that it is the risen Christ who is the Good Shepherd. It is not just that Jesus was a good shepherd during his earthly ministry—through the resurrection "Jesus' cause continues."

FIFTH SUNDAY OF EASTER

Reading I: Acts 6:1-7

For the New Testament scholar, several problems are raised by this story. The main one is that although we are told that the seven men were appointed to "serve tables" in order to allow the apostles to give their undivided attention to the ministry of the word, nevertheless the only members of the seven whom we hear about after their appointment turn out to be themselves notable ministers of the word, namely, Stephen and Philip. Probably this confusion is due to the author of Luke-Acts, who sees in the appointment of the seven the institution of a subordinate ministry (deacons?—he uses the verb *diakonein*, meaning "serve" but does not actually call them deacons).

In actual fact, however, the seven must have been more than that. They must have been, in a real sense, leaders of the growing Greek-speaking part of the community. In that case, the real concern of the apostles in recognizing the seven would have been to prevent a split between the Greek-speaking and the Aramaic-speaking Christians (Hellenists and Hebrews). Perhaps even the act of ordination—laying on of hands with prayer—reflects the practice at the time Luke wrote rather than that of the earliest Church (see also Acts 13:3 and 14:23, which are probably equally anachronistic). Nevertheless, ordination by the laying on of hands with prayer must have been introduced in a Palestinian-Jewish environment, for it reflects the synagogue practice of ordaining elders—a fact that has even led some modern scholars to suppose that the seven were appointed presbyters (elders) rather than deacons. But this is improbable. The truth more likely is that we have here two levels of interpretation: (1) the original historical situation, that is, the tensions mentioned above and the recognition of the leaders of the Greek-speaking group by the Twelve, thus averting a breach between the two parties; (2) the origins of a subordinate ministry.

Responsorial Psalm: 33:1-2, 4-5, 18-19

As a psalm of thanksgiving for the mighty acts of God in salvation history, this selection is appropriate for the Easter season, particularly since the last stanza refers to deliverance from death. Originally, of course, this was a reference to deliverance from some natural calamity, probably famine, which is mentioned in the last line. In the context of this Easter liturgy, this can be given a full Christian sense. In his resurrection Christ has indeed delivered the souls (lives) of his people from death.

Reading II: 1 Peter 2:4-9

We recall that 1 Peter is full of baptismal references. Originally, perhaps, this passage was an instruction for baptismal candidates. It tells them the nature of the community into which they are being admitted. It is a temple (the place of God's presence) made up of living stones (that is, men and women). It is, like the people of the old covenant (Exod 19:6), a holy or royal priesthood, a distinct race and nation. Special stress is laid upon the priestly aspect of the community, for only this aspect is spelled out in terms of implied functions. The community expresses its priestly character by offering up spiritual sacrifices acceptable to God through Jesus Christ and declares the wonderful deeds of him who calls it out of darkness into light.

Between this exposition of the nature of the Church there is inserted a string of Old Testament quotations, connected by the theme of the stone (Isa 28:16; Ps 118:22; Isa 8:14-15) and applied to the person and work of Christ. These quotations were evidently suggested by the reference to the composition of the Church out of living stones. This reminds the author that Christians, as living stones, are joined together by Christ, who is the cornerstone. Remove the prosaic quotations and we have what may have been an early (baptismal?) hymn about the Church.

This is the *locus classicus* in the New Testament on the theme of the Church's priesthood. It was, of course, the passage that inspired the Reformers to reassert the doctrine of the priesthood of all believers. Though it was understandable, it was a pity that they had to assert it polemically against the late medieval doctrines of ministerial priesthood, obscuring therefore the priestly understanding of the ministry.

A book by an American Lutheran scholar, John H. Elliott, has sought to cut the ground from under this polemic by insisting that (1) there is a basic difference between the priesthood of the Church as predicated in Exod 19:6 and the cultic priesthood of Leviticus, and (2) the sacrifice offered by the Christian community is not cultic but ethical—the living of a Christian life in the world.

It is a helpful insight that the priesthood of the Church is based on Exodus rather than Leviticus. This protects the teaching of the letter to the Hebrews that Christ has once for all replaced the sacrifices of the Levitical priesthood by his redemptive act, and that any priesthood we predicate of the Church or its ministry can never abrogate the "once-for-allness" of his sacrifice and the uniqueness of his priesthood. Nor can it be denied that the author of 1 Peter sees the Exodus-type sacrifice of the Church as being actualized and made visible to the world in the quality of its ethical life.

Nevertheless, I wonder whether we can exclude cultic ideas altogether from this passage. The "spiritual sacrifices" offered by the Church do not exclude the "declaring" (or recital) of the wonderful deeds of God in salvation history. Here is the primary focus of the Church's priesthood, and this is what the Church does in the liturgy. Of course, this issues or should issue in a lifestyle in the world. But its cultic basis must be preserved or the whole conception of sacrifice will evaporate. The great Eucharistic Prayer (traditionally called the "canon" in the West and the "anaphora" in the East) is the occasion *par excellence* when we "show forth," "declare" or recite before God in thanksgiving his mighty acts of salvation. This is the primary work of the Church. For this we are baptized, and for this we renew our baptismal vows at Easter.

Gospel: John 14:1-12

What C. H. Dodd wrote some years ago about the First Epistle of John is equally applicable to the discourses in the Fourth Gospel: "The argument is not closely articulated. There is little direct progression. The writer 'thinks around' a succession of related topics. The movement of thought has not inaptly been described as 'spiral,' for the development of a theme often brings us back almost to the starting point—almost, but not quite, for there is a slight shift which provides the transition to a fresh theme."

This special pattern makes an analysis of a passage like today's gospel very difficult. A number of themes arise in succession:

1. Jesus' impending departure, that is, his death and exaltation.

2. (linked by the key word "way") Jesus as the revelation and the *way* to the Father.

3. Following this, a dialogue with Philip unfolding this Christological affirmation: Jesus as the revelation of the Father, a reference to the words and works of Jesus as the words and works of the Father, words and works that make him the revelation of the Father.

4. A challenge to believe Jesus, preferably because of encounter with his whole person or, if not that, at least because of his works.

5. The promise that believers will do even greater works because of Jesus' departure—which brings us back almost to where we started.

Obviously there is much in this passage that could be developed for a homily. The liturgical season, with Ascension Day approaching, suggests that we read it because of what it says about Jesus' departure to the Father. No doubt when the farewell discourse was first chosen in the traditional Lectionary for the lessons of the old "great forty days," our forefathers equated this departure with the ascension as a separate event and thought of the discourses almost as though they were delivered by the risen Christ during the great forty days.

Our understanding of the Easter event today, as well as of the farewell discourses, is more sophisticated. For us, the "going" of Jesus to the Father is the whole complex event, celebrated throughout the great *fifty* days— his resurrection, exaltation, appearances, and the gift of the Spirit. And the farewell discourses themselves, while doubtless enshrining the traditional sayings of Jesus, are meditations of the Johannine community upon the meaning of this total complex of events.

For us, the important message of today's pericope is that the risen, exalted Christ continues his words and works in his Church. Are these "greater works"—the word and the sacraments—greater because they will actually mediate the divine salvation, whereas the words and works of the earthly Jesus only pointed forward to, and prepared for, the central saving acts? His departure from earth was preparatory for his continual coming to his Church.

The Homily

It seems artificial to try and detect any single theme running through today's readings. Each theme is, of course, related to the others because of the Easter season. Here are various lines that could be developed, depending upon the homilist's knowledge of the local situation of the congregation:

1. The bridging of tensions between conflicting views or groups within the Church.

2. The need for adapting the apostolic ministry to the challenges of a new world.

3. The priesthood of the Church in liturgy and life.

4. The true meaning of Christ's "departure"—in order to be ever present with his community at all times in all places through the "greater works" that his Church performs.

SIXTH SUNDAY OF EASTER

Reading I: Acts 8:5-8, 14-17

The Acts of the Apostles is planned to trace the expansion of the Church's mission from Jerusalem, Judea, and Samaria to the ends of the earth (Acts 1:18). The campaign undertaken by Philip, one of the seven, after the martyrdom of Stephen marks, for Luke, a decisive stage in the execution of this plan (Samaria). Equally important for Luke is the concern that each successive stage should receive the imprimatur of the original Jerusalem community and its apostles. Hence the curious anomaly that in this story baptism does not convey the gift of the Spirit, as is normally the case in Acts, but has to await the arrival of Peter and John to lay hands on the Samaritan converts.

In later times, especially in Anglican thought during the past century and in revisions of the Book of Common Prayer produced in the 1920's, this passage was taken as the Magna Charta for the episcopal confirmation of children baptized in infancy. This exegesis has thus passed into the theology of the average Anglican parish priest without question. Let it be said with all emphasis that such an interpretation has no foundation in this passage, in the rest of the New Testament, or in the early Fathers. The author of Luke-Acts knows nothing of "confirmation" as a separate rite, distinct from baptism, performed by the apostles or their successors (however justifiable such a development may have been in later times, granted the practice of infant baptism). Rather, he is concerned with one of his major theological themes—the maintenance of the ties between the expanding mission of the Church and the Mother Church at Jerusalem as the center of salvation history.

Responsorial Psalm: 66:1-3a, 4-7a, 16, 20

Precisely the same selection of verses from Psalm 66 is used on the fourteenth Sunday of the year in series C. The only variation here is the optional substitution of the Easter Alleluia for the refrain. However, this is an excellent example of the way in which the liturgical use of Scripture is itself an exegetical act.

482

The psalm originally celebrated some historical deliverance of the nation. It picks up the traditional language of the Exodus: "He turned the sea into dry land; men passed through the river on foot" (stanza 3). Now, in this season, the mighty acts thus described as an exodus become the resurrection of Christ and our participation in it through baptism.

Reading II: 1 Peter 3:15-18

The baptismal material in the first part of 1 Peter, which runs through 4:12, includes warnings of possible persecution (after 4:12 the tone changes and the persecution becomes actual). The references to persecution in the present passage are contingent in character: "Always be prepared . . . *when* you are abused . . . *if* that should be God's will." The newly baptized, thrilled at their admission to all the privileges of the people of God as detailed in last Sunday's second reading, are here reminded that it will not be smooth sailing all the time. They must know what they are in for. Indeed, how could it be otherwise, since the Christian life is a following in the footsteps of Christ? That is why the passage ends with a quotation from an early Christian hymn about the death and resurrection of Christ (the hymn continues beyond the present reading through verse 22).

The words "the righteous for the unrighteous" are thought to have been added to the hymn so as to adapt it to its present position (see vv. 14, 16), in which the passion of Christ is treated as an example for the persecuted Christians to imitate. In this way we see how a hymn receives new applications by being taken up successively into new contexts, namely (1) into a baptism homily; (2) into a letter warning Christians for whom persecution is an impending reality; (3) as used in today's liturgy, where the whole passage receives yet another interpretation.

Gospel: John 14:15-21

We see here the same kind of spiral thought that characterizes the farewell discourse throughout and of which we spoke in our comments on last Sunday's gospel. The points made are:

1. Love of Christ means obedience to his commandments.

2. The promise of the Paraclete (rsv: "Counselor") sent by the Father in response to the prayer of the Son.

3. The Spirit, whom the world cannot receive, will dwell in the community.

4. The coming of the Spirit is equivalent to the return of the Son and almost completely fulfills the primitive expectation of the parousia.

5. The world will no longer see the Christ, but the community will (a) see him, (b) live because he lives, (c) know the mutual indwelling of Christ with the Father and of Christ with the community.

6. This indwelling is a relationship of mutual love that includes obedience to Christ's commandments.

It will again be noted how point 6 brings us full circle to where we were at point 1. Yet, the spiral leads to an enrichment of understanding. The Christian life is not an external observance of Christ's commandments but an intense relationship of the community to the three Persons of the Trinity, each with a specific role to play in this relationship. The Spirit conveys the presence of the Son, who reveals the Father. But this intense personal relationship is not dissolved into mere emotion; it is concretely and soberly manifested in a life of obedience to Christ's commandments.

The departure of Jesus does not mean that he is now absent. It means his ever-renewed presence through the coming of the Spirit to the community. That is the Easter message of this gospel reading.

The Homily

In the latter part of the Easter season we move from the contemplation of the resurrection appearances to meditation upon the continued presence of the exalted Christ with his Church through the Spirit. Thus, the first reading and the gospel can be linked together. The Church is a community in which the Spirit is given and shared. This means (a) a unity with the apostolic community and the Jerusalem church, which was the center of salvation history; (b) communion with the risen Christ, and through him with the Father—a Trinitarian experience; (c) not an ecstatic experience necessarily (though such experiences may be granted *ubi et quando visum est Deo*), but keeping the commandments is the touchstone of the love of Christ and the indwelling of the Spirit.

These themes could be related to the charismatic renewal and/or the phenomenon of the underground Church where these are relevant to local conditions.

ASCENSION

First, let us remind ourselves that Ascension Day should not be thought of as a historical commemoration. The New Testament treats the ascension as an integral part of the Easter event. In fact, the earlier Easter narratives depict the appearances as manifestations of the already risen and ascended One. Hence Paul could include his Damascus experience among the appearances in 1 Cor 15.

The later appearance narratives (Luke and John) show a tendency to separate the resurrection and the ascension, but still they are not regarded as two successive events. They are separated in order to contemplate the meaning of two aspects of a single, indivisible event. When this separation occurs, the ascension seems to be variously located: in Luke 24, on Easter Sunday evening or, at the latest, the next day; in John 20, sometime between the appearance to Mary Magdalene (who is told not to touch the risen One because he has not yet ascended) and the appearance to Thomas (who is invited to touch him); in Acts 1, after the forty days (which, however, are symbolic of the time of revelation; there may be no intention to suggest that the ascension actually "occurred" on the fortieth day). For several centuries the Church did not, either in its writings or in its liturgy, treat the ascension as though it actually "occurred" on the fortieth day. With the revised Church calendar, we still keep it on the fortieth day as a matter of convenience (and that this is not an absolute rule is indicated by the rubrical permission to transfer the observance to the following Sunday). This allows us to isolate for contemplation one aspect of the total Easter event.

Reading I: Acts 1:1-11

It is curious that in his two-volume work Luke tells the story of the ascension twice (Luke 24; Acts 1). Each narration brings out a different aspect of the truth. The version in Acts looks forward to the future, to the inauguration of the Church's mission and the final return of the ascending One. Luke's perspective on salvation history represents an adjustment. Salvation history, already in the Old Testament , is constantly readjusted in the light of earlier events. The earliest Church looked for only a brief interval between the ascension and the parousia, an interval that would be marked by the apostles' mission to Israel and by persecution and martyrdom. Now salvation history is greatly extended. Paul already had modified it to include the mission to the Gentiles. Now, for Luke, the Church is here to stay, with a mission to the whole civilized world. But the hope of the parousia is still maintained, and the Church's mission is viewed as a preparation for the end.

Responsorial Psalm: 47:1-2, 5-8

This is one of the enthronement psalms, which, according to some scholars, were sung at a (hypothetical) annual feast at which the king was enthroned to symbolize Yahweh's kingship over his people. As the king took his seat upon his earthly throne, the whole people would have chanted this psalm in celebration of the kingship of Yahweh. The Church in its liturgy has associated this psalm with, and transferred it to, the ascension of Christ. Ascension Day is the feast of Christ's enthronement. Henceforth God exercises his sovereignty over the universe through his exalted Son.

Reading II: Ephesians 1:17-23

Ephesians, whether written by Paul himself or, as now seems more likely, by a close disciple steeped in the thought of his master, begins, like most of Paul's letters, with an opening thanksgiving and prayer. This prayer reproduces the pattern and phraseology of a liturgical hymn.

The first part of our passage prays for the Church's growth in wisdom and knowledge, and looks to the risen and ascended Christ for the power to foster this growth. The hymn then goes on to elaborate on the exaltation and kingship of Christ. The New Testament views Christ's kingship as exercised in two concentric circles. The inner circle embraces the Church, where his kingship is known and acknowledged; the outer circle embraces the world, where he is de facto king but his kingship is as yet unrecognized

(O. Cullmann). The Church's function is to extend that inner circle to cover more and more of the outer one.

Gospel: Matthew 28:16-20

As we noted in our introduction to this feast, the earlier Easter narratives saw the appearances as manifestations from heaven of the already risen and ascended Christ. This is still the situation in Matthew's story of the final appearance in today's gospel. It is the ascended One who says, "All authority in heaven and on earth has been given to me." It is the ascended One who commissions his apostles and sends them out into the world in the great missionary charge (see Eph 4:8-13, where the apostolate appears as the gift of the ascended Christ).

The final appearance takes place on a mountain. This, for Matthew, has theological significance. The great sermon had been preached on a mountain. The transfiguration took place on a mountain, as in the other Synoptists. And now the great appearance also takes place on a mountain. This is, in fact, the only appearance that Matthew records, apart from the personal and private one to the women (28:9-10). All the meaning of the resurrection appearances is, for Matthew, compressed into this single story. Such a device was probably suggested to him by the angel's charge to the women in Mark 16:7 to tell the disciples to go to Galilee, where they would see the risen Lord. The primary significance of the appearances is that they are *revelations* of the risen One. Because they are revelations, they can be doubted as well as believed. But those who do believe respond in adoration (v. 17).

In his opening words about his authority, the risen One echoes the language about the Son of man in Dan 7:14 in the wording of the Greek Old Testament, a fact that suggests that this story must have crystallized in the Greek-speaking Church.

The declaration of authority is followed by a missionary charge in three parts:

1. The disciples are commanded to "make disciples" of all nations. This is typically Matthean phraseology (cf. Matt 13:52; 27:57). The longer ending in Mark, which has "preach the gospel" (16:16), probably represents the earlier tradition, which Matthew has reworded to suit his own interests. The association of the appearances with the command to mission goes back to the earliest tradition, as the word "apostle" itself shows, as do the terms in which Paul speaks of his own call on the road to Damascus (Gal 1:16).

2. As in Mark 16:16, the call to mission includes the charge to baptize. All our evidence agrees that baptism was practiced by the Church

right from the outset, and this despite the fact that baptism had not been a feature of the Lord's public ministry. This remains true even if there was an earlier period when Jesus worked side by side with John the Baptist and during which he too baptized.

There can be no doubt that it was the impact of the post-resurrection appearances that led to the revival of baptism by the earliest Christians. Baptism became the way in which those who had not had a firsthand encounter with the Christ-event were brought into its sphere. The command to baptize given by the risen One in Mark and Matthew (see also the allusions to the forgiveness of sin in the appearance stories of Luke and John) is a verbalization of this experience.

In the earliest community and for some time, baptism was administered in the name of Jesus. It is only in this passage of Matthew and in the *Didache,* a Christian writing probably dating back to the end of the first century, that we hear of the threefold formula. One may say, however, that the use of Jesus' name alone as a baptismal formula implies the threefold name, for baptism in the name of Jesus implies the confession of him as the Messiah ("Jesus is Lord" was probably the earliest baptismal confession), and in Jewish context Messiah means the agent of God's final salvation, while the bestowal of the Spirit is a consequence of messianic salvation.

Hence, we may say that from the earliest date the Jewish Christians would have understood baptism in an implicitly Trinitarian sense. The development of the threefold formula would have become necessary in Gentile communities, where the implications of the primitive confession of Jesus as Lord were no longer understood and had to be spelled out. This does not mean that we should now go back to the single formula of earliest times. That would have quite a different meaning now—the repudiation of what was implicit in the earliest use of the single formula.

3. The command to baptize is followed by a charge to teach. It is not clear whether this teaching means post-baptismal instruction. "Baptizing" is a present participle in the Greek, as in the English translation, and this could suggest teaching accompanying baptism, that is, catechetical instruction.

After the charge to teach comes a final promise of the permanent presence of the ascended Christ from now until the parousia. This is a far cry from the perspective of the earliest community, which thought of the interval between the ascension and the second coming as a period of Christ's temporary absence (Acts 3:21). The wording of this promise thus verbalizes the experience of Christ's presence, an experience made possible for the Church through the gift of the Spirit and in the cultus during the intervening period.

The Homily

There is a wealth of material here for the preacher, and the selection must be guided by local conditions. Perhaps the strongest point of emphasis this year, as one compares Matthew's story of the ascension with Luke's, is the great missionary charge. We live in a time when Christians are ready to bend over backwards to be nice to people of other religions. Dialogue rather than evangelism and conversion is the contemporary watchword. There is a biblical justification for this, insofar as we should see the truth that is in other religions as the revelatory work of the Logos that became incarnate in Christ.

But Christian faith cannot remain content merely with dialogue. Somehow or other that dialogue must be steered to the confession before persons of other religions that "what they ignorantly worship, that we declare" to them. The same word that has spoken in their own religious experience has finally spoken in the flesh of Jesus. The mode of following the imperative to go into all the world may change. For Matthew, it had already come to mean "make disciples" rather than "evangelize," that is, the emphasis was on catechetics. But the imperative must, in one way or another, be obeyed.

SEVENTH SUNDAY OF EASTER

Reading I: Acts 1:12-14

These verses form a link between the ascension story and the election of Matthias. They presuppose the Lucan scheme, in which the ascension is depicted as an event distinct from the resurrection, and the coming of the Spirit as yet another distinct event, forty and fifty days respectively after Easter.

The "upper room" was certainly historical (see the Last Supper account and Peter's return to the house of John Mark's mother in Acts 12:12). There are four lists of the Twelve in the New Testament: Mark 3:16-19; Matt 10:2-4; Luke 6:14-16; and the present passage, Acts 1:13. They contain slight variations both in the names themselves and in their order. Even between the list in Luke's Gospel and that in Acts there is one variation: in Acts, John is placed before James, probably because he is to appear later in Acts as Peter's right-hand man.

By adding "and children" after "women," the Western text took "women" to mean "wives." Some think that the Western text was correct in its understanding of "women." We know from Paul that Peter and other apostles were married. This is the last appearance of Mary, the mother of Jesus, in the New Testament. It is striking that our last picture of her should be as a member of the believing community engaged in waiting and prayer.

Granted the Lucan schematization, which separates the resurrection, exaltation, and coming of the Spirit, today's reading is eminently suitable for the period between the liturgical observance of Ascension and Pentecost. This period Karl Barth once designated a "significant pause." It is a pause between the actions of God, a pause in which all the community can do is to wait and pray. It may seem paradoxical, but although the Spirit came, in Johannine language, "to abide with you [the community] for ever," the Church nevertheless has to pray constantly, *Veni, Creator Spiritus.* The gift of the Spirit is never an assured possession but has to be constantly sought anew in prayer.

Responsorial Psalm: 27:1, 4, 7-8a

A somewhat different selection of verses from this psalm is used on the second Sunday of Lent in series C. The first and third stanzas are the same, but the second stanza is new and the refrain is different (with Alleluia as an alternative, as always in the Easter season). These changes throw the emphasis on the idea of waiting for God to act (the refrain) and on the notion of life in a praying community in the pause between Ascension and Pentecost.

407

Reading II: 1 Peter 4:13-16

The theme of waiting for the Spirit, which used to be expressed in the old epistle for this Sunday (1 Pet 4:7-11 in the Roman Missal and the Anglican and Lutheran books) is unfortunately lost in this selection. One wonders what is gained by the change.

This passage, unlike the old one, takes us into the second half of the letter, which appends to the baptismal homily a warning of imminent persecution. It comes from a period (under Nero? Domitian? Trajan?) when it was beginning to be considered a crime to be a Christian. Christianity was by now recognized as a religion distinct from Judaism but was not classified as a *religio licita.* Consequently, Christians now had to suffer "for the name" at the hands of the state.

Gospel: John 17:1-11a

This reading is taken from the so-called high priestly prayer attributed to the Johannine Christ at the Last Supper. Some commentators, including Westcott and Hoskyns, have preferred to call it the "prayer of consecration" because in it the Johannine Christ is consecrating himself for his redemptive death. He is offering himself to the Father as an obedient sacrifice, for in John "hour" means the hour of the passion. Also, he prays that through his death the Father and the Son may be glorified—in other words, that the Father's redemptive purpose may be accomplished in the Son. This redemptive purpose is defined as the giving of eternal life to those whom the Father has "given" to the Son. A parenthesis or a sort of footnote by the evangelist himself further defines eternal life as knowledge of the Father and the Son. In the Johannine concept of eternal life, the emphasis lies not on that life's duration but on its quality—a life in communion with the Father and the Son.

After the parenthesis the prayer resumes with the theme of glorification in the typically Johannine spiral fashion. But the idea is enlarged to include the earlier life of Jesus, prior to the cross, and the further thought that the glory Christ receives at his exaltation is a resumption of the glory of his preexistent state. Thus, the glory of the cross cannot be seen in isolation but must be held together with the whole incarnate life, of which it is the ultimate expression, and with the preexistent life, which was a continuous act of God's self-communication and revelation.

In its second paragraph the prayer continues to look back on Christ's earthly work, especially the revelation that he had given to his disciples. In the Johannine scheme, this must specifically refer to the farewell discourse at the Last Supper, since it is here that John gives Christ's teaching to the disciples, though it may also include, to some extent, the signs in which the disciples saw his glory (John 2:11; 6:68-69). But it is the words of Jesus that constitute the main content of his revelation. These words are the words that the Father had given to him previously. In receiving these words as the words of the Father, the disciples have come to believe that Jesus is sent from the Father, that is, their response to the revelation that they have received takes the form of a Christological affirmation.

All this is couched in Johannine language, yet it accurately reproduces what is true of the synoptic tradition, and indeed of the historical Jesus. Historically speaking, Jesus proclaimed the kingdom of God. This was the message he had received from his Father in his baptismal call. And when men and women responded to it in faith, they "confessed" him, that is, acknowledged his divine mission.

The last part of our excerpt turns from Jesus' ministry to the fate of the disciples after Jesus' departure. Having received Christ's revelation, they no longer belong to this world, but they still have to live in it. This expresses in Johannine language the same idea as the synoptic Jesus' eschatological saying at the Last Supper: "I will no longer drink of the fruit of the vine [implying that he was to leave them and that they would stay behind] until I drink it new in the kingdom of God [that is, his glorification]." In that saying he consecrated himself in his departure from them as the effective means of their participation in the kingdom of God. Then, exactly following the pattern of the Johannine discourses, the prayer comes full circle, ending as it began. The opening words spoke of the hour of passion; the conclusion speaks of Jesus' coming to his Father.

The Homily

It would seem most appropriate on this Sunday before Pentecost to take the picture of the disciples waiting in the upper room for the outpouring of the Spirit that is the result of Jesus' departure to the Father and his ensuing glorification. This departure and the outpouring of the Spirit enable his disciples to be at once *in* the world, not *of* the world, yet *for* the world, as Jesus had been during his earthly life. This picture should then be related to the life of the contemporary Church, and the prayer *Veni, Creator Spiritus* should be made our prayer today.

PENTECOST VIGIL

Many parishes will in effect observe Pentecost on the Saturday evening before the feast and use the vigil readings. Hence our comments here.

Reading I: Genesis 11:1-9; or Exodus 19:3-8a, 16-20b; or Ezekiel 37:1-14; or Joel 2:28-32 (NAB: 3:1-5)

The Lectionary provides four alternatives for today's first reading: the tower of Babel (Genesis); the theophany at Mount Sinai (Exodus); the vision of the dry bones (Ezekiel); the prophecy of the outpouring of the Spirit (Joel).

The first two passages were undoubtedly in the mind of the author of Luke-Acts when he wrote the Pentecost account. He sees the preaching with tongues, which he interprets as the gift of foreign languages, as a sign of the gospel's transcendence of the divisions among humankind that resulted from the building of the tower of Babel. The gospel speaks to all people in their own language and so restores the unity that had been broken by human sin. The catholic Church is the advance guard of reunited humanity.

The Exodus theophany is probably alluded to in the symbolism of the tongues of fire and the rushing wind. The feast of Pentecost was interpreted in later Judaism as the celebration of the giving of the Law. The early Church sees a contrast between the giving of the Law and the outpouring of the Spirit, a contrast already suggested by Jeremiah and Ezekiel and expounded systematically in the Pauline writings.

The prophecy of Joel is expressly cited in Peter's speech at Pentecost (Acts 2:17-21 = Joel 2:28-32). In the prophet's vision, the descent of the Spirit was probably conceived in somewhat narrow, nationalistic terms. "All flesh" meant, for Joel, all of Israel. His point is that in the renewed, eschatological community the Spirit will not merely descend occasionally upon charismatic leaders, like the judges, kings, and prophets of old, but will be shared by all members of the community.

It is surprising that the passage from Ezekiel is never expressly utilized in the New Testament, though it seems to underlie much of the New Testament thought on the Spirit. Paul in particular associates the Spirit with resurrection—both Christ's resurrection (Rom 1:4) and the future resurrection of the faithful (Rom 8:11). But nowhere does the New Testament speak explicitly of the resurrection of the community as an event within history effected by the gift of the Spirit. Yet, there can be no doubt that the New Testament does understand the Christian community as the people of God, eschatologically renewed. This is evidenced by its appropriation of the titles and prerogatives used in the Old Testament for the community of the old covenant. The vision of Ezekiel has a special appeal today, when there is so much concern for the Church's renewal.

Responsorial Psalm: 104:1-2a, 24 and 35c, 27-28, 29bc-30

This is a hymn of praise to God for his works in creation. The dominant theology of the Spirit in the wisdom literature ("the Spirit of God fills the world") stresses the work of the Spirit in the created order. By contrast, the New Testament concentrates almost exclusively on the eschatological work of the Spirit. The pneumatology of the New Testament is conditioned by its Christology. When the psalmist speaks of the "renewal" of creation through the Spirit, he is probably thinking of no more than the renewal of nature at springtime. But in Christian use it can be reinterpreted to mean the eschatological renewal of creation, a renewal of which the Church is the first fruits.

Reading II: Romans 8:22-27

The first paragraph of this reading picks up the suggestion of the cosmic dimensions of the Spirit's work emphasized in the refrain of the responsorial psalm: "Lord, send out your Spirit, and renew the face of the earth." The Christian community is described as those who have the first fruits of the Spirit, which seems to indicate that the whole cosmos is destined ultimately to be renewed by the same Spirit. But because Christians still exist in the body, they are still part of this creation, and as such they share its groanings, its longing for redemption. The passage does not explicitly say so, but it would be consistent with Paul's apocalyptic expectations elsewhere to infer that the redemption of our bodies means being clothed (2 Cor 5) with the spiritual body (1 Cor 15) and will coincide with the renewal of the whole cosmos, the new heaven and earth.

It is surprising to find Paul here equating "sonship" with the final redeemed state instead of thinking of it as a status already granted in baptism (contrast Gal 4:5-7). At first sight this looks like a flat contradiction, but Paul probably means that the final redemption will make plain what is true of the believers already here and now, though in a hidden way (see 1 John 3:2).

The second paragraph turns to the work of the Spirit within the community here and now. The Spirit helps the infirmity of our prayers by making intercession for us. What does Paul mean by "sighs too deep for words"? Some see here a reference to speaking in tongues—glossolalia— like that at Corinth. Another, more plausible interpretation is that the Spirit takes our inarticulate petitions, translates them into the divine language, and presents them to God as prayer in his name and according to his will.

Gospel: John 7:37-39

On the last day of the feast of Tabernacles, there was a ceremony of drawing water, accompanied by the reading of Isa 12:3. Some commentators think that this provides the background for Jesus' invitation: "If any one thirst, let him come to me and drink."

Two other interrelated questions are much discussed in connection with this passage: What is the source of the quotation in verse 38 ("Out of his heart shall flow rivers of living water"), and whose heart is referred to in the quotation—the believer's or Christ's? It seems best, with Raymond Brown, to take the "his" as Christ's and to see an allusion to Moses' striking the rock to produce water in the wilderness (see 1 Cor 10:4: "the Rock was Christ"). This brings the whole pronouncement into line with John's doctrine of the Spirit. The farewell discourses tell us that Jesus dies to make the Spirit available to his own. When his side is pierced after the crucifixion, water as well as blood comes out in symbolic fulfillment of this promise, while his conferral of the Spirit upon the Eleven after his glorification on Easter Sunday night is its actual fulfillment. This gospel reading reminds us that the gift of the Spirit at Pentecost is the outcome of Christ's redemptive work. Easter and Pentecost are inseparable.

The Homily

There is obviously a wealth of material for the homilist's use, all of it connected with the Spirit. Here are some of the possibilities, depending to some extent on the option selected for the first reading.

1. The gift of the Spirit as the reversal of Babel suggests the universality of the Spirit-filled community. In a day of great international tensions, the Church of Jesus Christ is the one fellowship that *can* transcend all human divisions—yet that affirmation comes as a judgment as well as a promise.

2. Spirit versus law. This topic can be highly relevant to our current discussion of situation ethics.

3. The Spirit as the power of the Church's renewal (Ezekiel's vision).

4. The "democracy" of the Spirit. It is not a gift for occasional leaders or outstanding persons in the community. It is not confined to the hierarchy but is for "all flesh"—sons and daughters, old and young, menservants and maidservants, the simple believer as well as the most exalted church leader (Joel). (Recall the title of Newman's pamphlet: "On Consulting the Laity in Matters of Doctrine.")

5. The natural and cosmic dimensions of the Spirit's work (responsorial psalm and the first paragraph of the second reading).

6. The Spirit as the organ of Christian prayer (second paragraph of the second reading).

7. The Spirit as the outcome of Christ's whole redeeming work, symbolized as the provision of living water (gospel).

The homilist will have to judge which of these suggested themes is relevant to local needs.

PENTECOST SUNDAY

Pentecost originated as a final celebration of the ingathering of the grain harvest, which had begun at Passover. Later Judaism transformed it into a feast of salvation history celebrating the giving of the Law at Sinai and the establishment of Israel as God's people. All these associations were carried over into the Christian feast that marked the conclusion of the great fifty days. The grain harvest and the Law are replaced by the gift of the Spirit, and the constitution of the old Israel is replaced by the constitution of the new. The feast of the Law becomes the feast of the Spirit.

Reading I: Acts 2:1-11

There is no unanimity in the New Testament about a single outpouring of the Spirit. The gospel of the day, as we shall see, places the gift of the Spirit on Easter Sunday evening, while Acts 2 puts it on Pentecost. Originally, perhaps, the gift of the Spirit was associated with each of the resurrection appearances, and perhaps the Pentecost story corresponds to the otherwise unknown appearance to the five hundred (1 Cor 15:6).

Historically, this appearance marks the foundation of the Church as a wider community than the original Twelve and the beginning of the kerygma. Perhaps, as a later part of this story suggests (the crowd's suspicion that the apostles were full of new wine), the beginning of the kerygma was marked by an outburst of glossolalia such as Paul describes as taking place at Corinth (1 Cor 12–14). This earlier concept of glossolalia has been overlaid with a new symbolism (whether due to Luke or to his tradition, we cannot say) in which Pentecost reverses the effect of Babel.

Responsorial Psalm: 104:1ab, 24ac, 29bc-31, 34

For commentary on this psalm, see the vigil.

96

Reading II: 1 Corinthians 12:3b-7, 12-13

Paul's Corinthians were very keen on glossolalia, but its effect on the community was questionable. It led to divisiveness—those who spoke in tongues treated those who did not have this particular gift as second-class citizens.

In reply, Paul insists on several things here. First, to have the Spirit means to confess that *Jesus* is Lord. Here Paul's use of the name Jesus is especially nuanced. "Jesus" means the earthly Jesus, Christ crucified. The Corinthians regarded the death of Christ as a mere episode of the past and put all their money on the purely spiritual, ethereal Christ. Paul recalls them to the centrality of the cross, pricking the bubble of their enthusiasm.

Second, the gifts of the Spirit take different forms, not just the one form of speaking in tongues. Each gift, however unspectacular, has to be used for the common good.

Third, the gift of the Spirit must not lead to individualism but to the building up of the corporate body of the community. The Church is one body through a common baptism and a common "drinking of one Spirit." The latter is probably a reference to the baptismal Eucharist rather than to a rite analogous to the later rite of confirmation (see "supernatural drink" in 1 Cor 10:4). Here is a further suggestion that 1 Corinthians was written for the paschal feast.

Gospel: John 20:19-23

We have already seen that John places the giving of the Spirit on Easter day, and we have discussed the historical and theological grounds for this. Here, as in Acts, the Spirit empowers the Church for its mission ("even so I send you"). The mission is defined here, however, not as kerygma but as the forgiving and retaining of sins. The traditional Catholic and High Anglican interpretation of this has seen it as a reference to the sacrament of penance, but this is probably an anachronism as far as the evangelist is concerned. In the New Testament, forgiveness of sins is baptismal language (see Luke 24:47), and what we have here is the Johannine version of the tradition, which includes in the appearance stories the command to baptize. Our text speaks of the giving or withholding of baptism consequent upon faith or unbelief at hearing the gospel message. Only derivatively and insofar as the sacrament of absolution is a renewal of the baptismal status can this text be stretched to cover the traditional interpretation.

If our new interpretation be sustained, it is significant that both the second reading and the gospel speak of baptism, for in patristic times Pentecost was the day when those who for some reason had missed their baptism at Easter were baptized. Baptism was not continually administered at any time of the year because its corporate significance was paramount.

The Homily

The strong connection between the gift of the Spirit and holy baptism, to which we called attention in our comments on the gospel reading, might suggest that the homilist treat this connection in the Pentecost homily. One of the extravagances of the charismatic renewal, for all its good points, is the suggestion sometimes made that those who were baptized in infancy need a second baptism of the Holy Spirit. One even hears of water baptism being *repeated* after such an experience. It cannot be too strongly emphasized that this is quite contrary to both Scripture and Tradition. When baptism is administered in infancy, full sacramental initiation occurs. If a person later receives a special experience of the Spirit, this can only be understood as a spelling out of the full meaning effectually symbolized in the original baptism, not a *donum superadditum*, a gift additional to what was already received when the person was first baptized.

The homilist might confront the accounts of the giving of the Spirit in Acts and John with each other, pointing up the different theologies that underlie their different chronologies. By tying the gift of the Spirit to Easter, the gospel emphasizes that the Spirit is the gift of the risen One, and as such conveys the benefits of Christ's death and resurrection. The Pentecost story emphasizes the replacement of the Law by the gift of the Spirit as the basis of the life of the new community.

The reading from 1 Corinthians deals with the problems of a local congregation in which there is a great deal of enthusiasm for the *charismata*, or gifts of the Spirit. If this is the case in the homilist's own church, this is a good opportunity to echo Paul's warnings and to speak of the Pauline criteria.

[END OF THE EASTER SEASON]

Sunday after Pentecost
TRINITY SUNDAY

The doctrine of the Trinity, as distinct from triadic formulas and the triadic structure of the biblical experience of God, is implicit rather than explicit in Scripture. What is true of the New Testament, namely, that the Spirit brings believers to faith in Jesus as the one in whom God has acted, is also true, *mutatis mutandis*, of the Old Testament. We see this in the theophany that is the subject of today's first reading.

Reading I: Exodus 34:4b-6, 8-9

The first paragraph speaks of the theophany itself (Yahweh's proclamation of his name), while the second paragraph relates Moses' response to this theophany.

Later Judaism would have boggled somewhat at the suggestion that Yahweh himself "descended" and "passed before [Moses]" in making this proclamation. Such crudely anthropomorphic ideas seemed inconsistent with Yahweh's transcendence. Accordingly, various intermediaries were proposed as the agencies of divine revelation—angels, the *memra* (word) or the Logos, the wisdom or the Spirit of Yahweh. These intermediaries paved the way for the Christian understanding of the incarnation and the Trinity. In revelation—whether the revelation of Sinai or the revelation in the Christ-event—the transcendent Deity goes forth in self-communication out of the depths of his own being. He also creates the response to his self-revelation. This is the triadic pattern of events that we find in the story of the theophany on Mount Sinai: (1) Yahweh in his own essential being; (2) Yahweh going out of himself in self-communication; (3) Yahweh creating within the heart of Moses the response to this self-communication.

This triadic pattern corresponds to the New Testament formulation of God as Father, Son, and Spirit. It is important for the Christian understanding of the Old Testament that Yahweh is not to be equated with the first Person of the Trinity in Christian doctrine but with all three

Persons. Or, in the words of the so-called Athanasian Creed (note that Yahweh-Lord!):

> The Father is Lord, the Son Lord , and the Holy Ghost Lord.
> And yet there are not three Lords but one Lord.

Responsorial Psalm: Daniel 3:29-34 (NAB: 3:52-56)

This canticle, taken from the deuterocanonical portions of the Book of Daniel (and familiar to Episcopalians as the *Benedictus es*) is part of the Song of the Three Young Men, put into the mouths of Shadrach, Meshach, and Abednego (=Ananias, Azarias, and Misael) as they moved unscathed through Nebuchadnezzar's fiery furnace. The second half of the song is the *Benedicite, omnia opera*, also familiar as a canticle. It survives only in Greek, and it is impossible to say for certain whether it is of Hebrew or Aramaic origin. In any case, both parts of the song are impregnated with the liturgical language of the Old Testament psalms.

The first stanza picks up the theme of the "name of God" from the first reading. As we sing this song today, we must remember that for us that name is the threefold name of Father, Son, and Holy Spirit. This could be brought out by adding as a final couplet:

> Blessed art thou, O Father, Son, and Holy Spirit,
> to be praised and highly exalted for ever.

Reading II: 2 Corinthians 13:11-13

The Pauline letters were written to be read out at the Christian assembly. Here, as at the end of 1 Corinthians, this intention becomes perfectly clear—the conclusion of the letter leads into the celebration of the Eucharist. Hence the exhortation to be at peace with one another and to express this by exchanging the "holy kiss" (which, in earlier times, as in some recent revisions of the liturgy, preceded the offertory instead of following the canon). The triadic benediction would therefore fall naturally into place as the introduction to the Eucharistic Prayer (like the salutation before the *Sursum corda* in later times).

There are several places in Paul's letters where a triadic understanding of Christian experience is presupposed (for example, 1 Cor 12:4-6), but only here does Paul deliberately use a triadic formula. Elsewhere (*Anglican Theological Review*, April 1961) I suggested that this triadic formula has its roots in the so-called apocalyptic trinity. Jewish apocalyptic writings sometimes speak of God, the Son of man, and the angels, and this formula is carried into Christian usage as the Father, the Son (of man), and the angels (see Mark 13:32).

Note, however, that the Pauline formula is not a bald dogmatic statement but keeps close to the Christian experience: the *grace* of Christ, the *love* of God, and the *fellowship* (*koinōnia*) of the Holy Spirit. It speaks of the experience of grace, love, and fellowship. The order—Son, Father, Spirit—is striking and again reflects the order of Christian experience. It is in Jesus Christ and his gracious life and death that we encounter the love of God, and this encounter leads to our incorporation into the redeemed community, in which we participate in the common life of the Spirit.

Gospel: John 3:16-18

This lesson was traditionally associated with the Pentecost season, having been used (including verses 19-25) in the old Lectionaries on Monday in Whitsun Week. It is a welcome reform to have this important pericope read on a Sunday at least once every three years, for 3:16 is a succinct summary of the whole Gospel in characteristic Johannine idiom.

Some may feel that its use on Trinity Sunday implies a "binitarian" rather than a Trinitarian conception, for it mentions only the Father and the Son. A similar objection could have been raised against its traditional use on Whit Monday. But it is impossible to dissociate the gift of eternal life, which is the outcome of the sending of the Son, from the Spirit, who is the Giver of life.

As a concluding comment on this passage, we cite some words from an essay on the liturgical sermon written by Canon M. R. Newbolt in the influential volume of Anglican essays called *The Parish Communion* (1937):

"On a spring evening, as I passed through the Abbey gate at Chester, a street evangelist was declaiming his gospel in stentorian tones. 'God so loved the world that he gave us His Son, His only Son. That is what I have to say to you people of Chester. I do not know what you are going to do about it. God gave His Son! Eternal life!'—words hammered by the speaker into his audience with rhythmic, persistent repetition. 'Why,' I thought, 'can we not get this kind of simple gospel appeal inside the Cathedral? Must this message be given in the street, with an implied challenge to the official Church, outside the House of God, under its very walls?'

"Two days afterwards, while we were singing the solemn eucharist in the choir on Whit Monday, the nave of the Cathedral was packed with tourists, casual sight-seers, taking in the Cathedral as part of their day's outing. It happened that I remembered the street preacher; his words were still running in my head, but I had forgotten the opening of the Gospel for the day. It came with a shock of surprise when the Deacon from the chancel steps intoned 'God so loved the world that He gave His only-begotten Son.' These very words, surrounded by what may have been unusual pageantry of lights and coloured vestments, may well have rung in the ears of some excursionist from the Potteries on that very Bank Holiday, as the street missioner's had done in mine."

The Homily

All three readings suggest that the homilist should expound the triune name, not as an abstract formula, but as the basis of the biblical experience of God, both in the Old Testament and in the New. Archbishop William Temple once remarked how the conclusion of the *Veni, Creator* suggests at first sight that the be-all and the end-all of Christian experience is the apprehension of a dogmatic formula:

> Teach us to know the Father, Son,
> And thee of both to be but one.
> That through the ages all along,
> This may be our endless song:
> Praise to thy eternal merit,
> Father, Son, and Holy Spirit.

But then, as Temple meditated on the Christian experience as expounded in John's Gospel, he came to discover that the *Veni, Creator* is talking about our participation in a rich life, the life in which God, as he is in himself, discloses himself in Jesus Christ and enables those who accept him to participate in the *koinonia* of the Holy Spirit. This is the kind of thought the homilist will want to impress upon the congregation today.

Thursday after Trinity Sunday or Sunday after Trinity Sunday
CORPUS CHRISTI

Where the solemnity of Corpus Christi is not observed as a holy day, it is assigned to the Sunday after Trinity Sunday.

Anglicans have certain reservations about this Sunday's provisions. Many of them would use a set of propers provided for the Thanksgiving for the Institution of Holy Communion on the previous Thursday, but few would want its propers to replace those of this Sunday. They also express some reservation about doctrinal feasts (but see Trinity Sunday!) as opposed to the anamnesis of events in salvation history.

Nevertheless, the very genius of Scripture ensures that the readings set forth saving events rather than doctrines. And whatever the final disposition of *An Agreed Statement on Eucharistic Doctrine,* published in 1971 by the Anglican-Roman Catholic International Commission, may be, one can at least go forward with the confidence that many of us talk what is very largely a common language about this subject.

Reading I: Deuteronomy 8:2-3, 14b-16a

This passage comes from a recital of the events of the Exodus and of the wanderings of the Israelites in the desert. It recalls especially the trials to which the people were exposed—hunger, thirst, fiery serpents, and scorpions—and the provisions that Yahweh made to relieve them: the water from the rock and the manna. Paul himself treated the water from the rock and the manna as types of the two great Christian sacraments of baptism and holy communion (1 Cor 10:1-4); and in the discourse of the bread from heaven in John 6, part of which will be read as the gospel of this day, the manna is likewise treated as a type of the Eucharistic Bread.

Responsorial Psalm: 147:12-15, 19-20

The same selection of verses from Psalm 147 is provided for the second Sunday after Christmas. It is appropriate for any festal occasion, but its particular relevance to Corpus Christi is found in the second line of the second stanza: "he fills you with the finest of wheat."

Reading II: 1 Corinthians 10:16-17

One might have expected that the second reading for this solemnity would be 1 Cor 10:1-4, in which Paul interprets the manna of Deut 8 typologically of the Eucharist. Instead, we have a Eucharistic passage from a later point in the same chapter.

It is becoming the commonly accepted view that in verse 16 Paul is quoting a traditional Eucharistic formula. This is indicated by the quite Jewish expression "the cup of blessing." The verb "we bless" is also Jewish (*berakah*) and contrasts with Paul's usual preference for the Greek equivalent, *eucharistein,* "to give thanks." The idea of "participation [*koinōnia*] in the body/blood is probably also Pauline, though Hellenistic, and represents an exegesis of the words over the bread and the cup. *Koinōnia* has not merely a symbolic but a strong realistic sense. "Body and blood" refer not to things in themselves but to an event and a person—to Christ giving himself in his redemptive death. In holy communion he offers real participation in himself as he gives himself to his sacrificial death. This language draws out explicitly the meaning of his words and actions at the Last Supper.

People have often wondered why the usual order—bread/cup—is reversed here and have sometimes speculated that there were early communities that celebrated the Eucharist in this order. This is hardly likely, for Paul himself cites another traditional formula in chapter 11 with the normal order—bread/cup. The reversal must be explained from the fact that Paul wishes to give further comment of his own upon the bread/body word and drops the cup/blood word out of the picture. For verse 17 has to be seen as Pauline comment. And it involves a remarkable shift of sense. The word "body," used Christologically and sacramentally in the traditional formula, is now taken up in an ecclesiological sense. The body is now not the bread but "we," the community that participates in Christ's sacramental body in the Supper. "Participation in Jesus and his (sacramental) body" becomes identical with incorporation into the Church as the Body of Christ (Ernst Käsemann).

Doubtless Paul is led to this exegetical step because of the difficulties at Corinth, which he will elaborate upon in the next chapter. The Corinthians held an all too individualistic attitude toward the Eucharist. For them, it was a guarantee of personal salvation. For Paul, however, it binds one not only to Christ but also to one's neighbors, to the Christian community, with all the obligations that entails. The Eucharist has a horizontal as well as a vertical direction.

It was this passage that inspired St. Augustine to write his well-known words: "If you wish to understand the body of Christ, hear the Apostle speaking to the faithful: 'Now you are the body and members of Christ.' If you, then, are the body and members of Christ, your mystery is laid on the Table of the Lord, your mystery you receive" (Letter 272).

Gospel: John 6:51-58

The bread discourse from John 6 has been much discussed in recent years. The problems are: (1) Is the whole discourse Eucharistic? (2) Are only verses 51c-58 Eucharistic? (3) Are verses 51c-58 a later addition to the text?

It is clear that verse 51c ("and the bread which I shall give for the life of the world is my flesh") represents a turning point in the discourse. The first part speaks throughout of the bread from heaven as typified by the manna. "Eating" is then a metaphor for faith. The word "flesh," introduced for the first time in verse 51c, *could* also refer to the incarnation rather than to the Eucharist, though the words "shall give for the life of the world" extend the thought beyond the incarnation itself to the atoning death. But when we get to verse 53, which speaks not only of eating the flesh but also of drinking the blood of the Son of man, the Eucharistic reference is beyond all doubt. This led Bultmann to regard verses 51c-58 as an interpolation by an ecclesiastical redactor.

In the view of the present writer, the discourse is to be viewed as an integrated whole, without resort to the interpolation hypothesis. The background of the whole chapter is the early Church's celebration of the Eucharist proper in the context of a meal. The first part of the discourse, down through verse 51b, which focuses on the bread from heaven, is, we would suggest, a meditation on the agape. The second half, verses 51c-58, is a meditation on the Eucharist proper and is based on a Johannine tradition of the institution narrative.

Looked at from another perspective, the whole discourse outlines the events of salvation history, the coming of the Christ as the bread from heaven into the world in the incarnation (vv. 26-51b), the surrender of himself in his atoning death (v. 51c), the availability of his surrendered life as the nourishment of the faithful in holy communion (vv. 53-58). John does not regard the sacrament as a thing in itself, detached from the total saving event of Christ, but as the means by which this saving event is constantly made available for present participation in the life of the Church.

We note, too, how in Johannine idiom the double aspect of the Eucharist expressed in the earlier institution narratives (Paul and the Synoptists) is preserved. The Eucharist makes the past present for participation ("flesh" and "blood" referring back to Christ's death on Calvary), and it makes the future ("I will raise him up at the last day"; "will live because of me"; and "will live for ever") equally present ("has eternal life"). Note also that the Eucharistic part of the discourse does not lose sight of the manna typology: "not such as the fathers ate and died."

The Homily

Two possibilities suggest themselves. The theme of manna runs like a thread through the Old Testament reading, the psalm, and the gospel. This can be related to the idea of the Church as the pilgrim people of God for whom holy communion is indeed a viaticum, as the manna was for the Israelites.

Alternatively, the homilist could address the Pauline passage and speak of the Lord's Supper as creative of community. Post-medieval Western piety—whether Reformation, Counter-Reformation, or pietistic—had in various ways individualized the Eucharist in theology and practice. In one tradition, the Mass became the occasion for individual recitation of the rosary. In another, the "quiet early service" was the occasion when the devout individually "tanked up" with grace. In yet another tradition, the Lord's Supper became a duplicate of penance and absolution.

Much of the resistance to the recent liturgical changes is due to the fact that these changes seek to express the corporate dimension of the Lord's

Supper. Our participation in the sacramental body of Christ means that we must express ourselves as his ecclesial body. We who are many become one body in him. The Pauline teaching on the corporate nature of the Eucharist—the two senses of Corpus Christi—needs to be brought out in many places today, while in other places it has been overworked at the expense of personal devotion.

SEASON OF THE YEAR

SECOND SUNDAY OF THE YEAR

Reading I: Isaiah 49:3, 5-6

The readings for this Sunday continue the theme of Jesus' servanthood and its manifestation in the baptism. This accounts for the selection of the first reading, the second of the servant songs in Second Isaiah.

When we compare the second servant song with the first, which we read last week, we note two points of difference. First, the second song states that God formed his servant "from the womb." This consciousness of predestination is characteristic of the Hebrew prophets (see Jer 1:5) and recurs in Paul (see Gal 1:15). Such an idea of predestination must not be allowed to harden into an abstract dogma but must be allowed to remain what it is in the Bible—a doxological expression of faith in a concrete situation. It is this fact that expresses itself in the annunciation and infancy narratives of the Gospels.

The second point to notice is the enhanced emphasis on the universal scope of the servant's mission. The first song simply included the phrase "a light to the nations." The second expands on this. "It is too light a thing" for the servant's mission to be confined to Israel: "I will give you as a light to the nations, that my salvation may reach to the end of the earth."

Responsorial Psalm: 40:1, 3ab, 6-9

This is a personal psalm of thanksgiving for deliverance from tribulation. The psalmist is determined to give thanks not only with his lips but also in his life. He offers his will in obedience to the will of God. This, he says, is what God desires, not sacrifice and burnt offerings or sin offerings. While this looks like a total repudiation of all cultic sacrifice, we have to remember that this psalm was recited precisely as an accompaniment to the offering of just that—a cultic sacrifice. What the author must mean is that self-oblation must accompany cultic sacrifice, not that the latter must be abandoned in favor of the former.

Yet, as the author of the letter to the Hebrews perceived (Heb 10:5-10), this critique of cultic sacrifices points forward to their abolition by Christ's own sacrifice of himself in perfect obedience to the Father. The sacrifices of the old covenant were permitted to last for several centuries as a witness not only to their own inadequacy but also to the impossibility of a human being's offering the perfect oblation of his/her will. It would have been all too Pelagian to suppose that a human being could. So the sacrifices and the prophetic critique of them had to carry on until the appearance of the one true sacrifice.

The use of this psalm in Hebrews sanctions its Christological inter-pretation, and it is in this sense that it is used in the liturgy today. This is a song of Christ the servant offering himself in his baptism to a life of total obedience to the Father's will, a life that will lead him to a ministry to the poor and the outcast, the sick and the suffering, culminating on Calvary. All this will be the subject of the gospel readings in the coming months.

Reading II: 1 Corinthians 1:1-3

Today we begin the reading of extracts from 1 Corinthians in course. Here we have the introductory greeting in the conventional style of all ancient letters: "A to B, greeting." But, as usual, Paul Christianizes the epistolary convention. He is Paul, "called by the will of God to be an apostle of Christ Jesus." His addressees are the Church of God, those sanctified in Christ Jesus, called to be saints. And his greeting is a Christian blessing: Grace and peace.

The most striking feature in this heading, however, is Paul's emphasis on the universality of the Church. He reminds the Corinthians that they are the Church of God "which is at Corinth." They are the local embodi-ment of the universal *Ecclesia*. There can be only one people of God, and each congregation is nothing by itself but is only a manifestation of that one people.

Paul reminds the Corinthians that they are not alone—they are called to be saints together with all those who in every place call on the name of the Lord Jesus Christ, and that that Lord is the Lord of those other churches as well as their own. The Corinthians were engrossed in their own spiritual progress and their own problems. They were congregational in a bad sense, in that they thought they were the whole people of God, living on their own. A local church can, of course, be congregational in a good sense if it realizes the supreme dignity of its vocation to be the representative and embodiment of the universal Church. Again and again as Paul takes up point by point the practical and theological problems that beset the Corinthian church, he will trace back their faults to the supreme mistake of identifying their own congregation with the Church catholic, of isolating themselves from the whole body.

Congregationalism in the bad sense is not confined to the denomination that bears that name. In fact, Congregationalists often exhibit congregationalism in the positive sense. But it is a disease that appears to be endemic to the American religious scene. It has been attributed to the frontier situation, in which a group of pioneers get together and start a church on their own. In such an atmosphere, it is difficult to foster a sense of the givenness and universality of the Church. Church seems to be something you get together and start on your own. Hence, it is of great importance to proclaim the true, biblical, Pauline view of the congregation. "It is not that the *ekklēsia* divides up into *ekklēsiai*. Nor does the sum of the *ekklēsiai* produce the *ekklēsia*. The one *ekklēsia* is present in the places mentioned" (K. L. Schmidt).

Gospel: John 1:29-34

This gospel departs from the normal rule of reading Matthew's Gospel during series A, presumably because of the importance of Jesus' baptism to the Epiphany season. The fourth evangelist avoids a direct narrative of the baptism of Jesus, probably because of claims of the "baptist" sect, which led Matthew to insert the dialogue between Jesus and John, as we saw in last week's gospel. To narrate Jesus' baptism would have made him appear too much like the subordinate of John. This impression the evangelist is at pains to correct, from the prologue on through the early chapters of the Gospel, and not least in the present passage ("a man who ranks before me, for he was before me"). Instead, the Baptist bears witness to the theological meaning of the baptism as it was expressed in the voice from heaven and in the descent of the dove. The latter is explicitly mentioned (v. 33). The voice from heaven is clearly alluded to in the words "This is the Son of God," and perhaps also in the reference to the "Lamb of God, who takes away the sin of the world." This too may be an allusion to the identification of Jesus with the servant of Yahweh of Second Isaiah.

If we ask what this Johannine account of the meaning of the baptism adds to the synoptic accounts, two points spring to mind. One is that John makes even clearer than the Synoptists (especially if we follow the variant "elect" in verse 34) that the theological meaning of the baptism is to be sought exclusively in the manifestation of Jesus as the servant of Yahweh. The second point is that Jesus' mission as servant will include his bearing (or taking away) the sin of the world (Isa 53). In this way the post-Epiphany season begins to point beyond itself to Passiontide.

The Homily

Taking the Old Testament reading, the psalm, and the gospel together,

the homilist might continue from last week the theme of Christ as the servant of the Lord, chosen for his role from the womb, called to take it up
at his baptism, carrying it out in his ministry of preaching the kingdom
of God, teaching God's will, eating with the outcast, healing the sick and
demon-possessed, and finally dying on the cross. This mission is continued
in the life of the Church, and that consideration should lead to the question: How are we continuing that mission in our locality, in our nation,
and in the world today?

A second possibility for the homily would be based on the second
reading and would take the form of an exposition of true versus false congregationalism. What priorities are expressed in our budgetary decisions?
Do we, for instance, attach more importance to getting a new organ for
our church than to meeting a crying need for missionary or social activity
beyond the parish boundaries?

THIRD SUNDAY OF THE YEAR

Reading I: Isaiah 9:1-4

This reading overlaps with the first reading of the midnight Mass at   *15*
Christmas. The verses about the birth of the Davidic king are dropped
at the end, but the reading starts with the reference to "the land of Zebulun
and the land of Naphtali" and "Galilee of the nations" (or Gentiles). This
passage will be taken up in the gospel of the day, where Matthew introduces it as a formula quotation to mark the beginning of the Galilean
ministry. This shows how the same passage is capable of different applications. Read on Christmas night, it relates to the nativity of Christ; it was
then that light dawned in the darkness. Read now, it refers to the beginning of Jesus' ministry. It is with his coming to Galilee and the launching
of his proclamation that the light begins to shine. Yet, as we have already
remarked, the nativity and the ministry cannot really be separated because
both are aspects of the single Christ-event, the coming of light into the
darkness of the world.

Responsorial Psalm: 27:1, 4, 13-14

Another arrangement of this psalm is used on the second Sunday of Lent   *407*
in series C. Here its use is more apt, for it is more suggestive of Epiphany
themes. "The Lord is my light" picks up the light/darkness motif of the
first reading, while "the beauty . . . and the goodness of the Lord" may
naturally be referred to the manifestation of God in Christ.

Reading II: 1 Corinthians 1:10-13, 17

In the first part of 1 Corinthians, Paul takes up several points that had been reported to him orally by Chloe's people. He is writing from Ephesus, and it appears that these emissaries of Chloe (one is tempted to speculate that she was a wealthy Christian woman in whose house the Corinthian Christians used to meet) have given the Apostle a verbal report of what was happening at Corinth. Other reports came in a letter sent by the congregation and delivered by Stephanas, Fortunatus, and Achaicus (1 Cor 7:1; 16:17). So it is interesting to note that some of the more painful questions were passed over in the letter in silence, and Paul got to know of them only through the oral report of Chloe's people.

The most damaging feature at Corinth was the dissension in the community. There is no indication that this was caused by doctrinal differences, for Paul does not take issue with them on that score. Rather, the Corinthians appear to have split into cliques, each claiming the patronage of one of the great leaders of the Church. It is not clear whether "I belong to Christ" represents a fourth clique (a sort of non-party party!) or whether this is Paul's own rejoinder: "I will have no truck with any of your parties. I belong to Christ." Paul meets their dissensions head-on by pointing out that they deny the baptismal reality. One is baptized in the name of Christ, not in the name of any human leader, however exalted.

Gospel: Matthew 4:12-23

Matthew begins the ministry of Jesus by summarizing Mark's "Day in Capernaum." This is an epitome of the ministry: Jesus proclaimed the coming of the kingdom; he called disciples and worked miracles of healing. All of this is placed under the rubric of the formula quotation from the ninth chapter of Isaiah (see the first reading). By means of this quotation, Matthew, who, despite some exclusivistic sayings such as 10:5, is not himself an exclusivist, underlines the universality of the gospel: it begins, not in Judean territory, but in Galilee of the Gentiles, and is therefore intended for all.

The Homily

If the homilist chooses to preach on the Old Testament reading, it might be instructive to compare the differences in Isaiah's message when used at Christmas and when used today. The context in which Scripture is read—the different context of the audience—is, in part at least, determinative of the meaning of any passage of Scripture, and this is a good example of that fact.

Although the passage from 1 Corinthians comes in course on this Sunday, it occurs providentially in the week of prayer for Christian unity (January 18–25). This gives the homilist a magnificent opportunity to speak about the unity of the Church and the great dangers of our unhappy divisions, which obscure the Christological and baptismal reality.

Taken together, the Old Testament reading, the psalm, and the gospel continue the theme of last week—the preaching of the gospel, the calling of all people to discipleship and ministry. But today's readings, especially the gospel, put special emphasis on the universality of that mission.

FOURTH SUNDAY OF THE YEAR

Reading I: Zephaniah 2:3; 3:12-13

In the Christian Church, Zephaniah has always been one of the least known and least used Old Testament prophets. This was so from the beginning, for he is cited only once in the New Testament (Matt 13:41). He prophesied during the reign of the reforming king Josiah and was therefore roughly contemporary with Jeremiah. But he does not seem to have been interested in Josiah's reform. He was filled with a sense of impending doom—he had much to say about the day of the Lord, and for him, as for Amos, this day would be a day of darkness and not light, a day of judgment for Israel.

In view of this impending judgment, Zephaniah in today's passage urges Israel to "seek righteousness, seek humility," for only righteous and humble people will escape that day. Zephaniah's single contribution to Old Testament religious thought was his emphasis on God's concern for the *'anawim,* the "poor," an idea that will be taken up in the first beatitude in today's gospel.

Note that this reading is a composite one, bringing together two passages separated by more than a whole chapter. This combination of texts is wholly justified, since both passages advocate humility as the only ground of security on the day of the Lord.

Responsorial Psalm: 146:6c-10

A slightly different selection of verses from this psalm is used on the twenty-sixth Sunday of the year in series C. On that occasion the psalm is meant to reinforce the theme of social justice; here it emphasizes the kindred theme of Yahweh's—and therefore the Church's—concern for the poor. Note the refrain from the first beatitude.

507

Reading II: 1 Corinthians 1:26-31

Last week we saw how Paul wrote to the Corinthians in reply to, among other things, the verbal information brought to him by Chloe's people about the divisions among the congregation. As usual, Paul goes to the theological root of the matter. The trouble with the Corinthians was that they were too sure of themselves. They boasted about their wisdom. They believed, like the later Gnostics, that through their initiation into Christ they had been made partakers of a heavenly wisdom. They were already on cloud nine! They thought themselves superior to other people who had not had this experience, and hence their cliquishness, which Paul was so concerned about in last week's reading.

In today's passage Paul seeks to "take them down a peg or two." They think themselves wise and strong, whereas actually they belong to what the outside world would regard as the dregs of society: "not many wise according to worldly standards, not many powerful, not many of noble birth." They have nothing to boast about in themselves before God. It is not their own spiritual endowments, achievements, or experiences that are the ground of their salvation, but only God's saving act in Jesus Christ, a fact that should humble them. If they must "glory," all they can glory in is the Lord—the saving act of God in Christ.

There is a remarkable parallel here to the way in which Paul dealt with the Judaizers in Galatians. The Judaizers sought salvation through the Jewish law, while the Corinthians believed that they were saved through their own wisdom. In each instance Paul sees the same basic fault. Each party tries to find something in themselves to boast about, some endowment or qualification to give them security vis-à-vis God. Being a Christian, however, means surrendering all this boasting, of whatever kind. For Paul, boasting is the supreme expression of human sinfulness. Thus, the gospel gets under the skin of both Jew and Greek, the religious and the irreligious, for both are exposed to the same temptation.

Gospel: Matthew 5:1-12a

The beatitudes form the opening of the "Great Sermon." In Matthew, it is the Sermon on the Mount; in Luke, the Sermon on the Plain. Matthew's reason for choosing this location is that he understands the teaching of the sermon as the new law, corresponding to the old law given on Mount Sinai, and for him Jesus is the second Moses, the giver of the new law.

Each beatitude consists of two parts. The first part describes the humiliation of the present, the second the glory to come. The beatitudes are not addressed to all people indiscriminately, but to the disciples, to those who have left all to follow Jesus. Note that in Luke the beatitudes are all in the second person plural. Here Luke is probably original, for the "you" style has survived in the last of Matthew's beatitudes. So Jesus is addressing those who have left all to follow him. *They* are the poor— in spirit, as Matthew correctly explains. *They* are the ones who realize that spiritually they are the have-nots, who have no righteousness of their own and therefore hunger and thirst for (God's) righteousness.

The second group of beatitudes is more activistic. It is the merciful, the pure in heart, and the peacemakers who are pronounced blessed. Faith, if it is genuine, works through love, as Paul put it. It is those who combine both the passive and the active sides of a true relation to God who are pronounced already here and now to be blessed and who are promised future participation in the kingdom of God.

It has often been observed that the beatitudes describe the life of Christ himself. He was all the things and did all the things that the beatitudes enumerate. And that brought him to the cross, and beyond that to his resurrection.

The Homily

There is a clear theme running through the readings of this Sunday, and that is the theme of the poor: "In your midst I will leave a humble and a lowly people" (caption, first reading); "Happy the poor in spirit; the kingdom of heaven is theirs!" (refrain, responsorial psalm); "God chose what is foolish . . . weak . . . low and despised" (second reading); "Blessed are the poor in spirit" (gospel). These quotations, however, only go to show what a complicated question the place of the poor is in Christian thinking. Are they the economically and materially handicapped (the stanzas of the psalm), or should the whole notion be spiritualized (first beatitude)?

This is a very acute question today. The Church is challenged on all sides to identify with the economically deprived. Yet, the quotations cited above give us reason to pause. Dare we listen to some words of Hoskyns on this question? In a sermon at Cambridge in 1932, he said:

"I fear lest we Christians have gone materialist and that we are nowhere in so grave a danger of materialism as at the moment when we utter the word 'poor' or 'weak,' and that we are in this danger despite the phrase which meets us at the beginning of the Sermon on the Mount, the 'poor in spirit,' a phrase introduced for the express purpose of preventing us from thinking of the poor or of the weak *merely* [my italics! Hoskyns does not say we should *not* think of them in those terms] in terms of lack of money, or lack of robust physical health."

He goes on to suggest that the poor might also be found in the most unlikely quarters, which are hardly calculated to evoke much sympathy today any more than they were in 1932: the Tory landowner striving to preserve his estate not merely for his own family but for the good of the whole village that is economically dependent on the estate; the French statesman of the thirties who was responsible for the security of his country against another 1914; the officials of the British War Office who, remembering the horrors of Flanders, "dare not behave as though peace were assured." So Hoskyns challenges his hearers: "Are you quite certain that those whom you call the strong are not in fact the weak? Human life is strangely kaleidoscopic. The strong at one moment are the weak at another. The poor (in the biblical sense) are not a fixed, easily recognizable quantity of men and women."

But here we must be careful. We must not so spiritualize the notion of the poor that we turn our back on the physically poor. It is precisely because the poor are the poor in an economic sense that we are to see in them especially the poor in spirit whom the Lord pronounces blessed. For to be poor in the gospel sense is to be a have-not standing before God, dependent on him alone for deliverance.

Yet, we have to see the poor also in many whom the world, which sees only on the outside, sees as the rich. There is as much poverty, in the biblical sense, in Westchester County, Main Line Philadelphia, or on Chicago's North Shore as there is in Harlem, Roxbury, or Watts. All people have to be brought into the presence of God and see themselves as the weak and the poor. The Church should indeed identify itself with the economically poor because it sees in them a parable of the plight of all people before God. And the Church should engage in humanitarian action on behalf of the poor because such action is a parable of the love of God in Christ, who "for our sakes became poor, that we through his poverty might become rich" (2 Cor 8:9).

FIFTH SUNDAY OF THE YEAR

Reading I: Isaiah 58:7-10

This passage is more familiar as a Lenten reading. The verses immediately preceding this excerpt pose the question of true fasting. Today's verses give the answer: True fasting is sharing our bread with the hungry. But the preceding question is omitted today, since we are not in the Lenten fast. The effect is to throw the emphasis on the *consequence* of sharing one's bread: "Then shall your light break forth like the dawn . . . . then shall your light rise in the darkness." This makes the reading appropriate for the post-Epiphany season, which is concerned not only with the epiphany of God in Christ but also with the Christian life as an epiphany of God's love for us. The theme of the Christian as a light in the world's darkness is then taken up in the refrain of the responsorial psalm and in the gospel.

Responsorial Psalm: 112:4-7, 8a, 9

Psalm 112 sets out the characteristics of the just or righteous person in the style of the wisdom literature. It is to be noted that the refrain, though based on verse 4a of the psalm, does not say quite the same thing. When the psalm itself speaks of light, this means the reward the upright person receives for well-doing—a state of general well-being as contrasted with "darkness," that is, affliction. The refrain, however, distinguishes between the just and the upright person in a way the psalm does not, and makes the former a light—that is, a source of well-being—for the latter.

When analyzed, the thought of the refrain is really far from clear, though its intention is obvious, namely, to relate the psalm to the Old Testament reading and the gospel, both of which speak of the righteous as a source of light. One may hope, in the interests of clarity and of faithfulness to the text of Scripture, that this refrain will be reconsidered when the Lectionary comes up for review.

Reading II: 1 Corinthians 2:1-5

It has often been thought that Paul changed his preaching at Corinth because of his failure at Athens (Acts 17). In preaching to the Stoics and Epicureans there, he had tried to use sophisticated philosophical arguments, replete with literary allusions. So when he got to Corinth, he abandoned this style and concentrated on the message of the cross. This is unlikely because in writing up Paul's visit to Athens, the author of Acts probably followed the custom of ancient historians, composing the Areopagus speech himself and putting it on Paul's lips. It is a sample of the Christian apologetic customary at the time Acts was written.

Accordingly, we must suppose that at Athens, as at Corinth, Paul followed his usual practice of preaching Christ crucified. At Athens his message was refused because the cross was a stumbling block to the Jews and folly to the Gentiles. Intellectuals did not, and still do not, want to hear about human sin and divine salvation through the cross of Jesus Christ—that is both the folly and the stumbling block.

The Corinthians' present behavior—their cliquishness and their pride in wisdom—is wholly inconsistent with the gospel of the cross as they had received it through Paul's preaching. The cross of Christ was the *Umwertung aller Werte,* the denial of all human wisdom and its accompanying pride. The way the Corinthians are now behaving, one would think that Paul had not preached the message of the cross but lofty and plausible words of human wisdom, like the wandering preachers and charlatans so common in the Hellenistic world. Paul has only his weak words, yet God made these words the vehicle of his "Spirit and power." And, after all, they did bring the Corinthians to faith.

Gospel: Matthew 5:13-16

The band of disciples, the nucleus of the future Church, is described under three metaphors: salt, a city on a hill, and a light in the world. The passage concludes with the well-known exhortation especially familiar to Anglicans as the first of Cranmer's invariable offertory sentences and so constantly heard Sunday by Sunday for three centuries: "Let your light shine before men . . . ."

The Sermon on the Mount does not say that the disciples are to *become* the salt, that they are to become like a city on a hill or make themselves a light amid the darkness of the world. They *are* all those things, and that because Jesus has called them and they have responded. Rather, they are expected to manifest what they are: "Let your light so shine before men." How is this done? By good works. Our text does not specify what these good works are. It is more concerned to insist that good works are not the meritorious deeds of the disciples themselves, for the world that sees them does not praise the disciples for them, but the heavenly Father. The good works of the disciples point away from themselves to the grace of God through which they were wrought.

The Homily

For this Sunday the homilist would seem to have two possibilities. The dominant theme of the readings (first reading, psalm, gospel) is the Christian community as the light of the world. The homilist should start from the gospel, which shows that Christians *are* the light of the world. They do not have to become that light through their own good works but rather should show what they are by the good works that are the fruits of God's grace. Then the first reading and the psalm can be used to illustrate what these good works might be, especially in a Christian concern for the poor.

This theme can in turn be related to the epiphany motif. Not only is Christ the epiphany of God, but the Christian community has to be the epiphany of Christ in the world.

SIXTH SUNDAY OF THE YEAR

Reading I: Sirach 15:15-20

This is the clearest statement in all of the canonical and deuterocanonical Old Testament writings on the subject of human free will. It is even clearer than Deut 30:15, whose teaching it echoes. Taken by itself, this passage would seem to be unadulterated Pelagianism. It does not recognize the bias toward sin that characterizes humanity in its fallen state. The human person appears to be a *tabula rasa,* having complete freedom to choose either good or evil ("fire and water"), and there is no apparent recognition of the human need for grace.

The author's main thrust, however, is to exonerate God from all responsibility for the evil in the world—God never told anyone to be godless or gave anyone license to sin. The caption to this reading picks this out as the point of the whole passage. If we want a complete doctrine of human free will and the limitations imposed upon humans by their fallen nature, we must take into consideration not only this passage but also passages such as Rom 7:7-25.

Responsorial Psalm: 119:1-2, 4-5, 17-18, 33-34

Psalm 119, the longest in the psalter, is a skillfully constructed acrostic poem in praise of the Torah. Every verse in the twenty-two sections of eight verses begins with the same letter of the Hebrew alphabet, in order throughout the alphabet. Today's responsorial psalm is constructed from the first (aleph), third (gimel), and fifth (he) letters of the alphabet.

The psalm often sounds highly legalistic in its understanding of piety, but we have to remember that Torah meant all that we mean by God's revelation of himself to humankind. We may therefore say that this psalm represents the Torah as an epiphany of God to human beings, and a passage from it is therefore appropriate for use during this season.

Reading II: 1 Corinthians 2:6-10

In last week's passage, 1 Cor 2:1-5, Paul repudiated wisdom and claimed that he preached only Christ crucified. Now he appears to take back much of what he had said. He does not entirely repudiate wisdom after all. There *is* a legitimate sense in which it can be used in Christian theology. In making this point, the Apostle picks up the "Gnostic" language that the Corinthians (wrongly) used about themselves: "wisdom," "mature," "mystery" (the word that the RSV translates as the adjective "secret"), "depths of God." He even quotes an apocryphal verse that would have especially appealed to the Corinthians (v. 9).

But there is a profound difference between Paul's use of these words and the Corinthians' use of them. The Corinthians were talking about a spiritual revelation into which they claimed to have been initiated when they became Christians. They thought that their very reception of it made them "mature." Paul, on the other hand, is talking about the meaning of the cross in salvation history (v. 8). The "mystery" is that the crucified One, precisely as the crucified, is the Lord of glory, or, to put it in our modern theological jargon, the cross is the eschatological act of God.

The Corinthians thought otherwise. For them, the cross was an unfortunate episode of past history; the less said about it, the better. All that mattered now was that Christ was risen. He was now spirit and, as such, had conveyed to them the esoteric gnosis or wisdom by means of which they were "in." They thought they were mature, but in fact, by displaying their ignorance of the cross, they were showing their immaturity.

One further point calls for comment. Paul says that it was "the rulers of this age" who "crucified the Lord of glory." Who were these rulers? Pontius Pilate and Herod, or the demonic powers? Perhaps, as so often, it is not a question of either/or, for the political rulers who executed Jesus may well, in Paul's thought, have been acting as the earthly agents of the powers of evil. These powers would then have blinded the rulers and prevented them from realizing that they were crucifying the Lord of glory. They, of course, thought that he was a mere messianic pretender. Perhaps this is also a sly dig at the Corinthians. By refusing to recognize the Lord of glory in the crucified (as opposed to the risen) One, they were aligning themselves with Pontius Pilate and Herod, and so acting as agents of the powers of evil.

Gospel: Matthew 5:17-37 (long form); 5:20-22a, 27-28, 33-34a, 37 (short form)

The shorter form helps us to see more clearly the structure of the longer form. In the Sermon on the Mount, Jesus enunciates the new law of the kingdom of God, or, better, the new interpretation of the old law that is to prevail in the kingdom. This new interpretation is illustrated by a series of antitheses, as they are commonly called. These antitheses follow a common pattern. First comes the formula "You have heard that it was said [that is, that God said] to the men of old." This formula introduces a verbatim quotation of one of the commandments of the old law. Then comes Jesus' reinterpretation, introduced by the formula "But I say to you."

Both the short and the long form reproduce the first three antitheses. The prohibition of murder is enlarged to embrace anger, the prohibition of adultery to cover lustful glances, and the prohibition of false oaths to include any kind of swearing, since a simple yes or no should be just as binding. The longer version includes further illustrative material and adds to the prohibition of adultery the prohibition of divorce. (Since the latter is attested elsewhere in the gospel tradition, it has clearly been added to the antithesis at some point in the transmission of the tradition.) The continuation of chapter 5, not included here, gives two more antitheses, one on revenge and the other on love of the enemy.

The better righteousness that the kingdom of God requires covers not only overt behavior but also inner motive. God's demand for obedience is absolute and total, claiming the whole person in the entirety of his or her relations.

It has been said that the Sermon on the Mount by itself is bad news, a sharpening of the demands of the law to the point of the impossible. Thus enunciated, it throws a person back on the need for grace (and so advertises the Pelagian suggestions of the first reading, taken by itself). But in the kingdom, grace is given to enable one to advance toward the goal of absolute obedience.

The Homily

For today's homily we offer three suggestions. First, one could take the first reading and the gospel together. The passage from Sirach offers an either/or choice: good or evil, life or death. But it appears to assume too easily that human beings can choose and pursue the good by their own unaided power. The antithesis puts before us the "better righteousness," which is beyond the unaided powers of human beings to attain and therefore points to their need of grace.

The second possibility is to apply one of the antitheses to a current ethical problem. The three antitheses included in today's gospel touch upon acute contemporary problems such as war and pacifism, sexual morality and marriage (the latter only in the longer form), and the credibility gap of public institutions. But the relation of the absolute demand of God to the relativities of human life is a tricky business. The preacher will need some sort of ethical methodology like that of the "middle axioms," just as the voltage of a high-power line has to be transformed downward for ordinary consumption.

The third homiletical possibility is even more difficult. It is to relate the second reading to the contemporary theological situation. Here the homilist would have to penetrate into the basic theological stance of the Corinthian gnostics and seek to discern an analogous stance in the Church and in the world today, and then confront it, as Paul does, with the "mystery" of the cross. It would have to be shown that the supposed contemporary theological maturity (humanity come of age?) is, in fact, immaturity, that the cross provides a radical critique of this supposed maturity and leads the believer on to a very different, God-centered kind of security.

SEVENTH SUNDAY OF THE YEAR

Reading I: Leviticus 19:1-2, 17-18

Leviticus 19 is a miscellaneous collection of laws, some of them thought to come from a primitive form of the Decalogue. Verses 1-2 serve as an introduction to the whole collection, and therefore they fittingly preface verses 17-18 in today's excerpt.

Holiness means separateness, distinctiveness, from the world. It was first of all the quality of Yahweh. Then, by making Israel his people, Yahweh made them holy, too. This is not expressed here but is presupposed by the context of the Old Testament law, given as it is after the Exodus; it is however made clear, as far as the Christian Church is concerned, in the second reading: "God's temple is holy, and that temple you are."

Holiness is first of all indicative: You *are* holy. But then it is also an imperative: You *shall be* holy. The distinctiveness of the people of God is to be shown in, not established through, their behavior. This behavior is summed up in the command to love the neighbor. In the Old Testament and in Judaism, "neighbor" meant fellow Israelite. Jesus reaffirmed the centrality of this commandment but widened the concept to embrace the enemy in today's gospel.

Responsorial Psalm: 103:1-4, 8, 10, 12-13

This is perhaps the best known of all the thanksgiving psalms of the whole psalter. The psalmist, speaking of his own individual experience of the purpose of God, transforms his personal gratitude into a corporate hymn of praise. What precisely that personal experience was is difficult to say, but perhaps the reference to delivery from "the Pit" (sheol) in stanza 2 suggests that he had been very ill and at the point of death. In his own personal experience he sees mirrored the experience of Israel throughout its salvation history (see verse 7, not used in this selection). The psalm praises God for his kindness and mercy, manifested particularly in the forgiveness of sins.

Reading II: 1 Corinthians 3:16-23

The context of 1 Cor 1-4 is the divisions that afflicted the church at Corinth. People were saying, "I belong to Paul," "I belong to Apollos." Each group boasted of the "knowledge" (gnosis) it had received from its purported leader.

Paul begins this section by reminding the Corinthians of what they already know: "Do you not know . . . ?" This is not, therefore, new teaching, not a further elaboration of Paul's foundational message, but part of his original teaching. Such divisions and such pride in the peculiar advantages possessed by each group represented a defilement of God's temple, that is, the Church. Paul uses many images for the Church (garden, building, etc.), but here he uses the image of temple for the first time in his writings. "Temple" brings out the point that the Church is the place where the Spirit of God is present. The Church does not consist of bricks and mortar but of people; nor is it primarily an organization or institution.

Later on, in 1 Cor 6:16-17, Paul will apply the same figure to the individual Christian. There we will learn that it is immorality that defiles the individual Christian as God's temple; here it is disunity that defiles the whole congregation. How does this square with Matt 16:18, which says that the gates of Hades cannot prevail against the Church? Answer: Local or even regional churches (e.g., North Africa) *can* be destroyed. Each local church is a manifestation in microcosm of the universal Church. But the Church as a whole cannot be destroyed.

In the second part of our reading (vv. 18-23), Paul brings to a head the discussion of the Corinthian cliques and divisions, and the discussion of wisdom and folly. The knowledge (gnosis) that each group claims to possess is a purely human wisdom. True wisdom, God's wisdom, is the gospel of the cross of Christ. Human wisdom leads to boasting in human leaders. The apostles are not human leaders of this sort. They are not lords over God's people but servants of Christ and servants of his people. There is indeed an "authority of the laity," as the Spirit-filled body, which balances the authority of the ministry. But this authority is not free and independent; it is subordinated to Christ, as Christ in turn is subordinated to God (Paul's Christology here is functional and historical, not ontological or metaphysical, as it became in later Christology, in which "subordinationism" was rightly repudiated as a heresy).

Gospel: Matthew 5:38-48

This reading continues the Sermon on the Mount from last week. It is the part known as the "antitheses": "You have heard that it was said . . . but I say to you." Here two antitheses are drawn out. The first is taken from the Torah: "an eye for an eye and a tooth for a tooth" (Lev 24:19). The second is a maxim that combines the commandment to love the neighbor from our first reading with an injunction not found anywhere in the Old Testament but representing much of what is taught or assumed there, namely, that one should hate the enemies of God and of Israel. Jesus is not contradicting the Old Testament but is radicalizing it, going much further though in the same direction. For the "eye for an eye" injunction was not meant to sanction revenge but to restrict it. Now Jesus rules it out altogether.

Jesus' injunction was probably formulated in opposition to the policy of the Zealots, who advocated armed rebellion against the occupying Roman power. The evangelist later redirected the prohibition of vengeance, applying it to the persecutors of the Christian Church (v. 44). In our own day, Mahatma Gandhi and Martin Luther King, Jr., applied Jesus' teaching of non-violence to successive situations of a very different kind. But claims that have been made to enlist the support of Jesus' teaching for violent revolution can hardly be used to support an absolute pacifism, even though that may be the vocation of Christian individuals. Jesus was addressing his disciples, not those who had the responsibility for government. The teaching of Rom 13, which allows the state to bear the sword for the enforcement of law and the prevention of evil, still stands as part of the canon.

The Homily

Today's gospel reading suggests an exposition of the relevance of Jesus' command of non-violence to the political and social questions of the day. Numerous resources are available, particularly the U.S. bishops' pastoral letter "The Challenge of Peace: God's Promise and Our Response." It must be remembered that the Sermon on the Mount is directed to the disciples and their behavior, both as individuals and—at least at the level of the evangelist's redaction—as a community, not to the state as such nor to those who bear authority and responsibility in the state. Its relevance to the state is only indirect at most.

The second reading provides another opportunity to deal with cliques and divisions in the congregation. Disunity is seen as a defilement of the holiness of God's temple, the place of his tabernacling presence. It sets up altar against altar and prompts Paul's question: "Is Christ divided?"

EIGHTH SUNDAY OF THE YEAR

Reading I: Isaiah 49:14-15

Today's selection from Second Isaiah is a song of consolation. Israel has been in exile in Babylon. Zion has felt forsaken by Yahweh during those seventy years. But Yahweh cannot and will not forget his people. Sooner would a mother forget the child she has borne and nursed. The evangelical poet William Cooper drew on this passage in the verse:

> Can a woman's tender care
> Cease toward the child she bear?
> Yes, she may forgetful be,
> Yet will I remember thee.

(See *The Hymnal 1940 Companion,* p. 284. This stanza is omitted in *Hymnal 1940.*)

This is one of the few examples in the Bible of female imagery used for God—today a welcome corrective to the predominant use of male imagery.

Responsorial Psalm: 62:1-2, 5-8b

This selection forms three stanzas, of which the first two are almost identical in thought and wording. This psalm is an expression of individual trust in God, matching the message of the gospel. Note the repetition of "alone . . . only . . . alone" in the first two stanzas. It is a devotional expression of the first commandment: "You shall have no other gods before me." The quiet trust of this psalm forms an impressive contrast to the anguished, feverish appeals of so many of the psalms of lament. God alone and no worldly thing or person is worthy of ultimate trust.

Reading II: 1 Corinthians 4:1-5

Behind the divisions in the Corinthian church lay a wrong attitude toward their apostolic leaders. The Corinthians regarded them as exalted personages who had some special mystical religious knowledge (gnosis) that they imparted to those whom they initiated into the Christian faith.

Paul insists that the apostles are nothing in themselves, only servants. The Greek word is *hypēretēs,* not the usual *diakonos.* It was a common word for the secretary of a religious society. But the Christian servant is a servant primarily of Christ, not just a secretary in the employ of a human society. The other word that Paul uses for the apostles, namely, "stewards," suggests that they are the people entrusted with the administration of someone else's property—in this case, God's. What exactly are "the mysteries"? The term is commonly interpreted to mean the sacraments, but in the New Testament its usual meaning is secret truths revealed by God, primarily the gospel, though of course that would also include the sacraments.

Paul then takes up the notion of stewardship and develops the theme of fidelity as the steward's primary duty. The Corinthians expected the apostle to show initiative and to exercise personal authority. They were criticizing Paul for not measuring up to their expectations. He did not appear as a successful "divine man," like the false apostles Paul fulminates against in 1 Corinthians. When Paul says that he has nothing on his conscience, this must not be generalized. All he means is that he knows he has stooped to emulate the successful divine men or wandering preachers (they were something like the successful television evangelists of our day). Paul is content to await the final evaluation of God on the last day.

Gospel: Matthew 6:24-34

This section of the Sermon on the Mount deals with the disciples' attitude toward material possessions. It is absent from Luke's Sermon on the Plain (Luke 6) but is found later in Luke (12:22-31), and therefore comes from Q. Matthew is thought to have preserved the wording of Q better, though Luke probably has it in its original sequence in Q.

Verse 24 serves as the title to the whole section. God demands our ultimate allegiance; there can be no other ultimate allegiance, for then God would not be the ultimate.

Anxiety arises from making something other than God our ultimate concern. The ensuing passage instances concern for food, drink, and clothes—the most elementary of human needs. The argument is from the lesser to the greater: "If the birds, the grass, the flowers . . . how much more you?" Behind the argument rests faith in God as Creator. This faith is not just a matter of subscribing to the doctrine that the universe was originally created by God some thousands or billions of years ago; rather, it is a matter of present, immediate experience. We receive the world from God at this moment and at every moment of our lives as his gift. Anxiety is the result of listening to the serpent's temptation of Adam and Eve: "You shall be as gods." It is attempting to be our own gods, to usurp God's function as Creator.

The Homily

The most obvious choice today would be the gospel with its call "Do not be anxious." The homilist should be careful to point out that Jesus does not advocate abandonment of life's responsibilities. Anxiety is a concern that goes beyond the responsibilities imposed upon us by our station in life. It is making the things of this life our ultimate concern. That is to dethrone God and to put either these earthly things or ourselves (by thinking that our own efforts can provide them) in his place. "Seek first the kingdom of God and his righteousness." Our ultimate concern must be God's salvation and his will, and we must trust him to provide what we need in carrying out that will.

NINTH SUNDAY OF THE YEAR

Reading I: Deuteronomy 11:18, 26-28

The opening verse (cf. 6:8, where the same instruction is given) was later taken literally and gave rise to the practice of wearing phylacteries, mentioned in the sayings of Jesus (Matt 23:5). Whether it was taken literally in Deuteronomic times we do not know. This verse provides a setting for verses 26-28, the choice between blessing and curse. Such blessings and curses were customarily attached to covenants as sanctions for their enforcement. From these primitive origins the idea passed into the "Two Ways" of Jewish ethical teaching (*Manual of Discipline,* 1 QS 4) and was taken over in the catechesis of the early Church (see *Didache* 1:1). The same idea appears in the parable of the two houses at the conclusion of the Sermon on the Mount, which forms the gospel reading for today.

Responsorial Psalm: 31:1-3, 16, 24

Psalm 31 is an individual thanksgiving, praising God in the temple for deliverance from sickness and trouble. Today's selection combines several verses that speak of God as the source of security and refuge.

In Christian usage (see Luther's *Commentary on the Psalms*), such psalms are to be read as thanksgivings of the sinner who has been justified by the grace of God. If interpreted otherwise, they are sentimentalized and trivialized. This suggests that we treat the curse in the first reading to mean specifically the curse of the law (Gal 3:10), under which all people live apart from Christ and from which Christ by his redeeming work has saved us (see the second reading).

Reading II: Romans 3:21-25a, 28

The word "now" represents a major turning point both in the argument of Romans and in the history of salvation. In Rom 1:18–3:20 Paul has established that "all," whether Jew or Greek, godly or ungodly, "have sinned." Now, however (*nyn de*), the situation has been dramatically changed by God's intervention in Christ. First, Paul repeats in the same terms as in Rom 1:16 his definition of the gospel as the revelation of God's righteousness, and into this he weaves his conclusion, drawn from the preceding analysis of the human situation before God, namely, that all, whether Jews or Gentiles, have sinned.

Next, Paul cites what is widely recognized today to be a pre-Pauline formula, with glosses of his own that express his distinctive emphasis on the role of faith, as opposed to the works of the law, in the process of justification. Here is the formula, or rather the part of it included in this reading, with the gloss in parentheses:

> through the redemption which is in Christ Jesus,
> whom God put forward as an expiation by his blood,
> (to be received by faith).

The reading ends with a summary conclusion of Paul's understanding of the gospel: "For we hold that a man is justified by faith apart from works of law." The pre-Pauline fragment is concerned with the Christ-event in itself. Paul himself is concerned with our appropriation of it by faith.

The meaning of the passage may be best grasped by a study of the key words:

"Righteousness" here is not a moral quality, as in Matthew or James, but God's saving act, as in Second Isaiah (for example, Isa 51:5, where it occurs in synonymous parallelism with "salvation"). The law and the prophets (that is, the Old Testament canon) bear witness to the coming of this salvation, for the Old Testament is an incomplete book pointing forward through type and prophecy toward its fulfillment. That God should act to save through Christ is therefore not something unheard of but the key to the true meaning of the Old Testament.

"Apart from law" and "through faith" go together. A righteousness dependent upon the law would be one that sought to secure God's favor by fulfilling the law, which Rom 1–3:20 demonstrated to be beyond the capacity of sinful, fallen human beings. Instead, it comes through faith, that is, it can only be attained by receiving it "as a gift" (v. 24a).

"Justified," aptly rendered by the Old English word "rightwised," means being put right with God. This is the quest, conscious or unconscious, of all human religion.

"Redemption," a word that comes from the pre-Pauline formula, is an Old Testament term, where it is used of God's saving act in bringing Israel out of Egypt. Later in the Old Testament it signifies the looked-for deliverance at the end (Dan 4:30c [LXX ed. Swete[4] 1912/1930] = Dan 4:34 [LXX ed. Rahlfs[7] 1935/1962]: "At the end of the seven years the time of my deliverance came . . . ."). In early Christianity it refers specifically to the deliverance from sin and death that Christ's death has accomplished.

"Expiation" (Greek: *hilastērion*) is one of the most controverted words in the New Testament. Three meanings have been held: (1) the traditional interpretation—propitiation. Here the actor is the human person, the object is God, and the presupposition is that the person must do something to satisfy God and appease his wrath. Since human beings are unable to do this by themselves, God undertook to do it in Christ, and so Christ propitiated the Father. (2) A modern view—expiation. Here God is the subject, and the object is sin. God, in Christ, undertook to wipe away human sin. Finally (3) the mercy seat, that is, the place where atonement is wrought. The first interpretation is supported by the use of the Greek word *hilastērion;* the second has the support of the Old Testament verb that underlies the Greek words derived from the root *hila-;* the third is linguistically possible.

Perhaps we should opt for "expiation," without excluding all notions of propitiation. "We can hardly doubt (since Paul says that God set forth Christ in this capacity) that expiation rather than propitiation is in his mind; though it would be wrong to neglect the fact that expiation has, as it were, the effect of propitiation: the sin that might justly have excited God's wrath is expiated (at God's will), and therefore no longer does so" (C. K. Barrett).

"Blood" is a term derived from the cup-word in the Last Supper tradition. It does not mean the physical stuff as such but the saving event of Christ's death considered as a sacrifice. Probably the pre-Pauline hymn that Paul cites was designated for use in connection with the Eucharist (at the Christian Passover?).

Gospel: Matthew 7:21-27

Matthew's Sermon on the Mount ends with a series of sayings directed by the evangelist against the charismatic prophets and healers (divine men) who were troubling the Church in his day. The test at the End will be, not their charismatic achievements, but their obedience to the new righteousness set forth in the great sermon.

It is realized today that Matthew was fighting on a double front. On the one hand, there was strict Pharisaic Jewish orthodoxy, consolidating itself after the fall of Jerusalem, and on the other hand, there were the charismatic enthusiasts. Against both groups and in different ways, Matthew sets forth an understanding of Christianity that, while not denying God's redemptive act in Christ (consider his interest in Christology and in prophecy fulfillment), emphasizes that after the Christ-event has been appropriated, its effects must be shown forth, not in charismatic achievements or in observance of the minutiae of the rabbinic law, but in works of love and mercy. So the Christian, like the wise man who built upon rock, is the one who "hears these words of mine and does them." This is a presentation of Christianity that is very different from that which we find in Paul and is much closer to that in James, but both are valid and there is a right time for each.

The Homily

What does the congregation today most need to hear? Is it Paul's message that "we are justified by faith [Luther added "alone"; it was not in the Greek, and he probably should not have done so, though it can be held that he captured Paul's true intention] apart from the law"; or is it Matthew's message, which insists that the Christian must not only hear Christ's words but do them? Could we preach both Paul's version—that we are justified by faith (alone)—and also the version of Matthew-James—that we are justified by works and not by faith alone—and see that both are true, each at its own time?

TENTH SUNDAY OF THE YEAR

Reading I: Hosea 6:3-6

As the caption indicates, this passage was chosen because of its final couplet: "For I desire steadfast love and not sacrifice . . ., which is cited in the gospel.

The prophets denounced the practice of sacrifice unaccompanied by obedience, but they did not denounce sacrifice as such. "I desire A and not B" is the Hebraic way of saying what the priorities should be: "I desire love more than sacrifice." It is noteworthy that despite the prophetic protest, sacrifices still went on—in fact, they were actually elaborated after the Exile. Both the prophetic protest and the sacrifices were necessary, and the continuance of both side by side witnessed to important elements of the truth.

What God really wants is obvious—the total commitment of a person's life to him. But it is less obvious that a person cannot achieve this by himself or herself. The continuance of the sacrifices was a witness to the need for the provision of the perfect sacrifice that would make possible the obedience that the prophets demanded. It pointed forward to the justifying deed of God of which the second reading speaks.

Responsorial Psalm: 50:1, 8, 12-15

Psalm 50, like Psalms 40 and 51, reflects the prophetic protest against sacrifices divorced from moral obedience. But as with Hos 6, it is very easy to misconstrue its meaning. At first glance it looks as though God does not want any cultic sacrifice at all, but only heartfelt thanksgiving, as Hosea seemed to imply when he said that God wanted only "steadfast love." But again we are confronted with a Hebraic manner of speech. The protest is not against sacrifice as such but against crude ideas of sacrifice— as though sacrifices could somehow secure the favor of God, as though, even more crudely, God needed sacrifices for his physical sustenance. In place of this, the psalmist proposes that what God really looks for is the "sacrifice of thanksgiving." This is the peace offering of the Old Testament (Lev 3:1-16, etc.) accompanied by heartfelt thanks.

Reading II: Romans 4:18-25

In this section Paul is offering scriptural support for his doctrine of justification by faith (shorthand for justification by the grace of God manifested in Jesus Christ and apprehended by faith). He does this by taking the story of Abraham as an example.

When God promised Abraham that he would become the father of many nations, Abraham was one hundred years old and his wife, Sarah, was ninety years old. But Abraham took God at his word, being "fully convinced that God was able to do what he had promised." Similarly, faith in the gospel means faith in God's ability to do for us what we cannot do for ourselves, that is, put ourselves right with him, make ourselves justified in his sight. This justifying faith accepts the fact that, in the death and resurrection of Jesus Christ, God has done for us what we could not do for ourselves.

Gospel: Matthew 9:9-13

There are two unique features in Matthew's version of this story as contrasted with that of Mark. (It is usually in these unique features—the evangelist's "redaction," as it is referred to nowadays—that the evangelist's distinctive message is found, and it is on such points that the preacher will want to focus attention.) The first feature is the alteration of the name Levi to Matthew. Of course, to the precritical approach this occasions no problem: Levi and Matthew were both names of the same person, and the author was simply referring to his own call. But the modern critical approach sees the Gospel of Matthew as the outcome of a long process of oral tradition and as a combination of earlier documents, not as direct eyewitness. So Matthew must have had some theological reason for changing the name. Now the name Matthew occurs in Mark's list of the Twelve (Mark 3:18). It seems, therefore, that Matthew wants to interpret this story as the call of one who subsequently became a member of the Twelve, and one of the Twelve was a social outcast. To be an apostle is a matter of *sola gratia.*

The second change that Matthew makes in his Marcan source is the addition of the citation of Hos 6:6 in 9:13. Commonly this is taken to mean here that God wants us to keep the moral law but does not care about the ritual. However, not only does that do violence to the original Hosea (see above; in any case, the New Testament sometimes does not scruple to do violence to the original meaning). More than that, "the inferior assessment of the ceremonial law is foreign to Judaism" (G. Barth).

What, then, is the meaning? It is surely that Jesus' action in eating with the outcast is an actualization of God's mercy (Hebrew: *chesed*). It is the ultimate answer to all that the Jewish law of sacrifices had stood for: the utter helplessness of human beings before God, their inability to achieve their own salvation. Thus, the three readings and the responsorial psalm all fit together in a remarkable way.

The Homily

It is clear that this Sunday's homily text should be: "I desire steadfast love (mercy), not sacrifice." The homilist should guard against the anticultic interpretation of the prophetic protest against sacrifice, showing that God did intend the sacrifices of the old law to continue, but accompanied by obedience and true devotion. Yet, people were unable fully to offer the sacrifice of obedience that God really required, so Christ offered this sacrifice by enacting the mercy of God in his eating with the outcast and by dying for our sins and rising for our justification.

When these ideas have been gathered from all three readings, they can be applied as a critique of that kind of Pelagianism that recurs in one form or another in every generation and is so common today—that God does not particularly care whether we go to church or not, so long as we live a decent life. It is not so much a matter of going to church but of receiving the justifying mercy of God that alone makes it possible for us to offer that mercy (steadfast love) to others.

ELEVENTH SUNDAY OF THE YEAR

Reading I: Exodus 19:2-6a

We have noted previously that on the Sundays in ordinary time, the Old Testament reading is usually selected to go with the gospel. All three readings today contain interesting and significant material, but there does not seem to be any common theme running through them. The nearest we can get to such a theme is that the people of God is presented under a series of images: a kingdom of priests and a holy nation (first reading); the sheep of God's flock (responsorial psalm); a people reconciled to God through the death of his Son (second reading); and a people established by the mission of the Twelve (gospel).

The passage from Exod 19 provides the Old Testament background of the hymn about the Church that is embedded in 1 Pet 2:1-10, which was treated in our commentary for the fifth Sunday of Easter this year. *83* Taken together, these passages from Exodus and 1 Peter form a classical treatment of the priestly nature of the whole Church, about which the New Testament has more to say than about the priestly character of the Church's ministry.

Responsorial Psalm: 100:1-2, 3, 5

This is a psalm sung upon entering the sanctuary, a call to praise and thank Yahweh. Some commentators are of the opinion that it is an enthronement psalm, that is, it was sung at the entrance to the temple when the king was enthroned. But there is no mention of Yahweh as king, as one might expect on such an occasion. At the same time, the image of Yahweh as shepherd is suggested by the reference to Israel as his sheep. This image prepares for the gospel reading, in which Jesus sends out the Twelve on their mission, because he sees that the people are as "sheep without a shepherd."

Reading II: Romans 5:6-11

The opening verse of this passage was very important for Nygren's *Agape and Eros.* This was a one-sided book, but it had a real point. It contrasted the two concepts of love denoted by the two Greek words in the title, *agape* being biblical, and *eros* pagan. *Agape* means the love entirely uncaused by the attractiveness of its object, whereas *eros* is essentially a love evoked precisely by the object's attractiveness. The one is completely selfless, the other essentially self-regarding. Although we would not, with Nygren, exclude *eros* from the human-divine relationship (it is surely capable of being redeemed), what he says about the love of God in the light of our reading is profoundly true: God sent his Son to die for the ungodly, while we were yet sinners.

Another point, which Bultmann emphasized in connection with this passage, is the event-character of God's love. It is not just a vague idea or a benevolent sentiment, not just a vague conviction that God will keep us free from harm. It happened concretely in the event of the cross. It is not an inference about the universe. In fact, what we observe about the universe may very well appear to contradict the love of God. Only through the cross, only through our justification and reconciliation by his blood, by the event of his self-giving death, do we know that God is love. Charles Wesley's well-known hymn "Jesus, Lover of My Soul" is about Christ's self-giving on the cross as the event of our justification and reconciliation.

The passage concludes with a double *a fortiori* argument. First, since we have already been justified and reconciled, how much more shall we be saved (at the day of judgment) from the wrath of God! "Wrath of God" does not mean capricious anger but alienation from a holy God, which is the consequence of sin, a process that reaches its culmination at the day of judgment. The fact that we are already justified and reconciled gives us confidence that we shall not be finally and eternally alienated from God. The second *a fortiori* argument concerns life between now and the last judgment—we may continue to rejoice in God who has reconciled us through Christ.

Gospel: Matthew 9:36–10:8

The historicity of the disciples' mission during Jesus' lifetime has been recently questioned, on the supposition that it involves a reading back into the lifetime of Jesus the missions of the post-Easter Church. Certainly the Church's interest in this story and its preservation must have been due to the fact that it continued such missions after Easter. But their historicity to the early ministry of Jesus is clinched by the fact that the message the disciples are given to preach is the message of the earthly Jesus ("The kingdom of heaven is at hand"), not the Church's post-Easter message of Christ's death and resurrection. Yet, the restriction of the mission to Israel *may* reflect the hesitations of the post-Easter Jerusalem church over the extension of the mission to the Samaritans and Gentiles (see Acts).

For Matthew, this restriction was only temporary and limited to Jesus' earthly life. He ends his Gospel with the great missionary charge, "Go and make disciples of *all* nations" (28:19). Thus, he has the same perspective as the Fourth Gospel, which has the saying "And I, *when I am lifted up* from the earth, will draw all men to myself" (12:32), and Ephesians, which says that it is only through the cross that the barrier between Jew and non-Jew is broken down (Eph 2:14-16). Historically speaking, this was in fact so: Jesus' earthly mission was confined almost exclusively to his own people, as even Paul admits (Rom 15:8). Only after the death of the Messiah did the mission become universal in scope.

The Homily

The lack of any clear, consistent theme in today's readings makes the homilist's choice a difficult one. Here are some suggestions.

If the homilist did not develop the theme of the priesthood of the whole Church on the fifth Sunday of Easter this year, that might be done today. This would provide an opportunity to relate the ministerial priesthood to the priesthood of all believers.

The reading from Romans offers an opportunity to clear up some popular confusion about what Christianity means when it speaks of the love of God. This is not a deduction about the way the universe is ordered but a confession of faith arising from our confrontation with the death of Christ on the cross as the ground of our justification and reconciliation. Sir Edwyn Hoskyns used to say that the first letter of John was able to make the great affirmation that God is love only at the end of the New Testament period, only after what he (Hoskyns) loved to call "the turmoil" of the letter to the Romans. It is not a self-evident truth or a premise of the faith.

The gospel offers an opportunity to speak about the mission of the Church. A Church that claims to be apostolic is a Church "sent out" to preach and to bring all people liberation from their ills. The homilist has a chance to identify what the mission of the Church should be on the local scene—precisely at what points men and women and children locally cry out for liberation.

TWELFTH SUNDAY OF THE YEAR

Reading I: Jeremiah 20:10-13

This reading has clearly been chosen to match the gospel, which speaks of the persecution that the apostles will encounter on their mission. Jeremiah was preeminently the prophet who suffered persecution because of his prophetic activity. His fate influenced the development of the later Jewish view that rejection, persecution, and martyrdom were inseparable from the prophetic vocation, a view echoed in a number of dominical sayings (Luke 11:51; 13:33-34; Mark 12:1-9).

To be a bearer of the word of God means to suffer, because that word inevitably encounters hostility and rejection. It is illuminating that apparently, according to the sayings of the Lord referred to above, Jesus regarded his own fate as the culmination of the rejection of the prophets and their message. But it was Paul, more than any other New Testament figure, who regarded Jeremiah as a model for his own apostleship. Certainly Paul regarded suffering as the supreme manifestation of the cross in his own apostolic ministry (see especially the catalogues of his sufferings in 2 Cor 4:7-12; 6:3-10; 11:22-33).

Responsorial Psalm: 69:7-9, 13, 16, 32-34

Psalm 69 is one of the great passion psalms of the Old Testament, second only to Psalm 22 in its influence upon the passion narratives of the Gospels. The final couplet of the first stanza of this responsorial psalm is cited by the Fourth Gospel (2:17) in connection with the cleansing of the temple. If the Church applied it to the Lord's passion, it is equally applicable to the fate of Jeremiah in today's liturgy.

Reading II: Romans 5:12-15

In Rom 5-8 Paul is expounding the liberating effect of Christ's redemptive deed—it brings freedom from wrath, from sin, from the law as a means of salvation, and from death. Here the Apostle enunciates our liberation from sin and death by a comparison of Christ and Adam. Each wrought a deed with momentous consequences.

Adam	*Christ*
disobedience (=trespass)	obedience (death on the cross)
sin ⎫	⎧ free gift, grace
⎬ spreading to the many	⎨
death ⎭	⎩ life

Although there is an antithetical correspondence (Adam is called the "type" of Christ), the correspondence is transcended in a "much more." The caption at the head of the reading is unfortunately ambiguous: "God's gift to us is nothing like our sin against him." This could suggest that our sin is much greater than God's grace. But Paul means it the other way around: God's grace is much greater than our sin. It was easy enough to introduce sin and death upon the *tabula rasa* of human life, but much more difficult to eradicate them after they had been introduced.

We have to guard against reading later theological ideas into Paul's statement about the fall. He does not say that Adam introduced into human life a hereditary trait that is henceforth transmitted biologically. Death, we are told, spread to all members of the human race, not because

Adam sinned or because they sinned "in Adam," but because all sinned like Adam. Adam, as it were, opened the door to sin and death; ever since, sin and death have been prowling around, and all persons have fallen under their clutches because they have succumbed to sin. Adam created the environment in which all would sin and would therefore come under the dominion of death.

Nor must we interpret the passage so as to mean that physical death is, in a crude and mechanical sort of way, a punishment for sin, even for actual sin. (If it is punishment for "original sin," such a view is even more deterministic, and ultimately Gnostic.) Rather, "death" is to be understood theologically as the *theological consequence* of sin. Death means separation from God, and separation is the consequence of sin. Physical death is not a punishment but a biological inevitability. For human beings, however, it is existentially the final revelation of their utter aloneness in a world in which they have cut themselves off from God by sin.

Gospel: Matthew 10:26-33

This is a continuation of the Matthean missionary charge to the Twelve, the beginning of which we read last week. As already indicated, this is a challenge to fearless proclamation in the face of persecution and an assurance of God's care for his witnesses and of their ultimate vindication.

The first saying ("nothing is covered") occurs in various contexts in the Synoptists. Here it is applied to the apostolic preaching. Its original application (see Mark) was probably eschatological: the kingdom of God, which is operative in a hidden way in Jesus' ministry, will at the end be made visible to all who see.

Matthew is rather fond of the body/soul contrast, which is not typical of Scripture. It represents popular Hellenistic language, not a systematically thought-out anthropology. Who is the one who can cast into Gehenna (RSV: "hell")? The Father? Christ? Satan? All three interpretations have found their advocates. The context, however, suggests that Matthew refers it to the Father, for it is the Father who is able to let the sparrows fall to the ground. The protection of the witnesses is contingent upon their faithful testimony. "You are of more value" is not a general statement about the value of human personality; it is an assurance for the messengers. While they are on duty delivering their message, they will be guarded, but even this does not exclude martyrdom. One way or another, the message will be delivered. That is what is important.

In other synoptic versions of the final saying (v. 33), a distinction is drawn between Jesus and the Son of man, though the relation between the two figures is one of functional identity. For the earlier tradition, Jesus was a figure on earth, and the Son of man was a transcendent figure in heaven. The resurrection revealed their identity, and Matthew carries this to its logical conclusion by substituting "I" for the Son of man on the transcendent side. The apostle's testimony on earth, whether given or shirked, will determine his fate at the end. The whole section is an exhortation to faithful and courageous testimony even in the face of suffering and persecution, presumably a very relevant message for Matthew's Church.

The Homily

Two possibilities for the homily can be proposed. One is the integral relation between witness and suffering (Jeremiah in the first reading, the apostles in the gospel). A Church built upon the foundation of the prophets and apostles must be a witnessing and, if necessary, suffering Church.

The second possibility is much more theological. It would be an exposition of what Paul really says about the sin of Adam and its consequences for us, an attempt to disabuse people of crude notions of physically transmitted taint that leave little room for individual responsibility for sin and, on the other side, a Pelagian denial that human beings are seriously tainted by a fallen nature. To prepare for this subject, the preacher would have to study some modern systematic theology. Among Protestant authors in this field, we would recommend Brunner's *Man in Revolt* or Niebuhr's Gifford Lectures, *The Nature and Destiny of Man.*

THIRTEENTH SUNDAY OF THE YEAR

Reading I: 2 Kings 4:8-11, 14-16a

The provision of hospitality by the Shunammite woman for the prophet Elisha is one of the more engaging episodes of the Old Testament. The caption to the reading fails to indicate the evident reason for its selection this Sunday. Clearly it was chosen because it illustrates the dominical saying in the gospel: "He who receives a prophet because he is a prophet shall receive a prophet's reward."

What the historian of the Book of Kings means when he speaks of a "holy man of God" is shown by the other woman's reaction to Elisha's predecessor, Elijah, after he had restored her son to life: "Now I know that you are a man of God, and that the word of the Lord in your mouth is truth" (1 Kgs 17:24). In other words, to be a holy man of God in the Old Testament does not signalize mystical achievement but means to be the bearer of God's word—a word that is "truth," that is, not that it passes the test of doctrinal orthodoxy, but that it effects what it says on the plane of history. Similarly, Elisha is a holy man of God, not because of the achievements of his piety, but because he, like his predecessor, was entrusted to proclaim to his generation the effective word of Yahweh.

Responsorial Psalm: 89:1-2, 15-18

These verses come from one of the great messianic psalms of the Old Testament that portray the coming of the ideal Davidic king. Understandably, it is a psalm that Christian tradition has associated with the Christmas season. It provided the offertory for the third Mass of Christmas in the Roman Missal, and it has always been the proper psalm at one of the offices of Christmas Day in the Book of Common Prayer.

The last stanza alludes to the messianic king. But this aspect is not stressed today. It is simply a hymn of praise for the steadfast love and faithfulness (*chesed wĕmeth*, very important Hebrew words characterizing Yahweh's being and actions). No doubt the Shunammite woman regarded the visits of Elisha to her home as signs of Yahweh's steadfast love and faithfulness.

Reading II: Romans 6:3-4, 8-11

This passage is used in full at the Easter Vigil. While the references to the Christian's dying with Christ are all in the past tense, the references to resurrection are future and conditional. The new life in Christ is something that has to be constantly implemented. The Christian life means more than aspiring after an elusive ideal. What happened to us in baptism cannot be made to "unhappen," however often we stumble and fall. The reality of baptism is always there. Luther, when he was tempted to despair of his faith, used to repeat "Baptizatus sum." That is something we, too, can always draw upon. So the Christian life is fitting oneself into that which we have already been made by baptism: "Werde das, was du bist" (Become what you are!).

Gospel: Matthew 10:37-42

This is the last installment of the Matthean missionary charge to the Twelve. It embraces three complexes of material: the warning that discipleship may involve the breaking of family ties; the saying about taking up the cross; a group of three sayings about the reception given to messengers.

The first two clearly go together. Both concern the cost of discipleship. They appear in various contexts in the gospel tradition, and only in this passage as part of a missionary charge. The first saying in the third group is found in both Matthew and Luke (in a different context in Luke); the second is peculiar to Matthew; the third is found also in Mark.

The fact that the second saying (about receiving a prophet, v. 41) governs the choice of the first reading suggests that this is the saying to which we should pay particular attention today. It is a challenge to those who hear the message of the envoys to receive them properly, not for the sake of their persons, but because they are the bearers of the divine message. What this passage has in mind may be illustrated from the words that Paul used when speaking of his reception by the Thessalonians: "And we also thank God constantly for this, that when you received the word of God which you heard from us, you accepted it not as the word of men but as what it really is, the word of God, which is at work in you believers" (1 Thess 2:13).

The Homily

The emphasis thrown upon the latter part of the gospel by the choice of the first reading suggests what the subject today should be: the proper reception of Christ's messengers. Priests and ministers must be trained to preach. This involves particularly the study of biblical exegesis, so that the sermon may become, not the utterance of human opinions, but the authoritative declaration of the word of God enshrined in Scripture. But a responsibility is laid upon the hearers also. They have to be trained as to what to look for in a sermon, to apply the right criteria, to listen, not for eloquent speech, but for a clear declaration of the word of God based upon a sound exegesis of the text. A homily on the responsibility of listening would be in order today.

As an alternative, the homilist might take up the Pauline teaching on baptism in the second reading and stress the nature of Christian life under the rubric "Become what you are."

FOURTEENTH SUNDAY OF THE YEAR

Reading I: Zechariah 9:9-10

This passage is often associated with Palm Sunday, for obvious reasons. Here it is used to complement the pericope called "The cry of jubilation," which forms today's gospel. When our Lord rode into Jerusalem on Palm Sunday, his action was not a sudden inspiration but something wholly in character with his previous ministry—his self-identification with the lowly.

Responsorial Psalm: 145:1-2, 8-11, 13c-14

The same selection of verses from Psalm 145 is used on the thirty-first Sunday of the year in series C. If it was not chosen here as a general psalm of praise, it must have been selected as a response to the challenge in the first reading: "Rejoice greatly, O daughter of Zion! . . . Lo, your king comes to you," which is taken up in the words "I will extol thee, my God and King." This would mean transferring to Christ what, in the Old Testament, is addressed to Yahweh, but there is ample New Testament precedent for such procedure.

520

Reading II: Romans 8:9, 11-13

It is important to know what Paul means by "flesh" and "spirit." The New English Bible has perpetuated the misunderstanding of flesh as "lower nature." It is not lower nature (a Greek rather than a biblical concept), but unredeemed nature, which includes what the Greeks would have called the higher nature (hence Paul can speak of the "mind of the flesh"). The whole person, with the so-called higher nature as well as the lower, stands in need of redemption. Also, "body" does not mean body as opposed to soul, but the whole person, subject to sin and death, yet open to the possibility of redemption. "Lower nature" would suggest that there is a part of our nature that is beyond redemption, just as "higher nature" suggests that there is a part of us that does not need redemption.

Gospel: Matthew 11:25-30

The first half of this reading, through verse 27, is also found in Luke and apparently comes from the common source shared by both evangelists. It is, therefore, a quite early tradition and is sometimes called "the synoptic thunderbolt from the Johannine sky." It looks so different from most of the synoptic material and is highly reminiscent of the discourses and the prayers of the Fourth Gospel, especially the theme of the mutual knowledge of the Father and the Son. It is probably best understood as a liturgical fragment celebrating the knowledge of God that has come through Jesus Christ, and is a halfway house toward the development of the Johannine discourses. But it is deeply rooted in our Lord's self-understanding, as registered by his use of the word *Abba* for his Father. This betokens a unique relationship, which he invites others to share through his word.

The second part of the reading is peculiar to Matthew. It echoes the invitation of wisdom found in Sir 51:23-26 and is also found in a shorter (and perhaps earlier) form in the Gospel of Thomas: "Jesus said: Come to me, for easy is my yoke and my Lordship is gentle, and you shall find repose for yourselves." It is another liturgical fragment. In it Jesus is represented as the mouthpiece of the wisdom of God. This is an early type of Church Christology, which again has its roots in the self-understanding of Jesus.

The Homily

The combination of the Old Testament reading and the Matthean form of the cry of jubilation with the Savior's invitation highlights the theme of Jesus' humbling of himself to bring the wisdom of God to humankind. A meditation on the humiliation of the incarnation would be in order, and perhaps an extension of this motif to the interpretation of the Church as the bearer of the revelation of God's truth in the world today. If the Church is to follow the pattern of its divine Master, it must witness to the truth, not by authoritarian demeanor, but by humble testimony and suffering for the truth's sake.

An alternative for the homilist would be an exposition of Paul's doctrine of the human person. This should seek to correct the common misunderstanding of flesh as lower nature, and to emphasize that the whole person is both in need of redemption and redeemable.

FIFTEENTH SUNDAY OF THE YEAR

Reading I: Isaiah 55:10-11

It is a little surprising that the caption to this reading calls attention solely to the pictorial half of our passage. This is not a piece of teaching about the natural order; rather, the natural order is here used to provide an analogy for the supernatural: "As the rain . . . so my word." This passage provides an Old Testament prototype for the parable of the sower, which consists of the same pictorial and material sides: "As the seed . . . so the word."

Responsorial Psalm: 65:9-13

This psalm, as the response indicates, forms a link between the Old Testament reading and the gospel. It picks up the pictorial side of the analogy and praises God for the gift of the rain.

Commentators are divided over the original use of this psalm. Some have associated it with the autumn harvest festival (see the first line of stanza 3), and indeed it is still so used in many churches. It is more likely, however, that it was intended for the beginning of the barley harvest: the rains are still falling (stanzas 1 and 2), and the grain is still standing in the fields (stanzas 3 and 4). It is certainly very fitting for use at this time of year. In the parched land of Judah, the rain served as an obvious symbol of the grace of God.

Reading II: Romans 8:18-23

Here Paul expounds his view of the created order. It is, as the Old Testament affirms, the creation (*ktisis*, v. 19), that is, it owes its being to God and is therefore good. But it became subject to "futility" (v. 20); it is in "bondage to decay" (v. 21) and "groans" (v. 22).

Paul is not a romantic nature worshiper but a realist who recognizes "nature red in tooth and claw." He attributes this lamentable state of affairs to Adam's fall. The basis for this assertion lies in Gen 3:17, where the ground is cursed because of Adam's sin. The creation, Paul says, was thus subjected, "not of its own will, but by the will of him who subjected it in hope." Most commentators identify "him" here with God, but some refer it to Adam. In the latter case, Adam, through his fall, dragged down the whole created universe with him.

Some commentators would remove the semicolon after "hope" and translate the word *hoti* as "that" instead of "because." The whole sentence could then be paraphrased: "the creation was subjected to futility, not because of any wrong it had done itself but by the [disobedience] of Adam, who thereby dragged it down into subjection. But there was still a hope of its ultimate liberation."

Where did this hope come from? It must lie, not in Gen 3, but in the apocalyptic expectation of a new heaven and a new earth. So the whole creation waits with eager longing. Just as its fall, its state of corruption and decay, was the consequence of the human fall, so the hope of its redemption is bound up with human redemption. Its longing, therefore, is for the redemption of humanity, for the "revealing of the sons of God" (v. 19), for the redemption of their bodies (v. 23).

Now, this longing has been given substance—believers, as a result of Christ's finished work of redemption, have the first fruits of the Spirit.

In them the process of redemption, for which the whole creation yearned, has already been initiated. But meanwhile they have to live in the tension between the "already" and the "not yet," and therefore they too still share the groaning of the whole creation. (With some ancient manuscripts, we omit "adoption as sons" in verse 23, for elsewhere Paul regards adoption as a present reality [Rom 8:15; Gal 4:5]. At the moment their sonship is hidden, visible only to faith; but it will be revealed for what it is at the end, not brought into being only then for the first time [see v. 19; also 1 John 3:2].)

This picture of the unity between human destiny and the destiny of the universe is magnificent, but is it tenable? Certainly there are mythological elements in it—for example, it depends upon a literal acceptance of the story of the fall and of the cursing of the ground as its consequence. Is the perishability and decay of the universe really a consequence of human sin? And does human redemption lead to the redemption of the universe from this decay?

This much we may affirm: As a result of the disturbance of the divine-human relationship, the relationship of human beings not only to one another but to the whole created order is disturbed. People either deify nature (pantheism, romanticism) or they treat it with contempt (pollution!). When the relationship of human beings to God is restored, then not only is their relation to one another rectified as in the sacramental community, but they also recover their harmony with the created order. This much of truth we can discern in Paul's daring picture. Western thought, especially since the Reformation, has tended to concentrate upon the salvation of the individual; our passage is a powerful reminder of the cosmic dimension of redemption.

Gospel: Matthew 13:1-23 (long form); 13:1-9 (short form)

The short form of the gospel substantially represents the parable as originally told by Jesus. The discussion about the purpose of parabolic teaching (vv. 13-17) and the allegorical interpretation of the sower (vv. 18-23) are later interpretive additions. Most, though not all, New Testament scholars would agree that this is so. The arguments for this position have been vindicated by the discovery of the Gospel of Thomas, which has the parable without any interpretation. That being the case, the short form offers an opportunity to deal with the original interpretation.

To understand the shorter form, we must entirely disabuse our minds of the allegorical interpretation and look at the total impression the story creates. What we see is a tremendous harvest, despite the loss of some of the seed. The climax comes at the end and, as so often in Jesus' parables, contains an element of deliberate absurdity—a hundredfold yield is fantastic, the usual yield being in the neighborhood of seven and a half, with ten as an outside possibility. The point of the parable is miraculous success in spite of apparent frustration.

But this is not a general lesson; it bears quite concretely upon the situation of Jesus and his hearers. There was much frustration in Jesus' ministry. Only a few followed him. He encountered much hostility from the authorities of his day. He was misunderstood by the crowds. Even some of his closest followers left when he deliberately broke with the crowds (John 6:66). Jesus is confident, nevertheless, that his ministry will result in the eventual triumph of God's kingdom.

The allegorical interpretation (vv. 18-23) adapts the parable to a missionary situation, most likely that of the Greek-speaking Church prior to Mark. It warns new converts of the perils that beset the life of discipleship and urges upon them the need for perseverance.

The central portion on the purpose of parabolic teaching appears to have been first inserted at this position by Mark, although it represents earlier tradition and is possibly an authentic saying of Jesus. It referred originally, not to the teaching in parables, but quite generally to the kingdom of God mysteriously present in the words and works of Jesus.

Mark constructs a theory of his own about parabolic teaching. He holds that parables were told deliberately to create misunderstanding and to mystify the hearers, producing hardness of heart and unfaith. The parables are riddles to outsiders, and their meaning is entrusted to an inner group of disciples, who will be able to make the meaning plain only after the resurrection. This is all part of Mark's messianic secret. Only after Jesus' death and resurrection can his messiahship be safely proclaimed; during his earthly life it remains a mystery. This was not a piece of abstract theologizing, but Mark's answer to a Christology that overemphasized the miracles of Jesus and minimized the cross.

Matthew has taken over the parable and its allegorical interpretation from Mark without any substantial changes. But he has introduced considerable changes into the central section, and this is obviously the most important part to study if we are following the longer form of the gospel. Matthew makes the following major alterations:

1) Verse 11: Instead of Mark's "to you is given the mystery of the kingdom of God," Matthew has: "To you it has been given to *know the secrets* . . . ." The fact that Luke has the same wording shows that both evangelists are following a second, non-Marcan source at this point.

2) Verse 12: Matthew adds this from Mark 4:25.

3) Verse 13: Matthew alters Mark's scandalous *hina* ("in order that") to *hoti* ("because").

4) Verses 14-15: Our present text includes a citation from Isa 6, which was already alluded to in verse 13. There is a growing opinion among scholars that this is a post-Matthean addition to the text.

5) Verses 16-17: "Blessed are the eyes" from Q (par. Luke 10:23-24).

To get at Matthew's theology, we will ignore the fourth point and concentrate on the other points. Matthew has edited this section to bring out two antithetical points: (a) the disciples (that is, the Church) are the bearers of the new revelation, hoped for by the Old Testament worthies and now fulfilled (v. 17), and will be rewarded at the end; (b) the old Israel has rejected the new revelation and will be rejected at the end. The motivation behind these redactional changes comes from Matthew's own situation. The mission to Israel has finally failed, leading to a debate between the Church and the synagogue over which is the true people of God.

The Homily

Much will turn on whether the shorter or the longer form of the gospel is read. If the shorter, then attention is drawn to the parable as it was originally told by Jesus. It envisaged a situation of frustration and sought to assure the disciples of the ultimate triumph of the kingdom. Such a message could be quite easily transferred to the Church's situation today, when once again there are many frustrations and apparent failures. The assurance of abundant success despite these failures is the message for today, a message in thorough conformity with the gospel's *theologia crucis.* Allusion may be made to the other readings, for instance, the rain yielding fruit (first reading and psalm) and the groaning of the community with the whole created universe (second reading).

If the long form of the gospel is used, it directs the preacher to an exposition of the great privileges of the Christian community as the bearer of God's truth in the world. One would not, in our changed situation, want to point to the synagogue as the community that once had the truth but rejected it, but the longer gospel could perhaps be used as an indictment of our secularized, once Christian civilization. The hope for the final vindication of Christianity in verse 12 could be related to the similar thought of the final cosmic vindication in the second reading: "the revealing of the sons of God" and "the redemption of [their] bodies."

SIXTEENTH SUNDAY OF THE YEAR

Reading I: Wisdom 12:13, 16-19

The caption to this passage highlights the idea of repentance. From the parables in today's gospel, however, it appears that the real reason for the choice of this passage was to reinforce the notion of God's forbearance: "Thou who art sovereign in strength dost judge *with mildness,* and *with great forbearance* thou dost govern us" (v. 18). God's care, it says, is for all people, and even for the tares among the wheat. "Thy sovereignty over all causes thee to spare all" (v. 16).

Responsorial Psalm: 86:5-6, 9-10, 15-16a

This psalm of individual lament is remarkable for its confidence in the faithfulness and steadfast love of Yahweh, a confidence unshaken by present distress. If God's forbearance is the main theme of this day, this is a highly suitable psalm to go with the Old Testament reading and the gospel.

Reading II: Romans 8:26-27

We note that two verses (24-25) have been omitted between the end of last week's reading from Romans and the beginning of today's selection. This is because verse 26 picks up from verse 23. The inward groaning of those who possess the first fruits of the Spirit is assisted by the Spirit, who intercedes for us "with sighs too deep for words" (v. 26; the word for "sighs" is akin to "groanings"). Herein lies the clue to Paul's meaning. It is not that speech of the Holy Spirit is in itself encompassed with infirmity and therefore itself groans or sighs in an unintelligible fashion (in glossolalia, for instance); rather, Paul's thought is that the Spirit condescends to take up our infirm prayers and to bear them up to God and to present them before God in the form of intelligible speech. Here the Spirit acts as a Paraclete or Advocate, as in the Fourth Gospel, although Paul does not actually use the word.

We habitually think of prayer in terms of "me down here" speaking to "God up there." But when I pray as a believer, it is not just "me down here"—it is the Spirit of God within me praying to "God up there." Thus, immanence and transcendence are both acted out in the activity of prayer. Thus, too, prayer is an activity in which the believer participates in the mystery of the Holy Trinity.

Gospel: Matthew 13:24-43 (long form); 13:24-30 (short form)

We continue today with another parable from Matt 13. Like the parable of the sower, the parable of the tares has undergone allegorization, and once again the short form gives the non-allegorized version, which is very probably close to the form in which Jesus originally spoke it. There is a further similarity: in the long form, the parable and its allegorical interpretation are separated by other materials. In this case, the intervening material consists of two parables found elsewhere in the Gospel tradition, namely, the parable of the mustard seed, which occurs in Mark and Q (Mark 4:30-32; Luke 13:18-19); and the parable of the leaven, which is found in Q (par. Luke 13:20-21). These little parables are followed by a shortened form of Mark's conclusion to the parables (Matt 13:34-35; par. Mark 4:33-34) and a fulfillment from Ps 78:2, which is both unique to and typical of Matthew.

We thus once more have three levels in the tradition: (1) the parable of the tares, substantially as told by Jesus; (2) the parable of the tares with its allegorical interpretation; (3) the insertion of the complex of other materials between the parable and its interpretation, and the shift of the latter from a public to a private location. The meaning of each of these levels may be constructed as follows:

1) Jesus is criticized by his purist contemporaries for inviting the outcast to eat with him as an anticipation of God's salvation. He answers by saying that it is for God to make the separation and that he will do so only at the end. Then it will be clear who are the wheat and who are the tares. Doubtless there will be some surprises in store.

2) The allegorical interpretation applies the parable to the Christian community. There are tares as well as wheat in the Church now. The Church is a *corpus permixtum*, and there need be no premature attempt to separate the wheat from the tares in its present life.

3) By sandwiching the intervening material between the parable and its interpretation, and especially by shifting the scene from public to private teaching just before the interpretation, Matthew has applied this complex of material to the situation of his own Church. As we saw last week, that situation is marked by disappointment over the failure of the mission to Israel. Now the Church is assured that when the gospel came to Israel, it came as a *parabolē*, a *mashal*, a riddle (Ps 78:2). Only the Church comprehends the riddle. The tares are presently indistinguishable from the wheat, but at the end God will separate them. The Church must meanwhile be patient.

There is a remarkable amount of continuity between the three interpretations—more so than in the case of the sower. At each level the point remains the forbearance of God. What changes is the identity of the wheat and the tares. For Jesus, it was the outcast and the authorities of his people. For the Church tradition, it was the good and the bad within the Christian community. For the evangelist, it was non-believing Israel and the members of his Church.

The Homily

The main point of today's readings is obviously the forbearance of God. The Old Testament reading, the psalm, and above all the parable of the tares at its successive levels of interpretation all make this point. The preacher is free to identify those areas in which the people need to recognize this forbearance in action in their midst, what group they are tempted to treat as tares. Having made the identification, the preacher can use the scriptural materials to speak to that situation.

Or the preacher may find it more appropriate to take the second reading, with its teaching about the Holy Spirit as the power of God within believers; the Spirit takes their inarticulate prayers and renders them intelligible before the throne of God. If there are prayer groups in the parish or if there is a great concern with the problems of prayer, this would be a fitting theme for a homily.

SEVENTEENTH SUNDAY OF THE YEAR

Reading I: 1 Kings 3:5, 7-12

In the Hellenistic tradition, wisdom meant philosophical speculation. In the Old Testament tradition, on the other hand, wisdom had much more mundane significance. It included a practical know-how in various areas of life as well as the knowledge of God and of good and evil.

Chapters 3 to 11 of 1 Kings demonstrate Solomon's wisdom in many different spheres: as practical psychologist in the case of the two prostitutes (3:16-28); as administrator (ch. 4); as builder (chs. 5-7); as merchant (ch. 9). Our passage today relates how he acquired this wisdom in a dream in which he prays for wisdom rather than for riches or for length of days. Wisdom is thus the supreme value of human life.

This reading was evidently chosen because of the parables of the treasure and the pearl, which represent the kingdom of God as the supreme value for which no sacrifice is too great.

Responsorial Psalm: 119:57, 72, 76-77, 127-128, 129-130

The wise person (note the last two lines in the final stanza) is the one who knows and keeps the commandments of Yahweh. The psalm is thus linked to the first reading, for the wise person loves the commandments of God "above fine gold" (third stanza), as Solomon chose wisdom rather than riches, and as Jesus in today's gospel urges the crowd to seek the kingdom of God the way a person would spare nothing to get hold of a treasure trove or a pearl of great price. Thus, the psalm is also linked to the gospel reading.

Reading II: Romans 8:28-30

In the readings from Rom 8 that were read on the previous Sundays, Paul has been speaking primarily of the suffering, the transitoriness, and the infirmities of human existence, including Christian existence. But again and again the hope of ultimate transformation and vindication keeps breaking through.

This week's reading forms a transition from the shadowy side of human and Christian existence to the glorious destiny that awaits the redeemed. Verse 28 states a proposition that was known to Paul's readers ("We know") and was apparently a religious maxim in Judaism. He then bases this maxim on the realities of Christian experience. It is not just pious make-believe to say that everything will turn out all right in the end; it is an assurance based upon what the believers have already experienced from God: he foreknew them, predestined them to be conformed to his Son's image, called them, justified them, and, surprisingly—for we would expect this to be reserved until the final fulfillment—glorified them. In other words, the Christian eschatological hope is not for something totally different from what we already have ("pie in the sky when we die") but the ultimate fruition of our present life in Christ.

Gospel: Matthew 13:44-52 (long form); 13:44-46 (short form)

The long form of this gospel contains the twin parables of the treasure and the pearl, followed by the parable of the dragnet and the concluding saying of the Christian scribe. The short form stops after the twin parables. It is a pity that it has also dropped the saying about the Christian scribe, for this saying is closely related to the twin parables (the kingdom of God as the supreme value, of which the Christian scribe is the custodian). It also provides an important clue to Matthew's self-understanding as an evangelist. The evangelist takes "what is old," that is, the gospel tradition as he has received it, and reapplies it to the new situation that confronts him and the Church at his time. We have already seen him doing this in his treatment of the parables of the sower and the tares (his "redaction," as New Testament scholars call it).

This process of reinterpreting the tradition of Jesus' words and works has continued ever since in the ongoing life of the Church. The latest chapter in the history of exegesis (which is really what Church history is all about) is accomplished when the preacher stands up on a Sunday and delivers the homily. The test of faithful exegesis is whether it enables the old to be said today in a new situation. This cannot be done simply by repeating the old as it stands, but only by reproducing the old in a new way so that it can say what it said in past situations and not something different. In other words, the saying about the Christian scribe describes the task of hermeneutics.

Important as these considerations are for the self-understanding of the homilist and the self-understanding of the evangelist, they are not the main point that today's readings propose for our consideration. As the first reading and the psalm show, the intention of this gospel is to speak of the kingdom of God as the supreme value to be preferred above all else, as a person would even cheat (by hiding the treasure) in order to acquire some treasure trove of the owners of the field in which it was found. Here we see an example of Jesus' propensity to use unattractive human behavior in his parables, as in the case of the Lucan parables of the unjust steward and the unjust judge. This serves as a warning against treating the parables merely as moral lessons; rather, they light up worldly behavior as worthy of imitating in quite a different context. The kingdom of God is of such great value that the most drastic action is worth taking to gain it.

The parable of the pearl is of a rather different type. It involves no discreditable conduct. But like the parable of the hidden treasure, it holds up for our emulation in quite a different context the behavior of a man who was prepared to take drastic action to secure the object of his desire. Matthew, of course, relates these pictures to the life of the Church in his day. It was a Church threatened by antinomianism (disregard of the moral law), by false prophets, and by persecution. In that situation Christians must be prepared to take drastic action to be accepted among the righteous at the last day. Hence, Matthew appends to the twin parables the further parable of the dragnet.

The Homily

The key note of today's readings is struck by the twin parables we have just discussed. To them, as we have seen, the picture of Solomon's choice and the psalmist's devotion to the Law are closely related. Persecution may not be a peril for the Church in this country today as it was in Matthew's time, but doctrinal and moral laxity certainly are. The believer is urged to take drastic action to remain faithful to God and his kingdom.

EIGHTEENTH SUNDAY OF THE YEAR

Reading I: Isaiah 55:1-3

Having announced the return of God's people to their homeland as the culminating event of Israel's salvation history, Second Isaiah concludes his prophecies with an invitation to the eschatological banquet. This banquet imagery continues to develop along a trajectory both in the wisdom literature and in Jewish apocalyptic. It is taken up in the New Testament and underlies the accounts of the feedings, one of which forms the gospel of this day.

Responsorial Psalm: 145:8-9, 15-16, 17-18

The second stanza, linking as it does with both the Old Testament reading and the gospel, explains the psalm's presence here. Note particularly the verb "satisfy" both in verse 16 and in the gospel (Matt 14:20). The Greek word is not the same, however, in these passages. The psalm has "filled"; the gospel has a rather coarse word meaning "stuffed full." But the notion of repletion, however expressed, figures frequently in descriptions of the eschatological banquet.

Reading II: Romans 8:35, 37-39

In this concluding selection from Rom 8, Paul rises to great heights of eloquence. It is almost a hymn of triumph. In both paragraphs, as arranged in the Lectionary, the word "separate" occurs. The first paragraph is a question : "Who [not "What"] shall separate us . . . ?" Paul regards the seven forms of suffering he is about to enumerate as quasi-personal powers, perhaps because they are earthly manifestations of the cosmic-demonic powers enumerated in the second paragraph, which is in the form of a statement, not a question. Here Paul names ten cosmic powers that cannot separate us from "the love of God in Christ Jesus." This last phrase corresponds to "the love of Christ" in the first paragraph. The two are essentially the same thing, the same love.

For Paul, this love is not an abstract quality but an event that happened, namely, the cross. The cross was the obedience of the Son (see Phil 2:8) and at the same time the redemptive act of the Father (2 Cor 5:19). In this passage, then, Paul is interpreting the death of Jesus as a victory over the demonic powers, who can do no ultimate damage to believers. Paul does not say that believers are already immune to the onslaughts of these powers, but he is sure that amid all demonic onslaughts the believers are "superconquerors."

Gospel: Matthew 14:13-21

The feeding of the multitude occurs more frequently than any other episode in the four Gospels—six times in all. This testifies to its importance for the early community, an importance due to its connection with the Eucharist. Whereas we tend to see the origin of the Eucharist exclusively in the Last Supper, the early Church laid at least as much stress on Jesus' eating with his disciples in Galilee, to say nothing of the post-resurrection meals. The telling of the story has been shaped by the Eucharistic customs of the community: "taking the . . . loaves," "blessed," "broke," "gave," "ate." The words "he looked up to heaven" may also be Eucharistic, though not attested elsewhere in New Testament Eucharistic texts.

Note, however, the complete absence of any reference to Passover, covenant, or sacrificial motifs. There is no mention of the "words of institution." There is no cup; instead of wine, fish figure twice in the early part of the narrative, though they disappear later on. Clearly the account has in mind the early Christian rite of the breaking of the bread, celebrated daily (Acts 2), rather than the covenant-sacrifice meal, which was probably, in the earliest days, a single, annual Christian Passover celebration.

This daily breaking of the bread had eschatological associations: it was an anticipation of the messianic banquet. The Church's Eucharist today combines, or should combine, both the sacrificial and the eschatological associations. In the recent past, emphasis has been placed more on the sacrificial than on the eschatological aspect, but the imbalance is now being redressed.

All this applies to the meaning of Jesus' feeding the multitude in the oral tradition. What of the evangelist's redaction? As we compare Matthew's account with its parallel in Mark 6:30-44, not only do we find Matthew's account abbreviated, but we also see that the role of the disciples in the episode differs considerably, and this must in fact be Matthew's chief redactional concern. In the opening dialogue between Jesus and the disciples (vv. 15-18 of our reading), Mark portrays the disciples as lacking in understanding, whereas in Matthew they understand well enough but are deficient in faith (H. J. Held).

In the actual feeding (the final paragraph of our reading), the disciples' role is more prominent, and what happens to the multitude is less prominent. The disciples bring the bread to Jesus at his command (v. 18). Matthew explicitly states that the disciples "gave" the bread to the crowd. The evangelist seems concerned to underline the functions of the ministry as they are developing in his Church.

The Homily

The Old Testament reading and the psalm slant our attention to the gospel reading, toward the level of the oral tradition rather than toward Matthew's redaction. This suggests that the most obvious line for the homilist to take would be to expound the Eucharist in terms of the eschatological banquet. Of course, he/she may also emphasize, with Matthew, the role of the Church's ministry in providing the food for the banquet. The ministers have an important role to perform, but it is Christ who really acts in the meal, giving the bread of life through their ministry.

The reading from Romans provides an opportunity to deal with a perennial pastoral problem—that of suffering. People often expect Christian faith to serve as an insurance policy against suffering. The words of Jesus about taking up one's cross and the words of Paul in the second reading show that there is no justification for this view. Both Jesus and Paul hold out to Christians a power that will enable them to cope with suffering and to triumph over it. The Christian "solution" to the problem of suffering is not an intellectual argument but practical help in facing it.

Among the various kinds of suffering the Christian has to face is death itself. The New Testament pictures of what is to happen to the Christian after death are derived, for the most part, from Jewish apocalyptic and are therefore mythological in their imagery. They cannot as such, therefore, be the objects of Christian faith, for Christian faith cannot consist in holding extraneous mythological ideas. Rather, these ideas are used to express Christian faith. What that faith is, Paul expresses in non-mythological terms when he says that nothing, not even death itself, can separate us from the love of God that we have experienced in Christ. That is the Christian "answer" to the problem of death. Is the love of God in Christ so real to us that when faced with death we ask only his assurance?

NINETEENTH SUNDAY OF THE YEAR

Reading I: 1 Kings 19:9a, 11-13a

This passage has obviously been chosen to match the gospel story of the appearance of Jesus to his disciples on the lake. In each story an encounter with God/Christ takes place after the stilling of the storm.

Elijah has slain the prophets of Baal, and Jezebel has threatened his life in revenge. He retreats to Mount Horeb to commune with God, as Moses had done before him (there are distinct parallels in the narrative— the forty days and the lodging in the cave). Yahweh is not in the storm, the earthquake, or the fire, but in the gentle breeze after the storm. The place of encounter with God is not in the awesome events of nature but in the word of revelation. At the same time, however, after the encounter of revelation has occurred, the storm, earthquake, and fire can be seen as the harbingers of God's revelation.

Responsorial Psalm: 85:8ab, 9-13

The use of this psalm as a response to the passage about Elijah is evidently suggested by the first two lines of the first stanza: "Let me hear what God the Lord will speak, for he will speak peace to his people."

The origin of this psalm is in dispute, and its original reference is uncertain. Its affinities (see its soteriological vocabulary) seem to be with Second Isaiah, and a reasonable assumption would be that it refers to the impending return from exile. In the Christian liturgy it is used most frequently in Advent and at Christmas.

Reading II: Romans 9:1-5

In our readings in course from Romans, we now reach the section in which Paul wrestles with the problem of the place of Israel in salvation history (Rom 9-11). Israel's rejection of Jesus as Messiah has been a great shock to Paul, and he uses very strong language in praying for their salvation (Rom 9:3).

From verse 4 on, Paul lists the great prerogatives of Israel in salvation history—eight of them, culminating in the Messiah himself and ending in a doxology. The reading of the RSV margin is followed here. The RSV text inserts a period after "Christ" and relegates the doxology to a separate sentence, thus: "God who is over all be blessed for ever." Both renderings are possible renderings of the Greek, but it is unlikely that Paul would have called Christ "God" without qualifications, as in the RSV margin. The whole subject has been well discussed by Bultmann in his essay "The Confession of the World Council of Churches."

In his attitude toward his fellow Jews, Paul strikes a mean between two diametrically opposite attitudes that have characterized Christian thought at different periods—anti-Semitism and a complete "ecumenical" acceptance of Judaism as a valid religion and an abandonment of any hope for their conversion to faith in Jesus Christ. Both attitudes are seemingly a betrayal of the gospel as Paul understands it. His attitude is in continuity with both Moses (Exod 32:32) and Elijah (see the sequel to the first reading in 1 Kgs 19:14ff).

Gospel: Matthew 14:22-33

Since Matthew has taken over the walking on the water from Mark, we must pay special attention to Matthew's alterations. Two major changes may be noted: (1) the addition of the dialogue between Peter and Jesus, and the walking of Peter on the water; (2) instead of ending with the disciples' misunderstanding of Jesus, the story now ends in a confession of faith: "Truly you are the Son of God." It is reasonable to suppose, with G. D. Kilpatrick, that Matthew is drawing upon a special Petrine tradition, akin to the material he has added in 16:17-19. In that case, the Peter episode may be another part of a story of Jesus' resurrection appearance to Peter.

The effect of these changes is to alter completely the thrust of the pericope. In Mark it was an element in the evangelist's theme of the disciples' misunderstanding, designed to play down the interpretation of Jesus' miracles as epiphanies in opposition to a "divine man" Christology. This is no longer an acute problem for Matthew, so he has altered the interpretation of the scene. It becomes a paradigm of discipleship. The boat represents the Church; the storm, the persecution through which Matthew's community is passing. Jesus appears and challenges Peter, the disciple *par excellence,* to trust him. Peter is afraid and cries out, "Lord, save me." Jesus, half rebuking, half encouraging him, says: "O man of little faith, why did you doubt?" The Lord brings Peter to safety, and all the disciples make the adoring confession "Truly you are the Son of God."

The Homily

Probably the most obvious choice would be to take Matthew's alterations to Mark's story of the walking upon the water and treat it as a paradigm of discipleship. To be the Church is to be in a storm-tossed bark. Christ comes and rebukes us for our little faith, and encourages us to trust in him. He stills the storm and brings us to safety. The realization of his present help in trouble should lead to adoration and a confession of faith.

A relevant alternative would be to take the second reading as the basis for a discussion of the very tricky question of Christian-Jewish relations. There are centuries of anti-Semitism for which the Church must repent, and it has probably lost the right today to seek to "convert" the Jews. The credibility gap is far too great, and it is the Church's own sin that this is so. But on the other hand, the Church cannot cease to pray with the Apostle that the Jews may come to know Jesus as the Messiah—in their own way, perhaps, and not in ours.

TWENTIETH SUNDAY OF THE YEAR

Reading I: Isaiah 56:1, 6-7

This passage comes from Third Isaiah, the postexilic portion of that work. It is founded on the teaching of Second Isaiah, as the opening verse of the reading shows: it uses the same terms, "justice" and "righteousness." On the other hand, there is a new twist to these words: justice and righteousness are not exclusively Yahweh's mighty acts in bringing his people out of exile but are demands upon human conduct. Third Isaiah thus gives a moralistic slant to the teaching of his mentor.

Verses 6-7 deal with an acute practical problem that arose after the return and the restoration of the temple. Prior to the Exile, foreigners had been allowed to perform certain functions in the temple precincts. Ezekiel had objected to allowing uncircumcised foreigners around the place. Third Isaiah now stipulates the conditions under which they may serve: they must observe the Sabbath and keep the covenant, as far as it is applicable to non-Israelites.

This is not unqualified universalism. But it is, at least in a symbolic way, a prophecy foreshadowing the universalism of the gospel. It points to the time when the temple of God will be a house of prayer for all people; it thus points forward to the effects of Christ's redeeming work. Mark, or the tradition before him, puts these words on Jesus' lips as an interpretation of his cleansing of the temple (Mark 11:17). John further interprets that event by taking it as an act of prophetic symbolism, declaring the replacement of the old temple by the temple of Jesus' body (John 2:19-21). It is there that the text of Isa 56:7 comes to its final fulfillment.

This passage was chosen today because of the universalist implications of the episode of the Canaanite woman in the gospel reading.

Responsorial Psalm: 67:1-2, 4-5, 7

Psalm 67 combines thanksgiving for the harvest with prayer for continued blessings. It serves as an appropriate thanksgiving for the continuation of the benefits the Church enjoys and as a prayer for the spread of these benefits to all nations, in keeping with the universalist implications of the Old Testament reading and the gospel.

Reading II: Romans 11:13-15, 29-32

This passage occurs toward the end of Paul's discussion of Israel's place in salvation history, the opening part of which we read last week. Paul believes that the pattern of salvation history will run like this: First, the gospel is proclaimed to Israel by the earliest apostles. But Israel rejects it, so Paul is called to proclaim it to the Gentiles. This step will provoke Israel to jealousy, and Israel will then hurry to gain acceptance before the end.

Paul's view of salvation history causes difficulties for us today. For one thing, he expected the end to come very soon. He did not think in terms of several millennia of history. Already Matthew was compelled to adjust the early Christian perspective on salvation history. He contemplated the failure and abandonment of the mission to Israel and, as a consequence, saw the necessity of concentrating in the future on the mission to the Gentiles. Matthew had no hope, as Paul did, that Israel would be provoked to jealousy and would want to come in. This adjustment of perspective need not surprise us. As Cullmann has shown, it is characteristic of the understanding of salvation history in both the Old and the New Testaments that it should constantly be adjusted in the light of later events.

For us, what is of permanent validity in this passage is not Paul's particular scheme of salvation history (which had to be corrected already by Matthew), but rather the great principle enunciated in verse 29 and highlighted in the caption: the gifts and calling of God are irrevocable. That must be the basic principle as we wrestle today with the place of Israel in salvation history.

Gospel: Matthew 15:21-28

Matthew took over the story of the Canaanite woman from Mark, but with several important changes:

1. The woman is called a Canaanite instead of a Syro-Phoenician.

2. There is considerable expansion of the dialogue material in the body of the story (vv. 22-24).

3. Jesus praises the woman for her faith (v. 28).

4. Matthew removes Jesus' saying that the children (that is, Israel) must be fed first.

5. The narrative of the woman's return home to discover that her daughter was cured of the demon is reduced to a brief statement that the girl was indeed healed (unlike Mark, Matthew is not interested in the fact that the healing was performed from a distance).

It may well be that Matthew had access to an alternative version of the healing, perhaps a more primitive one (so Bultmann and Lohmeyer). In any case, Matthew's alterations have a theological rather than a historical motivation. He shifts the interest away from the miracle to the woman's faith. As a Canaanite, she is a stranger to the covenants of Israel (see the Old Testament conflicts between Israel and Canaan). Jesus takes the barrier very seriously. He first refuses to answer her, then announces that he was sent only to the lost sheep of Israel. It was the woman's faith that finally overcame the barrier.

Mark and Matthew wrote for a different public at different periods. Mark wrote for Gentile Christians, showing them that salvation was first for the Jews only and then for the Gentiles. Matthew wrote for Jewish Christians, showing them that faith, and faith alone, breaks down the barrier between Jew and Gentile.

The Homily
On this Sunday a unitive theme runs through all the readings. The homilist should wrestle today with the twin facts of the particularity and universalism of the gospel. Israel has a unique place in salvation history, and the gifts and call of God are irrevocable. At the same time, the temple of Christ's body is a house of prayer for *all* nations. All the nations will come and praise Yahweh, and faith—faith alone—opens up salvation to the Gentiles.

TWENTY-FIRST SUNDAY OF THE YEAR

Reading I: Isaiah 22:19-23
In this passage Isaiah denounces one Shebna, the prime minister ("who is over the household"), and predicts his replacement by Eliakim. The passage is notable for its use of the "key," which is taken up in the gospel today, the *Tu es Petrus* saying.

Responsorial Psalm: 138:1-3, 6, 8bc
Slightly different selections of verses from this psalm are used on the fifth   *459*
and seventeenth Sundays of the year in series C. Today's refrain ("Lord,   *489*
your love is eternal") suggests that God's purposes are not defeated by the infidelity of his human instruments. God can replace a faithless agent with another who is faithful to him.

Reading II: Romans 11:33-36
This magnificent doxology comes at the end of Paul's discussion of Israel's place in salvation history. Theology is an attempt to reflect on the ways of God in salvation history. This is precisely what Paul has been doing in Rom 9–11. But the theologian must always confess the inadequacy of his or her work. The riches and wisdom of knowledge of God are always

too deep to penetrate, his judgments and his ways are unsearchable. No theologian has ever known the mind of the Lord. No theology, however venerable, can claim to be absolute. There comes a time when the theologian must lay down the pen and confess the relativity of all his or her formulations. Theology is therefore always subject to change. And theology is best done in the context of liturgy. It must be doxological.

Gospel: Matthew 16:13-20

Matthew has introduced considerable alterations into his Marcan source. The words "Son of the living God" are added to Peter's confession. In Mark, Jesus almost ignores Peter's confession and enjoins the disciple to silence. He then proceeds at once to speak of the necessity of his passion. Peter protests and is met by the rebuke "Get behind me, Satan." Matthew has placed the prediction of the passion, Peter's objection, and Jesus' rebuke in a separate pericope following the confession. Instead, Jesus pronounces Peter blessed and gives him the name Peter, "Rock." Then comes a series of promises: the building of the Church on the foundation of Peter; the assurance that the powers of death shall not prevail against that Church; the promise of the keys; and the saying of the binding and loosing.

There seems to be a growing consensus that the original situation of these words to Peter was not in the earthly life of Jesus but in a post-resurrection setting; that the whole passage, verses 17-19, enshrines very early material going back to the Aramaic-speaking Church; and that the Rock on which the Church is to be built is Peter himself, not his faith, as some patristic and most Reformation exegesis has supposed.

But there is division among exegetes along confessional lines over the question of the continuation of Peter's function in the Church. Protestant exegesis sees the fulfillment of the saying about the Rock in the once-and-for-all role that played such a large part in the foundation of the Church after the first Easter and resurrection appearances (Cullmann), and sees the power of the keys and of binding and loosing as continued in the Church as a whole, though capable of being entrusted to particular officers by the community (Marxsen). Anglican exegetes tend to agree with the Orthodox that the power of the keys and of binding and loosing is shared by the whole episcopate, though many of them would be prepared to allow the Bishop of Rome a special place in this collegial office. Catholic scholars naturally maintain that the Petrine office is vested in the papacy.

Nonetheless, it is significant that on all sides there is growing Christian awareness that one aspect of the Petrine office—witness to the resurrection—belongs to the events of the Christian beginnings and is therefore inalienable. At the same time, its other aspects—keys, binding and loosing—continue in the Church. This continuity is a sign of the faithfulness of God.

The Homily

We suggest two possibilities. Following the second reading, the homilist could speak of the nature of the theological task, drawing out the provisional, tentative, and inadequate character of theology, its being subject to revision, and its doxological-liturgical character. True theology emerges from liturgy and returns to it.

More likely the homilist will want to speak of the Petrine office in the Church, distinguishing between its once-for-all aspects and its continuing aspects.

TWENTY-SECOND SUNDAY OF THE YEAR

Reading I: Jeremiah 20:7-9

Of all the Old Testament prophets, Jeremiah comes closest to the New Testament understanding of what it means to be a bearer of God's word. He foreshadows the truth, first emphasized in the New Testament by Paul, in opposition to the wandering preachers, who set great store in their own miraculous powers and visionary experiences, that witness means suffering. This theme was then taken up by Mark (followed, as we see in today's gospel, by Matthew) in his redaction of the Jesus tradition. It is this aspect of today's passage from Jeremiah that the caption rightly emphasizes: "The word of the Lord has meant derision for me."

Responsorial Psalm: 63:1-5, 7-8

Many of the psalms are intensely personal, but when they were adopted into the liturgy of the temple, they acquired a corporate meaning, the "I" of the psalmist being expanded to embrace the whole people of God. In the person of Jesus Christ, who is the true Israel, the psalm is narrowed down again to a single person, the "I" of Christ himself. But then it expands once more to include the body of Christ, which in him can take these words to itself.

The people of God on their pilgrimage pass through a dry and weary land where there is no water. But in the sanctuary, as they assemble to celebrate the liturgy, they have a pledge and assurance of the ultimate vindication of Christ's cause. They feast together on "marrow and fat" and praise God with joyful lips, even in the midst of the dry and weary land.

Reading II: Romans 12:1-2

It is a pity that the text as printed omits a tiny yet crucial word—"therefore" (Greek: *oun*): "I appeal to you *therefore*, brethren." It is crucial because chapters 12–15 of Romans present Christian ethics as "therefore ethics," that is to say, Christian ethics is a response to what God has done in Christ. Only after expounding the redemptive act of God in Christ and setting it in the context of salvation history could Paul go on to discuss ethical problems. This ethic is seen as the true Christian worship. In a celebrated essay, Ernst Käsemann suggested that Paul is in some way anti-cultic, that for him true Christian worship is to be seen in ethical behavior, not in the cultus. This is the kind of either-or that appeals to the German mind, but it does less than justice to the inclusiveness of the biblical material.

No one doubts that liturgy must penetrate life, but life must first find its focus in liturgy. We present our bodies as a living sacrifice in the liturgy (Cranmer included this phrase in the Eucharistic Prayer, and it has remained a feature of Anglican liturgies ever since) precisely in order that we may go out into the world and present them in life.

Christian ethics is not primarily expressed in a code. Paul will give something that looks like a code in Rom 12–15, with many single commandments. But these are meant as *illustrations* (Dodd) of what a renewed mind, not conformed to this world, will lead to. In an apt illustration, Bishop John A. T. Robinson has spoken of the Christian's "antennae," which should enable one to discern the will of God in a given situation and which arises out of a transformed mind. Such transformation takes place through hearing the word of God and through offering oneself to God in union with Christ's suffering. This takes place quite concretely in the liturgy.

Gospel: Matthew 16:21-27

As we noted in the comments for last Sunday, Matthew has detached this section from Mark's pericope and placed it by itself. As in the second reading today, a tiny but significant word has been left out at the beginning—the word "then" (Greek: *tote*): "Then Jesus began to show his disciples." This word detaches this section and yet links it as a sequel to the foregoing pericope.

The other major alteration Matthew has made in the Marcan text is in the final verse (27), which he has converted into a scene of the parousia-last judgment: "The Son of man is to come with his angels in the glory of his Father, and then he will repay every man for what he has done." For Mark, the court of the Son of man will vindicate the Church and pass judgment upon the believing world. For Matthew, it is the Church that will be judged—a theme that he hammers home again and again, right up to the parable of the sheep and the goats. The Church will be judged according to the fidelity of its discipleship, even at the cost of taking up its cross and following Jesus, in its readiness to lose its life for his sake.

The Homily

Once again, the gospel determines the major message of today's readings. The challenge to the Church to take up its cross and to lose its life for Christ's sake takes on a new form in every age. In Matthew's time it meant, quite literally, persecution, since the Church could no longer come under the umbrella of Judaism as a *religio licita*. It is the same in many parts of the world today. The homilist must determine what form that challenge takes today for the Church in this country (maybe also in the parish) and deliver the challenge of Jesus' words accordingly. Allusion might also be made to the fate of Jeremiah.

Another possibility for the homily is offered by the second reading. Here the homilist has an opportunity to expound the distinctive characteristic of Christian ethics as "therefore ethics," the ethics of response, involving, not the meticulous observance of a detailed code, but the expression in each new situation of a mind renewed and not conformed to this world. Then, too, the text could be treated from the perspective of cultus versus life.

TWENTY-THIRD SUNDAY OF THE YEAR

Reading I: Ezekiel 33:7-9

This passage comes from a chapter in which Ezekiel sets down the responsibilities of the prophet as he envisages them after the restoration from exile. One of the images under which he defines that role is that of the watchman, a familiar figure in the defense system of Palestine. Watchmen were posted on the hills to warn of the approach of a foreign invader.

Verses 1-6 are a parable; verses 7-9 (today's reading) are its application to the prophetic role. It is characteristic of Ezekiel that he conceives the prophet's function as concerned with individuals. This was a result of the destruction of the nation as a corporate entity at the time of the Exile. Henceforth all that the prophet can do is to speak to the individual. If the prophet fails to deliver the warning, it is his own responsibility. If he does deliver it and the individual refuses to pay heed, it is not the prophet's fault. He has discharged his responsibility.

Ezekiel's picture of the prophet as watchman has been selected to go with the gospel, which speaks of mutual concern in the eschatological community, in which we all share the gift of the Spirit.

Responsorial Psalm: 95:1-2, 6-9

The *Venite* consists of two parts: the first a call to worship, the second a warning against neglect of the word of God. The first part is very popular among Anglicans as the invitatory canticle of Morning Prayer, but in most recent revisions the stern warnings of the second part have frequently been omitted. Yet, it was this second part that the author of Hebrews (Heb 3:7–4:13) took up and expounded as especially relevant to his Church. The situation of the people of this Church was that they were growing stale instead of advancing in the Christian life (the medieval sin of acedia), just as Israel grew tired in the wilderness.

The refrain, "If today you hear his voice, harden not your hearts," is singularly apt after Ezekiel's parable of the watchman.

Reading I: Romans 13:8-10

As we saw last Sunday, chapters 13–15 of Romans consist largely of ethical exhortation. Here Paul presents the second table of the Decalogue. Note the unusual order (Hellenistic-Jewish): 7, 6, 8, 10, according to the Reformed and Anglican enumeration; 6, 5, 7, 9-10, according to the Roman and Lutheran enumeration. Paul then summarizes its single injunctions in the all-embracing command of Lev 19:18: "You shall love your neighbor as yourself." Note the logical structure of this passage:

1. An imperative (v. 8a).
2. The grounds for the imperative (v. 8b).
3. The second table (v. 9).
4. A deduction from the imperative given in verse 8 (v. 10).

Evidently Paul is drawing upon an established pattern of catechesis. This pattern was probably derived from Hellenistic Judaism, as is shown not only by the order of the commandments but also by the typically Hellenistic attempt to discover a single unifying principle behind the separate injunctions.

The teaching of this passage is that there is really only one commandment which is universal and covers every situation, and to which we are always obligated—the commandment of love. The separate commandments of the Decalogue are no more than illustrations of what love may mean in particular situations.

Gospel: Matthew 18:15-20

This gospel reading is closely connected to last week's. These are the only passages in all four Gospels in which the term "church" (*ekklēsia*) occurs. Both passages include the promise about binding and loosing; in Matt 16 it is addressed to Peter only, and in Matt 18 to the disciples generally.

It would seem reasonable to suppose that Matthew has taken both passages from a common source that formed a commentary of Church origins: (1) a community rule (vv. 15-17), paralleled at Qumran; (2) the promise about binding and loosing, which in our opinion comes from a resurrection story, as is indicated by its combination with the *Tu es Petrus* saying in Matt 16 and by the parallel tradition in John 20:19-23.

In its original form this tradition was evidently a saying of the risen Lord empowering the Twelve to admit or exclude men and women from the kingdom according to whether they accepted or rejected the kerygma. By combining it with the saying about fraternal correction, Matthew's source has converted it into a Church rule. Binding and loosing now become the function of the whole community, and their character is changed to the administration of discipline within the community.

The Homily

As usual, the Old Testament reading, the psalm, and the gospel go together. The homilist has the opportunity to speak of Church discipline and the role of priest and community in discharging their joint responsibility. The widespread rejection of traditional forms of Church discipline in postconciliar Catholicism and the total breakdown of any kind of Church discipline in Protestantism do not mean that there is no place for it in the Church. The gospel text, which is part of canonical Scripture, suggests that it is an essential aspect of Church life. The Reformed tradition lists discipline along with word and sacraments as essential signs of the Church. There is something for us all to learn from that.

The second reading suggests a consideration of the relation between the separate injunctions of the Decalogue and the basic law of love.

TWENTY-FOURTH SUNDAY OF THE YEAR

Reading I: Sirach 27:30–28:7

Sirach is one of the deuterocanonical (or in Reformation parlance, "apocryphal") books. Until recently it was known only in a Greek translation, although we knew from the prologue that it was originally written in Hebrew. Fragments of the Hebrew original have been discovered at Qumran. The author was Jesus ben Sirach, who wrote it about 180 B.C. It was translated into Greek by his grandson about 130 B.C. It is, therefore, a late book, not too far removed from the New Testament period. The teaching of our excerpt reaches a height not far from the New Testament in what it says about forgiveness (see the Sermon on the Mount, the Lord's Prayer, and today's gospel about the unforgiving servant).

Responsorial Psalm: 103:1-4, 9-12

Slightly different selections of verses from this psalm are used on the third Sunday of Lent and on the seventh Sunday of the year in series C. The reason for its choice today is that human forgiveness is meant to be patterned after divine forgiveness, as both the first reading and the gospel testify.

410
464

Reading II: Romans 14:7-9

The context of this passage is a discussion about the relation between the strong and the weak members of the Church. Recent work on Paul's letter to the Romans suggests that this discussion was occasioned by tensions in Rome between Gentile Christians who were liberal in their attitude toward the law and Jewish Christians who were scrupulous about legal observances; they were the strong and the weak, respectively. Paul urges mutual toleration. The strong in particular should respect the scruples of the weak.

As so often, Paul moves from specific practical problems to the underlying theological principles. The fundamental principle here is that no Christian exists by himself or herself, but only in relation to the Lord (the risen and exalted *Kyrios*, that is, Christ), and therefore in relation to other Church members, who are equally related to the *Kyrios.*

This excerpt looks very much like a baptismal hymn. This is indicated by the "we" style common in hymns and by the way the hymn goes beyond the point immediately at issue, namely, the relation between weak and strong, to speak of the living and the dead. As Lord of the living, Christ is the Lord of both groups within the Church.

Gospel: Matthew 18:21-35

The parable of the unforgiving servant is found only in Matthew's Gospel. We do not have to deal, therefore, with a redaction of a known source like Mark or Q. Matthew's redactional contributions are: (1) attaching the parable to the saying about forgiving seventy times seven, with the connecting link "therefore"; (2) placing this whole complex at the conclusion of the community discourse, thus making the parable a moral exhortation for the community; (3) adding the final saying, which draws the moral.

Note the typically Matthean phrase "my heavenly Father" (v. 35). Also note that the saying of verse 22 and the teaching of the parable do not really fit together. The parable does not inculcate repeated forgiveness but rebukes refusal to show mercy on the part of those who have received mercy from God.

There is no reason to doubt that this is an authentic Jesus parable. It fits in perfectly with the situation in his ministry. Jesus has offered God's eschatological forgiveness to his hearers already here and now. If they do not share in this forgiveness with other people, God will revoke that forgiveness at the last judgment. This parable was told by Jesus, not as a moral exhortation about life in the Church, but to shame the consciences of his hearers.

The Homily

On this occasion all the readings can be taken together. They deal with the necessity of forgiveness as the basis of relationships within the community. This, of course, necessitates taking the gospel at the redactional level. Perhaps the homilist could identify groups within the community that are in tension with one another, like the strong and the weak at Rome.

The necessity of forgiveness toward other Church members is grounded upon the fact that all members live under the forgiveness of God—beginning with baptism and renewed in absolution and in each reception of holy communion—and upon the fact that Christ died and rose again not only to achieve forgiveness of sin but also to be the Lord of all the living and the dead.

TWENTY-FIFTH SUNDAY OF THE YEAR

Reading I: Isaiah 55:6-9

The hymn contained in Isa 55:1-11 was used as the fifth reading at the Easter Vigil, where it received comment. Here only the second of its three stanzas is used. The reason for its selection is indicated by the caption, which calls attention to the last two verses: "For my thoughts are not your thoughts, neither are your ways my ways, says the Lord." These words underline the teaching of the parable of the laborers in the vineyard in today's gospel.

Responsorial Psalm: 145:2-3, 8-9, 17-18

A somewhat different though overlapping selection of verses from this
psalm is commented on for the fourteenth Sunday of series A and the
thirty-first Sunday of series C. The second and third stanzas, especially
the latter, match both the Old Testament reading and the gospel today.
Again, as we shall see, the difference between God's thoughts and our
thoughts, according to the parable of the laborers in the vineyard, is that
God's justice is not a *quid pro quo* affair but is characterized by mercy
and forgiveness.

142

432

Reading II: Philippians 1:20c-24, 27a

This week we turn from Romans, which we have been reading for the
past several Sundays, to Philippians. The latter was written while Paul
was in prison. Traditionally this imprisonment was identified with that
at Rome (Acts 28:30-31). There is, however, a growing consensus among
scholars today that the imprisonment in question must have occurred during Paul's stay at Ephesus (ca. 52–55, though the absolute chronology of
Paul's life is somewhat conjectural). It was during this supposed imprisonment (of which there are hints in some of the letters, for example 1 Cor
15:32) that the great controversial letters were probably written: Galatians, 1 Corinthians, much of 2 Corinthians, and Philippians.

The view is also gaining ground that Philippians, like 2 Corinthians,
is a compilation from two or three short letters written by Paul to the
community at Philippi over the space of several months. These fragments
were subsequently put together when they were edited for the later use
of the Church. The letters may be identified as follows:

Letter A, 4:10-23. Paul's thank-you for the "care packet" sent by the
Philippians to him in prison by a messenger from Philippi named
Epaphroditus.

Letter B, 1:1–3:1; 4:4-7. News about Paul's welfare and prospects in
prison. Epaphroditus' recovery from illness while with Paul; Paul's desire
to send Timothy to Philippi soon; and warnings against the possible arrival of false teachers.

Letter C, 3:2-4:3, 8-9. An attack on the false teachers after their arrival at Philippi.

Today's reading thus comes from Letter B. Paul faces the possibility
of martyrdom. If we are right in placing the imprisonment at Ephesus in
52–55, we know that his worst fears at this time did not come true: he
was released and was able to visit his churches once more before he was
arrested again, this time in Jerusalem, and transported to Rome. Our
reading consists of the Apostle's vivid meditation on the prospects of life
and death. He is in a state of tension, pulled both ways. Whether he lives

or dies, Paul is convinced that Christ will be honored in his body, that is, either by Paul's labors for the gospel (see the catalogues of sufferings in 2 Cor 12, etc.—that is what being an apostle meant for Paul) or by actual martyrdom.

In either case, it is not Paul's own personal salvation that is at stake. He does not simply want to escape from his labors into personal bliss with Christ; rather, he believes that his martyrdom will in some way contribute, perhaps even more effectively than his apostolic labors, to the fulfillment of God's purpose in salvation history. "To live is Christ"—the great Pauline saying highlighted in the caption to this reading does not mean simply the enjoyment of mystical communion between the believer and the Lord but the execution of the apostolic mission.

Gospel: Matthew 20:1-16

As we have noted in previous discussions of our Lord's parables, there are three possible levels of exegesis: (1) the parable as taught by Jesus; (2) the parable as modified in the oral tradition; (3) the parable as presented by the evangelist in the context of his Gospel.

At the level of Jesus' own teaching, the parable of the wicked husband-man must have concluded with the question "Do you begrudge my generosity?" The context in which it was originally told must have been a complaint of Jesus' opponents that he was paying more attention to the outcast than to the respectable members of society. Jesus takes a situation as familiar in daily life then as now—long lines of unemployed waiting for a job. But he depicts the behavior of the employer in a quite surprising way. Out of pity for the unemployed and their families, the employer generously gives a full day's wages to everyone. That is what God is doing in Jesus' ministry—giving the tax collectors and prostitutes an equal share with the righteous in his kingdom. Obviously, the parable is not a moral lesson about labor relations!

At the level of the oral tradition, the proverbial phrase "the last will be first, and the first last" has been added. This looks like a reapplication of the parable to the situation of the post-Easter community. Israel has rejected the gospel, so Gentiles have been drawn in.

The evangelist shows his own understanding of the parable by appending it to the discourse, Matt 19:23-30. Here Peter, as the spokesman for the Twelve, proudly claimed that they, unlike the rich whom Jesus was criticizing, had left everything to follow Jesus. They will indeed be rewarded, for they will sit on twelve thrones with Christ, receive a hundredfold, and inherit eternal life. But then comes a warning: "many that are first will be last, and the last first" (19:30). In Matthew, this does not mean that the disciples are the last who will turn out to be the first, whereas the rich are the first who will turn out to be last. What Matthew means— or makes Jesus mean—is that those who forsake all and follow Jesus, and who are therefore the first, may turn out to be the last.

The parable of the laborers in the vineyard follows right upon this as a warning to the Christians in Matthew's Church not to hanker after rewards. Rewards are not denied, but they are not the purpose of toil for Christ and his kingdom. They always come as a surprise. Paul, in the second reading, exhibits precisely the kind of attitude Jesus is enjoining in Matthew's presentation.

The Homily

The most obvious choice today would be to take the gospel at the Jesus level, emphasizing the generosity of God, and link it with the first reading ("My thoughts are not your thoughts") and with the responsorial psalm ("The Lord is good to all"). This should not be presented as a general religious lesson but should be applied, where possible, to some quite concrete situation in the life of the community—for instance, where pious people are grumbling because of the Church's concern for the poor and the outcast and thinking that more time should be spent on themselves.

Less obvious, and requiring very careful preparation, would be to link Paul's contemplation of martyrdom with the parable at the level of the evangelist's presentation. Like the disciples in Matthew, Paul has left all and followed Jesus, delivering his apostolic witness precisely through his sufferings. In such a situation, it would be tempting for the Apostle to look for a reward when he departs through martyrdom. His longing to "be with Christ" could be regarded in such a light. But Paul resists the temptation. His martyrdom, like his continuing earthly life, is all part of his apostolic ministry, not a personal escape. The question is, which— martyrdom or continuing labor—is God's will for him?

TWENTY-SIXTH SUNDAY OF THE YEAR

Reading I: Ezekiel 18:25-28

Ezekiel is well known for his insistence upon individual responsibility for sin. In earlier days Israel had barely recognized a distinction between a person and the community. The overall picture was one of communal solidarity, with emphasis upon the corporate consequences of individual guilt (e.g., "visiting the iniquity of the father upon the children to the third and fourth generation" in the Decalogue).

The destruction of Israel's national institutions during the Exile accelerated a new emphasis on the individual, though it had begun to appear even earlier: "Every man shall be put to death for his own sin" (Deut 24:16; cf. 2 Kgs 14:6). The change must, of course, be understood precisely as one of emphasis—not as a denial of the older idea of solidarity but as a corrective. Both aspects—individual responsibility and corporate solidarity—have to be held together in tension, and it requires a finesse to know just when one or the other aspect has to be given priority.

These verses bring out another aspect of Ezekiel's doctrine of responsibility. This is that a person is free at any time to turn from wickedness to righteousness and vice versa. In each case, that person will be judged by the new life to which he or she has turned, not by his or her previous life. This is perhaps an oversimplification, but it fits in with the parable of the two sons in today's gospel.

Responsorial Psalm: 25:4-9

This psalm is an individual lament. The psalmist is oppressed by his enemies but is equally aware of his own sin. He calls upon God to deliver him from his enemies by remembering not his own sins but God's own mercies, and to lead him in the right way after deliverance.

This psalm forms a suitable response to the reading from Ezekiel. Both passages view a person's life as bisected into past and future by the present moment. The past is characterized by sin, the future is filled with hope for righteousness. In the present moment a person is thrown utterly upon the mercies of God—an aspect of the matter that Ezekiel, in his emphasis on personal responsibility, tends to overlook. The psalm corrects this.

The refrain, "Remember your mercies, O Lord," calls attention to the very important biblical conception of remembrance. In modern parlance, to remember means simply to recall mentally an event of the past. In the Bible, when God remembers, he does not merely recollect a past event but brings it out of the past and makes it effective in the present. Thus, the mercies that God performed in the past become renewed as present realities.

This concept is very important for our understanding of the Eucharist. "Do this in remembrance of me" means not only that we recall in our minds the messianic sacrifice, the supreme act of God's mercy, but that in response to the Church's action, God will make present that sacrifice. As was well said by the Anglican-Roman Catholic International Commission in 1971:

"The notion of *memorial* as understood in the passover celebration at the time of Christ—i.e., the making effective in the present of an event in the past—has opened the way to a clearer understanding of the relationship between Christ's sacrifice and the eucharist. The eucharistic memorial is no mere calling to mind of a past event or of its significance, but the church's effectual proclamation of God's mighty acts. . . . In the eucharistic prayer the church continues to make a perpetual memorial of Christ's death; and his members, united with God and one another, give thanks for all his mercies, entreat the benefits of his passion on behalf of the whole church, participate in these benefits and enter into the movement of his self-offering" (reprinted in *Worship*, January 1972, 46:3–4).

The refrain "Remember your mercies, O Lord" is thus a highly suitable chant for the Eucharist.

Reading II: Philippians 2:1-11 (long form); 2:1-5 (short form)

The longer form of this reading includes the great Christological hymn which, following ancient tradition, is read on Passion Sunday (the reader will find comment on the hymn there). Whether we opt for the longer or the shorter form, it seems clear that today both comment and homiletical treatment should concentrate upon the ethical exhortation that it is the purpose of the hymn to reinforce.

But we cannot ignore the hymn entirely. Apart from the interpretation of the hymn itself, there is a controversy among contemporary exegetes over its relation to the exhortation. Does the hymn merely present Christ as an example? In that case, the drift of thought is: Let your relationship with other Christians be marked by unity, love, humility, consideration for the interests of others. In so doing, you must display the same attitude that Christ showed when he humbled himself to become man and to die on the cross.

That is the way in which the passage has normally been taken. Karl Barth, however, popularized—at least among the Germans—another interpretation. It depends upon a different rendering of the final phrase in the short form of the reading: instead of "which was in Christ Jesus," it reads "which you have in Christ Jesus." Such a variant rendition is possible because there is no verb in the Greek for "was" or for "you have"; it simply reads "which in Christ Jesus," allowing the reader to understand either "was" or "you have." If we understand "you have," it gives a different meaning to "in Christ," namely, the characteristic Pauline sense of "in Christ," sometimes called "mystical," though Barth himself would have repudiated the term. In this interpretation the pattern of Christ's life, namely, the pattern of humiliation-glorification, is not a model for Christians to imitate but a pattern with which Christians are brought into conformity by their incorporation into Christ and their life in him.

It is difficult to decide which is the correct interpretation. Barth's at

55

least has the advantage of giving to "in Christ" its normal Pauline sense of treating Christ not merely as an external example but as the source of redemptive life.

Gospel: Matthew 21:28-32

The second part of the saying (v. 32) is paralleled in Luke 7:29-30, and therefore it must have become attached at some stage in the tradition to the saying about the tax collectors and prostitutes (v. 31b). It is clear that the latter phrase, which occurs in both sayings, attracted the saying about John the Baptist to the comment on the parable. Then coalescence of the two sayings must have taken place prior to Matthew, because Matthew is responsible for placing the whole pericope in sequence with the question of authority (Matt 21:23-27), connecting them by means of the catchword "John the Baptist" (vv. 25, 32).

We thus have three levels of exegesis: (1) the Jesus level, consisting of the original parable of the two sons with Jesus' comment, 21:28-31a; (2) the oral tradition, consisting of the parable with an extended comment, 21:28-32; (3) the evangelist's understanding, indicated by his combination of the parable plus extended comment with the pericope about the question of authority, 21:23-27 + 28-32. The exegete has to try to interpret the parable on all three levels.

Jesus evidently told this parable (some have thought that this was the original nucleus of the parable of the prodigal son) to vindicate his proclamation of the good news of the kingdom against his critics: "The tax collectors and prostitutes who receive me now will enter into the kingdom of God at the last judgment rather than you who criticize me for consorting with them." The parable is a proclamation of God's mercy for sinners.

The addition of the saying about John the Baptist gives the parable a surprising and not altogether apt twist. Matthew, however, has straightened out this awkward state of affairs by sandwiching the pericope between the question of authority and the wicked husbandman. By doing so, he makes it one of a series of three comments upon the Jewish authorities' response to God's purpose throughout salvation history. This response was one of constant rejection, from the time of the prophets through John the Baptist to Jesus himself (and of course also, in Matthew's own perspective, to the post-resurrection mission of the Church). For Matthew, it justifies his own Church's abandonment of the mission to Israel and its concentration on preaching to the Gentiles (Matt 28:16-20, and see especially Matt 21:43, added by Matthew to the third of his three pericopes in 21:23-45).

The Homily

There are several choices before the homilist today. The simplest one—though it involves fastening upon an incidental feature in today's readings—would be to take up the refrain of the responsorial psalm, expound the biblical conception of remembrance, and relate it to the Eucharist. This would give the homilist an opportunity to transcend the Reformation/Counter-Reformation antithesis over the relation between the Eucharist and Calvary and would have an important ecumenical significance.

A second possibility, especially if one accepts Barth's interpretation of Phil 2:5, would be to speak of Christian ethics as formation (see Bonhoeffer's *Ethics*).

But the intention of the compilers of the Lectionary was to highlight a theme derived from the gospel, the first reading, and the responsorial psalm. Unfortunately, this choice is complicated by the three levels at which the parable of the two sons may be interpreted. If we choose Matthew's salvation-history level of interpretation, we would do best to drop all reference to the first reading and the psalm. We could, however, give the parable a highly relevant interpretation by relating it to the widespread rejection of Christianity in the Western world (the son who said he would go but did not) and the apparent eagerness, for example in Africa, for the gospel (the son who said he would not go but then went). This theme, however, could be left for next week. The traditional level of interpreting the parable yields little contemporary meaning. The Jesus level, which can be readily combined with the first reading and the psalm, suggests an appeal to repentance addressed to backsliders and conventional Christians.

TWENTY-SEVENTH SUNDAY OF THE YEAR

Reading I: Isaiah 5:1-7

The song of the vineyard, it is thought, was composed by the prophet Isaiah during the early part of his ministry and was sung at vintage festivals. Only the last stanza equates the vineyard allegorically with Israel, thus turning a happy little song about country life into an expression of God's judgment upon his people. This represents a clever turn on the part of the singer, who has engaged the attention and approval of his hearers up to this point. The parables of Jesus are clearly in the same tradition.

Why this reading was chosen for today is obvious (see the gospel).

Responsorial Psalm: 80:8, 11-15, 18-19

As in Isa 5 and other passages in the Old Testament, the vine appears in this psalm as a symbol for Israel. The psalm, however, is not used for purposes of denunciation but as a prayer for deliverance.

Reading II: Philippians 4:6-9

According to the partition theory (see our comments for the twenty-fifth Sunday), verses 6-7 form the conclusion of Letter B, verses 8-9 the conclusion of Letter C. This would explain the sudden shift from a blessing to a final exhortation (one would expect these to be in the reverse order at the end of a letter). It further eases the position of the word "finally"— some fifteen verses before the actual end of the present "letter" (of course, we all know preachers who go on for fifteen minutes after saying "finally," but Paul was probably not among their number, at least on this occasion!). It also explains why Paul seemingly repeats himself in verses 7 and 9 ("peace of God," "God of peace"). 169

The partition theory also enhances the understanding of the two paragraphs in our pericope. The first paragraph comes at the end of the thank-you note for the help Paul has received from the Philippians. The exhortation may be a reassurance in view of the possible arrival of false teachers at Philippi. Verse 7 will be the concluding blessing. Verses 8-9 will have followed originally upon 4:3. Paul has been denouncing the false teachers who have by now arrived in Philippi (3:2-21). They were probably some kind of enthusiasts who believed that they were already in heaven and had attained perfection, ignoring the "not-yet-ness" of Christian existence, and who did not take seriously the place of the cross in Christian life. Like the opponents in Galatia, they may have demanded the circumcision of Gentile Christian converts (see "whose glory is in their shame"—3:19). In a final exhortation Paul seeks to direct his readers to higher things. In order to do so, he draws upon the ethical teaching of Stoicism: things true, honorable, just, pure, gracious, excellent (virtuous), worthy of praise—all these are the categories of Stoic ethics; there is nothing distinctively Christian about them. But, in Paul's thinking, they are none the worse for that.

Finally, the Apostle reiterates what he said in 3:17, though in somewhat different words, holding himself up as an example for his converts to imitate. At first sight, this idea looks rather embarrassing, even contrary to Paul's repudiation of justification by works. But Paul understands his life as an apostle, especially his sufferings, to be a manifestation of the cross of Christ. Therefore, in asking the Philippians to imitate him, he is not asking them to copy his good works but inviting them to pattern their lives on Christ as he is made manifest in his (Paul's) apostolic existence. This interpretation is borne out by what Paul says about himself in 3:12-16, where he disclaims any notion that he has already achieved ethical perfection.

Gospel: Matthew 21:33-43

In Matthew (and Mark, the source Matthew follows here), the parable of the vineyard is heavily allegorized. Luke and the recently discovered Gospel of Thomas contain traces of an earlier form of this parable that is shorter and less allegorized. In this earlier form, there are no echoes of Isa 5 in the opening of the parable (v. 33). The emissaries prior to the son are reduced to two or three single ones, without any suggestion that they are identified with the Old Testament prophets. The Christological upgrading of the son is missing, and the parable must have concluded with his murder.

For the original meaning, we have to ignore all the secondary allegorical features and consider the story by itself. As in the Lucan parables of the unjust steward and the unjust judge, Jesus draws a surprising lesson from an utterly discreditable piece of human behavior. See, he says, how these vinedressers stopped at nothing. They even murdered the heir to get hold of the vineyard. You must be just as resolute in laying hold of the kingdom of God!

It was all too easy for the Church to allegorize this parable. The vineyard became Israel; the vinedressers, its religious leaders; the successive emissaries, the Old Testament prophets; the son, Jesus the Messiah; his murder, the crucifixion. This interpretation was then clinched by combining with it the testimonium from Ps 118:22, so that the parable closes with Jesus' resurrection. Matthew goes further and adds verse 43, so that it closes with the prediction of the mission to the Gentiles following Israel's rejection of the gospel. All this is not wrong; it is simply the constant reapplication of the parable to new situations in the community's life.

The Homily

By combining Matthew's version of the parable of the wicked husbandmen with the reading from Isa 5 and Psalm 80, the Lectionary intends us to hear the parable with its allegorical interpretation. The preacher's most obvious course would be to adapt this theme: the vineyard as God's people; the vinedressers as their religious leaders; the son as the gospel message of Jesus Christ; his murder as the rejection of that message by the chosen people and their leaders; the threat that the kingdom of God will be given to a nation bringing forth fruits thereof as a threat to the

Church today—perhaps the Church in the Western world—and a threat that the leadership of the Christian cause will pass, say, to Africans?

If this seems too much like dynamite, the homilist could fall back on the original form of this parable as told by Jesus and preach a challenge to the hearers to seize hold of the gospel.

There remains the second reading. Here there are two possibilities: the conclusion of Letter B in Phil 4:6-7, which would lead to an exhortation against anxiety and an assurance of the peace of God that surpasses understanding; or the conclusion of Letter C, which holds up the finest ethical ideals of pagan philosophy as worthy of Christian imitation. Should we take Stoic ethics today, or should we, by analogy, hold up virtues, say of humanists or Marxists, for imitation?

TWENTY-EIGHTH SUNDAY OF THE YEAR

Reading I: Isaiah 25:6-10a

Just as the vineyard became, since the song in Isa 5, an accepted symbol for Israel as the people of God in salvation history, so our present reading made the great banquet a classic symbol of the consummation of God's saving purpose in history. But this idea of the eschatological banquet was not created by Isaiah. Its roots can be traced back to earlier Canaanite literature. The Qumran community took up this symbolism in the institution of their daily meal, and Jesus also put it to various uses: in his conduct in eating with outcasts; in his parable of the great banquet, which forms the gospel for today; and above all in the saying at the Last Supper that he would no longer feast with his disciples until he could do so in the consummated kingdom of God.

Responsorial Psalm: 23:1-6

It is instructive to compare the use of this psalm here with its use on the sixteenth Sunday of the year in series B. There the emphasis is indicated *328* by the refrain, which focuses on the image of the shepherd. Here, since it is in response to the reading from Isaiah on the messianic banquet, the emphasis lies upon the Lord's house or temple, where he prepares the banquet table and invites his people to share the blessings of his kingdom. The third stanza marks a shift in imagery from God as shepherd to God as host at his banquet.

Reading II: Philippians 4:12-14, 19-20

According to the partition theory, these excerpts from Philippians would be from Letter A, the thank-you note for the relief they had sent to Paul while he was in prison, probably at Ephesus (see the commentary on Reading II for the twenty-fifth Sunday of the year in series A).

169

Paul seems a trifle embarrassed to accept any gift at all. C. H. Dodd spoke of Paul's "sturdy bourgeois independence," which made him a little too proud to accept help readily in this way. Or was it just stoic detachment (v. 12a)? Perhaps it is more theologically based than that. Paul knows that the existence of an apostle is marked by the sign of the cross—in facing hunger and want as readily as plenty and abundance.

There is a slight undertone suggesting that the Philippians had inadvertently deprived Paul of boasting in his sufferings. But Paul is too gracious to say so, and although admitting that he could have gotten along very well without it, he nevertheless thanks them for their kindness. It is a pity that verse 18 has been omitted, for there Paul gives the Philippians' charitable act a theological meaning: it was a sacrifice acceptable and pleasing to God.

Gospel: Matthew 22:1-14 (long form); 22:1-10 (short form)

It is interesting to compare the long and short forms of this gospel. The long form really consists of two parables spliced together—the parable of the great banquet and the parable of the man without a wedding garment. That the combination is secondary is shown by Luke (14:16-24) and by the Gospel of Thomas, where the great banquet occurs on its own, without the addition of a wedding garment. The combination produces an unrealistic effect, for one inevitably asks, How could the poor man have been expected to have a wedding garment if he had been hauled in unexpectedly from the street? The answer is that in the original parable he had not just come in off the street. In its original form the parable stood on its own. The original opening of it was then lost when it was joined to the parable of the great banquet.

Although it is difficult to be certain, it seems likely that the evangelist was responsible for combining the two parables. He interprets the gathering in of the ragtag and bobtail from the streets allegorically as Jesus' prediction of the subsequent Gentile mission, and adds the second parable as a warning against their admission on too easy terms.

It is unlikely that the evangelist was requiring the circumcision of the Gentiles, since that issue had been settled long before at the apostolic conference (Gal 2; cf. Acts 15). Matthew may be inserting a bit of propaganda in favor of the apostolic decrees which, according to Acts 15, were promulgated at the council, but which in all probability were enacted at a later conference while Paul was away (see Acts 21:25). As an original parable of Jesus, the story of the man with the wedding garment, like many other parables, would be an exhortation to readiness in face of the coming kingdom of God. The invitation came sooner than the man expected, and it caught him unprepared. Woe to a person in such a case!

The shorter form, as we have noted, consists of the parable of the great banquet by itself. A study of the parallels in Luke and in the Gospel of Thomas shows that the version in Matthew is highly allegorized. Again, the allegorization has produced some quite unrealistic features. It is most unlifelike—and Jesus' parables are lifelike, even if they often end on a note of surprise. What invited guest would not only spurn the invitation but actually kill the servants who brought it? And what host would send out his troops not only to destroy those murderers but to burn down their city? Clearly, these details reflect the events of A.D. 66–70, the Jewish war and the destruction of Jerusalem. With these accretions, the parable is used by the post-A.D. 70 Church as an interpretation of the debacle of those years—they were a punishment of Israel for rejecting the gospel, for persecuting the Christian messengers, and for putting them to death.

But this is not the end of the allegorization. Comparison again with Luke and the Gospel of Thomas shows that in Matthew the parable has been transformed in other ways. In the other versions it is simply a great banquet given by a private individual; but in Matthew it is the story of a wedding feast given by a *king* for his *son*. The king is equated with God, and the son with Jesus, the Messiah. This, of course, is an entirely natural post-Easter reinterpretation, but if we want to ask what Jesus meant when he told the parable, we have to disregard these later elements. It is a judgment on Jesus' contemporaries who rejected his invitation to the coming kingdom, and an assurance to the outcast, with whom Jesus celebrated the great banquet in advance.

The Homily

People are often puzzled by the longer form of today's gospel, and although the pulpit is not the place to air scholarly problems and solutions, experience has shown that it does help to introduce a little "higher criticism" to relieve the difficulties of this particular passage. The accompanying first reading and the psalm, however, divert attention from the secondary allegorical features and accretions to the image of the great banquet. If we take the longer form of the gospel, it would be convenient to take up the second parable—the man without a wedding garment—and to speak about preparedness for the Eucharistic banquet. An exhortation composed to be read before holy communion in the Book of Common Prayer at the time of the Reformation, though little used today, alludes to this little parable in the following words:

"Which [i.e., the holy sacrament] being so divine and comfortable a thing to them who receive it worthily, and so dangerous to them that will presume to receive it unworthily; my duty is to exhort you in the mean season to consider the dignity of that holy Mystery, and the great peril of the unworthy receiving thereof; and so search and examine your own consciences . . . that ye may come holy and clean to such a heavenly Feast, in the marriage garment required by God in Holy Scripture, and be received as worthy partakers of that Holy Table."

The renewed emphasis on the banquet aspect of the Eucharist would make this teaching singularly appropriate today, when it often appears that the banquet emphasis has deprived the liturgy of the awesomeness it once had.

If the shorter version of the gospel is used, we would again recommend disregarding the allegorical additions and concentrating on the image of the banquet, this time emphasizing that "everything is ready." "God fulfills his promises and comes forward out of hiddenness. But if the 'children of the kingdom,' the theologians and pious circles, pay no heed to his call, the despised and the ungodly will take their place; the others will receive nothing but a 'Too late' from behind the closed doors of the banquet hall" (J. Jeremias). Can we discern something like this happening in our world today?

TWENTY-NINTH SUNDAY OF THE YEAR

Reading I: Isaiah 45:1, 4-6

In Second Isaiah we find a remarkable treatment of the Persian emperor Cyrus. Although he is a pagan king, he is saluted as the anointed of Yahweh, his servant raised up to conquer Babylon and to restore God's people to their homeland:

> For the sake of my servant Jacob,
>   and Israel my chosen,
> I call you by your name,
>   I surname you, though you do not know me.

This inaugurates a line of Jewish teaching about the state, including the pagan state, that culminates in Jesus' pronouncement about the payment of tribute money (today's gospel) and in Paul's teaching about the Roman state under the emperor Nero as the servant and minister of God.

Responsorial Psalm: 96:1, 3-5, 7-10ac

Another selection from this psalm is used on the second Sunday of the 447
year in series C. It is one of the enthronement psalms, which, according
to some scholars, were sung at a (hypothetical) annual feast in which the
king was enthroned in order to symbolize Yahweh's kingship over his
people. As the king took his seat upon his earthly throne, the whole people
would have chanted this psalm in celebration of the kingship of Yahweh.

This psalm (which, incidentally, tends to be overworked in
Anglicanism because, I suspect, of the Book of Common Prayer's
mistranslation of the first line of the third stanza as "worship the Lord
in the beauty of holiness") has close affinities in theological outlook with
Second Isaiah. It emphasizes the sovereignty of Yahweh over all nations
and thus forms a fitting response to the proclamation of God's appointment of Cyrus.

Reading II: 1 Thessalonians 1:1-5b

This letter to the Thessalonians is the earliest written document in the New
Testament. It was written by Paul during his stay at Corinth in A.D. 50.
Paul had founded the church at Thessalonica not very long before. He
had had to leave it hurriedly, and, in his anxiety over his recent converts,
he sent Timothy to see how things were going. The report Timothy brought
back was largely favorable—hence the warm tone of the opening
thanksgiving, which forms the main part of today's reading. But there
were also a few problems in Thessalonica; we will meet them on the thirty-
second and thirty-third Sundays.

Gospel: Matthew 22:15-21

Apart from a few stylistic changes, Matthew has taken over this pericope
substantially in its Marcan form. He also retains the Marcan context, where
it precedes the question of the Sadducees about the resurrection (Mark
12:18-27 / Matt 22:23-33), though Matthew has inserted the parable of
the great banquet between the parable of the vineyard and the present
pericope. Also, Matthew has rewritten the introduction so as to speak
of a *plot* to entrap Jesus. The result of these changes is to emphasize that
the episode of the tribute money was part of Jesus' conflict with his opponents. It thus is part of the material with which Matthew seeks to speak
directly to the situation of the Church in his day, locked as it was in mortal combat with the Jewish leaders of Jamnia over the question of what
was true orthodoxy and who were the true people of God.

The Pharisees' question about the tribute money is a classic example
of the so-called pronouncement story, with its threefold form of setting,

action, and pronouncement. Everything in this story is subordinated to the punchline: "Render therefore to Caesar the things that are Caesar's, and to God the things that are God's."

This pronouncement has been interpreted in many different ways in the course of Christian history. Often, like Rom 13, it has been construed in the interests of a conservative throne-and-altar theology as in Lutheran orthodoxy, which reached its tragic climax in the German Christian movement during the Nazi period. Exegesis in Germany has swung to the other extreme today: "Only a penny for Caesar, everything else for God."

A more reasonable interpretation would be that Caesar has his own legitimate but limited sphere, and even that he holds it under God and is responsible to God for its proper governance. This does not necessarily mean—though in certain circumstances it has meant and could mean again—that the state itself has to profess Christianity. It means that the state must be what it is and perform the proper functions of a state in maintaining law and order and promoting the welfare of its citizens. But when it oversteps the mark and puts itself in the place of God, Christians are in the last resort absolved from obedience. We must give to Caesar the things that are Caesar's and not the things that are God's. We must obey God rather than human beings.

The Homily

The obvious basis for today's homily is the gospel, supported by the first reading and the psalm. This requires a treatment of the proper biblical attitude toward the state and what this entails today. Such a theme provides a suitable occasion to discuss the Christian attitude toward war in as concrete a way as possible, or the Christian's duty in an election year.

The opening of 1 Thessalonians offers several possibilities. For example, one could give a meditation on the Christian greeting "Grace and peace," relating it to the sign of peace in the liturgy; or a meditation on faith, hope, and love as the criteria by which the Apostle measures Christian growth; or again, the gospel as coming not only by word but in the power of the Holy Spirit.

THIRTIETH SUNDAY OF THE YEAR

Reading I: Exodus 22:21-27

This reading is an excerpt from the "book of the covenant" (Exod 20:22–23:19). The materials in this book are akin to many legal codes of the Ancient Near East, the most famous of which is the Code of Hammurabi (twentieth century B.C.). The biblical code was apparently crystallized in the ninth century B.C.

Today's reading comes from a section of the code dealing with laws of social conduct. They inculcate a social ethic based upon compassion. Abstract justice is not enough, especially for the underprivileged. This lesson was obviously chosen to go with the summary of the law, which forms today's gospel reading. The effect is to slant the summary in a social direction.

Responsorial Psalm: 18:1-3, 46, 50ab

This is a royal psalm of thanksgiving for victory in battle, possibly written by David himself. The selected stanzas make an appropriate hymn of praise for any occasion, but it is difficult to discern any specific connections with the other readings here, except perhaps in the refrain, which takes up the thought of the love of God found also in the summary of the law.

Reading II: 1 Thessalonians 1:5c-10

This week we continue Paul's thanksgiving for the progress of the Thessalonians in the gospel. This passage is particularly important for the hints it gives of what Paul had preached at Thessalonica on his foundation visit: "you turned to God from idols, to serve a living and true God, and to wait for his Son from heaven, whom he raised from the dead, Jesus who delivers us from the wrath to come." From this it may be inferred that Paul's gospel to Gentile audiences would have comprised:

1. an apologetic for monotheism;

2. a proclamation for the deliverance wrought by Jesus through his (death and) resurrection;

3. the prospect of Jesus' impending return.

In his evangelistic preaching to pagans, Paul could take less for granted than when preaching to the Jews. He had to start with faith in the one God. We shall see later how the promise of the parousia would lead to serious problems for the Thessalonians when some of their number died before it occurred.

Gospel: Matthew 22:34-40

The summary of the law is not original with Jesus. Its two parts represent a combination of Deut 6:5 and Lev 19:18. Nor is the combination itself original to Jesus, for it is found in at least one earlier Jewish work, the Testaments of the Twelve Patriarchs, an amalgam of wisdom and apocalyptic materials. Jesus' thought was similarly cast in both molds, wisdom and apocalyptic, and the summary of the law represents the wisdom facet of his teaching. Jesus undoubtedly appeared not only as the final apocalyptic preacher but also as the authoritative declarer of God's wisdom.

In the Jewish parallels, the two commandments stand side by side, as a convenient summary. Jesus understands the interlocking of the two commandments in a new and quite radical way. You cannot have one without the other. Without the love of neighbor, the love of God remains a barren emotion; and without the love of God, love of neighbor is but a refined form of self-love.

The Homily

Today the homilist's obvious choice would be to propound the summary of the law, pointing up the intimate connection between the love of God and the love of neighbor and, in the light of the Old Testament reading, giving love of neighbor a social slant, thus proclaiming a politics of compassion.

The reading from 1 Thessalonians might give the homilist an opportunity to stress the importance of monotheism over against idolatry, which today can be demythologized as a false ultimate concern.

THIRTY-FIRST SUNDAY OF THE YEAR

Reading I: Malachi 1:14b–2:2b, 8-10

The caption to this reading provides a fair summary of the first paragraph of this denunciation, which is addressed to the priests of Israel. The prophetic book of Malachi (the name means "my messenger" and is taken from 3:1; the work is really anonymous) was written after the return of the exiles, and is directed against the abuses that marked the restoration of the sacrificial system.

The priestly caste was particularly at fault in this matter. We generally think of the Old Testament priests as offerers of sacrifices. Malachi, however, lays greater stress on instruction, a priestly function no less important. The relationship between the Old Testament priesthood and the ministerial priesthood as it is known in Catholic Christianity is not a direct one, for Christian priesthood can only be understood from the priesthood and sacrifice of Christ. Nevertheless, teaching is a function of both the Old Testament and the Christian priesthood. The Old Testament priests were guardians of the Torah, and just as sacrifice and instruction went on hand in hand in the old dispensation, so sacramental ministrations and teaching go hand in hand in the Christian ministry.

An old-fashioned Anglican dogmatic theologian has written: "The priest's highest duty is to consecrate the Eucharist, and the next, to give absolution. But the Eucharist must be accompanied by counsel. Therefore, the priest must be a man of holiness, of learning, with a knowledge of human nature; he must know his Bible, and the art of teaching" (C. B. Moss, *The Christian Faith* [1943] 394).

Despite the caption, however, it appears that this pericope was chosen because of the final paragraph and its opening question: "Have we not all one father?" This question is echoed by our Lord's statement in the gospel reading: "you have one Father."

One often hears it said in Christian circles that the teaching of the fatherhood of God was new with Jesus and is unique to Christianity. This is not fair to the Old Testament, as our text from Malachi indicates, or to Judaism. There is some precedent for Jesus' teaching on the fatherhood of God in the Old Testament, though it must be admitted that it is not the dominant aspect of its doctrine of God as it was for Jesus, nor does it have the unique features that it has in his teaching.

Responsorial Psalm: 131:1-3

This is one of the psalms expressing the individual's trust and confidence in Yahweh. It is a beautiful testimony to the piety of the "poor" in Israel.

Usually we have found that the responsorial psalm is what its name suggests—a response to the Old Testament reading. This time, however, it appears to introduce the second reading. The psalmist rests in Yahweh like a child on its mother's bosom, and in a similar image Paul speaks of himself, in his pastoral ministry among the Thessalonians, as being "like a nurse taking care of her children" (see next reading).

Reading II: 1 Thessalonians 2:7-9, 13

This passage comes from the part of 1 Thessalonians in which Paul gives thanks to God and recalls his missionary preaching at Thessalonica and his converts' response to his preaching. This preaching was accompanied by a deep pastoral concern for the Thessalonians; his preaching of the gospel was not of a "take it or leave it" kind.

Part of this pastoral concern was shown in Paul's refusal to be an economic burden to the infant community. He worked night and day, he says, to earn his living rather than make demands upon them. The Book of Acts explains that Paul worked as a tentmaker. This behavior, of course, is no universal prescription for the ministry, and Paul himself knew the dominical precept that the laborer is worthy of his hire, but he had special reasons for not availing himself of this privilege.

Practice in this matter has varied in the history of the Christian Church. In the Western world we are mostly familiar with the "clergyman," a member of a paid profession. But circumstances are changing, and the idea of tentmaking priests is being seriously discussed again, and even beginning to be practiced to some extent. There was also the priest-worker experiment in France. Such a shift would not in itself be contrary to either Scripture or ancient tradition. As for Paul, it must be a matter of expediency—whatever best serves the preaching of the gospel and continued pastoral care.

The third paragraph of this reading contains a whole theology of preaching. The Thessalonians received the proclamation of Paul and his colleagues, not as the word of human beings, but for what it really was— the word of God. Preaching is the word of God given in and through the words of human beings. It requires, on the part of the preacher, fidelity to the apostolic witness to Jesus Christ (Paul, as an apostle, is a fountainhead of that witness) and prayer that God will take the feeble words of the preacher and make them vehicles of his word. On the part of the listeners, preaching requires the discernment of faith, that they may hear the word of God given in and through the human words of the preacher, and prayer that the word of may bring forth fruit in their lives. Both preacher and congregation need to pray for the Holy Spirit.

Gospel: Matthew 23:1-12

Matthew 23 is a lengthy denunciation of the Pharisees. It makes very painful reading, and we wonder today—especially since Pope John XXIII's laudable attempt to improve relations between the Christian Church and the Jewish community—how Jesus could have indulged in such vitriolic condemnation of religious leaders who, as Jewish scholars are constantly reminding us, were for the most part good people.

Several considerations must be kept in mind. First, Matt 23, as it stands, was compiled by the evangelist himself; it is not a speech actually delivered by Jesus. The cumulative effect is created not by Jesus but by the evangelist himself.

Second, Matthew was involved in the struggle between his own Jewish-Christian Church and the rabbis, who after the fall of Jerusalem were consolidating their authority in Judaism. It is that struggle that is reflected here.

Third, condemnation of one's opponents as hypocrites was not confined to the Christian side. The rabbis frequently retorted in kind.

Fourth, in compiling this speech, Matthew drew on traditional material. He started with the quite short rebuke of the *scribes* (not the whole Pharisaic party!) in Mark 12:30-40. Some of the woes against the Pharisees come from the source common to Matthew and Luke (Matt 23:13 par.; 23 par.; 25-27 par.; 29-31 par.). But much of it comes from Matthew's special source, which reflects the views of a Jewish-Christian community rather than those of Jesus himself. There was certainly an element of anti-Pharisaic teaching in Jesus; he denounced *some* Pharisees, particularly the Pharisaic scribes, for hypocrisy. But, as Luke's special tradition also shows, he could take a quite favorable view of other Pharisees, and they could be friendly toward him. We must keep the whole thing in proportion and see this chapter in its historical context. An element that was present in Jesus' teaching has been exaggerated out of all proportion for historical reasons that no longer obtain.

In applying such material to the life of the Church today, we have to remember that, to quote the title given to a course of sermons by Hoskyns, "*We* are the Pharisees." We must allow such denunciations to be addressed as warnings to us, especially to those of us who exercise a leadership role in the Church—the clergy and, in particular, the bishops. We, like the rabbis, are the guardians of tradition, only ours is the apostolic tradition and theirs was a tradition going back to Moses. We also are in constant danger of not living up to our own teaching. We enjoy ostentation, flattery, special insignia, and honorific titles. (The attempt to reduce episcopal regalia in the Roman communion is a move in the right direction and to be applauded; it has hardly hit the Anglican episcopate yet, apart from a mild suggestion at the Lambeth conference that English bishops should drop the title "My Lord.")

Non-Catholics are often puzzled by the seeming contradiction between Matt 23:9 and the practice of addressing priests as "Father." We should not dismiss their puzzlement too lightly. If "Father" is insisted upon as a personal distinction by the priest himself, or if the person using it does so without remembering that it means that the priest is the sacramental sign of the presence of God himself as Father, then such a usage would come under the condemnation of Matthew's injunction (it is hardly from

Jesus himself). Anglicans should note that the Book of Common Prayer uses the ministerial title "Father" very sparingly—only in address to the bishop in a liturgical context when he is clearly acting as the sacramental embodiment of the fatherhood of God. Should it not therefore be used only in a functional context?

The Homily

Today's readings are joined together by the overarching theme of priesthood and ministry. The Old Testament reading emphasizes that teaching and instruction must accompany the performance of liturgical duties. The psalm and the second reading highlight the notion of pastoral care: the pastor is like a nurse. The gospel emphasizes the guardianship of apostolic tradition and the necessity of a life in conformity with the teaching, and warns against regarding the ministry as grounds for personal pride rather than as a sacramental sign of God's presence in word and sacrament.

A second theme, shared by the Old Testament reading and the gospel, is the fatherhood of God. This could provide alternative material for meditation. Here it should be stressed that the fatherhood of God is not a general, universal truth but a covenant relationship.

THIRTY-SECOND SUNDAY OF THE YEAR

As we approach the end of the Church year and Advent draws near, the mood of the liturgy changes perceptibly and becomes eschatological. This is in accord with tradition, for in ancient times Advent started earlier and lasted longer.

Reading I: Wisdom 6:12-16

This excerpt comes from the conclusion of the first part of the Book of Wisdom. The theme of that part is that wisdom is the gateway to immortality. Hence the overall context—though it is hardly visible from our extract—is eschatological. The pericope itself is a concluding exhortation to seek wisdom, an assertion of its accessibility (cf. Prov 8). Bearing in mind its eschatological context, we can relate this reading to the other readings. Those who seek and find wisdom will have acquired something that will survive the last judgment, which Paul describes in the second reading, while the gospel speaks of the "wise" virgins—those who sought after wisdom. Also, compare the emphasis on vigilance in verse 15 of this reading with Matt 25:13, the last sentence of our gospel reading.

Responsorial Psalm: 63:1-7

The first part of this psalm (through verse 8) falls in the category of an individual lament. The soul expresses its thirst for communion with God in the temple, and its delight when communion is established. We may link this with the search for the divine wisdom (first reading) and with the virgins' longing to meet the bridegroom (gospel).

Reading II: 1 Thessalonians 4:13-18 (long form); 4:13-14 (short form)

The short form is apparently permitted not merely on the grounds of brevity but because it omits the highly bizarre eschatological imagery of the long form. Such imagery is certainly difficult for the modern Christian and requires demythologizing if its message is to be rightly heard.

Paul's converts had received from him the impression that the second coming was imminent (see 1:9). Meanwhile, some of them died—before the parousia. First Paul urges the Thessalonians not to grieve and then states his grounds for not grieving: since Jesus died and rose again, the believers who die will likewise rise again. Then he seeks to prove this from a "word of the Lord." Scholars are divided as to whether this means a saying of the earthly Jesus (cf. perhaps Mark 9:1) or a saying received from the risen Christ through a Christian prophet, like the sayings in the Book of Revelation.

How are we to demythologize, that is, not eliminate but interpret, the imagery for faith? The clue lies in Paul's final word: "so we shall always be with the Lord." The ultimate hope of the believer is Christological, and it is corporate. It is Christological because it is not merely a hope of individual survival after death but of being with the risen Christ in his transformed resurrection existence. It is not attained through any intrinsic quality of one's own, such as an immortal soul, but solely because Jesus entered into resurrection existence before us and will enable us to enter it, too. It is corporate, for again the Christian hope is not for individual salvation but for the restoration in Christ of humanity, indeed of the whole cosmos. Paul was time-conditioned in his apocalyptic imagery and mistaken in his belief that the parousia was imminent, but he asserts an abiding truth. And because of that truth, the Christian is enabled to transcend the grief of bereavement, unlike the "others who have no hope."

Gospel: Matthew 25:1-13

The parable of the ten virgins (rsv: "maidens") would appear to have a long history behind it. Like many other parables, it may be interpreted at three different levels of tradition—Jesus, the oral tradition of the early post-Easter Church, and the evangelist's redaction.

It is often argued that this parable is an allegory and therefore could not have come from Jesus. But it is not a pure allegory even in Matthew. Any allegory concocted by the early Church would surely have made the bride central to the story, for in the early Church's ecclesiology the Church was the bride of Christ. But the bride is never mentioned.

If the parable comes from Jesus, it must be a story taken from real life. True, it contains several puzzling details: Whose house was the groom entering—the bride's or his own—and in whose house did the marriage feast take place? What made the groom arrive so late? Would a wedding feast have taken place after midnight? Were the virgins bridesmaids, and if so, why did they have to escort the groom? The fact is, we know too little about marriage customs of that time to answer all these questions and must assume that the whole story is true to life, though possibly with one element of surprise on which the whole meaning of the story turns, namely, the astonishingly late arrival of the groom.

In order to understand what the story could have meant on the lips of Jesus, we must forget all the allegorical equations (the groom = the Son of man; his return = the parousia; the virgins = good and bad Christians or believers and unbelievers; the wedding feast = the messianic banquet) and let the parable make its own point as a story from life. Those who hear Jesus' message of the dawning kingdom and respond with repentance and faith will be accepted when it finally comes, while those who reject his message will find out their mistake too late.

The early Church (see Luke 13:25) began to give allegorical interpretations to the individual elements in the story in order to adapt the parable to its own situation. The Jewish community by and large had rejected the Church's preaching of Jesus as Messiah, while others had accepted it.

Finally, Matthew places the parable in the framework of his Gospel. The introductory word "then" in verse 1 (omitted in the incipit of the Lectionary) links the parable to the foregoing chapter, the so-called synoptic apocalypse, which culminates in the coming of the Son of man for the last judgment. At the end Matthew adds a floating saying in the Jesus tradition: "Watch therefore, for you know neither the day nor the hour."

Viewed in the overall context of Matthew's Gospel, the parable now acquires a fresh meaning. The division between the wise and the foolish virgins becomes the division between those in Matthew's Church who keep the commandments of Christ, the new lawgiver of the Church, and those who hear his words but fail to do what he commands. Note also that Matthew follows the parable of the ten virgins with the parables of the talents and of the sheep and goats. All three parables make pretty much the same point.

The Homily

Today's readings clearly invite the homilist to proclaim the eschatological message of the gospel. Three possible accentuations of this message are suggested—one by the Old Testament reading and the psalm, one by the second reading, and one by the gospel.

If the Old Testament reading and the psalm are chosen, the homilist will speak of the heavenly wisdom that alone can satisfy the human religious quest and that alone will stand us in good stead at the final judgment. The lives of Christians will be judged according to whether they sought and found this wisdom or rejected it. Here an allusion to the wise and the foolish virgins could also be introduced.

If the second reading is chosen, the homilist will have an opportunity to demythologize Paul's picture of the parousia. This must be done in answer to the questions of the Thessalonians, which are also asked today: Where are our dead? What has become of them? Will we see them again? The homilist will seek to express Christian hope, which is both Christological and corporate. If there are people in the congregation who hanker after "spiritism," Christian hope as set forth by Paul should render that particular answer to a legitimate question unnecessary, for the ground of Christian hope is not that we can communicate with the dead but that Jesus died and rose again.

If the homilist chooses to preach on today's gospel reading, we would suggest that he/she follow Matthew's redactorial interpretation and equate the wise and foolish virgins with two types of Christians—those who hear the word and keep it, and those who hear the word but do not keep it. But since the same point comes up in the parable of the talents next Sunday, the homilist may find it best to preach on one of the other readings today and plan to preach on the parable of the talents next week.

THIRTY-THIRD SUNDAY OF THE YEAR

Reading I: Proverbs 31:10-13, 19-20, 30-31

Proverbs' picture of the virtuous woman is a beautiful one, though it is hard to see its connection with today's other readings. Perhaps the last verse will help us: "Give her of the fruit of her hands," a thought that is found also in the parable of the talents: the profitable servants are given a share in their earnings. But to concentrate on this point detracts from the main thrust of both readings. The first reading is a picture of a gracious wife and mother who practices love for both God and neighbor in that state of life into which it has pleased God to call her.

Responsorial Psalm: 128:1-5

The second stanza fits in admirably with the Old Testament reading. It also balances the picture: the God-fearing wife (Prov 31:30) is matched by a God-fearing husband (Ps 128:1, 5). Note the typically Old Testament concern with the community. Its ideal is not just the happiness of an individual family—the welfare of the family enriches the life of the whole community. The same thought was present in the second stanza of Prov 31. The graces and virtues of the good housewife are not confined to the home but are extended to the community at large through concern for the poor. The marriage services emphasize that a Christian home should not be self-centered but should reach out in blessing to the community around it.

Reading II: 1 Thessalonians 5:1-6

Paul is apparently replying to a question from his correspondents concerning "the times and the seasons," that is, the precise date of the parousia, which Paul's original preaching had led them to expect imminently. Paul rejects the inference. There is one thing they need to know: the end will come suddenly (cf. Mark 13:32 and Acts 1:8). Despite these warnings of Scripture, however, curiosity over the date of the end has continued to exercise the minds of Christians ever since, and ignorant and unscholarly fanatics claiming to know the date of the parousia can always win a ready hearing. But the Book of Revelation is about events in the first century, not the twentieth century or any other. The experience of history shows that announcements of the exact date of the end have invariably been proven wrong. As fundamentalists, such fanatics should take 1 Thess 5:1-6, Mark 13:32, and Acts 1:8 to heart!

Jesus' parable of the thief in the night (Mark 13:35 par.; Luke 12:39f) is one that the Thessalonians apparently knew already (v. 2)—an interesting indication that Paul may have transmitted more Jesus tradition than the letters suggest. By citing this parable, Paul elevates the parousia hope from one of curious speculation to one of existential attitude. The Christian must always live on tiptoe, as if the parousia were coming at any moment.

But there is more to it than "as if." In a manner typical of his teaching (cf. Rom: 13:11-14), Paul insists that the end has in some sense already come. Christian believers are already children of the light and the day. The imperative is based on an indicative: Be what you are, children of the light and the day. Here is the final answer to the fanaticism of parousiac excitement. It is not a matter for idle curiosity but one of living here and now in the power of the future that we have already begun to participate in through baptism.

Gospel: Matthew 25:14-30 (long form); 25:14-15, 19-20 (short form)

When I read the short form of this gospel, I rubbed my eyes in astonishment. Is the reading meant to stop at verse 20? Surely it should at least include verse 21. Otherwise the caption refers to nothing in the text. Hopefully the long form will be used lest the reading lose its whole point.

As with the parable of the ten virgins, we may distinguish three stages in the history of the tradition:

1. At the Jesus level it was a story told from life. The owner of an estate had to go on a long journey, so he left his money to three servants in trust, lest it remain idle during his absence. Two of them put it to wise use, made capital gains, and were commended by the master on his return. But a third servant carefully hoarded it and, on the master's return, gave him back the exact sum he had been entrusted with. Instead of commending the third servant for his caution, the master rebuked him and handed the money over to the most enterprising of the three servants.

When Jesus first told this story, he must have applied it to something quite concrete in his ministry. Perhaps he was condemning the Jewish religious authorities. They were like the third servant, so carefully bent on preserving in its purity the tradition with which they had been entrusted that they lost their openness for new things and refused to accept Jesus' message.

2. In the early community the parable was moralized by the addition of the maxim "To every one who has will more be given, and he will have abundance; but from him who has not, even what he has will be taken away." In addition, the parable was allegorized. The master was equated with Christ, his departure with the ascension, and his delayed return with the delay of the parousia. The words "enter into the joy of your master" are inserted so that the reward becomes participation in the messianic banquet.

3. Matthew places the parable in his sequence of parables following the synoptic apocalypse, which culminates with the Son of man coming to judge the *Church.* The faithful servant now stands for those Christians who hear the teaching of Christ and follow it; the unprofitable servant represents those who do not keep the new law enunciated by Jesus for the Church.

The Homily

The homilist, if prepared to drop today's eschatological note, could take the first reading and its responsorial psalm as the basis for an exposition of Christian marriage and family life. He/she should stick closely to the text, emphasizing particularly the responsibility of the family toward the community at large, and illustrating this from the marriage rites. If, however, the homilist wishes to preserve the eschatological aspect, three alternatives may be proposed. The choice between them will depend upon the preacher's knowledge of the congregation and its needs.

The second reading provides an opportunity to dampen curiosity about "the times and the seasons" and to direct attention to the existential attitude of vigilance, living "as if" the Lord is to come at any moment, and Christians' responsibility to be what they were made in baptism—children of the light, children of the day.

The gospel reading suggests two possibilities, depending on whether we take it at the Jesus level or at the level of the evangelist. At the Jesus level, there is a possible analogy between the servant who hid the talent in the ground and Church people who oppose all change. Of course, the genuine values of the past must be preserved, but clinging to past customs may indicate a desire for false security and a lack of adventurous obedience to the will of God here and now.

At the level of the evangelist's redaction, the homilist could take the line suggested last week in connection with the parable of the ten virgins, but here equating the faithful servant with Christians who hear the word and keep it, and the unprofitable servant with those who hear the word and do not keep it.

Last Sunday of the Year
CHRIST THE KING

The liturgy now sets Christ's kingship in an eschatological context, as does the Bible. His enthronement at the ascension is the opening act of his final eschatological reign, and his continued heavenly rule between the ascension and his return marks the progressive defeat of the powers of evil. For he must reign until he has "put all his enemies under his feet" (second reading).

Reading I: Ezekiel 34:11-12, 15-17
There is a close connection between the images of king and shepherd, a connection presumably going back to the figure of David.

Ezekiel prophesied during the Babylonian Exile. In the earlier part of chapter 34, he delivers a strong indictment against the pre-exilic kings of Judah who had been false shepherds. Because of this, Yahweh himself will henceforth take over the shepherding of his people (v. 15). He will seek out the lost and bring back the strayed (vv. 12, 16), an allusion to Israel's return from exile and resettlement in the Holy Land (see v. 13, omitted here). The verses suggest that Ezekiel envisaged a theocracy, for the monarchy was not to be restored. Later on in chapter 34, however, Yahweh says that he will set over them David, who will be a shepherd and prince among them. The apparent contradiction is resolved if the Davidic king is the agent and representative of Yahweh, a concept that carries over into the messianic hope.

The same *prima facie* contradiction occurs in the Gospels. In the synoptic parable of the lost sheep, which is undoubtedly authentic to Jesus himself, it is Yahweh who seeks out the lost sheep, though he does so implicitly through Jesus. But in the Johannine allegory of the good shepherd, Christ is the good shepherd, not alongside of nor in addition to Yahweh, but as the representative of the Father. It is in Jesus Christ, therefore, that the prophecy of Ezekiel comes finally to rest.

The last verse introduces the note of judgment. The shepherd will distinguish between sheep and goats. This links the first reading with the gospel (see the caption).

Responsorial Psalm: 23:1-3, 5-6

A slightly different arrangement of verses from this psalm was used on the fourth Sunday of Lent this year. Here the psalm is much more suitable, for it forms an obvious response to the passage from Ezekiel.   47

Reading II: 1 Corinthians 15:20-26, 28

Many important passages are raised in this passage, such as the concept of Christ as the first fruits, the Adam/Christ typology, the importance of "order" in the resurrection process and its relation to the Corinthians' Gnostic view that Christians were already raised. But today's theme, the kingship of Christ, as well as the caption, suggests that we should concentrate on verse 24: "Then comes the end, when he delivers the kingdom to God the Father after destroying every rule and every authority and power."

One fact calls for comment, and two problems for discussion. The fact in question is that, according to Paul, Christ's reign is to be of limited duration. He reigns "until . . . ." It is destined to be replaced by the kingship of God himself when Christ delivers the kingdom to the Father.

The first of the problems is the period covered by Christ's reign. Verse 25 is one of the passages to which "chiliasm" or "millenarianism" appeals. Its chief basis is Rev 20. The Book of Revelation speaks of a first and a second resurrection. At the first resurrection, only the faithful Christians will arise, to reign a thousand years with Christ (the millennium). This is to be followed by a second, or general, resurrection. 1 Cor 15:26 is then interpreted by means of Rev 20. This interpretation is untenable for two reasons: first, it takes the events of the Book of Revelation to be successive rather than as varying descriptions of the same event; second, it allegorically harmonizes Revelation and 1 Corinthians.

It seems quite clear from 1 Corinthians that the reign of Christ is inaugurated with the resurrection-ascension (vv. 20, 27) and is destined to last until the second coming (vv. 23-24a). The kingdom of Christ is thus coterminous with the period of the Church. "In chronological respect (not in spatial) the kingly rule of Christ and the Church completely coincide" (O. Cullmann). It is important to note that Christ's kingdom is a period of perpetual warfare with the "enemies" that will still be under his feet (v. 25). "The present kingdom of Christ is not a period of peace, but of glorious warfare" (H. L. Goudge).

The second problem is the idea of Christ's delivery of the kingdom to the Father and his subjection to him. What can this mean? It means that during the period of Christ's kingdom, the period of the Church, God acts toward the world not directly but through Christ. That is to say, every act that he does toward the world or the Church is an extension of the act that accomplished once and for all the history of Jesus of Nazareth. But after the redemptive work of Christ has been completed at the consummation, God's relationship with the redeemed universe will become a direct one. "Now we see God and experience His action through the God-man who represents Him to us; then Christ will have brought us to the Father; we shall enjoy the Beatific Vision, and immediate union with God himself. . . . God will be all in all, not only in Christians but in the whole realm that Christ restored to him."[1]

Gospel: Matthew 25:31-46

This pericope is often called the "parable" of the sheep and goats or of the last judgment. But such a designation is inaccurate. Except for the comparison in verses 32-33, the whole story remains on the level of direct description. Its literary genre is that of an apocalyptic revelation. But there is a history behind the tradition. The parable is a combination of four elements:

    1. Verses 32-33, the simile of the sheep and goats.

---

[1] I quote from H. L. Goudge's commentary on 1 Corinthians (Westminster Commentaries, 1915, fourth edition revised). I would call attention to this Anglican scriptural scholar, whose work antedated biblical theology in Germany. Goudge was Regius Professor in the University of Oxford between the World Wars. His work has been much neglected, even by Anglicans. Here is a subject for a master's thesis!

2. A series of sayings about the reception accorded to Jesus' disciples (vv. 35-39, 40b, 41-45).

3. The combination of 1 and 2 to provide an allegorical interpretation of the simile.

4. Introduction (v. 31) and conclusion (v. 46) and the placement of the whole in its Matthean setting.

We will discuss each of these elements in turn.

1. The simile of the sheep and goats. Following J. A. T. Robinson, we reconstruct this as follows:

It is with the kingdom of God as with a shepherd who separates the sheep from the goats. He will place the sheep on his right and the goats on his left.

There is no reason why this should not be an authentic parable of Jesus. There is nothing allegorical about it. The kingdom is compared, not to a shepherd nor to the sheep and goats, but to the act of separation. The story is similar to the parables of the wheat and tares (Matt 13:24-30) and of the good and bad fish (Matt 13:47-50), both undoubtedly authentic parables of Jesus. The message is characteristic of Jesus' eschatology: acceptance or rejection at the end. It is a story taken from Palestinian life. During the daytime the sheep and goats are all mixed up. At night the shepherd separates them because the goats need shelter from the cold, whereas the sheep are hardy enough to stay out all night (J. Jeremias). Since sheep are white and goats black, their separation can imply an act of judgment, enabling the parable to be applied to the kingdom of God in a way characteristic of Jesus. Acceptance or rejection of this message will determine which side one will be on at the last judgment—among the saved or the condemned. The final separation is being anticipated in Jesus' ministry.

2. The sayings.

I was hungry,   and you gave me food,
I was thirsty,   and you gave me drink,
I was a stranger   and you welcomed me,
I was naked   and you clothed me,
I was sick   and you visited me,
I was in prison   and you came to me.
When did we see you hungry and fed you or thirsty
    and gave you drink?
When did we see you a stranger and welcomed you
    or naked and clothed you?
When did we see you sick or in prison and visited you?

Amen, I say to you, as you did it to one of the least of
these, you did it to me.

Like other critics, T. W. Manson commented on the whole pericope
that "it contains features of such startling originality that it is difficult to
credit them to anyone but the Master himself." But, as J. A. T. Robinson
has rightly observed, when critics talk like that, they are really speaking
of these sayings, not the whole pericope. It is these that have the ring of
the "Master himself." But what do they mean? They are commonly used
by Church preachers and by secular humanitarians as a piece of ethical
teaching, inculcating concern for the victims of famine and oppression.
God forbid that we should deny the necessity of such concern. But we
must question whether this is the true exegesis of this passage, and whether
therefore it should be so used homiletically. It is closely akin to Mark 9:37
par.; Mark 9:41; and Luke 12:8f par. (Q); cf. Mark 8:38 par. Comparison
with these sayings shows that the passage under examination, far from
being a humanitarian lesson, is an assertion of the "shaliach" principle,
according to which the acceptance or rejection of an accredited agent involves the acceptance or rejection of the sender, and the further assertion
that acceptance or rejection of the accredited agent, like acceptance or
rejection of the sender, will be validated at the last judgment. The life situation in which this passage would have been spoken by Jesus would
therefore have been when he was sending his disciples out on a mission.

3. That this was how Matthew himself understood these sayings is indicated by his addition of "my brethren" to the words "one of the least
of these" (v. 40, not in v. 45). "Brethren" in Matthew always means
disciples. Hunger, thirst, etc., symbolize the weakness and poverty of the
disciples, and the relief given to them symbolizes the acceptance or rejection of them and their message, exactly as in the saying about the cup
of cold water in Mark 9:41. This interpretation will disappoint, perhaps
even anger many, but we are responsible for a genuine exegesis of the text,
not to make it say what we want to hear.

In the post-Easter Church, the shepherd is equated with a king (v. 40),
that is, God. Thus, the parable became an allegory of the last judgment.

4. Finally, the evangelist takes up the allegorically interpreted parable
and inserts the apocalyptic coloring, especially in verses 31 and 36. As
a result, the king of verse 40 became identified, somewhat unusually and
awkwardly, with the Son of man of verse 31. Matthew probably also inserted "all the nations" in verse 32, equating the judged with the nations
to which the disciples will be sent to preach the gospel in all the world
(Matt 28:16-20).

The Homily

The homilist will be very tempted to take the gospel in the popular, humanitarian sense, linking it with today's theme of Christ the King. Unfortunately, however, as we have seen, a proper exegesis of this passage forbids us to do this. In preaching, we must adhere to the exegesis of the text; otherwise our preaching would be our own words, not the word of God.

If the preacher does want to give a humanitarian message, he/she had better stick to the first reading, for Ezek 34:16 will fit the bill. The caritative service of the Christian Church can thus be expounded as an expression of the Christly care as king and shepherd. Psalm 23 could also be related to this.

Other aspects of Christ's kingship expressed in today's readings are: Christ's kingship as the continued warfare with the powers of evil, and the Church as the agent of that warfare (second reading); Christ as judge over the nations of the world, which will be judged by the reception they have given to the Church's proclamation of the gospel.

Series B

ADVENT SEASON

In series B the gospel readings are taken from the Gospel of Mark, supplemented by the Gospel of John. This is necessary because Mark's Gospel, being the shortest, requires supplementing. Also, in the three-year cycle, John is otherwise read only at certain seasons (especially Lent and Eastertide) in series A and C.

Let us first remind ourselves of the structure of the Advent season. The theme of future eschatology—the Christian hope for the final consummation of history—dominates the concluding Sundays of the year and reaches its climax on the first Sunday of Advent. On the following three Sundays, other themes preparatory to the celebration of Christmas and the first coming of the Messiah gradually take over. Thus, each succeeding liturgical season dovetails into its predecessor.

FIRST SUNDAY OF ADVENT

Reading I: Isaiah 63:16b-17; 64:1, 3b-8

This passage is a selection of verses from the psalm of lament covering Isa 63:7–64:11. It has been described as "one of the jewels of the Bible" (*Jerome Biblical Commentary*). The exiles had returned from Babylon with high hopes enkindled by Second Isaiah's prophecies. But then nothing seemed to happen. The temple still lay in ruins:

> Our holy and beautiful house
> where our fathers praised thee
> has been burned with fire,
> and all our pleasant places have become ruins (64:11).

This is the historical context of the lament. The psalmist confesses his sins and the sins of his nation, which he sees to be the cause of the delay in the restoration of Jerusalem: "all our righteous deeds are like a polluted garment." He thus anticipates Paul's insight that every person's virtues are tainted with sin. The prophet cries out for God to intervene:

O that thou wouldst rend the heavens and come down,
that the mountains might quake at thy presence!

These words were undoubtedly in the mind of the earliest evangelist when he recorded the story of Jesus' baptism. Mark 1:10 states that the heavens were "rent," a word that the rsv unfortunately obscures by translating it "were opened," thus assimilating it to the other Synoptics and missing the point. This cry for divine intervention has long been associated with Advent. Many will remember that it provided the Introit for the fourth Sunday of Advent. *Rorate coeli desuper* was one of those Latin tags that everyone knew in the Middle Ages.

Though we see, with Mark, the fulfillment of the psalmist's prayer in the Christ-event, the Church still looks for a final rending of the heavens when the Son of man will come again. Indeed, the Church experiences a rending of the heavens in each liturgy, when Christ comes down in his sacrament to visit the people in their need.

Responsorial Psalm: 80:1ac, 2b, 14-15, 17-18

This psalm is a community lament, similar to the first reading, and thus a fitting response to it. As the refrain shows, it too is a cry for divine intervention.

In the last stanza, "man" and "son of man" stand in synonymous parallelism, common in Hebrew poetry. Both lines of the stanza are a petition for God to come to the aid of his human creation. But the man in question is the king of Israel ("man of thy right hand"), for the king is the ideal embodiment and representative of humanity. Although there is no direct connection between this figure and the Davidic Son of man, it is possible to give the verse a Christological interpretation, since passages referring to the earthly king of Israel may be transferred to the messianic king. In that case, "man of thy right hand" and "Son of man" become references to Christ, and the stanza becomes a petition for God to intervene by sending his Messiah. That would make the psalm particularly appropriate for Advent.

Reading II: 1 Corinthians 1:3-9

This reading is the opening blessing and thanksgiving of 1 Corinthians (actually this was not the first letter that Paul wrote to that community, for he tells us in 1 Cor 5:9 that he had written them a previous one). The thanksgiving is something of a *captatio benevolentiae.* Paul thanks God for the variety of charismatic gifts that have been manifested in the Corinthian community—their speech and knowledge (gnosis)—but later on he will have much to say in criticism of the way they are using these gifts, though never for a moment does Paul doubt that in themselves they are genuine gifts of God.

Note how Paul immediately sets the charismatic gifts in an eschatological context. He reminds the Corinthians that in spite of all their present knowledge, they are still waiting for the revealing of the Lord Jesus Christ. They need to be sustained by him to the end and to be preserved guiltless in the day of our Lord Jesus Christ. Here are three reminders of the "not yet," which the Corinthian charismatics were so much in danger of forgetting in their intoxication with the gifts they already had. It is these reminders that make this passage appropriate for Advent. Paul's substantive criticism of the Corinthians' use or misuse of the charismatic gifts will be developed later in the letter, especially in chapters 12 and 14, which may be regarded as an unfolding of the implications of the eschatological pointers in the opening thanksgiving.

Gospel: Mark 13:33-37

As in the other years of the three-year cycle, the requirements of the first Sunday of Advent make it necessary to begin the gospel readings, not with the opening of each Gospel, but with the future-eschatological material in the synoptic apocalypse. This apocalypse in all three Synoptics concludes with a series of eschatological parables. Today's reading is one of these—the parable of the doorkeeper.

This parable has a long and complicated history in the synoptic tradition and, as it stands in Mark, has acquired secondary features, as comparison with the Lucan form (Luke 12:35-38) will show. These secondary features are: (1) "a man going on a journey"—a phrase taken from the parable of the talents; (2) "puts his servants in charge, each with his work"—a phrase taken from the parable of the faithful and unfaithful servants (Matt 24:45 and Luke 12:42). The insertion of (1) applies the parable clearly to the departure of Christ at his ascension and identifies his return with the parousia. The second feature (2) applies the parable to the whole Christian community. It thus becomes a parable of the post-Easter Church waiting for the delayed parousia. It is also likely that the fourfold division of the day (evening, midnight, cockcrow, morning) is an accommodation to Roman usage, replacing the Palestinian division of the first, second, and third watches.

The original parable as told by Jesus will therefore be something like this: "A man goes out [for a dinner party] during the evening and commands the doorkeeper to be on the watch so that when he comes back and knocks on the door, he may open it at once and let him in." The parable concludes with an exhortation: "Watch, therefore, for you do not know when the master of the house is coming, whether in the first or the second or even in the third watch."

We cannot be certain exactly what the original application of the parable was on the lips of Jesus. Joachim Jeremias thinks that it was probably addressed to the religious leaders of Israel, the scribes. But it could just as well have been addressed to Jesus' disciples or to the crowd. In any case, it was originally a warning to be prepared for the final eschatological crisis which, as Jesus saw it, was soon to overtake his people as a result of his ministry. "It was not spoken to prepare the disciples for a long . . . period of waiting for the second coming, but to enforce the necessity for alertness in a crisis now upon them" (Dodd).

The Church had to adapt this parable to the post-Easter situation. Now there was not one final crisis but a phased process: the ascension of Jesus, his waiting in heaven, and his final return. The exhortation to watchfulness is now applied to the waiting Church, and a series of fresh allegorical touches is added to the original parable in its various forms.

The Homily

The major emphasis today is on waiting for the divine intervention. This theme runs through all the readings. Nevertheless, the context of this waiting varies. In the Old Testament reading and the psalm, it is a context of disappointment and frustration. The history of God's people has run into a bad patch. High hopes have remained unfulfilled. This could perhaps be directly related to the present situation of the Church. The past years have seen great efforts at renewal and reform. Yet, the drift away from the Church has been growing apace, despite its efforts to respond to the world's need. In this situation the Church raises the Advent cry "O that thou wouldst rend the heavens and come down!"

The charismatic renewal has gripped the Church in many places. As Paul did, so we must welcome it with thankfulness. Christian people are being enriched with all speech and knowledge; many are lacking in no spiritual gift. But those who have the gifts must be warned of the "not yet." They must still wait for the revealing of the Lord Jesus Christ. They still see through a glass darkly. They need to be sustained to the end and preserved guiltless to the day of the Lord Jesus Christ.

The gospel could be expounded either at the Jesus level, in which it is a warning to stay alert in the crisis caused by his coming, or at the Church level, in which it is a warning to be alert for his return. The latter would be appropriate this Sunday and could be well fitted either to the first reading and the psalm or to the second reading.

SECOND SUNDAY OF ADVENT

Reading I: Isaiah 40:1-5, 9-11
This is the best known of the prophecies of Second Isaiah. Indeed, it is one of the best known passages of the Old Testament, if for no other reason than its use by Handel in the three opening numbers of *The Messiah.*

Of course, the unknown prophet of the Exile was not consciously thinking of the Christ-event. He had in view the restoration of Israel from the Babylonian Exile around 538 B.C. Cyrus of Persia had won his preliminary victories and the power of Babylon was waning. The prophet himself, then, is the voice crying in the wilderness. He, according to the reading of the RSV margin (anticipated by the English text of *The Messiah* and certainly to be preferred) is the bearer of good tidings:

> Get you up to a high mountain,
>   O herald of good tidings to Zion;
> lift up your voice with strength,
>   O herald of good tidings to Jerusalem.
>
> (RSV margin)

"Good tidings"—in the Hebrew original this is a verb that later gave us the noun "gospel" in its New Testament sense. The good tidings here is the good news of the impending divine intervention in history bringing about the return from exile.

The prophet envisages this return as a second Exodus, in which miracles similar to those of the first Exodus will be repeated:

> Every valley shall be lifted up,
>   and every mountain and hill be made low;
> the uneven ground shall become level,
>   and the rough places a plain.

One might call Second Isaiah the father of typology. Henceforth the Exodus event becomes the type of expected eschatological event and is taken up into the New Testament as the type of the Christ-event itself. It was in this latter sense that this prophecy was applied in the text of *The Messiah,* and it is in the same sense that we read it today. Typology is based upon the conviction, not that history repeats itself, but that God's mighty acts in history follow a consistent pattern because God is true to himself and his purpose.

The eschatological event is defined as the revealing of God's glory, a thought that will have profound significance in New Testament theology (see, for example, John 1:14). "Glory" becomes a word of salvation history; it is an event, the event of the active, saving presence of Yahweh. Yahweh "comes with might."

If the expected event becomes, in Christian interpretation, the Christ-event, so too, according to the New Testament, the prophet of the Exile foreshadows John the Baptist. He is the "voice" (John 1:23, to be read next week) that cries: "In the wilderness prepare the way of the Lord" (see today's gospel). His preparatory work that will make a highway for the advent of the Messiah will be his preaching of repentance.

Responsorial Psalm: 85:8ab-13

No one knows for certain when this lament was composed or what concrete siutation it had in view. It is not unlikely, however, that the psalm was more or less contemporaneous with Second Isaiah. Like the Old Testament reading, the lament looks forward to the intervention of Yahweh in history. It picks up many of the themes of Second Isaiah: "salvation is at hand," "that glory may dwell in our land." The second stanza is a veritable compendium of theological terms for the eschatological event: "steadfast love," "faithfulness," "righteousness," "peace." The third stanza also speaks of the coming of Yahweh as being heralded in advance:

> Righteousness will go before him,
> and make its footsteps a way,

reminding us how the exilic prophet described his mission and how this terminology is taken up in the New Testament and applied to the Baptist.

Reading II: 2 Peter 3:8-14

The second letter of Peter is commonly thought nowadays to be not only a pseudonymous work but also the latest document in the New Testament, written perhaps after A.D. 125. The unknown author appeals to the authority of Peter and to certain Petrine traditions in order to convey to his Church a message that, he is convinced, is precisely what Peter would have said had he still been alive.

The author is faced with false teachers, perhaps of a Gnostic character, who have no place for belief in the second coming of Christ. As in 1 Corinthians, these Gnostics emphasize the "already" at the expense of the "not yet." They dismiss the Church's traditional teaching about the second coming by pointing scornfully to its failure to occur, despite constant teaching that it was just around the corner.

In answer, the author appeals to Psalm 90: "A thousand years in thy sight are but as yesterday when it is past, or as a watch in the night." God's time scheme is different from ours. But the author still seeks to retain the existential vitality of the parousia hope. The dominical parable of the thief in the night is cited to show that Christians must always expect the day of the Lord to come at any moment. This gives a motivation for holiness and godliness of living (v. 11). It is therefore not true to say, as some have said, that this letter, like other early catholic writings in the New Testament, has relegated the parousia to the last chapter of dogmatics and deprived it of significance for the Christian life.

The following points in this pericope seem to still speak to contemporary Chistianity:

1. Christians must always live as though the end were to come at any moment. Watchfulness is a part of Christian living.

2. Rightly understood, the imminent hope in Christianity is a motivation for the pursuit of holiness and godliness of life.

3. However much we demythologize the New Testament pictures of the end, the hope of a new heaven and a new earth as the final goal of history is something that can never be surrendered.

Gospel: Mark 1:1-8

Following the established pattern of Advent, John the Baptist occupies the forefront of our attention on the second and third Sundays. He marks the inauguration of the Christ-event, and therefore the inauguration of the gospel. It is unclear whether Mark means "gospel of Jesus Christ" to be taken subjectively (the gospel preached by Jesus, the good news of the kingdom, as in Mark 1:14) or objectively (the gospel about Jesus). The subjective sense makes good history, for it is an incontestable fact that Jesus' mission grew out of the Baptist's. In some sense the one was a continuation of the other, in others a breakaway. John's accent was on judgment, Jesus' on salvation. This difference is expressed in the parable of the children in the market places (Matt 11:16-19).

Mark (v. 3) picks up the Deutero-Isaian prophecy of today's first reading and prefaces it with a prophecy of Malachi (3:1), which he alters significantly. "*My* face" becomes "*thy* face," so that it is addressed to Christ. Both techniques—the combination of two widely separated texts and the alteration of a text—are now familiar to us from the Dead Sea Scrolls.

As reported by Mark, John's preaching consists of two aspects: first, the preaching of repentance and baptism and the forgiveness of sins;

second, the announcement of the coming of the mightier One who will baptize with the Holy Spirit.

In recent years there has been something of a "quest for the historical Baptist" for reasons similar to those that motivated the "quest for the historical Jesus." Both historical figures have been subject to reinterpretation in the light of post-Easter Christian faith. There can be no doubt that the "historical Baptist" did baptize; this is attested not only by the New Testament but also by the Jewish historian Josephus. The latter gives a non-sacramental interpretation to it; he regards it merely as a sign of conversion from sin to righteousness that had already taken place. This we may suspect, however, as an attempt to debiblicize the Baptist for the benefit of Josephus' pagan readers.

But did John also speak of the stronger One who was to come after him? Josephus says nothing of this, but it is generally agreed that he did, although he was not consciously predicting the coming of Jesus. The stronger One whom the Baptist expected was either Yahweh himself or a very different kind of Messiah from what Jesus turned out to be—a Messiah whose accent, like John's own, would be on judgment rather than on salvation (see "fire" in Matt 3:11/Luke 3:16). In that case, "Holy Spirit" will be a Christian reinterpretation of "fire" from the perspective of Pentecost, but a wholly legitimate one.

The Homily

As we have seen, the dominant theme of today's readings is John the Baptist's work as the forerunner of Christ. As the *beginning* of the gospel of Jesus Christ, John could be regarded simply as a figure of the past, of historical interest only. But then he would not be the beginning of the *gospel.* John the Baptist is part of the good news, the beginning part, and therefore of permanent relevance in the life of the Church.

The Church must allow John the Baptist to perform his distinctive ministry of forerunner in its midst today . How is he to do this? By the preaching of repentance. Unless people are first convicted of sin, they cannot know the need for a Savior. It is easy to quote Bonhoeffer against this (see his strictures on what he called "methodism" in *Letters and Papers from Prison*—"despair or Jesus"). No doubt this was a legitimate protest against many things, including Lutheran sermons that preached despair for forty minutes and Christ as a possible way out in the last five! But the New Testament, including John the Baptist, our Lord, St. Paul, and the author of the Fourth Gospel, each in his own way, insists that repentance—the abandonment of any attempt to save ourselves—is the essential precondition for faith, which means allowing God to do for us what we cannot do for ourselves. The preaching of John the Baptist on this Sunday means the preaching of repentance as the indispensable *preparatio evangelica* and an indispensable preparation for the celebration of Christmas.

If the homilist is drawn rather to 2 Peter, this would be an opportunity to drive home the existential vitality of the hope of an imminent parousia as the motif of the quest for holiness.

THIRD SUNDAY OF ADVENT

Reading I: Isaiah 61:1-2, 10-11
Responsorial Psalm: Luke 1:46-50, 53-54

This is one of the most familiar passages from Third Isaiah (56–66). It is akin to the servant psalms of Second Isaiah (40–55), for although the prophet does not explicitly call himself the servant, he describes his mission in terms of servanthood. This passage appears to have profoundly influenced Jesus' understanding of his own mission. Even if—which, however, is by no means certain—the sermon at Nazareth (Luke 4:16-22) is a Lucan composition, Jesus himself alluded unmistakably to this text in his answer to John (Matt 11:2-6/Luke 7:18-23), whose authenticity is beyond reasonable doubt.

The Christological interest of this text, however, would be more appropriate for the Epiphany season (a slightly different selection from Isa 61 is used in the Episcopal Church's adaptation of the Lectionary on the third Sunday of Epiphany in series C). Today's caption highlights the theme of *joy* in face of the impending advent of God's salvation, a theme that is reinforced by the responsorial psalm (the *Magnificat* and the refrain taken from its two opening words). This, it will be noted, is in accordance with the tradition of the Roman Missal, where this Sunday was known as Gaudete Sunday, from the opening word of the Introit. In the Book of Common Prayer, this theme belonged, as generally in the medieval rites of Northern Europe, to the fourth Sunday of Advent. We might note that the *Magnificat* is particularly associated with Advent, Bach's *Magnificat*, for instance, being frequently performed on one of the Advent Sundays.

Reading II: 1 Thessalonians 5:16-24

The opening of this reading continues the Gaudete theme. However, the caption underlines the second paragraph, with its references to the parousia. As we have already noted, the theme of the second coming is replaced after the first Sunday of Advent by that of the first coming, but there are occasional echoes of the earlier theme on later Sundays. Such is the genius of Advent. It refuses to contemplate the first coming apart from the second, or the second apart from the first.

Gospel: John 1:6-8, 19-28

This gospel reading represents an ingenious combination of two separate passages. The first paragraph is a prose comment that the evangelist inserted into the Logos hymn. Bultmann thought that the Johannine prologue was first composed as a hymn to John the Baptist by his followers, who regarded him as the bearer of the eschatological revelation. Perhaps it was, even earlier than that, a hymn to Wisdom, successively adapted for "baptist" and for Christian use. In any case, the evangelist's prose insertion is clearly designed to counter a false estimate of the Baptist: he is not the light but only a witness to the light.

The same tendency ostensibly to downgrade the Baptist continues in the second paragraph of our pericope. John is here presented as entirely repudiating all messianic or quasi-messianic titles. He is neither the Christ, the prophet-Messiah, nor (contra the Synoptics) Elijah, but only the "voice" of Isa 40.

This disagreement with the synoptic interpretation should not worry us unduly. In the Synoptists' environment, it was perfectly safe to interpret John as an Elijah redivivus. But for the Fourth Gospel, in its different situation, Elijah could well have been too high a title, suggesting that he was actually the Messiah, the immediate forerunner of Yahweh. Perhaps John reflects an earlier state of Christology than that of the Synoptists, a stage when Elijah was still preempted for Christ himself—the stage that Bishop John A. T. Robinson characterized as the view that Jesus was his own Elijah, in the sense that he was the forerunner of the apocalyptic Son of man and was himself exalted to heaven to fulfill that role.

The Homily

The major theme today is again the mystery of John the Baptist as the forerunner of Christ. The reading from the Fourth Gospel emphasizes the self-effacing character of John's ministry. This self-effacing character reaches its climax in a later passage of the Fourth Gospel in which the Baptist compares himself to the best man who must give way to the bridegroom when the task is done: "He must increase but I must decrease." Here John is the pattern for the Church's ministry, a parallel that was suggested by the Book of Common Prayer in the collect for this Sunday (written by John Cosin in 1661, though unfortunately addressed to the second Person of the Trinity):

"O Lord Jesus Christ, who at thy first coming didst send thy messenger to prepare thy way before thee: Grant that the ministers and stewards of thy mysteries may likewise so prepare and make ready thy way by turning the hearts of the disobedient to the wisdom of the just, that at thy second coming to judge the world we may be found an acceptable people in thy sight, who . . . ."

Karl Barth was fond of illustrating the self-effacing character of the Baptist's ministry from the Isenheim altarpiece, in which the Baptist is portrayed with a large index finger pointing to Christ on the cross, the Lamb who takes away the sin of the world.

Another possible idea for a homily might be suggested—the Gaudete theme from the first reading, the responsory, and the second reading. It is instructive to compare the three types of joy represented by Gaudete, Laetare, and Jubilate Sundays—the joy of Advent, of mid-Lent, and of Easter. Advent joy is the joy of anticipation; mid-Lent joy is that of reaching an oasis in the desert; and the joy of Easter is that of sorrow that has been turned into joy.

FOURTH SUNDAY OF ADVENT

As we draw nearer to the Christmas festival, the Advent readings take us to the brink of the incarnation. The whole series of Old Testament prophecies, culminating in John the Baptist and his message, reaches its fulfillment in the Christ-event. The move from John the Baptist's ministry to the Blessed Virgin Mary and the annunciation looks at first sight like a step backward, chronologically. But theologically it is not, for John sums up the whole of Old Testament prophecy and announces the impending Christ-event, and Mary is the appointed agent through whom the Christ entered into the world. She thus brings us to the fulfillment of Advent hope in her role in the annunciation.

Reading I: 2 Samuel 7:1-5, 8b-12, 14a, 16

This passage gives classical expression to the Davidic-messianic hope in the Old Testament. It is not the only type of the messianic hope, but it later became dominant in many circles, for example among the Pharisees, as we see from Ps Sol 17; among the covenanters of Qumran, who looked for both a Messiah of David and a Messiah of Levi; and among the simple pious folk of Judea and Galilee, as we see from the Lucan infancy narrative.

In its original intention, however, 2 Sam 7 was an expression of royal ideology. The promise was that the Davidic dynasty would last forever.

Note how David's original intention is reversed by the prophet's later word. David indicates his intention of building a house for Yahweh, that is, a temple. At first, Nathan approves of the king's proposal but later corrects this in the light of a further word from the Lord received in the night. Instead of David's building a house (temple) for Yahweh, Yahweh covenants to maintain the "house" (dynasty) of David in perpetuity.

Strictly speaking, then, this is not a messianic prophecy in the later sense, for it does not speak of the coming of the ideal Davidic king. But after the destruction of the Davidic monarchy, this promise could only take the form of the coming of a Davidic Messiah, and in Christian perspective the promise has been fulfilled in the coming of Jesus the Christ, whom the New Testament (as in the Lucan annunciation story that forms the gospel reading today) proclaims as the Son of David.

Responsorial Psalm: 89:1-4, 26, 28

This psalm makes a perfect response to the first reading, for, as the *Jerome Biblical Commentary* points out, the two passages should be read in conjunction. Only the second and third stanzas deal directly with the Davidic-messianic hope. The first stanza comes from the opening of the psalm, which is a general hymn of praise to Yahweh. But the first stanza is not unrelated to the messianic hope, for the faithfulness of Yahweh is exhibited precisely in his faithfulness to his covenant with David. Note how the second stanza refers quite specifically to the covenant of 2 Samuel.

Reading II: Romans 16:25-27

In the manuscript tradition, this doxology appears at three different places: after Rom 14:23; after Rom 15:33; and in its canonical position here. Some have thought that it is a Marcionite gloss, for it seems to assume that the God who revealed himself in Jesus Christ had been silent through the Old Testament period, as Marcion taught. However, this is untenable for two reasons. First, Origen explicitly informs us that Marcion did not read these verses in his text. Second, Marcion would never have allowed that the writings of the Old Testament prophets were instruments through which the Christian revelation was proclaimed, even in the Christian era.

The doxology actually has close affinities with the style and thought of Colossians and Ephesians (cf. especially Col 1:26-27; Eph 3:9-10) and is therefore probably the work of a Deutero-Pauline editor of Romans. Judging from the various places where it appears in the manuscript tradition, it was probably added as a conclusion to Romans in the three different versions that were current in early times—ending respectively with chapters 14, 15, and 16.

The statement that the revelation was kept secret before Christ does not mean that the Old Testament God is a different God from the God and Father of our Lord Jesus Christ, as Marcion thought, but that it is only with the coming of Christ that the Old Testament prophecies acquire their true meaning. The movement from silence to revelation is a good Advent theme.

Gospel: Luke 1:26-38

Annunciation stories are a regular literary form of Scripture. There are a number of such stories in the Old Testament (for example, the births of Isaac, Samson, and Samuel), and of course Luke has already recorded the annunciation of John the Baptist.

We should make full allowance for this literary form in assessing this narrative. The purpose of annunciation stories is to acquaint the *readers* with the role that the person about to be born is to play in salvation history. It is thus a device to effect this end, not a historical narration. At the same time, there are elements in the story of Jesus' annunciation that surpass the other annunciation stories. The usual situation is that of a miraculous birth granted to a barren couple—in the case of Isaac, to parents who were even past the age of begetting and bearing children. In the case of Jesus, it is an annunciation to a young woman without a husband. The emphasis rests on the creative act of the Holy Spirit rather than on the virginal conception *per se*, which is its presupposition.

All that the historian can say with certainty is that the basic elements in this tradition are earlier than Matthew or Luke, for the name of Mary, her virginity, and the function of the Holy Spirit are common both to Matthew and Luke, who are otherwise entirely independent of one another at this point. Many would also argue that these traditions can be traced back to the earliest Palestinian stratum of Christianity. Beyond that point, however, the historian *qua* historian cannot go. The exegete must deal rather with the meaning. What is the kerygmatic thrust of the annunciation? It is that the history of Jesus does not emerge out of the stream of ongoing history. As Adolf Schlatter put it, it expresses the transcendental origin of the history of Jesus. Or, as Sir Edwyn Hoskyns put it, the incarnation is "a dagger thrust into the weft of human history."

Our response to the annunciation story should be not to accept it as an entertaining story or even to insist merely on its historicity and leave it at that. As such, it would still be "flesh," which profiteth nothing. Our response should rather be the affirmation of faith in the transcendental origin of Jesus' history.

The role that the Child to be born is to play in salvation history is defined in terms of Davidic messiahship. Thus, the gospel reading is linked with the Old Testament reading. Christian faith sees the promise to, and covenant with, David fulfilled in the coming of Jesus Christ.

The Homily

The most obvious subject for today's homily would be the annunciation. The homilist should be careful to remain within the framework provided by the liturgy and remember that this is still Advent and not yet Christmas. We stand on the verge of the fulfillment of the messianic hope, and the tension of waiting for it that is characteristic of the Advent season should not be relaxed today. Israel's hope could be related to the hopes of humanity in general and of modern men and women in particular, and Christ could be proclaimed as the One who comes to answer those hopes.

There are two other possibilities. One would be to draw out the kerygmatic sense of the dogma of the virginal conception, dealing with any difficulties the congregation may feel about it (though refraining from putting into their minds difficulties they do not feel). The other possibility would be to speak of the mystery of the revelation of God (second reading), how it had been kept secret until the incarnation, and how it is only in the "preaching of Jesus Christ" in word and sacrament that this revelation can still be received.

CHRISTMAS SEASON

CHRISTMAS

Since the readings are the same each year, we shall summarize what we wrote for series A.

14

The Christmas festival is not primarily a historical commemoration of the birth at Bethlehem but the celebration of God's eschatological self-disclosure in the Christ-event. The commercialization and sentimentalization of Christmas in the secular world, and their effects on the Church, make it advisable to deemphasize the historical aspect of Christmas and to stress its theological aspect.

MASS AT MIDNIGHT

Reading I: Isaiah 9:2-7

Originally this was a coronation anthem. Every new Davidic king was welcomed in the hope that he would be the ideal king. The joy of the occasion is expressed in two comparisons: the joy of harvest and the joy of victory on the field of battle (v. 3). The new reign ushers in the three freedoms—from want, from oppression, and from war. In the original use of the anthem, the birth of the child (v. 6) was the enthronement of the king, interpreted in the court theology as God's adoption of the monarch as his son (cf. Ps 2:7). The newly enthroned king is hailed by a series of honorific titles; he is even called "God." This bold ascription of divinity, common enough in the ancient Near East, is rare in the Old Testament (see Ps 45:7) and should probably be interpreted in a biblical sense to mean the sovereignty of Yahweh.

In the perspective of Christian faith, this hope for the ideal Davidic king comes to fulfillment in the coming of Jesus Christ. In him all blessings of salvation—freedom from want and oppression, and the realization of peace on earth—are given to humanity. We hail this Child as the One who will be enthroned in his ascension. To him all the messianic titles will be rightly given, including that of God, though not as *Deus in se*, which in later dogmatic language would be the first Person of the Trinity, but as *Deus pro nobis,* the second Person of the Trinity, God turned toward us in his grace and salvation.

Responsorial Psalm: 96:1-3, 11-13

This is the greatest of the enthronement or royal psalms. The theme of the "new song" can be traced throughout the two Testaments. The original song was the song of Moses and Israel by the Red Sea (Exod 15). This song is continued in the liturgy of the tabernacle and the temple. Then the temple was destroyed, the song of the liturgy ceased, and Israel cried out: "How shall we sing the Lord's song in a strange land?" The idea of a new song thus became part of Israel's eschatological expectation. In the New Testament, the Book of Revelation tells us that the new song is sung by the redeemed in celebration of the victory of the Lamb. The angelic hymn at Bethlehem is the overture to this new song, and the Church's liturgy its anticipation and partial realization.

Reading II: Titus 2:11-14

This reading speaks of the first and second comings of Christ (vv. 11, 13). Thus the Advent theme of the second coming is carried right into Christmas. The first coming is an anticipation of the second, and it is celebrated at midnight because at midnight, according to New Testament imagery, the second coming will occur (see Matt 25:6).

Gospel: Luke 2:1-14

The infancy narratives of both Matthew and Luke raise a number of difficult historical problems. But, in the words of the *Jerome Biblical Commentary,* "the details of the narrative are symbolic and biblical; they communicate the mystery of redemption, not a diary of earthly events." It is as a communication of the mystery of redemption that we should listen to this gospel reading at the first Mass of Christmas.

In first-century Palestine, shepherds belonged to a despised trade, like tax collectors and prostitutes. They should not be romanticized. The angelic announcements are a biblical device expressing the meaning of an event in salvation history. The first announcement, by a single angel, tells of the birth itself; the second, by "a multitude of the heavenly host," proclaims the blessings that will result from that birth: glory to God and peace (that is, messianic salvation) on earth. The words "among men with whom he is pleased" translate a biblical idiom that means "among all people, who are now made the objects of God's favor." It does not mean "people of good will" in the secular sense of the phrase.

The Homily

The homilist has a wealth of possibilities here. A combination of the Old Testament reading and the angelic annunciation would suggest the message of peace, to which the homilist must be careful to give a biblical interpretation (*shalom*). Or the homilist could take the theme of midnight as the time of Christ's first and second comings. Again, he/she could concentrate on the nativity story itself, bringing out the fact that the shepherds were members of a despised trade, that the incarnation is especially intended for the poor, the despised, and the oppressed, and therefore encourages Christian sensitivity to their needs. Yet again, the homilist could contrast the words "people of good will" (who quickly become people of ill will once Christmas is over!) and the biblical notion of God's favor toward humankind in the incarnation.

MASS AT DAWN

Reading I: Isaiah 62:11-12

This passage from Third Isaiah originally spoke of the joy that marked a Jewish festival (perhaps the feast of Tabernacles). In the present liturgical context, it speaks of the joy of the new Israel at the birth of its Savior, the advent of messianic salvation.

Responsorial Psalm: 97:1, 6, 11-12

This is another of the enthronement psalms. The second stanza and the refrain underline the dawn of the light—imagery that has passed into the lore of the season and is expressed in so many Christmas carols.

Reading II: Titus 3:4-7

This passage is very similar to the second reading of the midnight Mass, except that it speaks only of the first coming of Christ. Also, instead of leading to an ethical exhortation, it speaks of the salvific consequences of the incarnation—our regeneration and renewal, or rebirth as children of God. This is a traditional theme of Christmas: the Son of God became human that we might become children of God.

Gospel: Luke 2:15-20

This is a continuation of the gospel for the midnight Mass. Impelled by the angelic message, the shepherds go to Bethlehem and visit the newborn Babe. The picture is familiar. What matters, however, is its inner significance. The shepherds make known not only what they have seen but what they had been told, that is, the angelic message that this was the divine salvation come into the world.

The Homily

The Old Testament reading has a pregnant phrase: the people of God are "sought out." The incarnation is God's search for his human creation (K. Barth). As such, it is the answer to all human religion, which is the search of human beings for God. The Church is the outcome of this search, not merely an institution for the cultivation of human religion. The Church is the place where God's search for his people continues.

The second reading suggests the theme of filiation. Only Christ is the Son of God by nature; our divine filiation is by adoption and grace. The Bible knows nothing of the modern humanistic idea that all human beings are children of God; they are only potentially such until they are incorporated into Christ.

The gospel, with its interpretation of the nativity scene as a sign and its insistence on the thing signified—the coming of messianic salvation into the world—is another protest against the sentimentalizing of Christmas.

MASS DURING THE DAY

Reading I: Isaiah 52:7-10

This passage from Second Isaiah is similar in tone to the Old Testament reading for the Mass at Dawn and to the enthronement psalms read at all three Masses this day. "Your God reigns" is an announcement of the return from exile, but these words were also used at the sovereign's enthronement. This proclamation is described in a verb as bringing good tidings—the verb from which the Christian word "gospel" (*euangelion*) is ultimately derived. Paul took up this text and applied it to his own apostolic work of preaching the gospel, and it probably also influenced the formulation of Jesus' own message of the kingdom of God.

In today's liturgy the good news can be referred specifically to the angelic proclamation at the nativity. In the incarnation the Church discerns the return of Yahweh to Zion (v. 8) to comfort his people (v. 9). At Bethlehem Yahweh bares his arm and the people see the coming of his salvation (v. 10).

Responsorial Psalm: 98:1-6

This psalm is very similar to Psalms 96 and 97, used in the first and second Masses of Christmas respectively. Its applicability to the nativity is obvious. Note the link between "arm" in the first stanza and "holy arm" in the Old Testament reading.

Reading II: Hebrews 1:1-6
The first part of Hebrews seeks to establish Christ's superiority over the angels—perhaps in a situation in which a form of Jewish Gnosticism was leading Jewish Christians to think of Christ as only one among other angelic mediators. The opening section of Hebrews is prefaced by a hymn to Christ similar to the Johannine prologue, which is read in the gospel of this Mass. The hymn in Hebrews seems to be based on an earlier Jewish hymn to the wisdom of God and follows a regular pattern. Wisdom is described as preexistent with God from eternity. She is the agent of creation and preservation, and manifests herself to people on earth and returns to heaven.

This pattern was adapted by Christianity to express its own Christological faith. Christ is identified with preexistent Wisdom. As such, he is the agent of creation and preservation. He appears on earth and returns to heaven. Note that here the incarnation is presumed rather than expressed in the words "when he had made purification for sins." This is an idea that is wholly Christian and has nothing to do with the Wisdom hymn. Only in the series of scriptural quotations is the entry of Christ into the world explicitly stated. After his return to heaven, Christ triumphs over the angels, conceived here, as elsewhere in early Christianity, as hostile powers.

One further point should be noted about the writer's treatment of this hymn. He sets it in the context of God's revelation throughout Israel's salvation history. In the Old Testament period, God had spoken through the prophets "in many and various ways"—a phrase that in the Greek expresses the fragmentary, partial character of his self-revelation in the Old Testament. The hymn, placed in this context, now expresses the finality of God's self-revelation in Christ.

Gospel: John 1:1-18 (long form); 1:1-5, 9-14 (short form)
The shorter version of this gospel is arrived at by omitting the prose comments inserted by the evangelist into an already existing hymn (see above). The anti-John the Baptist polemic is hardly relevant to Christmas.

The function of the hymn in relation to the Fourth Gospel as a whole is to provide the eternal background of the ministry, life, and death of Jesus. This whole ministry was the revelation of the Word-made-flesh, the embodiment of the fullness of God's self-revelation. This self-revelation (Word, Logos), however, did not begin with the Christ-event but with creation (see Heb 1:1-4). God created the universe in order to communicate himself to it in love (John 1:1-2). He communicated himself throughout human history (vv. 4, 9-10), especially, though not exclusively, in Israel's salvation history (v. 11). Wherever it is received, this revelation restores human beings to their adopted status as children of God.

It is often debated where precisely the prologue moves from the preexistent Logos to the incarnate Christ. Clearly it has done so by verse 14. Yet, the parentheses have the effect of changing the earlier statements about the work of the Logos into statements also about the incarnate Christ. This makes the whole prologue a comment on the rest of the Gospel. The entire life of Christ is the story of the Word becoming flesh.

The Homily

The homilist should look up last year's sermon and choose another theme today. He/she may decide to take the second reading and the gospel—the two Christological hymns—together. Both speak of the Christ-event as the culmination of God's revelation or self-communication to the world in creation, to humankind in general, and to Israel in particular. Thus it will be possible to relate the final revelation of God both to the Old Testament revelation and to human religion in general. All religions contain fragmentary and partial disclosures of God; but what was fragmentary and partial is now finally and fully disclosed in Christ.

Sunday in the Octave of Christmas

HOLY FAMILY

The readings are the same as in series A, except for the gospel and the optional readings. Our comments here, therefore, summarize what we said in series A, with new comments provided for the gospel and the optional readings.

Reading I: Sirach 3:2-6, 12-14

This passage forms a commentary on the fifth (fourth) commandment, "Honor thy father and thy mother." That the keeping of the commandment atones for sin is a typical idea of later Judaism, but we should not take this with full theological seriousness. For the New Testament, atonement for sin is through Christ alone. Sirach's statement should be taken merely as an incentive to obedience. In a loose, non-theological sense, one could say that love of parents makes up for many sins.

Responsorial Psalm: 128:1-5

This psalm presents piety as the true foundation of family and social life and of economic prosperity, in a manner reminiscent of Deuteronomy. Naive though it may seem, this should not be too lightly dismissed. Where there is a wholesome respect for God and his will, there is a better chance for human relationships to be well ordered and harmonious. Those who fear the Lord are not tempted to put themselves in God's place, are therefore free to love their neighbor, and make it easier for the neighbor to love in return.

Reading II: Colossians 3:12-21

This reading is taken from the parenetic section, or ethical exhortation, of Colossians and, as is widely thought, reproduces the pattern of an early Christian catechism. This catechesis begins with a list of virtues to be "put on"—an echo of the vesting of the candidates as they come up out of the baptismal waters. Sometimes another imperative, "put off," precedes, recalling the stripping of the candidates before baptism. Then comes a "household code," a list of the duties of the members of a family and of society in their several states. These codes were apparently already taken over by Hellenistic Judaism from Stoicism, and passed thence into Christian usage. Their subordinationist tone is thus not distinctively Christian but is derived ultimately from Stoicism. The distinctive Christian elements are to be found in the words "in the Lord"; in the injunction to husbands to *love* their wives; in the earlier definition of love as forgiveness; and in the motivation of that forgiveness in Christ's forgiveness of the sinner.

Gospel: Luke 2:22-40 (long form); 2:22, 39-40 (short form)

The caption at the head of both the long and the short form, as well as the text of the short form itself, puts the stress on the growth of the Christ-child to maturity and on the fact that he was filled with wisdom. The presentation scene and the encounter between the Christ-child and Simeon, the *Nunc dimittis,* and the encounter with Anna are important kerygmatically, but they receive their proper due on the feast of the Presentation of the Lord (February 2), when the same gospel is read. Our comments today will therefore be confined to the growth of the Christ-child.

Three points may be made here. The first is a dogmatic one. The Christ-child is fully human, and as such he has to grow not only physically but also mentally and spiritually. If we are to understand the incarnation in scriptural terms, we must not think of it as entailing complete maturity from the outset. Rather, Christ is perfect man with the perfection that belongs to each stage of human growth. At each stage, too, he is the perfect manifestation of God in a manner appropriate for that stage.

The second point is that this growth to maturity takes place in the context of a human family. Apart from the story of the visit to the temple when Jesus was twelve years old, this is the only verse in the New Testament that speaks of his life in the Holy Family. Scripture is very reserved about that life, unlike the later apocryphal gospels. But this verse is a priceless gem, for it contains all that we really need to know about the Holy Family. First, it was the divinely provided context in which the Christ was prepared for his saving mission. Second, the Holy Family is the paradigm for all Christian family life, for the Christian family is the divinely provided context in which the Christian child may grow to physical, mental, and spiritual maturity.

The third point is typological. This verse points back through Luke 1:80 to 1 Sam 2:26. Jesus stands in the prophetic succession. He is the last and the greatest of the prophets but transcends them all, for he is the eschatological prophet. But he is still a prophet.

The Homily

It is clearly the Church's intention today that the life of the Holy Family should be held up as the pattern of Christian family life. The readings provide different ways of doing this. The gospel suggests that the family is the divinely provided context for growth to physical, mental, and spiritual maturity. The second reading suggests that the pattern of Christian family life is based on mutual forgiveness, while the Old Testament reading emphasizes the importance of the fifth (fourth) commandment—a tricky subject to tackle in the contemporary world!

OPTIONAL READINGS

Reading I: Genesis 15:1-6; 21:1-3

God has promised Abraham that his descendants will become a great nation. This seems a most unlikely prospect. He and his wife are childless; she is well past the age of childbearing, and he is a very old man. In this situation Abraham is provided with an assurance: if Yahweh can make all the stars of heaven, he can certainly make Abraham's descendants just as many in number. In verse 6 Abraham takes Yahweh at his word. This is quoted by Paul as one of the pivotal verses in his exposition of the righteousness that comes through faith (Rom 4:3, 9-22), that is, a right relationship with God.

The second part of the reading, from Gen 21, speaks of the fulfillment of the prenatal promise in the birth and naming of the child. This whole story line is repeated in the narratives of the birth of Jesus in Matthew and Luke—the promise of (supernatural) birth, the birth, and the naming.

Responsorial Psalm: 104:1b-6, 8-9

Excerpts from this psalm were used for the vigil of Pentecost in series A, which the reader may wish to consult. The response highlights the theme of covenant, an image not actually present in the Old Testament reading, though the first part of it (Gen 15:1-6) is followed immediately by a covenant ceremony. *96*

Reading II: Hebrews 11:8, 11-12, 17-19

Hebrews 11 is often called "the roll call of the heroes of faith." Yet, strictly speaking, the Bible knows no heroes, for heroes are witnesses to their own achievements, whereas in Heb 11 the great figures of salvation history from Abraham to the prophets and martyrs of the old covenant are adduced, not for their heroism, but precisely for their "faith," which is, in the author's thought, closely linked to hope. Faith is taking God at his word when he makes promises for the future. Thus, the Old Testament figures become examples for the new Israel, the new wandering people of God. The new people has also in each succeeding generation had to imitate Abraham, who "went out, not knowing where he was to go," and his family, who lived in tents because they had no abiding city here, but "looked forward to the city which has foundations."

January 1
SOLEMNITY OF MARY, MOTHER OF GOD

Since the readings for this occasion are the same each year, we will confine ourselves here to summarizing the comments given in series A. *26*

The title of this solemnity is suggested by two sentences in today's readings. In the second reading we hear: "God sent forth his Son, born of woman," a sentence that has direct bearing on the title "Mother of God." Then in the gospel we hear: "Mary kept all these things, pondering them in her heart." These words have no direct bearing on the title; rather, they treat Mary as the paradigm of faith and therefore a paradigm of both the Christian believer and the true Israel. Despite the title, the main thrust of today's readings is the birth of Christ, in which the saving act of God is inaugurated. *Theotokos* is, of course, primarily a Christological title.

Reading I: Numbers 6:22-27

The Aaronic blessing is a remarkable Old Testament anticipation of the Church's Trinitarian faith (cf. the threefold "holy" in Isa 6). The caption calls attention to the last verse: "So shall they put my name upon the people of Israel, and I will bless them." In the Bible, the "name," whether it be of God or of a human being, is very important. The name stands for the whole person, his/her character and personality. The name of God is his Being, all that he has manifested himself to be in salvation history. Hence, to bless in God's name is to invoke upon the faithful all that God is and all that he has done for his people. In the act of blessing, the name of God is passed on, in the sense we have defined, from age to age.

Responsorial Psalm: 67:1-2, 4-5, 7

As the refrain shows, this psalm picks up the theme of Yahweh's blessing of Israel.

Reading II: Galatians 4:4-7

Recent exegesis regards this passage as a pre-Pauline creedal formula, expanded with the Pauline phrase "born under the law, to redeem those who were under the law." Without the expansion, the hymn would read:

> God sent forth his Son
> (born of woman)
> that we might receive adoption as sons.

The purpose clause follows directly upon the sending clause, thus linking the incarnation with our existence. The coming of the Son of God into the world is not merely a fact of history but an event of direct existential significance for believers today. The Son of God became human in order that human beings might become the children of God (see second reading, Mass at Dawn, Christmas).

Paul's addition about the law points toward the event mentioned at the end of today's gospel reading, the circumcision of Jesus, in which he is shown to be born "under the law." The incarnation means that Christ entered into a human life with all its limitations, including the restrictions of human freedom that characterize human life. The law was one of these restrictions—it told people what to do but left them powerless to do it. Only by such complete submission could Christ liberate people, for only he remained truly free and therefore able to pass on the "contagion" (Van Buren) of that freedom to others.

Gospel: Luke 2:16-21

This pericope received comment at the Mass at Dawn on Christmas. Today's selection, though, begins one verse later (v. 16) and continues through verse 21 to include the circumcision and naming of Jesus. Thus, it is these two events that are highlighted today.

The Homily

We suggest three possibilities. Following the Old Testament reading and the psalm, the homilist might deal with the biblical concept of blessing. Karl Barth's reflections on this subject in *Church Dogmatics* III/2 are particularly helpful here. He says: "Blessing is regarded in the Old Testament as the epitome of all the good things which the father can pass on to the son and the son receive from the father. A blessing is the word which has divine power to pass on good things" (p. 580). The homilist might expound the biblical concept of blessing, then relate it to the priestly blessing in the liturgy, and finally apply it to the situation in which we stand this Sunday—at the threshold of a new civil year.

The second possibility would be to link the second reading ("born under the law") with the circumcision of Jesus and proclaim the liberation from the bondage of the law that results from Jesus' submission to it. In view of the present-day interest in liberation (which, it has been suggested, is the contemporary equivalent of salvation), this might be a relevant topic.

Thirdly, the homilist could take up the biblical concept of "name" from the Aaronic blessing in the first reading and the naming of Jesus in the gospel. In the case of the name Jesus (=Yahweh saves), this sets out in advance the whole program of his life. Each of us is given a baptismal name that sets before us a program and a goal for our lives, not in a Pelagian sense of having to do it in our own strength but because of the name that Christ has already received and lived out for us.

[*In countries where the feast of Epiphany is transferred to the Sunday between January 2 and January 8, inclusive, the* SECOND SUNDAY AFTER CHRISTMAS *is omitted.*]

January 6
or the Sunday occurring between January 2 and 8, inclusive
EPIPHANY

Since the Epiphany readings are the same each year, we will summarize the comments we gave in series A.

Epiphany originated in the Eastern Church, where it was primarily a celebration of our Lord's baptism. This was interpreted as the first of his

28

epiphanies, or manifestations; other epiphanies, such as the miracle at Cana, were added later. When this feast spread to the West, it assimilated some of the associations of the Western Christmas. Hence, it became primarily a commemoration of the visit of the Magi. Next, the Magi came to be regarded as a type of the Gentiles (see the collect and the epistle of the Roman Missal and the Book of Common Prayer). Finally, Epiphany became associated, especially in Lutheranism, with overseas missionary work. The current readings attempt to restore the original emphasis on the revelation of God in Christ and to subordinate all these secondary features to this primary theme.

Reading I: Isaiah 60:1-6

This reading falls into two halves: verses 1-3, the fulfillment of Isa 40ff in the return of the exiles from Babylon to Jerusalem; and verses 4-6, a prediction of the eschatological pilgrimage of the Gentiles to Jerusalem after the rebuilding of the city. In Christianity generally, and as used on this day especially, each half is reinterpreted. Verses 1-3 now refer to the Christ-event, which supersedes the return from Babylon as the salvation event ("light" and "glory). In verses 4-6 the Gentiles respond to that revelation by coming to Christ, a response symbolized in the journey of the Magi.

This passage (see "gold and frankincense" in verse 6) has clearly influenced the narrative of the Magi in Matt 2:1-12 and has also contributed to its later legendary development (see "camels" in verse 6).

Responsorial Psalm: 72:1-2, 7-8, 10-13

Originally composed for the coronation of a Davidic king, this psalm has been applied by Christian faith to Jesus Christ. It emphasizes the milder, pastoral attributes of kingship—concern for justice and compassion for the poor. The psalm further complements the Old Testament reading, adding what was missing there, namely, the figure of the messianic king.

Christian faith, again, sees this picture fulfilled in the mission of Christ and in the universality of the gospel. Again, too, this fulfillment is symbolically expressed in the visit of the Magi (who "bring gifts" and "fall down before him"). And like the Old Testament reading, this psalm has contributed to the legendary development of the Magi story, in which they became the "three kings."

Reading II: Ephesians 3:2-3a, 5-6

This reading combines the same two themes as the Old Testament reading, namely, the revelation or epiphany of God (v. 3) and the Gentiles' participation in the messianic salvation (v. 6).

Ephesians was written (probably after Paul's death by an unknown genius of the Pauline school) when the unity of Jew and Gentile in the Church, a goal toward which the Apostle had worked hard, was an accomplished fact. Matthew's story of the Magi likewise takes for granted the success of the Gentile mission.

Gospel: Matthew 2:1-12

Many different traditions from early Christianity have provided the ingredients for the Magi story. First, there is the primitive kerygmatic assertion of Jesus' Davidic descent, which qualified him, in Jewish eyes, for the messiahship (see Rom 1:3). This element in the kerygma explains the importance attached in the infancy narratives of Matthew and Luke to Jesus' birth at Bethlehem.

Second, there is the dating of Jesus' birth, common to Matthew and Luke, toward the end of Herod the Great's reign (4 B.C.), a fact that is historically plausible.

Third, there is the folk memory of Herod's general character and particularly his pathological fear of assassination and usurpation in his closing years, not unlike that of Queen Elizabeth I.

Fourth, there is the use of the star as a messianic symbol (see Num 24:17, which, surprisingly, Matthew fails to cite, and the Dead Sea Scrolls).

Fifth, there are the frankincense and myrrh, suggested by the first reading and the responsorial psalm, neither of which is cited by Matthew. Only the formula quotation from Micah (v. 6) can be attributed to the evangelist with any degree of certainty, though it is unusual for such a quotation to be put in the mouth of a *dramatis persona*. The fact that the Magi were Gentiles is not emphasized in the narrative, though it is present in the Old Testament scriptures that form the background of the story.

The Homily

It is important to note that the Magi story does not stand alone but that its context is set by the first two readings and the responsorial psalm. The major themes of today's readings are the revelation of God in Christ and the universality of that revelation. The Magi story is a symbolic expression of these kerygmatic truths. It may be taken as an expression of the religious quest of human beings. Indeed, the Magi were probably astrologists and magicians rather than astronomers and philosophers. Their gifts of gold, frankincense, and myrrh may have been the tricks of the trade that they surrendered (see *Matthew*, Anchor Commentary, p. 13). This interpretation would give the homilist an opportunity to relate the story to the contemporary religious quest in some of its stranger manifestations.

BAPTISM OF THE LORD

Except for the gospel, the readings today are the same as those commented on in series A.   *31*

Gospel: Mark 1:7-11

The first paragraph consists of John's messianic preaching; the second is Mark's version of the baptism of Jesus.

The content of John's messianic preaching can be discussed at two levels: at the level of the "historical Baptist" and at the level of post-Easter Christian interpretation. At the historical level, John pointed to the coming of a stronger one (Yahweh himself or a distinct messianic figure?—the answer is not clear), and he spoke of this stronger one as a judge (baptism with fire in Q; Mark's "Holy Spirit" is clearly a Christianization, but "Spirit" could mean "wind," another image for judgment). It is historically unlikely that John recognized Jesus as the Coming One (see the Baptist's question in Matt 11:3 and parallels, and note also the modern critical view that Jesus' earthly life was only implicitly messianic, the expressly messianic interpretation of his person having arisen only after Easter).

Similarly, we can discuss the significance of Jesus' baptism on the historical level. That Jesus was baptized by John is a fact beyond all reasonable doubt (although it has occasionally been questioned), for it caused much embarrassment to the early Christian community, especially in controversies with the continuing followers of the Baptist. The clue to its interpretation lies in Jesus' subsequent conduct. After his baptism he broke away from John and embarked upon a career of eschatological preaching and a healing ministry distinct from John's mission. Historically, therefore, Jesus' baptism must have meant for him a call to this mission. In various ways Jesus alludes to the decisive significance of his baptism (see, for example, the question of authority in Mark 11:27-33 par.).

In Mark's Gospel, these two traditions—John's messianic preaching and Jesus' baptism—have been Christianized. First, the two traditions have been tied closely together. This shows that for Christian faith, Jesus in his baptism is marked out precisely as the stronger one whose coming the Baptist had predicted. Second, the stronger one becomes, even in John's preaching, a savior rather than purely a judge; he baptizes with the Holy Spirit rather than with fire. Third, the baptism of Jesus is interpreted in an explicitly messianic sense by two narrative devices: the descent of the Spirit like a dove and the voice from heaven. Here many Old Testament passages have contributed to the narration: the rending of the heavens, Isa 63:11; the descent of the Spirit upon the Messiah, Isa 11:2; the voice from heaven, Ps 2:7 and Isa 42:1. The Christology of the voice from heaven combines the motifs of the messianic Son of God and the suffering servant.

Mark, unlike Matthew and Luke, still describes the descent of the Spirit and the voice from heaven as inner experiences of Jesus rather than as objective events. Yet, he intends his readers to overhear the voice and share the vision. It is therefore improbable—though many have interpreted the passage this way—that Mark thought in adoptionist terms. The voice *declares* rather what Jesus *is* in his ensuing history. In all that Mark proceeds to narrate about him, Jesus shows himself to be the Son and the servant of God. Thus Mark means us to read the baptism of Jesus as the first in a series of secret epiphanies, revealing to us, though not yet to Jesus' contemporaries, the significance of the whole story that is to follow. That story is the account of God's eschatological act in Jesus, in his ministry and his death.

The Homily

In preaching on the baptism of Jesus in series B, it would be appropriate to stress that Mark relates this event as an inner experience of Jesus—his call to a unique eschatological ministry—but that at the same time Mark, by recording it in his Gospel, makes it for his readers an epiphany of who Jesus was. In the coming weeks we shall read of Jesus' words and deeds, culminating first in his transfiguration, and then, after the move to Jerusalem, in his passion. The baptism of Jesus puts us in the right frame of mind to hear these stories, the whole story of our redemption. This liturgical pilgrimage with Jesus from Galilee to Jerusalem is a paradigm of our whole Christian life of discipleship, which was inaugurated for us at our baptism.

LENTEN SEASON

The purpose of the Lenten readings is to prepare the people of God for participation in the paschal feast. The Old Testament readings focus on Israel's salvation history as the presupposition of, preparation for, and in some respects a prefigurement of, the redemptive act of God in Christ. The New Testament readings are either expositions of the meaning of the cross or of the believers' participation in salvation through baptism. The gospel readings of series B begin with the Marcan temptation and transfiguration stories on the first two Sundays, which are traditionally associated with those events. Then follows a series of readings from the Fourth Gospel containing predictions of Christ's death on the cross and interpretations of its meaning. These gospels would form an admirable basis for a series of homilies on the subject of the cross.

ASH WEDNESDAY

Since the readings on Ash Wednesday are the same each year, the reader is referred to our comments on them in series A.

FIRST SUNDAY OF LENT

Reading I: Genesis 9:8-15

This reading comes from the P (Priestly) version of the flood story. The J (Yahwist) story speaks of the divine promise, P of the divine covenant as the outcome of the flood. It is characteristic of P that it postulates a series of covenants, whereas J and E (Elohist) feature only the one basic covenant (J: Sinai; E: Horeb). The covenant with Noah is distinguished from other Old Testament covenants in that it is made not with Israel only but with the whole human race. In this covenant God promises never again to destroy the earth by a flood. This is a pictorial statement of the biblical faith in divine preservation. It is God's will ultimately not to destroy the earth but to redeem it. As usual in the Bible, the covenant is accompanied by a token or sign. In this case it is a God-given sign—the rainbow. The ancients, of course, were unaware of the laws of the refraction of light. Therefore this feature of the flood story is in part an "etiological myth," that is, a story designed to explain the origin of an enigmatic phenomenon.

These two features of the story—the universal covenant of preservation and its accompanying sign—are important theologically in their own right. However, the point of this reading today, as the second reading shows, lies in the fact that Noah's flood is treated in Christian thought, and already in the New Testament, as a type of baptism.

Responsorial Psalm: 25:4-5b, 6, 7b-9

A slightly different arrangement of these verses was used on the twenty-sixth Sunday of the year in series A. Here the refrain suitably matches the flood story, with its reference to Yahweh's covenant and to his love and truth, of which the rainbow is a sign.

172

Reading II: 1 Peter 3:18-22

Behind this passage there probably lies an early Christological hymn:

```
1 [Christ] suffered once for our sins
2        that he might bring us to God,
3 being put to death in the flesh
4        but made alive in the spirit,
5 in which also he preached to the spirits in prison
6        and having gone into heaven sat down
             at the right hand of God
7 angels and authorities and powers having been
             made subject to him.
```

The first two lines express the early Palestinian and Pauline doctrine of the atoning efficacy of Christ's death. It was "for our sins" and it "brings us to God." The third and fourth lines use Hellenistic language of the two spheres—the "flesh" (the earthly sphere) and the "spirit" (the heavenly sphere; see Rom 1:3-4 and 1 Tim 3:16). Since by the end of line 4 we have already come to the resurrection, it follows that the preaching to the spirits in prison is performed by the already risen Christ. It has nothing to do with a *descensus ad inferos* between the death and the resurrection, as in the Apostles' Creed. It expresses the early Christian interpretation of the death and exaltation of Christ as a triumph over the powers of evil.

This means, further, that the spirits in prison are not the dead but cosmic powers of evil. Hence, what Christ preaches to them is not the gospel of God's redeeming love, so that they may have a chance to repent, but the announcement of their final defeat. Line 6 speaks of the ascension, and line 7 is a résumé of the subjection of the powers first mentioned in line 5.

The first part of 1 Peter (to 4:11) consists of a baptismal homily. The author has taken the traditional hymn and adapted it to his baptismal purpose by a somewhat complex insertion. He understands the "spirits in prison" to refer, not to the cosmic powers, as in the original hymn, but to the disobedient spirits at the time of Noah. This could mean either the wicked angels of Gen 6 or the wicked of Noah's generation, who were destroyed in the flood. As a result, the "preaching" now becomes a preaching of salvation. The dead are given a chance to repent. By introducing the reference to Noah, the author acquires an opening for a typological treatment of Noah's flood with reference to Christian baptism.

This insertion, as noted, is complex, and not easy to interpret. "Saved through water" may mean either that Noah and his sons passed through the water and so escaped, the water being a hostile element that might have drowned them; or it can mean that water was the means whereby the ark was brought to safety. In view of the analogy drawn between the waters of the flood and the water of baptism, the second meaning seems preferable. There is, in fact, a double typology here: the first between the flood and the water of baptism, and the second between the eight persons in the ark and the Christian community. Many medieval fonts in England portray Noah's ark as a type of the Church, and the notion may already be present here.

Finally, the author adds an interpretation of Christian baptism (v. 21b). The stress on water, he insists, must not be taken in a materialistic sense, as though the whole meaning of baptism resided in the physical washing. Baptism is not the removal of dirt from the body but, literally, "the answer of a good conscience toward God." The RSV translation indicates that there is uncertainty over the meaning of this phrase. We would take it to mean an answer given to God and proceeding from a good conscience. At baptism there was scrutiny of the candidate, eliciting the fact that he/she came to baptism with a good conscience, that is, with repentance of sins and faith in Jesus as Savior.

One might be surprised that the author does not replace the materialistic interpretation of baptism with a sacramental interpretation. He speaks, not of what God does in and through baptism (though this is implied when he speaks of the type where, in our interpretation, the waters of the flood are a means of salvation), but of the candidate's part in baptism. The effect, however, is to give a comprehensive instruction on baptism that emphasizes both God's part (in the type) and the response of the candidate (in the antitype).

Gospel: Mark 1:12-15

The Marcan form of the temptation narrative is extremely brief. Both Matthew (whose version we are more familiar with from the traditional pericopes) and Luke expand the story from their common source (the Q material). Mark lacks the threefold temptation and the statement that Jesus fasted. It is even possible that he intends to suggest that the angels fed Jesus during the forty days (note that the Greek word for "ministered" is in the imperfect tense, suggesting an action over a prolonged period). This in turn hints at a Moses/Elijah typology (the manna in the wilderness is called "the bread of the angels" in Ps 78:25, and Elijah is sustained by ravens during his forty-day fast).

The mention of the wild beasts suggests a further piece of typology. In Ps 91:11-13 we are told that the righteous person will be protected by the angels and will be immune from the attacks of wild beasts. Even more striking is a passage from *The Testament of Naphtali* (from the intertestamental collection known as *The Testaments of the Twelve Patriarchs*). Here the patriarch Naphtali says to his sons:

> The devil shall flee from you
> And the wild beasts shall flee from you . . .
> And the angels shall cleave to you.

Here we get the same three features as in the temptation story—the devil, wild beasts, and angels. Perhaps there is even the thought here that Christ is the second Adam, who restores the harmony of nature previously destroyed by Adam's fall. Satan put in his usual claim to a son of Adam, but this time he met his match.

Thus, for all its brevity, the Marcan form of the temptation narrative is particularly rich in meaning. Mark is not interested in the psychological experience of Jesus but in proclaiming him as the new Israel, the new Moses, the new Elijah, the righteous man of God, and the new Adam, through whom the powers of evil are defeated and the peace of paradise restored.

The Homily

Either the gospel or the first reading can determine the homily. If we take the gospel, we can link it with the hymn enshrined in the second reading in its original form, as reconstructed above. Taking both readings together, we can proclaim *Christus victor*—Christ victorious over the powers of evil. This may be illustrated from pastoral experience, in which we can find examples of the continuing power of Christ to overcome the evil in human life. We can conclude by urging the faithful to seek the power of

Christ to overcome evil in their own lives, especially the power of temptation.

If, however, we take our cue from the Old Testament reading, the story of the flood can be linked to Christian baptism, as is done by the author of 1 Peter in his redaction of the early Christian hymn (see above). The two sides of baptism can be emphasized: what God does and what the candidate does. God saves "through water," although, as Luther insisted, *Wasser tut's freilich nicht*—that is, it is not the water in itself that effects salvation—God uses the water as the means of his saving action. The candidate, for his/her part, repents and makes a profession of faith. The whole purpose and climax of Lent is the renewal of our baptismal vows at the Easter Vigil. This treatment of today's readings can help prepare for that.

SECOND SUNDAY OF LENT

Reading I: Genesis 22:1-2, 9, 10-13, 15-18

The sacrifice of Isaac provided the early Church with one of its types for the death of Christ. Indeed, it probably underlies Paul's statement in today's second reading, also highlighted in the accompanying caption: "God did not spare his own Son but gave him up for us all."

The interest of the story about Isaac lies not so much in its primitive origins, which were connected with the abandonment of human sacrifice, nor with its meaning as it stands in the Pentateuch; it lies, rather, with its later development in Judaism.[1] The upshot of this development of interpretation was that whereas in the Old Testament, interest was concentrated exclusively on the testing of Abraham's faith (see Heb 11:17), in later Judaism this interest was often combined with an emphasis on Isaac's voluntary surrender of his life. To this voluntary surrender was attributed atoning significance, and the sacrifice of Isaac was further connected with the Passover lamb.

Responsorial Psalm: 116:10, 15-19

A different selection of verses from this psalm is used at the Mass of the Lord's Supper on Holy Thursday. There its primary reference is naturally to the Eucharist. Here the focus is on the deliverance of the just person from affliction, recalling the deliverance of Isaac. Note especially the phrase "Thou hast loosed my bonds." In later Judaism the story of Isaac was called the *Akedah*, or "binding of Isaac."

[1] See J. Massingberd Ford, *Wellsprings of Scripture* (New York: Sheed and Ward, 1968) 25–35.

Reading II: Romans 8:31b-34

Last week we suggested that a possible theme for preaching might be the power of God in the lives of believers to enable them to overcome evil and to surmount temptation. This is what Paul is speaking about here. He raises a series of rhetorical questions. The rsv text (see, however, the rsv margin) takes the last of the sentences in our pericope also as a question. The sense must then be: "Is it (*sc.*, No, of course, it cannot be!) Christ Jesus who condemns us, Christ Jesus who died, was raised, who is at the right hand of God and who intercedes for all?" Paul emphasizes the absurdity of the rhetorical questions by citing all that God, in Christ, has done and is doing for us—this in a series of traditional formulas derived from the kerygma and liturgy of the early community:

1. God did not spare his own Son but gave him up for us all (see Rom 8:32).
2. Christ died (see 1 Cor 15:3).
3. He was raised from the dead (see 1 Cor 15:4).
4. He is at the right hand of God (see Acts 2:33, etc.).
5. He intercedes for us.

Only points 1 (the Isaac typology) and 5 (the statement about the heavenly intercession) are not otherwise directly paralleled in the kerygma. But their style (the relative "who" and the "we" style) and their content (the basic assertions of salvation history) suggest that we have here also traditional formulas.

Gospel: Mark 9:2-10

We commented on another version of the transfiguration narrative on the second Sunday of Lent in series A, and so we will confine our remarks here to the peculiarities of the Marcan version. These are as follows:

1. Mark says nothing about the change of Jesus' *face.*
2. He emphasizes the whiteness of Jesus' garments (v. 3b) .
3. He places the name of Elijah *before* that of Moses (v. 4a).
4. He emphasizes Peter's bewilderment and lack of understanding (v. 6).
5. He states that the three disciples were also bewildered about Jesus' allusion to the resurrection of the dead (v. 10)—this following the command to keep silent until after the resurrection, a command that Matthew also has but that Luke omits.

The first four points are almost certainly taken by Mark from his tradition. Mark's redaction is to be found in points 4 and 5. He emphasizes the difficulty the disciples had in understanding Jesus, and the command to silence (here it is applied to the disciples; in the earlier chapters, to the demons and those healed). What is the point of this command? The answer seems to be that Mark is trying to formulate a particular Christology, that is, an understanding of the person of our Lord, over against another Christology current in his day but which he rejects. This other Christology saw in Jesus a direct epiphany of divine power displayed in his miracles and culminating in the transfiguration. Against that Mark asserts his Christology of the suffering Son of man. Hence, neither the true Christology nor the transfiguration can be disclosed until after the resurrection.

Why do the disciples constantly misunderstand? They represent, I think, Mark's Church, which is very attracted to the epiphany Christology of Mark's opponents, but, like the blind man in chapter 8, they gradually come to see that Jesus is not merely the Christ, the epiphany of God, but the suffering Son of man, who attains to his glory only through the passion. This final disclosure of the true disciples comes only after the resurrection (14:28; 16:7), when they see the risen Lord in Galilee. If they disclosed the transfiguration before the death and resurrection, it would be an expression of a wrong Christology, involving glory without the cross. The oblique message of Mark's version of the transfiguration is: No cross, no crown.

The Homily

In different ways, all of today's readings focus upon the cross. The cross can be treated in several ways:

1. It is the act in which the Father gives the Son up to death for the benefit of sinners (first and second readings). Here the homilist could emphasize the continuity of action between the Father and the Son. The cross is not the act of the perfect Man appeasing the wrath of an angry Deity, as in some doctrines of the atonement, but an act of God himself to which the Son freely assents (both Isaac and Christ exhibit this).

2. The cross is not just an event of A.D. 30. Its benefits are constantly being applied to us by the Lord's intercession in heaven (second reading), which finds it externalization on earth in the Eucharist.

3. It is not in the miracles or even in the transfiguration of itself that we behold the glory of God in the face of Jesus Christ, but only in the crucified One. It is only when we have faced the cross with Jesus that we can proclaim the earthly life of Jesus to the world as the epiphany of the glory of God.

The homilist must be guided by the needs of the congregation in choosing a theme.

THIRD SUNDAY OF LENT

Reading I: Exodus 20:1-17 (long form); 20:1-3, 7-8, 12-17 (short form)

The short version of the Decalogue is attained by the omission of those parts that have a rather narrow and temporary application, namely, the prohibition of idolatry in the first commandment (according to the Latin-Lutheran enumeration, but the second commandment according to other traditions) and the abbreviation of the third (fourth) commandment. Anglicans are further accustomed to the abbreviation of the ninth-tenth commandments as "Thou shalt not covet," a procedure that could have been followed here with advantage.

The Decalogue appears in two places of Scripture: here and in Deut 5. The two versions differ mainly over the grounds for the Sabbath commandment. The content of the second table (duty to the neighbor) is paralleled in many primitive legal codes. The first table (duty to God) is unique to Scripture. Both tables also differ from other codes in form. They are apodictic: "You shall." The other codes are conditional: "If you do so and so, the consequence will be so and so." Thus, the natural law is taken up and transformed by the insights of Yahwism.

It has been much debated whether, historically, the Decalogue originates from Moses. Contemporary scholarship looks rather more favorably on the traditional ascription. If it is correct, then Moses probably reinterpreted earlier codes in the light of the ethical monotheism for which he stood. Obviously they have undergone at least two later recensions— the one Deuteronomic (Deut 5), the other priestly (Exod 20).

With the exception of the third (fourth) commandment, all of the ten words have a timeless validity. The New Testament quotes the second table in several places and clearly regards it as valid for Christian believers. The Decalogue was a constant element in medieval catechesis, and is expounded in the Reformation catechisms as the summary of Christian moral obligation. It has been frequently used as a form of self-examination before communion. In Christian use it has to be understood, of course, in the light of our Lord's teaching as given in the Sermon on the Mount.

Responsorial Psalm: 19:7-10

Psalm 19 falls into two distinct halves. The first part, through verse 6, is a nature psalm celebrating the revelation of God in creation. The second part is a hymn of praise to the law of God, similar to much of Psalm 119. It is from the second part that today's selection is taken. It forms an excellent response to the reading of the Decalogue.

Reading II: 1 Corinthians 1:22-25

Paul had had a great deal of experience in preaching to both Jews and Gentiles. He had found again and again that the Jews wanted a sign, that is to say, a legitimating miracle (as in today's gospel—John 2:18) to authenticate his apostolicity and the truth of his message. The Greeks, on the other hand, looked for wisdom, that is to say, they were prepared to accept Christianity if it was presented as "wisdom," or "gnosis"—that is, if it brought a convincing understanding of the universe and of the place of humanity in it, so that one could thereby be released from the trammels of earthly existence and reunited with one's heavenly origin.

It was wisdom rather than signs that the Corinthians, who were mainly Gentiles, desired at this time. Later on, however, by the time 2 Corinthians was written, they would be impressed by Jewish-Christian preachers who came along offering signs. Paul does not altogether repudiate the religious quest of either the Jew or the Gentile, but he corrects it by the message of the cross. The cross is power (*dynamis*, the word frequently used for "miracle" and corresponding to "sign") and wisdom. But it is a paradoxical kind of power and wisdom—a foolishness (note the chiastic construction) in human eyes that is wiser than human beings, and a weakness that is stronger than them. Only believers can penetrate the wisdom behind the folly, and the power behind the weakness. For all unbelievers the message of the cross remains a scandal (for Jews) and folly (for Greeks).

Gospel: John 2:13-25

The Fourth Gospel has a version of the cleansing of the temple that is parallel to, but independent of, the synoptic version. John's tradition combines two elements found separately in the Synoptics: (1) the cleansing of the temple (Mark 11:11 par.); (2) the prediction of the temple's destruction (Mark 14:58 par.). There are other features not paralleled in the Synoptics: (1) the whips: a greater degree of force used by Jesus (a feature that has been taken up in recent theologies of revolution); (2) the citation of Ps 69:9: this was a psalm traditionally used in the early Church's passion apologetics; (3) the interesting statement that the incident took place when the temple had been forty-six years in building—pointing to the date A.D. 28. We take it that these features were already present in the Johannine tradition.

The evangelist himself seems to be responsible for the following features: (1) the shift of the cleansing of the temple from Holy Week to the beginning of the ministry. (Does that mean that he is also responsible for the remark about the forty-six years? Alternatively, following Raymond Brown, we may suppose that the saying about the destruction of the temple belonged to this year already before John, and that John has shifted the cleansing to the earlier date and thus combined the originally separate traditions of the cleansing and the prophecy.); (2) the statement that Jesus was referring to his body in the saying about the destruction of the temple.

We will concentrate on the meaning of these two redactional features. (1) The reason for the shift of the incident to the beginning of the ministry will be a programmatic one. John wants to make Jesus lay out all his cards on the table right at the outset. The destruction of the temple, that is, the end of the Jewish dispensation and its worship, is the ultimate purpose of Jesus' whole ministry. (2) Closely connected with this is the second redactional feature. This expresses the positive side of Jesus' program, just as the destruction of the temple expresses its negative aspect. The old order of worship is to be replaced by a new one—an order focused no longer on the old temple but on the body of Christ.

In what sense is "body of Christ" used here? Does it mean the ecclesial body in the Pauline and Deutero-Pauline sense? Or is it the glorified humanity of Christ? The second sense seems closer to Johannine theology elsewhere (see John 1:14), but we cannot altogether rule out overtones of the Pauline meaning.

The Homily

If on the previous Sundays of Lent texts that expound the cross were used, the homilist could well take the second reading and the gospel together and speak of the cross as a sign—not a legitimating sign but the expression of the wisdom and the power of God (second reading) that inaugurates a new dispensation and a new worship (gospel).

The other possibility would be for the homilist to deal with the interpretation of the ten commandments as a summary of duty to God and neighbor, perhaps highlighting those commandments that seem to be most relevant to the needs of the congregation.

FOURTH SUNDAY OF LENT

Reading I: 2 Chronicles 36:14-16, 19-23

In his priestly rewriting of Israel's history, the Chronicler now reaches the Exile and the return. He offers his explanation of the Exile as a divine punishment along lines similar to 2 Kings, but, significantly, from his standpoint, he stresses that it was a punishment of the preexilic *priests*, as well as the people, for not listening to the preexilic prophets. He compresses the burning of the temple and the destruction of Jerusalem into a single verse, and interprets the seventy-year exile as a sabbath for the land of Judah, during which it lay desolate. The last three verses, a verbatim reproduction of Ezra 1:1-3, were, it is generally agreed, added here by a later editor because 2 Chronicles was the last book in the Hebrew canon and the editor did not want the Old Testament to end on a negative note!

As we noted before, the Old Testament readings in Lent point up the highlights of Israel's salvation history. This reading features the Exile.

Responsorial Psalm: 137:1-6

This psalm, the lament of the exiles in Babylon, fittingly follows the first reading. The theme of Jerusalem was a tradition on this day, the old Laetare Sunday. The psalm presents Jerusalem to the exiles as a memory to be kept alive until better days when the people will be restored to their homeland.

Reading II: Ephesians 2:4-10

If, as is widely held today, Ephesians is a Deutero-Pauline composition, that is, written by a disciple of Paul and a member of the Pauline school after the Apostle's death, this passage certainly captures the spirit of the Apostle himself. As in so many New Testament writings of the subapostolic period, we have here a citation from a hymn, evidently a baptismal hymn (note the relative "who," the concentration on the basic facts of the kerygma, and the liturgical "we" style) in verses 4-6. Note also the parenthetical insertion in verse 5, which changes from the first person plural to the second person plural. Note further the connection between this hymn and that in Col 2:12, as well as Paul's exposition of baptism in Rom 6.

All of these passages associate baptism with the death and resurrection of Christ. But there is a difference. In Rom 6 the genuine Paul is careful to say that while we have died with Christ in baptism, nevertheless our rising with him lies in the eschatological future and is a challenge to ethical realization in the present. In Colossians both death and resurrection are experienced already in baptism. The hymn in Ephesians goes further: not only are we risen with Christ but we have already been translated into heaven with him. This approaches Gnosticism (see 2 Tim 2:18). Probably Romans and Colossians are drawing upon the same hymn that Ephesians quotes. We thus have a trajectory: (1) primitive Hellenistic-Christian baptismal hymn; (2) Rom 6; (3) Col 2:12; (4) Ephesians; (5) second-century Gnosticism.

Being in heaven with Christ is not a matter for self-congratulation or for a false sense of security, so the author inserts the parenthesis: "by grace you have been saved." Christian initiation is not simply, as it was for the Gnostics, an illumination about one's true, innermost nature. The author expands this Pauline affirmation very precisely in verse 8 ("by grace . . . through faith"). He then introduces his second anti-Gnostic point: the Christian life is not an intoxication with being in heaven already, but a constant call for strenuous moral effort. It means doing the good works that God has prepared for us to walk in. This again is good Paulinism. Paul excludes works from any role in justification but insists that they are its consequence.

Gospel: John 3:14-21

The conversation with Nicodemus is the first discourse in the Fourth Gospel. It is typical of this evangelist's procedure. He takes an incident in the life of our Lord from his tradition, here an encounter between Jesus and Nicodemus (there is good reason to think that this encounter, as a historical occasion, belonged to the later part of the ministry, shortly before the passion). He then has Nicodemus ask three questions (vv. 2, 4, 9), each of which elicits a pronouncement from Jesus. Some of the material in these pronouncements, for example, the saying about being born again in verse 3, comes from the sayings tradition and is paralleled in the Synoptists. The rest is an elaboration of Johannine theology.

The first part of the discourse enunciates the necessity for rebirth as the essential prerequisite for entry into the kingdom of God. The second part, from which our passage is taken, explains that this rebirth can only come as a result of the "lifting up" of the Son of man, that is, his death and glorification. As the quotation marks indicate, it is only the saying about the serpent and the Son of man that is represented as a saying of Jesus. Verses 16-21 are presented as a meditation of the evangelist and look back on the coming of Christ and his saving work as an already accomplished event.

In the opening saying about the serpent and the Son of man, we have an interesting interpretation of the cross. There are several presentations of the atonement in the New Testament, but the one given here is frequently overlooked. It is almost an Abelardian interpretation. The very sight of Christ lifted up on the cross has power to bring men and women to faith and repentance, just as the contemplation of the serpent lifted up on the pole by Moses (Num 21:9ff) was able to heal the Israelites who had been bitten by fiery serpents. Paul seems to envisage a similar interpretation of the power of the cross when he reminds the Galatians that Christ had been placarded before their eyes as the crucified One (Gal 3:1).

This may not be a very satisfying doctrine of the atonement intellectually, but from a devotional point of view it has great power. It is saved from being a purely exemplarist interpretation by the ensuing meditation, which asserts most emphatically that the cross is an act of divine love: "God so loved the world that he gave his only Son." This also picks up the words at the opening of the second reading: "God, who is rich in mercy, out of the great love with which he loved us."

The Homily

The most obvious choice of a theme for today's homily is that which is expressed in the second reading and the gospel: the cross as the ultimate manifestation of God's love. The preacher should try to so hold up Christ crucified before his/her hearers as Paul placarded the Crucified before the eyes of the Galatians, so that they realize the love of God for sinners and are led to repentance, faith, and devotion. The homilist might also speak about the devotional value of the crucifix—not the "triumph crucifix" so popular today, but the medieval crucifix that portrays the suffering Christ.

The Old Testament reading does not seem to yield very much appropriate material for a sermon, but the homilist might like to depict the Jews in Babylon and their memory of the songs of Zion; comparison could then be made with the liturgical situation of the new people of God in Lent, with a reminder of the joy of the festal liturgy in which they hope to share at Easter.

FIFTH SUNDAY OF LENT

Reading I: Jeremiah 31:31-34

Jeremiah is prophesying to the Jews in Babylon. He interprets the unfaithfulness for which the Exile was a punishment as a breach of the old covenant made at the Exodus. The prophet looks forward to a new covenant that Yahweh will make with his people. This time God will write his law, not on tablets of stone, but in the hearts of his people. All of them will then "know" him, that is, live in obedience to his law.

From the time of Paul, Christians have seen the fulfillment of this prophecy in the covenant that was established by the blood of Christ and that led to the outpouring of the Spirit into the hearts of believers (2 Cor 3:6ff). As has often been pointed out, this is the one passage in the Old Testament where the idea of a New Testament is expressly mentioned.

Responsorial Psalm: 51:1-2, 10-13

This psalm, the *Miserere*, is the most famous of the penitential psalms. It takes up and turns into a prayer Jeremiah's prophecy that under the new covenant the hearts of believers will be inwardly transformed, so that their sins will be forgiven and they may walk in the law of the Lord.

Reading II: Hebrews 5:7-9

The letter to the Hebrews alternates between ethical exhortation (parenesis) and theological exposition, the one reinforcing the other. The theological exposition deals with Christ as the heavenly high priest. The author does not really get down to his major theological theme until chapter 7. Before that he prepares the ground for his treatment. He must show that our Lord, despite his lack of Levitical descent, was indeed a high priest—a high priest after the order of Melchizedek.

The author enunciates this theme several times before he develops it. The passage that forms today's reading is sandwiched between two such enunciations (vv. 5-6, 10). In this section the author wishes to prove that our Lord has the requisite qualifications for high priest. He does this by arguing that no high priest appoints himself to the office but is chosen by God. He takes the Gethsemane scene as an illustration that this is true of Christ. At Gethsemane, Christ did not seek honors for himself but dedicated himself unreservedly to the will of God. But the Gethsemane prayer was heard. Not that Jesus was saved from death, as he prayed ("Father, let this cup pass from me"); rather, through death and resurrection he was made perfect—God brought him to "perfection." "Perfect" here means reaching a goal or destiny, not moral perfection. His destiny was to become our high priest. To this office he was divinely appointed at the resurrection. He thus becomes the source of eternal salvation to all who accept the gospel.

Gospel: John 12:20-33

Like the story about Nicodemus that we read last week, a traditional incident is used today as a springboard for a Johannine discourse. We are not told what happened to the Greeks—whether they really got to see Jesus or not. Doubtless in the earlier tradition the story came to a natural conclusion. The Johannine discourse, with its two great pronouncements, develops the theme of the cross: (a) a grain of wheat must die if it is to bring forth fruit; (b) only by being lifted up will Christ draw all to himself.

These pronouncements are not unconnected with the Greeks' request. They cannot "see" Jesus—that is, experience messianic salvation—until after he has been crucified. Historically this was so. The contacts of Jesus during his earthly ministry were almost exclusively confined to his own people (see Rom 15:8), and his contacts with Gentiles were strictly exceptional (the Greeks in this story, the Syro-Phoenician, a woman in Mark, and the centurion in Q—each time there is a reluctance on the part of Jesus to break the barrier). It was only later that Hellenistic Christians began preaching to Gentiles (Acts 11).

But there was also a theological reason why Jesus restricted his contacts to the Jews. It was only after the wall of partition had been broken down—that is, the Jewish law as a barrier between Jew and Gentile—that the Gentile mission could begin. Thus, the grain of wheat has to die before it can bring forth fruit (win Gentile converts), and the Son of man has to be "lifted up" (Johannine language for the crucifixion-resurrection) before the Gentiles can be brought in.

The discourse is followed by a prayer of Jesus often called "the Johannine Gethsemane."

The Homily

Today's readings are again focused on the cross and provide various approaches to it. With the Old Testament reading, the homilist can expound the cross as the means whereby a new covenant was established between God and humankind, a covenant in which God's law is written, not on tablets of stone, but by the Spirit in the heart. The responsorial psalm is a prayer for such a renewed heart.

The second reading portrays the Gethsemane prayer of Jesus as the supreme renunciation of ambition for office, rewarded in the resurrection by his exaltation precisely to the supreme office. If the homily is based on this reading, the homilist could also bring in the concluding part of the gospel, the "Johannine Gethsemane."

The main part of the gospel speaks of the necessity of the death of Christ for universal salvation. Only by the surrender of his life could Christ bear fruit, that is, bring all people to salvation.

PASSION SUNDAY (PALM SUNDAY)

The Procession with Palms: Mark 11:1-10 or John 12:12-16

Jesus' entry into Jerusalem, while doubtless the major theme of this Sunday in popular estimation, is both historically and liturgically merely a subsidiary theme, serving only as a prelude to the passion. Any homily dealing with the entry into Jerusalem should make this clear.

As usual in the exegesis of the Gospels, we have to distinguish between three levels of meaning in this pericope: the *historical* level, that is, what actually happened in the life of the earthly Jesus and what he intended by it; the *tradition*, or the way the episode was shaped and interpreted in the early communities; and the *redaction*, or the use to which the evangelists put the tradition.

1. *The historical level.* Jesus went up to Jerusalem to deliver his final eschatological challenge to Israel at the very heart of its corporate and religious life. His entry into Jerusalem to cleanse the temple was a symbolic expression of this eschatological challenge. The final salvation and judgment of God were breaking through. Israel must decide. If it accepts its salvation, all well and good; if not, then (as the cleansing of the temple indicates) the present order of things will be replaced by God's new, eschatological order.

As Jesus approaches Jerusalem, he expresses this challenge by riding on a colt (a horse or an ass? Linguistically, "horse" would be possible and more expressive of the challenge, but asses were—and are—more common in Palestine). Two features suggest that the entry may have taken place at the feast of Tabernacles (or at the Dedication) rather than at Passover: the palms and the singing of Ps 118:25. "Blessed is he who comes" in that case would not originally have had a messianic significance but was merely a welcome to the pilgrims indiscriminately.

2. *The level of tradition.* Jesus' triumphal entry was messianically "overexposed" (Bornkamm). His work undoubtedly evoked messianic hopes and fears, and therefore he may even have been greeted at the entry as the prospective Messiah in a politically Davidic sense. But it is hardly likely that he intended to create this impression overtly.

The Church, however, reinterprets the story in the light of Easter faith. It makes Jesus act as sovereign "Lord" (v. 3), directing the whole proceeding. The miraculous discovery of the ass suggests to the earliest Palestinian community the supernatural foresight of the prophet-man of God, and in the Hellenistic Church that of the "divine man." It is probable that the community further added to the original Hallel psalm the words of verse 10a as an expression of its faith. The term "our father David" would be unusual in Judaism, and the whole phrase looks like a liturgical acclamation of the early community. At the level of tradition, then, the entry is an overt expression of Jesus' messiahship conceived in terms of the Davidic Messiah, the eschatological prophet, the *Kyrios* (Lord), and the divine man.

3. *The redaction.* Mark in turn attaches the story to his passion narrative. The effect is to say that the messianic images (son of David, eschatological prophet and man of God, Lord and divine man) are predicable of Jesus only because, and precisely because, he is the crucified One. Moreover, the divine-man motif—namely, miraculous foresight displayed in the discovery of the ass—now serves to bring home to the reader that Jesus, as the Son of man who is to suffer, knows beforehand the whole saving plan of God and sets the whole plan in motion by his own initiative.

We take John's version of the story to be, not a fuller redactional modification of Mark or of the other Synoptists, but an independent version derived ultimately from the same tradition used by Mark, though at a very early stage of its development. It lacks the miraculous discovery of the ass, showing that this motif had come into the pre-Marcan tradition somewhat later. In John, furthermore, Jesus finds the ass *after* the acclamation of the crowd. It is difficult to decide whether this is the earliest tradition (which would make Jesus' decision to ride on an animal a response to the crowd's acclamation) or a later theological reinterpretation (Jesus wishing to correct expectation of the Davidic Messiah with a suffering-servant concept).

John has the crowd come out of the city to meet Jesus. Only John mentions that the branches were of palm. If the entry occurred at the feast of Tabernacles or the Dedication, this could be historical. The second half of the crowd's acclamation ("even the King of Israel") is worded differently, supporting our view that this second part is a later expansion. John, like Matthew (though in a different form, so that John is not using Matthew) but unlike Mark and Luke, has the citation of Zech 9:9, thus indicating that the proof text came into the tradition later. Compare also John's explicit statement (v. 16) that the disciples did not realize the applicability of the text from Zechariah until after the resurrection.

At the level of John's redaction, the following points suggest themselves. This was not Jesus' first visit to Jerusalem. Hence, the crowd comes out to meet him because of his previous words and works at Jerusalem, especially the raising of Lazarus (v. 18). The entry in John introduces the episode of the Greeks at the feast (John 12:20-22). This makes Jesus the King of Israel, not in a narrow, nationalistic sense, but in a universalistic sense (see, in John, the title on the cross in three languages). It is in this sense that we must understand the revelation of Jesus as the resurrection and the life in the raising of Lazarus. He is that for all people.

John alone tells us that the true meaning of the entry did not dawn upon the community until after the resurrection, thus conforming to our contention that there was a development and reinterpretation of the incident in the post-Easter community.

Finally, we must note that both Mark and John, by placing the story before the passion narrative, emphasize what the liturgy itself emphasizes, namely, that the entry is not an isolated episode but is introductory to, and subordinate to, the passion.

Reading I: Isaiah 50:4-7

See Passion Sunday in series A for comments. 53

Responsorial Psalm: 22:7-8, 16-17a, 18-19, 22-23ab

Again, see series A for comments. This psalm is particularly appropriate 53 for the Marcan passion, impregnated as the latter is with its language. We will bring out certain elements of this psalm in our discussion of the Marcan passion account.

Reading II: Philippians 2:6-11

See Passion Sunday in series A for comments. Scholars today generally 54 regard Phil 2:6-11 as a pre-Pauline Christological hymn with Pauline interpretations, particularly the words "even death on a cross." This interpretation was meant as Paul's corrective of a Christological trajectory that otherwise might have gone off course and developed into a Gnostic-type myth: the Redeemer from heaven who briefly sojourns on earth and returns to heaven. Paul thus secures the truth that the incarnation and death of Jesus are not transient episodes but abiding, living truths in the life of the believing community. We will bring out in our discussion of the gospel reading certain features of the Christology of this hymn that appear in Mark's passion.

Gospel: Mark 14:1-15:47 (long form); 15:1-39 (short form)

The passion accounts are the only parts of the Gospel material that existed from the first in the form of continuous narratives. They were probably constructed as Christian Passover haggadahs, or cult narratives for liturgical recital. Each passion has its particular timbre and theological emphasis.

The suggestion has sometimes been made that Mark's narrative combines two earlier narratives of the crucifixion. Recently a similar suggestion has gone further and proposed that the two pre-Marcan crucifixion stories that the evangelist combined in Mark 15:20b-41 express two different theologies of the passion. It will be helpful for our understanding of Mark to follow up this suggestion.

The first and earlier narrative, it is suggested, consisted of 15:20b, 22, 24, 27. It would read as follows: "And they led him away to crucify him. And they brought him to the place called Golgotha. And they crucified him, and divided his garments among them, casting lots for them, to decide what each should take. And with him they crucified two robbers, one on his right and one on his left."

This crucifixion report, it is suggested, is very early. It is impregnated with echoes of Psalm 22 and Isa 53 (the parting of the garments and the numbering with the transgressors). This earlier crucifixion narrative represents the stage at which the passion story was formulated in apologetic terms. How could the righteous, innocent servant of God have suffered crucifixion, the type of execution reserved for the worst criminals? Answer: That is precisely the picture of the righteous servant of God in Psalm 22 and Isa 53.

The second and later tradition of the crucifixion has been found in Mark 15:25, 26, 29a, 32b, 33, 34a, 37, 38. This tradition would read as follows: "And it was the third hour when they crucified him. And the inscription of the charge against him read, 'The King of the Jews.' Those who passed by derided him. Those who were crucified with him also reviled him. And when the sixth hour had come, there was darkness over the whole land until the ninth hour. And at the ninth hour Jesus cried with a loud voice [uttered a loud cry] and breathed his last. And the curtain of the temple was torn in two, from top to bottom."

This narrative interprets Jesus' death, not as that of an innocent, righteous suffering servant of God, but as an agonizing conflict between the powers of light and the powers of darkness. This is an apocalyptic interpretation. The loud cry of Jesus is an announcement of triumph of the power of light (and implicitly Jesus' exaltation), and the rending of the temple curtain a symbolical expression of that victory. We have here an interpretation of the death of Jesus that recalls the hymn in Phil 2:6-11. Jesus is the divine Redeemer who has emptied himself of his divine glory, and therefore it is concealed from the powers of darkness, who are his enemies. They therefore crucify the Lord of glory (1 Cor 2:8). His death leads to his exaltation and triumph over the powers.

Mark does not deny the validity of either interpretation but combines them, allowing the one to correct the other. Jesus' death is not just that of the righteous, innocent suffering servant, for that could be misunderstood as a mere ethical example (see 1 Pet 2:21-25). His death would then have had no cosmic significance as the triumph over the powers of darkness. On the other hand, the triumph over the powers of darkness could be misunderstood as mere mythology unless it was insisted that this triumph was wrought out in a real, flesh-and-blood history, in an act of obedience (see Paul's interpolation of "even death on a cross" in Phil 2:8).

It is this combination of the ethical and the cosmic-eschatological that creates the unique tone of the Marcan passion.

The Homily

The homilist has the option of taking the entry into Jerusalem as the prelude to the cross or of taking the Marcan passion narrative by itself, using the other readings with it.

If the Marcan form of the entry is chosen, the homilist can speak of the messianic enthusiasm of the multitude and the way Jesus corrects this by riding on an ass, thus foreshadowing the humiliation of the cross. It is only as the suffering servant that Jesus is the King.

If the Johannine version of the entry is read, then the homilist has an opportunity to oppose the nationalist implications of the entry with its universalist understanding. Jesus is King, not in a narrow, nationalistic sense, but because he is the resurrection and the life of all, and because in dying on the cross he is the light of the world, drawing all to himself.

If the homilist chooses to concentrate on the Marcan passion narrative, he/she has an opportunity to bring out Mark's distinctive understanding of the passion (see the first reading and the psalm) with the apocalyptic victory concept (see the pre-Pauline hymn in Phil 2:6-11). As the servant, Jesus is not merely ethical example but *Christus Victor*. But he is *Christus Victor* precisely in and through his obedient suffering on the cross. Mark superimposes the suffering crucifix on the triumph crucifix. Each by itself fails to comprehend the full meaning of the cross and is in danger of imbalance.

Perhaps this is not so much the occasion to try and give a relevant message to the contemporary world as an occasion to assist the people as they begin "in the meditation of those mighty acts whereby God has brought" us salvation and life.

EASTER TRIDUUM

HOLY THURSDAY

Mass of the Lord's Supper

All of the readings (Exod 12:1-8, 11-14; 1 Cor 11:23-26; John 13:1-15) are
the same each year, so we will summarize the comments given in series A.

58

Three principal mysteries are celebrated in this Mass: the institution
of the Eucharist; the establishment of Christian priesthood; and the commandment to love one another.

1. *The institution of the Eucharist.* Institution does not mean the enact-
ment of a new rite but a reinterpretation of Jewish custom, whether the
Last Supper was an actual Passover or an ordinary Jewish meal. The institution is the investment of an existing rite with new meaning. The variation between the Eucharistic narratives in the Gospels and that given in
1 Cor 11 shows that there was no fixed tradition of what Jesus said on
that occasion. There was probably a liturgical expansion of an original
nucleus, the precise contours of which, however, are hard to determine.
The words "my body" said over the cup and the words "covenant" and
"blood" appear in all accounts and must belong to the earliest core. So,
too, does some eschatological reference to the effect that the present meal
looks forward to the eschatological banquet. There are thus both
backward- and forward-looking aspects to the Eucharist.

2. *The establishment of Christian priesthood.* This theme requires great
caution in handling. It is oversimplistic to say that Jesus, by commanding
the Twelve to celebrate the Eucharist, was consciously instituting the Christian priesthood, which developed later in succession from the apostles to
the Christian priests, the bishops and presbyters of the Church. The command "Do this" is addressed to the whole community, and the Eucharist
is the focal act whereby the community expresses its priesthood (1 Pet
2:1-10). The Eucharistic president performs a priestly role inasmuch as
he expresses the priesthood of the whole community. It might also be said
that in his actions the priesthood of Christ is exhibited to the community.
But the priesthood of the Church and the priesthood of the ministry derive
their priestly character primarily from the nature of the Eucharist.

3. *The commandment to love one another.* This theme is given by the footwashing and the Lord's words accompanying that act in John's Gospel. The theme of love emphasizes the horizontal, as distinct from the vertical, aspect of the Eucharist, that is, the relation expressed and cemented between the members of the community as distinct from the relation between the believer and the Lord. The exchange of peace by all members of the congregation is a current attempt to emphasize this horizontal aspect.

In choosing between these three suggested themes, the homilist will be guided by the concrete needs of the congregation as he/she knows them.

GOOD FRIDAY

The readings for Good Friday are always the same. Additional comments will be found under series A and C.

61

420

Reading I: Isaiah 52:13–53:12

This, the fourth servant song of Second Isaiah, contributed three features to the primitive Church's understanding of the crucifixion: Christ's suffering was innocent, vicarious, and redemptive; it is for all persons; and the suffering servant will be vindicated (that is, Isa 53 offered a way of understanding the resurrection in relation to the cross).

It is a matter of unresolved debate among New Testament scholars whether the earthly Jesus himself appropriated Isa 53 for the understanding of his mission. The sayings in which the references to Isa 53 occur are sparse and probably represent later additions (the ransom word in Mark 10:45; the addition of "for many" in the word over the cup in Mark 14:24, absent in 1 Cor 11:25). Some of the passion predictions, especially Mark 9:13, *may* echo Isa 53, but in their present form they have clearly been colored by the details of the passion narrative.

If Isa 53 was first used in the post-Easter Church, that should not disturb us, for it relieves the passion of being a mechanical fulfillment of a preconceived dogmatic scheme. It is the culmination of the whole earthly mission of Jesus. In his ministry he had identified himself to the utmost with sinners, thus breaking the barrier between human beings and God. He stood for God on the side of sinners. It was because the primitive Church saw the cross in the light of this identification with sinners that Isa 53 was taken up as an almost perfect prediction of the passion and as a quarry for theological affirmations about the cross. But these statements are not abstract theologoumena; they are an attempt to capture in words, for the benefit of those who did not "see," the meaning of a real piece of history, wrought out in flesh and blood by God himself for us and for our salvation.

Responsorial Psalm: 31:1, 5, 11-12, 14-16, 24

This psalm was used in Jewish evening prayers as it is used at Compline in the Christian Church. Verse 5 provided Luke (or his special tradition) with an alternative "last word" from the cross. Luke evidently preferred it to Ps 22:1, which he would have found in Mark. While lacking the profundity of the assertion of Jesus' God-forsakenness (the nadir of his self-identification with sinners), it conveys something of the Godward dimension of the cross. The cross is not only the act of God for the salvation of sinful human beings, but it is also their perfect offering of obedience to God. This idea is taken up in the second reading.

Reading II: Hebrews 4:14-16; 5:7-9

This passage is the third enunciation of the major theme of Hebrews—the high priesthood of Christ. That priesthood is characterized in three ways: as sympathy for human weakness consequent upon Jesus' having shared our earthly experiences; as God's answer to the Gethsemane prayer; and as Jesus' learning of obedience through suffering.

As we suggested above, the doctrine of Christ's high priesthood expresses the Godward direction of the cross. The real sacrifice that God demands of human creatures is the perfect offering of themselves in obedience to the divine will. Since they are sinners, they cannot offer that sacrifice, for all their acts, even their righteous deeds, are still the deeds of sinners. While the Levitical sacrifices could not take away sin, they acted as a constant reminder of the sacrifice that God really wanted (see Psalms 40 and 51). The Old Testament sacrifices were continued until God undertook to do for human beings what they could not do for themselves, that is, offer the sacrifice of perfect obedience to God. This God did in sending his Son. But human beings are not thereby relieved of their obligations. They can now be taken up into Christ's own sacrifice and are enabled to offer themselves, soul and body, in union with that sacrifice, so that the imperfection of the believers' self-oblation is transformed by the perfection of Christ's self-offering.

Gospel: John 18:1–19:42

John tends to pack his theological interpretation into the discourses, culminating in the farewell discourse and the high priestly prayer. When he reaches the passion narrative, he lets the facts speak for themselves. Only three overt "Johannine" theological points are made in the passion narrative. One is the definition of Christ's kingship in terms of witness to the truth (18:37-38). The second is the last Johannine word from the cross, "It is finished [consummated]," in 19:30, announcing the completion of the sacrifice of the Lamb of God, which had been foreshadowed by the Baptist early in the Gospel. These first two points indicate the two-way direction of the cross: God's saving act for us, and our offering to God. The third Johannine touch, perhaps added by a redactor, establishes the disciple at the cross as the witness for the Johannine tradition (19:35).

The Homily

The twofold direction of the cross—God's saving act for us, and our perfect offering to God—corresponds to the twofold office of Christ, the *duplex munus* (as it was called in traditional dogmatics) of king and priest, which in turn follows the pattern of the yet older dogmatic formula of the two natures, human and divine. As king, he comes from God, exercising his saving power among sinful human beings, identifying himself unreservedly with them. He stands where they are, and in so doing brings to them the saving compassion of God. The cross is the nadir of Christ's kingly service of God toward his people.

Christ is also priest. At his baptism he accepted the call of the Father, and at each moment of his ministry he offers himself anew in perfect obedience. Thus, the Father's words become his words, and the Father's works his works. The cross is not a meaningless, tragic end to a life of surrender to the will of God.

On Good Friday the doctrine of the atonement should be proclaimed. This can be done at various levels. The cross can be interpreted as the culmination of God's search for humanity that took place in Jesus' identification with sinners, in his baptism, in his eating with the outcast. It can at the same time be interpreted as the culmination of a life of perfect obedience to the Father.

At the level of the tradition of the post-Easter Church, the cross can be interpreted as the fulfillment of the mission of the suffering servant vicariously dying for us and for our salvation.

At the level of the evangelist's presentation, the homilist can take the theme of kingship as witness to the truth, linking this with the title on the cross.

EASTER VIGIL

This is the archetypal liturgy of the Church year. It has four parts: (l) the service of light, with the Easter proclamation; (2) the liturgy of the word; (3) the liturgy of baptism; (4) the liturgy of the Eucharist. The homily follows the gospel and leads into the baptisms.

The readings are the same each year, except for the gospel. Therefore, the reader should consult series A for comment on the seven Old Testament readings and the epistle, while comment on the gospel follows here.

65

Gospel: Mark 16:1-8

The nucleus of historical fact behind this tradition is that Mary Magdalene (and other women? Their names vary; only Mary Magdalene figures in all accounts) visited the grave of Jesus on Sunday morning, and claimed to have discovered it empty. We cannot get back behind the women's testimony. All we can do is to take their report at their word, as the first disciples did. For the disciples and Peter welcomed their report as congruous with the conviction they had formed (in Galilee, as we should maintain) as a result of the appearances. The community then shaped the women's report into a vehicle for the proclamation of the Easter kerygma by means of an angelic message (Mark mentions a "young man," but his white clothing is generally understood to suggest an angelic figure). This, of course, is not historical description but theological interpretation. The women's response was a typical biblical reaction to an epiphany—fear, wonder, and silence.

To this traditional account Mark has added an element (16:7) that somewhat dislocates the story (cf. 14:28, a complementary addition from the evangelist), but serves to point to the appearances in Galilee, first to Peter and then to the Twelve. Why does Mark make these additions and yet does not relate the appearances? In my opinion, he could not do so because he had no appearance stories available in his community. All he knew was the tradition that the risen One appeared first to Peter, then to the Twelve (see 1 Cor 15:5), and he indicated this by his addition of 16:7 to the angelic message. Why did Mark do this? Because it is in the Easter revelation that all the misunderstanding of the disciples, so emphasized by Mark, is cleared up—their forsaking of Jesus and, in the case of Peter, denying him. The disciples are finally restored and commissioned to proclaim the gospel (Galilee in Mark's symbolism means the place where the proclamation of the message begins; see Mark 1:14-15).

The Homily

The homilist thus has three levels at which to treat this gospel: the historical level, the level of the tradition, and the level of Mark's redaction.

At the historical level, we must deal with the place of the empty tomb in Christian faith. The belief in the resurrection of Christ does not rest primarily upon the empty tomb. The resurrection is not identical with the empty tomb, but the tomb does play an essential role in the New Testament witness. The empty tomb is a symbol that the resurrection appearances are not spiritualist séances. Christ's resurrection is no mere survival. In the resurrection, death has been overcome; our destiny is opened up beyond death and the grave.

At the level of the tradition, the operative verse is 16:6, the angelic proclamation: "He is risen, he is not here." "He"—the Jesus who lived and walked and taught and suffered and died on earth is not "here"—not to be sought in the past, in Palestine in A.D. 1–30. "He is risen"—his saving work is an ever-present reality in the community of the believers.

At the level of the redaction, Easter restores the disciples and commissions them as apostles to proclaim openly the saving act of God in Christ, in his death and resurrection, a mission that the Church continues today.

EASTER SEASON

EASTER SUNDAY

Once again we would remind the reader that the Easter Sunday Mass is not itself the paschal liturgy; that has already been celebrated at the close of the Easter Vigil. Rather, Easter Sunday is the first of the great fifty days—the Easter season. The revised calendar has reverted to the older pattern, in which the Easter season is a single period of fifty days rather than forty days of Easter followed by ten days of Ascensiontide as a distinct period. During these fifty days we are bidden to reflect upon the post-resurrection appearances of the risen Lord, the consequences of the Easter event in the life of the Church, the gift of the Spirit, and the promise of eternal life.

The readings are the same for series A, B, and C. The homilist may refer to our comments in series A; we will confine our remarks here to a few pointers.

Reading I: Acts 10:34a, 37-43

This passage comes from the kerygmatic speeches in the early part of Acts. Note the emphasis on the importance of the apostolic "witness," a word occurring no less than three times in the passage. This witness covers both the earthly life of Jesus and the post-resurrection appearances. The latter were—and are—problematic because, unlike the earthly life, the appearances were not public, verifiable events but were confined to a few. This is the only "evidence" we have for the resurrection. No one else can see the risen Christ as the original witnesses saw him. Subsequent visions there have certainly been, but they are different in function, if not in character, as subjective experiences.

Paul has both a post-resurrection appearance and subsequent visions, but he distinguishes sharply between them (cf. 2 Cor 12:1-9 with 1 Cor 15:8). Psychologically, no doubt, both fall into the category of visions, but in meaning they are very different. The Easter appearances are revelatory encounters that founded the Church and launched the Christian mission. As such they belong to the *eph hapax*, the once-for-all-ness of the original saving events, and are unrepeatable. Our Easter faith depends in the first place solely upon the testimony of the first witnesses. We just have to take them at their word when they proclaim that God raised Jesus from the dead and made him manifest. But this is not an irrational leap of faith. Once we accept the testimony of the original witnesses, everything begins to fall into place. Our acceptance of the witness will find confirmation in our Christian experience.

Responsorial Psalm: 118:1-2, 15-16a, 17, 22-23

Psalm 118, with its reference to the stone rejected and subsequently made the cornerstone, was perhaps the earliest Old Testament passage that the primitive community applied to the death and resurrection of Christ. It was the basic Old Testament text for the "no-yes" interpretation of the earliest kerygma.

Reading II: Colossians 3:1-4 or 1 Corinthians 5:6b-8

Both of these readings emphasize the ethical consequences of Christ's resurrection and our participation in it. Although baptism effectively symbolizes and initiates our dying to sin and rising again to new life in Christ, our own resurrection has to be constantly implemented by obedience. Hence the imperatives: *seek* the things that are above, *set* your mind on them; *cleanse* out the old leaven, *celebrate* the festival with the unleavened bread of sincerity and truth.

Gospel: John 20:1-9

This story seems to consist of two separate traditions: (1) the visit of Mary Magdalene to the tomb and her subsequent report to the disciples; and (2) Peter's visit to inspect the tomb (cf. Luke 24:12). To this the evangelist has added his distinctive motif of the race between Peter and the Beloved Disciple. The latter functions here in a way similar to that of the angelic interpreter in the synoptic accounts (R. E. Brown).

The Homily

The homilist has two alternatives: (1) How do we come to Easter faith? *Answer:* Through the report of the first witnesses, who themselves "saw and believed" (Acts and today's gospel). (2) The ethical consequences of Easter and baptism (second reading).

SECOND SUNDAY OF EASTER

Reading I: Acts 4:32-35

Each year readings from the Book of Acts replace Old Testament readings during the Easter season. These readings show the continued work of the risen Christ in his Church. This passage features two aspects of the life of the new community: the sharing of all things in common and the apostles' preaching of the resurrection with great power (*dynamis*, a word that calls attention to the charismatic nature of the early Christian preaching). This section is anticipated by the picture of the life of the earliest community given in Acts 2:42-47. Indeed, there is something to be said for the view that the author has combined two different accounts of the same thing from two different sources.

As we pointed out in series A, this so-called early Christian communism was not based on an economic doctrine but was a spontaneous expression of Christian *agape*, necessitated by the move from Galilee to Jerusalem. In New Testament times it was not treated as a law for all the churches. Paul gave the same principle a different expression in his collection for the Jerusalem church. Some centuries later Benedictine monasticism was yet another expression of *koinonia*. But whatever form it may take, in any given society there must always be some expression of this principle in the life of the Christian community if it is to retain its integrity.

Responsorial Psalm: 118:2-4, 15c-16a, 17-18, 22-24

We have said before that Psalm 118, with its reference to the rejection of the stone and its subsequent elevation to be the chief cornerstone, was perhaps the earliest Old Testament passage that the primitive community applied to the death and resurrection of Christ. It was the basic Old Testament passage for the "no-yes" interpretation of the death and resurrection: the death of Jesus as Israel's (and all humanity's) no to Jesus, and the resurrection as God's vindication of him, his yes to all that Jesus had said and done and suffered during his earthly life.

Reading II: 1 John 5:1-6

This reading overlaps with the traditional epistle for the old Low Sunday, which was 1 John 5:4-10. By beginning with verse 1, the reading latches on to the paschal theme of baptism: "Jesus is Christ (Messiah)" was a primitive baptismal confession, and it is in baptism that believers become children of God. This carries with it the responsibility to love God and neighbor. Then, in the typical "spiral" style of the Johannine school, the author reverts to the theme of baptismal rebirth and adds a new point, namely, that through baptism we overcome the world. "World" in Johannine thought means unbelieving human society organized in opposition to God and subject to darkness, that is, sin and death. The writer then makes the tremendous statement that Christian faith overcomes the world. As he immediately makes clear, the faith he is talking about is not a dogmatic system but an existential trust in Jesus Christ as the Son of God, the revelation of God's saving love. Such faith points beyond itself to its object—the saving act of God in Christ. That is the real victory that triumphs over unbelief.

This point is reinforced by the final paragraph, the perplexing passage about the three witnesses: the Spirit, the water, and the blood. A clue here is that the statement has a polemic thrust—it refutes those who say that Jesus Christ came by water only, not by water and blood. "Came by water" is probably a reference to Jesus' baptism; "came by blood," to his crucifixion. There were false teachers in the environment of the Johannine Church who asserted that Christ was baptized but not crucified. This may refer to a Gnostic teaching that Jesus was a mere man on whom the divine Christ descended at his baptism, then left him before his crucifixion. A modern analogy would be those who base their whole theology on the incarnation and ignore the atonement.

Gospel: John 20:19-31

The traditional Low Sunday gospel is used every year on the second Sunday of Easter. It contains two appearances. The first is that to the Twelve, a tradition that goes back to 1 Cor 15:5 and is developed in various forms in Matthew, Luke, and here in John 20. Perhaps the appearance to the seven disciples in John 21 is another variant of the same tradition. Luke and John 20 locate this appearance in Jerusalem. Matthew (see Mark 16:7) in Galilee, while in 1 Cor 15 no locality is given. Galilee seems to be the earliest tradition of its location, though this is much disputed.

The second appearance, resolving the doubt of Thomas, is peculiar to John and represents a manifest concern of the subapostolic age—how is it possible to believe in the risen Lord if one has not seen him? The answer is that even to see him is no guarantee of faith (consider Thomas). Even the disciples had to make the leap of faith when they saw him. It is therefore possible for those who have not seen him to make that same leap. This does not mean that seeing the Lord was not necessary for the original witnesses. They had to see him precisely in order that they might become witnesses, and through their witness enable those who had not seen him to believe.

The Homily

This Sunday offers at least three possibilities for the homily. Taking the reading from Acts, the homilist might expound the community life of the early Christians, who had all things in common, and raise the question of how this concern could be appropriately expressed in the life of the contemporary Church.

The second reading suggests the theme of Christian faith as the power that overcomes the "world." This could be connected with two points in the gospel reading: (1) the risen Christ's greeting of peace (*shalom*), which includes the notion of victory ("The Christian church cannot speak of peace save in the context of the death of Christ, in the context of victory over evil"—Hoskyns); (2) the theme of doubting Thomas—how in an age of widespread loss of faith and hope can doubt and despair be replaced by the faith that overcomes the world?

THIRD SUNDAY OF EASTER

Reading I: Acts 3:13-15, 17-19

Few scholars today would defend the speeches in Acts as representing what Peter or others said on any given occasion. As they stand, these speeches are the compositions of the author of Luke-Acts and represent his theology. At the same time, however, they frequently enshrine very early Christological materials. Here, for instance, Jesus is called by the very early title "the Holy and Righteous One," which describes him in his earthly life as the righteous servant of Yahweh. The title "Author of life" is probably very ancient. The Greek word for "author" is *archegos*, "captain" or "leader," and portrays Jesus as the new Moses. As the first Moses led God's people into the land of Canaan, so the new Moses leads the faithful into life, the kingdom of God, the new Canaan.

Note, too, the primitive picture of the death and resurrection as humanity's no and God's yes (see the comments on last Sunday's responsorial psalm).

On the other hand, the second paragraph introduces some typically Lucan themes: the Christ must suffer as the Scriptures foretell (see the gospel).

Responsorial Psalm: 4:1, 3, 6b-7a, 8a

This psalm is an individual lament in which a pious Israelite calls out for deliverance and receives an answer in the form of vindication from his/her enemies. Thus vindicated, the plaintiff can lie down and sleep peacefully.

Since Christ is "the Holy and Righteous One," this psalm can be applied to his death and resurrection. He was in distress and called upon the Lord, who raised him from the dead and vindicated him. His work thus accomplished, he can sit down at the right hand of God.

Reading II: 1 John 2:1-5a

To apply to Christ the words "I will lie down and sleep" (responsorial psalm) does not imply that he is inactive. He is our "advocate" ("paraclete," literally "helper") in heaven. Sin still occurs in the Christian life (when 1 John was written, the Gnostics were perfectionists who believed that proper Christians were sinless), but the exalted Christ still pleads our cause with the Father. He is the "expiation" for our sins—a better word than "propitiation," which suggests that God was an angry Deity who required appeasing. Rather, the exalted Christ acts as our advocate before God by applying the benefits of his death to our sins, cleansing and removing them so that we can be restored to the right relationship with God. The Gnostics, with their slogan "we know him," not only maintained that they no longer sinned and therefore required no continuing work of Christ to expiate their sins, but they also believed that they were dispensed from the need for moral effort. However, the true test of our "knowing God"—that is, of religious experience—is that we keep his commandments.

Gospel: Luke 24:35-48

This gospel represents a departure from the norm in series B, which is to follow a course of readings from Mark, supplemented by John during Lent and the Easter season. On the third Sunday of Easter in series A, the Emmaus story was read, and today's selection completes the Lucan appearance stories with the account of the appearance to the disciples in the upper room. It is the counterpart of John 20:19-23, which we read last week. The location—in the upper room in Jerusalem—is the same; the risen Lord's greeting is identical. The emphasis on the physical is similar.

In John this emphasis on the physical takes the form of the invitation to touch the body of the risen One, while in Luke it takes the form of a demonstration by eating a piece of broiled fish. This detail is doubly interesting. The presence of fish suggests an original Galilean setting for this appearance story, while the meal context suggests the association of the original resurrection appearances with the Eucharist.

These primitive elements were developed (probably by the pre-Lucan tradition) for apologetic purposes similar to those which were at work in John. Luke simply takes these elements over from his tradition. His real interest is to be found in the final paragraph—the instruction of the risen Lord to his disciples. This is again rooted in earliest tradition and has parallels in John and Matthew, for it includes the command to mission (forgiveness of sins also includes the notion of baptism; cf. Matt 28:19). But in Luke there is a unique emphasis on the scriptures: "'Everything written about me in the law of Moses and the prophets and the psalms must be fulfilled.' Then he opened their minds to understand the scriptures, and said to them, 'Thus it is written . . . .'" The same themes, as we have seen, recur in the final paragraph of the reading from Acts. Clearly we have here a theological concern of Luke.

The Homily

The combination of the kerygmatic speech from Acts and the risen Lord's instruction to the apostles is like two searchlights focusing on the same target: the scriptures announce that Christ must suffer. Therefore, repent and receive forgiveness. Can we make something of this for today's homily? How do the scriptures foretell Christ's suffering? Not in a mechanical way, but in their insight into God's way with human beings. Those who fulfill God's mission, particularly as prophets, have to suffer at the hands of a godless world—Moses, Jeremiah, the suffering servant of Second Isaiah. But God vindicates them, and their suffering proves to be an expiation for the sins of the people.

This could be linked to the theme of the second reading. The homilist could then bring forth contemporary analogies to the expiatory value of suffering. The themes of bloodshed, expiation, victory, and peace belong to Easter, as they belong to the life of the body politic. They are "words which have been formulated out of the stuff of which human life is made" (Hoskyns).

FOURTH SUNDAY OF EASTER

Reading I: Acts 4:8-12

In the Book of Acts we can sometimes discern a pattern similar to that of the Fourth Gospel. A miracle takes place and is followed by a discourse expounding the theological significance of the miracle. Our present passage occurs after the healing of the crippled man in chapter 3. Peter moves from the immediate fact of the healing to a proclamation of the thing signified, namely, the power of the gospel of Jesus Christ crucified and resurrected. The affinity between the sign and the thing signified is more obvious in the Greek than in the rsv translation—"healed" in verse 9 and "salvation" in verse 12 come from the same Greek verb, *sōthēnai*, "to be saved" or "to be made whole."

Note that Luke has once more incorporated into a speech of his own composition some very primitive material. This consists of (1) the "no-yes" interpretation of the cross and the resurrection (*you* crucified Jesus—*God* raised him); (2) the use of the passage about the stone rejected from Ps 118:22, one of the earliest pieces of Christian apologetic. The "name" of Jesus was probably used by early Christian exorcists as a formula to heal sick people. Luke takes up this formula of exorcism and applies it to "healing" in an ultimate, salvific sense. It is in the "name" of Jesus that eschatological salvation is made available, and in that name alone. In other words, eschatological salvation comes solely as a result of the death and resurrection of Christ.

Responsorial Psalm: 118:1, 8-9, 21-23, 26, 28-29

Selections from Psalm 118, as we have seen before, are frequently used in the Easter season. This particular selection highlights the "stone" testimony quoted in Peter's apologia in the first reading.

It has been suggested by Old Testament scholars that this psalm was originally used at the annual enthronement festival in Israel. As the king entered the temple in triumph and mounted the steps of the throne, "it was as if a new and highly decorative coping stone had been added to the cornice, which the builders had failed to beautify completely" (Barnabas Lindars). The exaltation of Jesus is the eschatological fulfillment of the enthronement festival in ancient Israel. He is the new coping stone of the eschatological community.

Reading II: 1 John 3:1-2

In his earthly life our Lord had admitted his disciples to the privilege of calling God "Abba, Father." This same privilege was made available to those who were baptized after the resurrection (Rom 8:15; Gal 4:6). The language used here ("Father," "children of God") is derived from the same background. The "world"—that is, human society organized in opposition to God—did not know "him," that is, probably Christ rather than God (so Dodd). This is reminiscent of Paul's statement that the rulers of this *world* did not know Christ, for otherwise they would not have crucified the Lord of glory (1 Cor 2:8). In Johannine thought, the Jews who crucified Jesus similarly symbolize the unbelieving world that rejects the revelation of God in Christ. This links the second reading with the first reading, with its assertion that "you" (Israel) crucified Jesus Christ of Nazareth.

Next another Johannine theme appears. As the world hated the Revealer, so it will hate the believers (see John 15:18). The world can see no more in the Church than one religious organization among others. It can classify the Church sociologically, and legitimately so on the world's own level. But it cannot perceive in the Church the eschatological community that it is. For its true character is as yet hidden: "it does not yet appear what we shall be." It is only when Christ appears at the parousia that we shall see him as he is—the Son of man exalted in his glory. Only then shall we be like him, transformed into the same eschatological glory that has been his since his resurrection.

Gospel: John 10:11-18

In series A, B, and C we read an excerpt from the good shepherd discourse (John 10) on the fourth Sunday of Easter, which replaces the old Good Shepherd Sunday (second Sunday after Easter). The present passage forms the interpretation of the second of the two sheep parables (the first is John 10:1-3a; the second, that interpreted here, is 10:3b-5).

Two applications of this second parable are given (vv. 11-13, 14-18), each headed by the same declaration, "I am the good shepherd" (vv. 11, 14). Each interpretation makes the basic point that the good shepherd lays down his life for the sheep (vv. 11b, 15b), and then proceeds to give this point a different actualization in the life of the Church. The first application connects this with the defense of the sheep against "wolves," a traditional image for false teachers, which the evangelist probably applies to the Gnostics. The second application speaks first of the inner life of the Church (the shepherd knows the sheep by name) and then of the Church's missionary outreach; the other sheep would be the Gentiles.

The Homily

A great wealth of themes is presented in today's readings. The homilist can narrow down the possibilities by bearing in mind the liturgical season for which these readings are provided—that of Easter. Hence, they all speak of the risen Lord and his continued work within the Church.

The reading from Acts speaks of the risen Lord performing his saving work in the world, manifested symbolically by the healing of the crippled man. The "name" that saves is the name of the risen One. The Church offers the world that which can be attained through Christ alone. The heart of the gospel lies in this little word "alone." Christian theology is going through a period when we would like to jettison this word and, entering into dialogue with other religions in a spirit of broadmindedness, recognize that they too offer their devotees salvation. Against this we must place our text and the interpretation of it in Article xxviii of the Church of England, entitled "Of obtaining salvation only by the Name of Christ." It reads:

"They also are to be accursed that presume to say, That every man shall be saved by the Law or Sect which he professeth, so that he be diligent to frame his life according to that Law and in the light of Nature. For Holy Scripture doth set out unto us only the Name of Jesus Christ whereby man must be saved."

In modern words, this article condemns the view that it is good to have a religion but it doesn't matter which one. The biblical exclusiveness that underlies the mission of the Church can be linked with the second aspect of the interpretation of the parable of the sheep and the shepherd: "I have other sheep, that are not of this fold; I must bring them also, and they will heed my voice. So there shall be one flock, one shepherd. Perhaps, too, the "wolves" against which the good shepherd defends his flock are those broadminded Christians today who hold that salvation is through any religion, not through Christ alone. This exclusive claim is made because only Christ has been raised from the dead. Only he has passed through death to our final destiny, and therefore we can attain our final destiny only through him.

A somewhat different though not unrelated homily could be composed on the basis of the second reading. In that case we would emphasize the "not-yet-ness" that characterizes our present participation in the risen life of Christ: "It does not yet appear what we shall be." This is a major theme in the theology of hope.

FIFTH SUNDAY OF EASTER

Reading I: Acts 9:26-31

At first sight this passage seems to be a straightforward piece of historical narrative, creating no problems of interpretation but yielding very little material for preaching. A comparison of this account of Paul's first visit to Jerusalem with his own account in Gal 1:18-19 reveals, however, certain major discrepancies.

Paul's own account emphasizes his entire independence of the Jerusalem apostles. On his first post-conversion visit, he merely saw Cephas and accidentally ran into James during his fifteen days' stay. Luke gives a very different account: Paul was anxious to join up with the apostles, who in turn were reluctant to receive the ex-persecutor; only when their scruples were overcome by Barnabas did they agree to accept him. Once introduced, however, Paul "went in and out with them," a phrase that in Luke means intimate companionship. "By the very fact that he—known to many in Jerusalem as the Christian-baiter—allowed himself to be seen walking arm in arm, as it were, in the streets and lanes of the city with the leaders of the Nazarene sect . . . Saul made open confession of his faith in Jesus" (Zahn).

We must certainly allow for some one-sidedness on Paul's part in Gal 1:18-19. Obviously he *was* dependent up to a point on the tradition he had received from those who were Christians before him. His visit to Cephas may have been precisely for the purpose of obtaining information about Jesus, for in 1 Cor 15:3-7 Paul makes it clear that he did depend on tradition for certain Christian traditions about events that happened before his apostolic call.

Luke's account must for the most part be regarded as an expression of Lucan theology rather than purely historical narration. For Luke, Paul is a model for the Church in his own day, in the subapostolic age. It is only when the Church remains in fellowship with the apostles—walking arm in arm with them, as it were—that it remains apostolic, preaching the same gospel as the apostles preached. The final paragraph suggests that it was not the expansion of the Church in itself that concerned Luke, but the fact that the apostolic message of the resurrection of Christ was spread so far and wide. It is not growth that matters, but what kind of growth.

Responsorial Psalm: 22:25b-27, 29-31

Psalm 22, as we know, is the passion psalm *par excellence.* But it is really a passion-and-resurrection psalm. Verses 1-21 are about the suffering of the righteous servant of God, verses 22-31 about his vindication. Originally, when Christians' *Pascha* was a unitary festival, the whole psalm could be sung at one go, with a highly dramatic change of key at verse 22. (I had this burnt upon me as a Church of England choirboy by the shift of the Anglican chant from a minor to a major key at this point.) The psalm expresses both the humiliation and the vindication of God's righteous servant. With the split-up of Passion Week and the Easter season, we now have to split the psalm. But we must remember that the Easter part that is sung today speaks of the vindication of the righteous One precisely in his suffering. The reference to the "afflicted" in the first stanza will help us to bear this in mind.

Reading II: 1 John 3:18-24

This passage is exceedingly difficult to summarize. C. H. Dodd suggests that the author has thrown together some notes he had never had time to develop. The same scholar discerns six different points here: (1) Only if we love one another are we assured of our standing as Christians.

(2) If we are uncertain about this standing, we may nevertheless trust that God knows us better than we know ourselves. (3) If our conscience is clear, we are free to live a life of prayer and of obedience to God's commandments. (4) God's expectation of us can be summed up under two headings: faith in Jesus Christ and love for one another. (5) The external test of mystical union with God (mutual indwelling) is whether or not we keep the commandments. (6) The internal test is the gift of the Spirit.

What impresses one in this passage is the way in which the Johannine author succeeds in holding together things that are often separated from one another in our thinking—faith *and* works, belief *and* obedience, the prayer of union with God *and* the love for one another. It is not a matter of either/or but of both/and.

Gospel: John 15:1-8

One is tempted to suppose that the earliest tradition behind the Johannine allegory of the vine was a genuine parable of Jesus, running something like this: The vinedresser takes away from the vine every branch that bears no fruit and prunes every branch that does bear fruit in order that it may bear more. The branches that are cut off wither. They are then gathered and thrown into the fire.

That would be a parable of judgment. Its Johannine allegorization is similar to that of the parables of the shepherd and the door in chapter 10. The vine is equated with Christ, the vinedresser with the Father, the branches with the disciples, the cutting away of the unfruitful branches with the excommunication of the unworthy. This cutting away of the unfruitful branch may have been earlier applied to Judas. For the evangelist, however, it means the Gnostic heretics. The pruning of those who remain means the future persecution of the disciples. The equation of Christ with the vine was doubtless suggested by the language of the Eucharist, such as "I am the bread of life," while the extension of the allegory to include the disciples as branches is reminiscent of the Pauline doctrine of the Church as the body of Christ.

We should not argue for John's direct dependence on Paul; perhaps both concepts were Christian adaptations of a common Gnostic theme. Added to this is the typical Johannine motif, already encountered in the second reading, of mutual indwelling.

The Homily

The fact that the second reading and the gospel both feature the theme of mutual indwelling constitutes a strong invitation to the homilist today. This mutual indwelling is not established by keeping God's commandments, as the second reading at first sight suggests. Rather, we must first dwell in the vine, that is, the risen Christ, partaking of the life that flows from him through the word and the sacraments. Thus, believing in the name of the Son, living the life of prayer, and having the assurance of a forgiven conscience and the indwelling Spirit, we must proceed to show forth our Christian standing by loving one another in deed and truth, keeping God's commandments, and bearing much fruit.

If the homilist should prefer to preach on the reading from Acts, he/she will have to be careful to treat it primarily as an expression of Lucan theology, not as a historical report. Luke's concern is that the Church in postapostolic times should remain in fellowship with the apostles, as Paul did. Some have tried glibly to contrast apostolic succession with apostolic success. If we understand apostolic succession to mean fidelity to the apostolic message of the resurrection of the crucified One as the event of redemption, then the only success that is apostolic is the success that follows upon that fidelity to the apostolic message. That is the relation between the two paragraphs of the first reading. Such a thought could be linked up with the second and third stanzas of the psalm, which speak of the worldwide acknowledgment of Yahweh consequent upon the vindication of his servant.

SIXTH SUNDAY OF EASTER

Reading I: Acts 10:25-26, 34-35, 44-48

For the believer, the most important consequence of the resurrection is the gift of the Spirit. Although the day of Pentecost is the primary celebration of the outpouring of the Spirit, the whole period of the fifty days includes this as one of its motifs, just as the fifty days in Judaism were a celebration of the enjoyment of the fruits of the Promised Land. It is thus appropriate, especially in the latter part of the Easter season, that we begin to think of the work of the Spirit in the Church. The same shift of theme was still perceptible in the traditional Lectionary.

Luke presents the Cornelius episode as the decisive step in the launching of the Gentile mission. Its decisiveness is emphasized by the length and detail of the narrative in chapter 10, of which today's reading forms the closing part, by the repetition of the story in full when Peter reports back to the Jerusalem church in chapter 11, and by Peter's reference to the episode at the apostolic council in chapter 15.

This emphasis is a clue to Luke's theology. Historically, the mission to the Gentiles is more likely to have begun, almost in a fit of absence of mind, by anonymous Hellenistic Jewish Christian missionaries of the Stephen party (see Acts 11:19-20). Luke's interest is that every step forward in the Christian mission must have the sanction of the Jerusalem church (see his interpretation of Paul's first visit to Jerusalem in last Sunday's first reading). Of course, Luke did not invent the Cornelius story—there is no need to doubt that Peter did convert a Gentile God-fearer. But this was not really the beginning of the Gentile mission, for Cornelius already had one foot in the Jewish camp. It is the significance of the event that Luke has blown up out of all recognition.

One striking feature of the story is that the Holy Spirit falls upon Cornelius and his companions *before* they are baptized. Usually, both in Acts and in the New Testament generally, the Spirit descends after baptism, with or without the laying on of hands. Luke's point is that the Spirit here takes a fresh initiative where the Church was too timid to follow. Hence this episode has been aptly called the "Pentecost of the Gentiles." Why, then, would baptism still have to follow? What would have been the status of converts who had received the Spirit but who had not yet been baptized? The best answer to this question is that the Spirit has, in this unique instance, gone beyond the confines of the Church and bestowed its blessing on outsiders. They are then brought into the circle of the people of God through baptism. Normally one is brought into the Church and there receives the Spirit.

Responsorial Psalm: 98:1-4

Psalm 98 was one of the enthronement psalms, celebrating the victory of Yahweh as manifested in the enthronement of Israel's king. Here in the Easter season we celebrate the victory—the resurrection—in which God triumphed over the powers of sin and death.

Reading II: 1 John 4:7-10

The Johannine author has been insisting over against his Gnostic opponents that the love of others is the acid test of the claim to "know" God. After a digression, the writer returns to this theme: Only the person who loves others "knows" God as the Gnostics claimed to know him. Then comes the tremendous statement that the reason for this is because "God is love." This affirmation is frequently repeated out of context, as though it were a general, self-evident truth. Sir Edwyn Hoskyns was fond of saying in his lectures that the statement "God is love" occurs in only one passage of the New Testament, and only after the "whole turmoil of the Epistle to the Romans." That God is love is a confession of faith from those who have encountered the love of God in action in his Son Jesus Christ, not a philosophical presupposition. So here, in this very passage, the Johannine author goes on at once to say that we know God to be love only because he has sent his Son into the world, and sent him to be the expiation for our sins. Only on those grounds—because of the incarnation and the atonement—do we affirm that God is love. It is not a general truth about the universe. Hence we cannot ask, Why does a God of love allow this or that to happen? As Bultmann said of grace, God's love is an event.

Gospel: John 15:9-17

The gospel reading widens our understanding of the theme of love, already broached in the second reading. We encounter the love of God in Christ because, first of all, the Father has loved the Son and the Son has loved the Father. The word for "loved" in each case is in the aorist tense—that is to say, it refers to a single, concrete act. God loved the Son in calling him and sending him. The evangelist is not speculating about the timeless love of the Father and the Son but is saying what happened. God called Jesus at his baptism and called him to a saving mission. The Son obeyed the Father and kept his commandments, that is to say, he concretely fulfilled the mission laid upon him; his obedience to the Father's commandment was consummated in his death on the cross.

By his death Jesus has constituted the disciples as a society of "friends." One might almost say that this is the Johannine doctrine of the Church as opposed to the institutional, organizational understanding of the Church that was gaining the upper hand at that time. The disciples are friends, not first of one another, but of Jesus. Only because of that are they friends of one another. The life of this society is characterized by joy (Hoskyns: "the delightful merriment of Christians"), bearing fruit, that is, keeping the commandment of love. All these things are the outcome of the death and resurrection of Christ and characterize the life of the Christian community.

The Homily

Taken together, the second reading and the gospel provide an opportunity to wrestle with the theme of love. The homilist could start with the great affirmation "God is love" and go on to point out how this is not a general truth but an event. Then he/she could characterize that event and draw out its effects—abiding in the love of the Father and the Son, and manifesting this mutual indwelling by the keeping of God's commandments, which in turn means love of one another. The homilist might speak of the Church as a society of "friends," a truth to which the Quakers have borne witness and which is a judgment of much of our ecclesiasticism.

An alternative would be for the homilist to take the episode about Cornelius as the Pentecost of the Gentiles, speaking perhaps of how the Spirit sometimes takes a leap forward where timid Christians are afraid to tread, and ask whether there are signs of something like this happening in the Church today.

ASCENSION

Apart from the gospel, the readings on Ascension Day are the same every year and were commented on in series A. This year we will repeat our general remarks on Ascension Day and proceed to comment on the gospel reading, on the assumption that the homilist will choose to preach on this.

Ascension Day, let us recall, is not to be thought of merely as a historical commemoration. In fact, there is no clear single event of the ascension in the New Testament. There was always a doctrine, or rather kerygma, of the ascension from the earliest days. Christ was always proclaimed as resurrected and ascended.

The pre-Pauline tradition in 1 Cor 15:3-8 and Phil 2:6-11, Paul himself, and the two earliest evangelists, Mark and Matthew, make no distinction between the resurrection and the ascension as events, but regard the appearances as appearances of the resurrected and already ascended One. When the desire to portray the ascension as a separate event emerged in the later stages of the tradition, the dating of it varied. Luke 24:51 appears to place it on Easter Sunday evening. John 20 seems to suppose that the ascension occurred on Easter Day between the appearance to Mary Magdalene and that to the disciples in the upper room. Only Acts 1 records the familiar story of an ascension forty days after Easter Day, and even there the number forty is probably to be taken symbolically as a holy period of revelation.

The ascension story is the dramatization of a universal element in primitive Christian proclamation and faith. It is fitting, so long as we remember this, that particular concentration should be given to this facet of Easter faith on one day in the Easter season. That is the rationale for the continued observance of Ascension Day.

Gospel: Mark 16:15-20

It is now universally acknowledged that the earliest texts of Mark end at 16:8 and that verses 9-20 are a later addition. But that is not to say that they are worthless. In any case, they form a part of the canonical Scriptures as the Church has received them (hence the term "canonical

88

ending"). Also, the ending is a compilation of many traditions, some of them earlier than anything we have elsewhere in the Easter narratives. The older view that it was an artificial summary of the other Gospel stories is now being increasingly abandoned. For instance, the command to preach the gospel and to baptize is presented in what is assuredly an earlier form than the more developed tradition at the end of Matthew. At the same time, the second paragraph of our reading is clearly a summary based on the end of Luke and the beginning of Acts (note the separation of the ascension from the resurrection and the location of the appearances between them). But unlike Luke and Acts, the sitting at the right hand of God is explicitly mentioned.

The Homily

The homilist would naturally want to draw out what is distinctive about this canonical ending of Mark's Gospel. Following the suggestion of the caption to this reading, he/she might speak about Jesus' sitting at the right hand of the Father. This, of course, is a figure of speech. To quote Calvin, it does not say that Jesus Christ is in a definite place but that he has entered upon a particular function, which is to be prophet, priest, and king.

Then, too, the homilist may wish to expound the missionary command and the command to baptize, and to speak of the mission that the Church has received from her ascending Lord and under the imperative of which she still stands today. This should be related quite concretely to the mission of the Church in the particular place where the homilist and the people are.

OPTIONAL READING

Reading II: Ephesians 4:1-13 (long form); 4:1-7, 11-13 (short form)

Ephesians 4:1-6 receives comment on the seventeenth Sunday of the year in series B, so we will concentrate here on the second part of the reading, verses 7-13 (verses 7, 11-13 in the short form). First, however, the reader is reminded that 4:1 marks the beginning of the hortatory or parenetic section of the letter, introduced, as in Rom 12:1, with the Greek particle *oun* ("therefore"). The ethical exhortations arise as consequences from the doctrinal exposition. The first part of the reading is an exhortation to maintain the unity of the Church.

Verses 7-13 address the themes of Ascension Day more directly. The maintenance and upbuilding of the unity of the Christian Church depend primarily upon the work of the apostolic ministry, that is, through the

330

proclamation of the word. The deutero-Pauline author of Ephesians sees the ministry in subapostolic perspective. Whereas Paul saw the charisms of local ministry welling up, as it were, in the congregation from below (though always to be exercised under the ultimate control of the apostles), this author sees them as gifts to be conferred from above by the ascended Christ. Whether they were conveyed sacramentally through ordination is not made clear, but that is certainly the case by the time of the later deutero-Pauline Pastorals. On the whole subject see Raymond E. Brown, *The Churches the Apostles Left Behind* (1984).

The catchword "gifts" leads to the citation of Ps 68:19, though in a version differing from both the MT (Hebrew) and the LXX (Greek): "gave gifts to" instead of "received gifts from." Actually, however, there is precedent for this change in the Targum, a paraphrasing commentary on the Hebrew text from rabbinic sources, composed in Aramaic. There the text is modified to apply to Moses' ascending Mount Sinai and receiving the Torah to give to the people of Israel. Our author Christianizes this Targum (perhaps with polemical intent), making Christ the subject, as he ascends to heaven to receive the ministerial charisms to confer upon his Church below.

Verses 8-10, omitted in the short form of this reading, are a Christological excursus, reflecting on the psalm text and applying it to Christ's ascension (it is odd that the short form omits the verses that deal with the basic theme of the day, but no doubt the argumentation was thought to be too rabbinic). The fact that Christ has ascended denotes that he had previously descended "to the lower parts of the earth." Commentators are about equally divided as to whether this means his descent at the incarnation (as in the Fourth Gospel) or his descent into Hades at the time of death. But the message of Ascension Day does not depend on our deciding the question, for the emphasis today is on verse 10. The point the author intends to make is that only one who had previously descended could be said to have ascended again, and therefore the text applies more fittingly to Christ than to Moses. At his ascension Christ achieved two results: (1) he triumphed over the heavenly universe (the principalities and powers?); and (2) he henceforth rules the universe with his dominion, that is, he is exalted to universal lordship. Ascension Day is his coronation.

Having commented on "ascended" from the psalm quotation, the author then picks up the word "gifts" from the second part of the text and defines these gifts of the ascended Christ as Church offices. In this list it is clear from Eph 2:20 and 3:5 that "apostles and prophets" belong to the foundation period of the Church now past, while evangelists, pastors, and teachers are features of the Church in the author's present.

Evangelists are probably the immediate successors of the apostles, like the writer himself, who exercise authority over more than just local churches, while the pastors and teachers (probably a single office, since the definite article covers both nouns) form the local ministry—the same officers referred to later by the standardized term "presbyters" (elders). At this early subapostolic period the permanent ministries succeeded the earlier apostles and prophets in many of the functions, though not in actual office. Whether or not the author thinks of them as having been ordained in an actual rite of prayer and laying on of hands (as in the Pastorals), this passage offers the scriptural warrant for believing that every ordination is the sacramental act of the ascended Christ in his Church.

SEVENTH SUNDAY OF EASTER

Reading I: Acts 1:15-17, 20a, 20c-26

In the narrative of Acts, the choice of Matthias occupies the twelve-day interval between the ascension and the day of Pentecost. It is therefore appropriately read on this Sunday, thus breaking the consecutive order in which the excerpts from Acts have been read during the Easter season.

This passage, like so many of the pericopes in Acts, combines earlier tradition with the author's redaction. There is no reason to doubt that the basic factual nucleus is historical. The number of the Twelve has to be made up after the defection of Judas by choosing one from among those who had received a resurrection appearance (one of the five hundred in 1 Cor 15:6?). Later tradition brought in the citation from Psalm 69 as an apologetic text for Judas' defection. Luke then wrote up the whole to express his own doctrine of apostleship.

The original function of the Twelve was distinct from that of the apostolate (see 1 Cor 15:5, 7). The Twelve had been appointed by the earthly Jesus as a *sign* of the eschatological community, the new Israel, which was to be the outcome of his work. As recipients of the second resurrection appearance after Peter, they became the *foundation* of the eschatological community. The choice of the twelfth man would have preserved this eschatological significance.

Later tradition tended more and more to make the Twelve as such apostles. The apostles, on the other hand, were originally missionaries, sent out to proclaim the gospel. The Twelve and the apostles formed overlapping circles. Luke carried further the later tendency, already discernible in Mark and Matthew, to make the Twelve as such apostles by practically confining the apostolate to the Twelve. He also defines the function of the apostolate as witness to the original saving history of both the earthly ministry of Jesus and his resurrection. The apostles thus serve as a bridge between the earthly Jesus and the ongoing life of the Church, a paramount concern of Luke's.

Responsorial Psalm: 103:1-2, 11-12, 19-20b

This psalm of thanksgiving is used on a number of occasions. Today the final stanza is highlighted by the response, "The Lord has set his throne in heaven," thus making the psalm one of thanksgiving for the ascension of Christ.

Reading II: 1 John 4:11-16

This reading follows immediately upon the second reading of last Sunday, and in typical Johannine fashion it repeats the themes of the earlier passage with slight variation: the love of God; the duty of love for one another; the mutual indwelling of God in the faithful and of the faithful in God; the definition of God as love, in the sense of the saving event. As usual in such Johannine repetition, a new point is made. That new point is that this mutual indwelling is exhibited in the confession of Jesus as the Son of God.

Gospel: John 17:11b-19

We spoke in series A of this chapter, the high priestly prayer of Christ at the Last Supper or, as it has been called by some exegetes, the prayer of consecration. In a way it represents the Johannine equivalent of the words of institution, in which Christ consecrates himself as the messianic sacrifice and offers the benefit of his sacrifice for the disciples to partake of in advance. In the Johannine prayer he consecrates himself so that his disciples may be consecrated for their mission and be preserved in unity and truth amid persecution.

At first sight, it might be thought that this reading would be more appropriate for Holy Thursday. It would certainly not be inappropriate there, but we have to recall that in Johannine parlance "I am coming to thee" refers to the whole process of the death, resurrection, and ascension of Christ, and so it is just as meaningful today. As a result of Jesus' departure, the mission of the apostles is inaugurated. So the prayer looks forward to Pentecost and beyond, to the mission of the Church.

The Homily

It is possible to link all three readings together under the rubric of apostolic mission. The ascended Christ sends his apostles out into the world to bear witness to the redemptive event. Thus, Matthias is chosen to be with the rest of the Twelve as a witness of the whole Christ-event. The first letter of John speaks of the confession as expressed focally in liturgy but also implemented in the internal life of the community ("love one another") and in its unity (the high priestly prayer that all may be one) and in the confession of Jesus as Son of God to the outside world. The homilist may choose to emphasize the mission itself, the necessity of confession, or the need for unity in mission.

PENTECOST VIGIL

Four alternative passages are provided for the Old Testament reading, in keeping with the concept of a vigil service. They are: the tower of Babel (Genesis); the theophany at Mount Sinai (Exodus); the vision of the dry bones (Ezekiel); the prophecy of the outpouring of the Spirit (Joel).

Reading I: Genesis 11:1-9; or Exodus 19:3-8a, 16-20b; or Ezekiel 37:1-14; or Joel 2:28-32 (NAB: 3:1-5)

The first alternative (Genesis) forms a counterpart to the Pentecost story in Acts. The preaching in tongues, interpreted by the author of Luke-Acts as the gift of foreign languages rather than as ecstatic speech, as in Paul and elsewhere, symbolizes the overcoming of the divisions among humankind, for which the building of the tower of Babel serves as an etiological legend.

The second alternative (Exodus) is the theophany to Moses, which provides the Pentecost account with its imagery of the tongues of fire and the rushing wind. This establishes a Law-gospel typology, which Paul developed theologically.

The fourth alternative (Joel) provides the major text for Peter's sermon following the outpouring of the Spirit in the Lucan Pentecost story. The expected outpouring of the Spirit will include everyone, not only outstanding charismatic leaders as under the old covenant. And whereas "all flesh" meant, for Joel, the whole of Israel, in Peter's speech it means all of humanity.

The third reading (Ezekiel) is the only one of the four alternatives that has no direct relation to the Pentecost story in Acts. It is surprising that it is never used in any of the New Testament texts on the Spirit. Indeed, nowhere in the New Testament is it explicitly asserted that the Church is the old Israel renewed by the Spirit, an idea that Ezekiel 37 might have suggested. Yet, the New Testament clearly understands the Church as the eschatologically renewed people of God, and it would seem legitimate to use the passage from Ezekiel as a parable of what happened at Pentecost.

Responsorial Psalm: 104:1-2a, 24 and 35c, 27-28, 29bc-30

This psalm has traditionally been associated with Pentecost. It speaks of the wisdom of God as the power that creates, sustains, and renews the earth. The wisdom concept bifurcated in Christian tradition, providing materials both for the doctrine of the person of Christ and the doctrine of the Spirit. Thus, the psalm may be interpreted as a hymn to the work of the *Creator Spiritus.*

Reading II: Romans 8:22-27

Here Paul draws upon Jewish and early Christian apocalyptic traditions. Apocalyptic extended the earlier nationalistic eschatological hope of the Old Testament to include the whole of human history and the whole cosmos. God was bringing the cosmos and, in the center of it, his covenant people to a final goal, a goal described under various symbols— here the symbol of the redemption or adoption. Early Christian understanding of the Spirit was set in this framework of apocalyptic expectation. Indeed, Ernst Käsemann has called apocalyptic the matrix of early Christian theology. The Spirit was an anticipation of the final apocalyptic goal: the Spirit is the first fruits (see the similar term, *arrhabōn,* used by Paul elsewhere, meaning "down payment"), the first installment of the blessings of the final state of things.

In this passage Paul is careful to insist, against all false spiritual enthusiasm, on the element of "not-yet-ness" that characterizes the Spirit's activity. We have only the first fruits. We are still in travail with the rest of the cosmos. Our full adoption as children, the redemption of our bodies, lies in the future. What the Spirit gives us can best be characterized as hope.

In this situation the Spirit impels us forward to the realization of that hope, helping the weakness of our prayers when, for example, we pray "Thy kingdom come." Our prayers are weak because we are still here and have not yet reached the ultimate goal. We have to pray for a goal we cannot yet comprehend, since we have not yet seen it. But the Spirit knows what that goal is, since the Spirit is part and anticipation of that goal. So the Spirit can take up our weak prayers and present them effectively to the Father.

Gospel: John 7:37-39

Many commentators take this scene as an allusion to the ceremony of the drawing of water that was a feature of the last day of the feast of Tabernacles. The Johannine Christ invites people to come to him to partake of the water of life. "His heart" is best taken as the heart of Christ, and the scripture quoted as an allusion to Moses' striking the rock in the wilderness so that water gushed out. This provides a type for what happened at Pentecost: the Spirit was poured forth from the heart of Jesus, that is, as a result of his redemptive work.

The Homily

There is an almost bewildering variety of themes for the homilist on this occasion. We mention the following:

1. The gift of the Spirit as the reversal of Babel suggests the universality of the Spirit-filled community. Here is the only power that can transcend all the divisions that human history has created between people and nations.

2. Sinai and Pentecost suggest the contrast between law and the Spirit and raise the question of the place of law in the Christian life. Here the so-called third use of the law—the law as guidance for sanctification—is brought into consideration.

3. Ezekiel's vision of the dry bones and the refrain of the psalm suggest the Spirit as the power of renewal in the Church.

4. The passage from Joel suggests that all members of the community share the Spirit. It is not the monopoly of the ordained, any more than it is the monopoly of gifted charismatic leaders, as it was under the old covenant.

5. The psalm and the first paragraph of the second reading invite our consideration of the cosmic dimensions of the Spirit's work of renewal, a theme about which our Orthodox friends have much to teach us.

6. The Spirit is the foundation of Christian hope. A helpful analogy is suggested by Rubem Alves in his *Theology of Christian Hope*—the Spirit is an aperitif, whetting our appetites for the ultimate fulfillment.

7. The second paragraph of the second reading prompts consideration of the Spirit as the organ of Christian prayer.

8. The Spirit flows from the heart of Jesus, that is, it is the outcome of his redemptive work.

The homilist should consider carefully the needs and situation of the local church and decide which of these points speaks most to those needs and that situation.

PENTECOST SUNDAY

Again, the readings are repeated each year. We will summarize the comments we gave in series A.   *98*

Reading I: Acts 2:1-11

This day is not merely the commemoration of a single historical event. Indeed, while Acts locates the outpouring of the Spirit on the day of Pentecost, John in today's gospel places it on Easter Sunday evening, each for theological rather than historical reasons. The important point is that the giving of the Spirit is the outcome of the work of the risen Christ. Nor should we think of the outpouring of the Spirit as a single event. Even the Book of Acts speaks of successive outpourings. We must avoid historicizing the Lucan presentation in this reading. The historical nucleus behind the Pentecost story is the beginning of the kerygma.

Responsorial Psalm: 104:1ab, 24ac, 29bc-31, 34

The responsorial psalm is a different and more appropriate selection of verses of the psalm used at the vigil service (see the second stanza, which   *277* is taken up by the refrain both here and at the vigil).

Reading II: 1 Corinthians 12:3b-7, 12-13

This passage deals with the specific gifts of the Spirit in the community (*charismata*). At Corinth there was great emphasis on speaking in tongues. Paul will not suppress this activity (see 1 Thess 5:19) but would have the Corinthians be aware of its dangers by applying the criterion of true confession. If the person speaking by the Spirit acknowledges Jesus (the "Jesus" is emphatic: the incarnate, crucified One, over against the Gnostic idea that the incarnation and crucifixion were at best transient episodes), then the charism is genuine.

Another point that Paul makes is that there are other gifts besides speaking in tongues, and each has a necessary contribution to make. And this leads to his third point: The gifts of the Spirit must not produce individualism but must be placed at the service of the whole body. In effect, there are three tests or criteria for the *charismata*: (1) right confession; (2) the renunciation of exclusive claims; (3) the placing of the gifts at the service of the whole community.

Gospel: John 20:19-23

The gospel reading associates the gift of the Spirit with the apostolic mission, here defined, not as the proclamation of the kerygma, but as the forgiving and retaining of sins. The primary reference here is probably to baptism rather than to the sacrament of penance. It can be extended to cover the latter only secondarily and derivatively. The forgiving and retaining will then be a reference to giving or withholding baptism on the grounds of faith or its absence as a response to the hearing of the kerygma.

The Homily

The homilist might confront the accounts of the giving of the Spirit in Acts and John with each other, pointing up the different theologies that underlie their different chronologies. By tying the gift of the Spirit to Easter, the gospel emphasizes that the Spirit is the gift of the risen One, and as such conveys the benefits of his death and resurrection. The Pentecost story emphasizes the replacement of the Law by the gift of the Spirit as the basis of the life of the new community.

The second reading deals with the problems of a local congregation in which there is a great deal of enthusiasm for the gifts of the Spirit. If this is the case in the homilist's own church, there is an opportunity here to echo the Pauline warnings and to speak of the Pauline criteria.

OPTIONAL READINGS

Reading II: Galatians 5:16-25

This passage comes from the parenetic section of Galatians. Since Paul is drawing upon traditional catechetical teaching, we must not suppose that he has formulated the teaching with the situation in the Galatian churches specifically in view. We should not, for instance, infer, as some commentators have done, that there were two parties in Galatia, one Judaizing and the other libertinist, the former being addressed in the doctrinal section of the letter, and the latter in the parenesis. At the same time, however, the Apostle seems to have selected items from his catechetical tradition that have special bearing on the situation in the Galatian churches. These churches were seriously divided over the question of whether or not Gentile Christians should be circumcised. It is not clear whether they were Judaizers who wanted to impose Jewish law in its totality upon the Gentile converts or whether they were syncretists who included circumcision among other extraneous elements. Probably the latter, since Paul has to remind his addressees that circumcision implies the obligation to observe the whole law. Hence the Apostle emphasizes those works of the flesh that cause divisiveness, and those virtues that promote unity.

It is most important to note that the "flesh" is not our lower nature (so, erroneously, the NEB), but our unredeemed, self-centered ego. "Flesh" includes the mind as well as the body; and the sins of the mind, such as pride, are as serious as sensuality. Equally, "Spirit" should be capitalized, for it means, not some innate "higher" nature than humanity, but the Holy Spirit of God, released through the Christ-event and made over to the believers in baptism.

Paul next introduces a second contrast, between the law and Spirit. In Galatians, law generally means law misunderstood as the way to salvation. Human beings in their autonomy mistakenly think that they can achieve salvation by their own efforts, whereas this is possible only through the Christ-event and the consequent bestowal of the Spirit. In later Judaism the feast of Pentecost celebrated the giving of the law. It may have been this fact that led the author of Luke-Acts to introduce typology from the Sinai event into his story of the giving of the Spirit (the wind and the tongues of fire), and led Paul to draw the theological contrast between law and Spirit.

A third contrast drawn by Paul is between "works" and "fruit." Works are, as already suggested, achievements of the self-seeking natural human being, whereas fruit is that which grows through the outside influence of grace or of the Holy Spirit. What we have to do is to open ourselves to that influence and trust the possibility of this growth. Again, "works" is plural, whereas "fruit" is singular. It is a frequently made mistake to speak of the "fruits" of the Spirit, a mistake that enjoys the exalted precedent of Archbishop Cranmer in the Litany of the Book of Common Prayer. "Works" pull us this way and that; "fruit" expresses inner unity of character.

Finally, there is the implied contrast between the *fruit* of the Spirit and the *gifts* of the Spirit listed by Paul in 1 Corinthians. Is there a real difference between the two? Not too much, for love appears in 1 Cor 13 as a gift (charism), while here in Galatians it is a fruit. Yet there is a difference. A gift is granted as an initial endowment at baptism or ordination, whereas fruit is what eventually grows within the believers through the subsequent influence of the Holy Spirit.

Gospel: John 15:26-27; 16:12-15

Today's (optional) gospel reading combines the third and fifth of the five Johannine Paraclete sayings. They are closely related, for both speak of the teaching function of the Holy Spirit, of the way in which the content of the Spirit's teaching is derived from Jesus, and therefore, since Jesus is the truth, of the Spirit as the Spirit of truth.

The first of our Paraclete sayings (the third in the Gospel of John) is closely paralleled in the synoptic tradition (Mark 13:11; Matt 10:19-20; Luke 12:12; cf. Luke 21:15) and is perhaps the original saying out of which the other ones in John developed. As in the Synoptists, this saying is set in the context of persecution predicted for the disciples. This promise is attested so widely and in such a variety of contexts (see above) that it has a high claim to authenticity. Jesus promised his disciples that they would have the divine assistance of the Holy Spirit as they bore witness in a situation of rejection and persecution. Perhaps this promise originally applied to their missions while Jesus was still on earth. Since Jesus' preaching of the kingdom of God was itself empowered by the Spirit, may we not at least suppose that the apostles' preaching during Jesus' earthly life was similarly empowered, although, of course, they did not receive the Spirit as a permanent endowment until Pentecost? In the light of the Pentecost experience, the Gospel tradition, both synoptic and Johannine, will then have transferred this promise to Jesus' farewell discourse (Mark 13, Luke 21, and John 14–16).

The coming of the Spirit is closely tied to the person of Christ. In this passage it is "I" (=Jesus) who will send the Spirit. That is why some of us believe that the present movement underway in the Anglican communion to remove the *Filioque* from the Nicene Creed as a gesture to the Orthodox is misguided, despite the wording of verse 26b ("proceeds from the Father"). At least it should be asserted that the Western Church showed a sound theological instinct in adding "and the Son," and that that addition was true to this verse ("*I* will send you"). If it be objected that the Nicene Creed is talking about the immanent as opposed to the economic Trinity (the external relations of the three Persons rather than their function in salvation history), we reply that that is not what the Fourth Gospel is talking about here (see Raymond Brown, *ad loc.*). Perhaps the best formula would be "who proceeds from the Father *through the Son,*" which is what the *Filioque* probably intended to assert.

The most important feature of this text, though, may be its insistence on the concurrent witness of the apostles and the Spirit. The apostles and the apostolic Church after their deaths are witnesses of the Word, but the Word without Spirit may be dead, while the Spirit without Word may run wild. Word and Spirit, apostolic witness and witness of the Spirit— these must be held together, though they have often been separated in the history of the Christian Church.

The second part of our reading, as already noted, comprises the fifth Paraclete saying. Its point is very similar to our last remark on the third saying. If the apostles are to bear witness, they must constantly be guided back to the Jesus tradition. The Spirit brings no new revelation but does bring a constantly renewed and ever deeper understanding of the original revelation. To suppose that there can be any additional revelations over and above that which was revealed in Christ is to deny the eschatological character of that revelation.

It is puzzling, however, to read further that the Spirit "will declare to you the things that are to come" (16:13). This has suggested to some commentators new apocalyptic revelations like those of the Johannine Apocalypse. Can this be the intention of the fourth evangelist (who, despite other affinities, is so different in his eschatological outlook from the Seer who wrote Revelation)? It is more likely that our passage means "interpreting to each generation the contemporary significance of what Jesus has said and done" (R. Brown), thus reinforcing the general import of these two Paraclete sayings.

[END OF THE EASTER SEASON]

Sunday after Pentecost
TRINITY SUNDAY

The doctrine of the Trinity, contrasted with the triadic formulas and the triple structure of the biblical experience of God, is implicit rather than explicit in Scripture. By "triple structure" of biblical experience we mean that in both the Old Testament and the New, God is experienced as going forth out of himself (from his "aseity") in revelation and redemptive action, and also creating in human hearts a believing response to his revelatory and redemptive action.

Reading I: Deuteronomy 4:32-34, 39-40
We can experience this triple experience of God in the first reading. It speaks of God "in heaven above and on the earth beneath," that is, of his aseity (he is Yahweh, God who is); of his transcendence (in heaven above); and of his immanence (on earth beneath). It speaks, too, of God going forth out of himself in his acts of revelation and redemption. The first revelatory act of God specified is the original act of creation ("the day that God created man upon the earth"); the second is his speaking out of the fire in the giving of the Law on Mount Sinai. The redemptive act it speaks of is the Exodus, when God took a nation for himself by signs and wonders, which he did before the eyes of his people in Egypt. This redemptive act, of course, provides the supreme type for his eschatological redemption in Christ, in which God brought into being a new people for himself by the "signs and wonders" of the Christ-event.

Finally, our passage speaks of the response that God creates in the hearts of his people—their faith in him who is, who reveals and redeems, and their obedience to his statutes and commandments.

Responsorial Psalm: 33:4-6, 9, 18-20, 22

Today's psalm highlights the Old Testament concept of the "word of the Lord," which is one of several concepts that contributed to the Johannine conception of the Logos. In the priestly narrative of creation (Gen 1), God brings the universe into existence by uttering his fiat: "Let there be light," etc. It is to this action that the psalmist is referring when he says that God created the heavens through his word. But with this formal affirmation the concept of the word is well on its way to becoming hypostatized, thus preparing the way for John 1:1 and forming part of the ingredients for the formulated doctrine of the Trinity.

Reading II: Romans 8:14-17

When the letter to the Romans was read in course during the early summer of series A, these verses were skipped. They are eminently appropriate today, for they speak of God the Father (Abba); of the Christ, with whom we are co-heirs; and of the Spirit, who leads us as children of God. This supports our contention that the triadic formula is primarily a deposit of Christian experience. The Christian believer knows that he/she has been adopted through Christ in baptism, and in the Eucharistic liturgy is enabled by the Spirit to invoke the Father (for "Abba" is certainly a liturgical cry, derived from the ecstatic worship of the Aramaic-speaking Church).

Here, as in Gal 4:6-7, Paul assumes that divine adoption is not a natural datum of human existence but an eschatological gift, made possible by the Christ-event and conveyed to believers through the operation of the Spirit (that is, word and sacrament).

In his controversies with the Corinthians, Paul had never denied the ecstatic gifts of the Spirit but always emphasized that the real test of the Spirit was not ecstasy but suffering in the way of the cross—hence the last point in this reading, the proviso that we must suffer with Christ now if we are to finally share his glory.

Gospel: Matthew 28:16-20

This was the gospel for Ascension Day in series A, where fuller comment can be found. Here, of course, the emphasis rests upon the baptismal command, the clearest instance of the New Testament triadic formula that provided the basis for the later doctrine of the Trinity.

90

In the earliest Palestinian Church, baptism was administered in the name of Jesus (see Acts and Paul). The triple formula arose only toward the end of the first century, and then outside of Palestine (see the *Didache*). Yet, from the earliest days baptism was understood to mean translation into the eschatological existence made possible by the Christ-event and participation in the gifts of the Spirit. In a completely Jewish environment it would have gone without saying that if Jesus was the Messiah, he was the one in whom God had acted eschatologically, and if God had inaugurated the messianic age in Jesus Christ, this involved also the gift of the Spirit. Thus, baptism was always implicitly Trinitarian.

The Homily

We need to guard against the notion that the Holy Trinity is a mysterious formula or still more a perplexing and complicated dogma, intelligible only to theologians. We must therefore interpret the experience of believers, particularly their prayer and sacramental experiences, in such a way that they see that they are themselves constantly involved thereby in the life of the Blessed Trinity. As Thomas Hancock, a nineteenth-century Anglican divine, said: "Thus the rudest man or woman who cannot reason about the Trinity may *know* the Trinity more perfectly than some acute theologian who has by heart all the writings of St. Athanasius or St. Augustine and all the controversies of the first six centuries."

Thursday after Trinity Sunday or Sunday after Trinity Sunday
CORPUS CHRISTI

Where the solemnity of Corpus Christi is not observed as a holy day, it is assigned to the Sunday after Trinity Sunday.

Thomas Hancock, whom we cited above, expressed the reserve of many Anglicans (a reserve which the present writer shares) about the propriety of a Sunday devoted to Corpus Christi. "The feast of the Trinity," he wrote, ". . . and not Corpus Christi (as some amongst us dream) ought to be the latest of the catholic feasts. Beyond God, what can there be to know? It is the completion of the order of festivals, for the Holy Spirit has led the Church, ritually and liturgically, to the Father." At best, Corpus Christi should be regarded as a coda, rather than as a climax, to the festivals.

Reading I: Exodus 24:3-8
Two passages from the New Testament have made this section from Exo-

dus central to the understanding of Christian redemption and its representation in the Eucharist. The first is Mark 14:24: "This is *my* blood-of-the-covenant." Here the covenant blood of Christ is contrasted with the blood that Moses sprinkled against the altar and over the people. The second New Testament passage is Heb 9:15-21, especially verse 20, which actually cites Exod 24:8. (It is curious that the second reading stops short of this verse. When the Lectionary is reviewed, the desirability of extending it accordingly should be considered.)

Why was it necessary in the Bible for a covenant to be ratified in blood? The idea seems to be that the death of the victim has a finality about it that makes it, and therefore the covenant that it ratifies, irrevocable. Sacrifice is expressive of the offerer's total commitment to carry out the terms of the covenant.

This passage suggests a way in which the Eucharist can be related to the atonement. Before the covenant is complete, the people have to become participants. In the Sinai covenant this is achieved when Moses sprinkles the people with half of the blood, after applying the other half to the altar, representing Yahweh himself. Similarly, in Christ's sacrifice the sacrificial death is completed, on God's side, when the Son presents himself to the Father ("blood" = his life surrendered in obedience unto death). On the human side, it is completed when the communicant receives the Eucharistic cup in communion. The Eucharist, understood thus, becomes an integral part of the once-for-all sacrifice of Calvary.

Responsorial Psalm: 116:12-13, 15, 16bc-18

These same verses were used on Holy Thursday, the only difference being the refrain, which today is from verse 13 instead of from 1 Cor 10:16. This psalm is very appropriate after the Old Testament reading, for, as we suggested above, it is in our partaking of the Eucharistic cup that the typology of Moses' sprinkling the people with the blood is fulfilled. It is the "cup of salvation," in the sense that by drinking of this cup we partake in the saving event.

Reading II: Hebrews 9:11-15

Although this passage is going to lead up to the quotation of Exod 24:8, the background is not what Moses did there but what the high priest did annually on the Day of Atonement. It may be said that the Day of Atonement provides a better analogy for Christ's role in his sacrifice, for it suggests the once-for-all event in which Christ entered into the presence of God at his exaltation, as the high priest entered the Holy of Holies on the Day of Atonement. On the other hand, the Exodus analogy suggests more strongly the mode in which the *people* partake of this sacrifice, and therefore provides a closer type for holy communion. By fulfilling the work of the high priest on the Day of Atonement, Christ puts himself in the position in which he can fulfill the work of Moses when he sprinkled the people at the ratification of the covenant. For this reason we would renew our plea for the extension of this reading through verse 20.

Note: In verse 11 the rsv translates "high priest of the good things that *have come.*" Other manuscripts have "of good things that *are to come.*" The latter reading is preferable not only on text-critical grounds but also theologically, for it emphasizes that Christ's work is a piece of anticipated eschatology, thus leaving open (1) the idea of ultimate consummation, and (2) the continual anticipatory realization of this in the Eucharist.

Gospel: Mark 14:12-16, 22-26

This passage combines two Marcan pericopes—the preparation for the Passover and the institution of the Eucharist. Two points may be noted from Mark 14:12-16. (1) It is here, not in the institution narrative, that Mark identifies the Last Supper with the Passover meal. As is well known, the Johannine account of the Last Supper dates it on the fourteenth of Nisan, a day before the Passover, which began at sundown on the fifteenth. We are not called upon here to decide which dating is historically correct, still less to try to harmonize the discrepancy; rather, each account must be asked for its theological intent. Mark wishes to assert that the Eucharist is the Christian Passover meal. (2) Jesus is depicted in Mark 14:12-16 as the eschatological prophet (an early Christological interpretation) by his supernatural foreknowledge, indicated by the direction to the disciples to meet the man with the water jar. Similar powers were ascribed to Old Testament prophets, especially Elijah and Elisha.

The institution narrative is not a description of the Passover meal but is restricted to those aspects of the Supper that were liturgically important to the early communities. What we really learn here is how Mark's Church celebrated the Eucharist rather than precisely what Jesus did and said at the Supper, though, of course, what Mark's Church did is ultimately derived from what happened in the upper room.

Apparently, in Mark's Church the Eucharist was celebrated at the conclusion of a common meal (in Paul's earlier account in 1 Cor 11, the bread precedes the meal, and the cup follows it). Seven actions were performed:

1. Taking the bread.

2. Blessing (of God for the bread; note, not of the bread; this accords with Jewish custom).

3. Breaking of the bread so that the congregation could share the one loaf in communion.

4. The administration (note that the words are words of administration rather than of consecration; consecration, in accord with Jewish ideas, was effected by thanksgiving).

5. Taking the cup.

6. Giving thanks over the cup (a Hellenistic word for the Hebrew act of blessing, retained for the bread).

7. Administration.

Three important words are spoken by Jesus in Mark's account: (1) the bread word, (2) the cup word, and (3) the eschatological saying.

In the light of the first and second readings, exegesis today should concentrate upon the cup word: "This is my blood-of-the-covenant, which is poured out for many." The trend in contemporary scholarship is to regard this version as a later rewording of the cup word in 1 Cor 11 due to liturgical development. Once the intervening meal had been brought forward to the beginning, and the bread and the cup consequently brought together at the end, the tendency was for the two sets of words to be assimilated. So we get: "This is my body. This is my blood." Mark's tradition interprets the blood as the blood of the covenant on the background of Exod 24. Thus, what the cup conveys is not a thing (blood) but a participation in the event of salvation history, the new covenant.

The Homily

The obvious procedure for the homilist today would be to concentrate upon the cup word at the Eucharist in its Marcan form, relating it in turn to Exod 24, the refrain of the psalm, and Heb 9:11ff. It should be shown how the cross and the Eucharist are not to be detached from one another but how the Eucharist forms an integral part of the salvation event.

SEASON OF THE YEAR

SECOND SUNDAY OF THE YEAR

Reading I: 1 Samuel 3:3b-10, 19

The call of Samuel serves as a type of the infancy narratives. Note particularly the echo of verse 19 in Luke 2:52. This Sunday, however, a rather different typology is suggested. Today's gospel, while not a direct narrative of Jesus' baptism (something that the Fourth Gospel studiously avoids), contains John the Baptist's witness to Jesus. This witness is probably based on the heavenly voice at the baptism of Jesus. In his baptism Jesus responded to his Father's call to take up the mission of the eschatological prophet. Thus, the call of Samuel, which is a call to be a prophet, serves as a type of Christ's baptism. Like Jesus in his baptism, Samuel hears the call of God and responds with the words "Speak, Lord, for thy servant hears." So, too, the Fourth Gospel frequently speaks of the Son hearing the Father's words.

Responsorial Psalm: 40:1, 3ab, 6-9

This psalm, commented upon on the second Sunday of the year in series A, is used today as a response to the reading of Samuel's call, and this reinforces the typological interpretation we offered above, for this psalm was applied to our Lord by the author of Hebrews. It is Christ who says the words of the refrain: "Here am I, Lord; I come to do your will." Hebrews pictures Christ as saying these words when he "came into the world." This "coming" need not be narrowly confined to the moment of his birth; his coming covers his baptism, in which he embarked upon his messianic mission, and indeed every moment of the incarnate life, in which he responds constantly to the Father's call.

Reading II: 1 Corinthians 6:13c-15a, 17-20

The context of Paul's argument here is a discussion of immoral sexual behavior in the Corinthian community. Paul is not so much concerned with the guilty parties (perhaps some kind of temple prostitution was involved; it was a question of a hangover from their previous pagan life) but with the failure of the Corinthians to discipline the offender. As "gnostics," they used the slogan "All things are lawful for me"—anything goes. They felt this way because as gnostics they believed that their Christian experience enabled them to transcend the realities of the material world.

Against this gnostic position Paul argues that the Christian experience, rather than delivering the soul from the body, brings the whole person, body and soul alike, under the lordship of Christ. Paul drives home his point with two figures. The first pictures the individual believers as members of Christ. Here, for the first time in Paul's letters, we meet the figure of the Church as the body of Christ, a figure that will be developed in chapter 12. Since sexual immorality involves the whole person, it deprives Christ of his rightful property. It is worth noting that Paul's first use of the concept of the ecclesial body of Christ is ethical.

The second figure is of the Church as the temple of the Holy Spirit. Sexual immorality desecrates the temple of the Lord. This figure is particularly appropriate if temple prostitution was the point at issue.

Gospel: John 1:35-42

This is the Johannine version of the call of the first disciples. The Fourth Gospel connects the call very closely with the ministry of John the Baptist. The evangelist, interpreting his tradition of the baptism of Jesus (which, as we have seen, he suppresses because of his polemic against later members of the "baptist" sect), has the Baptist point out to his disciples the presence of the "Lamb of God." The terminology may be a reflection of the heavenly voice, "Thou art my beloved Son, the object of my favor." This voice, in its synoptic form, points to the figure of the servant of Yahweh, and it is not improbable that the title "Lamb" is connected with the title "servant," whether as a word-play in Aramaic or as an echo of the comparison of the servant to the lamb led to the slaughter in Isa 53.

Thus, the message of this passage will be: True followers of John the Baptist, those who really listen to their master, leave him and follow Jesus.

The true disciple of John, therefore, comes to Jesus with the question "Where are you staying?" In the Fourth Gospel, to "stay" means more than just to lodge in a house overnight; it is the same word as is used for "abide" in those Christological passages that speak of the Son's abiding in the Father. This is what the two disciples really come and "see" (another theological word, meaning to perceive with the eye of faith the mystery of the Word in the flesh). In this encounter the new disciples make a Christological confession: "We have found the Messiah." And because of this confession, Simon is renamed Cephas. Here the evangelist telescopes into a single scene a whole process of revelation and response that, historically speaking, covered a much longer period, extending from the baptism of Jesus through Peter's confession and the Easter appearances. The evangelist's concern is to present a theological interpretation of history, not a mere chronicle of historical events.

The Homily

A common thread seems to run through the first reading, the psalm, and the gospel. This is the mystery of Christ's person, conceived in terms of his response to his Father's call. This mystery is something that we, like Andrew and Simon, can "see" if we, like them, come and follow Christ. In this post-Epiphany season it would be appropriate to offer an interpretation of the incarnation that replaces the traditional language of "divine and human natures" with the language of dynamic relationship between the Father and the Son, a relationship of call and response. This pattern is prefigured in the call of Samuel and, if we may coin a word, is meant to be "post-figured" in the life of the Christian believer.

The second reading offers the homilist another possibility—the Christian requirement of sexual purity, a highly relevant theme in this permissive age. Note that Paul does not simply issue a series of don'ts but goes to the heart of the matter—the whole person in the totality of his or her being, including bodily existence, belongs to Christ. He/she is a member of Christ's body and therefore must live responsibly in that relationship.

THIRD SUNDAY OF THE YEAR

Reading I: Jonah 3:1-5, 10

The Book of Jonah is not a normal prophetic book consisting of the prophet's oracles in poetic form. Ostensibly it is a prose narrative about the activity of the prophet himself. In reality, however, it is a kind of tract (almost a propagandist historical novel like those of Dickens or Kingsley), intended to put across the author's universalistic views as protest against the narrow nationalism of postexilic Judaism.

The unknown author has used as the basis of his tale a saga that had grown up around the figure of the prophet Jonah mentioned in 2 Kgs 14:25. The first part of his work (chs. 1–2) concerns the prophet's unsuccessful attempts to escape from the task Yahweh imposed upon him, namely, preaching to the Ninevites. The prophet thought that God could not possibly care for such Gentiles as they were! The story of Jonah in the belly of the great fish occurs in this part and represents Yahweh's refusal to let the prophet run away from his mission. He was rescued at sea in order to preach. Our passage comes from the beginning of the second part (chs. 3–4), where Jonah carries out his preaching of repentance to the Ninevites.

Jesus used Jonah's ministry as a type of his own but claimed that with him something (*sic:* neuter) greater was present, namely, the presence of the kingdom (Luke 11:29-30). Matthew gives a different interpretation of this typology, taking Jonah's sojourn in the fish for three days and three nights as a type of Christ's resurrection. Since our passage comes from the second part of Jonah, only the former typology is relevant to its interpretation. This is also indicated by the correspondence between this reading and the gospel, which provides a summary of Jesus' eschatological preaching. Jonah is thus presented to us in today's liturgy as a type of Christ in his preaching of the kingdom.

Responsorial Psalm: 25:4-5b, 6, 7b-9

A different selection of verses of this psalm was used on the twenty-sixth Sunday of the year in series A and received comment there. Both Jonah and Jesus figure today as preachers of repentance. But repentance must be followed by obedience to the will of God, a point not featured in the Jonah story (nothing is said about the Ninevites' subsequent behavior) but strongly emphasized in the gospel, where Jesus' preaching of repentance is followed by the call of the disciples.

172

Reading II: 1 Corinthians 7:29-31

In 1 Cor 7 Paul has been dealing with problems of sex and marriage that the Corinthians had raised in a letter they had written to him. He concludes the first part of his answer with a general discussion about the Christian attitude toward the world, which for him is determined by his expectation of an imminent parousia. In view of this, Paul recommends living in the spirit of *hōs mē* ("as if not"), that is, in a spirit of detachment from the world.

It would be tempting to dismiss Paul's injunction of detachment as no longer relevant now that the expectation of an imminent parousia has been abandoned. But his injunction still has existential validity, for it is still true that the form of this world is passing away. All its structures and relationships are provisional and must not be treated as if they were ultimates. They are only penultimate values, not because this world is unreal, in a Platonic sense, but because as a result of the Christ-event, the kingdom of God has become a present reality awaiting its consummation. Our Lord taught the same eschatological detachment in the Ser-

mon on the Mount when he enjoined his disciples to seek first the kingdom
of heaven. It may sound a little brutal to apply this counsel even to marriage, but even the marriage relationship is only penultimate, for in the
consummated kingdom of God "they neither marry nor are given in marriage" (Matt 22:30).

Gospel: Mark 1:14-20

The Matthean parallel to this pericope—the beginning of Jesus' preaching
in Galilee and the call of the first disciples—was used on the third Sunday
of the year in series A. Mark's version lacks the formula quotation from *113*
Isa 9:1-2 ("The land of Zebulun and . . . Naphtali . . ."), which was
highlighted in the caption and the short form of the Matthean gospel. The
absence of the quotation thus calls attention to Mark's summary of Jesus'
preaching, a point that is further emphasized by the caption here and by
the selection of the passage from Jonah for the Old Testament reading.

As we have just noted, this summary is "compositional," that is, composed by Mark himself. To some extent Mark has picked up the missionary
language of the Hellenistic Church ("believe in the gospel") and of the
earliest post-Easter period ("The time is fulfilled"). But the central phrase
("the kingdom of God is at hand") undoubtedly reproduces Jesus' own
message (see Q-Matt 10:7 par.; also Q-Matt 12:28 par.). The exhortation
to repent was part of Jesus' message and was taken over by him from John
the Baptist, though with somewhat different overtones. John's message
was that God was to act soon.

Jesus' message is that God is beginning to act eschatologically—with
his own appearance—and will consummate that action in the not too dis-
tant future. This implies that "the time is fulfilled," that is, that the event
to which the Old Testament looked forward is now beginning to happen.
The challenge to repent, therefore, means much more than to be sorry
for one's individual sins. The Greek word for "repent" is *metanoiein,* which
literally means "to change one's mind." But Jesus must have used the
Hebrew *shûbh,* or its Aramaic equivalent, which means to turn around
180 degrees, to reorient one's whole attitude toward Yahweh in the face of
his coming kingdom. It therefore includes within it the demand of faith.
So Mark's addition of "believe in the gospel," despite the later missionary
origin of this particular language, brings out the force of Jesus' challenge
to repent. This is how it differs from John the Baptist's use of the same
word.

It is important to remember that Mark is not summarizing Jesus'
preaching simply out of historical interest. He places this summary as a
kind of title to his whole connected account of Jesus' ministry. "Gospel"

is the characterization that Mark gives to his whole work (see Mark 1:1), which includes Jesus' way to the cross and, beyond that, his resurrection. It is in this whole story that the kingdom or reign of God draws near and is inaugurated, and will surely be consummated.

The call of the disciples that follows serves to illustrate what it means to repent and believe in the gospel. It does not mean to accept certain timeless truths but to be attached to the person of Jesus, to go along with him in his way—a way that will lead to the cross, as will become clear at Caesarea Philippi.

The Homily

The first reading, the psalm, and the gospel suggest the theme of Jesus' preaching of repentance. The homilist could differentiate between the common moralistic understanding of repentance and the New Testament notion of turning around and reorienting one's whole attitude toward God. This in turn results in a personal attachment to Jesus like that of the disciples and following him in his way (here the refrain of the psalm can be picked up) through the cross to the resurrection.

If the homilist is attracted to the second reading and to the theme of eschatological detachment, this theme could be related to the call of the first disciples, whom Jesus detached from their earthly avocations in order to follow him. For some, discipleship will mean literally this; for others, it will mean remaining in the world and its structures but living in the spirit of eschatological detachment from it.

FOURTH SUNDAY OF THE YEAR

Reading I: Deuteronomy 18:15-20

In the original intention of the Deuteronomic author, the "prophet" whose coming Moses predicts stood for the prophetic office as such, exercised by a whole series of prophets in Israel. They were understood by the Deuteronomist as standing in a charismatic succession from Moses. Later on this text was interpreted eschatologically in certain circles of pre-Christian Judaism, as we see from the Dead Sea Scrolls (1 QS 7) and from the evidence of the Fourth Gospel (see John 1:21; 6:14; 7:40). In these circles Deut 18:15 was interpreted as a prediction that God would send one final prophet (the "eschatological prophet," as modern scholars call this figure) before the End.

Jesus' own self-understanding, though perhaps not quite so explicit, was in line with this, for he understood his mission in terms of proclaiming the dawning of God's kingdom, and himself as the last messenger before its consummation. It was apparently left to the earliest post-Easter community to work out an explicit Christological interpretation of Jesus in terms of the eschatological prophet like Moses (see especially Acts 3). As originally intended, this was a high Christology, emphasizing not only Jesus' authoritative teaching but also his agency of redemption, just as Moses had led the Israelites out of Egypt as the agent of God's earlier act of redemption. When Christianity moved to the Hellenistic world, this early Christological title seemed inadequate and was replaced by such titles as Kyrios, Son of God, and Logos.

The selection of Deut 18:15-20 for today seems to have been determined by the allusion to Jesus' teaching with authority in the gospel reading.

Responsorial Psalm: 95:1-2, 6-9

The *Venite* consists of two parts: a call to worship and a warning against neglect of the word of God. The first part is very popular among Anglicans as the invitatory canticle of Morning Prayer, but in most recent revisions the stern warnings of the second part have often been omitted. Yet, it was this second part that the author of Hebrews (Heb 3:7–4:13) took up as especially relevant to his Church. The situation of the people of this Church was that they were growing stale instead of advancing in the Christian life, just as Israel grew weary in the wilderness.

These same verses are used on the third Sunday of Lent in series A 44 and on the eighteenth Sunday of the year in series C. Today the refrain 492 serves to pick up the warning to give heed to the prophet like Moses.

Reading II: 1 Corinthians 7:32-35

One can only speculate what motives led to the choice of the caption, which speaks of the advantage of the unmarried state to women and, unlike the text, says nothing about men! Paul's views on marriage and celibacy cut right across the views commonly held by Christians today. He commends celibacy for both men and women, but regards marriage as perfectly lawful and proper for *any* Christian. At the same time, however, he has a distinct preference for celibacy. Both states have their advantages and their perils, but on balance, according to Paul, the celibate, whether man or woman, is less likely to be distracted from the service of the Lord.

At the same time, certain points of difference have to be noted about Paul's teaching on celibacy compared with that of later times. Paul refuses to lay down a hard and fast rule (v. 35: "not to lay any restraint upon you"). The celibate life requires a charism that not every Christian has (see v. 7). Yet, against much contemporary post-Freudian opinion, Paul clearly believes that celibacy is the higher state. This is seen from what he says in other parts of this chapter (vv. 6, 8, 25, 38).

Gospel: Mark 1:21-28

This passage follows immediately upon last week's gospel reading. After the call of the first disciples, Mark has Jesus embark upon his public ministry in Galilee. The first item of material that Mark selects for inclusion from his material is an exorcism. Perhaps the miracles he includes from 1:20 to 3:12 are from an earlier collection of miracle stories that he edited and supplemented with other non-miracle material.

One special feature of this editorial work is the evangelist's emphasis on Jesus' teaching, though without indicating the content of that teaching. The effect of this is to play down the one-sided emphasis on the miracles that such a pre-Marcan collection of miracle stories might have created. The Marcan tradition saw the miracles as displays of Jesus' authority. The Greek word for "authority" in the "choric ending" of the exorcism story is *exousia.* This word also has the connotation of power, particularly in this context of miracle. Mark does not deny that Jesus displayed both authority and power in his miracles, but for him the miracles were only one aspect of Jesus' authority. The primary emphasis rests upon his teaching: "he taught as one who had authority [*exousia*—the word is picked up by the Marcan redaction from the body of the exorcism story], and not as the scribes." The exorcism follows merely as an illustration of the power of Jesus' teaching with authority. "In Jesus' word heaven breaks in and hell is destroyed. His word is deed" (Eduard Schweizer).

The Homily

The first reading, the psalm, and the gospel concentrate upon Jesus' teaching with authority. Jesus is the prophet of the end-time, whose word is the very word of God himself. He is the "bearer of the word" (Rudolf Bultmann). Rightly understood, this description is not a minimizing Christology but a very high one. The prophets said, "Thus says the Lord." The scribes quoted earlier rabbinic authorities. Jesus says, "I say unto you," and this puts him in the place of God. Jesus is thus "aut Deus aut vir non bonus," as the old quip has it. An exposition of the word-Christology might be in order today.

As an alternative, the second reading would offer an opportunity for a consideration of celibacy in the light of Paul's teaching. This teaching corrects a legalistic interpretation of celibacy but at the same time offers a critique of the "muscular Christianity" common in many Protestant circles. Celibacy is a charism, but where that charism exists it is a call to a life of less distracted devotion to the service of the Lord. Paul does not advocate celibacy because of a Manichean dualism. Celibacy means the surrender, not of a state that is evil, but of one that is good, for a higher end, for a more completely devoted service of the Lord.

FIFTH SUNDAY OF THE YEAR

Reading I: Job 7:1-4, 6-7

The Book of Job is rarely used in the Lectionary, so a word of introduction is in order. Job belongs to the third group of Old Testament books, called the "Writings." It begins with a prose narrative in which Job, a hitherto prosperous paterfamilias, is suddenly overcome by calamity, both domestic and economic. There follows a poetic dialogue between the unfortunate hero and his three friends, who seek to comfort him with platitudes. Job is thus led to wrestle with the problem of suffering.

Suffering can no longer be interpreted as it was in Deuteronomy, namely, as a direct punishment for sin, for Job has been righteous and has maintained his integrity. What Job has to learn in the end is that a person's righteousness gives him or her no claim upon God. The book closes with a prose epilogue in which the fortunes of Job are restored to him. The Book of Job can best be understood as a forerunner of the Pauline doctrine of justification by the grace of God alone.

Today's reading comes from the early part of the poetic dialogue. Job has just responded to the opening sally of his friends and then trails off into a soliloquy on the miseries of human life.

It is not too easy to see why this reading was chosen for today. Since the Old Testament readings usually fit the gospel, we may presume that Job's reflections on the miseries of human life are meant to provide a background for the healing work of Christ, of which the gospel speaks. It is from such miseries as Job speaks of that Christ comes to save us.

Responsorial Psalm: 147:1-6

The first stanza shows the original context for which this psalm was probably composed, namely, the rebuilding of Jerusalem and the return of the exiles from Babylon. It is a hymn of praise. Our verses are derived from the first of the three sections of which this psalm is composed and praise God for his mighty acts in the creation of the world and in Israel's salvation history. The refrain highlights the opening lines of the second stanza and prepares the way for the gospel, thus supporting our interpretation of the relation between the Old Testament reading and the gospel.

Reading II: 1 Corinthians 9:16-19, 22-23

This ninth chapter looks like a digression from the concerns of the preceding chapters—the problems of community life raised by the Corinthians in their letter to Paul. Chapter 9 is not introduced by the formula "Now concerning . . .," which signalizes the questions the Corinthians have raised. For that reason some have thought that chapter 9 is part of another letter in which Paul was defending his apostleship against the attacks of his opponents; other parts of the letter are thought to be found in 2 Corinthians. There is perhaps more to be said for this view than is commonly thought. Compare, however, next week's reading, which is linked to today's passage by the idea of being all things to all people.

Paul has been criticized by his opponents for not letting his converts pay him for his preaching. They accuse him of lack of confidence in his authority as an apostle. Paul agrees that he has a perfect right to ask for payment. Although he does not say so here, he did actually accept money from the churches of Macedonia. But there were special reasons for his not doing so in Corinth. It was part of his becoming all things to all people in order that he might by all means save some.

Why would receiving support hinder Paul's goal? We know that very soon after this letter—perhaps already when these words were being written, if it is part of a slightly later letter—false teachers turned up at Corinth, sponged on the congregation, and nearly won over their allegiance. Paul does not want the Corinthians to take him for a wandering preacher like his opponents, for then the Corinthians would misunderstand his gospel. They would take it for the preaching of "another Christ," maybe a miracle-worker, not Christ crucified as Paul preached him. For Paul, to preach the gospel means quite concretely and specifically to preach Christ crucified.

Gospel: Mark 1:29-39

Mark opens his account of Jesus' ministry in Galilee with a day of healing in Capernaum. After the first miracle of freeing the demoniac of an unclean spirit, which we read last week, comes the healing of Simon's mother-in-law, followed by a generalized summary of miracles at sundown and Jesus' attempt to flee in order to carry on his mission elsewhere.

It is possible that these Capernaum miracles had already been combined together in a pre-Marcan miracle catena. It has been suggested that Paul's opponents at Corinth, of whom we spoke in the preceding comment on the second reading, used such miracle catenae in order to support their own claims and to propagate their own false Christology. Just as Paul countered their claims with his preaching of Christ crucified, and himself as a suffering rather than a wonder-working apostle (see the second reading on the ninth Sunday of the year in series B), so by composing this Gospel Mark seeks to correct the false Christological inferences that could easily be drawn from these collections of miracle stories.

In today's passage Mark makes his point by showing that Jesus got up very early in the morning, first to pray and then to move elsewhere. Jesus flees from the crowds, despite Simon's plea that he should continue in a campaign that had brought so much success, and insists that he must move on. The words "that is why I came out" may refer, not to Jesus' departure from the house in Capernaum early that morning, but to the whole purpose of his mission in the world. In other words, Jesus regards his miracles as only a subordinate feature of his ministry. His main purpose is to preach (see Paul!) the good news of the coming kingdom. In this way Mark has corrected the pre-Marcan miracle catena, which presented the miracles as the principal feature of Jesus' ministry.

The silencing of the demons, a common motif in Mark, works in the same direction. The demons "knew him," as in other stories they recognize him to be the "Holy One of God." But to call him by that title simply because he is a wonder-worker would be dangerously misleading. Hence, the demons are enjoined to silence. Only the centurion at the foot of the cross can rightly confess Jesus as the Son of God, for the Jesus he sees is not the wonder-worker but the crucified One.

What role, then, do the miracles play in Mark? They are now seen as prefigurations of the ultimate messianic miracle, which is the cross and the resurrection. They are preliminary acts of healing that foreshadow the greatest act of healing.

This, then, provides the true context of meaning for today's responsorial psalm. It is not just that Jesus healed Simon's mother-in-law or the concourse of patients at sundown; it is that by his death on the cross, in whose benefits we partake at every Eucharist, he continues to heal the broken-hearted.

The Homily

Taken together, all the readings of this day are a proclamation of the healing power of Christ crucified. First the preacher can use the reading from Job to depict the misery of human life; then he/she can connect this with the healing ministry of Jesus in the gospel reading, and show that according to Mark these healings are foreshadowings of the supreme miracle, in which the broken-hearted are healed—the miracle of the cross. It was to preach Christ crucified that Paul, too, became all things to all people.

These readings might give the homilist an opportunity to impart a renewed understanding of anointing as a sacrament of healing.

SIXTH SUNDAY OF THE YEAR

Reading I: Leviticus 13:1-2, 45-46

The Book of Leviticus embodies much early legislation, but in its final form it is the work of the priestly school (P) after the Babylonian Exile. Today's reading is the beginning and the end of the section dealing with leprosy. This disease was not precisely what modern medicine classifies as Hansen's disease but included many other skin diseases that were temporary in character. Such diseases were serious not merely because of their contagious character, assumed or real, but because they were thought to make the patient spiritually unclean and therefore unfit to participate in the community's worship. Rules were set up for quarantine. The patient had to report to the priest, who diagnosed the malady, not as a physician, but as the minister of the Torah, and decided on the length of the quarantine, which involved a second visit to the priest—the one referred to in today's gospel. Obviously, this passage was selected as background reading for the gospel story.

Responsorial Psalm: 32:1-2, 5, 11

Psalm 32 is one of the traditional seven penitential psalms. Today it is regarded rather as a wisdom psalm (see the beatitudes of the first stanza) incorporating a thanksgiving. This psalm plays a key role in Paul's argument about justification and was prominent in the controversies of the Reformation (see the word "imputes" in the first stanza). Evidently this psalm is used today because leprosy serves as a symbol for human sin. Just as the leper reports to the priest, so the sinner comes and confesses to Yahweh (second stanza) and receives forgiveness from him (first stanza).

Reading II: 1 Corinthians 10:31–11:1

The context of these rather general-sounding remarks is a discussion of a further problem raised in the Corinthians' letter, namely, the question of eating things sacrificed to idols. Christians at Corinth invited out to dinner were often offered meat that had been previously used in pagan sacrifices. The butchers would naturally stock such meat. Was it permissible to eat it? As instructed Christians, the Corinthians knew that the idols to which the meat had been sacrificed were non-existent.

Paul insists, however, that the Christians should not vaunt their knowledge over against their weaker Christian brothers and sisters who had scruples (Jewish Christians, perhaps) or their pagan neighbors who took a malicious delight in making an issue of the matter to embarrass their Christian guests. So Paul lays down certain rules. It is not the food or drink in themselves that are holy, unholy, or neutral but the effect that the Christians' behavior will have on other persons. The scrupulous might be scandalized, and an opportunity to bear witness before one's pagan neighbors might be lost. So the general rule is: Do everything to the glory of God and try to please all people (in the sense of not giving them offense).

As a final rule of thumb, Paul says, "Be imitators of me." He can ask the Corinthians to do that without a trace of arrogance because he himself imitates the behavior of Christ. This must mean more than just following an external ethical example (Paul shows little knowledge of, or interest in, the earthly Jesus or the Jesus tradition). Rather, it must be something like what Paul hints at in Phil 2:6-11—an imitation of the path of Christ when he came down from heaven and humbled himself in his death on the cross. In his life as an apostle, Paul reproduces the same pattern of self-emptying, humiliation, and suffering. His whole life as an apostle is thus an epiphany of Christ.

Gospel: Mark 1:40-45

This short miracle story follows the basic threefold pattern common to all such stories. (1) The diagnosis: this is quite briefly indicated by the simple statement that the man was a leper and requested healing. (2) The cure: by word and touch. (3) The demonstration: the command to go and report to the high priest in accordance with the Levitical law (see the first reading).

The third point has been overloaded with the motif of the messianic secret, a fact that shows it to be Marcan redaction. The cured leper is told to say nothing to anyone, but he disobeys this command and his cure becomes the talk of the town. The result is that Jesus withdraws (unsuccessfully) to the country.

Mark adds this motif because of his polemic against the understanding of Jesus as merely a wonder-worker (see our comments on last Sunday's gospel). We saw that Mark uses commands to silence (there it is a command to the demon, here to the cured leper) in order to forestall the misunderstanding of Jesus and to point forward to the supreme miracle of the cross.

A puzzling feature here is the fact that the command to secrecy is disobeyed. The man goes out and freely talks about his cure (cf. similar features in Mark 1:34; 3:13; 5:43; 7:36; 8:26). Evidently we are dealing with a characteristic element in Mark's theory of the messianic secret. It is being repeatedly penetrated. Since we are dealing with a Marcan construction rather than a historical fact, we have to ask, not what Jesus' purpose was in giving an injunction he must have known would be broken, but what Mark intends theologically by these injunctions to secrecy and their constant breach. The answer would seem to be that Mark wants to show that while the messiahship of God is a mystery that must not be prematurely exposed (because it is rightly understood only in the light of the cross), yet because it is the mystery of God's presence at work in Jesus' words and works, it cannot really be suppressed but must come out. It comes out, for Mark, in the proclamation of the post-Easter Church, which the irresponsible gossip of the healed leper is meant to foreshadow. The difficulties disappear when we realize that at this point we are dealing not with history but with an artificial theological construction of the evangelist.

The Homily

The fact that leprosy symbolizes sin, like Mark's device of the messianic secret, compels us to take the first reading, the responsorial psalm, and the gospel as a proclamation of the power of the cross to cleanse from sin. It is this cleansing power that is mediated in the sacrament of absolution and experienced in the Eucharist. Here is the ultimate purpose of the epiphany of God in Jesus Christ. The homilist thus has an opportunity to deal with the sacrament of absolution.

The second reading provides material for ethical exhortation dealing with the theme "All things are lawful, but not everything is expedient," that is, the right use of Christian freedom and the need for respect for the scruples of the weaker brothers and sisters. The homilist might know of some concrete situation in the congregation to which this teaching could apply.

SEVENTH SUNDAY OF THE YEAR

Reading I: Isaiah 43:18-19, 21-22, 24b-25

To understand the very concrete meaning of this passage, we need to recall the situation in which Second Isaiah uttered his prophecies. The exile by which God had punished his people for their sins was about to end, and there would be a return to the holy land, conceived in terms of a second Exodus.

"The former things" refers to the first Exodus. Not that Exodus but a new one, the return, must henceforth be the focal point of the remembrance (anamnesis) in Israel's liturgy. But Israel's new liturgy is reared on the foundation of the confession of sin (vv. 22, 24b). As Hoskyns remarked in respect to Bach's Mass in B Minor, the *Kyrie eleison* provides the ground base for the liturgy. Nevertheless, in the midst of the anamnesis and the confession of sin, there breaks through Yahweh's word of forgiveness: "I am He who blots out your transgressions . . . and I will not remember your sins" (v. 25).

This reading was chosen to match the gospel reading, the story of the paralytic. This shifts the concrete application away from the original context to the Christian Exodus—the Church's experience of forgiveness of sin in Christ.

Responsorial Psalm: 41:1-4, 12-13

This psalm is a thanksgiving for a recovery from sickness. It is not obviously suitable as a response to the theme of the new Exodus from Babylon of which the first reading speaks, but when that reading is reinterpreted in the light of the healing of the paralytic, it becomes more fitting.

The first stanza consists of two beatitudes (cf. the psalm for last Sunday). The second stanza recalls the prayer for forgiveness uttered by the afflicted one. The third stanza returns to the theme of thanksgiving and closes with a doxology that does not belong to this particular psalm but forms the conclusion of the first book of the psalter. The refrain has the effect of calling attention away from the thanksgiving to the sick person's prayer. It thus prepares our minds to focus upon the plight of the paralytic, and therefore upon our own plight as sinners.

Reading II: 2 Corinthians 1:18-22

The second letter to the Corinthians is widely regarded today, not as a single letter written by Paul on one occasion, but as a collection of various letters written in the course of a major crisis in Paul's relations with the Corinthian community. According to this theory, our present passage comes from the letter Paul wrote when the crisis was over and the relationship with the community had been happily restored. During the crisis Paul had twice changed his plans. First he had paid a lightning visit to the Corinthians, a visit that had ignominiously failed to bring them around. Then he had postponed visiting them again to give Titus time to straighten things out. This frequent change of plans gave rise to the charge that Paul was fickle and unstable.

Paul defends himself (not, however, with the passion with which he had earlier defended his apostleship, but rather with a calm explanation) by arguing that his behavior has always been consistent. As usual, he goes back to first principles. His behavior was affirmative because it was an expression of the gospel, which is itself affirmative. The gospel is God's affirmation of all his promises. This affirmative action of God comes to each Christian personally in the moment of sacramental initiation, to which Paul now refers. In this, God has established and commissioned us, put his seal upon us, and given us his Spirit as a down payment (*arrhabōn;* RSV: "guarantee") of our final salvation.

Gospel: Mark 2:1-12

The healing of the paralytic has a long history behind it. We need not doubt that Jesus did cure a paralytic at some time in his ministry, and that the story therefore rests ultimately on an authentic reminiscence. At first it was probably told as a straightforward miracle story, with a *diagnosis* (the helplessness of the man, requiring the supreme effort of his friends to bring him to Jesus, vv. 1-4); the *cure* by Jesus' word (v. 11); the *demonstration* (the cured paralytic takes up his bed and walks home under his own power, v. 12); and the "choric ending." At a later stage in the tradition, the saying about the man's faith and the declaration of the forgiveness of sins must have been added (vv. 5, 10). Thus the story is made edifying. Simultaneously an independent dialogue developed between Jesus and his critics about his authority to forgive sins, reflecting the debates between the Christian community and the Jewish authorities over the Christian claim of imparting forgiveness of sins through the sacraments.

Finally, the evangelist combined the two traditions, inserting the conflict dialogue into the miracle story and thus making it serve his polemic against an interpretation of Jesus as being merely a wonder-worker. To sum up, Jesus heals the man as a sign of the ultimate messianic miracle— the forgiveness of sins through his death on the cross (Mark 10:45; 14:24).

The Homily

It is noticeable how clearly the readings in series B signalize the transition from the post-Epiphany season to Lent. First we had a series of readings in which there is an unmistakable pointer to the cross. Now today we have readings that call particular attention to the forgiveness of sins. This theme should be dealt with not so much in a Lenten way, with emphasis on human wretchedness, but rather as an extension of the Epiphany theme. The cross is the culmination of the supreme epiphany, of which the epiphanies in the life and ministry of Jesus are prefigurations. The purpose of Jesus' manifestation in his incarnation was precisely in order to take away our sins. The meaning of the incarnation does not lie in itself; it took place in order to make possible the atonement, which is the heart of the Christian message. This would seem to be the major theme for the homilist today.

The second reading suggests a different theme, and a somewhat intractable one—the affirmation of the divine promises in Christ. This theme can only come alive where the promises of God in the Old Testament are a vital issue for faith. Perhaps this notion could be translated today into the sense that modern people have of the "pull of the future" (Ernst Bloch). People have hopes and aspirations for a better world, and unless life is ultimately meaningless, these hopes will be ultimately fulfilled. The eschatology of the gospel proclaims that God has in fact given us, in Jesus Christ, the assurance of the fulfillment of our hopes for redemption. Christ is the affirmation of God's "promises"; he is the affirmation of the future that is the content of our highest aspirations.

EIGHTH SUNDAY OF THE YEAR

Reading I: Hosea 2:14b, 15b, 19-20

The burden of Hosea's prophecy (the precise date is uncertain; it is somewhere between 750 and 721, the fall of Samaria) is that the northern kingdom has been faithless to Yahweh and has succumbed to Baal worship. Partly because the Baal cult focused on the idea of the sacred marriage between the deity and its worshipers, and partly because of his own marriage experience (he married Gomer, who was unfaithful to him), the prophet pictures the relationship of Yahweh and his people in terms of a marriage. Yahweh had married Israel in the desert, but Israel had been faithless and had gone a-whoring after Baal. Yahweh, however, will woo Israel back, renew his covenant with her in the wilderness, and remain betrothed to her forever. Such is the import of our passage. Its selection was determined by the appearance of the same marriage metaphor in the gospel reading of today.

Responsorial Psalm: 103:1-4, 8, 10, 12-13

This is perhaps the best known of all the thanksgiving psalms in the whole psalter. The psalmist, speaking of his own individual experience of the purpose of God, transforms his personal gratitude into a corporate hymn of praise. Precisely what that personal experience was is difficult to say, but perhaps the reference to delivery from "the Pit" (sheol) in the second stanza suggests that he had been very ill and at the point of death. In his own personal experience he sees mirrored the experience of Israel throughout its salvation history (see verse 7, not used in this selection). The psalm praises God for his kindness and mercy, manifested particularly in the forgiveness of sins. It therefore serves as a fitting response to the reading from Hosea.

Reading II: 2 Corinthians 3:1b-6

This part of 2 Corinthians comes from Paul's so-called first apology. After he had sent off the first letter to the Corinthians, he got bad news from Corinth. False apostles had shown up there, and his converts had succumbed to their blandishments. These interlopers sought to undermine the Corinthians' confidence in Paul, already strained by the factions in his congregation (see 1 Corinthians), by discrediting Paul's apostolic authority. He therefore writes the first apology to defend himself against these attacks.

One of the charges leveled against Paul by the false apostles was that on his first visit he had brought no letters of recommendation with him from the other churches, a sure sign that he was no true apostle. It was customary for itinerant preachers in the Hellenistic world to secure such letters from the communities they visited and to carry them to their next port of call (see "to you, or from you" in verse 1). These letters would record the miracles they had performed, the ecstasies and visions they had displayed, and their ability to speak in tongues. Paul admits that he has no letters of commendation as his opponents do; he refuses to compete in that league. His true commendation, the true proof of his apostleship, is the converts produced by his preaching. Their faith is a "letter from Christ . . . written with the Spirit of the living God" on their hearts, not in pen and ink.

In the second paragraph Paul still has his eye on his opponents. They boasted of their miracles as personal achievements. They operated in a spirit of self-sufficiency. In his preaching of the word of the cross, however, Paul has no sufficiency of his own but relies wholly on the enabling power of God. The final phrases of our reading introduce a new idea. The discussion shifts from the contrast between the letters of recommendation and the work of the Spirit in the hearts of the believers to a new contrast between the written code and the Spirit. Again, we must suppose that Paul's opponents made much of the "written code." This is probably a reference to their allegorical interpretation of the Mosaic Law. To this, Paul opposes the "Spirit," which for him must mean the proclamation of Christ crucified.

Gospel: Mark 2:18-22

This pericope consists of a pronouncement story and two appended parables—the new patch and the wineskins. The pronouncement story has the usual threefold form: (1) the setting: John's disciples and the Pharisees are fasting; (2) the action: the people come and ask Jesus a question: "Why don't your disciples fast like John's?" (3) the pronouncement: "You don't fast at weddings." This is undoubtedly an authentic incident in the life of Jesus. In his reply he expresses the complete newness of what has come in his ministry: the joy of the kingdom of God is already breaking through.

The appended parables may have belonged to the original pronouncement, but it is more likely that they circulated independently before being joined to it. In any case, they fit their context perfectly, for both the pronouncement and the parables speak of the new bursting through the confines of the old.

The one saying that does not fit into the context is the assertion that the bridegroom will be taken away and then they will fast. Critics regard these words as a later addition. First, they identify the bridegroom allegorically with Jesus—an explicit post-Easter Christology. Second, they presume knowledge of Jesus' death. Third, they presuppose the reintroduction of the practice of fasting in the post-Easter community. "That day" may even refer quite specifically to the fast before the Christian Passover, in which the Church mourned for the giving up of the Savior to death.

By inserting this pericope here, Mark intends that the cross should overshadow the gospel narrative almost from the very beginning of the ministry. In this way he converts the Jesus tradition from a miracle saga into the proclamation of the cross.

The Homily

The context of the passage from Hosea (Gomer) justifies the homilist in expounding human marriage as a parable of the relation between Yahweh and Israel in the Old Testament, and Christ and the Church. Remember, though, that in doing so we are treating the question of the fasting pericope at the level of the evangelist's redaction, not at the level of the original Jesus tradition, and the homilist should be careful to present the nuptial theology as the teaching, not of the earthly Jesus, but of the early community. This theme can then be related to the Eucharist as the marriage supper of the Lamb.

The second reading provides many different lines of thought. The question of the false apostles is probably not immediately relevant to the contemporary life of the Church, but there are two other themes that are always relevant for meditation. The first is the idea that the true commendation of a parish minister is not in external success but is to be measured by the converts he or she has been instrumental in winning, the souls trained for the kingdom of heaven. The second theme is that the sufficiency of the Christian pastor comes not from self but from God, and what this means for each individual's prayer.

NINTH SUNDAY OF THE YEAR

Reading I: Deuteronomy 5:12-15

The fourth (third) commandment of the Decalogue is read today in preparation for the gospel reading, which consists of Jesus' conflicts with his opponents over his breaches of the sabbath.

It is to be noted that in Deuteronomy the fourth commandment is not merely a legal ordinance enacted as a ritual taboo. It is set in the context of remembrance (anamnesis) and is Israel's grateful response to the Exodus, the foundation event of its salvation history. In the Judaism of New Testament times, as we can see both from our Lord's ministry and from Paul, this "evangelical" setting of the Law was widely forgotten. Note that a different theological motivation for the observance of the sabbath is given in Exod 21, where it is interpreted as a memorial of Yahweh's rest after the six days of creation.

Responsorial Psalm: 81:2-7a, 9-10b

This is a psalm designed for liturgical use at the feast of Tabernacles (Passover is less likely). Like the weekly sabbath in Deuteronomy, the two annual feasts of Passover and Tabernacles were memorials of the Exodus. Hence the appropriateness of this psalm as a response to the reading of the fourth (third) commandment in its Deuteronomic version.

Reading II: 2 Corinthians 4:6-11

Like last Sunday's second reading, this passage comes from Paul's defense of his apostolate, the so-called first apology. He has been attacked for preaching a "veiled gospel" (4:3), probably because he does not prove his authority by spectacular miraculous displays. Paul concedes that sometimes his gospel is veiled, but in that case it is the fault, not of his gospel, but of his hearers; if they receive his words in faith, then his gospel is a manifestation of light, that is, authentic revelation. For the God who brought light out of darkness at the creation has also brought light in the new creation, the Christ-event (v. 6). Paul is perhaps recalling his own personal experience on the road to Damascus. The light of Christ shone in his heart to give him knowledge of the saving presence of God in the person of Jesus Christ.

But Paul is afraid that he has conceded too much to his opponents in speaking like this of the revelation of light in his ministry, so he hastens at once to qualify what he has just said. The treasure of God's revelation is committed to earthen vessels—the frail human personalities of his apostles. How frail they are is shown by the catalogue of Paul's apostolic sufferings, one of three such catalogues in 2 Corinthians (the others are in 6:4-10 and 11:22-33). Each of these catalogues has to be seen in contrast to the boasting of Paul's opponents. As we have mentioned, they claim that their miracles, their ecstasies and visions, their eloquence and brilliant allegorical exegesis of the Old Testament were epiphanies of the divine power. Paradoxically, Paul asserts the counterclaim that it is his apostolic sufferings that are the epiphanies of Christ. This is because for him the center of the gospel is not Jesus the miracle-worker but Christ crucified. Paul's apostolic sufferings are a manifestation of the crucified One. It is in the cross that light shines in the darkness.

Gospel: Mark 2:23–3:6 (long form); 2:23-28 (short form)

The two pericopes that make up the long form are linked by the common motif of our Lord's breach of the sabbath rule. The first episode is a pronouncement story with the usual threefold structure: (1) the setting: the disciples are walking through the grainfields and plucking ears of grain on the sabbath; (2) the action: the Pharisees object to this disregard of the sabbath regulations; (3) the pronouncement: Jesus defends his disciples' conduct by comparing it to David's eating of the showbread during his flight from Saul (note that in the Old Testament Abimelech, not Abiathar, was the high priest; the other evangelists understandably omit the name). The renewed introduction "And he said to them" suggests that the two further sayings about the sabbath are independent logia that were added later.

Let us first take the original pronouncement. We regard this as authentic to Jesus because it asserts an implicit rather than an explicit Christology. Jesus does not say that he is the Son of God or the Messiah but draws an analogy between the situation in David's time and that in his own. Each situation, David's and Jesus', was one of emergency and crisis in which the normal rules were suspended. David was in flight from Saul; in Jesus' ministry the kingdom of God is breaking through. Therefore, sabbath regulations must give way in both cases. Implicit is the thought that something (and therefore someone) greater than David is present.

The saying "The sabbath was made for man, not man for the sabbath" we take to be an authentic Jesus saying (it differs so completely from anything possible in contemporary Judaism and is perhaps also too radical for the early Church, for both Matthew and Luke omit it), but originally independent of the story to which it has been attached. We infer this from the overloading of the pronouncement and the new introduction given in verse 27, "And he said to them." Its radicality, however, must not be understood in a humanistic sense. It is not that all institutions, including religious ones, are for human use, to be observed or broken as best serves humanitarian interests; rather, the saying is evangelical in thrust. In contemporary Judaism the sabbath was regarded as a sign of the eschatological salvation intended by God, and now that that salvation is present in the ministry of Jesus, the sign that has pointed to that salvation must give way to the reality.

The last part of the saying, "so the Son of man is lord even of the sabbath," is problematical. It uses "Son of man" as a self-designation of the earthly Jesus in a way that many modern scholars find difficult to accept as authentic. While Jesus spoke of the coming Son of man in judgment and glory, and implicitly identified himself with that figure, he probably did not use the title as a direct self-designation. We are therefore inclined to think that this saying is an explanatory note added by the evangelist. Mark wants to guard precisely against a humanistic misunderstanding of the previous verse. It is only because Jesus dispenses his disciples from the sabbath regulations with messianic authority that they can break them and get away with it. They cannot take matters into their own hands.

The Homily

The Old Testament reading, the psalm, and the gospel suggest the theme of the sabbath—its Old Testament institution as a memorial of the Exodus and its New Testament fulfillment by the coming of the messianic salvation. This raises the question of the Christian understanding of Sunday. Sunday is not itself the sabbath—a misconception which first filtered into Christianity after the emperor Constantine made Sunday a weekly rest from toil and which reached its apogee in the Puritan sabbatarianism of Britain and New England. Rather, Sunday is the *fulfillment* of the sabbath. It is a day, not for legalistic prohibitions, but for joyous participation in the eschatological salvation to which the Old Testament sabbath looked forward. The Church has to face the challenge of thinking out anew the theology of Sunday. Today's readings give the homilist an opportunity to tackle this problem.

TENTH SUNDAY OF THE YEAR

Reading I: Genesis 3:9-15

The man and the woman had been tempted by the serpent and, contrary to God's command, had eaten of the forbidden tree. Note that in Genesis the serpent is not identified with Satan. That interpretation was developed in later Judaism and taken over into Christian theology. Our Lectionary assumes this later identification by coupling this reading with the Beelzebul controversy (gospel). Originally the serpent stood simply for the power of temptation. After the man and the woman have succumbed to temptation, God calls them to account and passes sentence on all three parties, including the serpent.

The story is in part a profound expression of the psychology of temptation and in part a primitive etiological myth, that is, a story explaining why things are as they are—why a serpent, unlike other animals, crawls on its belly, eats dust, and is hostile to the human race; why human beings, unlike animals, wear clothes and have a sense of shame. By the time of the Book of Wisdom, the serpent had come to be identified with the devil (Wis 2:24). In early Christianity (perhaps as early as 1 Tim 2:13-15), the seed of the woman was identified with Christ. Only in the most general way can the original text support this later development. What it tells us is that in the conflict between evil and humanity, humanity will finally win. It does not tell us how (we know that it happened in the Christ-event). The text shows "at the outset of redemptive history the note of promise and hope" (Ottley).

Having acquired this later interpretation, the text became known as the *protevangelium*, the first proclamation of the gospel in the Bible. That is why it is the first of the lessons read in the service of nine lessons and carols broadcast from the chapel of King's College, Cambridge, every Christmas eve.

Responsorial Psalm: 130:1-8

This psalm is both the cry of the individual in the depths of sin and death and also the cry of the people of God (note the shift at the end of the third through the fourth stanza from the individual to the community) for restoration from exile in the land of darkness and the shadow of death. This hoped-for corporate redemption occurred in the restoration from exile. As a response to the story of the Fall, the psalm is read today as a universal cry for salvation.

Reading II: 2 Corinthians 4:13–5:1

This passage, like those of the two previous Sundays, comes from the section of 2 Corinthians in which Paul is defending his apostleship against the attacks of the false apostles who showed up at Corinth. The false apostles relied on their own personal qualifications and achievements, such as they were. Paul relies only on his faith and that in which he believes. Paul first believes the gospel himself before he preaches it to others.

The faith of which Paul speaks is very simple: it is faith in God who raised Jesus from the dead, a faith that also carries with it the hope that God will raise both Paul himself and his converts. This hope is what makes Paul's sufferings as an apostle bearable. His apostolic labors result in an increase of grace, that is, more people are converted to faith and more bring forth the fruit of the Spirit. And all this, Paul says, is "to the glory of God."

In the second paragraph Paul reverts to the theme of his apostolic sufferings. They are taking a toll on his physical health, but Paul knows that his "inner nature" (the new Adam in him, the divine image) is being renewed in preparation for the final resurrection of the body. We do not yet, as the false apostles supposed, have resurrection life, but we have something that is starting in our inner nature—the renewal of the core of our ego, which will eventually be clothed by the resurrection body. It is this resurrection life that Paul is referring to when he contrasts the things seen and the things unseen, and says that the former are transient and the latter eternal. This must not be understood in a Platonic sense, as though there were two permanent orders of reality. The things that are eternal are partly future (the glorious resurrection life) and partly present (the inner transformation that is already taking place).

The third paragraph (5:1) is the beginning of a new section describing the resurrection hope. It is, however, logically connected with the preceding paragraph by the opening word, "For." It is because we know that we have a resurrection body awaiting us, says Paul, that we do not lose heart amid our present sufferings.

Gospel: Mark 3:20-35

This reading is one of the well-known "sandwiches" that occur in Mark's Gospel, that is, passages in which one event is inserted into another (cf. 5:21-43; 11:11-21; 14:53-72). In this case the two events are the coming of Jesus' "own" to take him home, with the consequent pronouncement about who are the true family of Jesus, and the Beelzebul controversy with the scribes. The purpose of these sandwiches is twofold. First, on a more superficial level, the event inside the respective sandwich provides time

for the other event to take place. Here Jesus' "own" have time, after setting forth from home, to reach him where he is. The second, more substantive purpose is to allow the one event to interpret the other. Both Jesus'
"own" and his scribal opponents misunderstand him, and he reacts to their
misunderstanding.

Let us take the Beelzebul controversy first. The structural pattern of
this story is that of a chiasm (abb'a'):

a) The scribes charge Jesus with being possessed by the devil.

b) The scribes charge that he casts out demons by the prince of demons.

b') Jesus answers the second charge (b) with the parabolic saying of
a house divided against itself.

a') Jesus answers the first charge (a): he is the stronger one who is
binding the strong one (Beelzebul) so that he may later plunder his goods.
This refers to Satan's overthrow when the kingdom of God finally comes.

Tacked on to the Beelzebul controversy is the very difficult saying
about blasphemy against the Holy Spirit, a saying that has played a
somewhat macabre role in the history of Christian piety. People have had
fantastic ideas that they have somehow inadvertently committed this un-
forgivable sin, and that in so doing they have condemned themselves un-
wittingly to everlasting damnation. Our text has nothing to do with such
fantasies. Nor does it, as more recent exegetes have often contended, have
the purely general meaning of calling evil good and good evil ("Evil, be
thou my good"). Rather, it has to do quite specifically with Jesus' exorcisms and his implicit Christological claim. To blaspheme against the Holy
Spirit is to fail to see that Jesus' works are the acts of the eschatological
power of God at work in his person. It is to deny the "theology of Jesus"
(to use Schillebeeckx's term, meaning what Jesus believed God was doing
in himself) or Jesus' implicit Christological self-understanding.

Now we turn to the outside of the sandwich (vv. 20-21 and 31-35).
In the RSV text as printed in the *Lectionary for Mass* (1970), we read that
Jesus' "friends" came to seize him. The Greek is *hoi par' autou*, which
literally means "those who customarily were around him." Since verses
31-35 are a continuation of this story, the phrase in question is elucidated
by verse 32: "Your mother and your brethren"—hence the RSV 1971
"family."

There is further ambiguity in the phrase "for they said, 'He is beside
himself'" (v. 21). Who are the "they"—the family of Jesus themselves or
other people? This is where the sandwich arrangement helps to interpret
the ambiguity. There is a deliberate correspondence between the role of
Jesus' family and that of the scribes. Both in various ways misunderstand
Jesus and his mission. The one party thinks that he is mad, the other that

he is in league with Beelzebul. This may shock those who take the birth stories in Matthew and Luke as literal facts. Such readers would object that Jesus' family, or at least his mother, already knew who he was from the start. But we must not harmonize Mark with Matthew and Luke in this way but must take Mark's text as it stands. The point of the saying in verse 35, "Whoever does the will of God is my brother, and sister, and mother," is that Jesus' "eschatological family" replaces his earthly family. To do the will of God means to respond to Jesus' eschatological message and to follow him. In this interpretation we follow the task force on Mary in the New Testament (see the report of that name, edited by Raymond E. Brown et al., p. 59). It is worth adding that in a footnote the task force observed: "However we cannot say that Mark means to exclude the family permanently from following Jesus. Presumably family members could become disciples of Jesus on the same basis as anyone else."

The Homily

The combination of the *protevangelium* from Gen 3 and the Beelzebul controversy from Mark 3 slants the reception of today's readings toward the proclamation of Jesus' victory over the powers of evil. This victory may be completely misunderstood (as Jesus' family did) or maliciously misinterpreted (as the scribes did). One needs the discernment of faith to see in Jesus the working of the Spirit of God. So, too, one needs the discernment of faith to behold in Jesus' disciples the eschatological family of God.

Today's homily could aim at producing the discernment of faith in Christ as the agent of God's saving action, and the Church as God's eschatological family. But, as the second reading reminds us, such discerning faith cannot remain hidden: "We believe, and so we speak." The congregation should therefore be urged to speak of their faith to others and to invite them to look at the things that are not seen, the true meaning of human life.

ELEVENTH SUNDAY OF THE YEAR

Reading I: Ezekiel 17:22-24

Together with the more usually cited Dan 4:9, 20-21, Ezekiel's allegory of the cedar tree is a source of the imagery of the mustard bush in the gospel reading. The cedar stands for the restoration of the Davidic monarchy after the Exile. The shoot or twig (see Isa 11:1) refers to a descendant of Jehoiachin, the last Davidic king before the Exile. The beasts and birds represent the nations of the earth. This indicates that the prophecy expects the kingdom after the return from exile to be more than just the mere restoration of the status quo before the Exile; in fact, it is to be the realization of the messianic kingdom. It is therefore legitimate to say that this prophecy finds its ultimate fulfillment in the kingdom of Christ, of which the Church on earth is a foretaste.

Responsorial Psalm: 92:1-2, 12-15

This psalm of thanksgiving is preoccupied with the theme of moral retribution. Yahweh is praised for his mighty acts, especially in rewarding the righteous with prosperity, so that they become like fruitful trees. According to the Mishnah, this psalm was used at the morning sacrifice, particularly on the sabbath. It expresses the Deuteronomic theology, a viewpoint that has to be balanced by that of other works such as Psalm 73 or the Book of Job, which recognize that the righteous do not always prosper and that reward often seems to go to the wicked.

Reading II: 2 Corinthians 5:6-10

We are still in that part of 2 Corinthians where Paul is defending his apostleship against the attacks of the false apostles. His emphasis on his apostolic sufferings had led him to speak about his confident hope of resurrection. Despite the fact that the gospel is committed to frail earthen vessels, there is no room for despondency. In speaking once more of his hope, Paul drops the metaphor of a "tent" for this frail earthly existence and speaks directly of the body. He can, he says, face the dissolution of the body, already presaged in his apostolic sufferings, with confidence because God will replace it with the resurrection body. And that will be a great gain, for in this present body we are absent from the Lord; we are certainly "in" Christ already as members of his body but not yet "with" Christ (as the false apostles taught, overemphasizing the "already").

In the letters of his middle period, Paul is coming to take seriously the possibility of his own death before the parousia. This hope of resurrection is not just a dreaming about "pie in the sky when I die" but provides a powerful motivation for life now—to please the Lord. It must be our aim now to please the Lord because at the parousia we will all have to appear before the judgment seat of Christ. This belief in a last judgment according to our works is not a hangover from Paul's earlier Judaism, nor is it inconsistent with his message of justification by faith and grace alone. Faith must, if it is genuine, work in love. We are responsible for our sins and failures even if our good works are the fruit of the Spirit. If we receive a reward for our good works, this reward is not a prize for good behavior but the fulfillment of our human destiny.

Gospel: Mark 4:26-34

This reading consists of two little parables—the seed growing secretly and the mustard seed—and a generalizing conclusion to the collection of parables in Mark 4. This collection of parables, probably made already at the pre-Marcan stage, was concerned with seed and sowing. They are strung together with the formula "And he said."

Each parable, it will be remembered, contains one main point, which is its basic message. The parable of the seed growing secretly seeks to inculcate trust on the part of Jesus' disciples that the kingdom, already hiddenly at work in Jesus' ministry, will in God's good time become manifest and be consummated. It is possible that the parable was originally a polemic against the Zealot policy of armed rebellion against Rome as a means of bringing in the kingdom. It is most important to avoid interpreting this parable by emphasizing the idea of growth, appealing though that may be to modern botanical knowledge and modern evolutionary ideology. The ancients did not understand the process of growth as we do; they thought only of the contrast between the seed and the grown plant or tree. Hence, the basic point of the parable is the contrast between the insignificant beginnings of Jesus' ministry and the final cosmic event of the coming of the kingdom of God.

In interpreting the second parable, that of the mustard seed, the same considerations apply. It does not speak of the evolutionary growth of the kingdom or the Church. The only difference between the two parables is that the first emphasizes that the farmer can do nothing to produce or hasten the end of the process, whereas the second emphasizes exclusively the contrast between the small beginnings and the final consummation.

The Homily

As long as we avoid the notion of evolutionary growth and the unqualified identification of the Church with the kingdom of God (the Church is not the kingdom of God but the place where the kingdom of God is proleptically manifested), it would be admissible to see the great tree under whose shade birds of every sort can nest as a picture that is proleptically realized in the catholicity of the Church, the society of human beings on earth in which peoples of all races, classes, and nations come together.

There is a wealth of themes to be gathered from the second reading, but the caption helps us to zero in on the idea of future judgment as a motivation for present Christian living—to be well pleasing to the Lord. It could be pointed out that the hope of heaven is not a narcotic or a drug that immunizes us against concern with the affairs of this world or with our own behavior in daily life, but it provides a sound motivation for upright behavior in dealing with those affairs.

TWELFTH SUNDAY OF THE YEAR

Reading I: Job 38:1, 8-11

Each of Job's comforters has had his say, and Job has responded to their arguments. None of them answered his basic problem: how could this suffering be explained in view of the fact that he had walked uprightly with God. Now Yahweh himself finally speaks to Job "out of the whirlwind"—a typical device to denote a theophany. Yahweh's answer is to assert his utter transcendence and the inapplicability of all human criteria to judge his ways. Job was not present at creation! Our reading selects the creation of the sea, with its assertion of God's sovereignty over it (v. 11), thus preparing for the gospel reading about the stilling of the storm.

Responsorial Psalm: 107:23-26, 28-31

In this psalm four different groups of persons are invited to give thanks to God. The fourth group consists of those who have been rescued from a storm at sea. Thus, the psalm matches the first reading and the gospel. The key words linking the psalm with the gospel occur in verse 29: "he made the storm be still." In fact, this verse is held by some to be part of the literary background for the gospel reading.

Reading II: 2 Corinthians 5:14-17

We have to see this passage in the context of Paul's first apology, which we discussed over the past few Sundays. Paul is contrasting the motivation of his own ministry with that of the false teachers by whom the Corinthians are captivated. This impelling motivation is the love of Christ, concretely actualized in his death upon the cross. Hence, it produces a pattern of apostolate that is itself marked by the cross: Paul, like all true Christians, but unlike the false teachers, lives no longer for himself but for him who died and was raised.

The meaning of the second paragraph is much controverted. What does Paul mean when he speaks of regarding Christ from a human point of view? The fact that he acknowledges that he himself had once shared this point of view has led many to find the clue in Paul's pre-conversion conception of Christ. If "Christ" is used here as a proper name, the meaning would then be that Paul, before his conversion, had known Jesus in the flesh but now knows him as the risen Lord. The trouble with this interpretation is that it makes Paul treat the earthly history of Jesus as an episode of the past in a way that was characteristic of the Corinthian Gnostics in 1 Corinthians. It is no wonder that one critic (Schmithals) suggested that it is a Gnostic gloss added to the text.

An alternative view is to take "Christ" here, not as a proper name, but as "Messiah." Paul is then saying that as a Jew he accepted Jewish (political?) notions of messiahship, but when he became a Christian he rejected the view in favor of the message of the crucified and risen One. This interpretation has more to commend it, but it requires taking the words "from a human point of view" adjectively, as a modifier of Messiah. In Paul, however, this phrase, when used pejoratively, as it clearly is here, is used adverbially. If we keep in mind the concrete situation in which the first apology was written, everything seems to fall into place perfectly. Paul calls the Christology of his opponents a way of knowing Christ "from a human point of view." They view Christ as a "divine man" or a wonder-worker and claim that this is to regard him from a superhuman point of view. Paul, however, castigates this view of Christ as fleshly, sarkic (that is, "a human point of view"). To regard Christ as merely a wonder-worker is precisely that. He is rather the crucified and risen One, and only as such has he opened the new age.

The apparent contradiction between this realized eschatology of 2 Corinthians and the rejection of realized eschatology in 1 Corinthians (where the Corinthians asserted that in baptism they had already been raised) is explained once we realize that the situation in 2 Corinthians is completely different from that in 1 Corinthians. There the problem was the local Gnostics; here the problem is the wandering preachers who interpret Jesus as an earthly divine man.

Paul's theology is thus intensely situational. In response to one situation he can make a point that is completely contradicted when he faces another situation. It shows how careful we must be in trying to systematize Paul's theology—or any New Testament theology, for that matter.

Gospel: Mark 4:35-41

First, let us try to reconstruct the history of the tradition of this pericope. What historical nucleus underlies the story? Three things we can say for certain are historical facts: (1) the general scene—Jesus and his disciples crossing the lake in a boat and encountering a storm; (2) the impression of authority that Jesus gave in all that he said or did; (3) the data about Jesus' family.

The story has, however, been developed in the tradition along lines that were already familiar from the Old Testament, where Yahweh stills the raging sea and where prophets still storms (see Jon 1:15). The story is now told to evoke an answer to the question "Who is this?" The answer is that Jesus is the eschatological prophet in whom Yahweh (see the first reading and the psalm) is epiphanously present.

Mark in turn has redacted this story. First, he has linked it to the parable collection in chapter 4 (note the opening words, "On that day . . . said to his disciples"—"that day" is the day of parabolic teaching when Jesus promised the disciples that the mysteries of the kingdom of God would be disclosed to them). The stilling of the storm is part of the disclosure. But the disciples do not yet understand. Hence the insertion of the typically Marcan words "Why are you afraid? Have you no faith?" This reproach to the disciples and the fact that they raise a question without being answered point the reader to Peter's confession in chapter 8, where an incomplete faith is expressed, and beyond that to the cross and the resurrection, when the disciples will finally come to realize who Jesus truly is (Mark 16:7).

The Homily

The Old Testament reading, the psalm, and the gospel are linked together by the motif of the stilling of the storm. The homilist could relate this to the storms through which the Church (which already in the New Testament is typified as a boat) is passing and proclaim the power of Christ to still these storms today if we truly cling to him.

The second reading suggests that the homilist might identify some contemporary ways of regarding Christ from a human point of view (for example, Superstar?) and proclaim him as the one who died and was raised, through whom we too become a new creation.

THIRTEENTH SUNDAY OF THE YEAR

Reading I: Wisdom 1:13-15; 2:23-24

The controlling reading, as usual the gospel, is the raising of Jairus' daughter, with its proclamation of Christ as victor over death. The reading from Wisdom provides the Old Testament presuppositions for this victory (Protestants can be assured that although this reading comes from one of the "apocryphal" books, the doctrine it asserts is an interpretation of Gen 1–3, consonant with Paul's teaching).

The world as God created it was essentially good (Wis 1:14; see Gen 1). Humans, in particular, were created to be immortal (Gen 3 contrariwise seems to assume that they were created mortal), but Wisdom deduces from the fact of their creation in God's image (Gen 1:26) that they were created immortal, and Paul seems to share this assumption when he speaks of death, as does the last phrase in Wis 1:14 here, as an alien intruder into the world, consequent upon sin (Rom 5:12). Finally, Wis 2:24 equates the serpent in Gen 3 with the devil. This is the first known instance of this identification, which is found also in the New Testament, including Paul (see 2 Cor 11:3), though not mentioned in Rom 5.

The doctrine of this passage appears at first sight to conflict with the self-evident truth that death is a biological fact. It is arguable, however, from the connection of immortality with righteousness (see Wis 1:15), that the author is speaking of moral and spiritual death, as Paul undoubtedly does in Rom 5. In that case, biological death has more than a merely physical meaning; it is the ultimate sign of human beings' alienation from God, the "sacrament of sin" (P. Althaus). It is death in this sense—not physical death *per se,* as Christians still have to die—that Christ overcomes by his death on the cross.

Responsorial Psalm: 30:1, 3-5, 10-11a, 12b

According to its title, this psalm was originally associated with the restoration of the temple in the time of the Maccabees in 164 B.C. In that case, the original reference to "death" would be the catastrophes of the desecration of the temple by Antiochus Epiphanes and the Jewish war of independence. It thus becomes a psalm of national thanksgiving. Here, however, it is a psalm celebrating Christ's victory over death, as adumbrated in the gospel reading.

Reading II: 2 Corinthians 8:7, 9, 13-15

As usual, the second reading has no direct connection with the other readings but simply appears in course. Chapter 8 of 2 Corinthians is concerned entirely with Paul's collection for the Jerusalem church. He had undertaken to raise this money several years previously at the apostolic conference (Gal 2) and had faithfully carried out his side of the agreement. Accordingly, he had proposed to the Corinthian converts that they take part in the collection and suggested how it could be organized (1 Cor 16:1-4).

Meanwhile, however, the great crisis in the relations between Paul and the Corinthians had supervened, the result of the appearance of the false prophets in Corinth. In the ensuing fray (involving a sudden and disastrous visit to Corinth by Paul), the severe letter, identified by many with 2 Cor 10-13, a visit by Titus, the Corinthian *volte-face,* and the writing of the letter of thanksgiving (2 Cor 1:1-2:13; 7:5-16), the collection had been forgotten. Now that the crisis is over, Paul can return to the subject (2 Cor 8; 9, thought by some to be two separate communications on the subject). In the course of this correspondence, Paul musters every argument he can think of to encourage the Corinthians to proceed with their fundraising drive. The strongest motivation for Christian giving is specified in verse 9—gratitude for the riches Christ has brought through his self-emptying in the incarnation (for the doctrine, see Phil 2:6-11).

Gospel: Mark 5:21-43 (long form); 5:21-24, 35-43 (short form)

It is characteristic of Mark's Gospel for one pericope to be inserted in the middle of another. Here the story of the woman with the hemorrhage is inserted into the narrative of the raising of Jairus' daughter. It is disputed whether this insertion is due to the evangelist's redaction or whether it came to him in this form from the tradition.

The older form critics took the latter view, supposing that the insertion was a device to explain the delay between the arrival of the messenger from Jairus and Jesus' arrival at the house, a delay that meant that the little girl was dead by that time. Later redaction critics are inclined to see in the insertion an attempt by the evangelist to allow one miracle to interpret the other. The healing of the woman with the hemorrhage is interpreted as an act of salvation (vv. 28, 34); so also is the raising of Jairus' daughter. Each is therefore a prefigurement of Christ's salvation from death. The shorter reading simply omits the insert.

We first offer a reconstruction of the history of the tradition of the two stories. On the historical level, we may suppose that Jesus *healed* the daughter of Jairus from a critical but not fatal illness (v. 23). In the tradition the narrative was then modeled on the raisings by Elijah and Elisha and served to proclaim Jesus as the eschatological prophet. The background of this story seems to be thoroughly Palestinian.

The story of the woman with the hemorrhage, on the other hand, seems to be more Hellenistic. The woman's action in touching the healer's garment suggests that she thought of Jesus as *theios anēr* ("divine man"). This aspect is enhanced by Luke, who adds that Jesus knew that power (*dynamis*) had gone out of him when the woman touched him. Mark seeks to correct this notion by transforming the woman's superstitious act into an expression of faith, and the whole episode into a personal encounter with the Savior.

In addition, by combining the two episodes Mark inserts at the end of the raising his motif of the messianic secret (v. 43a). From a historical point of view, the command to keep silent about the raising would be absurd, but as a theological device it makes sense. What Mark is saying is that the true significance of the act of raising is not yet apparent. It is only at the resurrection that the veil of secrecy over Jesus will be lifted (see Mark 9:9), and therefore it is only then that Jesus will be seen as victor over death. The raising of the little girl is not itself Jesus' victory over death (the girl had to die sometime, and certainly did). It was only a parable or prefiguration of the act by which Jesus overcame death in its existential sense. The healing of the woman with the hemorrhage prefigures Christ's death as a cleansing from sin.

The Homily

The gospel, together with the Old Testament reading and the psalm, has the strongest claim on the homilist's attention today. This would involve (1) an existential interpretation of physical death as the sign and seal and sacrament of sin; and (2) the proclamation of Christ as the one who by dying on the cross on our behalf has cleansed us from our sin and deprived death of its sting, thus restoring us to communion with God and to life that cannot be destroyed by physical death (see Rom 8:35-39).

The second reading would suggest a homily on the topic of Christian stewardship and its motivation in the generosity of God in Christ, who became poor that we might be rich.

FOURTEENTH SUNDAY OF THE YEAR

Reading I: Ezekiel 2:2-5

The choice of this reading is governed by the gospel, which presents Jesus as a prophet rejected by his own people. Ezekiel likewise was sent to his own people and was warned that they might reject him. This passage comes from the first of four different accounts of Ezekiel's call. He marks a new departure in Old Testament prophecy. Ever since the first prophet (Amos), the concept of the "Spirit" had been avoided by the prophets. It was originally too much associated with ecstatic prophecy and Baal worship, but by Ezekiel's time it could safely be brought out and used, for by now it had been purified of its older, questionable associations. Henceforth, endowment with the Spirit will be a characteristic of Yahweh's prophets. Then it will pass into New Testament usage. "Son of man" simply means "man"; it is not a messianic title. It denotes a man in contrast to God, the human bearer of the divine message.

Responsorial Psalm: 123:1-4

This is a community psalm. A representative of Israel pleads for mercy on behalf of the whole community. What concrete situation is envisaged is no longer determinable. It is a beautiful cry for help (note especially *servant/master, maid/mistress* as parables of Israel's relation to Yahweh). But it is not easy to see precisely what connection the psalm has with the reading from Ezekiel. Perhaps the point lies in the final stanza, in which case it can be taken as a lament on the part of the prophet that his message is rejected and he receives nothing but contempt from his hearers.

Reading II: 2 Corinthians 12:7-10

This passage is from the so-called severe or tearful letter (2 Cor 10–13), written at the height of Paul's controversy over the false apostles who were undermining his influence among the Corinthians. It thus takes us back to an earlier stage in the story of Paul's relationship with the Corinthians than that envisaged in the previous weeks' readings.

Paul had been unfavorably contrasted with the false prophets, who boasted of their ecstasies, visions, miracles, etc. The Apostle replies that whenever he was tempted to preen himself like his opponents, he was pulled up short by a "thorn in the flesh" to keep him from being elated. There has been much discussion about the precise meaning of Paul's affliction. Here he speaks of being "buffeted" (the RSV "harass" is weak). This has often been taken to imply epilepsy, whose convulsions would throw him to the ground. Others have deduced from Gal 4:14-15 that Paul had some sort of ophthalmic condition. The trouble is, as Lietzmann remarked, that the patient has been dead for nineteen hundred years! This makes diagnosis difficult.

The two references contradict each other and should probably be taken metaphorically. The Galatians would have given Paul their most valuable physical organs, that is, they would have done anything for him in his illness. The sickness did not literally throw him to the ground but left him depressed. Karl Bonhoeffer, the father of Dietrich and a medical authority, thought that it might have been chronic depression, a phenomenon often accompanied by spells of supranormal activity. The elder Bonhoeffer characterized it as the result of a "hyperrhythmic temperament." It seems safest to leave it at that. Paul does not complain about it but uses it positively. It brings home to him that the grace of God, and only that, is all he needs to carry out his apostolic labors. His life is thus an epiphany of the cross of Christ. That is what it means for him to be an apostle.

Gospel: Mark 6:1-6

Once again we must try to reconstruct the history of this pericope. It was claimed by the earlier form-critics that the whole episode was constructed as a vehicle for the saying about the prophet being honored everywhere except in his own country. But other features of the story have a ring of historicity. Jesus was more than a prophet to the early Christian community, and therefore it is unlikely that they would have constructed a scene for such a saying without modifying it in the light of their post-Easter Christology. The family relationships of Jesus also are surely based on historical reminiscence. Moreover, it is unlikely that the post-Easter Church would have recorded that Jesus *could* do no mighty work in his hometown unless this had been the case. So we may presume an authentic memory of an occasion when Jesus was rejected in his own native town. The memory was then cast into narrative form by the primitive community in order to reassure itself when the kerygma was rejected by their own people. Their Master had suffered a like fate.

Finally, Mark takes the story, adds verse 1 as an introductory link and verse 6b as a generalizing conclusion. The exceptive qualification in verse 5b has clearly been added to mitigate the offense in verse 5a, though it is unclear whether this addition was made by Mark or by the pre-Marcan tradition.

By inserting this pericope in its present position (Luke has another version of the same episode right at the beginning of the ministry), Mark introduces one of his reminders of the impending passion into the early part of his narrative (see 3:6, which, like this episode, also occurs at the end of a major structural section of the Gospel). Mark is thus telling his readers that Jesus was not merely a successful wonder-worker; even his miraculous deeds led to his rejection and to the cross.

The Homily

The first reading and the gospel give us the theme of rejection. If the Church is true to its mission, it will inevitably encounter rejection. Of course, we must not put unnecessary stumbling blocks—for example, outmoded terminology, philosophical concepts, etc.—before modern men and women and prevent them from hearing the Christian message. But there are limits to our accommodation of the gospel to fit modern conditions. The scandal of the cross must never be mitigated. The gospel must never be watered down so that "Jones can swallow it" (a memorable phrase coined by the late Monsignor Ronald Knox in his Anglican days). The basic responsibility of the Church is not to win converts on any terms but to proclaim the Christian message faithfully "whether they hear or refuse to hear" (first reading).

The second reading prompts a consideration of the way a Christian should face depression. Paul suggests that it can be used positively, driving the believer to rely solely on the grace of God and to find in him strength in his or her weakness.

FIFTEENTH SUNDAY OF THE YEAR

Reading I: Amos 7:12-15

This reading appears to have been chosen to go with the mission of the Twelve in the gospel. Amos is sent to God's people in Israel (the northern kingdom) as the Twelve were sent to God's people in Galilee.

The passage places before us two contrasting conceptions of religion— one represented by Amaziah, priest of Bethel, and the other represented by the prophet Amos. Amaziah thought of religion in "civil" terms. It existed to promote loyalty to the status quo—the royal house and patriotism. Bethel was the king's sanctuary and the temple of the kingdom, a sort of national cathedral. Amaziah thought of his own role as that of a court chaplain, whose job was to prophesy "smooth things."

Amos, however, was not a card-carrying member of the prophetic guild (whose members viewed their duties much as Amaziah did his); he was an outsider whom God had called to denounce the government for its injustices and inhuman policies. We do not get the substance of Amos' message here, only his basic attitude. It is to deliver the word of the Lord, not to take the professional line of the court chaplains and spokespersons for an uncritical patriotism.

Responsorial Psalm: 85:8ab, 9-13

In commenting on this identical selection on the nineteenth Sunday of the year in series A, we pointed out that the original context of this psalm is uncertain, but that its theology reminds one of Second Isaiah and that its plausible context is the impending return from exile. While suitable for any occasion, it does not appear to have any particular connection with today's readings.

156

Reading II: Ephesians 1:3-14 (long form); 1:3-10 (short form)

The opening thanksgiving of Ephesians (which we regard as Deutero-Pauline) is suggested by Paul's thanksgiving in 2 Cor 1:3ff, and is today widely thought to be made up from a liturgical hymn. This liturgical material runs through verse 14. The shorter version is obtained simply by lopping off the latter portion, which is printed as a separate paragraph in the rsv. In the Greek both parts consist of a simple sentence.

The contents suggest that these verses were taken from a baptismal hymn. They speak of (1) the election and predestination of the believer before the creation; (2) the Christ-event; (3) the gnosis conveyed in Christian experience; (4) the definition of gnosis as the cosmic scope of salvation history; (5) the distinction between "we" (Jewish Christians) and "you" (Gentile Christians), and the sealing of the latter with the Holy Spirit in their initiation. It may reasonably be conjectured that the distinction between Jewish and Gentile Christians has been introduced into the hymn by the author of Ephesians, thus adumbrating his major theme throughout the letter. That theme is the unity of both parties in the one Church. Thus, the hymn would have concluded with a celebration of the sealing of all the newly baptized. It will be seen that the short form omits an essential part of the hymn.

Gospel: Mark 6:7-13

It was claimed by some of the early form critics that the synoptic missions were creations of the post-Easter community. If this were so, one would have expected Jesus' charge to reflect the Church's post-Easter Christological kerygma, whereas in point of fact the terms of their mission in both Mark and Q are exactly those of the earthly Jesus. Mark does not specify, as Q does, that they were charged to proclaim, as Jesus did, the inbreaking of the kingdom of God, but he implies it in (a) the eschatological haste (no bread, etc.); (b) the warning of possible rejection as Jesus' message was rejected; (c) the statement that they preached repentance (see Mark 1:14); (d) their performance of exorcisms and healings. "We must regard as authentic the commission to act like Jesus himself in proclaiming that God's kingdom has drawn near and in doing mighty works" (F. Hahn).

It is equally clear that the four forms of the charge (Mark, Q, Matthew, Luke) tended to expand or reduce the original nucleus in accordance with contemporary needs and practices. Thus, in Mark, as we have seen, we find that the reference to proclaiming the kingdom of God has been dropped (Mark knew only a Christological kerygma in his Church), and the reference to exorcism and healing is extended to include a specific mention of oil (see Jas 5:14 for this Church practice).

What function does this charge play in Mark? Mark clearly is very interested in the Twelve. They are sometimes presented in a highly negative way, as blind and unperceptive to the mystery of Jesus and his mission. Here, however, they are presented in a positive light. They are entrusted with the same message and mission as the Master himself. Clearly, Mark wishes to hold before his Church this twofold possibility. In Mark's Church the successors of the apostles are simultaneously warned and encouraged. They may misunderstand Jesus and, in the supreme hour of persecution, fail their Lord, as the disciples forsook him and fled; or they may become true witnesses to the gospel message, as the disciples did briefly in Jesus' earthly lifetime and as they did for good after the risen One had commissioned them in Galilee (Mark 16:7).

The Homily

The first reading and the gospel indicate a homily on the mission of the Church. The following points can be brought out: (1) What matters supremely, more than apparent success or failure, is the Church's fidelity to the gospel message. Amos failed at Bethel, and the Twelve were warned that people might refuse to hear them. (2) Particularly, the word of God must be delivered in the teeth of opposition from the advocates of "civil religion." (A possible case in point: Civil religion says that draft evaders must bear the full brunt of their punishment for life; the gospel proclaims forgiveness.) (3) There is an eschatological haste about the Church's message. The Church may be required to divest itself of much of its excess baggage accumulated over the centuries if the message is to be delivered in freedom.

The second reading, in either its short or long form, offers several possibilities for the homilist. One could speak about the ultimate purpose of God to unite all things in himself, drawing on the insights, perhaps, of Teilhard de Chardin, the theology of hope, and/or process theology. This ultimate hope of unity of all things must then be exhibited as the impelling motivation for present action in human society and in Christendom toward a closer approximation to the ultimate goal. (See also *Faith and Order*, Louvain, 1971).

One might also speak on various aspects of the baptismal mystery— the initial redemption conveying "the forgiveness of our trespasses," or the wisdom and insight we presently have into God's ultimate purpose for the universe, or the relation between the gifts of the Spirit and the final blessedness of the redeemed (longer form). If the homilist opts for the second reading, he/she must be careful not to be too abstract but must endeavor to relate the biblical message to the concrete situation of the congregation.

SIXTEENTH SUNDAY OF THE YEAR

Reading I: Jeremiah 23:1-6

The first reading is suggested by the observation in today's gospel that Jesus had compassion on the multitude "because they were like sheep without a shepherd." In ancient Israel, as in other cultures of the ancient Near East, the figures of king and shepherd were very closely associated. David the shepherd boy was taken from among the flock to be king over the united kingdoms of Judah and Israel. Although we should not sentimentalize the idea of shepherding (as talk of the "gentle Shepherd" might tempt us to do, although the Hebrew word for "shepherd" also means "to rule"), it is still true that the image of shepherd contains within it the notion of feeding and providing for the flock—in fact, much of what we associate with pastoral care.

Jeremiah, writing toward the end of the reign of Zedekiah just before the final captivity in 587, looks back over recent reigns and condemns the last kings of Judah as shepherds who have misgoverned their flock. The denunciation concludes with the promise of a "righteous Branch" ("The Lord is our righteousness" is a play on the name Zedekiah). This scion of the house of David will be the Messiah, the ideal king. Jeremiah, of course, was thinking purely in historical terms—of the restoration of the Davidic monarchy after a period of exile. But his words kindled a hope in Israel which, in the perspective of Christian faith, finds its ultimate fulfillment in Jesus the Christ.

Responsorial Psalm: 23:1-6

The first two stanzas of this psalm, the most familiar in the psalter, picture Yahweh as shepherd, while the third and fourth stanzas portray him as host at a banquet in the temple. The royal theology of Judah found no contradiction between the notion that both Yahweh and the king were Israel's shepherd, for the king was the sacramental embodiment of Yahweh's kingship and shepherdhood. Christian faith sees the same dual notion fulfilled in Jesus Christ. He is the one through whom God exercises his eschatological rule and shepherds his people. The second stanza suggests that it is particularly at the Eucharistic banquet that Christ exercises his shepherding function.

Reading II: Ephesians 2:13-18

This passage is the theological core of the letter to the Ephesians. Looking back over the career of Paul, the Deutero-Pauline writer contemplates the results of the Apostle's work. Jew and Gentile have been brought together into a single community, the body of Christ. Christ on the cross (that is, by his death as the event of salvation) has fulfilled and abolished the law, not as moral demand, but as the way of salvation. Christians now keep the law *because* they have been saved by grace, not *in order to* earn salvation. Now both Jew and Gentile have access in one body to the Father. "Access" is a liturgical term denoting the approach to God in worship. Note the Trinitarian character of the final sentence: through Christ in one Spirit to the Father. Note, too, that verse 13 alludes to Isa 57:19, while verse 17 cites and provides its Christian application. This indicates the sermonic quality of Ephesians.

Gospel: Mark 6:30-34

This excerpt is highly composite. Verses 30-33 form a link between the mission of the disciples and the feeding of the multitude. They bear clear signs of Mark's editorial work. Verse 30 points back to the mission of the Twelve (here only in Mark are the Twelve called "apostles," a term that was not originally a title but functional). Verse 31, often used in connection with retreats, points forward to the feeding. Verse 32 introduces a favorite theme of Mark's—teaching given in secrecy to the Twelve, though the fulfillment of this intention is delayed until chapter 8 (Caesarea Philippi). Verse 34 is the beginning of a new pericope, the feeding of the multitude (cf. the variant in 8:2). The reference to the shepherd motif is probably pre-Marcan and gives a special emphasis to the miraculous feeding. But the note about teaching looks redactional; Mark frequently emphasizes Jesus' teaching activity without giving the content of his teaching.

The Homily

It is the figure of the shepherd (first reading, psalm, and gospel) that dominates today's readings, and that is probably what the homilist will choose to expound. One could show how Christ still performs this function of shepherding in the liturgy. In the first part of the liturgy, Christ teaches his flock through his word, a notion that Mark emphasizes as an essential function of the shepherd. In the second half of the liturgy, Christ prepares a banquet for his flock (third stanza of the psalm). Thus the thought of Christ as shepherd can be shown to be the background of the Church's understanding of the ministry as pastoral. The pastor is not a substitute for the absence of Christ but the human vehicle through whose functions Christ renders himself present. The picture of Christ as the host at his table (third stanza of the psalm) provides a rationale for presiding behind the altar.

The second reading presents an opportunity to speak of the Church as transcending the distinction between Christian Jew and Gentile. The obvious contemporary application of this would be in the field of race relations. But this theme must be tackled theologically, not sociologically or humanistically. Everything said must be based on the understanding of the cross of Christ as the abolition of the law. Only in those terms has a Christian preacher the right to talk in the pulpit about race relations. Whatever happens in the secular world, it is clear that deliberate segregation in the Church is a denial of the gospel—in other words, heresy.

SEVENTEENTH SUNDAY OF THE YEAR

Reading I: 2 Kings 4:42-44

This little story from the Elisha cycle is not widely known, but it has become quite important in recent New Testament scholarship because it provides the literary prototype of the miraculous feedings in the Gospels. The pattern of the feeding narratives is largely the same: (1) food is brought to the man of God; (2) the amount of the food is specified; (3) it is objected that the quantity is inadequate; (4) behaving as master of the situation, the man of God ignores the objection and commands that the food be distributed; (5) the crowd not only have enough to eat but there is some left over.

Responsorial Psalm: 145:10-11, 15-18

Psalm 145 is used quite frequently as a responsorial psalm, but this is the only time this particular selection of verses is used on a Sunday. The second stanza obviously connects with the Old Testament reading and the gospel, and the common theme of both is further underlined in the refrain.

Reading II: Ephesians 4:1-6

In accordance with common critical opinion, we take Ephesians to be the work of a second-generation Paulinist thoroughly steeped in the Apostle's teaching. Ephesians follows a very clear division, chapters 1-3 being doctrinal and chapters 4-6 parenetical (that is, containing ethical exhortation), so that our reading is the beginning of the parenesis.

There is a close connection, however, between the two parts of the document. The first part sets forth the unity of Jew and Gentile in the one body, providing a look back at the achievement of the Apostle himself, while the parenesis begins with an exhortation to unity. But the exhortation to unity leads back into a further reminder of the theological grounds for the appeal. The "ought" is based on an "is." There *is* one body, one Spirit, one hope, one Lord, one faith, one baptism, one God and Father of all Christians, and therefore the writer, speaking in the Apostle's name, can exhort his readers to be what they are. As in Paul himself, the imperative rests upon an indicative. Unity is both a gift and a task (German: *Gabe* and *Aufgabe*). The imperative to unity is therefore like the imperative to individual sanctification: "Become what you are."

Gospel: John 6:1-15

As we have seen, part of the background for this familiar story is provided in the less familiar story about Elisha. The same points that we enumerated in the Elisha story reappear in the Johannine feeding and provide the basic framework for the narrative. But there are other motifs in John, such as the Eucharist and the eschatological or messianic banquet. Note the acts of Jesus: *took, gave thanks* (the Hellenistic equivalent of "blessed," which Mark still preserves in one place), *distributed.* And when the text says that the people were *filled,* we have a word that is used elsewhere for the repletion of the messianic banquet. In the ensuing discourse in the synagogue at Capernaum (see next Sunday's reading), the evangelist develops yet another aspect of the symbolism of this story, namely, the Moses/manna typology. But this typology is scarcely evident in the story itself as John received it from his tradition.

The concluding verse appears to enshrine a genuine historical reminiscence not recorded in the Synoptists. It is impossible to ascertain precisely what happened in the feeding, but it is clear from all the Gospel accounts that it represented a crisis in the Lord's ministry. We know that at some stage Jesus broke off his Galilean ministry and went to Jerusalem, and in all the Gospels the feeding is a pivotal point in the narrative. This shows that its central position is due not merely to Mark's arrangement but goes back to earlier tradition. In Mark's first version of the feeding, we are told that Jesus packed the disciples off in a boat while he dismissed the crowd. The reason for this becomes clear in John's note here: it was to prevent the disciples from being infected by the dangerous nationalistic-messianic enthusiasm of the crowd.

The Homily

As we have seen, the Johannine feeding admits of several theological interpretations (Jesus as the new Elijah, the messianic banquet, the miraculous meal as a type of the Eucharist). It would seem appropriate on this Sunday to take our cue from the responsorial psalm and its refrain: "The hand of the Lord feeds us; he answers all our needs." A consideration of this theme would lead to a treatment of the affluent nations' responsibility to provide for the impoverished peoples of the earth and to conserve the bounties of nature. The United States is the most wasteful country on the earth. Not only are we depriving the poorer nations of a fair share of the world's goods, but we are consuming our own resources at such a rate that there will not be enough left for our own descendants. A reflection on these serious matters would be in order today.

If the subject of Christian unity did not come up in January, the second reading offers an opportunity to deal with it today. Here, as we have suggested, the gift of unity must be stressed first, and then the obligation it places upon us to exhibit this unity. The homilist should ask how concretely this has to be done on the local scene.

EIGHTEENTH SUNDAY OF THE YEAR

Reading I: Exodus 16:2-4, 12-15

There are two accounts of the manna and the quail in the Pentateuch, the other being in Num 11. There the manna was provided first, and after the people "murmured" (a constant motif in the Exodus story), the quails were given. In this account greater emphasis is placed on the manna. Both are intelligible as phenomena in the Sinai desert, the manna being a sweet excretion from certain insects and the quail being migratory fowl that often drop dead from exhaustion in their flight over the Sinai desert.

Note how the final remark of Moses highlights the manna at the expense of the quail, providing the phrase "bread from heaven," which was destined to play an important role in later tradition.

Responsorial Psalm: 78:3, 4bcd, 23-25, 54-55b

The phrase "bread from heaven" is taken up in the refrain of the psalm. Psalm 78 is a long recitation of Israel's salvation history from Jacob to David. This section of it covers the Sinai period. The bread from heaven becomes the "bread of the angels," a further step on the road to its typological interpretation of the messianic banquet and the Eucharist.

Reading II: Ephesians 4:17, 20-24

Today's reading from Ephesians continues the parenesis, or ethical exhortation. The material is almost certainly derived from a primitive Christian catechism. Note first the reference to the teaching of Christ. Note secondly the pattern of renunciation and renewal. "Put off" and "put on" are suggested by the candidates' divesting themselves of their garments to go down into the baptismal waters and their vesting again with the baptismal robe after emerging from them. We cannot be sure that this symbolism was already applied at this time, but it is not improbable.

Running through this passage is the contrast between the old pagan life and the new Christian life. The word "likeness" in the RSV is not in the Greek, and we have no reason to speculate that the author is here thinking of human beings as having lost the divine likeness (though retaining the image) at the fall. Also, the word "nature" translates the Greek word for "human being." We might find it helpful here to use Tillich's term, the "new being."

Gospel: John 6:24-35

This is the opening section of the discourse on the bread of life. Like so many of the Johannine discourses, it is composed from traditional materials. The reference to "signs" recalls the discussion in Mark 8:11-13, and the figurative interpretation of bread recalls the dialogue in Mark 8:14-21.

The evangelist himself is not averse to the term "sign," but he polemicizes against a faith that does not penetrate beyond the sign to the thing signified. Hence the exhortation to labor not for earthly bread but for the "food which endures to eternal life." This introduces the theme of the bread from heaven. At the outset it is stated that the Son of man (that is, he who came down from heaven and who will ascend thither again) will give this bread.

The dialogue about the true work looks like a digression, but it serves to underline the nature of the bread from heaven. This bread has to be received in faith; that is the only way to labor for it. Having established the difference between the sign and the thing signified, the dialogue then proceeds to draw a second distinction, that between the type and its fulfillment, between the manna and the "true" (that is, eschatological) bread from heaven. Note how the evangelist draws both distinctions by means of the Johannine technique of misunderstanding. Each time the Jews misunderstand the Revealer, who then proceeds to give the correct interpretation. In the course of this dialogue, a shift occurs. First Jesus promises as Son of man to give the bread of eternal life, but later he says, "I *am* the bread of life."

There is a major dispute as to whether the evangelist already has the Eucharist in mind in this first part of the discourse or whether that theme does not really come to the fore until verses 51-58 (regarded by some as the addition of a redactor). Is Christ the bread of heaven already in the incarnation or only in the Eucharist? Is this bread made presently available in the proclamation of the word only or in the sacrament also? Are eating and drinking no more than metaphors for faith in the divine Revealer, or do they also include sacramental eating and drinking?

We would hazard two opinions on this subject. First, it would be wrong to draw a sharp line between the historical and kerygmatic, and the sacramental. All are part of one single act of revelation and redemption, with the historical coming of Christ decisive, and the preaching of the word and partaking of the sacrament complementary as re-presentations of the once-for-all revelatory and redemptive event. Therefore, it is not either faith in the word or sacramental eating and drinking alone, but both, the one informing the other but the one incomplete without the other.

Second—an even more hazardous opinion—since verses 26-51b speak exclusively of the bread of life, and only verses 51c-58 of the flesh and blood of Jesus, the background of the earlier part is the fellowship meal and preaching of the word, while the background of the later part is the Eucharist proper. If the later part is the addition of a redactor who is also of the Johannine school, it would mean that the evangelist had emphasized the agape meal and preaching, to the virtual exclusion of the Eucharist proper. But his rather "way-out" view was seen within the Johannine school to require supplementation. It is in that supplemented form that John's Gospel has been received into the canon by the Church. As the text now stands, it asserts that the incarnate Christ is present as the bread of life in the fellowship meal and in the word, and that in the Eucharist proper the crucified One gives his flesh and blood to be the food of the faithful.

The Homily

If last Sunday's homily dealt with our need for bread and with society's need for a just distribution and conservation of the earth's resources in order that the poor and the unborn will have enough to sustain life, there is an opportunity today to move on to our further need for the bread that comes down from heaven, for God's revelation in Jesus Christ.

If last week the homily dealt with the need of the Church to strive to exhibit that unity that it already possesses as a gift, today the homilist might go on to speak of individual sanctification under the rubric "Become what you are"—grow into the new being that you put on once for all in your baptism.

NINETEENTH SUNDAY OF THE YEAR

Reading I: 1 Kings 19:4-8

This is one of the stories from the Elijah cycle. Elijah has reached a crisis in his career; the opposition of King Ahab had driven him to flee. In his despondency, he requests that he might die, but he is supernaturally provided with food to sustain him on the journey to Horeb, the mountain of God, where he will receive a theophany.

In Christian usage this passage has a twofold interest: (1) it is a type of Jesus' fast in the wilderness and of the Church's Lenten fast (this passage forms the Old Testament lesson for Friday in the first week of Lent in *Lesser Feasts and Fasts* of the Episcopal Church); (2) it forms a type of holy communion considered as the food of pilgrims on their way to the mountain of God (it is used as the fifth alternative Old Testament reading for the votive Mass of the Holy Eucharist). On this Sunday it has obviously been chosen to parallel the continuation of the discourse on the bread from heaven in today's gospel.

Responsorial Psalm: 34:1-8

Of this psalm the *Jerome Biblical Commentary* states: "A wisdom psalm, though it is widely classified as a psalm of thanksgiving." Chiefly because of verse 8a, which serves as the refrain ("Taste and see the goodness of the Lord"), this psalm was used in the early Church during the time of communion. It goes suitably with the Old Testament reading and the gospel today.

Reading II: Ephesians 4:30–5:2

This passage continues the parenesis of Ephesians. The baptismal references are again clear ("the Holy Spirit . . . in whom you were sealed" and "put away"). Once again, the imperatives are grounded in indicatives. Christians are to forgive one another because Christ has forgiven them, and they are to walk in love because Christ loves them with a love that expresses itself in sacrificial terms.

Gospel: John 6:41-51

It is interesting to find the "Jews" (usually a symbol for the unbelieving world in the Fourth Gospel) "murmuring" at the discourse on the bread of life, just as the children of Israel did in the wilderness. The use of this same verb can hardly be accidental, and it calls further attention to the manna/Eucharist typology. They murmur because of another typical Johannine misunderstanding. They know where Jesus came from, they know his parentage. (The reference to Jesus as "son of Joseph" has no relevance to the question of the virginal conception; it simply reflects the undoubted fact that Jesus passed for the son of Joseph, whether this evangelist knew of the virginal conception or not.) The evangelist has worked in a tradition from the story of Jesus' rejection in the synagogue at Nazareth as given in the Synoptists.

Jesus' reply to the misunderstanding asserts that a knowledge of his heavenly origin is possible only to those who are "drawn to him" in faith by the Father. To be drawn is further defined as hearing and learning from the Father. The earthly origins of Jesus are not denied, but faith sees beyond them to his heavenly origin, just as the Creed asserts not only that Jesus was born of Mary but also that he was conceived by the Holy Spirit. The one level is historical fact, the other a confession of faith. Faith is not, however, just abstract, notional insight; it involves participating in "eternal life." Faith is also paradoxical: on the one hand it is a free decision, but on the other hand it involves an element of predestination (the Father must draw believers to the Son). The great "I am" is repeated twice here: "I am the bread of life" (as in verse 35) and "I am the living bread which came down from heaven." Once again there is a typical Johannine repetition of the manna typology (v. 49). The last clause of verse 51 introduces for the first time the theme of the flesh of Jesus, which, as we saw last Sunday, may be the beginning of the passage added by the Johannine redactor.

The Homily

If the homilist elects to continue the exposition of the Johannine discourse on the bread of life, there is a wealth of material from the gospel. First, there are the two levels of Jesus' being, the historical and the heavenly, a schema that will apply also to the sacrament. This would give an opportunity to speak of the mystery of the Eucharistic presence under the signs of bread and wine. There is also the paradox of faith and predestination. The first reading, however, suggests that the homilist should narrow down his/her treatment to the Eucharist as viaticum—the food of pilgrims on their way to the mountain of God.

If, on the other hand, the homilist is following a course on the Ephesian parenesis, he/she should first expound the indicative (Christ's love for us in offering himself as a sacrifice to the Father for our forgiveness) and then the imperatives that follow from it (forgiveness of others as we have been forgiven—see the Lord's Prayer). Some quite concrete instances where forgiveness is required in the life of the local community might be given.

TWENTIETH SUNDAY OF THE YEAR

Reading I: Proverbs 9:1-6

This is one of several Old Testament and, for others than Roman Catholics, apocryphal passages that speak of Wisdom's heavenly banquet. This concept forms part of the background of the discourse on the bread of life in John 6:35-51b (see R. E. Brown on the "sapiential theme in vv. 35-50" in *The Gospel According to John*, Anchor Bible Commentary, 1:272-273). It is perhaps a little unfortunate that this reading should be paired off with verses 51-58 (today's gospel), where the sapiential theme falls into the background somewhat (but see verse 58). On the whole, it would pair off better with the gospel reading of the eighteenth Sunday, the reference to Wisdom's wine preparing for the reference to "thirst" in John 6:35.

In the Book of Proverbs, the present passage forms the close of the prologue on Wisdom. Wisdom and Folly each invite their prospective participants to a banquet, and they are free to choose which to accept. Our present reading is Wisdom's invitation.

Responsorial Psalm: 34:1-2, 9-14

A different selection of verses from Psalm 34 was used last Sunday, but with the same refrain. As we noted there, this is a wisdom psalm. The last two stanzas of today's selection are strongly sapiential and fit beautifully with the first reading (note especially the similarity between the invitations of the third stanza and those of Prov 9:5).

Reading II: Ephesians 5:15-20

We now reach the second part of the parenesis of Ephesians. Here we have a section that, whether designedly or not, quite aptly fits the first reading and its context, namely, the contrast between Wisdom and Folly. Folly consists in *not* "making the most of the time" (literally "buying up the opportunity") and in drunkenness and debauchery. This exhortation has an eschatological background: the days are evil and the present age is under the domination of the evil powers, but their time is short (see Rom 13:11-14). Thus again, though less explicitly, the imperative is rooted in an indicative: the powers of evil are being vanquished; therefore, live as children of the new age. The author is then led to contrast intoxication from wine with Pentecostal ecstasy, which expresses itself here, not in glossolalia, but in the more sober manner of "psalms and hymns and spiritual songs"—one of the earliest pieces of evidence we have of the use of hymns in the early community.

This passage is thought by some to be part of the *Haustafel* (household code) that follows, for such catechetical patterns are sometimes prefaced by an exhortation to perform one's duty toward the gods (in the pagan *Haustafeln*) or to Yahweh (in the Jewish ones).

Gospel: John 6:51-58

Here at last we reach the definitely Eucharistic part of the discourse on the bread of life. We move from bread as such to the flesh and blood of the Son of man. As indicated above on the eighteenth Sunday, we tend to regard these verses as an addition by a redactor who is himself a member of the Johannine school. We suggested that the first part is a meditation on the agape-fellowship meal, and the added part a meditation on the Eucharist proper. The thought moves from the revelation of the incarnate One as the heavenly wisdom to his sacrificial surrender in the death of the cross.

The redactor seeks to balance the one-sidedness of the evangelist's Eucharistic theology. The evangelist appeared to emphasize the incarnation at the expense of the cross, and the agape-fellowship meal and the proclamation of the word at the expense of the Eucharist. The redactor's

334

additional material here is derived from the Supper tradition as it had circulated in the Johannine communities ("this is my flesh," "this is my blood," "eat," "drink," and the indication of the soteriological effects of sacramental eating and drinking).

The Homily

If we have been following the readings from the Johannine discourse on the bread of life, we can move today from a consideration of the presence of Christ in the fellowship meal and the preached word to the sacramental presence of his flesh and blood in the Eucharist proper. This is perhaps crude language from which many modern Christians shrink. (See the revision of the Anglican "prayer of humble access" in the first Trial Liturgy of the Episcopal Church, where the Johannine language about eating Christ's flesh and drinking his blood was replaced by the slightly more refined language of "partaking in his body and blood.") Hoskyns, however, insisted that flesh and blood in this context is language "by which Christianity stands or falls" (*Cambridge Sermons*, p. 137): "By our Christian language, by the express doctrine of the Church and its worship, we are being thrust into the whole relativity of human life, into the life where men are not God, where their ideas and notions are not the absolute Truth of God, where at best men speak in parables, and where their actions are not the righteousness of God, where in fact life passes to death. . . . Into this realm of death the Lord passes with eyes wide open, with inexorable purpose, and into this realm He draws His disciples with Him."

It would be very congenial to have a form of Christian worship consisting of a fellowship meal celebrating Jesus as the bread of life and a proclamation of him as incarnate wisdom. But our canonical John (whatever the evangelist may have originally planned) goes further than that and insists that the Christian liturgy moves further to an eating and drinking of the flesh and blood of Jesus, that is, to participating in the sacrifice of Calvary. At a time when the Eucharist is being stressed as a messianic banquet and the sacrificial aspect is being played down, it is good to be reminded of this other aspect and to seek to redress the balance.

TWENTY-FIRST SUNDAY OF THE YEAR

Reading I: Joshua 24:1-2a, 15-17, 18b

For the Old Testament scholar, Josh 24 is highly important in the history of Israelite traditions. It preserves remnants of an ancient liturgy for the renewal of the covenant at Shechem. This tradition stands in conflict with later Deuteronomic theology and its doctrine of the central sanctuary at Jerusalem. It is believed to have originated from a covenant between the earlier inhabitants of Shechem and the Israelite invaders. The former worshiped El-berith, while the latter worshiped Yahweh. The ceremony recalls the choice then made by the two parties. Henceforth Yahweh, the God of the invaders, would be worshiped by both groups.

The appointment of this reading for today is governed by the parallel between the choice made at Shechem and the choice confronting the disciples after the discourse in John 6. The challenge "Choose this day whom you will serve" parallels "Will you also go away?"; and the response "We will serve the Lord, for he is our God" parallels Peter's response, "Lord, to whom shall we go? You have the words of eternal life."

Responsorial Psalm: 34:1-2, 15-22

The refrain and the first stanza are the same as in last Sunday's responsorial psalm, while the rest of the stanzas are made up from verses not used last week. The new stanzas strike a different note, namely, God's vindication of the righteous sufferer. Some think that the fourth stanza (vv. 19-20) rather than Exod 12:46 is the source of the Old Testament quotation in John 19:36. If this view is correct, it would show that this psalm was used in the early Church's passion apologetic. The goodness of the Lord that we taste and see in the Eucharist is the goodness manifested in the suffering and vindication of Jesus, the righteous servant of God.

Reading II: Ephesians 5:21-32

Verse 22 marks the beginning of the household code of Ephesians. This code forms a major portion of the parenesis in the second half of the letter and runs through 6:9.

Verse 21 serves as a heading for the household code. The primary principle of the household codes is that of subjection. Early Christianity seems to have taken over these codes from Hellenistic Judaism, which in turn adapted them from the Stoics. The codes set forth the duties of wives, husbands, parents, children, masters, and slaves.

In the New Testament these codes are often given a Christian veneer, generally by the addition of the words "in the Lord" to the injunctions.

Occasionally, however, as in the present instance, the process of Christianization goes much further. Ephesians provides a unique elaboration of marriage as a parable of the relation between Christ and his Church. In this theological expansion of the code, the author of Ephesians has brought together a remarkable variety of traditions. He takes the statement about the unity of husband and wife in marriage from Gen 2:24. He portrays the Church in the language of Levitical purity. The command to love one's neighbor in Lev 19 provides the basis for verse 27. An early Christian kerygmatic formula is reproduced in verse 25, and a baptismal-liturgical formula in verse 26. In verses 23 and 29 the Pauline figure of the Church as the body of Christ reappears, but with Christ as the head of the body, a development that may be of Gnostic origin.

With these materials the author has skillfully interwoven two parallel themes—the duties of husband and wife, and the ecclesiological theme of the relation between Christ and the Church. We may sort out the two themes as follows:

22 Wives, be subject to your husbands	22 as to the Lord
23 The husband is the head of the wife	23 as Christ is the head of the Church
24 [a repetition of v. 22]	24 the Church is subject to Christ
25 Husbands, love your wives	25–27 as Christ loved the Church . . . without blemish
28 Husbands should love their wives as their own bodies. He who loves his wife loves himself. . . .	
29 A man loves and cherishes his own flesh	29 as Christ does the Church
	30 we are members of his body
31 Citation of Genesis 2:24	32 interpreted mystically of Christ and the Church

By presenting this passage in two columns, we get a clue to the author's procedure. He began with the duty of the wife to the husband as set forth in the household code with its slight Christianization ("as to the Lord"). He then expanded the code by drawing upon a number of kerygmatic, liturgical, and ecclesiological traditions, and then supplemented the household code itself by drawing upon the tradition on the other side of the column. As a result, the marriage relationship is transformed from one in which the wife is simply subjected to the husband without qualification into one in which the husband is to devote himself unreservedly to the love of his wife. Thus, the household code is turned upside down—the emphasis rests no longer on the duty of the wife to the husband but on the husband's love for his wife.

Finally, the two columns are clinched together by the citation of Gen 2:24. On the literal level, this text speaks of the union of husband and wife. But this is a *mystērion*. It has another, higher level of meaning, portraying the unity between Christ and the Church. The author's doctrine of the Church is not built up from below, from a natural understanding of marriage; rather, his understanding of marriage is built from above, from a theological understanding of the mystical union between Christ and his Church.

Gospel: John 6:60-69

This pericope forms the conclusion to the discourse at Capernaum on the bread of heaven. Following as it does verses 51-59, it appears to contradict that section, especially in verse 63. Having insisted in verses 51c-59 that the believer must eat the flesh and drink the blood of the Son of man in order to have eternal life, Jesus now tells his hearers that "the flesh is of no avail." But "flesh" here is not the Eucharistic flesh of verses 51c-59; as in John 3:6, it means "the natural principle in man which cannot give eternal life" (R. E. Brown). Similarly, "spirit" here means what it means in 3:6—the life-giving Spirit that will be given as a result of the ascension of the Son of man to where he was before (v. 62).

Our passage, therefore, is not speaking of the sacrament but of the reception of the revelation of Jesus as the heavenly wisdom, the bread from heaven. In other words, it refers back to verses 35-50, not to verses 51c-59, which, as we have seen, are best understood as a later redactional addition. It is Jesus' claim to be the revelation of God in verses 35-50 that many of the disciples find to be a hard saying, not the Eucharistic teaching of verses 51c-59. Yet, there are some who do accept his claim, namely, the Twelve. And in a scene parallel to the synoptic episode at Caesarea Philippi, the section concludes with a confession of Peter (vv. 68b-69). Thus, as throughout the Fourth Gospel, the division of spirits is determined by the acceptance or rejection of Jesus as the life-giving revelation of God. The evangelist, of course, is thinking not only of what happened in Jesus' ministry but of a similar division of spirits in his own community. The many disciples who abandoned Jesus, and Judas Iscariot, who was to betray him (v. 64; cf. vv. 70-71), typify the Gnostic Docetists in the evangelist's own day.

The Homily

The captions to the Old Testament reading and the gospel rightly focus our attention on the theme of decision in the face of the divine revelation. Can we perhaps see parallels in the life of the Church today to what the evangelist saw in the Church of his day? We could look to those who leave the Church (or cancel their pledges!) because of the contemporary Church's attempt to speak the word of God to the political and social realities of our day, or because the Church is seeking to update itself in order to become a better instrument for the proclamation of the gospel in the modern world.

The second reading offers the homilist an opportunity to speak of Christian marriage. It is important to bring out the chief purpose of the author. The Christian doctrine of marriage is acquired not merely by an empirical study of marriage as a human institution—valid as that is on its own level, like the original household code—but from an awareness of the relation between Christ and his Church. Hence, the Church must preach to the married that the more they know of the relation between Christ and his Church through their sacramental experience, the more they will understand the mystery of their own relationship.

TWENTY-SECOND SUNDAY OF THE YEAR

Reading I: Deuteronomy 4:1-2, 6-8

This passage comes from the prologue to the Deuteronomic law. The prohibition to add or subtract anything was a regular feature of ancient legal codes (cf. the Code of Hammurabi, where, however, the prohibition comes toward the end, not at the beginning as here). The second paragraph underlines the great privilege Israel enjoys through the possession of the law. The caption emphasizes the first paragraph, the prohibition to add or subtract from the law, and makes it clear that this reading was chosen to underline the distinction between the commandments of God and human traditions, which is the main point of the gospel reading.

Responsorial Psalm: 15:2, 3b-5

Almost the same selection of verses from this psalm is used on the sixteenth Sunday in series C. This is one of the so-called entry psalms, sung by pilgrims as they approached the temple. It describes the character of the pilgrim whom God will accept—a person of justice, sincerity, and integrity. The only difference in today's selection is the addition of the first line in the third stanza: "Who swears to his own hurt and does not change." Why is this line added today? Is it thought to have some special appropriateness in connection with the first reading? If so, the idea must be that Israel must not change in its allegiance to the law; it must not change the law by adapting it to new needs. Of course, in one sense this is precisely what has to be done. Fulfilling the legal code to the letter in a changed situation can result precisely in disobeying it. In that sense there must be change and adaptation. But it must be responsible change, change undertaken for the better observance of the law under changed conditions, not adaptation of the law to suit one's own interests.

Reading II: James 1:17-18, 21b-22, 27

For the next five weeks the second reading will be from the so-called Letter of James. Traditionally this letter has been accepted as the work of James the brother of the Lord, though the author simply calls himself "a servant [slave] of God and of the Lord Jesus Christ" (1:1). Critical opinion today is divided about the authorship and the date. Although some reputable scholars would defend its traditional authenticity and early date, it is to be noted that there were considerable doubts about it even in the early Church. Probably it was originally a Hellenistic Jewish document containing twelve exhortations based on the names of the twelve patriarchs in Gen 49 and slightly Christianized in the post-Pauline period by a Hellenistic Jewish Christian teacher. The letter enshrines a good deal of wisdom teaching and brings this to bear against the antinomians (Gnostics?) who in a later generation were appealing to a (wrongly interpreted) Paul. We would date the letter toward the end of the first century.

Today's excerpt is from the second exhortation, supposedly based on the name Simeon (*shamah*—doers, not hearers only). The sentence beginning "Of his own will . . ." is a place where the author has Christianized the exhortation by inserting a reference to baptism. It is then that the "word," that is, the gospel, is implanted, but it has to be constantly received anew and made the basis for Christian action. The word for "religion" is equivalent to "cultus." The true cultus, James insists, consists in ethical obedience. James does not intend to give an exhaustive description of such obedience but merely to illustrate it. He does not mean to decry the importance of liturgy—after all, he mentions baptism and the hearing of the word—but he insists that the performance of these must lead to a life of moral obedience and cannot be a substitute for it (see the Old Testament prophets).

Gospel: Mark 7:1-8, 14-15, 21-23

Like so many passages in the Gospel tradition, this pericope has a long and complicated history behind it. To begin with, the parenthesis in verses 3-4 is a note by the evangelist for the benefit of his Gentile readers, who were of course unfamiliar with Jewish customs. Other features in the passage point to the Hellenistic Jewish Christian community before Mark. The quotation of Isa 29:13 follows the Septuagint, not the Massoretic text used by our Lord and the earliest Palestinian community. The quotation does not altogether fit the situation, which is not a matter of honoring with the lips. Again, the distinction between the written law and the tradition does not adequately represent Jesus' teaching on the law, which is critical even of the law itself when it is used as a cloak for disobedience. It represents the rationalistic approach of Hellenistic Judaism. The situation may well be an authentic memory about Jesus' earthly activity, but the citation from Isaiah and the pronouncement of verse 8 are probably from the later Hellenistic Jewish community.

The second pronouncement (vv. 14-16), which is addressed to the whole people, has, however, every mark of an authentic parable of Jesus. It could have been his response to precisely the type of situation indicated in the introduction to the pericope. The disciples are accused of not washing before dinner, as the purity laws require. Jesus replies that it is not what people eat that defiles them; it is their inner purity, issuing in outward behavior, that matters.

Finally, the catalogue of vices (vv. 21-23) was a common teaching device in the catechesis, first of Hellenistic Jewish Christianity, and then of Gentile Christianity.

The Homily

It is clear from the captions to the first reading and the gospel that the Church recommends that the homilist deal with the antithesis between God's commandments and human ecclesiastical tradition. Our critical analysis has shown that this antithesis comes from the Hellenistic Jewish Church rather than from Jesus himself. This prevents us from assuming that the distinction between commandment and tradition is a complete answer to the question of radical obedience. It is, however, a distinction that has to be made where human traditions obscure the will of God, which is more clearly enunciated in the original commandments.

The second reading suggests cultus and ritual as one area where this distinction between the commandment of God and human traditions may be usefully applied in the interests of radical obedience. Cultic and ritual traditions have to be constantly under review lest in the course of time they actually impede the real end of cultus and ritual, which is to draw us to a more radical obedience to the will of God. The homilist might either (1) critically review inherited cultic or ritual observances at points where they no longer serve the higher end of obedience to the will of God;

or (2) interpret the abandonment, in recent years, of venerable cultic or ritual practices that had become barriers to obedience and ends in themselves.

TWENTY-THIRD SUNDAY OF THE YEAR

Reading I: Isaiah 35:4-7a

Although this passage occurs in the first part of Isaiah, among the prophecies of the preexilic Isaiah of Jerusalem, it breathes the spirit of Second Isaiah and, if not written by him, must be contemporary with him and from the same school. Its life situation is the impending return from exile (see especially verses 4b and 7b).

This passage was chosen for today because of verses 5 and 6, which speak of the healing miracles that will accompany the return from exile. When we remember that for Second Isaiah the return was the final redemptive act of God, we can understand how early Christianity saw this passage (like Isa 29:18 and 61:1-3) as a prediction of Jesus' messianic healings. This was clearly in the mind of Mark (or of his tradition) when he chose the highly unusual word *mogilalon* (literally: "with difficulty of speech") to describe the deaf-mute whose healing is recounted in today's gospel reading, for *mogilalon* is precisely the same Greek word used in the Septuagint for the word "dumb" in Isa 35:6. Thus, this passage is eminently fitted for use with today's gospel.

Responsorial Psalm: 146:6c-10

Selections from this psalm are used on other occasions in the Lectionary, but particularly noteworthy is the use of the same verses on the third Sunday of Advent in series A (but with a refrain more suited to Advent) as a response to Isa 35:1-6a, 10, which is almost the same Old Testament reading as today's. It is a psalm of praise for the healing power of Yahweh, especially for his opening of the eyes of the blind. Unfortunately, the psalm does not mention the opening of the ears of the deaf and the releasing of the tongues of the dumb, but that may be taken as implied.

Reading II: James 2:1-5

Continuing the exhortations based on the names of the twelve patriarchs in Gen 49 (see last Sunday), this passage is said to be based on the name Judah (= "Lord of glory"—Gen 49:8-12). It is an exhortation to the right treatment of the poor. Because the early Christians, for the most part, belonged to the powerless classes of the Roman Empire, the New Testament shows very little concern for social justice as compared with the Old

Testament prophets. But James' Church consists of rich and poor members, and a concern for the proper respect of the poor as persons surfaces immediately. Yet, there is no indication that the wealthy members of James' Church had any political power, and therefore there is little suggestion of a real social ethic. The utmost that this passage suggests is that the silence of the New Testament on such matters is no indication that the gospel has no social implications. It all depends on the conditions under which the Church has to operate, and these vary greatly in time and place.

Note how James, who on the surface looks so moralistic, again bases his exhortation on the truths of the gospel: wealthier Christians should show concern for the poorer members because (in baptism) God has chosen the poor to inherit the kingdom.

Gospel: Mark 7:31-37

This is one of the two miracle stories peculiar to Mark (the other is the healing of the blind man of Bethsaida in Mark 8:22-23). Both stories represent our Lord as employing a physical healing technique, and perhaps for that reason did not appeal to the later evangelists, who preferred to depict him as healing solely through a word.

Like so many other gospel pericopes, this story seems to have passed through a number of successive stages:

1. An original exorcism by Jesus (its exorcistic character is suggested by the words "his tongue was released").

2. The Palestinian Church, which interpreted Jesus in terms of the eschatological prophet-servant, wrote up the story as a fulfillment of Isa 35.

3. The Hellenistic Church, which interpreted Jesus in terms of the wonder-worker or divine man, preserved the foreign word "Ephphatha," thus creating an impression of the wonder-worker's mysterious power and emphasizing the physical means of healing (putting his fingers into the man's ears, spitting, and touching his tongue).

4. The evangelist gives a fresh meaning to the story by the place where he locates it in his continuous narrative. It symbolizes what is happening to the disciples (see Mark 8:22-26). They have been deaf to Jesus' word (7:18a) and are as yet unable to make any confession of faith in him. Eventually, however, at Caesarea Philippi, it will begin to dawn on them who Jesus really is, and Peter will make his confession of faith. Thus, the ears of the disciples will be opened, their tongues will be released, and they will speak plainly, declaring through their spokesman Peter, "You are the Messiah" (see next Sunday's gospel).

The Homily

The Old Testament reading, the psalm, and the gospel indicate the theme of the messianic miracle by which people come to hear the word of God and respond through a confession of faith. This is what happens in the liturgy.

Today's gospel passage used to occur in the Book of Common Prayer at Trinity 12, and in the Church of England that Sunday was popularly known as "Ephphatha Sunday," dedicated to a special concern for the deaf and dumb. The meaning of the Gospel miracles is not, of course, exhausted in humanitarian concern, for they proclaim the ultimate messianic healing, but as a parabolic expression of the meaning of the parable such humanitarian concern has a legitimate place.

The second reading provides an opportunity to speak of sensitivity to the poor as a continuing aspect of the Christian gospel, for God, in Christ, has chosen the poor to be heirs of his kingdom. It would be appropriate to explore the mode in which that sensitivity should be expressed in a democracy where Christians have political power (as opposed to their situation in the Roman Empire when the Letter of James was written).

TWENTY-FOURTH SUNDAY OF THE YEAR

Reading I: Isaiah 50:5-9a

The third servant song of Second Isaiah is used also on Palm Sunday, where it ends with verse 7, and is commented upon there in series A. The additional words included here run from "he who vindicates me is near" through "who will declare me guilty?" These words tie in with the prediction of the passion in today's gospel, where Jesus confidently affirms his certainty of vindication ("and after three days rise again").

53

Responsorial Psalm: 116:1-6, 8-9

On the other occasions when this psalm is used in the Sunday Lectionary (Holy Thursday, the second Sunday of Lent in series B, Corpus Christi), the verses chosen emphasize the theme of Yahweh's vindication of his servant. He was encompassed by the snares of death and the pangs of sheol (stanza 2) and cried to Yahweh, and God heard him (stanzas 1, 3, 4). The psalm thus speaks of death and resurrection.

59
234
286

The prediction of the passion in the gospel asserts that "the Son of man *must* suffer." This "must" is equivalent to the early Christian formula "according to the scriptures." It is not immediately obvious, however, which Old Testament scriptures speak of the death and resurrection of the Messiah, but the servant passages of Second Isaiah and the psalms about God's vindication of the righteous sufferer, of which this is one, provide a pattern of divine action that finds its fulfillment in Jesus Christ.

Reading II: James 2:14-18

This section on faith and works is said to correspond to Rachel, who here takes the place of Dan in the exhortations based on the list of patriarchs in Gen 49. Because of her barrenness (see Jas 2:17), Rachel gave her maidservant to Jacob, and Dan was the fruit of this association.

The kind of faith that James has in view is not the personal acceptance of God's saving act of which Paul generally speaks. With that kind of faith there could be no question of its dissociation from good works. Paul can speak of this kind of faith as naturally and inevitably working through love and producing the first fruits of the Spirit. James is thinking of a notional assent to orthodox formulas (see Jas 2:19). Such faith, if it is genuine, is bound to issue in good works, otherwise it is barren. Here James agrees with the best teaching of Judaism, with Jesus, and with Paul and 1 John.

Gospel: Mark 8:27-35

The Matthean version of the confession of Peter is used on the twenty-first Sunday of series A. Mark's version is clearly more primitive. Nevertheless, it too is the result of a process of development. To reconstruct the original historical event, we start with the fact that it is inconceivable that the post-Easter Church invented the Satan saying, given the fact that Peter was its most revered leader. Jesus must actually have called Peter "Satan." By why did he do so? As the text stands, he did so in response to the prediction of the passion: Peter could accept the idea of Jesus as Messiah, but not as a suffering Messiah. But the prediction of the passion is clearly a post-Easter creation. It makes Jesus identify himself openly with the Son of man and shows a clear knowledge of the events of the passion and the resurrection, reminiscent of the passion narratives in the Gospels. We take it, then, to be a *vaticinium ex eventu.*

The command to silence is a typical piece of Marcan redaction, reflecting his theme of the messianic secret. Remove these two elements—the charge to secrecy and the prediction of the passion—and the Satan saying follows directly upon Peter's "confession." Why, then, would Jesus reject it? He would do so if the term "Messiah" meant a political, nationalistic leader. Jesus consistently rejected that program as a diabolical attempt to divert him from his God-given mission. Given this meaning of Messiah—and this is the meaning that was current in Jesus' day, before it was appropriated for him after Easter—the Satan saying becomes intelligible. In the light of the post-Easter faith, however, Peter's confession became a positive confession, acceptable to Christ, and the Satan saying is therefore transferred to Peter's rejection of the idea of the suffering

161

Messiah by means of the passion prediction. Finally, Mark introduces the motif of secrecy to ensure that the confession "You are the Christ [Messiah]" can only be applied to the crucified and risen One, not to Jesus in his earthly ministry, which would make him merely a divine miracle-worker. Such seems to be the history of the tradition.

A second scene follows—the saying about the cost of discipleship. Some have thought that the saying about taking up one's cross must reflect a post-Easter situation, but the Greek word *stauros* probably meant originally not the gibbet but the taw (T) or chi (X), the sign of ownership with which cattle were branded. As such it means here God's seal or sign. In this sense it means "surrender of self-assertion before God and surrender of the autonomous freedom which directs itself against God" (Erich Dinkler). It thus becomes intelligible as an authentic saying of the earthly Jesus. After Good Friday, however, it acquires a new meaning: assuming one's cross, that is, the life of suffering and martyrdom in union with the cross of Christ.

If it is the evangelist Mark who has combined the two traditions—the confession of Peter and the saying about bearing one's cross—then the whole pericope as it now stands is directed against a wrong understanding of Christological confession and apostleship, one that interprets Jesus as a miracle-working divine man and conceives of apostleship likewise in terms of the divine miracle-worker. In place of this, Mark puts the confession of Jesus as Christ crucified, and apostleship as following him in bearing the cross, manifesting the dying of Jesus in our mortal bodies, as Paul phrased it.

The Homily

The Old Testament reading, the psalm, and the gospel focus upon the Christological confession of Jesus as crucified and vindicated, and the analogous understanding of apostleship. These are profound theological themes not easily translated into a homily for a contemporary congregation. Perhaps the simplest course would be to take Jesus' word about carrying the cross and to bring out the understanding of Christian existence that it implies: surrender of self-assertion before God and surrender of that autonomous freedom that directs itself against God. This is the pattern of existence exemplified by the suffering servant, by Jesus, and by Peter. It is also meant to be the pattern for all Christian existence.

The second reading gives the homilist an opportunity to deal with the question of faith and works. It should be made clear that there is no ultimate contradiction between Paul and James on this point. (The subject of justification is a more difficult problem and one that has divided the Churches of the Reformation from Rome, but fortunately that is not raised until the passage that follows today's selection.) The homilist should contrast the conception of faith that James has in mind (*fides quae creditur*) with Paul's dominant understanding (*fides qua creditur*) and should make it clear that where faith is interpreted in James' sense, it can easily become a moribund orthodoxy that needs to be quickened into life by a devotion to good works.

TWENTY-FIFTH SUNDAY OF THE YEAR

Reading I: Wisdom 2:12, 17-20

This figure in the Book of Wisdom shows close affinities with the righteous man of the psalms who is vindicated by God and with the suffering servant of Second Isaiah. In fact, verse 13, not used in this excerpt, actually calls the righteous sufferer God's *pais* ("son," though it could mean "servant").

The passage pictures the true Israelite, the tenor of whose life is a standing protest against the lawlessness of the ungodly (probably the apostate Jews of Alexandria), who are irritated by the silent protest of his life and conspire to kill him. Because of the parallels between this picture and Christ's passion (though see also Plato's *Republic*, which says something similar with Socrates in view), this passage has come to be regarded as a prediction of the passion. (In the Book of Common Prayer it is one of the lessons appointed for Morning Prayer on Good Friday.)

It is perhaps a pity that the excerpt here stops short of the proclamation of God's vindication of his righteous servant (v. 22). It was obviously chosen to go with Mark's second prediction of the passion, which occurs in today's gospel reading. That prediction speaks of vindication as well as suffering.

Responsorial Psalm: 54:1-4, 6

Psalm 54, which is appointed for Good Friday in the Book of Common Prayer, serves as a fitting response to the passage from the Book of Wisdom. The righteous person cries out to God for help against enemies and expresses confidence in divine vindication. For the Christian the psalm speaks of the resurrection of Jesus Christ and of every Christian from the grip of spiritual enemies.

Reading II: James 3:16-4:3

If we follow the division of the Letter of James according to the twelve

patriarchs (see the twenty-second Sunday above), we should make a rather   *343*
different division here, treating 3:13-18 as a single exhortation revolving
around the distinction between earthly and heavenly wisdom (Leah corresponding to earthly wisdom, and Rachel to heavenly wisdom), and
4:1-12 as an exhortation on false and true warfare (Gad). So the first
paragraph of today's reading will belong to the seventh exhortation, and
the second paragraph to the eighth. But the two exhortations are linked
by 3:18: those who follow heavenly wisdom will sow in a spirit of peace
and reap a harvest of righteousness. These words pave the way for the
exhortation on the wrong warfare (the ensuing part about the true warfare comes in verse 7: "Resist the devil and he will flee from you"), but
unfortunately it is not included here.

Gospel: Mark 9:30-37

The structure of this pericope is as remarkable as that of last Sunday's
gospel. First we have a prediction of the passion (the second of three in
Mark), followed by an exhortation to live out the cross in Christian life.
Here this exhortation is expressed in terms of servanthood and humility.
It is, of course, the evangelist himself, not historical reminiscence, that
is responsible for the ordering of the material. Mark is again polemicizing
against the false teachers of his time, who understood Christ as a divine
miracle-worker and themselves as his successors. Against this false
Christology and false concept of ministry the evangelist sets the ideal of
the suffering servant, of service and humility exemplified in the cross.

The Homily

Today's gospel invites reflection on the servanthood of the Church and
its ministry, based on the suffering servanthood of her Lord. The Second
Vatican Council sought to replace the ideal of a triumphalist Church with
that of the servant Church. How is this being implemented today in the
pattern of ministry and in the life of the congregation?

The second reading offers an opportunity to make a plea for peace
in the congregation if there is internal strife, to trace such strife to its roots
in jealousy, selfish ambition, covetousness (which includes the desire for
power as well as for money), and passion. One can avoid being merely
moralistic by rooting the exhortation to peace in the concept of the
heavenly wisdom that is the gift of God.

TWENTY-SIXTH SUNDAY OF THE YEAR

Reading I: Numbers 11:25-29

This is a somewhat confused story. Moses had appointed seventy elders to assist him in governing the people in the wilderness. The elders were given a share in some of the "spirit" of Moses to assist them. This resulted in a temporary manifestation of charismatic prophecy among the seventy elders. After it ceased, two men, Eldad and Medad, received a belated illapse of the spirit and likewise engaged in charismatic prophecy. (This is the confusing part.) It appears that Eldad and Medad were not members of the group of seventy elders, that is, not in the legitimate succession. An overzealous young man urged Moses to stop them from exercising an unauthorized ministry but Moses refused—the Spirit cannot be confined to regularly appointed offices. Its freedom to blow where it wills is a pointer to the day when the whole people of God will prophesy—an aspiration that Christian faith can see fulfilled at Pentecost.

The caption does not adequately express the reason for the choice of this reading. The question is not "Who decrees that all may prophesy?" but "Does God confine the gift of his Spirit to authorized channels?" That is the question raised in today's gospel.

Responsorial Psalm: 19:7, 9, 11-13

Although this psalm is used on other occasions (the Easter Vigil and the third Sunday of the year in series C), this is the only place in our Sunday series where this very fine prayer that we may be cleansed of our secret faults, especially the sin of pride, occurs. (I remember being told by the conductor of my pre-ordination retreat that this prayer should constantly be on the lips of a priest.) Its relation to the Old Testament reading is not immediately apparent, but perhaps if Moses had used his authority to stop unauthorized charismatics, it would have been an expression of the sin of clerical pride and a misuse of clerical power! 68 451

Reading II: James 5:1-6

This exhortation, the tenth in the series in the Letter of James, is allegedly based on the name of Asher (Gen 49:20). It is a warning to the rich against exploiting their employees. Like the selection for the twenty-third Sunday, this is one of the few New Testament passages that shows concern for social justice (the reasons for this comparative silence were indicated in our comments on the twenty-third Sunday). Again, the author is careful to provide a theological basis for his social ethic: the cry of the exploited has "reached the ears of the Lord of hosts." The divine title deliberately recalls the Old Testament prophets and their social teaching. 345

Gospel: Mark 9:38-43, 45, 47-48

[Note: The apparent omission of verses 44 and 46 is due to the fact that these verses are mere repetitions of verse 48 and do not appear in the earliest and best manuscripts.]

This passage combines two different traditions. The first is the pericope about the strange exorcist; the second, a series of warnings against offenses, which appear in a different context in Q (Luke 17:1-2), and in yet another context in the Matthean redaction of Q (Matt 5:29-30). Mark's arrangement has the effect of making the sayings against offenses a comment on the episode of the strange exorcist. To forbid the exorcist would be to cause one of these little ones to stumble, an effect to be avoided at all costs.

The Homily

The combination of the Old Testament reading, the psalm, and the gospel offers exciting possibilities. We have here a warning against clerical arrogance that refuses to recognize the charisms possessed by members of the Church (or indeed of people outside the Church's fellowship—see the gospel) and to see in their activities a genuine witness to the work of the Spirit and to the cause of Christ.

The second reading provides an opportunity to preach on social justice. In the United States, as in most Western countries, unions generally provide adequate insurance against the exploitation of employees by employers, although even here there are instances of abuse. And in some poorer countries there is evidence of serious underpayment (below the subsistence level) of laborers by American firms. The Christian Churches in this country should speak out and act as shareholders against this injustice, armed with the authority of Jas 5:1-6.

TWENTY-SEVENTH SUNDAY OF THE YEAR

Reading I: Genesis 2:18-24

As the reader is doubtless aware, this passage comes from the J (Yahwist) story of creation. It is an earlier tradition than the P (Priestly) creation story in Gen 1. Whereas the P story pictures man and woman as the culmination of creation, the J story makes the same theological point by picturing them as its center. Thus, in the P story human beings are created *after* the animals and in both male and female sexes. Here, however, man (male) is created first, the animals are then created to serve him (naming them indicates control over them), and finally woman is created from his "rib." The meaning of this word is uncertain, but it is intended to suggest the common humanity of man and woman (as the P story also does in a different way), as well as the derivative status of woman in relation to man.

Thus, it was the J story rather than the P story that provided the New Testament writers with materials to reinforce the then current view of woman's subordination to man (see 1 Cor 11:8-9; 1 Tim 2:13). However, the main thrust of Genesis is not the subordination of woman but her complementariness to man. Unlike the animals, she is a real consort—a help fit for him (the Authorized Version has "meet" for "fit," giving rise to the popular non-word "helpmeet."). Verse 24 is a conclusion drawn from the story of woman's creation as just described.

The little word "therefore" in verse 24 is the linchpin of the whole pericope. The story of the rib is an etiological myth designed to explain why it is that a man leaves his parents and marries a woman. It is because man and woman share a common humanity and are complementary to each other, and therefore neither is complete without the other. "One flesh" means more than merely physical union, though it includes that. "Flesh" in Hebrew means the whole human person in contrast to God, the human person in his/her humanness, with all its historical limitations (Paul will later add the notion of sinfulness to the word "flesh"). Flesh, therefore, includes the "spiritual" as well as the physical aspects of human nature.

Responsorial Psalm: 128:1-6

This psalm portrays an idealized picture of family life in Israel. It also breathes the spirit of Deuteronomy, with its rather naive belief that devotion to the Torah ("fears the Lord . . . walks in his ways") is rewarded in this world with prosperity and happiness. But the idea that piety and virtue are the foundations of family life is not obsolete. As used today, this psalm suits the Genesis story of the institution of marriage and the gospel's reiteration of Genesis, followed, in the longer form, by the pericope about Jesus' blessing of the little children.

Reading II: Hebrews 2:9-11

Today we begin a course of six readings from the Letter to the Hebrews. A few words about our critical presuppositions in dealing with this document will therefore be in order. We would date it about 85 and regard it as written to Greek-speaking Jewish Christians in Italy (probably Rome). These addressees (1) form an esoteric group within the Church; (2) have stagnated instead of grown to Christian maturity. The writer copes with this situation by an elaborate exposition of the theme of Christ's high priesthood, here used as the basis for a series of pep talks based on a typology of the Church as the "wandering people of God" (Käsemann). Just as the Israelites wandered in the wilderness between their departure from Egypt and their entry into the Promised Land, so the Christian community exists "between the times," between the Christ-event and the parousia. Israel stagnated in the wilderness and was punished. How much worse will it be for the Christian community if it neglects an even greater salvation effected through the priestly work of Christ!

In the readings of today and the next two Sundays, the author builds up the case for Jesus' eschatological high priesthood. Although not of the tribe of Levi, Jesus has all the qualifications for the job, including the sharing of our common humanity. He and we have a common origin, and he calls us brothers and sisters (v. 9).

This is, of course, only one side of Hebrews' Christology, for Christ has another origin too. He is also the preexistent Son through whom the world was created (Heb 1:1-3). Christ was even made perfect (!) through suffering. But "perfect" here does not mean moral perfection, as though he was not morally perfect at the outset but had to become so; rather, to become perfect means to achieve a goal or a destiny. It was only by suffering that the Christ could perfectly achieve our salvation and could become our high priest (which is a functional category, not an ontological one). In order to do his work effectively, that is, to plead for us before the Father, the high priest had to have an experiential knowledge of all human infirmities.

Gospel: Mark 10:2-16 (long form); 10:2-12 (short form)

The long form of this gospel comprises two pericopes—the first on divorce, the second on the blessing of children. A form-critical analysis would suggest that we have here part of an early catechism, built up of originally separate traditions about Jesus. A section on marriage would be followed immediately by a section on the family.

Jesus' prohibition of divorce is one of the most widely attested sayings in the tradition, being found in Paul (1 Cor 7:10), Mark-Matthew (the present passage and its parallel in Matt 19:3-9), and Q (Matt 5:31-32/Luke 16:18). The original Q form, best preserved by Luke, enunciates an absolute, unqualified prohibition. Paul, Mark, and Matthew modify the commandment in various ways. Paul introduces the "Pauline privilege" (making a Christian convert free to remarry if the non-Christian partner divorces him/her). By the device of secret teaching, Mark extends the prohibition of divorce on the part of the husband to divorce on the part of the wife, thus adapting Jesus' prohibition to Roman law, which, unlike Jewish law, allowed a wife to divorce her husband. Matthew in turn modifies the commandment by introducing into both his Marcan and Q sources the famous "Matthean exception," permitting divorce in the case of the wife's unchastity (*porneia*).

It is clear that when the Church came to treat Jesus' eschatological enunciation of the absolute prohibition of divorce as a community law, it was compelled to adapt and even to modify its absolute character in various ways. The Marcan version recognizes that divorce was allowed in the Mosaic period because of hardness of heart, that is, sin. Since sin is in principle done away with in Christ, a reversion to the condition before the fall, where divorce was unknown, becomes feasible. But the New Testament Church realized that despite the new life in Christ, people were still open to temptation and sin, and if Christ's absolute prohibition was to be treated as a law, concessions would have to be made. The point is not that the particular concessions made in the New Testament, and these only, are valid for all time, but that the New Testament grants to the Church the authority to make concessions that are pastorally necessary, while at the same time keeping Jesus' absolute prohibition before men and women and making it clear that anything short of radical obedience is sinful in the eyes of God, and therefore in need of forgiveness.

The pericope about the blessing of the children has its nucleus in the saying about receiving the kingdom of God as a little child, a saying also attested in a variant form by the Johannine tradition (John 3:3). The combination of this saying with the story of Jesus' blessing the children may have been taken as a justification for the early Church's practice of baptizing the children of Christian converts (so J. Jeremias).

The Homily

The combination of the Old Testament reading and the gospel permits a treatment of marriage as a state of life created by God himself. Marriage, in other words, is not a mere human ordinance that can be abolished at will, as many seem to think today. True, marriage as God intended it in creation can never be fully equated with the social institutionalization of it in any given period of history. It is often the current institutionalized form of marriage that many people are really rejecting, not marriage as intended by God. The Bible, however, affirms that marriage is not a human option but a divine creation. Christian theology has expressed this in various ways—for example, in terms of natural law, as an ordinance of creation, or as a divine mandate (D. Bonhoeffer).

The reading from Hebrews offers the homilist an opportunity to grapple with the full humanity of our Lord. Anyone who has read John A. T. Robinson's *The Human Face of God* may be moved to do this. The New

Testament is emphatic that the humanity of Jesus was full and undiminished, and that his divinity must never be taken as a presupposition into which our understanding of Jesus' human history must be forced. But at the same time, the divine that is manifested in Jesus is full and complete for its purpose at every stage of his mission. Note how Hebrews can allow 1:1-4 and 2:10 to stand side by side, without letting the one compromise the other: the heavenly origin of Jesus and of his history must be asserted along with his completely human origin.

TWENTY-EIGHTH SUNDAY OF THE YEAR

Reading I: Wisdom 7:7-11
The tradition of comparing wisdom and material wealth, to the disadvantage of the latter, goes back to Solomon's prayer in 1 Kgs 3:6-9. The comparison becomes a commonplace in wisdom literature (the price of wisdom is above rubies) and matches the gospel story of the rich young man.

Responsorial Psalm: 90:12-17
Little is known about the origin of this psalm, familiar to many generations of Anglicans from its use at funerals (but less used today). As the first stanza shows, it is influenced by wisdom theology ("that we may get a heart of wisdom"). This is its link with the prayer of Solomon, and one might have expected the refrain to highlight this point.

Reading II: Hebrews 4:12-13
The New Testament teaching about the word of God takes for granted what is said about it in the Old Testament. There God's word is an effective power that intervenes in human affairs, and particularly in Israel's salvation history. It effects what it says (Isa 55:10-11).

Today's passage from Hebrews deepens the Old Testament teaching. The word's effects extend to the very heart of the individual believer. And whereas in the Old Testament the word of God was primarily his word announced by the prophets—a word that had in the first instance to do with Israel's contemporary history, interpreting it as judgment or salvation—the word of God in the New Testament is the gospel message. This gives us the context of our present passage. The people to whom Hebrews is addressed are drifting away from the gospel through boredom and stagnation (their behavior is typified by the murmuring of the Israelites in the wilderness). They are warned that the gospel is not something to be trifled with. Failure to persevere in faith and to develop toward maturity incurs just as sharp a judgment as willful rejection of the gospel in the first place.

Gospel: Mark 10:17-30 (long form); 10:17-27 (short form)

The long form of this reading represents a combination of three units of material: (1) the rich young man (this is the usual name of the pericope, though only Matthew calls him a young man) in verses 17-22; (2) the comparison of entry into the kingdom of God to a camel going through the eye of a needle in verses 23-27; (3) the saying on the rewards of discipleship in verses 28-31. The shorter form is obtained by omitting the third unit.

These somewhat disparate pieces of tradition have been combined to form a sort of catechesis on the Christian attitude toward wealth. Of these items, the first is clearly the most important, and we will concentrate upon it. To begin with, we must dispose of a preliminary problem. It has long been a difficulty for piety and orthodoxy that Jesus should have rejected the address "Good Teacher" with the reply that "no one is good but God alone." Was not Jesus good and was he not God? Matthew already felt something of this difficulty, for he substitutes "Why do you ask me concerning that which is good?" Once more, however, we have to remind ourselves that we run into difficulties if we approach the Jesus of history with the presuppositions of Christian piety or later dogmatics. We have to approach him first as a real human being, reacting as a real human being—especially as a devout Jew would—to flattery or insincerity, and as a prophet confronting men and women with the goodness of God alone. Later on, piety and dogmatics will discover the sinlessness of Jesus and his deity in that true humanity.

In seeking to understand this episode, it is important that we divest ourselves of unconscious memories of Matthew's version. There Jesus presents the renunciation of wealth and personal discipleship as counsels of perfection: "If you would be perfect . . ." (Matt 19:21). In other words, it is not necessary to salvation to renounce all wealth and to follow Jesus in that particular way. Here, however, it is a challenge to radical decision in face of the coming of God's kingdom. This absolute challenge is far more in accord with Jesus' eschatological preaching.

Note, however, that the renunciation of wealth is not an end in itself but only a precondition for following Jesus. This particular man has to renounce what was an impediment for him in order to obey the command "Follow me." It is the life of discipleship, not the renunciation of wealth *per se,* that leads to eternal life. It is not enough to obey the Mosaic law in order to enter eternal life; beyond all that, it is necessary to accept Jesus' eschatological message and to follow him in the way of discipleship. This is one of the Gospel episodes that show the high degree of continuity between Jesus' proclamation of God's kingdom and Paul's preaching of justification.

The Homily

Once again we have a choice between the Old Testament reading and the gospel on the one hand, and the second reading on the other. The first of these choices confronts us with the subject of riches as an obstacle to Christian discipleship. For some this will mean a complete renunciation (monasticism). But such renunciation is not an end in itself but only a presupposition for a life of discipleship. To most it will mean, not renunciation, but stewardship of wealth. It is following Jesus that matters, and all Christians are called to do that.

The second reading provides an occasion to speak about the biblical understanding of the word of God. It would be all too easy to speak in abstractions, and the only way to avoid this is to pay close attention to the concrete situation in which the author of Hebrews is writing (see the commentary above). The situation of the Church today has certain analogies with the situation of the Church in Hebrews. We too are disillusioned. There is a certain loss of morale. Only by emphasizing the finality of Christ's claim and the dire consequences of backsliding can this state of affairs be overcome. Yet, the author of Hebrews knows that a mere pep talk is not enough; what is needed is an exposition of the finality of the Christ-event.

TWENTY-NINTH SUNDAY OF THE YEAR

Reading I: Isaiah 53:10-11

We commented on the fourth servant song before, especially in the readings of Holy Week. This extract was chosen because it contains the key word "many": "by his knowledge shall the righteous one, my servant, make *many* to be accounted righteous." In later Judaism, rabbinic comment interpreted "many" here to mean, not some, but all—that is, the nations of the world—thus ascribing universal significance to the servant's work (in rabbinic interpretation, the servant was not the Messiah but Israel). In the Christian application of this prophecy to Christ, the universality of his redeeming work is expressed by the use of "many" from the servant song, as in the gospel reading for today (Mark 10:45).

61
251

Responsorial Psalm: 33:4-5, 18-20, 22

Psalm 33 is a hymn of praise suitable for any occasion. The choice of verses for today does not appear to be motivated by anything in the readings, unless we are meant to have in mind the servant who waits for God's vindication of him and his unmerited sufferings (first reading).

Reading II: Hebrews 4:14-16

These verses take up the theme of Christ's full humanity, which was touched upon in the second reading two weeks ago. They affirm that Christ is fully qualified to be high priest because he shares our humanity, enabling him to sympathize with us in our weakness. He knows what we are from his own personal experience. More than that, he has been tempted "in every respect" as we are, "yet without sinning." Are we supposed to take "in every respect" literally? Several writers have seized upon this phrase and extended it to include sexual temptation. Now it is quite obvious that the author of Hebrews did not arrive at this conviction by examining every phase of our Lord's inner life. The evidence was not at his disposal anyway, for the Gospel tradition shows practically no interest in the psychological experience of Jesus. The case is similar to the ensuing phrase, "yet without sinning," a conviction shared by other New Testament writers and therefore part of the common early Christian tradition. No one ever examined every overt act that our Lord did and concluded that he was sinless.

The clue to the meaning of these statements is to be found in the temptation stories in the Gospels. Each of these temptations was concerned with the fulfillment of Jesus' role in salvation history—in post-Easter terms, with his messianic vocation. The temptations were temptations to abandon that role and to follow a different line. Jesus' sinlessness, accordingly, means his total commitment to his Father's call to perform this unique function in salvation history. Speculations as to whether Jesus underwent any temptations unrelated to his messianic vocation, though prompted by this rhetorical statement of Hebrews, is kerygmatically irrelevant for the New Testament. If we ask, Was our Lord subject to sexual temptation?, we are asking a question that the New Testament is not concerned to ask. That may be disappointing to our post-Freudian world, but perhaps that in itself is a judgment upon our contemporary obsessions.

Gospel: Mark 10:35-45 (long form); 10:42-45 (short form)

Two units of material comprise this passage—the Zebedees' question and the saying about true greatness. The shorter form contains only the second of these units. Before Mark, the Zebedees' question was probably an independent piece of tradition whose preservation in the Church was due to a biographical interest in the fate of John. Church tradition is ambiguous, part of it ascribing to John likewise an early martyrdom, the main stream identifying him with the author of the Johannine writings, who allegedly lived to a very old age.

Mark uses this traditional saying as an introduction to the saying on true greatness. It is part of Mark's use of the disciples throughout his Gospel as symbols of the dangers to which the Church in his own day was exposed. These dangers were twofold: a fascination with the "divine-man" Christology and dismay at the prospect of persecution. These two concerns provide the background for Mark's use of the two elements of material at this point. This story forms the climax of Mark's central section (Mark 8:22–10:45), in which he counters the twin heresies afflicting his Church with the proclamation of Jesus as the Son of man who is to be crucified (as opposed to Christ as the divine man or miracle-worker), and the Christian life as a challenge to take up one's cross and follow him.

The Homily

The Old Testament reading and the gospel set before us the picture of Christ the suffering servant as the model for Christian existence. Mark saw this as a rebuke to the "heresy" that afflicted his Church. It would be appropriate for the homilist to identify something in the life of the contemporary Church that parallels the heresy of Mark's Church (triumphalism? clericalism? something on the local level?) and suggest ways in which the Church must seek to become the servant Church.

The homilist who is following the readings from Hebrews might want to explore the implications of the statement that Christ was tempted in every respect as we are, yet was without sin, seeking to draw out first its Christological implications and limitations, and secondly its devotional value.

THIRTIETH SUNDAY OF THE YEAR

Reading I: Jeremiah 31:7-9

This passage is part of the second of a series of four poems celebrating the return from the Babylonian Exile. These poems are obviously akin to Deutero-Isaiah, though their exact literary relationship to that work is uncertain. Perhaps the four hymns are products of the Deutero-Isaianic school and somehow got attached to the prophecies of Jeremiah in an attempt to relieve that prophet's preoccupation with the decline and fall of the southern kingdom and the adjustment to life in exile.

However, Jeremiah was certainly hopeful of the eventual restoration of his people, as is indicated in his prophecy of the new covenant that comes later in chapter 31. Like a similar hymn of the return in Isa 35, this hymn stresses the presence of the weak, the blind and the lame, nursing and pregnant mothers among those returning from exile. In pictorial language this underlines the *sola gratia* aspect of the return. It is the mention of the blind here that doubtless influenced the choice of this passage to match the healing of the blind Bartimaeus in the gospel.

Responsorial Psalm: 126:1-6

It would be hard to find a more appropriate psalm to go with Jer 31:7-9, for like that hymn it celebrates the return from Babylon, and indeed the contrast between sorrow and joy is the theme of both passages. It is a pity that the psalm does not say anything about the blind, though, for that would tie in with the gospel too.

Reading II: Hebrews 5:1-6

Slowly the author of Hebrews is preparing for the exposition of his great theological theme—the high priesthood of Christ. Except for the reading on the twenty-eighth Sunday, all our passages through today's are concerned to establish Jesus' qualifications for high priesthood. Here the following qualifications are spelled out:

1) Due appointment by God.

2) The selection of Christ from among human beings to act as their representative before God in offering sacrifices for sins.

3) Sympathy for the ignorant and the wayward (a repetition from our earlier readings).

The later part of our reading takes up the first point—appointment by God. Jesus was appointed as Son and high priest at his resurrection (Pss 2:7; 110:4). Some may be surprised to see Ps 2:7 applied to the resurrection. It suggests an Adoptionist Christology (the heresy defined by a former colleague of mine as the view that Christ was a man who graduated in divinity with honors). But we are still moving within the orbit of Hebraic Christology, which is functional rather than metaphysical. Psalm 2 originally celebrated the king's coronation. From that point Christ embarked upon the functions of kingship, that is, the functions of the Son of God. So it is at his exaltation that Christ embarks upon his messianic functions, which include that of high priest. Incidentally, this shows that Christ's high priestly work is performed in heaven and that Calvary is only the preliminary to it.

Gospel: Mark 10:46-52

Normally the tendency of the synoptic tradition is for unnamed figures to acquire names, a process that continues in Church tradition (for example, the naming of the three wise men). Here, however, the process is reversed. The earlier evangelist, Mark, names the blind man, while Matthew and Luke drop the name. Bartimaeus must have been known later in the Christian community (at Jericho?) that first remembered and shaped the story. Probably he would have addressed Jesus simply as "Rabbi" (or "Rabbouni," v. 51; the rsv has "Master"). The post-Easter community would have used this story as a vehicle for its Davidic Christology by inserting the address "Son of David" (and is "have mercy on" liturgical?). Mark in turn received the story from the tradition, placed it here because of its geographical location (Jericho), and used it as a coda to his central section (8:22–10:45). That section thus ends as it had begun—with the healing of a blind man. This blind man follows Jesus in the "Way," a technical term for Christian discipleship. All this is part of Mark's answer to the "heresy that necessitated his Gospel" (the title of an important article by T. Weeden).

The true disciple is cured of Christological blindness—that is, of seeing in Jesus only the miracle-worker and not the suffering servant—and follows him in the Way of the cross.

The Homily

The homilist may want to take the gospel reading and feature the life of the contemporary Christian community, showing in what ways it can be characterized as blindness (its refusal to abandon false securities from the past?), and how the gospel of Christ crucified and the challenges to live a life in the way of the cross are a cure for that blindness.

The second reading could be used to examine the nature of priesthood: the representative nature of the priest's office ("chosen from among men"); appointment by God; the Godward direction of the priest's function on behalf of God's people. It could then be shown how all this is fulfilled in Christ and made visible in the life of the Church through the Church's own priestly character and through the ministerial priesthood.

THIRTY-FIRST SUNDAY OF THE YEAR

Reading I: Deuteronomy 6:2-6

The first paragraph of this reading forms an introduction. Israel is entering the Promised Land, and its side of the covenant is to keep the law of God from generation to generation. The second paragraph consists of the *Shema*, which became the daily Jewish prayer. God is to be loved in response to his prior revelation of himself as the one God. That divine unity was revealed through the Exodus event and, for the Deuteronomist, through the perpetual accessibility to his presence at the one central sanctuary. To love in this context means to trust solely in him and to reject the many gods of the heathens. In Hebraic thought, heart, soul, and strength do not mean separate human faculties but the person in the totality of his/her being. Thus, the radical nature of God's claim on Israelite obedience is emphasized.

Responsorial Psalm: 18:1-3, 46, 50ab

Psalm 18 is one of the royal psalms (note the third stanza), possibly going back to David. It is a thanksgiving for victory in battle. The refrain, taken from the first verse, forms an admirable response to the *Shema*.

Reading II: Hebrews 7:23-28

Having established the qualifications of Jesus to be high priest, the author at last embarks upon an exposition of his main theological theme. It consists of a point-by-point comparison of Jesus with the Levitical priests of the old covenant, demonstrating that at each point Jesus and the effect of his work are superior to them and the effects of their work. These are the main points of comparison in this excerpt:

Levitical Priest	*Christ*
many	only one
impermanent	eternal
subject to death	alive forever
sinner—had to offer for himself	sinless—no need to offer for himself
repeated sacrifices	once-for-all sacrifice
appointed by law	appointed by oath superseding law

Gospel: Mark 12:28b-34

The double commandment of love had a triple attestation. In Mark it is presented in a Hellenized form. The *Shema* is directed against pagan polytheism. The addition of mind/understanding to the list of faculties brings out the meaning of the Hebrew word for "heart" (*lebab*), which was the organ of intellectual activity, while the higher value placed on ethical obedience as contrasted with sacrificial cultus is typical of Hellenistic Judaism. Matthew's form lacks these features, and it is couched in a highly Semitic Greek. Hence it looks more primitive than Mark's. Luke's form, in our opinion, is an adaptation of the Marcan form and serves as an introduction to the parable of the Good Samaritan.

There has been much discussion about whether the double commandment is original with Jesus. Actually it is a combination of two different Old Testament passages, Deut 6 and Lev 19, so its contents cannot be regarded as original in themselves. But what about the combination of the two commandments, and what about their use as a summary of the whole Torah? The idea of summarizing the Torah under a single basic commandment was not unknown to rabbinic Judaism, which occasionally used the commandment to love one's neighbor in this way. But the rabbis never combined this commandment with the commandment to love God. However, the combination is found several times in the *Testaments of the Twelve Patriarchs*, and there are other hints of it in the writings of Hellenistic Judaism. In fact, it seems to be characteristic of Jewish wisdom tradition, both Palestinian and Hellenistic. It must have been from that source that it came to Jesus. Is there, then, anything distinctive about his use of it? Yes, for Jesus understands the interconnection between the two commandments in a quite radical sense. Love of God is illusory if it does not issue in love of neighbor, and love of neighbor is refined self-love if it does not proceed from the love of God.

The Homily

Today the homilist will probably want to deal with the double commandment of love as the summarization of Christian duty, bringing out the radical interconnection between the two commandments and illustrating it with examples from life. It should be emphasized that this is not merely an external, legal requirement but an existential response to God's revelation of himself as the one God (note the *Shema*, which prefaces the commandment in its Marcan form as in the Deuteronomic source).

If, on the other hand, the homilist is giving a course of sermons on Hebrews, today's second reading calls for an exposition of the nature of Christ's high priestly work—his offering of himself once for all and his pleading of that sacrifice eternally in heaven by making intercession for us. It is in the Eucharistic sacrifice that we find this heavenly intercession set before us as a concrete reality. In the words of the popular Eucharistic hymn composed by the Anglican hymn-writer W. Chatterton Dix but sung ecumenically:

> Thou within the veil hast entered,
> Robed in flesh, our great high priest;
> Thou on earth both priest and victim
> In the Eucharistic feast.

It is in terms of this concrete realization at the Eucharist that the homilist will find it most fitting to set forth the high priestly work of the ascended Christ.

THIRTY-SECOND SUNDAY OF THE YEAR

Reading I: 1 Kings 17:10-16

Both the Elijah and the Elisha cycles contain miracles involving the multiplication of food, and as such exhibit the literary genre to which the stories of miraculous feedings in the Gospels are conformed. This is their main importance for the New Testament.

The story of the widow's cruse, like the following story of the raising of her son, emphasizes the power of God's word in the prophet's mouth. In this story the power of that word is seen in the fulfillment in verse 16 of the promise given in verse 14.

Neither of these points, however, has determined the selection of the episode of the widow's cruse for today's reading. Rather, she is seen as a widow woman of the same character as the widow with the two coins in the gospel story. Both widows gave away all that they possessed.

Responsorial Psalm: 146:6c-10

This is the first psalm in the final group of Hallel psalms. God is praised for his loving-kindness toward the needy, including widows. Hence its selection here.

Reading II: Hebrews 9:24-28

This reading continues the exposition of the high priestly work of Christ in terms of a series of contrasts with the Levitical priesthood. Here are the points made this time, some of them repeated from last Sunday's passage, some of them new:

Levitical priest	*Christ*
scene of his work: a material sanctuary	the heavenly sanctuary, God's real presence
repeated offering (yearly)	once for all
offered blood of other creatures	offered his own blood

The last sentence of our reading seeks to elucidate the once-for-all character of human death. The reference to the parousia comes rather surprisingly here, but it is probable that all through this passage the author has in mind the ceremony on the Day of Atonement. After performing his priestly work in the Holy Place, the high priest came out of the temple and showed himself to the people, indicating thereby that the work of atonement had been accomplished. The parousia likewise will mark the completion of Christ's high priestly work. Note that the passages from Hebrews used last Sunday and today feature the two phrases that most clearly indicate the nature of Christ's high priestly work in heaven: "he always lives to make intercession for them" (7:25) and "now to appear in the presence of God on our behalf" (9:24).

Gospel: Mark 12:38-44 (long form); 12:41-44 (short form)

The longer form of this gospel combines two quite distinct traditions: Jesus' denunciation of the scribes and the episode of the widow with two coins. The denunciation of the scribes forms the conclusion to the series of Jerusalem conflict stories, whose function is to show the widening gulf between Jesus and the Jerusalem authorities, and so to prepare the way for the Sanhedrin's decision to get rid of Jesus. The episode of the widow is joined to the denunciation by the *Stichwort* principle (the word "widow" occurs in each unit). Also, Mark has located the conflicts in the temple, and the story of the widow is located there by its content.

Whether by design or not, however, the two stories, taken together in this way, provide a foil for one another, for the behavior of the scribes is contrasted sharply with that of the widow. Perhaps the story of the widow was used in catechesis to illustrate the duty of almsgiving.

The Homily

Today's readings invite the homilist to bring out the similarities in the behavior of the two widows: each was prepared to give up all that she had. Both, therefore, are examples of service and almsgiving.

If the homilist is giving a series of sermons on Hebrews, today's homily might be devoted to an exposition of the work of Christ in appearing in the presence of God on our behalf. Again, this could be related to the Eucharist as Christ's heavenly intercession was related to the Eucharist last Sunday.

THIRTY-THIRD SUNDAY OF THE YEAR

This Sunday marks the shift in the post-Pentecost season to the great themes of the End. This theme will be in the forefront from now through the first Sunday of Advent.

Reading I: Daniel 12:1-3

Apocalypses follow a regular pattern. The apocalyptist first recounts, under the guise of future prediction, a selected series of historical events up to the moment of writing, then indicates future historical events rather vaguely, and finally, becoming airborne as it were, foretells the cosmic events of the End: resurrection and the last judgment, the cosmic consummation.

Our present passage comes precisely at this last transition. "Trouble" is vaguely historical, but the deliverance that follows is the point at which history yields to cosmic eschatology. The deliverance takes the form of resurrection. Daniel 12 is notable as one of the earliest passages in the Old Testament that speaks of resurrection. Then follows the final judgment, in which the righteous and the wicked are separated, the former passing to eternal life, the rest to eternal "shame and everlasting contempt."

Note that the resurrection life involves a radical transformation: the redeemed will shine like the brightness of the firmament and like stars. This apocalyptic concept of radical transformation is taken up in the New Testament, where the synoptic Jesus speaks of it as a life like that of the angels in heaven (Mark 12:25 par.) and where Paul speaks of the spiritual body (1 Cor 15; Phil 3:21). It is important to note that the resurrection is understood, not as a resuscitation to the same mode of existence as in the present life, but as a complete transformation. What that life is like can only be described in poetic terms, as here, or in Paul's more abstract but question-begging phrase, a "spiritual body." It means entrance into a totally transcendental mode of existence.

Responsorial Psalm: 16:5, 8-11

This psalm expresses a devout individual's trust and hope in Yahweh to deliver him from Sheol and the Pit. It can hardly have meant resurrection from the dead in the apocalyptic sense, but, as so often in the Old Testament psalms, deliverance at death's door. Later this passage will be taken up into early Christian apologetic and applied to the death and resurrection of Christ (see the kerygmatic speeches in Acts 2 and 13). This is not a falsification of the psalm's original meaning but a deepening of it. It is in this latter sense that we are invited to understand the psalm as a response to Dan 12, though it is further extended to cover the hope of the general resurrection and not only Christ's resurrection.

Reading II: Hebrews 10:11-14, 18

Marking the conclusion of the theological core of Hebrews, this passage contrasts the high priesthood of Christ with the Levitical priesthood. The author reiterates his point about the repetition of the Levitical sacrifice. Last Sunday's reading, in making the same point, spoke of the yearly offering on the Day of Atonement; here the writer turns to the daily sacrifices offered, not by the high priest, but by the ordinary Levitical priests.

"He sat down" must not be pressed to mean that Christ has no further priestly work in heaven, as is suggested by some commentators. The heavenly session is only an image conveying one aspect of the truth, not an exclusive definition. In relation to his death, resurrection, and ascension, Christ's work is completed; therefore he can sit, waiting for the full effects of his victory to be gathered in at the parousia ("until his enemies should be made a stool for his feet"). But in relation to the ongoing life of the Christian community, his priestly work continues. He still makes intercession for us and still appears in the presence of God. That could be expressed by the image of standing (see Acts 7:56), which does not contradict the other image of sitting.

"Perfected" does not denote moral perfection. It means rather that the beneficiaries of Christ's sacrifice have been completely initiated. They are privileged, through Christ, to enter the heavenly sanctuary through liturgical worship while here on earth, and thus to attain already here, by anticipation, the goal and destiny of human life.

"There is no longer any offering for sin": Christ's sacrifice can never be repeated. But this does not rule out its constant application through his heavenly intercession and his appearing in the presence of God on our behalf.

Gospel: Mark 13:24-32

This excerpt from Mark's "Little Apocalypse" starts at exactly the same place as the reading from Daniel—at the point where the apocalypse moves from future historical events vaguely conceived (cf. Mark's "tribulation" with Daniel's "time of trouble") to a series of cosmic events. Here the latter are expanded with imagery drawn from other parts of the Old Testament: the failure of sun, moon, and stars. Then comes the last judgment; here Mark differs from Daniel in the role given to the Son of man (this figure has appeared earlier in Daniel, in chapter 7, a passage that will be read next week). Mark's portrait of the Son of man is, however, more precise than that in Daniel. In Daniel he appears as a symbol and personification of the people of God at the End, whereas in Mark he is an individual figure who performs the eschatological judgment.

Some seek to assimilate Mark's Son of man to Daniel's by harmonizing the two figures. They argue that the Son of man in Mark 13 does not descend from heaven to earth but, as in Dan 7, is manifested in heaven—in other words, it is not a parousia but an exaltation scene. However, in view of firmly established Christian tradition, discernible as early as 1 Thess 4:16, this seems most unlikely, and we are on surer ground if we take it to refer to the parousia. The Son of man comes from heaven to earth on the clouds with power and great glory, and sends out his angels, who accompany him to gather the elect and escort them to heaven. Clearly there has been a development of the myth of the Son of man between the Book of Daniel (165 B.C.) and the New Testament. Such a development is attested in Enoch 37–71, though it is not certain whether that part of Enoch predates the New Testament.

That Jesus himself spoke of the Son of man in this developed sense as the eschatological judge and savior is most probable, but that he painted elaborate apocalyptic pictures as in Mark 13 is improbable. Jesus proclaimed that the Son of man would judge people according as they accepted or rejected his own eschatological message. He thus reduced the Son of man to the status of a rubber stamp for his own word and work. After the resurrection Jesus was manifested as himself, the heavenly Son of man—in other words, as his own rubber stamp, ratifying his own word and work. The early Church then expanded the apocalyptic imagery to express its faith that the Son of man would come again as Jesus.

In the synoptic apocalypses there is a tendency for eschatological parables to be collected at the end, and so here we have the parable of the fig tree—undoubtedly a genuine parable of Jesus, which in its original setting spoke of his ministry as the dawning of the shortly-to-be-consummated kingdom. It is placed here to assure Mark's readers that the apocalyptic events just described are near at hand. Mark's Gospel was written in the sixties, before the hope of the imminent end had begun to fade, with a consequent deferral of the parousia.

After the parable come three sayings. The first (v. 30) could well be an authentic saying of Jesus in which "these things" referred to something other than the apocalyptic denouement—perhaps to the vindication of his own word and work. The second saying (v. 31), also probably authentic, expresses similarly Jesus' certainty about the validity of his eschatological message. Placed here by Mark, "my words" again refer to the apocalyptic events. The final word (v. 32) has caused much debate, centering on two questions: (1) the authenticity of the saying; (2) Jesus' disclaimer of knowledge about the date of the final consummation. As for (1), many would agree with Schmiedel, for whom this was one of the "pillar passages," that is, indubitably authentic precisely because of its frank admission of the Son's ignorance. But did Jesus explicitly call himself the Son? (That he had a unique filial consciousness is beyond doubt; see his use of "Abba.") This verse seems to lie somewhere along the trajectory leading from the cry of jubilation (Matt 11:25-26 par.) to the Johannine sayings about the Father and the Son. (2) Whether this saying goes back to Jesus or to the early post-Easter community, neither party shared the perspectives of Chalcedonian Christology. Therefore, we should not approach this text with the assumption of later Christology. Historically, Jesus' knowledge comprised what was sufficient for the performance of his eschatological mission, no more.

As we look back over the "Little Apocalypse" of Mark 13, we see that it was developed by combining authentic eschatological sayings and parables of Jesus with traditional apocalyptic material, for example the saying about the coming of the Son of man. Thus, a very different impression is created from Jesus' own proclamation that spoke of the inbreaking of the kingdom and the certainty of speedy vindication of his message. We may believe that this apocalyptic elaboration spoke meaningfully to Mark's Church, beset as it was by temptations of a divine-man Christology and by persecution.

The Homily

Apocalyptic material such as our first reading and the gospel passage creates a delicate problem for the homilist. Traditionally, the Church has ignored the biblical sense of imminence and has taken this material as a prediction of a remote consummation of history, appealing sometimes to Mark 13:32, with its admission that only the Father knows the date of the End. Apocalyptic thus became the last chapter of a dogmatic system, lacking any existential relevance for the present life of the Church. In the modern period, apocalyptic has more often than not been dismissed as "Jewish old clothes," representing the mistaken and eventually falsified ideas of early Christian days.

Is there a third way in which we can find a relevant word of God for the contemporary Christian community without falling into the trap of literal imminent expectation? Such an interpretation would have to recognize (1) the essentially mythological character of the apocalyptic material; (2) the cruciality of the imminent expectation. Imminent expectation is a mode of expressing certainty of conviction. Despite the troubles

(Daniel) and tribulation (Mark) that beset the Church at present, we have the certainty of Jesus' promise that there will come vindication and the final achievement of God's saving purpose. It is this conviction that the homilist must seek to put across to the congregation.

The second reading forms the conclusion of a course of readings on Hebrews. The homilist might want to relate Hebrews' insistence on the once-for-all, non-repeatable character of Christ's sacrifice to the Church's theology that the Eucharist is a sacrifice, in the sense that in and through its due performance the once-for-all sacrifice becomes a present reality for our participation. If we do not do this, the theology of Hebrews remains a remote transaction speaking of Calvary or the ascension, with no relevance to the life of the Church today.

Last Sunday of the Year

CHRIST THE KING

The feast of Christ the King, coming as it does at the end of the Church year, has acquired thereby an eschatological significance. Christ's enthronement at the ascension is the opening act of his final eschatological reign, and his continued heavenly rule between the ascension and his return marks the progressive defeat of the powers of evil.

Reading I: Daniel 7:13-14

As we noted last Sunday, the Son of man in Daniel stands for the people of the Lord, the saints of the Most High. We noted, too, that a development of this concept took place in Jewish apocalyptic, so that by the time of the New Testament the Son of man had become an individual, heavenly figure, the agent of final judgment and salvation.

It has been argued recently by a number of scholars that the New Testament, especially the Gospels (for example, Mark 14:62), finds the fulfillment of this prophecy in the *ascension* of our Lord. In other words, the coming is interpreted as a coming *to* the Ancient of Days and not *from* heaven. We reject this interpretation as far as the New Testament is concerned. Christian faith must read Dan 7, not as a prediction of what had already happened—that would be to ignore the "not yet" character of the Christ-event and make this passage more suitable for Ascension Day than for the last day of the Christian year; rather, we must read it as a proclamation (in mythological terms) of the final establishment of Christ's kingly rule. For we do not yet see all things subdued under his feet. Not yet do all peoples, nations, and languages serve him. That they will do so at the End is an inalienable aspect of Christian hope.

Responsorial Psalm: 93:1-2, 5

Psalm 93 is one of the enthronement psalms. Two points need to be observed today. (1) The psalm originally spoke of Yahweh's kingship, not predicting the kingly rule of Christ. (2) The kingdom of which it speaks is an eternal reality. But for Christian interpretation, many texts of the Old Testament that speak of Yahweh can be applied to Christ. It is through Christ, from the time of his ascension on, that the Father exercises his kingdom. Indeed, following the precedent of Paul's interpretation of the Old Testament (that the rock was Christ), we may say that already in the Old Testament, in the perspective of Christian faith, God was exercising his kingly rule through Christ, if by Christ we here mean not Jesus of Nazareth but God going out toward the world and toward human beings in his revelatory and redemptive work.

Reading II: Revelation 1:5-8

By starting at verse 5 instead of at the beginning of the sentence, our reading obscures the fact that this passage comes from the epistolary address of the Apocalypse. It is a greeting *from* Jesus Christ as well as from the Father and the seven spirits. Then a triple doxology follows. Point 1: Christ loves us—note the present tense: Christ's love is perpetual and goes beyond the historical event of the redemption (*Jerome Biblical Commentary*). Point 2: The historical event of the atonement, couched in a traditional creedal formula. Point 3: The effect of the redemption is to set up a community that shares Christ's kingly and priestly functions.

After the doxology there follows a proclamation of the imminent parousia, which is to be the theme of the whole apocalypse. This proclamation draws upon a combination of Old Testament *testimonia*, used elsewhere in the New Testament, from Dan 7:13-14 (our first reading) and Zech 12:10. The reading ends with a self-proclamation of Yahweh under three titles: Alpha and Omega (a Hellenized expression of the Old Testament's "first and last"); a second title asserting that God's being comprises present, past, and future (a reflection on the meaning of "Yahweh"?); and a third title, *Pantocrator* (a Greek rendering of *Sabaoth*, "hosts"). Combined, the three titles look like a meditation on the meaning of *Kyrios ho theos, Yahweh 'elohe sebaoth.*

Gospel: John 18:33b-37

It is beyond all doubt that Jesus was crucified on the charge of being a messianic pretender. This is established by the *titulus* on the cross, handed down in various forms but always agreeing on the essential core: "the King of the Jews" ("King" being the Roman equivalent of "Messiah").

It is not certain precisely what attitude Jesus took toward this charge at the investigation before the Sanhedrin and at his trial before Pilate. Some traditions present him as preserving a stony silence (pleading the fifth amendment, as it were), while others present him as not rejecting the charge but as being at pains to correct it (the answer "You say that I am a king" would be equivalent to "It's your word, not mine"). In the Johannine version of the trial before Pilate, Jesus explicitly corrects the charge by offering a reinterpretation of what kingship means for him. This is done by his answers to three questions put to him by Pilate.

First, Pilate asks him if he is a king. Jesus—in a reply that may be traditional, for it is devoid of Johannine theology—asks where Pilate got his idea. This is to establish the terms of the debate: Are we debating a charge trumped up by the Jewish authorities that I am a messianic pretender? Pilate indicates that the charge originated with the Jewish authorities and asks the defendant what basis there is for his behavior. Jesus' second reply is negative. He says what his kingship is not—it is not political in character ("of this world" is Johannine; "world" means human society organized on the basis of its unbelief). But Jesus insists that in a certain sense, not as yet defined, he is a king. Pilate therefore repeats the first question, thus giving Jesus a chance to state his own definition of kingship. He has come into the world to be the bearer of the divine revelation. Here, then, we have a complete redefinition of messiahship or kingship in terms of Johannine theology. "Truth" in Johannine thought means the reality of God as seen through his revelatory and redemptive action.

The Homily

Drawing on the first reading and the proclamation in Rev 1:7, the homilist might concentrate today on the second coming. If so, we would suggest that it be treated, not as the last chapter of Christian dogmatics, but as an immediate, relevant concern of Christian existence. Christian faith always lives "as if" the second coming were just around the corner, for it is so certain of its vindication.

The second reading suggests an exposition of the way in which the Christian community already here and now shares Christ's kingship and priesthood. We might point to the liturgy as the focal point where its priesthood is expressed and to secular life as the place where its kingship is exercised through service. But then it becomes necessary to insist that Christ's kingship is "not of this world," suggesting a consideration of the relationship between the Church and political power.

Finally, the homilist could concentrate upon the Johannine Christ's redefinition of kingship in terms of witness to the truth. Perhaps it is particularly relevant just now to refute recent attempts to portray Jesus as the paradigm of a political revolutionary.

Series C

ADVENT SEASON

FIRST SUNDAY OF ADVENT

Reading I: Jeremiah 33:14-16

These verses are an almost verbatim repetition of Jer 23:5-6 (see the sixteenth Sunday of the year in series B). In the precritical age, readers would have had no difficulty in supposing that Jeremiah spoke the same oracle on two separate occasions. The common opinion among scholars today is that Jer 23 contains the prophet's original oracle, and that Jer 33 is a revival of this oracle by one of his disciples in a later situation.

Jeremiah had predicted that the Davidic dynasty would be restored shortly after the fall of Jerusalem in 586. But the years of exile were prolonged and the promise went unfulfilled. The exiles were tempted to abandon their ancestral religion and adopt the religion of the surrounding nations. In this situation a later writer repeats Jeremiah's prophecy. No doubt its partial fulfillment was discerned in the return from exile, but Christian faith has seen in it a promise that was not fulfilled until the coming of Jesus, the real Messiah.

While we should not read into the phrase "The Lord is our righteousness" the full Pauline meaning of "righteousness," the use of the word here provides a background for Paul. Righteousness is not an ethical or moral quality but the saving act of Yahweh. The restoration of the Davidic monarchy after the Exile will be seen as Yahweh's mighty act of salvation. Christian faith will see the advent of Christ as God's final act of salvation.

Responsorial Psalm: 25:4-5b, 8-10, 14

Other verses of this psalm are used on the twenty-sixth Sunday of the year in series A, the first Sunday of Lent in series B, and the third Sunday of the year in series B. The idea of Yahweh's righteousness is picked up in the words "truth" (that is, God's fidelity to his promise) and "salvation" in the first stanza, and "steadfast love," "faithfulness," and "cove-

327

172
231
292

nant" in the third stanza. The psalm, accordingly, should not be interpreted moralistically. It speaks of patient waiting for the advent of Yahweh's righteousness.

Reading II: 1 Thessalonians 3:12–4:2

This reading straddles two halves of 1 Thessalonians. In the first half the Apostle reviews his relations with the Thessalonians to date. He is led to thanksgiving and an expression of his loving concern. This section concludes with a blessing or intercession. Paul prays that his converts may continue to grow in holiness until the parousia, the "coming" of Christ, which he expects to happen very soon. This is the first paragraph of our reading.

The second paragraph marks the beginning of the second part of the letter. This contains specific ethical exhortations and a discussion of several theological problems of concern to the young community. Before taking up specifics, Paul reminds his readers in general terms of the catechetical instructions that he had given them during his foundation visit. His original instructions were given "through the Lord Jesus." What precisely does this mean? Paul generally chooses his Christological titles carefully, with an eye on context. The catechesis of the Church rests upon the words of the historical *Jesus* perpetuated by the living *Lord* in his Church. Tradition is not something left behind by a Jesus now dead, but a process inaugurated by Jesus in his earthly life and constantly reenacted as a living word by the exalted *Kyrios*.

Gospel: Luke 21:25-28, 34-36

In series C we will be reading the Gospel of Luke in course. Today's selection, however, is out of course in order to present Luke's future-apocalyptic teaching on the first Sunday of Advent, where it is particularly seasonable.

Although Luke follows Mark in his location of the apocalyptic discourse (just before the passion narrative), he draws much of its content from his special material. Only in verses 25, 26b, and 27 does he follow Mark closely. The synoptic apocalypse was constantly adjusted so that it could speak to the ever-changing situation of the early Christian community. Luke's version, unlike Mark's, regards the Church as here to stay. This lengthy period is marked by "distress of nations" and by human fear and foreboding. And in the Christian community, slackness is setting in. There is dissipation, drunkenness, and the "cares of this life" (see the interpretation of the parable of the sower). In such a situation Luke calls upon his contemporaries to watch and pray.

The Homily

There is a remarkable similarity between the situation of the redactor in the reading from Jeremiah and that of the evangelist Luke. Both inherit traditions—the one from Jeremiah, the other from Mark (and ultimately, no doubt, from the historical Jesus himself)—that apparently have not been fulfilled. Both feel impelled to reiterate these traditions and to assure their readers that the promises of the oracles will be fulfilled despite the long haul. The homilist ought to be able to find analogies in the contemporary situation of the Christian community and to reassure the members that God is faithful to his promises. They should be exhorted to watch and pray (gospel) and to grow in holiness (second reading) during this Advent season.

SECOND SUNDAY OF ADVENT

Reading I: Baruch 5:1-9

The Book of Baruch is one of the deuterocanonical and pseudonymous Old Testament writings that are not found in the Hebrew Bible and that have been termed, in Reformation tradition, the "Apocrypha." Like the Book of Daniel, it is attributed to a figure of the past—Baruch was Jeremiah's secretary. The book presupposes for its situation the Babylonian Exile (586–538 B.C.), but it consists of various materials written later.

Today's passage comes from the last part of the book, comprising two prophetic poems modeled on Second Isaiah, and forms the concluding section of the second poem. The fictitious situation it assumes is that of Israel waiting to return from exile. It is difficult to be precise about the real situation, but the message was evidently written for Jews who later were living in the Diaspora. The miracle of the return is pictured in a series of supernatural events reminiscent of Isa 40 and, earlier still, of the Exodus itself.

This reading is a magnificent choice for this second Sunday of Advent. It matches the quotation of Isa 40 in the gospel and captures the Church's Advent stance in the thrilling words: "Arise, O Jerusalem, stand upon the height and look toward the east." The symbolism of salvation coming from the east like the dawn is deeply embedded in the Church's Advent lore.

Responsorial Psalm: 126:1-6

The identical arrangement of this psalm was used on the thirtieth Sunday of the year in series B, and, as we noted there, it celebrates the return from Babylon. It is equally appropriate as a response to the reading from Baruch, since the author of that poem pictures the deliverance of the Diaspora in terms of the return from Babylon as foretold by Second Isaiah.

Reading II: Philippians 1:4-6, 8-11

This passage comes from the opening thanksgiving (first paragraph) and intercession (second paragraph) of Philippians. If we accept the recent theory that Philippians is a compilation of three different letters sent by Paul to that community within a short period of time, this passage would come from the second letter. Paul is in prison at Ephesus (?). The Philippians' envoy, Epaphroditus, who has brought along a "care package" for the incarcerated Apostle, had fallen sick but has now recovered. Paul has also heard rumors that false teachers had either arrived or were about to arrive to stir up trouble in this faithful community, and so he is somewhat anxious about them. He sends his second letter (1:1–3:1; 4:47) to tell them the news about himself and Epaphroditus, and to exhort them to unity. These concerns are reflected in the thanksgiving and the intercession.

As in 1 Thessalonians (see last Sunday's second reading), Paul regards the "day of Jesus Christ" (that is, the parousia) as the terminal point of Christian maturation. Of course, he thought that he and his readers, the majority anyhow, would still be alive on that day and that therefore all spiritual growth would take place entirely within their earthly existence. Yet, by this time he had already written 1 Thessalonians and had faced the problem of Christians who had died before the parousia. It is therefore a reasonable extension of his meaning to suppose that the parousia remains the term of spiritual growth for all believers, including those already dead.

It is interesting that Paul characterizes Christian growth in the ethical terminology of Stoicism: "knowledge," "discernment," "approve what is excellent." Most interesting is the word for "discernment" (*aisthēsis*). Knowing that the will of God in concrete situations requires a kind of aesthetic sensibility, John A. T. Robinson once spoke of the Christian as having a set of built-in antennae to tell him or her what love requires in a particular situation. This, of course, is not the whole truth about Christian ethics, but it is an important factor and one to which the Apostle here gives countenance.

Gospel: Luke 3:1-6

On the second and third Sundays of Advent each year, the gospels focus on John the Baptist. In an elaborate dating (pointing probably to the year

27), Luke connects the appearance of the Baptist both to secular history and to salvation history as he brings the Baptist on stage in wording reminiscent of the appearance of the Old Testament prophets. Luke has a view of John the Baptist different from Mark's. Mark thought of the Baptist as the *archē tou euangeliou*, the "beginning of the gospel," the point at which the salvation event began. Luke, by contrast, places John *before* the beginning of the salvation event.

The Baptist sums up in his own person the whole salvation history of the Old Testament; he stands at the head of the Old Testament prophets and points, as they did, to the coming Christ. The one difference is that John is the last of the prophets and announces Jesus' impending arrival. Luke operates with two periods of salvation history—the Old Testament period, culminating with John, and the Jesus period, which is divided into two parts: the earthly history of Jesus (what he "began to do" [Acts 1:1]) and what he continues to do in the Church. This scheme is preferable to Conzelmann's three periods: the Old Testament, Jesus, and the Church.

John's baptism of repentance for the forgiveness of sins is, as the ensuing quotation from Isa 40 shows, essentially preparatory for the coming of the Messiah. Mark had already cited Isa 40, but Luke lengthens the quotation to include "all flesh shall see the salvation of God," which gives it a typically universalistic accent. This, incidentally, also shows that John foretells what is essentially a single period, for the universal mission of the Church is included in the salvation event. That event embraces the content of both Luke's Gospel and the Book of Acts.

The Homily

The homilist's purpose today must be to awaken a sense of tingling expectation, such as is characteristic of Advent. The reading from Baruch and the quotation from Isa 40 in the gospel will help to do this. Expectation for what? In Advent we focus on two events: we put ourselves in the time of preparation for the first coming of Christ, and we kindle anew our expectation of his second coming. The second coming has been in the forefront of our attention on the last few Sundays of the Church year and especially on the first Sunday of Advent. Then, from the second Sunday of Advent on, the first coming moves to the front of the stage; yet, the second coming is not ignored altogether, as the second reading shows.

The importance of Advent expectation for God to act lies in the fact that human beings cannot produce their own salvation. The resources for salvation do not lie within the possibilities of human history; they can only come from outside. Neither the incarnation nor the parousia can be thought of as a product of human evolution. The process theology currently in vogue sometimes seems to forget this. A few years ago human possibilities seemed limitless. Recent events, for example the ecological and energy crises, have made us aware of the very real possibility that we will exhaust all our sources of energy in the next decades. That should make us more receptive to the Advent message than we were in the sixties.

THIRD SUNDAY OF ADVENT

Reading I: Zephaniah 3:14-18a

Since this is the only occasion in the three-year cycle when a passage from Zephaniah is read, a few words about this minor prophet would be in order. Zephaniah's prophetic activity coincided with the earlier part of Josiah's reign (ca. 640-630 b.c.). He was probably located at Jerusalem. His prophecies are almost exclusively predictions of judgment. His message is the same as that of Amos: "The day of Yahweh will be darkness and not light." Today's excerpt comes from the only positive section of the work. It consists of a psalm inviting Zion to rejoice because salvation is at hand. The passage is so out of tune with the general tenor of Zephaniah's work that it has been thought to be an addition by a later editor.

Like last Sunday's passage from Baruch, this reading engenders an attitude of excited expectation for the intervention of Yahweh and is therefore fitting for the Advent season.

Responsorial Psalm: Isaiah 12:2-3, 4b-6

This week we depart from the usual practice of drawing upon the psalter for the responsorial reading and instead have an arrangement of the first song of Isaiah. It is uncertain whether this canticle is the work of Isaiah of Jerusalem. In fact, its tone rather suggests a situation at the return from exile.

In the Book of Common Prayer of the Episcopal Church, this song is provided as a canticle between the Old and the New Testament readings at the daily Office. The song gives thanks for the divine salvation that had been promised in the Old Testament and is now on the brink of fulfillment. This makes it equally suitable for Advent. Note particularly the emphasis on the presence of God in Israel (third stanza and refrain). The incarnation is the supreme realization of the coming of God to be present among his people.

Reading II: Philippians 4:4-7

If we accept the partition theory of Philippians, this passage will again come from Paul's second letter to the Christians of Philippi (see last Sunday's comments). This reading was the traditional one for the third Sunday of Advent and gave it the name "Gaudete Sunday." (In the Book of Common Prayer the reading was shifted to the last Sunday of Advent.)

As the caption ("The Lord is near") shows, the focal point of the passage is the statement that the Lord (the exalted Christ) is at hand. Advent is not a gloomy season (it does have a penitential aspect—see John the Baptist's message of repentance), despite the traditional use of the same liturgical color as is used for Lent. Rather, Advent is marked by a crescendo of joy. As the Lord comes nearer and nearer, we become more and more excited. The rhythm of Advent is well captured by the Advent wreath, which starts with one lighted candle and ends with four.

Gospel: Luke 3:10-18

This reading consists of two pericopes (in the form-critical rather than the liturgical sense of the word). The first (Luke 3:10-14) is called by the Germans (who always seem to have neat names for pericopes) the *Standespredigt* of the Baptist, that is, his preaching to various classes of people: the crowds in general, the tax collectors, and the soldiers. The second part is the Baptist's messianic preaching. He disclaims any suggestion that he is the Messiah (see the interpolations in the Johannine prologue). Both Luke and John may reflect the claims of continuing followers of the Baptist; their man, rather than Jesus, was the Messiah. In point of fact, the Baptist had pointed forward to the coming of another, the strong One ("he who is mightier than I"). Unlike the Baptist, who administers a baptism with water, the strong One will baptize with the Holy Spirit and fire. John's baptism is preparatory. The strong One's baptism will actually mediate the eschatological judgment, or salvation.

Mark had simply "Spirit," while Matthew and Luke add "fire." Probably "fire" alone is original and "Spirit" is a Christian addition reflecting the Pentecost event. Yet, the coming of the Spirit was part of Jewish eschatological expectation and was therefore implicit in the Baptist's words. Nor can we suppose that in speaking of the strong One the Baptist himself consciously had Jesus in mind; it is more likely that his conception of the Messiah was of one whose function would be more judgmental than salvific. It has been suggested that this is why later on in prison John asked whether Christ was the coming One or whether people were looking for another. Jesus turned out to be a very different kind of Messiah from what John had expected.

The Homily

John the Baptist is the obvious theme for the preacher again this Sunday.

One might concentrate on his disclaimer: he is not the Christ but only the one sent to prepare his way by preaching repentance (the *Standespredigt* shows what repentance concretely means).

In the Gospels, especially here in Luke and in the Fourth Gospel, there is great emphasis on the self-effacing attitude of John the Baptist. He points away from himself to the Other (the Isenheim altarpiece by Grünewald portrays the Baptist pointing to Jesus hanging on the cross). In the Book of Common Prayer, the old collect for this day drew an analogy between this self-effacing work of the Baptist and the work of the "ministers and stewards," whose function is to point men and women away from themselves to Christ, and so to prepare them for his coming, both at Christmas and at the last day, by preaching repentance. These considerations might lead the homilist to speak of confession and amendment of life in preparation for Christmas.

FOURTH SUNDAY OF ADVENT

Reading I: Micah 5:2-5a

As with Zephaniah last week, this is the only use of Micah in the Sunday Lectionary, so we will again provide some introductory information. Micah prophesied in the southern kingdom of Judah at the end of the eighth century, during the reigns of Ahaz and Hezekiah. Although he lived through a series of intense international crises, including the destruction of the northern kingdom of Israel and the invasion of Judah by the Assyrians, Micah took little note of these events (contrast Isaiah of Jerusalem) but concentrated rather on the denunciation of Judah for its social injustices (cf. Amos). Micah's work, like Zephaniah's, was later edited, and more positive promises were added. The oracle about the birth of the messianic king at Ephrathah ("Bethlehem" is thought to be an explanatory gloss) is probably one such addition.

The situation when Micah wrote seems to be that which prevailed at the end of the Exile, when hopes ran high for the restoration of the Davidic monarchy. Christian faith has, since Matt 2:6, seen the final fulfillment of this oracle in the birth of Jesus.

Responsorial Psalm: 80:1ac, 2b, 14-15, 17-18

This same arrangement of Psalm 80 was used on the first Sunday of Advent in series B. Note particularly the last two lines of the first stanza: "Stir up thy might, and come to save us!" It is hard to imagine a more appropriate Advent prayer. Its words are echoed in the ancient Advent collects that begin with "Excita."

202

The third stanza is a prayer for God's blessing on the Davidic king. Coupled with the first reading, this may be appropriately referred to Jesus Christ. Thus, we put ourselves in the position of ancient Israel waiting for the coming of the Messiah as we wait for the celebration of his coming at Christmas.

Reading II: Hebrews 10:5-10

This reading (beginning at verse 4) is also used on the feast of the Annunciation (March 25), a day with which this Sunday has much in common. It is one of the most important passages in Hebrews, for it defines Christ's sacrifice as the offering of his body (that is, the instrument of his will) in obedience to his Father. This, says the author of Hebrews, building upon Psalm 40, is the whole *raison d'être* of the incarnation. Christ took a body so as to have an instrument by which to offer this perfect obedience to the will of God. The choice of this reading today is a salutary reminder, needed particularly at this time of year, not to dissociate the incarnation from its supreme goal, the atonement. Bethlehem was the prelude to Golgotha.

Gospel: Luke 1:39-45

Since there are only two annunciation stories in the Gospels (see the fourth Sunday of Advent in series A and B), series C switches to the visitation. Today's reading in the Episcopalian Lectionary runs through verse 49, thus including the first four verses of the *Magnificat*, which has traditional associations with the fourth Sunday of Advent.

Three times in this pericope Mary is pronounced "blessed" (see also the second verse of the *Magnificat*; this is the scriptural ground for our calling her the "Blessed Virgin"). Two closely connected reasons are given for Elizabeth's calling her "blessed": Mary's faith (v. 45), which is the same as her obedience (Luke 1:38, the alleluia versicle), and her bearing of the Christ child (v. 42). So Mary is blessed, not for what she was or is in herself, but only in relation to the incarnation. The Mariology of Scripture is grounded in Christology.

In order to follow the evangelist's understanding of the annunciation, the conception of the Christ child, and the dialogue between Mary and Elizabeth at the visitation, we should avoid prematurely harmonizing Luke's presentation with the Johannine prologue. Luke does not operate with a preexistent Logos-Christology as the fourth evangelist does, any more than the fourth evangelist operates with a conception and birth narrative. For Luke, the virginal conception is not the way in which the preexistent divine Son assumes humanity, for he does not think in those terms;

540

11
211

rather, the miraculous conception is the supreme example of those Old Testament conceptions in which God raises up a person to perform a specific function in salvation history (Isaac, Moses [?], Samson, Samuel). Thus, Mary's miraculous conception of Jesus marks the birth of one who is to perform the eschatologically unique role in salvation history (Luke 1:32-33; note the future tenses, which speak of this child's future role, not of his "divine nature"). In Luke—and the same is doubtless true of Matthew—the infancy narrative is strictly *Vorgeschichte*, a historical prelude to a unique salvation history that begins with the baptism of Jesus and continues through his exaltation (see the qualifications for apostolic witness in Acts 1:22).

We shall discuss how this exegetical interpretation of Luke is to be squared with the Church's later ontological interpretation of the incarnation and shall propose a contemporary interpretation of it in our comments on the Johannine prologue at the third Mass of Christmas.

The Homily

Since the figure of Mary is central today, the homilist will probably want to explain why we call her "blessed," emphasizing that Mary's importance to Christian faith depends upon her faith and obedience as the preconditions that made the incarnation humanly possible, and upon the fact that she bore the Christ child. The homilist thus has an opportunity to propound a true and, it is to be hoped, ecumenically acceptable Mariology, one that is grounded solely in Christology.

The reading from Hebrews suggests a different line of thought: the final purpose of the incarnation was the atonement. This would give the homilist the occasion to relate Bethlehem to Golgotha.

CHRISTMAS SEASON

CHRISTMAS

Since series C has the same readings for Christmas as series A and B, we 15 shall summarize what we said there and offer some fresh comments on 215 the Johannine prologue (Mass During the Day), as promised last Sunday.

We should disabuse ourselves and our congregation of the notion that the primary thrust of Christmas is the historical occasion of Jesus' birth. (I have heard of Episcopalian clergy getting their church schoolchildren to sing "Happy birthday, dear Jesus," a fatuous misunderstanding of what Christmas is really about.) It is the celebration of God's eschatological self-disclosure in the Christ-event.

MASS AT MIDNIGHT

Reading I: Isaiah 9:2-7

Originally this was a coronation anthem sung at the enthronement of the kings of the Davidic dynasty. Each new king, it was hoped, would prove to be the ideal king. Christian faith finds this hope fulfilled in Jesus Christ. In him all the blessings looked for at each royal accession in Judah's history—freedom from poverty and oppression, the realization of peace— are given to Christian faith. The Davidic king was even hailed as God, that is, as the sacramental embodiment and representative of the divine presence. How much more is this true of Jesus Christ! He is God in the sense, not of *Deus in se*, but of *Deus pro nobis*, or, in Gogarten's words, "God turned to us" in his grace and salvation.

Responsorial Psalm: 96:1-3, 11-13

The "new song" is the celebration of messianic redemption, replacing the old song of Moses that celebrated the Exodus. The hymn of the angels at Bethlehem is the choral prelude to this new song. The Church's liturgy is its partial anticipation; its final realization awaits the heavenly liturgy described in the Book of Revelation.

Reading II: Titus 2:11-14

Note how the Advent theme of the two comings of Christ is kept right up to Christmas. The first coming anticipates the second. The midnight Mass of Christmas has symbolic significance, for the New Testament looks for Christ to come again at midnight (for example, Matt 25:6). Note, too, the traditional collect for Christmas: "Grant that as we joyfully receive him for our Redeemer, so we may with sure confidence behold him when he shall come to be our judge" (Book of Common Prayer; in the Roman Missal, Vigil of Christmas).

Gospel: Luke 2:1-14

We are not meant to take the birth stories as exact transcripts of historical events. It is vital to Christian faith that Jesus really was born into this world. And it is equally vital that his birth was "for us and for our salvation." But "the details of the narrative are symbolic and biblical; they communicate the mystery of the redemption, not a diary of earthly events" (*Jerome Biblical Commentary*, 2:121).

The shepherds were members of a despised class, like tax collectors and prostitutes. The evangelist is telling us that Christ came especially to the outcasts, an emphasis that will characterize Luke's Gospel throughout. Appearances of angels bringing messages to accompany events are the biblical way of expressing the meaning of salvation events as the acts of God. There are two such accounts in the birth story. The first appearance, by a single angel, announces the messianic birth; the second, by "a multitude of the heavenly host," interprets the saving significance of the birth: "Glory to God in the highest, and on earth peace among men with whom he is pleased." The words "men with whom he is pleased" translate a Hebraism that means "people who are the objects of God's favor," not "people of good will," in the secular sense of the phrase.

The Homily

Several possibilities suggest themselves: (1) the birth of Christ as a message of peace, in the rich sense of *shalom* (first reading and the angelic hymn); (2) midnight, the symbolic hour of the first and second comings of Christ; (3) the first Christmas came to shepherds, and so the incarnation is a message of hope for the poor and the oppressed, and a challenge to the Christian Church to become more sensitive to their needs; (4) the contrast between the civil notion of "people of good will" and the biblical concept of "people on whom God's favor rests." No Pelagian, do-it-yourself recipe but only the intervention of God's grace can cope with the fundamental predicament of human sin.

MASS AT DAWN

Reading I: Isaiah 62:11-12

This passage from Third (Trito-) Isaiah originally referred to one of the Jewish festivals (Tabernacles?). Read today, it speaks of the new Israel's joy at the advent of messianic salvation.

Responsorial Psalm: 97:1, 6, 11-12

This is another of the enthronement psalms. The second stanza and the refrain underline the dawn of the light—imagery that has passed into the lore of the season and is expressed in so many Christmas carols.

Reading II: Titus 3:4-7

Unlike the second reading of the midnight Mass, this one speaks only of the first coming of Christ. And it does not lead, as the earlier reading did, to an ethical exhortation but to an affirmation of the saving consequences of the Christ-event—regeneration and renewal, the rebirth of men and women as children of God. A traditional Christmas theme: the Son of God became a human being to make us children of God.

Gospel: Luke 2:15-20

This is a continuation of the gospel reading of the midnight Mass. The shepherds go to Bethlehem to visit the Christ child. The familiarity of the picture should not blind us to its theological significance. Here the divine salvation is disclosed to the outcast. The shepherds tell what they have seen (the Christ child) and heard (the angelic proclamation that God's salvation has entered the world)—they declare both fact and interpretation.

The Homily

The Old Testament reading speaks of the people of God as "sought out." This idea is fundamental to an understanding of the incarnation, which, as Karl Barth used to say, is God's *search* for humankind. The Church is the place, not merely where people search for God but where, through the word and the sacraments and witness to the world, God searches for his people.

The second reading invites a consideration of what it means to be a child of God. Christ alone is Son of God "by nature"; Christian believers become children of God only "by adoption and grace." The Bible does not say that all human beings are children of God; they are such only potentially until they are reborn in Christ.

MASS DURING THE DAY

Reading I: Isaiah 52:7-10

Compare the first reading of the Mass at Dawn and the enthronement psalms of all three Masses this day. The prophet proclaims the reign of God now being actualized by his mighty act. In his case this act was the return from exile; for us it is the birth of the Christ child announced by the angelic hymn. In that event the Church sees the return of Yahweh to Zion (v. 8) to comfort his people (v. 9). He bares his arm and all people see the event of salvation (v. 10).

Responsorial Psalm: 98:1-6

Other selections from this psalm are used on the twenty-eighth and thirty-   *511*
third Sundays of the year in series C. Compare also the enthronement   *526*
psalms used at the earlier Masses this day. They all praise God for his saving intervention and are thus applicable to the birth of Christ.

Reading II: Hebrews 1:1-6

Hebrews opens with a Christological hymn that was evidently drawn from an earlier tradition and was perhaps derived originally from a Jewish hymn in praise of divine wisdom. In any case, it reflects Jewish teaching. Wisdom is a hypostatized, or personified, entity preexistent with God from eternity, the agent of creation at the beginning of the world and its sustainer ever since. She is also the agent of divine revelation through all of Israel's salvation history. In the Jewish tradition, she seeks to dwell with people on earth and, when rejected, returns to heaven.

This wisdom myth was adapted in early Christianity as a vehicle to express its own faith in Christ. As early as 1 Corinthians (see 1:21, 23-24, 30; 2:6-7), he is identified with wisdom: he was the preexisting agent of creation and preservation and the agent of revelation in Israel's salvation history. He appeared on earth and then returned to heaven. The mythical pattern rarely appears in its entirety when applied to Christ. In Hebrews, for example, there is no mention of his descent in the incarnation or of his incarnate life. These are presumed in the mention of his having made purification for sins, an idea that of course is unparalleled in the Jewish wisdom myth.

Particularly noteworthy is the contrast between the partial, fragmentary revelations in Israel's salvation history ("in many and various ways") and the eschatological finality of God's self-revelation in Christ.

Gospel: John 1:1-18 (long form); 1:1-5, 9-14 (short form)

The short form omits the remarks about the Baptist, which today are often regarded as prose insertions into an earlier hymn to the Logos.

The evangelist intends the prologue to serve as a theological commentary on his Gospel as a whole. The Gospel relates the history of Jesus from his baptism until his glorification. The word "flesh" signifies the whole of human history, not just the humanity of Jesus considered in the abstract. This history, however, is the manifestation of the Logos, the self-communication of God. Now this self-communication did not begin with the Christ-event. In eternity God was already a self-communicating God. Creation (vv. 1-3), general revelation (human beings' natural knowledge of God—vv. 4, 9), and the special revelation to Israel (v. 11) were all activities of God in which he went forth in self-communication from his being-in-himself. Finally this self-communication culminated in the whole visible history of Jesus of Nazareth.

John is not thinking in terms of the ontological Christological dogma of Nicaea (325) and Constantinople (381). He does not combine the concept of incarnation with a birth narrative, though he is aware of birth traditions (see 7:41-42). No doubt he would have regarded these as *Vorgeschichte*, historical prelude, as did Matthew and Luke. He prefers to interpret the baptism of Jesus (which he does not directly narrate but which he clearly knows) as the point where the Word's becoming flesh was initiated as a dynamic process that occurs continually throughout Jesus' ministry. In this ministry Jesus is in constant communion with the Father and surrenders himself so completely to the Father's will that his words become the Father's words and his works the Father's works, so that in his history the Word continually becomes flesh. His coming into the world, or his coming down from heaven, is to be seen as the visible side of this dynamic process.

John does not think of the incarnation as a combination of two abstract entities, humanity and divinity, in a divine-human person. This is not to say that John's Christology was adoptionistic, in the later heretical sense. Historical adoptionism thinks in far more precise ontological categories than John does. Nor is it to say that the later ontological Christology was a mistaken development, for it was a translation of the New Testament proclamation into the Hellenistic categories of the fourth and fifth centuries. Exegesis, however, requires that we not read back these categories into John but let him speak for himself. Incidentally, this more dynamic understanding of the incarnation can probably speak more intelligibly to our day than later ontological categories. We need to interpret the latter by means of the former.

The Homily

Perhaps the homilist would like to take the opportunity to explore the Fourth Gospel's dynamic understanding of the incarnation so as to help the congregation grasp something of how God could communicate himself in a fully human life. Some useful hints may be found in *The Human Face of God* by John A. T. Robinson, although this work should not be read uncritically.

If this is too demanding, the homilist might at least point up the significance of the fact that we read Heb 1 and John 1 on Christmas Day. This shows that we are not just celebrating the birth of a human baby but the mystery of God's self-disclosure in the whole history of Jesus.

Sunday in the Octave of Christmas

HOLY FAMILY

The readings are the same each year except for the gospel. Accordingly, we will summarize our comments for series A and B and offer fresh comments on the gospel.

23
220

Reading I: Sirach 3:2-6, 12-14

The text offers a commentary on the fifth (fourth) commandment: Honor thy father and thy mother. The assertion that love of parents will make atonement for sins must be taken rhetorically as an incentive to obey the commandment, not as a serious theological statement. In the New Testament, atonement for sin is through Christ alone.

Responsorial Psalm: 128:1-5

Piety is the foundation of family and social life, and even of economic prosperity (see Deuteronomy). Perhaps we should not want to take this too naively today. Yet, it remains true that where people seek to fear God and to do his will, their relations with others stand a better chance of being on a sound footing. Those who fear God are less inclined to put themselves in God's place. That frees them for the love of neighbor and helps the neighbor to love them in return.

Reading II: Colossians 3:12-21

This passage is taken from the parenesis, or ethical exhortation, of Colossians, reproducing, according to a widely accepted view, material from an early Christian catechesis. It begins with a list of virtues. These are to be "put on," an idea suggested by the vesting of the candidates with new white robes as they emerge from the baptismal waters. This section of the catechism is sometimes preceded by a list of vices that are to be "put off" or renounced, an idea suggested by the disrobing of the candidates before their descent into the baptismal waters.

Following these two general exhortations, the New Testament letters often provide a *Haustafel,* or household code, listing various members of the household and stating their duties. It is thought that such forms were derived ultimately from Stoicism via Hellenistic Jewish catechesis. That will explain the subordinationist ethic characterizing them, which is Stoic rather than Christian. The distinctive Christian elements are the addition of the phrase "in the Lord" and the emphasis on love and forgiveness.

Gospel: Luke 2:41-52

The form critics classify this pericope as a "legend." This does not necessarily mean that the incident is wholly unhistorical, as indeed Dibelius was careful to point out. To call it a legend means that its purpose is not historical. There are many similar stories of the precocious childhood of a great person whose early life showed signs of coming greatness (for example, in the life of Buddha or Josephus).

We recognize certain redactional concerns of Luke: the legal piety of Jesus' home (see Luke 2:21-22), shown in the devout observance of Passover customs; the effect of these remarkable incidents on Jesus' mother (see Luke 2:19); and the emphasis on the human growth of Jesus (see Luke 2:40), though the last point may be modeled on the childhood of Samuel and may be designed to portray Jesus as the eschatological prophet. In that case it may even have been a feature of Luke's source.

That the core of the narrative is pre-Lucan is shown by the absence of any hint of the virginal conception ("his parents," "your father"). The answer of the boy Jesus in verse 49, with its reference to God as "my Father," seems to reflect the Church's Christology. The basic incident, however, is not only pre-Lucan but may well rest upon an authentic memory. And even the allusion to "my Father" may be pre-Christological, reflecting Jesus' growing historical awareness of his unique filial relation with God. This awareness will then be the basis and presupposition for his later submission to the Father's call and the acceptance of his unique eschatological role in salvation history. Thus, one hesitates to dismiss this story as entirely without historical worth, even if in the form-critical sense it should be characterized as a "legend."

Our real concern must be with the evangelist's purpose in including this story in his Gospel. It is evidently part of his picture of Jesus' family and its devout adherence to the Jewish law, which provided the environment in which Jesus developed, as Samuel had developed, so that he could later fulfill his role as the eschatological prophet and the bringer of redemption to Israel.

The Homily

The three readings provide different ways of treating the importance of family life in Christian nurture. The Old Testament reading emphasizes the importance of the fifth (fourth) commandment. The reading from Colossians, if we concentrate on its specifically Christian elements as opposed to the Stoic emphasis on subordinationism, sets a pattern of Christian family life based upon mutual forgiveness. The gospel suggests that the family is the context for growth to physical, mental, and spiritual maturity.

OPTIONAL READINGS

Reading I: 1 Samuel 1:20-22, 24-28

Here we have another Old Testament reading that provided a model for the narratives of Jesus' birth, particularly that in Luke's Gospel. Samuel's parents offer him to Yahweh "for ever," that is, for his whole life. We moderns would object that Samuel had not been consulted and should have been left to decide for himself when the time came. Such problems were alien to the ancient world. The parents in any case did not determine the child's destiny. They offered him for the service of the temple, but instead the child grew up to be a prophet who played a major role in the affairs of state. Like the birth of Jesus, Samuel's birth is narrated in the light of his subsequent destiny.

Responsorial Psalm: 84:2-3, 5-6, 9-10

It is strange that this familiar psalm has not been used before in the Sunday Lectionary. It is a psalm with affinities to the songs of Zion and to the pilgrim psalms, and speaks of the joy of worship in the temple. It would appear that it was designed for use at the autumn festival (Tabernacles). Its date of origin is sometime during the age of the monarchy (v. 1). The worshiper envies both the birds that live in the temple their whole lives long, having built their nests in its precincts, and the priests, whose work keeps them in the temple all the time. Thus, the psalm serves fittingly as a response to the reading about Samuel, who was dedicated to the service of the temple at Shiloh all his life.

Reading II: 1 John 3:1-2, 21-24

The overall context of this reading is the schism that has recently taken place in the Johannine community (see 1 John 2:19 ; 4:1). Certain members (we will call them "gnosticizing secessionists") have left the community because of their Docetic Christology and neglect of ethics (see 1 John 4:3; 4:20). The Johannine epistler seeks to assure the remaining members of the community that they, not the secessionists, are children of God. This is a status that has been conferred upon them by God's love, that is, by his act of revelation and redemption in Jesus Christ. The secessionists deny the full reality of that act and therefore do not share in that new status— they are not children of God.

It is noteworthy that the author, contrary to the practice of Paul, distinguishes between "Son of God," a term that he uses exclusively for Christ as a Christological title, and "children of God," a term for the derivative status of Christians. If this distinction were universally observed, it would ease the problem that such language causes for feminists nowadays.

Note how the author, in a manner this time closer to Pauline usage, preserves the "not yet" of this Christian status. Our being children of God is a reality, but it is visible only to faith. Lacking faith, the world cannot see or observe it. Only when the final consummation occurs will the Christian status of divine childhood become visible. This final consummation the epistler describes as the appearance, not of Christ, but of God. It will consist in the beatific vision of God.

The second part of the reading is the tail end of the most difficult parts of the New Testament. We take the "merciful" as opposed to the "severe" interpretation (see Raymond Brown's commentary *ad loc.*). Our own conscience may accuse us, but God is more merciful than we are with ourselves, and he will forgive us when our consciences accuse us. He will give us whatever we ask (the context suggests that what is being asked for is God's forgiving mercy). All this is promised because we—that is, the Johannine community, as opposed to the secessionists—are doing his will. His will is that we should believe in Jesus Christ, the Son of God (which the secessionists fail to do, since they deny the flesh of Jesus, the reality of his incarnation), and love one another (which the secessionists fail to do, since they do not love their fellow members in the community). They are cliquish and elitist. Note here the Johannine form of the double commandment of love. While it is through keeping these commandments that we abide in God, we know that we abide in him only through the Holy Spirit.

The Homily
Homiletical hints have been provided for this occasion above and in series

A and B. We might add that the Old Testament readings have been par-   25
ticularly chosen to provide the background of the New Testament por-   222
traits of the life of the Holy Family. What binds these accounts together,
in addition to the pattern of annunciation, birth, and naming, is that these
three elements of the story are related to the future role of the children
thus born in salvation history. The family life of Abraham and Sarah,
of Hannah and Elkanah, and of Joseph and Mary, and their dedication
of their children to Yahweh provide a model for Christian family life. All
these biblical parents do this out of a sense of responsibility toward God.
There is no hint of "letting the child make up his/her mind when he/she
grows up," which characterizes the religious indifferentism of so many
modern parents. Children today will of course make up their own minds
when grown up, but if they are exposed to the life of the Christian community in their childhood, they will have a basis on which to make their
decision.

January 1
SOLEMNITY OF MARY, MOTHER OF GOD

The readings are the same every year, and further comments on them will   26
be found in series A and B. The second reading and the gospel are tradi-   223
tional to the Christmas season. In the Book of Common Prayer, the second reading (Gal 4:4-7, following 3:23-25) is appointed for the first Sunday after Christmas Day, and while the gospel is the same, the day is entitled "The Holy Name of Our Lord Jesus Christ." The new Roman title
of the day is suggested by two verses in the second reading and the gospel,
namely, Gal 4:4c and Luke 2:19. These verses, however, emphasize Mary
not as *Theotokos* but as the paradigm of faith, and therefore of the Christian believer and the true Israel. But the main thrust of today's feast is
the birth of Christ as the inauguration of the saving act of God.

Reading I: Numbers 6:22-27
Note the threefold structure of the Aaronic blessing, which in a remarkable
way anticipates the Trinitarian structure of Christian faith (see below).
    The last verse is also important (see the caption: "They will call down
my name on the sons of Israel and I will bless them"). The concept of
the name is highly important in biblical theology. The name stands for
the whole person—what we mean when we speak of character and personality. The name of God means his being as disclosed in the salvation
history of the Old and New Testaments. By invoking God's name upon

the people, the priestly blessing confers upon them all that God is and all that he has done for Israel. For the Christian Church, the name of God further includes all that he has done in Jesus Christ. This is not an addition to the Aaronic blessing but, as its Trinitarian structure shows, its full explication. In the act of blessing, all that God is and has done is passed on from age to age.

Responsorial Psalm: 67:1-2, 4-5, 7

The refrain, "May God bless us in his mercy," shows how this psalm picks up the theme of the first reading. The "mercy" (*hesedh*) of God embraces all that he has done for Israel in his mighty acts—and for us also in Jesus Christ.

Reading II: Galatians 4:4-7

Comments on this reading can be found on the feast of the Solemnity of Mary, Mother of God (January 1) in series A. The reading emphasizes *27* that the purpose of the incarnation was the liberation of human beings from the law that they might become children of God.

Gospel: Luke 2:16-21

This reading is repeated from the Mass at Dawn on Christmas Day. To- *389* day, however, it continues through verse 21 to relate the circumcision and naming of Jesus. The circumcision ties in with the second reading ("born under the law"), and the naming of Jesus with the threefold name of the Aaronic blessing (first reading).

The Homily

The Scripture readings suggest three possible choices for the homilist. The first reading and the psalm invite a meditation on the theme of blessing. Valuable material on this will be found in Karl Barth's *Church Dogmatics* III/2, pages 578-587. On page 580 Barth sums up his exegesis in these words: "Blessing is regarded in the Old Testament as the epitome of all the good things which the father can pass on to the son and the son can receive from the father. A blessing is the word which has divine power to pass on good things." This biblical concept of blessing could be related to the priestly blessing in the liturgy, while the idea of passing on good things, that is, our Christian heritage, from generation to generation is an appropriate thought for New Year's Day.

A second possibility for the homily is the theme of liberation, suggested by Paul's explanation of the purpose of the incarnation and the connection between "born under the law" (second reading) and Jesus' circumcision (gospel). There is much talk today of liberation as a meaningful equivalent of the biblical word "salvation." The homilist might confront contemporary understanding of liberation with the biblical understanding of it.

A third possibility would be to take up the theme of the divine name in the Aaronic blessing and its connection with the naming of Jesus (=Yahweh saves). Jesus' name is a programmatic definition of the whole purpose of the incarnation. Similarly, our baptismal names are programmatic for us. They give us identity, meaning, and purpose in life. Such a reflection, however, needs to be guarded against a Pelagian misinterpretation, for our baptismal name is given "in the name of Jesus." His name—what he is and what he has done for us—alone makes it possible for us to realize the program denoted by our name. This, too, could be an appropriate reflection for New Year's Day.

[*In countries where the feast of the Epiphany is transferred to the Sunday between January 2 and January 8, inclusive, the* SECOND SUNDAY AFTER CHRISTMAS *is omitted.*]

January 6
or the Sunday occurring between January 2 and 8, inclusive
EPIPHANY

Since the readings for Epiphany are the same each year, the reader is referred to series A and B for additional comments.

28
225

In the Eastern Church, where today's feast originated, Epiphany was primarily a celebration of the baptism of Christ as the first of his "epiphanies," or manifestations. Other epiphanies in Jesus' earthly life were also associated with this day, especially the changing of the water into wine at Cana in Galilee. When the feast of Epiphany spread to the West, it assimilated some of the associations previously attached to Christmas, especially the story of the Magi. Since the Magi were presumed to have been Gentiles (a point not emphasized, however, in the Matthean pericope), the feast acquired a new emphasis as the manifestation of Christ to the Gentiles. This finally led, especially among the Lutherans, to an association of the feast with the mission of the Church in foreign lands.

Reading I: Isaiah 60:1-6
This passage is from Third Isaiah. The first part (vv. 1-3) announces the return of the exiles in language taken over from Second Isaiah (chs. 40–55).

The second part (vv. 4-6) foretells the eschatological pilgrimage of the Gentiles to the restored city of Jerusalem. The first part is typological of the birth of Christ; the second part, of the visit of the Magi.

Although Matthew (curiously, in view of his special interest in quoting Old Testament prophecies) does not cite this passage, it has clearly influenced the Magi narrative, as the reference to gold and frankincense in verse 6 shows. Other features from this passage, not noted by Matthew, were added by popular legend to the story of the Magi, namely, the fact that the Magi were Gentiles, to say nothing of the camels in verse 6!

Responsorial Psalm: 72:1-2, 7-8, 10-13

This psalm was originally a coronation hymn, composed for kings of the Davidic dynasty. Christian faith sees its fulfillment in Christ, for it emphasizes the "pastoral" aspects of kingship, such as the establishment of justice and compassion for the poor. The psalm also brings out a feature absent from the first reading—the figure of the messianic king.

We may suspect that this psalm, like the first reading, also influenced the Matthean narrative of the Magi. Once more we note the lack of any explicit quotation, yet the psalm speaks of the pilgrims bringing gifts and falling down in homage before the messianic king. Like Isa 60, the psalm has also contributed something to the legend of the Magi, namely, their identification as kings. That they were *three* kings was an inference from the three gifts specified by Matthew.

Christian faith sees Psalm 72 appropriately fulfilled in the coming of Christ as the messianic king who brings justice and compassion for the poor (fourth stanza), and in the universality of the acknowledgment accorded to the messianic king ("all nations" in the third stanza, echoed in the refrain).

Reading II: Ephesians 3:2-3a, 5-6

This reading is an explicit theological statement of the two themes adumbrated in the first reading: the revelation or epiphany of God in Christ (v. 3) and the universality of messianic salvation (v. 6).

Many modern scholars regard Ephesians as the work, not of Paul himself, but of a member of the Pauline school looking back, after the Apostle's death, upon his achievement in maintaining the unity of Jew and Gentile in the one Church.

Gospel: Matthew 2:1-12

This pericope gathers together early Christian traditions from different sources.

1. The primitive kerygma had affirmed Jesus' Davidic descent (Rom 1:3). According to Jewish expectation, this qualified him for messiahship. As a Christological affirmation, Jesus' Davidic descent explains the importance attached in the infancy narratives to his birth at Bethlehem.

2. A tradition common to Matthew and Luke dates the birth of Jesus in the reign of Herod (d. 4 B.C.). This dating is plausible and may well rest on fact.

3. There is the folk memory of Herod's cruelty, and especially the pathological fear of assassination and usurpation that marked the closing years of his reign.

4. The star was regarded as a symbol of the Messiah. It originated in Num 24:17 and was given a messianic interpretation as early as the Testaments of the Twelve Patriarchs. Matthew's failure to quote Num 24:17 is again surprising.

5. The gifts presented to the Christ child were suggested by our first reading and the responsorial psalm, although, again, Matthew does not cite them.

6. There is the *testimonium* from Mic 5:2 cited in verse 6. This passage was already interpreted messianically in Judaism (see John 7:42 and the fact that, unusually for Matthew, it is placed here on the lips of the scribes). It seems likely, therefore, that it was used as a *testimonium* before Matthew, though the structure of the pericope suggests that it was first inserted into the story by the evangelist.

7. Finally, although Matthew does not emphasize it, there is the tradition of *Gentiles* coming to see the messianic salvation, from the first reading and Psalm 72.

All these factors contributed to the shaping of the Magi story. The only certain historical facts behind the narrative are the names Jesus, Joseph and Mary; the dating of the birth; and perhaps the location of the birth at Bethlehem, although that tradition may have originated from Mic 5:2 and Jewish expectation about the Messiah. The significance of the story is almost entirely symbolical.

The Homily

The Magi story is set in the context of the first two readings and the responsorial psalm. This brings out the kerygmatic truths that the story symbolizes: the revelation of God in the messianic event and the universality of that revelation. It may be taken as an expression of the truth that the Christ-event provides the answer to the human religious quest, especially if the Magi were astrologists and magicians rather than astronomers and philosophers. Gold, frankincense, and myrrh may have been the tools of their dubious trade, offered not as tokens of homage but as "a declaration of dissociation from former practices" (Anchor Bible, *ad loc.*). This interpretation, if accepted, would provide the homilist with an opportunity to relate the story to some of the more bizarre manifestations of the contemporary religious quest. The gospel is the answer to the search of human beings for God, as well as its corrective.

Sunday after January 6
(transferred to Monday when it coincides with Epiphany)

BAPTISM OF THE LORD

The readings for today are the same every year, except for the gospel, which follows the account of the baptism from the synoptic Gospel read in course each year. This year it is from Luke's version. The comments on the first two readings and the responsorial psalm given in series A are summarized here; the comments on the gospel are new.

The baptism of the Lord was the primary mystery celebrated in the East on this day. The whole life of Christ was understood as a series of epiphanies, or manifestations, of which the baptism was the first and constitutive. In the West, the baptism was relegated to a subordinate place in the Epiphany season. It has now been restored to something of its former prominence by being assigned to the Sunday after January 6 if this Sunday does not coincide with Epiphany; if it does coincide, the baptism is transferred to the Monday after Epiphany. This arrangement helps to restore the emphasis to the theological aspect of the Christmas mystery, as opposed to its historical aspect, most of which seems to us to be legendary.

Reading I: Isaiah 42:1-4, 6-7

This passage, the first of the servant songs in Second Isaiah, has clearly been a major influence in the shaping of the synoptic baptismal narratives. The words "with thee I am well pleased" are almost certainly a rendering of "in whom my soul delights" (Isa 42:1b), and although the more obvious source of "Thou art my beloved Son" would seem to be Ps 2:7, it is possible, as some hold, that "son" is a translation of an ambiguous Aramaic word for "servant." Although in Second Isaiah the term "servant" has some other meaning (Israel, a faithful remnant of Israel, or an individual figure), for the New Testament and Christian faith the servant's role is fulfilled in Jesus, and it is as the servant, at least in part, that the baptismal story in the Gospels proclaims him.

Verses 2-3 describe the character of the servant, verses 6-7 his work. Both descriptions apply fittingly to Jesus and are useful introductions to the series of readings on the earthly ministry of Jesus that will occupy us from now until Lent.

Responsorial Psalm: 29:1-4, 9b-10

In part, this is an enthronement psalm of the familiar type (see the third stanza). The second stanza, however, may have been connected originally with Baal-hadad, the storm god of Canaan. The psalm is written in a meter reminiscent of Canaanite poetry as found in the Ugaritic texts. Whatever its origin, the psalmist has transferred it to Yahweh. The storm becomes an epiphany of his presence as the Creator-God. Like the first reading, the second stanza points to the heavenly voice at Jesus' baptism.

Reading II: Acts 10:34-38

This is part of the kerygmatic speech attributed to Peter in the Cornelius episode. As in Mark and John, the kerygma here begins the earthly life of Jesus with his baptism. In this rite he is anointed with the Holy Spirit and so prepared for a ministry of charismatic healing. Note that in summarizing the story of Jesus' ministry, the kerygmatic speech emphasizes what God did in Jesus.

It has often been observed that whereas Jesus preached the kingdom, the Church preached Jesus—with the suggestion that the Church was wrong. However, in preaching the kingdom and performing his exorcisms and healings, Jesus was proclaiming that God was acting eschatologically in his words and works. And in preaching Jesus, the Church proclaimed that in the earthly ministry of Jesus, God had been decisively at work. So despite the formal change, there is material continuity between Jesus and the Church's kerygma.

Gospel: Luke 3:15-16, 21-22

Luke has made five major alterations in his Marcan source:

1. He has prefaced his account of John's messianic preaching with the remark that the people were wondering whether John was the Messiah.

2. The second alteration is obscured by the Lectionary's omission of verses 19-20. Here, between the Baptist's messianic preaching and the baptism of Jesus, Luke has inserted the account of John's imprisonment, which Mark and Matthew placed after the temptation and just before the beginning of the Galilean ministry (Mark 1:14a par.).

3. Luke has suppressed the statement that it was John who baptized Jesus, and he has put the mention of Jesus' baptism into a subordinate

clause (a genitive absolute in Greek, a temporal clause in the RSV: "when Jesus also had been baptized and was praying").

4. Luke omits the statement that Jesus *saw* "the heavens opened."

5. Luke has added that the Spirit descended upon Jesus "in bodily form."

What is the point of these alterations? It could be that Luke prefers to follow an alternative version of the baptism narrative (Q? A special tradition?). In favor of Q is the fact of Matthew's and Luke's agreement, against Mark, in the words they use for the "opening" of heaven in verse 21 and for "upon him" in verse 22. At the same time, it is clear that Luke is seeking to play down John's role in the baptism of Jesus, for Luke, not his non-Marcan source, must have been responsible for placing the imprisonment of John before Jesus' baptism. Why did he do this? Perhaps for polemical reasons similar to those that operated in the Fourth Gospel. But Luke may have had weightier theological motives for suppressing any reference to John's role in Jesus' baptism. The Baptist, for Luke, is not the "beginning of the gospel," as he is for Mark; rather, the Baptist is the last of the Old Testament prophets, standing at the head of the old age and pointing to the coming One. Hence the line between the old age and the new runs between the first and second paragraphs of our reading as given in the Lectionary.

As we saw at Christmas, Luke presents the birth of Jesus as *Vorgeschichte*, preparatory history, the bringing into the world and the marking out of the One who was destined to be the epiphany and redemptive act of God. Thus, the angel at the annunciation promises that he will [future] be called the Son of God. This means that for Luke sonship is not an ontological status but a function that Jesus will embark upon later. The descent of the Spirit and the heavenly voice now inaugurate that function. Jesus will now embark upon a life of obedience to his eschatological mission, the function that the annunciation narrative had foretold.

The Homily

How do we preach about an event, the baptism of Jesus, that the gospel of the day hurried over with a genitive absolute? Clearly, we must emphasize, not the role of the Baptist, but the meaning of the descent of the Spirit and of the heavenly voice. Decisive for what Jesus was and did is not the part played in his life by his human contemporaries, but the act of God initiated in Jesus' history. The Lucan account of the baptism emphasizes this divine initiative. Is this just a *theologoumenon,* or does it have something to say to us today? We tend to think of Christianity as a cause that somehow we must support, and if it does not prosper, we become anxious about it. The Bible, however, is not concerned about Christianity but about the mighty acts of God, culminating in Jesus Christ. Our task is to respond to those mighty acts in faith and obedience, not to defend a human religious cause.

LENTEN SEASON

ASH WEDNESDAY

Since the readings for Ash Wednesday are the same every year, we refer
the reader to our comments on them in series A.

FIRST SUNDAY OF LENT

Reading I: Deuteronomy 26:4-10

This reading is normally associated, at least for Anglicans, with the Harvest
Festival or, in the United States, with Thanksgiving Day. When read at
the beginning of Lent, its emphasis shifts from the offering of the first fruits
to the confession of faith that accompanies the offering (vv. 5-9). For contemporary exegetes, this is perhaps the most important passage of the entire Old Testament, or at least of the Pentateuch, occupying a position
similar to that of 1 Cor 15:3-8 as the early Christian kerygma. What
Christ's death and resurrection are to the New Testament, the Exodus is
to the Old Testament. These are the basic messages of the two canons.
In each case the mighty acts of God lead to a confession of faith, a recital
of those mighty acts.

Responsorial Psalm: 91:1-2, 10-15

Psalm 91 is traditional on this Sunday, the old Introit having given the
day its name of *Invocavit.* It was this psalm that the devil quoted in the
temptation story—at the third temptation in Luke. The devil misapplied
the promise of angelic assistance, and verses 14-15 correct it. Only those
who set their love upon God can expect him to deliver them. For that
reason Christ was delivered: he, more than all others, set his love upon
his Father. He was delivered from the cross to resurrection.

Reading II: Romans 10:8-13

Here we have a New Testament confession of faith (v. 9) corresponding
to the Old Testament confession in the first reading. This confession
represents the subject matter of the catechetical instruction given to the

405

candidates before baptism and their profession of faith. Such simple confessions, as we find them in the New Testament, are the nucleus out of which grew, first the baptismal creed (for example, the Apostles' Creed), and later, conciliar creeds (for example, that of Nicaea). The same confession also forms the basic content of the great Eucharistic Prayer. The unity of the Church, despite the pluralism of its members (Jew and Greek); the unity of the New Testament, despite the variety of its expressions of the Christian message; the unity of the liturgy, despite the existence of different Eucharistic Prayers or Canons, lie in this common, basic confession: God has raised Jesus from the dead and made him Lord.

Gospel: Luke 4:1-13

The Lucan version of the temptation differs very little in wording from the more familiar Matthean form. The only notable differences are the rearrangement of the second and third temptations, and the statement that the devil left Jesus "until an opportune time" (v. 13). Hans Conzelmann saw in this a major clue to Luke's theology. The ministry of Jesus is the "Satan-free" period; the devil returns to assail Jesus in the passion (22:3). Thus, Luke deliberately links the temptation story with the passion.

There is an even more suitable link with the passion in the replies of Jesus to the three temptations:

> "Man shall not live by bread alone."
> "You shall worship the Lord your God,
>   and him only shall you serve."
> "You shall not tempt the Lord your God."

This threefold confession plots the future course of Jesus' ministry, culminating in the confession that he made before Pontius Pilate. It was this confession, this single-minded commitment to God's will for him (which is what the dogma of Christ's sinlessness really means) that characterized the whole course of Jesus' ministry and finally led him to the cross.

The Homily

Today's readings are linked by the idea of confession. The homilist could develop the place of confession in the life of the Christian community. Our readings suggest three types of confession: Eucharistic confession, baptismal confession, and Jesus' own confession in his temptations and on the cross.

Some Churches pride themselves on being "confessional" Churches, meaning that they have their own confession of faith, usually from the sixteenth century. Other Churches pride themselves on not being confessional Churches at all. Such differences are the products of different histories. Whether a Church is confessional or not, it belongs to the essence of the Church that it should be a *confessing* Church. If the Church is to be the Church, it must boldly confess its faith before the world in the face of persecution and when tempted to abandon its faith for the sake of accommodation to the spirit of the age.

At baptism we commit ourselves to this confession ("in token that hereafter he shall not be ashamed to *confess* the faith of Christ crucified"— Book of Common Prayer 1928, baptismal office). In the liturgy we set forth this confession at every Eucharist, and in life this confession must be lived out day by day. The 1967 *Liturgy of the Lord's Supper* of the Episcopal Church contained the noble petition, unfortunately dropped in the revised rites of 1970: "and grant that with boldness we may confess thy Name in constancy of faith." It is to this that the homilist will want to exhort the congregation today.

SECOND SUNDAY OF LENT

Reading I: Genesis 15:5-12, 17-18

This reading combines three different themes: Yahweh's promise of an abundant posterity to Abraham; his promise of the land to Israel; and the sealing of that promise with a covenant ceremony. The Book of Genesis contains several stories of God's establishment of his covenant with Abraham, all of them variants of the same tradition. In Abraham, God decisively intervened in human history to create a people for himself. God's choice is, on his side, a sheer act of grace; and faith is set, be it noted, not in the context of individual salvation, but in the context of a people's history. This is the context in which the Old Testament views *sola gratia, sola fide*. The apostle Paul discerned the fulfillment of God's promise to Abraham in the Christ-event and in the emergence of the new Israel, the Church (Gal 3; Rom 4).

Responsorial Psalm: 27:1, 7-9c, 13-14

This psalm serves as a link between the first two readings. The fourth stanza begins with the words: "I believe that I shall see the goodness of the Lord in the land of the living!" For Abraham this land was *eretz Israel*, the territory that his descendants were destined to occupy. For Christian believers this land is the kingdom of God, the "commonwealth of heaven" of which the second reading speaks.

Reading II: Philippians 3:17–4:1 (long form); 3:20–4:1 (short form)

Both the second reading and the gospel speak of a "change." The second reading speaks of the change of our earthly existence in the final consummation; the gospel speaks of the change of Jesus as he prayed on the holy mountain.

The term "glorious body," like the term "spiritual body," which Paul uses in 1 Cor 15, reflects the apocalyptic hope. According to this hope, the life of the age to come will not be merely a prolongation of this present life but an entirely new, transformed mode of existence. It was into this mode of existence that Christ entered at his resurrection. But his resurrection is not merely an incident in his own personal biography, as it were; he entered into that existence as the "first fruits" (1 Cor 15:20), that is, as the one who made it possible for believers also to enter into that new mode of existence after him. That is the Christian hope.

Gospel: Luke 9:28-36

The use of the transfiguration story on the second Sunday of Lent in the revised Roman Lectionary follows the tradition of the *Missale Romanum.* The Episcopal, Lutheran, and Methodist Lectionaries depart from the Roman Lectionary here and read the transfiguration story on the last Sunday after Epiphany. On that day it forms an admirable transition from the contemplation of the earthly ministry of Jesus as the manifestation of God in the Epiphany season to a contemplation of the passion as the ultimate epiphany. In the Roman Lectionary the transfiguration story serves the theme: "Behold, we go up to Jerusalem" (see below, The Homily).

That Jesus and his disciples ascended a mountain for solitude after the abrupt conclusion of his Galilean ministry, and that Jesus communicated to his disciples his change of plan—which was to go up to Jerusalem and challenge the religious authorities in the nation's capital—is historically plausible. This original nucleus of historical fact was then rewritten by the post-Easter community in the light of its Easter faith. There is some indication in the Gospels of an awareness that the events of Jesus' earthly life appeared in a different perspective after the first Easter (see John 2:22; 12:16). Thus, what happened on the mountain was rewritten with the use of Old Testament materials. The change in the appearance of Jesus' face is reminiscent of Moses on Mount Sinai (Exod 34:29). Moses and Elijah, both of whom figured in first-century Jewish apocalyptic as returning at the end, talk with Jesus about his "departure" (Greek: *exodos*), that is, his death and exaltation. The disciples were ready enough to accept Jesus as *one* of the end-time figures, along with Moses and Elijah, but not yet as a unique figure of the end-time. So a voice from heaven proclaims the finality of Jesus: "This is my Son, my Chosen; listen to *him*" (note the allusion to Deut 18:15). Then we are told that after this "Jesus was found alone." The story as retold by the post-Easter Church is rich in symbolism, proclaiming that Jesus is the Son of God, his final emissary, and the second Moses, who accomplishes the new Exodus.

The addition of the words "at Jerusalem" in verse 31 looks like a redactional addition, for it is one of Luke's major themes that the holy city is the focal point to which the ministry of Jesus moves. It is there that the saving event is accomplished, and it is from there that the proclamation of that saving event goes forth to the ends of the earth. The point of all this is that the gospel proclaims, not a timeless myth (see 2 Pet 1:16, also about the transfiguration), but something that actually happened at a particular time and place in history.

Gospel: Mark 10:32-45 (Episcopal Lectionary)

The Episcopal Lectionary curiously departs from the normal sequence of Lucan readings in series C and offers instead the third of the Marcan predictions of the passion, the question of Zebedee's sons, and the ransom saying (the last of these three items is omitted in the Lucan parallel). Mark has carefully constructed the whole section 8:27–10:45 to put across his conception of the suffering Son of man. There he corrects the earlier Christology of a mere wonderworker and braces the Church of his day to endure similar persecution.

Gospel: Luke 13:31-35 (Lutheran Lectionary)

This pericope has the merit of following the Lucan sequence and functions in much the same way as the transfiguration story and the complex pericope of the Episcopal Lectionary in that it points up the transition from Galilee to Jerusalem. It is probably the most historical of all three choices, for verse 33 has high claim to being an authentic saying of the historical Jesus. It indicates something of Jesus' historical intention in going up to Jerusalem, in the kind of terms he himself would have used. Thus, he speaks of himself as a prophet, whose purpose is to lay down his prophetic challenge at the heart of Judaism and face the consequences. He does not use a messianic title nor speak of his death as a ransom or a second Exodus. These were later, post-Easter interpretations of the meaning of Jesus' person and death, though, of course, true interpretations.

The Homily

Probably the most obvious theme today would be: "Behold, we go up to Jerusalem" (Mark 10:33). Quite a few Christians nowadays are fortunate enough to make this pilgrimage physically at least once in their lifetime. Each year the Church in its liturgy invites us to go on that same pilgrimage in heart and mind. Today the homilist has the opportunity of preparing the people to embark on that pilgrimage and of explaining the importance of Jerusalem as the center of salvation history.

Other possibilities for the homily would be: Abraham as the paradigm of faith and grace alone; or, taking up the common theme of the second reading and the transfiguration story, the concept of eschatological transformation, the Lord's and ours, his transformation being foreshadowed in the transfiguration ("an anticipation of his eschatology"—G. Kittel), and our transformation being symbolized at baptism and finalized at the consummation.

THIRD SUNDAY OF LENT

Reading I: Exodus 3:1-8a, 13-15

A single thread runs through today's readings. It is indicated by the name of God as revealed to Moses: "I am who I am," or, as many contemporary exegetes interpret it, "He causes to be what comes into existence." Our God is the God of Abraham, Isaac, and Jacob, not the God of the philosophers (Pascal)—that is to say, not an abstract, impersonal reality, but the transcendent One who intervenes powerfully in human history. God calls Moses and sends him to lead his people out of Egypt through the wilderness (second reading), refreshing them with water from the rock and bringing them into the Promised Land. Then finally he sends his Son, offering his people one last chance to repent and accept his salvation (gospel).

Once again the Exodus story functions in the liturgy as a type of the saving act of God in Christ. God sees the affliction of his people. He "comes down," that is, intervenes in history out of his transcendence, to deliver them from the slavery of sin and to bring them into the land "flowing with milk and honey," the kingdom of God.

Responsorial Psalm: 103:1-4, 6-8, 11

In this psalm we praise God for showing his ways to Moses, and his works to the people of Israel, as these ways and works are spoken of in the first reading. A psalm sung by Israel about the Exodus becomes a hymn of the Christian community celebrating the death and resurrection of Christ.

Reading II: 1 Corinthians 10:1-6, 10-12

The situation confronting Paul at Corinth is that the Christians there are supposing that the sacraments automatically confer the fullness of salvation here and now. Probably the Corinthians were under the influence of early Gnostic enthusiasm. Paul therefore has to stress the "not yet" aspect of the sacraments. They anticipate symbolically the fullness of salvation, but effectively they initiate and foster a process that looks to its final completion at the end. To illustrate his point, Paul draws an analogy with Israel in the wilderness and finds in the Exodus story types of the two major Christian sacraments of baptism and the Eucharist: the children of Israel were baptized when they passed through the cloud and through the Red Sea, and they were nourished with spiritual food and drink by the manna and the water from the rock in the wilderness.

It is probable that Paul did not invent this typology but took it over from earliest Christianity. It may well have had its origin in Jewish speculation about the messianic banquet and may have been taken up in pre-Pauline Christianity to interpret the eschatological banquets of the early community, such as those alluded to in Acts 2:42, 46. Certainly there is rabbinic influence present in the idea that the Rock *followed* the Israelites, an inference from the fact that it is mentioned *twice* in the Pentateuch (Exod 17 and Num 20; a modern commentator would regard these as doublets of the same tradition). More extraordinary is Paul's claim that "the Rock was Christ." Probably the basis for this identification is the equation of Christ with the divine "wisdom," the personified agent both of creation and of all God's acts in salvation history. "Wisdom" stands for God's going out of himself in self-communication and activity. For Paul, as for the New Testament as a whole, God's going out of himself culminates in his redemptive act in Jesus.

Gospel: Luke 13:1-9

Jesus here refers to two recent disasters, otherwise unknown to historians. One was the outrage of a tyrant, the other an accident involving construction workers in Siloam. From both events he draws a warning for Israel. Unless the nation repents, it too will perish. For Jesus, repentance means accepting his message of God's kingdom. The parable of the fig tree reinforces the challenge to repent. This provides a link with the second reading: "Let any one who thinks that he stands take heed lest he fall." Neither the old Israel nor the new dare presume upon a false sense of security.

The Homily

We tend to think of Lent as a time to increase acts of personal devotion and piety. The second reading and the gospel suggest that Lent addresses itself just as much to the Church as an established institution. Like all institutions, it is often threatened by a false sense of security. We have the warning example of Israel. In the wilderness the old people of God were lulled into a false sense of security when Yahweh, fulfilling his promise to Moses in the burning bush, brought his people out of Egypt through the cloud and the sea, fed them with manna, and quenched their thirst with water from the rock. We also have the warning example of the new Israel. The Corinthians were lulled into a false sense of security by their possession of the two sacraments of the gospel. The homilist should not find it difficult to apply these warnings to the contemporary Church as an institution today. "Unless you repent, you will likewise perish" (gospel).

FOURTH SUNDAY OF LENT

Reading I: Joshua 5:9, 10-12

Last Sunday's second reading interpreted the manna as a type of the Eucharist. Today's Old Testament reading tells us that the manna ceased when the first Passover was celebrated in the Promised Land. So, too, the Eucharist will cease when it finds its fulfillment in the messianic banquet of the kingdom of God.

Responsorial Psalm: 34:1-6

Comments on Psalm 34 can be found on the nineteenth, twentieth, and 335 twenty-first Sundays of the year in series B. 337
339

Reading II: 2 Corinthians 5:17-21

It is remarkable that Paul should appeal to the very people he calls a "new creation" to be reconciled to Christ. This is because the community's status as the new creation is not an assured possession but something that must constantly be worked at. To renew that status is the work of the apostolic ministry—the "ministry of reconciliation," as Paul calls it. God's saving act in Christ and the ongoing work of the apostolic ministry are not to be separated. The second is an extension of the first, part of the same salvation history.

This salvation history is inaugurated by an event in which "for our sake he made him to be sin who knew no sin." This bold affirmation can best be understood in the light of the Marcan-Matthean word from the cross: "My God, my God, why hast thou forsaken me?" Here Jesus enters the deepest consequences of human sin—our alienation from God. He takes his stand where we are as sinners, under the wrath of God, alienated from him, so that we may become what he, Jesus, is—the righteousness of God. The Greek Fathers were really saying the same thing when they asserted that Christ partook of our human nature in order that we might become partakers of his divine nature.

Gospel: Luke 15:1-3, 11-32

The second reading provides the right context for the interpretation of the parable of the prodigal son. This parable is often understood as a simple illustration of God's readiness to forgive in response to repentance, without the necessity of Christ's atoning death on the cross. "There is no place for Jesus in the parable of the prodigal son," it has been said. But the Jesus of the parables is never promulgating timeless truths of religion and ethics; he is always commenting on what is happening concretely in his own ministry.

The Pharisees were grumbling because Jesus was eating with outcasts (vv. 1-3: the Roman and Lutheran Lectionaries wisely start with this setting, while the Episcopal Lectionary less wisely omits it). The parable is a comment on Jesus' action in eating with outcasts. He is not left out of the parable for the simple reason that the parable presupposes and interprets his action. When Jesus eats with outcasts, it is not just humanitarian broadmindedness, as though the laws of God or the Pharisaic regulations did not matter; it is *God* breaking through the condemnation of his own law in order to reach out and save the lost.

The Homily

The homilist has a rare opportunity today to preach the atonement. The Pauline statement "For our sake he made him to be sin who knew no sin" can be linked, on one side, with the cross as interpreted in the Marcan-Matthean word and, on the other, with Jesus' action in eating with outcasts. In this way the cross will not seem to be an isolated event but the culmination of a whole life of self-identification with sinners, and the Pauline doctrine of the atonement not an abstract piece of theologizing but a fitting interpretation of Jesus' intention. The father in the parable came out to meet his son, to stand where *he* was in order to bring him back home; so, too, God in Christ came out to meet us as sinners.

FIFTH SUNDAY OF LENT

Reading I: Isaiah 43:16-21

In Second Isaiah, the impending return from exile in Babylon is depicted as a new Exodus. The "former things" and the "things of old" refer to the first Exodus. This is now replaced by a "new thing," the return from exile. In this new event the events of the first Exodus are repeated: "I will make a way in the wilderness and rivers in the desert." In Christian biblical theology, the proclamation of God's act of salvation in Christ picks up the same imagery. The "new things" are now the death and resurrection of the Messiah, and the "drink" that God provides for his people consists of the sacraments of the new covenant.

Responsorial Psalm: 126:1-6

The fourth stanza entitles us to apply the restoration of which the first and third stanzas speak and the "great things" of the second stanza to the death and resurrection of Christ:

> He that goes forth weeping,
>   bearing the seed for sowing,
> shall come home with shouts of joy,
>   bringing his sheaves with him.

"The metaphor of sowing in the Old Testament almost demanded a messianic application" (E. Hoskyns).

Reading II: Philippians 3:8-14

The third chapter of Philippians is a polemic against Paul's opponents. Whether they were Judaizers, that is, advocates of imposing the Jewish law on Gentile converts, or some kind of syncretists or "enthusiasts" is not certain, but current exegesis is inclining toward the latter (so not only the German Lutheran Schmithals but also the German Catholic Gnilka). As enthusiasts, these opponents would fondly imagine that through baptism they had "already attained" and were already perfect. Against their position Paul holds out his *theologia crucis*, not simply as an abstract doctrine but as a reality to which his whole life as an apostle is conformed. Only by becoming like Christ in his death, only by sharing his suffering and by living under the "not yet," can the Apostle know the power of Christ's resurrection now, and eventually attain the resurrection when Christ returns.

Gospel: John 8:1-11

The pericope about the woman caught in adultery, it is now agreed by most scholars, is not part of the original text of John, though, of course, it is part of the canonical text and, as such, has been rightly restored from the margin in the rsv Common Bible. The earliest manuscripts either omit it or place it somewhere else. Some place it after Luke 21:38, which is an interesting interpolation, for the story has a definitely Lucan ring. Despite its late attestation, it is certainly a very early and good tradition. Professor Bruce Metzger's verdict in his textual commentary is that it "has all the earmarks of historical veracity."

The Swedish New Testament scholar Harald Riesenfeld has offered an interesting explanation of why this story went underground, so to speak, for such a long time. It happened, he thinks, during the period when Church authorities were trying to enforce a strict discipline over Christian marriages. The story seemed at that time to encourage laxity in marriage standards. Actually, this was a false impression. After all, Jesus did say to the woman, "Go, and do not sin again." He recognized sin as sin. And in saying, "Neither do I condemn you," he was not condoning the sin but pronouncing the forgiveness of God. The scribes and Pharisees, however, come in for sharper condemnation and are put to shame. None of them could claim to be without sin. Here is a pictorial illustration of Jesus' saying, "Judge not, that you may not be judged" (Matt 7:1).

The Homily

The story of the woman caught in adultery provides the homilist with an opportunity to treat a very hot subject—Jesus' attitude toward sex and marriage, and particularly toward adultery. The homilist could contrast Jesus' attitude with (a) modern secular attitudes, and (b) the tendency of the Church in the past to regard sexual sins as the deadliest of all sins. As Dorothy Sayers and others have pointed out, the deadliest sin in the biblical-Christian ethic is the sin of pride.

An alternative possibility for the homilist would be to explore Paul's conception of apostolate as involving conformity to the cross. This is not an ethic for apostles only, but something that the Church proposes through its liturgy for all Christians, especially during Lent. The last stanza of the responsorial psalm could also be drawn into the presentation.

PASSION SUNDAY (PALM SUNDAY)

The Procession with Palms: Luke 19:28-40

Our Lord entered Jerusalem to go to his passion. That is how it turned out. Historically speaking, his motive was probably to lay down the final challenge to his people to accept the message and coming of the kingdom of God, with full knowledge that his action would almost certainly cost him his life. They rejected his message and brought him to the cross. As John's Gospel reminds us (12:16), the true meaning of Jesus' entry into Jerusalem did not dawn upon his disciples until after Easter. Then they came to see that the entry was paradoxically the procession of a king to his coronation (his crown would be of thorns, and his throne a cross).

Like Mark (contrast Matthew and John), Luke does not recall the prophecy of Zechariah ("Tell the daughter of Zion . . ."), but Luke's readers, who know their Greek Old Testament, are surely meant to recall that prophecy as they hear of Jesus riding on a "colt." A peculiarity of Luke's version is his paraphrase of *Hosanna:* "Peace in heaven and glory in the highest." This not only explains the Hebrew word for his Greek readers but also deliberately recalls the song of the angels at the nativity. Peace and glory were there proclaimed as a future promise that would become a reality only through the cross. Christmas cannot be detached from Good Friday and Easter except at the cost of trivializing and sentimentalizing it.

In the Mass for Passion Sunday, the readings are the same every year, except for the gospel. The reader, therefore, may refer to series A for comments on the first two readings and the responsorial psalm. Here we will offer comments only on the gospel and provide some ideas for the homily.

Gospel: Luke 22:14-23:56 (long form); 23:1-49 (short form)

The passion narratives, we are told by modern New Testament scholars, differ in form from the rest of the Gospel materials. Everything prior to the passion consists of "pericopes," that is, short units that were handed down in oral tradition as isolated units before they were combined in our written Gospels. The passion story, however, was from the start a continuous narrative. The Church has always understood the difference by redividing the Gospels into pericopes in its Lectionary and by reading the passion as a continuous narrative. One would hope that at least at the principal Mass today the long form of the passion narrative will be used intact. When read by three different persons, as the rubric suggests, the long form can sustain interest without boredom and accords more with the literary and pre-literary form of the material.

Each of the four evangelists has his own distinctive perspective on the passion. Mark emphasizes the isolation of Christ: betrayed, forsaken and denied by the disciples, mocked and tortured by his enemies, railed at by the brigands crucified with him, and, finally, bereft of the presence of his Father. Matthew brings out the royalty of Christ, but it is a paradoxical royalty, manifesting itself precisely in humiliation. John is also concerned with Christ's royalty, but it is a royalty visibly present. Luke takes a different line. It has been well said that he transposes the passion from the key of tragedy to the key of pathos. It is the story of a martyrdom (note the parallels with Stephen's martyrdom in Acts), of one who goes out in sympathy to others (for example, the "daughters of Jerusalem"; "Father, forgive them"; "Today you will be with me"). Note also the serenity of Christ's death ("Father, into thy hands . . . .") in each of the Gospels. The passion story is intended not merely to narrate what happened but to interpret it as good news.

The Homily

We would suggest three different possibilities for the homily today. First, the homilist may decide to give a course of sermons on the servant songs of Second Isaiah during Holy Week (the first song is used on Monday in Holy Week; the second on Tuesday; the third on Wednesday; and the fourth on Good Friday). The homilist could show how the prophet of the Exile meditated on the place of suffering in God's plan of salvation, how his insights found their fulfillment in the sufferings of Christ, and how his sufferings give meaning to all human suffering, especially that of his people.

The second possibility would be based on the *Carmen Christi.* Here the cross is viewed as the culmination of the path of humiliation that began in the incarnation of the Son of God and continued throughout his whole life of obedience. The hymn forms the theological basis for the exhortation to humility that Paul delivers to his congregation, keeping his eye on their particular problems. The homilist can do the same, keeping an eye on the particular problems of the local congregation.

The third possibility would be to bring out the unique features of the Lucan passion narrative, especially Christ's sensitivity to the needs of others, and finding in Christ's compassion the good news of the story of the cross.

EASTER TRIDUUM

HOLY THURSDAY

Mass of the Lord's Supper

We again remind our readers that the Roman Missal specifies three principal mysteries that are commemorated in this Mass and should be explained in the homily: the institution of the Eucharist, the institution of the priesthood, and Christ's commandment of mutual love. The readings are the same every year, and the reader is referred to our comments on them in series A. Here we offer some further comments on the three themes of this Mass.

1. *The institution of the Eucharist.* Although we habitually speak of the "institution" of the Eucharist, our Lord did not institute it in the sense of inventing an entirely new rite. Whether John or the Synoptists are correct in their dating of the Last Supper, that is, whether the Last Supper was a Passover meal or an ordinary Jewish religious meal, it is clear that the actions at the supper—taking the bread and wine, giving thanks, breaking the bread, and sharing the food and drink—were all well known and quite regular Jewish observances. What was new was the significance with which Jesus invested the familiar actions. Of course, we have to allow for a certain development in the interpretive words over the bread and the cup, as a comparison of the various accounts shows. The expansions should be attributed to the presence of the living Christ in his Church rather than to what the earthly Jesus said at the Last Supper. The meaning of the interpretive words lies in the fact that the Eucharist has both a backward- and a forward-looking significance. It looks back to the redemptive event of the cross, which it makes a present reality, and forward to the second coming, which it anticipates.

The German Catholic New Testament scholar Heinz Schürmann suggests one novel feature in Jesus' action at the supper. Instead of allowing each one present to drink out of his own individual cup, Jesus passes *his* cup around to all present. In Jewish meals, according to Schürmann, it was customary for the presider at the meal to pass his own cup to someone whom he wished to single out for special honor, thus allowing that guest

58

418

to share in the blessing he had said over the cup—a custom somewhat similar to our drinking a toast. Jesus shares his cup with *all* his disciples because he is making them all partakers in the benefits of his passion. This is an attractive suggestion, which, if correct, offers a notable enrichment to our understanding of what happened at the Last Supper and of what happens at the Eucharist.

2. *The institution of the priesthood.* This theme requires careful handling. It is too simplistic an interpretation to say that by commanding the Twelve to celebrate the Eucharist, Jesus made them priests, and that this commandment subsequently devolved in succession upon bishops and presbyters of the Church. The command "Do this" is given to the whole Church, and the Eucharist is the action in which the whole Church expresses its priesthood (1 Pet 2:1-10). The Eucharistic president acts as the representative and mouthpiece of the priesthood of the whole Church. Both the priesthood of the Church and the ministerial priesthood are derived from the very nature of the Eucharist. If we understand the Eucharist correctly, we will understand the priesthood both of the Church and of the ministry.

3. *Christ's commandment of mutual love.* This is expressed in the footwashing and in the accompanying words as given in the gospel. In our various traditions we have overemphasized the vertical relationship in the Eucharist—the communion of the soul with its Lord—and have underemphasized what the early Church expressed in making the Eucharist proper a part of a fellowship meal (called the *agape,* or love feast), thus underscoring the horizontal dimension.

The restoration of the exchange of peace by the whole congregation is one current attempt to recover this horizontal dimension. This restored practice has disturbed not a few of the devout, while on the other hand those who have found a new understanding of the horizontal dimension have in some places been driven underground in the so-called underground churches. This group has deprived the "established" churches of their enriched understanding of the social dimension of the Eucharist. They have fallen into the danger of detaching the horizontal fellowship from its roots in the vertical dimension of Christ's love for his people, a love exhibited in his sacrificial death and symbolized by the footwashing.

The Homily

The homilist will clearly have to choose one of these three subjects, guided not only by personal interest and predilection but by familiarity with the concrete needs of the congregation.

GOOD FRIDAY

Since the readings are the same every year, additional comments may be found in series A and B.

61
251

Reading I: Isaiah 52:13–53:12

When Philip the Evangelist discovered the Ethiopian eunuch reading this fourth servant song, the eunuch asked, "About whom, pray, does the prophet say this, about himself or about someone else?" (Acts 8:34). On the technical level of Old Testament scholarship, there is no consensus on the answer to that question. But for the New Testament, as for Christian faith, these words finally come to rest in the fate of Jesus of Nazareth. Echoes of Isa 53 occur in the earliest strata of the New Testament (Rom 5:25; 1 Cor 15:4) and have colored the Jesus tradition in the Gospels (Mark 10:45b; 14:24). How far Jesus explicitly applied this chapter to his own understanding of his mission is difficult to say, but he certainly understood his mission generally in terms of the Isaianic servant (for example, Matt 11:5 and par.). Isaiah 53 contributed three essential points to the understanding of Christ's death: his suffering was innocent, vicarious, and redemptive; it avails for all people (the rabbis equated the "many" with "all," including the Gentiles); the righteous sufferer is finally vindicated: "The will of the Lord shall prosper in his hand . . . ." (Isa 53:10).

Responsorial Psalm: 31:1, 5, 11-12, 14-16, 24

This is another psalm about the suffering and vindication of the righteous one. Though it has played a less important part in coloring the passion narratives, it provides Luke's version with its last word from the cross, "Into thy hand I commit my spirit." It is therefore particularly appropriate in this year of series C.

Reading II: Hebrews 4:14-16; 5:7-9

The author of Hebrews is like a musical composer—he enunciates his theme (Christ's high priesthood) several times before he fully develops it (7:1–10:18). This is the third enunciation. In it he characterizes Christ the high priest in three ways: he can sympathize with our temptations and infirmities because of his complete identification with us in his incarnate life; he prayed for deliverance and was heard (a clear reflection of the Gethsemane tradition, but note that "save from" does not mean "escape from" but "deliverance through"); he "learned obedience": the incarnation was so real that Jesus did not fulfill the Father's will as an automaton, but only through struggle and temptation and "learning experience." It was only after he was "made perfect," that is, had carried his earthly mission to its completeness, that he "became" the source of salvation, namely, by his high priestly work in heaven. All else—his incarnate life and its struggles, his obedience unto death—was but the prelude to the exercise of his high priestly office in heaven.

Gospel: John 18:1–19:42

As we have seen, each evangelist has his own particular perspective on the passion, and John's perspective is that the kingship of Jesus constantly shines through his humiliation. All the way through, Jesus is in command of the situation. He sets the passion in motion by voluntarily coming forward for his arrest. The temple police, awed by his personality, fall back. Peter would stop the arrest, but Jesus intervenes. On the cross Jesus makes his last will, bequeathing his mother to the disciple, and the disciple to his mother (John may regard Mary as a symbol of the Church). Finally, it is Jesus who decides on the moment of his death—he gives up his spirit. The passion narrative is a commentary on the saying: "I lay down my life, that I may take it again. No one takes it from me, but I lay it down of my own accord" (John 10:17-18).

Although the evangelist has packed most of his theology of the cross into his discourses, especially in the farewell address, at least two points of interpretation are brought out in the passion narrative. First, Pilate (like Caiaphas earlier, on the atoning death) bears unwitting testimony to Christ's kingship when he brings Jesus before the people and when he refuses to alter the inscription on the cross. Second, John the Baptist had proclaimed Jesus as the true paschal Lamb of God who takes away the world's sin, and now Christ dies as such at the moment when the Passover lambs are being slaughtered. Then at his death he announces the completion of his sacrifice: "It is finished" (John 19:30; the rsv translation is weak; the Vulgate's *Consummatum est* gets the point).

The Homily

Homiletical suggestions were offered for these readings in series A and B. Perhaps this year the homilist might choose to bring out the specifically Johannine understanding of the passion. The words from the cross in all four Gospels offer a useful handle to the respective evangelist's redaction (rather than treating these words as recordings of what the historical Jesus actually said). Of the three Johannine words from the cross, the last ("It is finished") offers the most theological meat. The homilist could dwell on the finality of Christ's sacrifice and on the anamnesis of it in the Eucharist, and then on the way in which believers are caught up into that sacrifice and called upon to show it forth in Christian living.

EASTER VIGIL

This is the archetypal liturgy of the whole Church year. It consists of four parts: (1) the service of light, with the Easter proclamation; (2) the liturgy of the word; (3) the liturgy of baptism; (4) the liturgy of the Eucharist.

Except for the gospel, the readings are the same each year. Therefore, the reader should consult series A for comment on the seven Old Testament readings, the responsorial psalms, and the epistle. Comment on the gospel follows here.

Gospel: Luke 24:1-12

None of the Gospels relates the actual resurrection, that is, the rising (or the raising by God) of Jesus from the dead. There are two reasons for this: (1) no one was present to witness it; there were witnesses to the empty tomb and to the appearances, but these were the aftermath of the event, not the event itself; (2) resurrection is transformation into an entirely new mode of existence, not mere resuscitation to the old life as in the raisings of Jairus' daughter, the widow's son at Nain, and Lazarus. The resurrection takes place at the point of intersection between this age and the age to come, between time and eternity. Only the this-side aspect of it ("He is not here") is open to this-worldly observation. Christ can only be revealed by God to the witnesses as already risen. So the gospel of the day gives us, not a narrative of the resurrection, but the witness of the empty tomb. In itself, an empty tomb is susceptible of diverse interpretations. The true meaning of it—and here lies the real *euangelion*, the Easter message—is conveyed by the "two men . . . in dazzling apparel" (angels, that is, communication from the beyond). "He . . . has risen."

The Church, believing this proclamation, can now proceed to baptize, to renew its baptismal vows, and to celebrate the paschal Eucharist, in all of which the past (Christ's death and resurrection) is "co-celebrated," that is, brought from the past into the present, and the future (the second coming of Christ) is anticipated. *Marana tha!*

The Homily

If we are going to bring out what is distinctive in the Lucan form of the story of the empty tomb, we will find it in the change that Luke has made in the angelic proclamation. Instead of telling the disciples to go to Galilee in order to see the risen Lord, the angelic messengers remind them of the prediction of the passion that Jesus had pronounced during his Galilean ministry. This ties together the disciples' pre-Easter experience and their post-Easter experience.

There is much discussion today about the relative importance of the pre-Easter Jesus and the post-Easter Jesus in the scheme of Christian faith. Some scholars seek to put all the emphasis on the pre-Easter One, others on the post-Easter One. The New Testament asserts that they are equally important. Without Easter, the earthly Jesus would be a figure of the past; without the earthly life, the resurrected One would be faceless. The Easter Jesus is the eternal presence of the One who walked in Galilee and who died on the cross in Jerusalem.

EASTER SEASON

EASTER SUNDAY

The Easter Sunday Mass is not itself the paschal liturgy. That was celebrated at the culmination of the Easter Vigil. Rather, this is the first of a series of Masses that belong to the great fifty days. In them we reflect upon the post-Easter revelations of the risen Christ and the fruits of our redemption in him.

The readings are the same every year. Comments on them can be found in series A and B, while here we will offer a few hints for the homilist. 72 256

The Homily

The readings suggest three different aspects of the Easter message. The first reading, taken from one of the kerygmatic speeches in Acts, is a proclamation of the death and resurrection of Christ as the final, redemptive act of God. This kerygma is at a primitive stage of development, before the full redemptive significance of the cross had been worked out. The whole life-story of Jesus is interpreted as "word," that is, an act of God's self-communication. The crucifixion was the radical calling into question of the validity of that word by Jesus' contemporaries. The resurrection in turn is God's vindication of the validity of that word. God set his seal on all that Jesus had said and done in his earthly ministry.

The resurrection does not mean that Christ's earthly ministry becomes a thing of the past, a phase now finished; rather, it is through the resurrection that all Christ stood for in his earthly life—his word, or self-communication of God; his bringing of healing and liberation to those in bondage to the devil—all this can now continue in the Church. It is not the continued influence of a figure in history through his teaching and example (as, for instance, in the case of Socrates), but the continuation of that same word and work. Part of the meaning of Easter is, as Willi Marxsen has put it, "die Sache Jesu geht weiter" ("What Jesus stood for continues"). That, of course, is not the whole message, but it is an important part of it.

The two alternative second readings (Col 3:1-4; 1 Cor 5:6b-8) suggest another aspect of Easter. Easter is not simply the recollection of a past event, or even its representation in word and sacrament. It also celebrates our own participation in the risen life, initiated in baptism and nourished in holy communion. This carries with it a present imperative.

Colossians 3:1-4	1 Corinthians 5:6b-8
1 *The Easter Baptisms*	1 *The Easter Eucharist*
You have died	Christ, our paschal lamb, has been
You have been raised	sacrificed
	Let us celebrate the festival
2 *The Imperative*	2 *The Imperative*
Seek the things above	Cleanse out the old leaven
Set your mind on the things above	With sincerity and truth

The story of the empty tomb from John 20:1-9 treats that pericope quite differently from the earliest tradition. It is clear that for the earliest Church the resurrection faith was grounded, not on the discovery of the empty tomb, but in the appearances. "To faith the empty tomb will be a sign of what has taken place. It will not, however, fight for the empty tomb as for an article of faith, because the truth of Easter does not in fact depend on the empty tomb" (E. Schweizer).

John's Gospel, however, following a late tradition, allows the "other disciple" to come to faith in the resurrection through the sight of the empty tomb, without an angelic proclamation, as in the other Gospels. Before that, Peter had seen but had not yet come to faith, while Mary Magdalene had seen the stone rolled away but concluded that the body had been removed by human hands. The empty tomb functions as a sign. But a sign is equivocal. It leaves open possibilities: *either* the body was somehow removed, *or* Jesus has been raised from the dead.

The homilist must distinguish between a sign and a proof. Even the arrangement of the linen cloths (v. 7) was not a proof for Peter. Only the other disciple came to faith, because he perceived the significance of the sign. A proof coerces; only a sign can produce the free decision of faith.

SECOND SUNDAY OF EASTER

Reading I: Acts 5:12-16

Here is a vignette of the apostles' ministry in the early community after Pentecost. It shows the power of the risen Christ at work in his Church. The apostolic preaching is not mentioned here, but there are never signs and wonders without the proclamation of the word.

The phrase "were added to the Lord" is very striking. New converts were "added," that is, they were brought into an already existing community. They did not hear the message and get together to form a community of their own; the community was already there. And they "were added"—a reverential passive denoting that it was *God* who added them; it was not the Church that added new members. The new converts did not become members on their own, but God translated them into the redeemed community.

Responsorial Psalm: 118:2-4, 22-27b

Psalm 118, with its reference to the rejection of the stone and its subsequent elevation to be the chief cornerstone, was perhaps the earliest Old Testament passage that the primitive community applied to Christ's death and resurrection. It was the basic Old Testament passage for the "no-yes" interpretation of the death and resurrection: the death of Jesus as Israel's (and all humankind's) "no" to Jesus, and the resurrection as God's vindication of him, his "yes" to all that Jesus had said and done and suffered during his earthly life.

Reading II: Revelation 1:9-11a, 12-13, 17-19

This is the opening vision of the Apocalypse, in which John the Seer sees the risen Christ and receives the messages for the seven churches. Some have held that this vision was a continuation of the post-resurrection appearances. It is true that the language of the vision is used about the original appearances (1 Cor 15:3-8), and that in the earliest tradition the appearances were appearances "from heaven" (Paul; Mark; Matt 28:18; John 21) rather than massive apparitions of a Christ still on earth, as in the later tradition (Luke 24; John 20). But Paul (1 Cor 15:8) is emphatic that the appearance to himself on the road to Damascus was last, not only in date but as a matter of principle. Paul himself had later visions of the risen Christ (2 Cor 12:1-4; note that there he pictures himself as being transported to heaven, rather than the risen Christ as appearing from heaven upon earth). Moreover, the resurrection appearances were revelations that formed the Church and gave it its mission in the world. Subsequent visions, like those of Paul in 2 Cor 12:1-4 and of John the Seer in our reading today, only continue what was begun at Easter. The auditory element here repeats, but does not add to, the original Easter revelations: Christ reveals himself as alive out of death.

Gospel: John 20:19-31

This, the traditional gospel for this Sunday, describes two appearances: to the disciples on Easter evening, which appears in various forms in Matthew, Luke, and here; and to Thomas a week later, which is peculiar to John. The element of doubt, which characterized the appearance tradition almost from the beginning and which proves that the appearances were not merely wish-fulfillment, has here been expanded for apologetic purposes, enabling the risen One to establish his identity. The earlier tradition had pictured the risen One in more spiritual terms; this later emphasis on the physical reality of the risen body preserves the truth of the identity-amid-change between the earthly Jesus and the resurrected One.

John, however, has given this story his own twist by taking up a concern of the later Church. How could a person believe in the risen One without having received an appearance? Answer: Seeing him is no guarantee of believing. Even disciples had to come to faith when they saw him; so those who have not seen him can still have the blessedness of faith through believing the testimony of the first witnesses.

The Homily

Apart from the fact that all three readings are relevant to the Easter season, there does not seem to be any obvious way of linking them together. Consequently, there are three choices for the homily. Taking the reading from Acts, the homilist might take up the thought suggested by the use of the word "added" and relate it to the adults baptized at the Easter Vigil (if there were any), showing them that they have not joined a club by their own volition, but that God, by his act, has "added" them to an already existing community.

The reading from Revelation suggests the possibility of drawing out the distinction between the resurrection appearances and subsequent visions of the risen Lord.

The gospel would provide the theme of seeing/not seeing and believing. Here the homilist could deal with the doubts of modern Christians and how those doubts can be replaced by the faith that overcomes the world.

THIRD SUNDAY OF EASTER

Reading I: Acts 5:27b-32, 40b-41

The apostles had been arrested for preaching while under orders to desist. In a tremendous gesture of defiance that has been the inspiration of the Church in all times of persecution, they replied, "We must obey God rather than men," and they started at once to preach to the Sanhedrin, enabling Luke to give us another fragment of the primitive Christian kerygma.

The most striking feature here is the concept, highlighted in the caption to this reading, of a double witness—the apostles and the Holy Spirit (cf. John 15:26). The Spirit and the apostolic word are both necessary. Without the Spirit, the word becomes a dead formula, no longer speaking meaningfully to the contemporary situation, while without the word, the Spirit becomes uncontrolled enthusiasm divorced from the original witness to the Christ-event.

Responsorial Psalm: 30:1, 3-5, 10-11a, 12b

The hope of a future resurrection is found only in some of the latest parts of the Old Testament and is absent from the psalms. When the psalmist speaks of being brought up from Sheol and restored to life, he is using metaphorical language to describe deliverance from earthly troubles (in this case probably illness). But Christian apologetic, followed by liturgical piety, interpreted the psalm Christologically—the "I" who speaks becomes Christ, and the deliverance becomes his resurrection.

Reading II: Revelation 5:11-14

This is John's vision of the heavenly liturgy, of which the liturgy of the Church on earth is a reflection (see the Eucharistic preface; in the picture the four living creatures and the elders suggest the participants in the Christian liturgy of the time). Christ is addressed as "the Lamb who was slain," that is, the paschal lamb, a tradition going back at least to 1 Cor 5. Is this actually a fragment of the early Christian paschal liturgy?

Gospel: John 21:1-19

This story, widely regarded as an appendix to John's Gospel but apparently composed by members of the Johannine school, is in surprisingly close contact with early tradition. It probably goes back to the first appearance of the Lord to the Twelve by the Lake of Galilee. Here it is set in the context of a meal. At some stage this primitive story was combined with the miraculous draught of fishes that figures in Jesus' earthly ministry (Luke 5). Some think that the story there is a retrojection of an appearance story into the earthly life, but the current trend is to regard John 21 as a projection of the earthly miracle in a resurrection context. The number 153 has symbolic significance, though the evangelist does not explain. Clearly it has some connection with the mission of the Church, which the apostles are commissioned to inaugurate.

In verses 15-19 we encounter another story that goes back to very early tradition, namely, the first appearance to Peter, in which the first of the apostles is entrusted with the pastoral care of Christ's flock (see also Matt 16:17-19 and Luke 22:31-32). To this early tradition has been added a final paragraph containing a prediction (regarded by New Testament scholars as *ex eventu*) of Peter's martyrdom. This is the earliest reference to that event and its only mention in the New Testament.

The Homily

Following the suggestion of the caption, the homilist might choose to take up from the first reading the concept of the double witness—the apostolic word and the Spirit. This might be helpful in a congregation where there is considerable charismatic enthusiasm, on the one hand, or in a congregation that is spiritually quite stagnant, on the other.

The reading from Revelation suggests an interpretation of the Church's liturgy as a reflection of the eternal worship of heaven. Here the homilist can draw out the familiar words of the Eucharistic preface.

The gospel reading provides the homilist with an opportunity to speak about the universal mission of the Church, suggested by the number 153—fish of all different sorts. Do we draw a line at welcoming people into the fellowship of the Church by thinking that they are not "our kind of people"?

FOURTH SUNDAY OF EASTER

Reading I: Acts 13:14, 43-52

The first reading continues to be taken from Acts instead of from the Old Testament. Acts shows us the Christian community in the first years after the Easter events, and thus mirrors the impact of the resurrection experiences on the apostolic Church.

Today's reading tells of the preaching of Paul and Barnabas at Pisidian Antioch during the so-called first missionary journey. The pattern of events is typical and is repeated in many cities during the missionary journeys: the apostles preach in the synagogue; a certain number of Jews and Gentile converts to Judaism believe, while others reject the message and stir up opposition against the apostles, who then declare their intention of turning to the Gentiles. The proclamation of the word of God has no promise of success, but the word must be proclaimed whether people hear or refuse to hear (Ezek 3:5). What matters is that the word is proclaimed faithfully. This matters even more than that it should be made to seem relevant by artificial stunts and gimmicks.

Responsorial Psalm: 100:1-3, 5

This Sunday, formerly called the third Sunday after Easter, was traditionally known as *Jubilate* Sunday, especially among the German Lutherans, because of the old Introit from Psalm 66. Now, in series C, we use another *Jubilate* psalm, Psalm 100. Easter is preeminently the season of joy. (Note also the last sentence of the first reading and the joyful tone of the hymn in the second reading.) Easter joy (*Jubilate*) is not the joy of anticipation, like that of Advent (*Gaudete*), nor the brief moment of relief like the joy of mid-Lent (*Laetare*), but the exuberance of sorrow that has been turned into joy (John 16:20-22, from the old gospel of this day).

Reading II: Revelation 7:9, 14b-17

We normally associate this passage with All Saints Day, but it is just as appropriate for Easter. The joy of the martyrs is also the sorrow that has been turned into joy. The martyrs have come out of "the great tribulation" (not merely tribulation, but *the* tribulation; the Seer regards their martyrdom as part of the messianic woes, a sharing of the cross of Christ). Paschal imagery is picked up in the phrase "the blood of the Lamb" (see last Sunday's second reading, with its reference to "the Lamb who was slain"), as also the image of the shepherd who will guide the martyrs to springs of living water, an image that will recur in the gospel.

Gospel: John 10:27-30

This gospel is not from the shepherd discourse proper, which comes earlier in John 10, but is an echo of it in the next section, Jesus' discourse at the feast of the Dedication. It is tempting, as some commentators have done, to rearrange the text and to put these verses back in the good shepherd discourse. But it is characteristic of John to return to an earlier theme and develop it further. The earlier explanations of the good shepherd parable dealt with the gate and the shepherd, while this one deals with the sheep, their relation to the shepherd, their enjoyment of eternal life already in the life of discipleship (following), and the thrice-repeated assurance that they shall not perish nor be snatched out of the shepherd's hand (at the final judgment).

While all this is stated in typically Johannine language, its substance correctly reproduces the teaching of the earthly Jesus as recorded in the Synoptists. To hear and to respond to Jesus' word on earth is the decisive factor that will determine acceptance by God at the last judgment (see Luke 12:8-9).

The concluding sentence about the unity of the Father and the Son gives the basis for the Nicene faith, but it was meant by the evangelist, not in an ontological or metaphysical sense, as in the later dogmatic formulas, but in the dynamic-historical sense of Hebraic thought. The Father and the Son are one because of the Father's call of the Son and his response in history, resulting in a complete alignment of the words and acts of the Father and the Son. The history, of course, has an external background in the relation of the Father and the Son, as the prologue makes clear (John 1:1-14).

The Homily

Again, it is difficult to connect the readings together by any common theme. The reading from Acts raises again the question of the Church's mission. When the Christian message is rejected in one place, it is carried to others. We see this happening today: while the Western world (Europe and America) is largely rejecting the gospel message, it is gaining a miraculous hearing in Africa. Where should we put our resources for mission?

The second reading invites us to paint a picture of the joy of the martyrs, a joy that is anticipated in the Easter liturgy.

The gospel reading presents us with an echo of the theme of the Good Shepherd. It is worth making the point that the risen Christ *is* our Good Shepherd. We do not believe that he merely *was* the Good Shepherd when he was on earth. He *gives* (note the present tense in verse 28) life to his sheep, and he does this as the risen Lord in his word and sacraments. This answers the question, How can we come to Easter faith now, when we can no longer see the risen Lord as the apostles saw him at the first Easter?

FIFTH SUNDAY OF EASTER

Reading I: Acts 14:21-27

On the homeward leg of the first missionary journey, Paul and Barnabas revisit the communities they had established on their outward trip. Current scholarship tends to regard the ordination of elders (presbyters) in Acts 14:23 as a Lucan anachronism. In Paul's churches, if 1 Corinthians is typical, the ministry was charismatic (1 Cor 12:4-11, 27-30). Here Luke describes an ordination service as he knew it in the Church of his day. But whether it is the charismatics of the Pauline age, the elders of Luke's time, or the threefold ministry of the second century and after, the function of all these ministries is to keep the Church on the foundation laid by the original apostles.

When the apostles return to the church in Syrian Antioch, they report, not what *they* had done, but what "God had done with them." It was he, not their own missionary strategy, that had opened a door of faith to the Gentiles.

Responsorial Psalm: 145:8-13b

This is another psalm of exuberant joy. The psalmist exults in God's mighty acts in creation and in salvation history. In the earlier part of the Old Testament, the kingdom of God is a timeless truth. Later it seemed that God's kingship was denied by the disasters that had befallen his people, and, as a result, the hope arose that God would eventually reestablish it. He was always king *de jure*, but at the end he would become king *de facto*. The New Testament message is that this has now happened—by the resurrection of Jesus Christ from the dead. So the deeds and works that the Church celebrates are comprised in the salvation history of Christ's death and resurrection. God's kingdom is now inaugurated *de facto* through the Easter events.

Reading II: Revelation 21:1-5a

This is John the Seer's vision of the new heaven, the new earth, and the new Jerusalem. These "new things" have been established in principle through the resurrection, and they are anticipated in the life of the Church. Now God does indeed dwell with his people, though only in the veiled form of the word and the sacraments. Here there is a foretaste of that joy. But not until the end will all tears be wiped away from the eyes of his people. Mourning and crying and pain are certainly not unknown in the Church, but faith knows that even now all things are being made new.

Gospel: John 13:31-33a, 34-35

It helps make sense of the opening passage, with its five bewildering references to the glorification of God and the Son of man, if we regard it, with some recent commentators, as an early Christian hymn. It celebrated the enthronement of Christ as Son of man at his exaltation and looked forward to his coming in glory. This explains the shift from the past tense to the future:

> Now is the Son of man glorified,
> and in him God is glorified [*at Christ's exaltation*];
> if [*since*] God has been glorified in him
> [*at the exaltation*],
> God will also glorify him in himself
> and glorify him at once [*at the parousia, expected shortly*].

In taking up this hymn, John has shifted the tenses backwards. The past tenses now refer to the glorifying that has taken place through the Son's revelation of the Father during his incarnate life, while the future tenses now refer to the glorification that will take place at once in the passion, death, resurrection, and ascension of the Son. Thus, the hymn becomes an expression of the basic themes of the Johannine theology of glory.

At his departure Jesus leaves his disciples a new "commandment" (see the covenant that Jesus bequeaths in Luke 22:29 and the institution of the Last Supper in the Synoptists). Some have criticized John's concept of love for being more restricted and introverted than that of the Sermon on the Mount. The Johannine Christ speaks of the mutual love of the Christian community, not of the love even of one's enemy. Could it be, though, that the command of love, which, as we have suggested, parallels the institution of the Last Supper in the Synoptists, is speaking explicitly to the agape meal of the early community? For the agape meal was the focal expression of love within the community.

The Homily

The reading from Acts suggests the theme of ordination. It is the risen Christ who makes new ministers in his Church, acting sacramentally through the bishops, the successors of the apostles.

The Seer's vision of the new Jerusalem could be the basis for a homily on the theme of urban renewal. It is the task of Christians to cooperate with one another and with secular people of good will in setting up advance signs of the new Jerusalem on this earth.

The gospel reading provides an opportunity to speak on the "new commandment" of love within the Christian community, not only as an external commandment but as a gift of the risen and glorified Christ to his Church.

SIXTH SUNDAY OF EASTER

Reading I: Acts 15:1-2, 22-29

This is Acts' version of the apostolic conference at Jerusalem. Paul's account of it in Gal 2:1-12 agrees to some extent. The *dramatis personae* (Paul, Barnabas, Peter, James) and the point at issue, namely, the circumcision of Gentile converts to Christianity, are the same. But the outcome is different. In Paul, the conference results in a "gentlemen's agreement": Peter will head up the mission to the Jews, Paul the mission to the Gentiles, and the law will not be imposed on the Gentile churches. In Acts, the conference concludes with the adoption of a compromise solution (the apostolic decrees): the Gentiles are spared the burden of circumcision but must observe a certain minimum of legal requirements. Acts has probably combined the results of two separate conferences. The first conference concluded as Paul said, but it left unclear what was to happen when Jews and Gentiles in mixed communities ate the Eucharistic meal together. Hence the subsequent fracas in Antioch described by Paul in Gal 2:11-14. It was to deal with this later problem that a second conference was apparently held, the results of which were communicated to Paul on his last visit to Jerusalem (Acts 21:25. If Paul was present when the decrees were promulgated, as Acts 15 alleges, why would James have to inform Paul of them in Acts 21?).

Responsorial Psalm: 67:1-2, 4-5, 7

Psalm 67 combines thanksgiving for harvest with prayer for continued blessings. It serves as an appropriate thanksgiving for the resurrection and for the continuation of the enjoyment of its benefits in the Church and the spread of its benefits to all nations.

Reading II: Revelation 21:10-14, 22-23

This is a continuation (in part a repetition and in part a further development) of the picture of the descent of the new Jerusalem. The descent is repeated, but a further description of the city is given—its radiance, its walls and gates, its foundations, its need of neither temple nor sun.

There is a partial correspondence between the holy city and the Church on earth. The Church, too, has a radiance—not the splendor of a worldly power (though it has often masqueraded as such since the time of Constantine), but the radiance of the word and the sacraments and the presence of the Spirit. The Church, too, has continuity with the old Israel, suggested by the symbolism of the twelve gates, angels, and tribes. Its foundation is the twelve apostles—their witness to Jesus Christ and his resurrection, perpetuated in the Church's Scriptures and expounded in its doctrine by the successors of the apostles.

But there *is* a temple in the Church, a visible place where God's presence is made known in word and sacrament. This is not because he is not everywhere, but because in this age and on this earth he wills to be manifested in a particular place, at a particular time, in a particular rite and a particular sacrament, this bread and this wine. Here is the scandal of the Church's particularity. To seek to abolish the temple in this age on this earth, as some kinds of secular interpretations of the gospel would like to do, is to ignore the "not yet" and to suppose that we are already in heaven. That is *Schwärmerei*, fanaticism.

Gospel: John 14:23-29

In the Easter season we tend to read the farewell discourses, with their promise of the coming of the Paraclete (rsv: "Counselor"), as discourses given by the risen and not yet ascended Lord during the forty days in preparation for the coming of the Spirit at Pentecost. For the evangelist, they are discourses of the earthly Jesus, placed in the context of the Last Supper. They look through and beyond the death of Jesus to his glorification, which releases the gift of the Spirit. Thus, in the early Church the whole of the fifty days included the celebration of the gift of the Spirit, not just the day of Pentecost.

We are here listening to a promise fulfilled at Easter. In the Fourth Gospel the risen Christ conveys the gift of the Spirit to his disciples on Easter Sunday evening (see the gospel of Pentecost Sunday). The Spirit is, as in Paul's letters, the gift of the risen Christ. In the gift of the Spirit, the risen Christ and the Father come and make their home with the disciples. The function of the Spirit is to "teach you all things, and bring to your remembrance all that I have said to you." It is not the work of the Spirit to convey ever new revelations, but to unfold in ever new understanding, interpretation, and application the once-for-all revelation of Jesus Christ ("all that I have said to you"). "His work is more than a reminiscence of the *ipsissima verba* of the Son of God; it is a living representation of all that he had spoken to his disciples, a creative exploitation of the gospel" (E. C. Hoskyns). This ongoing work of the Spirit gives the disciples peace and takes away their fear, because the Spirit is always there as their helper who stands by them in persecution and martyrdom.

The Homily

The story of the Council of Jerusalem in the first reading reminds us that in order to preserve the unity of the Church, and in order to keep within its fellowship people of diverse backgrounds and different understandings of the faith, it is often necessary to adopt compromise solutions. Such solutions are possible when the issue at stake can be relegated to the category of *adiaphora,* that is, things indifferent. There have been periods in the Church's history when unity has been confused with uniformity, and when such uniformity has been imposed upon believers at the cost of legitimate pluralism.

The second reading, as we noted, provides us with a continuation of the description of the heavenly Jerusalem. If the homilist related it to urban renewal last Sunday, today it might be related to the Church. In our earthly Jerusalems there is a need for a visible place where the presence of God is made known. There must be a Christian presence in the secular city.

Like so many of the Johannine discourses, the excerpt from the farewell discourses chosen for today's gospel offers a number of different themes. They include: the work of the Spirit as the Teacher who brings to our minds the teachings of Jesus and makes them relevant for the situation of the Church today; the peace of Christ compared with the peace of the world. The homilist should have no difficulty in selecting material from the gospel that will speak to the congregation today.

ASCENSION

Except for the gospel, the readings on Ascension Day are the same every year. Here we will give some comments on the gospel, and suggestions for a homily based on the gospel. For commentary on the other two readings and the psalm, the reader is referred to series A.

88

Gospel: Luke 24:46-53

This reading consists of two halves. The first half is Luke's version of the appearance to the apostles, which, like the story of the ascension in Acts, looks forward to the mission of the Church, and to the empowering of the Church with the Spirit for that mission. In the second half, the ascension is narrated as in Acts 2. In the Gospel the ascension narrative looks backward rather than forward. The ascension is here presented, not as the inauguration of the period of the Church—which it also is—but as the conclusion of the earthly ministry of Jesus. It is a farewell scene, as is indicated by the blessing. Henceforth Christ will be with his followers in a new way. "Jesus is not seen at all times by the believers in this position: even for the disciples it came to an end" (Schlatter). But unlike most partings, it leaves the disciples rejoicing—precisely because Jesus leaves them with his blessing. Such is the outcome and conclusion of his earthly ministry.

The Homily

This year the homilist might like to exploit the fact that in the first reading and the gospel we read two Lucan accounts of the ascension—the one from Acts taking place on the fortieth day after Easter, and the other taking place on Easter Day itself. This reminds us forcefully that on Ascension Day we are not commemorating a datable historical event; rather, we are dealing with an aspect of the total Easter mystery that Luke has chosen to verbalize in two different ways. The story in the gospel looks back to the earthly life of Jesus and reminds us that that life, including the post-Easter revelations of Jesus as alive after his passion, came to a definitive end. We can no longer know Christ as he was on earth. The story in Acts looks rather to the future, to the gift of the Spirit, and to the worldwide mission of the Church. The homilist could bring out these two aspects of the ascension and relate them to the concerns of the Christian community today.

OPTIONAL READING

Reading II: Hebrews 9:24-28; 10:19-23

The reader will find comment on Heb 9:24-28 given on the thirty-second Sunday of the year in series B. Our comments here will be confined to the second part of the reading.

366

Hebrews 10:19-23 stands at the beginning of the last major section of the work. In it the author applies the theological argument of the previous section (7:1-10, 18) to Christian life. Note the *oun* ("therefore," as in Rom 12:1 and Eph 4:1). The first part of today's reading can be regarded as a summary of the previous theological argument and as the basis for the ensuing parenesis.

The Christian life has its focus in the liturgy, in which we "draw near" to the presence of God by traversing the way that the ascending Christ has opened up through his sacrificial death ("through his blood"). We must enter that presence with confidence (because Christ has pioneered the way and also because of our baptism, v. 22b).

When the author speaks of Christ entering through the veil ("Thou within the veil hast entered / Robed in flesh our great High Priest"—the words of this well-known hymn are based on verses 20-21), he is drawing his imagery from the Levitical rite of the Day of Atonement, in which the high priest passed through the veil of the temple into the Holy of Holies. Perhaps the author had in mind the passion narrative of the Gospels, which elsewhere he shows signs of knowing (for example, in 5:7, with its echoes of the Gethsemane story).

The veil symbolizes the barrier between God and sinful humanity. But then the author curiously muddles the imagery by identifying the veil with the "flesh" of Jesus. Is the author treating the "flesh" as "the appointed means of approach" or as "the obstacle which hindered access" (Westcott)? The former interpretation would involve taking "flesh" with "way"; the latter, taking "flesh" with "veil." Both interpretations have patristic support, and modern commentators are divided. Whom should we follow? On the one hand, the flesh of Jesus is always spoken of positively in Hebrews. He took our flesh in order to identify completely with us and to be qualified as our great high priest, and he took that flesh with him, now glorified, as he ascended into heaven. On the other hand, the veil is something negative, the barrier between humanity and God. Accordingly, against many commentators, we would favor taking "flesh" with "way." Our access to God is through the glorified humanity of the ascended Christ.

The pattern of Christian worship set forth in this part of today's reading is succinctly expressed in the *Sursum corda* of the liturgy. As the Orthodox and Reformed traditions have in various ways reminded us, what happens in liturgy is not so much that Christ descends to earth, but that we ascend with him to heaven:

> Mighty Lord, in thine ascension
> We by faith behold our own.
>
> (Christopher Wordsworth, Hymnal 1940, no. 103)

SEVENTH SUNDAY OF EASTER

Ascension Day no longer inaugurates a new season, nor does it have an octave. The new name for this Sunday is yet another expression of what we have noted several times already, namely, that the fifty days are a continuous celebration of the Easter events, with different accentuations at different times. But this Sunday still continues the theme of Ascension Day itself: the enthronement of Christ at the right hand of the Father.

Reading I: Acts 7:55-60

At the moment of his death, Stephen is granted a vision of heaven, with the Son of man "standing at the right hand of God." There are two unusual features here: (1) the use of the title "Son of man"—the only time it is used by anyone other than the earthly Jesus himself (John 12:34 is only a partial exception, for here the Jews are merely repeating Jesus' *own* words. (2) Christ is described as standing rather than sitting at God's right hand. There is no universally accepted explanation of either of these features. Perhaps the title "Son of man" is used here because it suggests that the exalted Christ is pleading the cause of his first martyr, in anticipation of his function as Son of man at the last judgment (Luke 12:8-9; Mark 8:38), and is standing in order to welcome his martyr to heaven. In any case, Stephen's martyrdom is an appropriate gospel for this day, as it gives a vision of the ascended Lord.

Responsorial Psalm: 97:1, 2b, 6, 7c, 9

This is another of the enthronement psalms (see Ascension Day, series A). It is noteworthy that the earlier parts of the Old Testament do not deny the existence of other gods but assert that Yahweh is above them all (henotheism rather than monotheism). Similarly, in the New Testament, Christ at his ascension triumphs over the demonic forces of evil (Phil 2:10). Demythologizing the language, we might say that God in Christ is above all false absolutes that people choose for themselves.

Reading II: Revelation 22:12-14, 16-17, 20

This reading might seem more appropriate for Advent, and indeed this particular Sunday has always had about it something of an Advent character (see the old epistle, 1 Pet 4:7-11, with its exhortation to watchfulness in view of the impending end). As we noted earlier, the fifty days originally included the Advent hope—it is because Christ has been exalted that we can hope for his coming again: "What no eye has seen, nor ear heard, nor the heart of man conceived, what God has prepared for those who love him" (1 Cor 2:9).

The experience of Easter is of such a quality that believers know that there is more to come: the kingship of Christ, now inaugurated but hidden, must finally triumph universally. The final words, "Come, Lord Jesus" (*Marana tha*) are from the earliest liturgy of the Church. In the Eucharist the ascended Christ comes in anticipation of his final coming, and here he offers the thirsty the water of life without price.

Gospel: John 17:20-26

Traditionally the prayer of Jesus at the Last Supper has been called "the high priestly prayer." It represents not only what, according to the Fourth Gospel, was the substance of Jesus' prayer at the Last Supper, but also the prayer he continues to offer as the ascended high priest in heaven. It is a prayer "that all may be one." The unity for which he prays is not grounded on ecclesiastical joinery, for "it must not be supposed that the unity of the Church is to be attained by a long history of human endeavor" (E. C. Hoskyns). Rather, the unity of the Church is a unity based on the common sharing of word and sacraments, in which the act of God in Christ, the foundation of the Church's unity, is made ever present.

The first half of this Sunday's gospel concerns the life of the Church on earth. Its unity is a unity for mission, a unity whose aim is that the world may believe "that thou hast sent me." The second half of the gospel turns to the final destiny of the Church—what we traditionally call the Church Triumphant, but what John would rather call the Church Glorified. Even if Bultmann were right in assigning all the passages in John that express a future eschatology to the hand of an ecclesiastical redactor (for example, 5:28-29; 6:40), it is clear from this passage that John has not entirely eliminated the future consummation in favor of a realized eschatology. There *is* a future destiny for the Church: "That they may be with me where I am, to behold my glory." This future element chimes in perfectly with the future hope of the second reading, written, according to tradition, by the same hand as this gospel, but in any case the product of a mind from the same theological school.

The Homily

Since St. Stephen's feast comes just after Christmas, he often gets overlooked. Today's first reading provides a good opportunity to speak about the first Christian martyr. It was he who opened up the mission of the Church to the Greek-speaking world, and he reminds us that the Church can often get bogged down in its past and fail to adapt to the needs of a new age, to the "ever onward call of God to his people" (T. W. Manson).

The reading from Revelation offers the homilist an opportunity to stress the eschatological aspect of the Eucharist, linking it with the cry *Marana tha.* This is a long-neglected aspect of the Eucharist that has been given fresh emphasis in the recent revisions of the liturgy. The Eastern Orthodox have never lost this emphasis, and we can learn a great deal from them.

The first part of the high priestly prayer (today's gospel) provides another opportunity to focus on the unity of the Church. What does it mean to say that this unity rests, not upon human endeavors, but upon a sharing of word and sacraments?

PENTECOST VIGIL

The readings for the Vigil of Pentecost do not change from year to year and are commented upon in series A and B.   *95*
276

PENTECOST SUNDAY

Since the same readings are provided each year for Pentecost, the reader is referred to the homiletical suggestions given in series A and B.   *98*
279

OPTIONAL READINGS

Reading II: Romans 8:8-17

Chapter 8 forms the climax of the first, doctrinal part of Romans. In chapters 1-4 the Apostle had first prepared the way for, and then enunciated, his message of justification by grace alone through faith. Now, having dealt in chapters 5-7 with certain objections to that message, Paul is ready to move from justification to the new life in the Spirit that justification opens up for the believers.

Comment on 8:8-11 can be found on the fifth Sunday of Lent in series   *50*
A. These verses speak of the Spirit's indwelling the believers as a result of their baptism, making them participants in advance in the resurrection life and renewing their inner being daily in preparation for that resurrection life.

Verses 12-17 insist that baptism is only a beginning. Life in the Spirit is a life of freedom, but it is always a freedom struggling with constant temptation. For life in the Spirit means being under the lordship of Christ. The baptized are not under obligation to the "flesh" (our old, unredeemed nature, not some higher nature); therefore they must mortify the deeds of the body (remember, this will include pride as well as sensuality). They must be "driven" by the Spirit.

At this point notice how Paul appropriates and sanctions the language of the charismatic enthusiasts, which he had probably picked up at Corinth. But, significantly, he gives it an ethical twist. Not spiritual excitement and religious emotion but obedient Christian living is the supreme test of the Spirit's presence and activity. It is that, rather than overpowering emotion, that will entitle Christians to cry out in worship, "Abba, Father." And still that acclamation is characterized by a "not yet." Only at the final consummation will the believers really receive the "adoption" anticipated in baptism. For, as an Anglican theologian of the last generation, Oliver Chase Quick, used to teach, sacraments are both symbolic and instrumental. Baptism is symbolic of our final salvation, and it is instrumental in inaugurating the life in the Spirit that is to be consummated in that final salvation.

As we noted above, the freedom of the Spirit is a struggling freedom. This means that baptism inaugurates a life characterized by an element of suffering. Suffering is symbolized in baptism when the converts symbolically die with Christ; it is effectualized internally in mortification, and externally in persecution. Then, at the final consummation, the suffering will lead to glory, when the believers will inherit the kingdom of God with Christ (v. 17).

Gospel: John 14:15-16, 23b-26

Comment on 14:15-21 will be found on the sixth Sunday of Easter in series A, and on 14:23-29 on the sixth Sunday of Easter in series C.

87

435

[END OF THE EASTER SEASON]

Sunday after Pentecost

TRINITY SUNDAY

Reading I: Proverbs 8:22-31

The concept of the divine wisdom is mythological in origin but was taken up into the Yahwistic religion to express God's self-disclosure. This self-disclosure came to be hypostatized or personified as the divine wisdom. Wisdom means God's going forth from his "aseity" (his being-in-himself) in revelation and action.

The hymn in Prov 8 is somewhat rudimentary in its understanding of wisdom as divine activity, for, unlike later passages (Sir 24:1-24; Wis 7:22–8:1), it does not assign to wisdom an active role in creation; she is merely "around" when God creates. In its later development wisdom acquires a subjective role in human existence, becoming the organ of human religious experience. In this way "Wisdom" becomes the predecessor of both the Logos and the Holy Spirit. Thus, we may read this passage as a step on the road to the doctrine of the Trinity.

Responsorial Psalm: 8:3-8

This psalm puts into verse form the theological truth of the creation story in Gen 1. God is the creator of the whole universe, and human beings are the crown of creation, destined for glory and honor and invested with dominion over the created order. They exist in what Gen 1 calls the divine "image." God's name, whose wonder is proclaimed, is, in Christian understanding, a threefold name—a God who is in his own eternal being, who goes forth out of himself in creation and redemption and creates human beings' response to that creation and revelation. All this is latent in this psalm.

Reading II: Romans 5:1-5

This is one of those artless passages in which the Apostle exhibits the triadic structure of Christian experience. God is the source of our redemption, but it is through Jesus Christ that this redemptive act is performed, and through the Holy Spirit poured into our hearts that we come to experience that redemptive action.

Gospel: John 16:12-15

Here again the doctrine of the Trinity is implicit. The revelation that Jesus Christ brings is from the Father, and it is the function of the Spirit to make that revelation meaningful to each succeeding Christian generation. The Spirit does not convey new, independent revelation ("he will not speak on his own authority") but constantly updates our understanding of the once-for-all revelation of God in the Christ-event.

The Homily

As in other years, it will be the homilist's task today to help the congregation see that the doctrine of the Trinity is not the result of abstract speculation but interprets the very structure of Christian experience. This is true of our experience of the created order, as suggested in the first reading and the psalm. It is true of our experience of redemption, as indicated by the second reading. And, finally, it is true of our experience of revelation, as indicated by the gospel reading. In each case the God we experience is God who goes out of himself in self-communication and who creates within us a response to his self-disclosure.

Thursday after Trinity Sunday or Sunday after Trinity Sunday
CORPUS CHRISTI

Where the solemnity of Corpus Christi is not observed as a holy day,
it is assigned to the Sunday after Trinity Sunday.

As we observed in series A, it is a little difficult for an Anglican to ap-   *104*
proach this set of readings without at least some reservations. To many
of us it would seem more fitting to celebrate, with the early Church, the
event of the institution of the Eucharist, and to do this on Maundy Thursday, rather than to have a special day to commemorate a doctrine.[1] But
most churches of the Anglican communion provide a Eucharist in
"thanksgiving for the institution of holy communion," which may be used
at any suitable time. This is widely used on the Thursday after Trinity
Sunday, though it would rarely be used again on the ensuing Sunday.
But when one turns to the actual readings provided in the Lectionary, one
finds that, after all, by the very genius of Scripture, they are concerned
with saving events rather than with the later expressions of Eucharistic
doctrine.

Reading I: Genesis 14:18-20

It is striking that the letter to the Hebrews, which elaborates on
Melchizedek as a type of Christ's high priesthood, never mentions the
gifts—the bread and wine—that he presented to Abraham. This is all the
more surprising since these gifts were allegorically interpreted by Philo,
by the rabbis, and by the Church Fathers from Cyprian onwards as a type
of the Eucharist, especially in its sacrificial character.

Maybe we can remain true to the New Testament and still give the
text about Melchizedek a fitting interpretation for Corpus Christi. Westcott
suggests that Melchizedek is presented in Hebrews as a priest not in sacrific-
ing but in blessing, "that is, in communicating the fruits of an efficacious
sacrifice already made." This we can accept, as long as we also affirm
that the sacrifice made once for all becomes a present reality in the
Eucharist through the consecration and sharing of the bread and wine,
and, because of the presence of the sacrifice, communicates its fruits.

---

[1] It should be added that most contemporary Anglican theologians have little difficulty
with the doctrine of transubstantiation itself, rightly understood. We would recognize it as
a valid attempt, within the terms of a given philosophy, to express a doctrine that we too
accept, though it is not expressed in terms of a philosophy we would necessarily want to
use today.

Responsorial Psalm: 110:1-4

This is one of the royal psalms. Its date and original reference are in dispute. There is a trend to interpret it as a reference to the early kings of Judah in the Davidic line, though earlier critics regarded it as an attempt of the priestly family of the Hasmoneans to justify their claim to kingship as well as to priesthood. In either case, Melchizedek is taken as the prototype of the priest-king.

The author of Hebrews takes up this psalm because it enables him to develop his own teaching on Christ's high priesthood. In the earlier Church, the messiahship (kingship) of Jesus was firmly established. Now Hebrews develops the further Christology (implicit in the early Church's sacrificial interpretation of Jesus' death) that he is also priest. The psalm may remind us that in the Eucharist Christ is himself the true priest who presides over his Eucharistic banquet and gives himself as the sacrificial victim to the faithful. He "gives himself with his own hand" (St. Thomas Aquinas). The ministerial priest who presides at the earthly altar is the instrument by which Christ's true high priesthood is externalized.

Reading II: 1 Corinthians 11:23-26

This passage was the second reading for the Mass of the Lord's Supper on Holy Thursday (q.v.), suggesting that the feast of Corpus Christi is an extrapolation of the earlier occasion. On Holy Thursday we contemplate the institution of the Eucharist in its relation to the whole series of events of the sacred triduum. On Corpus Christi the Eucharist is isolated for contemplation as an ongoing rite in the Church.

Gospel: Luke 9:11b-17

Many motifs have shaped the narratives of the feeding of the multitude. On the historical level there can be little doubt that the meeting of Jesus and his followers in the desert marked the critical turning point in the Galilean ministry. (See John's note that Jesus' followers wanted to make him king, that is, a political Messiah, and Mark's enigmatic note that Jesus sent his disciples away while he dismissed the crowd. In the light of John's account, it is clear that Jesus did this to prevent the disciples from becoming infected with the crowd's dangerous political messianism.) There is no reason why this critical meeting should not have been accompanied by a meal, which, like all Jesus' meals with his disciples, would have eschatological associations as a foretaste of the eschatological banquet.

In earliest Christianity Jesus was interpreted as the prophet of the end-time, repeating Moses' gift of the manna (a theme that comes out most strongly in the Johannine discourse following this episode) and the miraculous multiplication of loaves by Elisha (2 Kgs 4:42-44).

Further, the language of the Eucharistic liturgy has colored the narrative: "sit down . . . taking . . . loaves . . . blessed . . . broke . . . gave . . . ate."

We generally think of the Last Supper as the institution of the Eucharist. But the New Testament sees two further bases for the rite: the meals of the earthly Jesus with his followers and the appearance meals after the resurrection. These meals emphasize an aspect that was certainly present in the Last Supper (Mark 14:25; Luke 22:16-18), namely, its eschatological character. The Eucharist is not only a feeding upon a past sacrifice made a present reality, but also a foretaste of the messianic banquet. The (optional) sequence of Corpus Christi shows that this eschatological significance of the Eucharist was not forgotten in the Middle Ages:

> Grant us with your saints, though lowest,
> Where the heav'nly feast you show
> Fellow heirs and guests to be.

The Homily

The two readings that stand out today are the Old Testament lesson about Melchizedek and the Lucan account of the feeding of the multitude.

A few years ago in Belgium I saw a triptych by an old Dutch master. The side panels portrayed four Old Testament types of the Eucharist. One of them was a portrayal of Melchizedek and Abraham (dressed as a medieval knight in black armor!). In the Middle Ages this scene was clearly regarded as a type of the Eucharist, typifying the offering of the bread and wine, first that it might become the sacramental body and blood of Christ, and secondly that the communicants might become partakers thereof. The homilist could expound this double offering and indicate what each means for our lives—the offering up of our lives in union with Christ's sacrifice and their transformation.

The Lucan reading suggests a stress on the Eucharist as the sharing of a banquet in anticipation of the eschatological banquet in the kingdom of God.

SEASON OF THE YEAR

SECOND SUNDAY OF THE YEAR

Reading I: Isaiah 62:1-5

This excerpt comes from a section of Third Isaiah that consists of songs celebrating the return from exile. The subject of the present song is the restored city of Jerusalem. God is now rejoicing over the city as a bridegroom rejoices over his bride.

While this reading comes from a section appropriate for any festival season, it is clearly intended to match the gospel (the wedding at Cana), for it uses nuptial imagery to depict the relationship between Yahweh and Israel—a familiar tradition since Hosea. The speaker in verse 1 is the prophet. His style and vocabulary suggest that he was a pupil of Second Isaiah. His master had prophesied the return from exile. That return had doubtless now taken place, but Jerusalem has not yet been rebuilt (see Haggai and Nehemiah). The prophet, however, is undaunted and is still convinced that his master's predictions will be completely fulfilled. So he refuses to keep silent or to rest (in intercession for Jerusalem) until God vindicates the city.

The writer then expresses the restoration of Jerusalem in three pictures: (1) It will be a crown and a diadem in the hand of Yahweh. It has been suggested that this image derives from the ancient Near Eastern practice of depicting the god of a city wearing a crown patterned after the city walls. (2) The city will be given a new name: "My delight is in her"=Hephziba, a girl's name in Hebrew. (3) The nuptial imagery already noted. Note the bold mixture of images: your sons will marry you (!); then Yahweh will rejoice over Jerusalem as a bride. We should not press this imagery too closely. The general idea is clear enough.

Responsorial Psalm: 96:1-3, 7-8a, 9-10ac

The first two stanzas of this psalm are used each year at the midnight Mass of Christmas, and practically the same selection of verses is used in a slightly different arrangement on the twenty-ninth Sunday of the year in series A. As well as being a psalm generally suitable for festivals, it has a strong missionary note, brought out here by the refrain: "Proclaim his marvelous deeds to all the nations."

Reading II: 1 Corinthians 12:4-11

This reading overlaps with the second reading on Pentecost Sunday. The selection for that day comprised three sections: (1) confession of Jesus as Lord; (2) the varieties of gifts [abbreviated]; (3) diversity and unity within the body. Today the first section is dropped; the second is given in full, specifying the varieties of gifts; and the third will form the beginning of next Sunday's second reading.

Note first the artless triadic structure of verses 4-6:

> charismata—the Spirit
> service [diakoniai]—the Lord [=Christ]
> workings [energemata=functions]—God

Paul's intention here is in part polemical, directed against the Corinthian Gnostics, who overemphasized the importance of some of the gifts, especially speaking in tongues. The Apostle prefers the term *charismata* to the term *pneumatika* ("spiritual things"), for it emphasizes that the gifts are gifts of grace (*charis*), not natural endowments to be proud of. The word "service" (*diakonia*) strikes a polemical note to be taken up later in the development of the image of the body. The Corinthians thought that the gifts existed for their own glory rather than for the service of the community. Since it is the same triune God who is at work in all of them, no gift can be exalted above any other.

Verse 7 then sums up verses 4-6 and serves as a heading for verses 8-10: every spiritual phenomenon is given for the common good. Verses 8-10 spell out the *charismata*, listing nine in all: (1) wisdom, (2) knowledge (*gnosis*), (3) faith, (4) healing, (5) miracle-working, (6) prophecy, (7) discernment of spirits, (8) tongues, (9) interpretation of tongues.

The gifts fall into three groups: (I) wisdom and knowledge; (II) faith, healing, and miracle-working; (III) prophecy, discernment of spirits, tongues, and interpretation of tongues.

I. Elsewhere in 1 Corinthians there is hardly any perceptible difference between wisdom and knowledge. Both refer to gifts that the Corinthian Gnostics claimed to possess, and criticized Paul for not having.

II. Faith here does not mean the faith by which all Christians respond to the gospel and so are justified, but a special gift confined to some. It is connected with miracle-working.

III. Prophecy does not require interpretation, for it is not unintelligible speech; but it requires the discerning of spirits—to see whether it is genuine or false prophecy. In verse 1 Paul has already set up the criterion: whether the prophecy confesses Jesus as Lord or says *anathēma Iēsous*.

Verse 11 rounds off the list by repeating the substance of verse 7 and prepares for the ensuing section on the churches as the body of Christ: *one* Spirit—*one* body.

Gospel: John 2:1-12

The view is gaining ground that the Fourth Gospel used a source consisting mainly of miracle stories, that is, an "aretalogy" (for the name see Sir 36:14: "wondrous deeds" in the RSV). Its purpose was to use a series of stupendous miracles to convince potential converts that Jesus was the Messiah (see John 20:30, probably the conclusion of the aretalogy). It was therefore a missionary writing. Its basic conception was that Jesus was the messianic prophet, recalling Moses, Elijah, and Elisha, as these were interpreted in later Judaism, that is, as "divine men." In short, it was designed as a missionary tract to convert Greek-speaking Jews to Christianity.

The evangelist, as distinct from the aretalogist, wrote at a later time, when Christians had been expelled from the Jewish synagogue. His purpose was not to convert but to force a decision upon Jewish Christians who were concealing their faith in order to avoid expulsion from the synagogue. So he incorporates the earlier aretalogy into his Gospel, adding glosses to the miracle stories, expanding them with dialogues and discourses, and combining the whole with a passion and resurrection narrative. In this way he sets before his readers the purpose of Christ's coming into the world—to bring about a *krisis*, a decision between light and darkness, truth and falsehood, life and death.

Unlike most of the other signs in the Fourth Gospel, the story of the wedding at Cana has no dialogue or discourse attached to it by the evangelist; rather, he has contented himself with a few extra touches. These may be identified as follows: verse 4 (especially "My hour has not yet come"); verse 6b ("for the Jewish rites of purification"); verse 11c ("and manifested his glory"). Each of these additions serves to link the Cana miracle with the passion story: the hour, for the evangelist, is the hour of the passion; the Jewish rites of purification are replaced by the messianic purification accomplished on the cross (see 1 John 1:7: "the blood of Jesus his Son cleanses us from all sin"); the cross is the supreme moment of Jesus' glorification.

In effect, what the evangelist is saying is that we are not to take the Cana miracle as a direct and complete epiphany of Christ's glory. Though the evangelist accepts the reality of the miracle, it has for him a further, symbolic significance, pointing toward what Jesus is to accomplish on the cross. There the old order will be replaced by the new. This is what the changing of the water into wine symbolizes. The real, final epiphany is the cross.

The Homily
It is usually possible to take the Old Testament reading and the gospel together. Today, however, the only possible connecting link is the nuptial theme. But this is not central to the gospel story, only its incidental setting. Hence the homilist will find it difficult to take these two readings together, and it would be better not to try.

If the homilist wishes to preach on the Old Testament reading, it would be best to take the nuptial theme from there and treat it on its own. This would provide an opportunity to interpret the Eucharist as the marriage between Christ and his Church. Here the Church knows herself to be Hephziba, the one in whom the Lord delights.

The second reading would allow the homilist to inculcate a balanced view of charismatic gifts in the community. This would be a fitting choice in places where the charismatic renewal is creating problems and tensions. It is necessary to remind ourselves that there are many gifts of the Spirit and that there is a fundamental unity between them all, for they are all equally the work of the one Spirit.

It is ironical that much homiletic exposition of the Cana wonder in the Epiphany season (it was read on Epiphany 2 in the old Roman Missal and in the Book of Common Prayer of the Church of England, and on Epiphany 3 in the American Book of Common Prayer) has been done on the level of the aretalogy. The changing of the water into wine has been taken as a direct epiphany of the glory of God in Christ. Compare Christopher Wordsworth's hymn:

> And at Cana, wedding guest,
> In thy godhead manifest.

But it is doubtful whether miracles carry the same convincing power today as they did in the ancient world or even in the eighteenth century (see Paley's *Evidences*). We are much more likely to be impressed by the symbolical significance that the evangelist has given to the story. Perhaps it would be appropriate to preach Christ today as the agent of change: as he replaced the old Jewish purificatory rites with the messianic purification wrought on the cross, so he is the agent of change in the renewal of the Church and in the world today. Yet, Christians are often so frightened of change and opposed to it.

THIRD SUNDAY OF THE YEAR

Reading I: Nehemiah 8:1-4a, 5-6, 8-10

The reason for the choice of this passage today is not clear. Probably a parallel is intended between Ezra's reading of the law and Jesus' reading of the prophecy of Isa 61 in the synagogue (see the gospel).

There is no reason to dispute the historicity of this narrative, but there has been much discussion among scholars about the identity of the book of the law. Wellhausen propounded the attractive theory that it was the completed Pentateuch brought back from Babylon. Internal evidence, however, indicates that the prescriptions for the celebration of the feast of Tabernacles follow D, not P.

This passage offers a model of synagogue worship: the reading of the Torah, with the people standing, and the "giving of the sense" of it (that is, its exposition) so that the people will understand clearly; and finally the response of worship. A similar liturgical order may be glimpsed in the synagogue at Nazareth and survives today in the Christian liturgy of the word, including the standing at the reading of the gospel, as the Jews stood for the reading of the Torah.

Responsorial Psalm: 19:7-9, 14

The first three stanzas of the responsorial psalm praise God for the perfection (first stanza), truth (second stanza), and purity (third stanza) of the Torah, while the fourth stanza contains the fine prayer that God's law may be the subject of our constant meditation, so that both our thoughts and our words may be acceptable in his sight.

It should be remembered that "law" (Torah) had a wider meaning than commandments, precepts, and ordinances, though of course it included these. This wider meaning embraced the whole range of God's revelation. For the Christian, the word or law of God is even more extensive. It embraces the revelation of the Word-made-flesh. Note that the refrain from John 6:63b refers to the teachings of Jesus, specifically to his discourse on the bread of life. Hence the psalm is not only a response to God's self-revelation in the law as proclaimed by Ezra, but also a response to Jesus' sermon in the synagogue at Nazareth, which will be read in the gospel.

Reading II: 1 Corinthians 12:12-30 (long form); 12:12-14, 27 (short form)

There has been much discussion among exegetes and biblical theologians over the sense of the Pauline image for the Church, the "body of Christ." Is it a metaphor, a simile, or an ontological reality? In this passage— briefly in the short form, at length in the long form—the term clearly stands for simile and for ontological reality. Paul starts with the simile: *"Just* as the body . . . *so* . . . ." But then one would expect him to say, "so it is with the Christian community." No wonder Calvin was surprised at this apparent equation of Christ and the Church. But Paul is probably expressing himself a bit loosely. What he really means by it is: As is the case with the human body, so it is with the body of Christ. This clearly shows that for Paul the body of Christ, though a simile, is more than that. It is an ontological reality. The point is clinched in verse 27, after the exposition of the simile: "you *are* the body of Christ," not "you as a community are like a body."

So Paul uses "body" in an ecclesial context both as an ontological reality and as a simile. Why does he do this? The answer lies in the probability that Paul did not himself coin the term "body of Christ," nor did he receive it from pre-Pauline tradition (in the New Testament it occurs only in the Pauline literature). Where, then, did he get it? Probably from the Corinthian Gnostics, who used it to express the solidarity between Christ and the baptized, as pre-Christian gnosis may have used the concept to express the solidarity between the Gnostic revealer-redeemer and the redeemed. For the Corinthians, "body of Christ" expressed a substantial identity between Christ and the believers. They shared a common *pneuma-*substance.

Paul accepts the truth behind this insight but tones it down. To affirm the ontological identity between Christ and the believers without qualification is to overlook the Christological distinction between Christ and the believers. He is risen but the believers are not yet risen. Therefore, their salvation is not an assured possession. They have to work at it through obedience to the *Kyrios.* Paul's corrected use of "body of Christ" means just this. To be the body of Christ means to be dependent upon Christ and subject to his lordship. Hence Paul picks up the Stoic comparison of human communities to a body, in which each member has its function to fulfill and in which each function is indispensable (vv. 14-26). Paul thus emphasizes the ethical implications of the term "body."

We may say, then, that for Paul, as for the Corinthian Gnostics, the term "body of Christ" was an ontological reality. But whereas for the Corinthians this ontological reality was a substantial one (of identity of substance, a *pneuma*-reality), for Paul it was a reality denoting Christological dependence: the lives of the believers shared a common determination by the saving act of God in Christ and were under the lordship of Christ. Consequently, they had to exhibit what they were in ethical obedience. It is significant that when Paul was not in dialogue with the Corinthians, and therefore not restricted to use their term, he substitutes the more satisfactory expression "one body in Christ" (Rom 12:5), which plays down the aspect of identity and conveys a stronger suggestion of sharing a common dependence on the Christ-event.

The long form of this reading goes on to elaborate the simile of the body. Like a human body, the Church has members, each with its special function:

1. apostles
2. prophets
3. teachers

---

miracles
· healings
helps
administrations
tongues

We confine ourselves to three observations about this list. First, it is the clearest evidence we have about the shape of ministry in Corinth and probably in the other Pauline communities, too. It was charismatic, not institutional. Second, in this setup apostles, prophets, and teachers were preeminent. They alone are enumerated (first, second, third). They are designated by personal titles, whereas the others are designated impersonally as gifts, a fact obscured in the rsv translation. Third, this ministerial setup is not prescriptive for all time. Later the free charismatic ministries developed into ordained institutionalized ministries. But one element remained permanent—the element of apostolic control. Paul exercised this control in the very act of writing 1 Corinthians, and with the canon of the New Testament a similar control was exercised by the episcopate in the second century.

Gospel: Luke 1:1-4; 4:14-21

Luke 1:1-4 is the preface to the two-volume work of Luke-Acts. It is curious to place this preface immediately before the sermon in the synagogue at Nazareth. Only here in the synoptic Gospels does an evangelist address the reader in his own name. The preface discloses a number of significant things about Luke's work as an evangelist. He is not the first in the field; "many" have written before him. This probably should not be pressed too much—all Luke is saying is that he has predecessors. We know that Mark, the author of the Q material, and the author or authors of the special Lucan material preceded him. Luke understands his work as a "narrative" rather than a gospel (contrast Mark 1:1), that is, it is intended as a historical work, a description of the beginnings of Christianity.

It is commonplace nowadays to say that the Gospels are not biographies. But this is only partly true of Luke, for his Gospel aims at being a *vita Jesu* rather than a proclamation of the Christ-event, as Mark's is. "The things which have been accomplished among us" (Luke 1:1) will include not only the life of Jesus but also the history of the early Church, which is covered in the Acts of the Apostles. "Us" means the Christian community from its inception. The Jesus tradition and the traditions about the early history of the Church have been handed down from eyewitnesses and ministers of the word, that is, the apostles and evangelists. Luke does not include himself among the eyewitnesses; he is a member of the second or perhaps even the third generation, dependent upon secondhand or thirdhand traditions for both the life of Jesus and the history of the early Church.

Luke's work rests upon his researches, not upon immediate inspiration: "having followed all things closely for some time past." His account is intended to be orderly ("to write an orderly account"), a criticism perhaps of the work of some of his predecessors. As we see from his actual work, however, his idea of being orderly is to follow one source at a time. His work is addressed to an individual, Theophilus, and is not designed, like the other synoptic Gospels, for liturgical use in a community. Its purpose is the instruction of catechumens.

The second paragraph of our reading (Luke 4:14-15) is an editorial link with the temptation story (note the phrase in brackets inserted in the Lectionary: "After forty days in the wilderness). The wording is based on Mark 1:14-15, but with two significant alterations. Luke emphasizes that Jesus' ongoing ministry was performed "in the power of the Spirit"—an idea taken up by the citation of Isa 61 in the sermon at Nazareth. Luke wants us to bear in mind that the whole of Jesus' ministry was inspired by the Spirit. Second, Luke suppresses Mark's summary of Jesus' eschatological preaching (Mark 1:15) and substitutes the statement that Jesus *taught* in the synagogues. This prepares for the next scene, too.

Luke has shifted the sermon in the synagogue from its later position in Mark (Mark 6:1-6) to the beginning of the ministry. He has done so for programmatic reasons. In the synagogue of his hometown, Jesus lays his cards on the table and interprets his role as that of the Isaianic servant. The servant's work will consist of preaching, the deliverance of the oppressed, and the performance of healings. All this has an eschatological significance: it is the fulfillment of Scripture. It is not certain whether Luke himself composed this material, which is absent from Mark, or whether it came from his special source. Probably the latter.

The Homily

Some will doubtless be tempted to apply Ezra's sermon in the square before the Water Gate to the political scandal of that name in recent U.S. history. If so, they should avoid treating Ezra's account as a direct prophecy, as the sects treat the Book of Revelation. Instead, they should concentrate on the call to the nation to hearken to the word of God and to obey his laws. For the Watergate crisis was the symbol of a moral rot in the nation as a whole, the consequence of its increasing secularization.

The second reading provides the homilist with an opportunity to talk about the Church as the body of Christ. That means the local community as well as the universal Church, for the local meaning was what Paul had primarily in mind. Particular stress should be laid on the obligations of each member to the others, for that is Paul's major concern in consenting to use the image at all.

The sermon in the synagogue is coming to be regarded as a Magna Charta of liberation theology. The homilist could prepare to preach on this by reading one or more of the works of that theology, but should not be uncritical of it and should ask how far it really squares with the text.

FOURTH SUNDAY OF THE YEAR

Reading I: Jeremiah 1:4-5, 17-19

Today's Old Testament reading consists of the first and last portions of the account of Jeremiah's call to be a prophet. The call, properly speaking, covers verses 4-10, 17-19, and it would have been more consistent with the structure of the text to divide the material thus, omitting only the two visions that interrupt the narrative of the call (vv. 11-16).

The call is related in the form of a dialogue between Yahweh and the prophet. Jeremiah was predestined from the womb to be a prophet—a characteristically biblical emphasis on the initiative of Yahweh in Israel's salvation history. "Consecrated" refers to the separation of the prophet for a distinctive role in that history. Jeremiah's call played an important role in Paul's understanding of his apostolic call (Gal 1:15). The liturgical selection today, however, treats Jeremiah's call as a type of Jesus' messianic call, for this passage was chosen to match the second half of the sermon in the synagogue at Nazareth.

Jeremiah's mission is not merely to Israel but to "the nations." Since the time of Amos, the prophets had a strong sense of God as the sovereign

Lord of all history, not just that of his people. This lordship was expressed more in his judgments than in his acts of mercy. The caption, "I have appointed you as prophet to the nations," calls special attention to this universality of Jeremiah's mission because of the Epiphany season and also because of the gospel reading, which invokes the stories of Elijah and Elisha as types of Christ's universal ministry. In these two types, however, the emphasis is on the salvation of Yahweh reaching out beyond Israel rather than on his judgment.

In the second paragraph of our reading, Jeremiah is warned of the opposition he will incur in Israel, which again links this reading with Jesus' rejection at Nazareth. There is a consistency both in God's dealings with his people and in his people's reaction to his word, a consistency that runs through both the Old Testament and the New.

Responsorial Psalm: 71:1-4a, 5-6b, 15ab, 17

This psalm is an individual lament, sung by an aged person in a time of sickness (third stanza). The afflicted one flees to God and prays for deliverance (first and second stanzas), and concludes with a vow to praise God henceforth (presumably in thanksgiving for delivery from sickness).

This hymn would be suitable for Christian devotion at any time, for the Christian's fundamental sickness is sin, and the delivery is forgiveness through the atoning work of Christ. However, the reason for its choice today seems to be that Jeremiah frequently fled to God for refuge in face of the hostility of the kings, princes, priests, and people of Judah (first reading).

Reading II: 1 Corinthians 12:31–13:13 (long form); 13:4-13 (short form)

Paul's hymn to charity falls into four parts: (1) verses 1-3; (2) verses 4-7; (3) verses 8-12; (4) verse 13: conclusion. The shorter reading consists of the second and third parts plus the conclusion. The longer reading reproduces the whole hymn plus 12:31, which indicates its context in the letter, namely, Paul's discussion of the *charismata*. The first and third parts refer to the *charismata;* the second part is more abstract and general in its characterization of *agapē*. The hymn's place in the letter is problematical. Verse 14:1 would follow directly upon 12:31a. Whereas 12:31b in the RSV [= 13:1 in the NAB] promises one "more excellent way," the hymn gives us the three virtues of faith, hope, and love, although love is acknowledged to be the greatest. These problems have led some to suppose that the hymn is a post-Pauline interpolation, but the first and third parts are too specifically related to the context, the discussion of the *charismata*, for that.

Striking, too, is the lack of any specific Christological reference in the hymn. But the triad of faith, hope, and love belongs to Christian tradition and occurs elsewhere in the Pauline letters, especially in the opening thanksgivings. Otherwise the hymn is akin in style to hymns in praise of wisdom and other virtues found in Hellenistic Jewish wisdom literature. It might be suggested that the second part of the hymn was preformed in Hellenistic Jewish Christianity or even in Hellenistic Judaism, and that Paul himself has adapted it to the context by adding the first and third parts. Note the difference of style: the first and third parts are written in an "I" style. This is not Paul's own ego speaking but refers to anyone or everyone. This use of the "I" style is characteristic of Hellenistic rhetoric (cf. Rom 7:7-25).

If the central paragraph originally stood on its own, before Paul used it here, and was modeled on Hellenistic Jewish material, we can see why *agapē* is treated simply as a human virtue without any reference to Christology, and why there is no clarification about its object—whether it is God's love for human beings or their love for God or for others. It is simply the description of an abstract virtue, like the praise of wisdom in the wisdom literature.

Gospel: Luke 4:21-30

As we have already noted, this is the second part of the sermon in the synagogue at Nazareth. The first part, read last Sunday, consisted of the text of the sermon (Isa 61) and the brief declaration in verse 21, with which today's reading also opens.

The synagogue congregation expresses its astonishment at Jesus' teaching and is perplexed because it knows his human origins. This material is similar to Mark 6, though the reference to Jesus' family is different, recalling John 7:41-42 and therefore suggesting a second source. Then comes the proverb "Physician, heal thyself" (not found elsewhere in the Synoptics) and the awkward reference to works already done in Capernaum—awkward because in Luke's Gospel Jesus has not yet worked there. This would suit the Marcan context better, but the reference to Capernaum is absent from Mark. Therefore the proverb and the reference to Capernaum must be a fragment of a non-Marcan version of the rejection that Luke has inserted here. Then comes the saying from Mark about the prophet's not being honored in his own country.

After this we have more material peculiar to Luke, namely, the references to the miracles performed for Gentiles by Elijah and Elisha. The style and vocabulary of this section are definitely Lucan, as A. R. C. Leaney notes in his commentary on Luke. The interest in turning to the

Gentiles after the rejection by Israel is also a characteristic Lucan theme. It is impossible to say for certain whether the whole of this section of the sermon is Lucan composition (Leaney leaves the question open). There is, of course, the possibility that the examples of Elijah and Elisha had already been used in Christian preaching before Luke, and that he has worked these traditional features into his composition, just as he formed the kerygmatic speeches in Acts out of earlier Christological formulas and Old Testament *testimonia.*

The story closes with a hostile attempt on Jesus' life. At first sight this looks like a Lucan expansion of Mark's statement (6:3) that the people of Nazareth were offended at Jesus because of his teaching. But the miraculous escape from a hostile crowd is paralleled in John 10:39, so it is hardly likely to be a Lucan creation. It seems, therefore, that Luke has a special source containing a version of the Nazareth episode differing from Mark's. This alternative tradition will include: (1) the citation of Isa 61; (2) the proverb about the physician and the reference to earlier works in Capernaum; (3) the attempt to stone Jesus. Luke will then have combined this narrative with Mark's, expanding it by his own composition and embodying the references to Elijah and Elisha. The effect of this Lucan redaction is to make the story programmatic to his two-volume work. Luke will repeatedly stress the fact that because of Israel's rejection of the Messiah, the gospel goes forth to the Gentile world.

The Homily

The more obvious choice for the homilist today would be to start from Luke's redaction of his two sources (Mark and special Luke) in the Nazareth episode. The homilist should follow Luke's understanding of salvation history. Those originally called reject the gospel, so it goes to others. Care must be taken, however, not to introduce an anti-Semitic note into a contemporary application. The more obvious application today is that while the Church is losing ground in America and Western Europe, it is making spectacular gains in some other parts of the world.

An alternative possibility for the homilist would be to speak of Paul's hymn to *agapē.* If the longer form of the second reading is used, this would suggest relating it quite concretely to the situation in Corinth (an excessive attachment to the *charismata*). There may be a parallel situation in the homilist's own congregation. If the shorter reading is used, it might be best to concentrate on part 2 of the hymn (the first paragraph of the shorter reading) and give a general meditation on the virtue of Christian charity.

FIFTH SUNDAY OF THE YEAR

Reading I: Isaiah 6:1-2a, 3-8

The vision and call of Isaiah form one of the most familiar parts of the Old Testament. Isaiah describes his vision of Yahweh in heaven with imagery derived from the earthly temple at Jerusalem, in which his experience takes place—the underlying conviction is that the Jerusalem temple is an external expression of the heavenly temple. One is led to suppose that the *Sanctus* was likewise part of the liturgy of the earthly temple, just as it in turn passed into the Christian liturgy.

The primary emphasis today, however, is not on the vision but on the call, which parallels the call of Peter in today's gospel. The vision of God's holiness, the *mysterium tremendum*, leads Isaiah to confess his sense of utter unworthiness. His call thus comes to him as a sheer miracle of grace. The prophet first receives forgiveness for his sin, is then called to "go for us," and responds by accepting the call. Note the contrast between his initial diffidence in reaction to the vision and the confidence with which he finally accepts the call.

Responsorial Psalm: 138:1-5, 7d-8

This is a psalm of praise and thanksgiving, following appropriately upon Isaiah's vision. It should be noted that whereas the combination of the Old Testament reading and the gospel highlights the call, the psalm highlights Isaiah's vision, as indicated by the refrain and the third line of the first stanza.

Reading II: 1 Corinthians 15:1-11 (long form); 15:3-8, 11 (short form)

This is one of the most important passages in the New Testament. Paul has to deal with the Corinthians' uncertainty and doubt about the resurrection of the dead. The older view was that the Corinthians held the Greek belief in the immortality of the soul as opposed to the Jewish-Christian belief in the resurrection of the body. More recently it has been supposed that as gnosticizers they believed that through the sacraments they were already raised and therefore did not require a further resurrection of the body.

In order to correct the Corinthians, Paul recalls the gospel that he had preached to them (about A.D. 50; 1 Corinthians was written a few years later). This gospel was encapsulated in a traditional formula, or more likely a series of formulas, which, Paul claims, he had received from those who were Christians before him. Since he mentions Cephas (Peter) and James (the brother of the Lord) by name, and since he met these two men at

Jerusalem on his first post-conversion visit there about the year 35, a substantial part of these formulas must be very ancient, taking us back to within five years or so of the events alluded to. The formulas embrace: (1) the death of Christ as a saving event; (2) his burial; (3) his resurrection as a saving event; (4) a list of appearances, including the appearance to Paul himself, in which he received his apostolic call (which, following Acts, we usually refer to as his conversion). The longer reading emphasizes the grace-character of Paul's apostolic call. The shorter reading follows the summary of the traditions with Paul's claim that his own kerygma and that of his predecessors were identical.

Gospel: Luke 5:1-11

The history of the tradition here is very similar to that of the gospel readings of the previous two Sundays. Luke again shifts the position of the Marcan pericope. This time the call of the first disciples is moved to a later point in the narrative. Again, too, Luke combines it with another tradition from his special material. This special tradition consists of the miraculous draught of fishes, a story found in a post-resurrection setting in John 21. It is much disputed whether this was originally a post-resurrection story later retrojected into the earthly life of Jesus or vice versa, and the weight of the arguments on both sides is about equal.

By combining this tradition with his Marcan source, Luke psychologizes the call of Simon Peter (the other disciples are only background survivals from the Marcan source). The call does not come like a bolt out of the blue, as in Mark. Simon had already witnessed the healing of his mother-in-law, and now he experiences the miraculous haul of fish. This creates in him a feeling of unworthiness: "Depart from me, for I am a sinful man, O Lord." Those who think that the post-resurrection setting was original can explain this as a reaction to the Lord's appearance after Peter's threefold denial. In Luke's narrative, however, it is a reaction to the *mysterium tremendum* of the miracle (cf. Isaiah's vision). The call comes in the metaphorical words about "catching men," as in Mark, but the wording is different, thus suggesting that it comes not from Mark but from Luke's special material.

The Homily

If the long form of the gospel is read, the homilist has the rare opportunity to take all three readings together—the calls of Isaiah, Paul, and Simon (Peter). In each case there is a sense of unworthiness that is later overcome in an act of grace and forgiveness, leading to a commissioning for a unique role in salvation history and to an immediate response. This seems to be a constant biblical pattern, and it would give the homilist an occasion to speak of vocation to Christian service in its various forms, whether ordained or non-ordained.

If the short form of the second reading is used, the emphasis rests upon the identity of Paul's teaching with that of his predecessors. The homilist could discuss what is basic to the Christian tradition (the proclamation of the central saving events of the cross and the resurrection of Christ) and the importance of agreement and unity in these basic traditions.

SIXTH SUNDAY OF THE YEAR

Reading I: Jeremiah 17:5-8

This poem of two stanzas consists of a woe pronounced upon those who trust in human beings and a beatitude upon those who trust in Yahweh. The woe and the beatitude are accompanied by two corresponding comparisons (a shrub in the desert and a tree by the waterside). The poem differs from the usual prophecies of Jeremiah because of its wisdom character and its corresponding lack of direct connection with Israel's salvation history. Whether Jeremiah wrote it or not is disputed by Old Testament scholars precisely because of its unique character in this respect, but there seems to be nothing in it that is contrary to Jeremiah's teaching elsewhere. Some scholars have tried to give the poem a concrete situation in Jeremiah's ministry but without success.

The choice of this reading for today seems to have been governed by considerations of form rather than of content, for the gospel reading consists of our Lord's beatitudes and woes from the Great Sermon (note, though, that they occur in reverse order). The people designated for blessing and woe, however, are not exactly the same as those in the reading from Jeremiah (but see below).

Responsorial Psalm: 1:1-4, 6

This psalm is an obvious choice to go with the poem from Jeremiah because it uses precisely the same comparison as the second stanza of the poem: the person who hopes in the Lord is like a tree planted by streams of water. In the third stanza of the psalm, however, the wicked are compared to chaff, not to a shrub in the desert, as in the poem.

But there is a far more significant difference between the psalm and the poem from Jeremiah. The psalm (first stanza) emphasizes the Torah (law) as the ground of human trust in Yahweh, while the poem says nothing at all about this. This shows that the psalm was written from a later, postexilic perspective than the wisdom poem.

Reading II: 1 Corinthians 15:12, 16-20

Having stated the kerygma, Paul first turns upon the Corinthians and reproaches them for their inconsistency. If they accepted the proclamation, or kerygma, of Christ's resurrection, how then can they deny the resurrection of the dead? What the Corinthians meant by denying the resurrection of the dead was discussed in last Sunday's comments. The bodily resurrection of Christ and that of the departed believers (this is what is meant by "the dead"; Paul is not expounding a generally valid anthropology) depend on one another. On the one hand, Christ's resurrection depends upon the validity of the Jewish apocalyptic hope, for to say that Christ has been raised from the dead makes sense only if we grant the validity of that hope (v. 16). Christ's resurrection is not an episode in his own individual biography but the first of the resurrections from the dead for which the apocalyptists had hoped and the one that determines all other resurrections. He is the first fruits of those who have fallen asleep (v. 20), and conversely, since he is the first fruits, the others will also be raised because of his resurrection.

Verses 17-20 merit particular attention. Here Paul is arguing existentially. To deny the resurrection of the dead is not to hold an incorrect theoretical philosophy of life; rather, it is to undercut the reality of our own present Christian existence: "your faith is futile and you are still in your sins" (v. 17). The Christian hope of resurrection is not a philosophical opinion but an inference from present Christian experience. We are forgiven sinners. We have been brought into a new relationship with God through Christ, a relationship that, if it is real, must issue in an ultimate consummation beyond this present existence. Faith in our resurrection cannot be argued on theoretical grounds; it depends on the reality of the present Christian experience of forgiveness. It is not just that we hope to go to heaven when we die or that we believe that the souls of all persons are intrinsically immortal. These things may or may not be true; they lie outside Paul's perspective. It is rather that God has forgiven us in Christ, and nothing, not even death itself, can deprive us of that new life.

Gospel: Luke 6:17, 20-26

In Luke (unlike Matthew) the Great Sermon is delivered "on a level place." If you go to the Holy Land, you will be shown the "Mount of the Beatitudes." This mountain, however, exists only in Matthew's redaction and is symbolical: the new law is given on a new Sinai. Luke probably follows his Q source in placing the sermon on a plain. The Sermon on the Plain is delivered "where cross the crowded ways of life"—where crowds are seeking to hear Jesus and to be healed of their diseases. Thus, verse 17 gives the Lucan setting for the sermon.

The sermon is addressed, not to the crowds, but to the disciples in the presence of the crowds (v. 20). This means that the ethics of the Great Sermon are not meant fo the world in general but for those who have already decided to follow Christ. They presuppose grace. This is not a general law but the demands upon those who have already been enabled by grace to fulfill them. Hence Jesus' lack of concern for whether his disciples will be able to fulfill such a demanding ethic. Only insofar as persons are "in Christ" (to use the Pauline equivalent of the synoptic "Follow me") will they reproduce this kind of life in their own lives.

In both Matthew and Luke, the Great Sermon opens with a series of beatitudes. There are nine in Matthew. But in Luke there are four beatitudes, followed by four woes. Each beatitude has its corresponding woe.

Beatitude	*Woe*
poor	rich
hungry	full
weeping	laughing
hated	spoken well of
(like prophets)	(like false prophets)

There is a sociological aspect to the beatitudes and woes in Luke, but we should not interpret them exclusively in sociological terms. The poor, the hungry, etc., include the underprivileged of society, but not them only. In the last analysis, Matthew is correct when he glosses "poor" with "in spirit," and "hungry" with "for righteousness," for ultimately it is a question of human beings' relationship with God. The poor and the hungry are those who know that they have nothing in and of themselves to entitle them to a right relationship with God. They know themselves to be the have-nots.

The Homily

The homilist might combine the Old Testament reading and the gospel by taking a cue from the opening words of the two stanzas of the wisdom poem in the first reading: "Cursed is the man who trusts in man," and "Blessed is the man who trusts in the Lord." These words interpret what the Lucan beatitudes and woes are about. Trust in human beings is the attitude of the rich, of those who are full, who laugh, and of whom people speak well. Trust in the Lord is the attitude of those who are poor and hungry, who weep and are hated, ostracized, and reviled. It appears that this curse and this blessing are being spoken dramatically by God over our affluent society, now threatened with chaos and dissolution.

The second reading offers the homilist an occasion to distinguish between Christian hope for a life beyond the present life and general notions of immortality and survival. Christian hope is characterized by: (1) its roots in Christology: only because of Christ can we be raised from the dead; (2) its existential character: only because of what we already are in Christ do we know that this existence is indestructible by death.

SEVENTH SUNDAY OF THE YEAR

Reading I: 1 Samuel 26:2, 7-9, 12-13, 22-23

First Samuel contains two versions of this episode, in which David spares King Saul after being hunted down by the king. The other version is in 1 Sam 24:1-22. The two versions differ considerably in detail, but both reflect one of the most attractive features of David's character—his magnanimity. Both versions, however, express something more, namely, the royal ideology according to which David is reluctant to put forth his hand against the Lord's anointed. This reading matches the gospel, an extract from the Great Sermon that inculcates Jesus' demand for forgiveness toward others, as God has forgiven us.

Responsorial Psalm: 103:1-4, 8, 10, 12-13

As would be expected, portions of this psalm are frequently used in the liturgy. The same selection of verses occurs on the seventh Sunday of the year in series A and on the eighth Sunday of the year in series B. In our comments for the latter, it is pointed out that Psalm 103 is an individual's thanksgiving after some personal trial (perhaps sickness—see the second stanza). It emphasizes the kindness and mercy of Yahweh (note especially the refrain: "The Lord is kind and merciful"). Today the psalm seems to be intended as a response to verses 22-23 of the first reading, although 1 Sam 26 speaks of God's *rewarding* human righteousness and faithfulness. We will discover the same quality of grace and reward in today's gospel reading.

123
305

Reading II: 1 Corinthians 15:45-49

Let us first remind ourselves of what we have frequently observed before, namely, that Paul's letters are not abstract theologizings but responses to highly concrete situations in his churches. Exegetes have long agreed that in this passage Paul is polemicizing against some other view. He asserts emphatically that the physical Adam was first, and the spiritual Adam second (v. 46). Commentators have contrasted this statement with Philo's exegesis of the two stories of the creation of man and woman in Gen 1 and 2. He took the human being created in Gen 1:26 to be the heavenly, archetypal human being, and the Adam of Gen 2-3 to be empirical, fallen humanity, and built up a dualistic anthropology of a Platonic kind.

More recently Philo's exegesis has been regarded as one form of a widespread Gnostic anthropology. This is what Paul is polemicizing against—in the form in which it was held by the Corinthian Gnostics. According to this view, the souls of the Gnostic elite consisted of divine sparks emanating from the heavenly Adam. These sparks had tragically become incarnated in the physical body of the earthly Adam. In this view the Christian gospel becomes a means of recovering one's heavenly origin, one's authentic selfhood. This recovery, the Corinthians believe, has already taken place for them through the communication of the Christian *gnosis*, or divinely revealed knowledge, and through the sacraments.

Paul reverses the order of the two Adams. The attainment of authentic existence is not the recovery of something innate but an eschatological possibility opened up by the death and resurrection of Jesus. Although to some extent we begin even here on earth to participate in the new being through the sacraments (a point Paul makes elsewhere but not here), we do not completely do so until the end. Hence Paul writes this passage to emphasize the eschatological reserve, the "not yet" that marks Christian existence. Only at the end "shall" we bear the image of the heavenly. Here some manuscripts read "let us bear the image of the heavenly," but this would push Paul somewhat in the direction of his gnosticizing opponents, something that, in the exigencies of controversy, he is at pains to avoid.

Gospel: Luke 6:27-38

The first two paragraphs of this reading correspond to the sixth and last antithesis in Matthew's presentation of the Great Sermon: "You have heard . . . But I say to you" (Matt 5:43-44). Such an antithesis is implicit in the Lucan form, since love of one's enemy was not current Jewish teaching. (Here "enemy" means "non-Israelite"; cf. the attitude of the Qumran community toward outsiders.) Note the golden rule at the end of the first paragraph, a saying that Matthew places later in the sermon (7:12).

Of special interest is the saying that concludes the second paragraph: "Be merciful, even as your Father is merciful." Matthew places this saying in the same context, right after the saying about loving one's enemy. But his version reads: "You therefore must be *perfect,* as your heavenly Father is *perfect.*" Matthew, of course, has a special interest in the idea of perfection, as his treatment of the rich young man indicates (19:16-22). Hence it is likely that Luke's form represents the earlier reading. This point is thoroughly biblical: a person's behavior toward others is to be the reflection of the treatment he or she receives from God. The biblical ethic is essentially one of response to God's treatment of his people—this is true both in the Old Testament and in the New. In the Old Testament the Decalogue is given in the context of response to God's act of deliverance in bringing Israel out of Egypt.

The third paragraph, against judging others, which comes later in Matthew's version (7:1-2), uses a series of "reverential periphrases," that is, roundabout ways of speaking about God and his action. Thus, "you will not be judged . . . condemned . . . forgiven" means that God will not judge you, etc. This paragraph seems to reverse the order of God's action and human action. In the previous paragraph the emphasis was on imitating God's treatment of us; here it is on God's responding in kind to our behavior. This apparent contradiction seems to run through much of Jesus' teaching, especially on forgiveness. The point must be that while God in Christ has initiated forgiveness toward us, we must continue to show forgiveness to others if we are to remain in that forgiveness. We should avoid any suggestion of a *quid-pro-quo* relationship between ethics and rewards.

In closing this passage on judging, Luke has strengthened the exhortation to generosity and forbearance by the addition of verse 38a. Verse 38b is found also in Matthew.

The Homily

As usual, the homilist is faced with two main alternatives. Taking a cue from the caption to the gospel, "Be merciful as your Father is merciful," he/she might expound the Christian ethic as an ethic of response. We are to behave toward others as God in Christ has treated us. The story of David and Saul could be used as an illustration.

Alternatively, the homilist could expound Paul's concept of the first and second Adams. If we are to be true to Paul in this text, we should emphasize, as he does, that our participation in the "new being" is marked by the eschatological reserve, the "not yet." At present we bear the image of the earthly Adam, and only at our resurrection shall we bear the image of the heavenly Adam, even if the outlines of that image have been traced over us in our baptism. Perhaps we should amplify the negative implication of Paul's rather one-sided polemic by insisting that we have in principle already begun to participate to some degree in the new being, and that it is the task of the Christian to seek to grow in that image (see Ephesians).

EIGHTH SUNDAY OF THE YEAR

Reading I: Sirach 27:4-7

Some parts of the wisdom literature are highly doctrinal and speculative; other parts consist of commonsense observations on human behavior and the moral imperative. Today's reading is of the latter kind. It spells out some of the dangers that threaten human integrity. The inner worth of human beings is to be assessed from their words and deeds, just as "the fruit discloses the cultivation of a tree." This is the same metaphor as occurs in today's gospel reading from the Sermon on the Mount.

Responsorial Psalm: 92:1-2, 12-15

This same selection of verses is used on the eleventh Sunday of the year in series B. As we commented there, this psalm of thanksgiving deals with the theme of moral retribution. Yahweh is praised for his mighty deeds, especially in rewarding the righteous with prosperity, so that they become like fruitful trees. The psalm expresses the Deuteronomic theology and must be balanced by that of other works such as Psalm 73 or the Book of Job, which recognize that the righteous do not always prosper and that reward often seems to go to the wicked.

315

Reading II: 1 Corinthians 15:54-58

This reading comes from the magnificent climax of Paul's chapter on the resurrection of the dead. The Corinthians, with their gnosticizing proclivities, believed that their initiation as Christians had already introduced them into the resurrection life, and that therefore there was no need for a resurrection after death. Paul argues that belief in Christ's resurrection carries with it a corollary belief in the resurrection of the dead, and vice versa. This is because Paul sets the resurrection of Christ in the framework of Jewish apocalyptic expectation. The Jewish apocalyptists expected a general resurrection at the end of history. The Easter event revealed that one resurrection had already taken place before the end of history—that of Christ, the "first fruits" (1 Cor 15:20, 23). His resurrection is not only the first instance of the final resurrection but also one that will make all other resurrections at the end possible. But there is an "order" in these resurrections (1 Cor 15:23).

Paul derives a second idea from Jewish apocalyptic, namely, the nature of the resurrection life. It is not a mere resuscitation, that is, a recovery of the old mode of existence before death; it is an elevation to an entirely new mode of existence. The resurrected will acquire a "spiritual" body. Paul illustrates this by a series of contrasts and by the analogy of the seed and the grown plant (1 Cor 15:35-44).

The metaphor shifts in verse 53. Instead of speaking of a transformation, Paul speaks of the resurrection body as a new garment—the same metaphor he will use later in 2 Cor 5. This shows that we should not press his metaphors into literal descriptions. When that transformation or clothing has taken place, then death, the last enemy, will be finally defeated.

In our reading today, Paul anticipates this final triumph in the lyrical terms of a text that combines Isa 24:8 and Hos 13:14 (vv. 54-55). In the original context of the Isaian quotation, death and sheol were being invited to do their worst for the punishment of God's people. Paul turns the text right around—it is no longer a challenge to death to come and do its worst, but a celebration of Christ's destruction of death's sting. The sting, Paul comments, is sin. That is to say, in the Christian perspective death is not simply a biological fact; it is a final expression of the consequences of sin, of complete and final separation from God.

"And the power of sin is the law" (v. 56). Here Paul recalls his arguments in Gal 3, Rom 5:13 and 7:7-25. The law came to increase the trespass. It did this by exposing sin for the reality that it is and, as Paul argues, actually increases sin. Why does Paul drag in this earlier theologizing about the law at this point? No doubt because the Corinthian enthusiasts believed that they were immune from sin and death. The victory over sin and death is already won, though only in principle. Christians stand between D-day and V-day. Yet so certain of V-day is Paul that he uses the present tense: "gives us the victory." With this assurance his converts can return to the workaday world, knowing that their labors contribute to the final victory and will be taken up into Christ's finished work.

Gospel: Luke 6:39-45

This reading is a continuation of Luke's Sermon on the Plain. Since only the aphorism about the log and the speck and the parabolic saying about the tree and its fruits appear also in Matthew's Sermon on the Mount, we may conclude that only these two items already occurred in the Great Sermon of Q. Luke has prefaced the little parable with the aphorism of the blind leading the blind and the saying about the disciple not being above the teacher, which have parallels elsewhere in Matthew. Luke appears to have derived them from Q but has redactionally transferred them to this position. The parable of the tree and its fruit thus becomes a commentary on the preceding sayings. Since the opening saying of the series (the blind leading the blind) is directed to Church leaders, we may presume that for Luke the rest of the passage is, too, including the parable of the tree and its fruits.

The Homily

This week it is possible to connect the parable of the tree and its fruit with the similar saying in the first reading and with the final saying about labors in the Lord in the second reading. These sayings could be expounded in two ways. First, they can be taken to refer particularly to the Church's leadership, as in Luke. A homily about the responsibilities of priests and ministers would be quite a good thing. Congregations need to know that their clergy are not being idle when they spend time in prayer, meditation, and the study of Scripture. It is like a tree drawing nourishment from the soil. Such devotional exercises are not mere human works—they are a means of allowing the power of the risen Christ to flood into our lives (see the second reading). But devotional exercises are meant to produce fruit in daily life. What Luke addresses primarily to Church leaders is equally applicable, however, to the whole people of God (as the sayings were perhaps applied in the Q source before Luke redacted it).

Note that the final verse of the second reading uses the word "labor," which Paul normally applies to the work of the apostles and his colleagues in the service of the gospel, and which is applied here to the behavior of the whole body of the faithful in their daily life in the world.

Of course, the homilist may prefer to speak about the resurrection of the dead, an especially apt subject if there has been a recent death in the congregation. (The passage from 1 Corinthians is the traditional reading in the Anglican burial office.) In that case the homilist will seek to preach the resurrection of Christ in such a way that it assures the listeners that those who have died in the Lord are still in him and are awaiting the resurrection in a new and glorious state at the final triumph of Christ over death. Then, in the end, it sends the mourners back into their daily lives, with the assurance that because of their resurrection hope, their life is redeemed from futility and meaninglessness.

NINTH SUNDAY OF THE YEAR

Reading I: 1 Kings 8:41-43

As the incipit shows us, this is part of Solomon's prayer at the dedication of the first temple. The wording is derived from a preexilic source that was edited during or after the Exile. It thus contains a mixture of Deuteronomic and Priestly theology. The concern for the stranger reflects, not the preexilic rules for resident aliens (their rights were governed by law), but a concern for pagans who had been attracted to Judaism during the Exile—the class of people later known as "God-fearers." One may perhaps conjecture that there was active missionary work on the part of these exiles, whose outlook would be reflected more in Second Isaiah than, say, in Ezra-Nehemiah.

Responsorial Psalm: 117:1-2

Psalm 117 calls upon all nations to praise the name of Yahweh. It is cited by Paul (Rom 15:11) to illustrate the universal scope of God's redemptive purpose in Christ.

Reading II: Galatians 1:1-2, 6-10

Paul always adapts the formal prescript of his letter to the particular occasion. The basic form is: "A to B, greeting," followed by a thanksgiving. In this letter to a church beset by false teachers who attacked Paul's gospel and questioned his apostolic authority, he incorporates into the mention of his own name as an apostle a defense of the divine origin of his apostolic authority: "not from men nor through men, but through Jesus Christ and God the Father, who raised him from the dead." As Paul will explain in next Sunday's reading, he was called to be an apostle by a resurrection appearance in which God revealed his Son to him.

Note, too, how abrupt Paul is in his address: "To the churches of Galatia." No hint of their being saints, of their progress in the faith, or of their charismatic gifts. True, he does pronounce an apostolic blessing (vv. 3-5, omitted from our passage). But then, just where the thanksgiving would normally come, he launches into a furious onslaught: "I am astonished that you are so quickly deserting him who called you" (v. 6). The Galatians are actually deserting God by listening to the Judaizers. "So quickly" need not necessarily mean "so soon after your conversion"; it could equally well mean "so soon after the false teachers arrived on the scene." That would make it possible to assume that the churches in question were in southern Galatia rather than in northern Galatia (there is no other evidence of churches in northern Galatia during the first century).

Thus, they were those founded on the so-called first missionary journey (Acts 13–14). This makes it possible to identify the apostolic conference referred to in Gal 2 with that of Acts 15 and yet to place Galatians after Acts 15, that is, during Paul's Ephesian ministry (Acts 19).

Paul says that the Galatians have fallen for a different gospel but then corrects himself. What the Judaizers were bringing was not the gospel, "good news," but bad news. Salvation, they said, had not really come through Christ—something extra was needed, namely, circumcision. This cuts right across the gospel as the proclamation of the free gift of God's grace. The very thought leads Paul to use strong language. Anyone who preaches any gospel different from the true one is "accursed" (*anathema*). Paul is not holding out for his private version of the gospel, for, as he tells us in 1 Cor 15:11, it is identical with the gospel preached by the original Jerusalem apostles. But not everyone would have drawn the same implications from that gospel as Paul did.

Paul knows that the Galatians will be offended by his strong line, but he cannot help that. He is not courting popularity as a minister of the gospel but is responsible to God and Christ alone (v. 10). As a true apostle, he seeks only to please God, whatever the cost to his own popularity.

Gospel: Luke 7:1-10

After the Sermon on the Plain, Luke begins a new section—a series of healings and other episodes indicating the kind of response Jesus evoked. The presentation of the Messiah in deed follows that of the Messiah in word.

The first episode is the response of a Gentile centurion to Jesus. This story comes after the Great Sermon, as it does in Matthew, and the sequence is therefore derived from Q. There is a similar story in John 4:46-53, the healing of the royal official's son, which looks like a variant of the same basic tradition. All three forms are healings performed at a distance, and all involve a son, child, or servant of a non-Jew. Luke's version is noteworthy in that it contains two sets of emissaries—Jewish elders and friends of the centurion. This enhances the tension and highlights the centurion's persistent faith, which is central to the story (v. 9).

It is also to be noted that for the most part Jesus confined his mission to Israel (see even Paul in Rom 15:8). His approaches to the Gentiles were strictly exceptional (for example, the Syro-Phoenician woman and the Greeks at the feast). This was not because Jesus was opposed to the Gentiles as such; he accepted the view of the more liberal of his apocalyptic contemporaries that the Gentiles would be given their chance at the end (see the verses that Matthew has inserted into this same story at 8:11; Luke records them in a different context, but they probably came from Q). The earliest post-Easter Church held the same view of salvation history. Then Hellenistic Jewish Christians of Stephen's circle found themselves at Antioch preaching to "Greeks," that is, non-Jews. It was left for Paul to provide a theology for what had happened, as he does in Rom 9–11. Since the gospel had been rejected by Israel for the time being, it must go forth to the Gentiles. This will provoke Israel to jealousy, and at the end they will come to salvation. Here is a revision of salvation history in the light of subsequent historical events, something that happens again and again throughout biblical history.

The Homily

Taken together, the Old Testament reading and the gospel open up the question of the universality of the Christian mission. That mission has to be constantly adjusted to new circumstances. In our day it is less a matter of Europeans and Americans sending out missionaries to convert the benighted heathen, and more a matter of partnership with indigenous churches in what used to be the mission field, and of finding the right means (dialogue?) to extend the Christian mission to those of other religions and cultures who have immigrated to North America and Europe.

The second reading suggests that the Church must take seriously the question of the truth of the gospel. A reaction against an older concern for complete theological orthodoxy can lead to the belief that today "anything goes." Creeds and conciliar definitions were not designed to express a complete system of truth, but to protect the truth of the gospel—and that is what the Church needs to recover today.

TENTH SUNDAY OF THE YEAR

Reading I: 1 Kings 17:17-24

This reading is from the cycle of Elijah stories, which present various exploits of the prophet, all of them miraculous. Tempting though it may be, it would be misleading to try to rationalize the miracles by giving them some purely naturalistic explanation. We should not, for instance, say that the child in our reading was not really dead but only in a coma. Such miraculous features belong essentially to the genre. Truth (God is Lord over death) is being conveyed by means of story rather than by means of history. It is the exegete's and homilist's task to bring out the truth rather than to retell the story as a historical report.

In verse 18 the woman complains that the prophet has come to "bring my sin to remembrance." This very important statement offers a clue to the biblical conception of remembrance (*anamnesis*). The late Gregory Dix, a well-known Anglican patristic scholar and liturgiologist, cited this passage as part of his evidence for the biblical idea of remembrance: "In the scriptures both of the Old and New Testaments, *anamnesis* and the cognate verb have the sense of 're-calling' or 're-presenting' before God an event in the past, so that it becomes operative *here and now by its effects* [italics Dix's]. . . . So the widow of Sarepta (1 Kings xvii 18) complains that Elijah has come 'to re-call to (God's) remembrance (*anamnesis*) my iniquity' and therefore her son has died."

The woman, of course, expresses the popular conviction that any calamity was a direct punishment for sin, a belief that Jesus seems to repudiate in the Fourth Gospel (John 9:3). But more important, she learns that the word of the Lord in the mouth of the prophet is "truth," that is, it does what it says. Note the biblical meaning of the word "truth." It is not just factual accuracy, nor is it truth in a philosophical sense. It means fidelity—here the fidelity of Yahweh to his promises, a fidelity shown by his acts. So the climax of the story—and here lies its theological point—is that the woman discerns that Elijah is indeed a man of God, and that the word of God is effective in deed.

Responsorial Psalm: 30:1, 3-5, 10-11a, 12b

Originally this psalm was the thanksgiving of an individual for deliverance from death (first stanza and refrain). Already in Israel, when it was taken up into the hymnbook of the temple, this psalm would have acquired a more corporate meaning. It is a psalm that might well have been sung by the woman of Zarephath when she received her son back alive, for it speaks of the transition from depression to joy.

Reading II: Galatians 1:11-19

Paul's Judaizing opponents in Galatia, who accused him of encouraging the Gentile converts to abandon circumcision and the keeping of the law, sought to undermine his authority by impugning his apostleship and his version of the gospel. They said that his gospel was secondhand, merely of human origin, and not firsthand from Christ, like that of the real apostles.

Here Paul takes up and elaborates the defense he had already adumbrated in the prescript of the letter (see last Sunday's second reading). Paul insists that his gospel came by a direct revelation from God in a resurrection appearance (cf. 1 Cor 15:8). This leads him to an autobiographical account of that call, a precious source of firsthand historical information. Of course, we must allow for a certain one-sidedness in Paul's account. In 1 Cor 15:1-8 he is more ready to admit that at least part of his gospel was transmitted to him through tradition. The fact of the matter is that Paul, not having been a witness of the earlier part of the Christ-event (Jesus' earthly life and death) and yet having received a resurrection appearance, was in a uniquely ambivalent position. In Galatians he emphasizes only one side of the facts, whereas in 1 Cor 15 he is more balanced.

As he usually does when reflecting on his call, Paul starts with his persecution of the Church. As he sees it, there was no gradual psychological preparation for that call. God intervened by sheer miracle, cutting right across Paul's previous behavior and turning him right around. Thus, his call involved a conversion. But the resurrection appearance is not to be equated with that conversion, as Edward Schillebeeckx seems to suggest in his book *Jesus*. Paul, in his pre-Christian, Pharisaic period, saw perhaps more clearly than anyone else that the gospel, as means of salvation, was antithetically opposed to the law: salvation comes either through the keeping of the law or through Christ. As a Pharisee, he was convinced that it came through the law. Therefore the gospel of Christ was the ultimate blasphemy, and the Christians had to be rooted out. Paul's conversion, therefore, came to him as a reversal of his previous position, and this colored his whole attitude in Galatians toward the Judaizers' demands for the circumcision of the Gentiles. If circumcision were a matter of ethnic custom, Paul would have no objection (according to Acts, he circumcised Timothy, who had a Jewish mother). But when it was imposed on Gentiles as a precondition for salvation, he found himself *in statu confessionis.*

Continuing his autobiographical account, Paul says that after his conversion he avoided all human contact and went straight into Arabia. We do not know what he was doing there—whether it was to think things out or to begin preaching the gospel. Acts presents his post-conversion behavior very differently by telling of his visit to, and his baptism by, Ananias in Damascus. Perhaps the resurrection appearance and his call, coming as it did directly from Christ, needed no supplementation by baptism.

Paul says that he "returned" to Damascus after that and did missionary work, and Acts agrees. His visit to Jerusalem three years later (probably two years according to inclusive reckoning) was for a visit to Peter and James, the Lord's brother (about A.D. 35). It is probable that here Paul received at least some of the traditions he mentions in 1 Cor 15, including the tradition of the two post-resurrection appearances to Peter and James.

But Paul is silent on this point in Galatians, an indication of the one-sidedness of this account.

Gospel: Luke 7:11-17

Much of the detail of this story is borrowed from the Zarephath story (first reading), which shows why that passage was chosen for today. Jesus goes to the town where a widow has lost her son. He resuscitates the dead man and gives him back to his mother. The crowd's response (v. 17) is reminiscent of the response of the widow of Zarephath. One or two other features are reminiscent of pagan stories of resuscitations: the miracle takes place on the road to the burial, and a great concourse of people witness it. Remove these borrowed features from the story and very little is left, except for the statement that Jesus was going to Nain.

The French Canadian Roman Catholic scholar Roché has analyzed the tradition of this story and concludes that it is a construction based partly on the story in 1 Kings and partly on pagan stories. He even questions one possible historical detail, the visit of Jesus to Nain. Whatever the origin of the tradition, it is a story intended to portray Jesus as the eschatological prophet, of greater power than the Old Testament prophets and the pagan miracle-workers. The Greek version of the narrative has a marked Semitic coloring, which, when coupled with the pagan contacts, suggests a milieu like Syria as its origin.

The Homily

If the gospel is chosen for today's homily, there will be the problem of dealing with a story that has little historical basis. The homilist, therefore, will have to handle it as an expression of kerygmatic truth. That truth is to be found in the two endings—the response of the widow of Zarephath and the response of the crowd at Nain. Here is rich material for proclamation. The word "visit" (Hebrew: *pqd*) is one of the great words of the Bible. Yahweh is essentially a God who visits, not only, as popularly thought, to punish but also to bring salvation. God's visit to Israel in the ancient prophets; his visit in the Christ-event, bringing life out of death; his extension of that visit through the word and the sacraments in the Church—that would be the theme of today's homily

If last week's homily was based on the reading from Galatians, the homilist will probably want to continue with Galatians today. In that case the homily should be about the divine origin of the gospel as preached by Paul, distinguishing what Paul received directly from the Lord and what he received from tradition. In the life of the Church today, the gospel we preach comes from tradition, but it has to be brought into life through the Holy Spirit. Tradition without the Spirit is dead; the Spirit without tradition runs wild.

ELEVENTH SUNDAY OF THE YEAR

Reading I: 2 Samuel 12:7-10, 13

This passage fits in neatly not only with the gospel but also with the second reading. All three readings proclaim the forgiveness of sin. The prophet Nathan acts as a father confessor to David. Nathan had previously stabbed David's conscience with the parable of the ewe lamb, confronting him with the brutal truth: "You are the man." David confesses, "I have sinned against the Lord," and Nathan declares that God has put away his sin. This is the classic Old Testament statement of the pattern of self-examination in the light of God's law, followed by confession of the sin as an offense against God and not merely against another person (see Ps 51:4: "Against thee, thee only, have I sinned"), and concluding with the confessor's declaration that God *has* put away the sin.

Responsorial Psalm: 32:1-2, 5, 7, 11

Instead of using the psalm which, according to picturesque tradition, David sang after his sin with Bathsheba (Psalm 51), we respond with another of the seven traditional penitential psalms. This is one that Paul used (Rom 4:7-8), preceded by the comment: "So also David pronounces a blessing upon the man to whom God reckons righteousness apart from works." Sacramental absolution is, like baptism and the Eucharist, a sacrament of justification through the grace of Christ alone, apart from the works of the law.

Reading II: Galatians 2:16, 19-21

This is one of the classic Pauline statements about justification. To be justified means to be in the right with God. The basic quest of religion— here Paul, Luther, and Trent are at one—is to be in the right with God. Paul had tried to get himself right with God by keeping the Mosaic law. In his encounter with Christ, he learned that this justification is something not to be earned but to be received as a gift through the Christ-event. It is not faith that is the primary cause of justification but the act of God in Christ, an act described by Paul as "grace," sheer unmerited forgiveness of the sinner. Faith is the subjective condition on the human side for receiving God's forgiveness. "Justification by faith alone" is shorthand for "justification by the grace-full act of God in Christ apprehended by the human being through faith alone."

That we are justified by faith and not by the works of the law does not mean that works have no place in the Christian life, for they are the fruit of faith. The justified sinner now "lives with God." This new life is a paradox. The Christian puts forth the utmost moral effort, and yet knows that it is not he or she but "Christ who lives in me" (see the similar paradox in Phil 2:12-13). This paradoxical understanding of the relation between faith and works should help us to transcend the antitheses of the Reformation.

But is the message of justification relevant today? Does the contemporary person, like Luther, seek a gracious God? Is not the modern question, as Martin Marty suggests, rather the question whether there is a God at all? Was Bonhoeffer right in rejecting the notion that people first have to be made sinners—which they do not feel themselves to be—before they can hear the gospel? Do we transcend the dichotomy between the Council of Trent and the Reformation by saying that both sides were concerned about an obsolete issue? Or is the question of justification not merely *one* approach to the Christian message but rather its central concern? Do we answer that question from an analysis of modern men and women or from a confrontation with the message of the New Testament? These are basic issues for contemporary theology, exegesis, and preaching.

Gospel: Luke 7:36–8:3 (long form); 7:36-50 (short form)

The crucial problem of this gospel is highlighted in the caption: "Her many sins were forgiven her, because she has shown great love." Taken at face value, these words suggest that the woman has earned forgiveness by her act of devotion and so was justified by works and not by faith. But a closer examination of the pericope shows that if this is the correct interpretation, it contains a glaring contradiction. The parable of the two debtors, which precedes our saying, makes love the *outcome* of forgiveness. To the question "Now which of [the two debtors] will love him more?" the answer comes, "The one, I suppose, to whom he forgave more." Later on it is stated that the person who is forgiven little, loves little. This means that we can only understand the woman's action in one way. Her extravagant act of devotion is a sign that her sins, "which are many," have already been forgiven. How were they forgiven? By Jesus' acceptance of her, sinner though she was.

The long form of the gospel, with its list of the women who also accompanied Jesus, might encourage the longstanding but erroneous tradition that Mary Magdalene was the woman whose many sins were forgiven and who therefore performed the extravagant act of devotion. There is nothing in the New Testament to warrant this identification. Moreover, our pericope may be a combination of two different incidents—that of a woman who anointed Jesus and that of a woman who washed his feet with her tears and dried them with her hair. The latter action is much more a sign of penitence than the former.

The Homily

Today's readings, concentrating as they do upon the single theme of the forgiveness of sins, offer a great opportunity to deal with the central message of the gospel—what Luther called the "article of a standing and falling Church"—and to relate this to the sacrament of reconciliation. Two thoughts suggest themselves. First, a better and more scriptural name for the sacrament of penance, a juridical concept, is "sacrament of absolution." It is an evangelical sacrament, a declaration of the gospel of God's forgiveness in a concrete situation. Second, consider the tremendous authority conferred upon the Old Testament prophet (first reading) and the Christian priest: they are not merely to *pray* that the sinner be forgiven but to pronounce the sinner forgiven on God's behalf. They cannot presume to do this because of some innate personal authority but because of their office and commission.

TWELFTH SUNDAY OF THE YEAR

Reading I: Zechariah 12:10-11

The original meaning of this passage from Deutero-Zechariah is highly uncertain, but one thing is clear: the New Testament Church (John 19:37 and Rev 1:7) took it as a messianic prophecy, referring either to the crowd's seeing the pierced Christ on the cross (John) or to the ungodly at the parousia (Revelation). It has been argued that this text underlies all the references to "seeing" the Son of man coming on the clouds of heaven (for example, Mark 13:26). In Christian interpretation, therefore, this text refers to the remorse that at the last judgment will overtake all who rejected Christ on earth.

It is arguable that this reading would be more appropriate for Advent or Holy Week. At this season of the year, when we think of the Christian life in the Spirit and of the pilgrimage of the Church from Pentecost to the parousia, it may serve as a reassurance to the community that the cause for which it stands—the gospel of Christ crucified—is certain of ultimate vindication.

Responsorial Psalm: 63:1-5, 7-8

Many of the psalms are intensely personal, but when they were taken over for liturgical use they acquired a corporate meaning, the "I" of the psalmist being expanded to embrace the whole people of God. In the person of Jesus Christ, who is the true Israel, the psalm is narrowed down again to a single person; but then it expands once again to include the body of Christ, which in him can apply the words to itself. God's people on pilgrimage pass through a dry and weary land where there is no water. But in the sanctuary, as they assemble to celebrate the liturgy, they have a pledge and assurance of the ultimate vindication of Christ's cause. They feast together on "marrow and fat" and praise God with joyful lips, even in the midst of the dry and weary land.

Reading II: Galatians 3:26-29

As we continue to read Galatians, we emerge from the long disputation on justification to something we feel we can really understand: the unity of the baptized in the Church, transcending all barriers of nationality, race, social standing, and sex. But Paul could never have written this purple passage unless he had argued through the whole question of justification. Only because baptism is the sacrament of justification are all these barriers of nature and history transcended; they are not transcended by being declared indifferent or due to misunderstanding. Only when a person receives the forgiveness of justification imparted in baptism are these very real differences of nature, history, and culture overcome. That people are one is an *eschatological* truth, a truth only "in Christ Jesus."

Gospel: Luke 9:18-24

Peter came to his confession "The Christ of God," not because he knew the correct doctrine of the incarnation in advance, but because of his encounter with the person of Jesus, watching him work and hearing him speak. The doctrine of the incarnation is not the presupposition and premise of our understanding of Christ but the conclusion of our encounter with him. That is why it is putting the cart before the horse to approach the Gospels with this kind of question: If Christ is divine, why could he not do (or say, or know) this or that? We hear first what he says and see what he does, and then, as we encounter the presence of God in him who is truly human, we confess with Peter, "You are the Christ of God."

For Jesus, however, to be the Christ was not a dignity to be claimed but a mission to be worked out, a mission that inevitably led him to the cross. And to follow him, to believe that he is the Christ, God present for us in human form, is to be called likewise to take up the cross "daily," as Luke alone of the evangelists says. We have to die daily with Christ in order that we may rise again with him.

The Homily

As so often, the Old Testament reading, the psalm, and the gospel suggest a common theme: that of the Church as a pilgrim people of God, called upon to take up the cross daily and to follow its Master on the road to Jerusalem. The thought of the pilgrim nature of the Church, so strongly emphasized at the Second Vatican Council against the triumphalism of an earlier era, is a suitable reflection in this season of "ordinary time."

The climactic statement of Galatians that in Christ all social distinctions are abrogated is a challenge to the congregation to examine its common life to see whether Paul's teaching is being implemented. "Jew nor Greek" stands for racial differences. A purely white church in a mixed neighborhood is a poor exhibition of catholicity. "Slave nor free" challenges us to ask whether we are like, for example, what used to be said of the Church of England—that it was the Tory party at prayer. "Male nor female" challenges us about the place of women in the Church. Are they being treated as second-class citizens?

THIRTEENTH SUNDAY OF THE YEAR

Reading I: 1 Kings 19:16b, 19-21

It is instructive to compare Elijah's call of Elisha with Jesus' call of his disciples as related in the gospel for this Sunday. Elisha said, "Let me kiss my father and my mother, and I will follow you." When Jesus called two would-be disciples, one said, "Lord, let me first go and bury my father." Elisha's call is one that could be added to already existing responsibilities. With Jesus' call it is different. All existing responsibilities have to be given up. They may be given back as part of the total call, but always as only part of it, enclosed within it, and subordinated to it.

The second difference is that Elijah's mantle falls upon Elisha. He can succeed him, become a prophet like his master when the latter finally departs (2 Kgs 2). But when Jesus ascends to heaven, his followers do not replace him. They remain followers, and he remains present as their living Lord.

Responsorial Psalm: 16:1-2a, 5, 7-11

The early Church seized upon this psalm as a prophecy of Christ's resurrection. In his Pentecost sermon as presented in Acts, Peter quotes verses

9-11. Once again, the "I" of the psalms is the "I" of the living Christ. But it also includes the members of his body, and so we may take this psalm upon our own lips and make it a prayer of praise for our inheritance, for our call into the life of Christ.

Reading II: Galatians 5:1, 13-18

Freedom is the hallmark of Christian existence. But this freedom is constantly threatened. For the Galatians it was threatened because they were succumbing to the blandishments of Paul's opponents and falling prey to some kind of syncretism that included circumcision. For Paul, this completely undermines the gospel. Christians are free because they do not have to acquire salvation by their own works; but because they have already been given salvation as a gift, they are free to work it out in obedience. This is the positive truth behind what gained popularity in the sixties as "situation ethics." There is one obligation for Christians, and that is the law of love. "The whole law is fulfilled in one word, 'You shall love your neighbor as yourself.'" Paul does not overlook the first and greatest commandment—the love of God; he is speaking to those who have already heard the message of justification, and who have therefore been brought into the love of God. Paul is talking about how that love of God can only express itself historically as love of neighbor. Love of neighbor should provide the Christian with a set of antennae (J.A.T. Robinson), enabling him/her to know in each concrete situation what that love requires, without a lot of rules and regulations. The guidance needed is provided by the "as yourself": Do to others as you would have them do to you.

"Flesh" and "Spirit" in the last paragraph are not our so-called higher and lower natures, though they are frequently thus misunderstood, even in modern translations. "Flesh" is our old, unredeemed humanity in its totality, including what we call our "higher nature." "Spirit," as the capitalization suggests, is the Spirit of God, the eschatological possibility that transforms our whole human nature, lower as well as higher, so called.

Gospel: Luke 9:51-62

The latter part of the gospel (the call of the would-be followers) has been sufficiently treated above under the Old Testament reading. Here we will concentrate on the former part.

The suggestion of James and John that fire should be called down from heaven to punish the Samaritans who would not receive Jesus "because his face was set toward Jerusalem" recalls their nickname, "Sons of thunder" (*Boanerges*). Recently attempts have been made to associate Jesus with the Zealots, the revolutionary liberationists of the day. That several of Jesus' disciples (for example, Simon the Zealot) had Zealot sympathies cannot be doubted. It seems probable that Jesus felt the constant temptation to seek an easy way out for his mission by adopting the Zealot line (O. Cullmann). But this was for him precisely that, a temptation, and one that he constantly resisted and that brought him, humanly speaking, to the cross. This recent controversy is a warning against the "peril of modernizing Jesus" (H. J. Cadbury). Every new movement of thought seeks to enlist Jesus on its side. But he remains himself, the judge of all human causes. He turns and rebukes James and John!

The Homily
We live in a world where violence and terrorism are common facts of life. The story of James and John in the gospel reading would provide the homilist with an opportunity to come to grips with the subject of violence and to pose the question, What is the Christian attitude toward it?

The second reading raises the related subject of freedom. This would give the homilist a chance to differentiate between the secular and the Christian concepts of freedom: freedom *from* as opposed to freedom *for*. The Christian is freed from sin in order to be free for the will of God.

FOURTEENTH SUNDAY OF THE YEAR

Reading I: Isaiah 66:10-14c
Originally this prophecy from Third Isaiah spoke of the joy following the restoration of God's people from exile. The returning exiles are received back by the holy city as a mother who consoles them at her breasts and dandles them on her lap. The metaphor is mixed, for it also speaks of Yahweh sending his "prosperity" (*shalom*, which the caption inadequately renders as "peace," presumably to establish a link with the gospel) like a river. (Note the reference to peace in the second reading also; otherwise there seems to be very little connection between the three readings.) This reading, however, is appropriate for the post-Pentecost season, in which the Church enjoys the fruits of redemption, particularly the gift of the Spirit.

Responsorial Psalm: 66:1-3a, 4-7a, 16, 20
This is a psalm of thanksgiving for a national deliverance, pictured in imagery derived from the original Exodus: "He turned the sea into dry land; men passed through the river on foot." The prophecies of Second Isaiah spoke of the return from exile in these terms, so the psalm forms a good

response to the first reading. It is a thanksgiving for all the blessings of redemption and, for us particularly, for the gift of the Spirit.

The latter verses of the psalm (here represented by verses 16 and 20) take a surprisingly individualistic turn. It is reasonable to suppose that at some juncture two originally distinct psalms were combined. The Christian sees a personal religious experience as part of the experience of the entire body, while the experience of the entire body is reflected in the experience of the individual. The gift of the Holy Spirit is at once corporate and individual. At times in the history of the Church one aspect has been emphasized at the expense of the other. Both must be held in balance.

Reading II: Galatians 6:14-18

It was Paul's custom to dictate his letters to an amanuensis, and then to take the pen himself and add a few concluding words. In these words he summarized and drove home the message of the whole letter. The purpose of Galatians is to dissuade his Gentile readers from lapsing into syncretism. They are probably not Judaizing in the strict sense, for Paul has to remind them that anyone who gets circumcised is obligated to keep the whole law, which would have been self-evident to a genuine Judaizer. Paul "glories," not in circumcision as his opponents do, but in the cross. What matters for him is that the believers have been re-created into a new existence, and in this new existence it is not the marks of circumcision but the marks of his apostolic sufferings, in which Christ crucified is manifested, that are important. Finally, the Apostle gives his readers his blessing in a style that suggests (as the conclusion of other letters, especially 1 Corinthians, suggest even more clearly) that his letters were written to lead into the celebration of the Lord's Supper.

Gospel: Luke 10:1-12, 17-20 (long form); 10:1-9 (short form)

All three synoptic Gospels record a mission of the Twelve during Jesus' earthly ministry. The mission of the Seventy (some texts have seventy-two) is peculiar to Luke. In chapter 9 Luke has already followed his Marcan source for the mission of the Twelve. Here he follows Q and his special material for the mission of the Seventy. The Q material is also used by Matthew in his mission charge to the Twelve. So it is clear that the idea of a mission of the Seventy was created, not by Q or Mark, but by Luke or his special material.

There can be little doubt that the number seventy is symbolic. The mission of the Twelve represents the Church's mission to Israel (twelve tribes); and the mission of the Seventy, its mission to the nations of the world (which, according to Jewish tradition, numbered seventy or seventy-two). Some critics maintain that the whole idea of missions during the earthly ministry is a retrojection of the post-Easter mission into the earthly life of Jesus. But it is noteworthy that the disciples are charged to proclaim Jesus' own message: "The kingdom of God has come near to you," not the Christological kerygma of the post-Easter Church. The mission is to be characterized by urgency and detachment. The exact expression of this urgency and detachment is conditioned by the circumstances of the time. But in some form or other, urgency and detachment must always characterize the Church's mission.

Two other features are worthy of note. First, it is not the disciples (and therefore not the Church) that initiate the mission. The initiative comes from the Lord of the harvest in response to the Church's prayer. The disciples return from their mission elated by their success, but Jesus at once dampens their elation: "Do not rejoice in this, that the spirits are subject to you; but rejoice that your names are written in heaven." There is an even more significant joy for the missionary: prior to their mission, they had been admitted to the privilege of partaking in the eschatological salvation. When they forget that, they are tempted to think that the mission is their own cause and that the success is their own achievement. Even an apostle or an evangelist is a justified sinner.

The Homily

Today's gospel reading calls upon the homilist to deal with the subject of Christian mission. When we compare the various missionary charges in the synoptic Gospels, we note that the early Church freely adapted our Lord's words to its altered circumstances. The question for us today is: How must the Church implement the call to mission in the post-Christian, secularized society of the West? How in the Third World? How in Communist countries? And above all, how in our own congregation and parish? This is not our mission but Christ's. He is the initiator of it, as the Lucan charge says, and we have to fit in with his plan. In the words of the second reading, we are called upon to witness to the cross of Christ, not to glory in circumcision—that is, our own religiosity or piety—and to impose that as a piece of propaganda upon others. It is Christ's mission and message, not ours.

FIFTEENTH SUNDAY OF THE YEAR

Reading I: Deuteronomy 30:10-14

This is part of Moses' farewell discourse in Deuteronomy. In fact, it is a liturgical sermon urging Israel to renew the covenant, and was probably composed in the time of exile. It suggests the concept of the law no longer written on tablets of stone but engraved on the heart, thus presaging the development of the wisdom tradition after the Exile. Paul picked up this passage (v. 14) and applied it to the gospel and the righteousness that comes by faith (Rom 10:5-8). As C. H. Dodd pointed out, Paul is not really doing violence to Deuteronomy, which is less legalistic than, say, Leviticus: "The deuteronomic code . . . bases righteousness on the love of God, to which we should be provoked by his grace towards his people."[1] Hence the first reading prepares us for the gospel of the day, which features the double command of love.

Responsorial Psalm: 69:13, 16, 29-30, 32-33, 35ab, 36

Like so many other psalms, this one begins as the prayer of an individual in distress and ends on a note of assurance. Psalms such as this reflect the pattern of Christ's death-resurrection and the Christian experience of sin and justification. Psalm 69 makes a fitting response to Deut 30:10-14, interpreted in the light of Rom 10:5-8.

Reading II: Colossians 1:15-20

This passage is a Christological hymn. The first part speaks of Christ in terms of the later Jewish concept of wisdom—the image of God personified as the agent of creation and preservation. The second part moves to the theme of redemption, but is patterned on the first part. As preexistent wisdom, Christ was the first-born of creation; as the risen One, he is the first-born of the dead. As the agent of creation he created the cosmic powers; in his exaltation he is their victor and the head of his body, the Church. The divine wisdom becomes incarnate in Jesus, and the incarnation reaches its climax in the cross, the source of reconciliation and peace.

It was a bold step for the New Testament to identify Christ with the preexistent "Wisdom." What led it to take this step? It was the conviction that the God who had revealed himself and acted in Jesus Christ was the same God who had created the world. Redemption is not redemption out of the world, but the restoration of the created world when it had fallen into sin. The implications of this for the Christian attitude toward the world

---

[1] C. H. Dodd, *The Epistle to the Romans* (New York: Harper and Brothers, 1932) 165.

are far-reaching. Christianity says a preliminary "yes" to the world as God's creation, and a preliminary "no" to it as subject to the powers of evil. But it says an ultimate "yes" to the world, because that world has been reconciled through the blood of the cross.

Gospel: Luke 10:25-37

The double commandment of love has come down in two different forms. In the Marcan/Matthean form, it is Jesus who gives the command in response to a question; in the Lucan form it is elicited from the "lawyer" in response to Jesus' counter-question. The content of the commandment is not original to Jesus, for it is a combination of texts from Deuteronomy and Leviticus. Nor is it certain that the combination is original to him, for it is also found in the Testament of the Twelve Patriarchs (although some scholars think that there it is a Christian interpolation).

It is arguable, however, that in Christian tradition the double commandment stems from Jesus and that Luke's form of it is a secondary adaptation to the dramatic exigencies of his pericope. Even if Jesus was not the first to combine love of God and love of neighbor, he understood that combination with a unique and radical seriousness (G. Bornkamm). There can be no love of God that does not express itself in love of neighbor. Conversely, there is no authentic love of neighbor that does not spring from love of God, for otherwise it is a refined, subtle form of self-love.

In Luke's dramatic construction, Jesus' acceptance of the lawyer's reply leads to a further question on his part. He wanted to "justify himself," to get the whole thing straight. He asks, " And who is my neighbor ?" The dramatic exchange is the springboard for the parable of the Good Samaritan. But the parable does not really answer the lawyer's question. It ends by reversing it: "Which of the three *proved neighbor* to him who fell among the robbers?" It is right here that the point of the parable lies. "You shall love your neighbor" does not mean that you may love some people but not others; rather, it means: be a neighbor to another, not just indulging in general sentiments of benevolence, but doing concrete acts for the person in concrete need. "Neighborliness is not a quality in other people, it is simply their claim on ourselves. We have literally no time to sit down and ask ourselves whether so-and-so is our neighbor or not. We must get into action and obey; we must behave like a neighbor to him" (D. Bonhoeffer).

The Homily

It seems an impertinence for the homilist to try to add anything to the parable of the Good Samaritan. More than any of Jesus' parables, with the exception of the parable of the prodigal son, it speaks its own message. Nevertheless, it is worthwhile trying to bring out the element of surprise involved when Jesus' hearers are told that the third passerby was not a layman but a Sadducee. It's like holding up a "Commie" or a hippie as an exemplar of the kind of behavior Christians ought to show but so often fail to.

If the homilist wishes to speak of doctrine rather than ethics, the Christological hymn of Colossians offers an opportunity to relate creation and redemption. The step that the early Church took in identifying Jesus with the Logos or Wisdom of God as the agent of creation meant that salvation is not *out of* the world but *of* humanity *with* the created order. The gospel is not a means of escape from the real world.

SIXTEENTH SUNDAY OF THE YEAR

Reading I: Genesis 18:1-10a

The annunciation of Isaac's birth to Abraham has no obvious connection with the thanksgiving for the Christian mystery in Colossians (second reading) or with Martha and Mary in Luke (gospel). Perhaps there is a thread linking the revelation of Isaac's birth to Abraham and the mystery hidden for ages and generations and now made manifest. God is a God who acts in history, his actions are constantly new, and accompanying his actions is the revelation of their meaning. Action plus revelation of its meaning equals mystery.

Annunciation scenes are a device to disclose the meaning of God's acts in salvation history. The birth of a major figure in salvation history (often a birth out of due course, a supernatural birth) is announced by an angel. The birth of Isaac was supernatural, because both Abraham and Sarah were too old to become parents. This and other similar birth stories (for example, Samson and Samuel) provide the Old Testament precedent for the annunciation of the birth of Jesus to Joseph in Matthew, and to Mary in Luke. For Jesus' birth is likewise supernatural. In other words, Jesus is not merely a product of human history but an intervention, indeed the final eschatological intervention of God in salvation history. The meaning of this history is disclosed to Joseph ("He will save his people from their sins") and to Mary ("He will be great, and will be called the Son of the Most High").

Responsorial Psalm: 15:2-4b, 5

This psalm is one of the "entry psalms" sung as the pilgrims entered the temple. It describes the character of the person whom God will accept as a worthy pilgrim—a person of justice, sincerity, and integrity. Abraham was known for his justice, and this psalm serves as a fitting response to the first reading.

Reading II: Colossians 1:24-28

The letter to the Colossians is one of the *antilegomena*, that is, a letter regarded, at least by more radical critics, as deutero-Pauline. If that is so, the present passage is remarkably close to what St. Paul would have written, and is the product of a mind thoroughly impregnated with the thoughts of the Apostle. It interprets the Apostle's self-understanding precisely as in Galatians, 1 and 2 Corinthians, and Romans.

Suffering is one of the hallmarks of apostleship. The Apostle fills up what is lacking in Christ's afflictions—a bold formulation, which, however, does not mean that something is lacking in the atoning power of Christ's death. The clue lies in the undoubted letters of Paul, which present his suffering as an epiphany, manifestation, or proclamation of Christ's cross. What is "lacking" is not the atoning power of the cross but its manifestation in the Church as a present reality. As in the undoubted letters, Paul's gospel is a "mystery" (1 Cor 2:1), the proclamation of a new saving act, a complete *novum* unheard of before. For Paul, this mystery has a particular nuance (see Rom 11:25): it involves admission of the Gentiles to the privileges of the end-time community.

There are also some differences between our passage and the undoubted letters. In the latter, Paul does not speak of the Church as the body of Christ *tout court* but employs that image as a metaphor or simile to express the unity of the Church amid the diversity of its members. Also, the undoubted letters either reject the notion that Christians already here in this time could be "mature" (*teleioi*, literally, "perfect") or use it ironically. Colossians and Ephesians speak of perfection as a goal toward which Christians should progress on their earthly pilgrimage. The differences are slight but significant. The *antilegomena* presuppose a later situation in which it is recognized that the Church is here to stay, to live in history and to produce a Christian culture.

Gospel: Luke 10:38-42

This well-known idyllic scene is placed by Luke immediately after the parable of the Good Samaritan (see last Sunday). In this position it corrects the activistic impression that might otherwise be deduced from Jesus' answer to the lawyer's question: "Do this, and you will live." Activism must spring from hearing the word of God. Most of us would feel that we have to combine Mary and Martha—hearing the word of God and going out into the world in active service. But we must recognize that some have a primary vocation to be Mary, others to be Martha.

The Homily

Probably the homilist will want to portray the two characters of Mary and Martha, pointing out how most of us have to be something of each— both the contemplative and the active.

Another possibility would be to base the homily on the reading from Colossians and to draw out the image of the Church as the body of Christ and the solidarity in suffering of all its members.

SEVENTEENTH SUNDAY OF THE YEAR

Reading I: Genesis 18:20-32

This is another reading from the Abraham cycle. Its context is clear: God is about to destroy Sodom and Gomorrah. The J (Yahwist) tradition from which this comes uses the occasion as an opportunity to reflect on the problem of divine justice, and casts its reflections in the form of a dialogue between Abraham and Yahweh. Abraham is the mouthpiece of the conviction that Yahweh, as a God of justice, would not destroy Sodom if it also meant the destruction of a few righteous persons along with the guilty majority. Pleading his case by a kind of Dutch auction, Abraham arrives at the point where he asks Yahweh if ten righteous persons would be enough to save the city and is assured that it would. The dialogue is then broken off, but the city is not spared. So in the Genesis narrative the dialogue throws the wickedness of Sodom into even sharper relief— there were not even ten righteous persons there.

Responsorial Psalm: 138:1-3, 6-8

As the reference to the temple in verse 1 suggests, Psalm 138 is a liturgical psalm of thanksgiving for deliverance. It forms a suitable response to the reading from Genesis, in which God is depicted as a God of mercy as well as of justice.

Reading II: Colossians 2:12-14

Here is another passage in which Colossians differs from the undoubted letters of Paul. In Rom 6 Paul says that in baptism we share the death of Christ but that our rising with him is conditional on our (daily) dying to sin and walking in newness of life. It awaits its final fulfillment at the final resurrection. Colossians abandons this reservation and speaks of the baptized as already risen, though a little later it emphasizes the necessity of implementing the resurrection by ethical obedience, so it is not so far removed from the position in Romans after all.

The picture of Christ's nailing to the cross "the bond which stood against us" is intriguing. A "bond" is a kind of I.O.U. The precise background of the metaphor is uncertain. Is the writer thinking of the *titulus* on the cross, so that "The king of the Jews" means that Jesus is king of his people because he forgives them their sins? Or is it derived from the *tropaion*, the post on which a triumphant military commander would hang the spoils he had taken from the enemy? If the source of the imagery is uncertain, the meaning is clear: in the cross Christ achieved the forgiveness of sin. All Christian experience throughout the ages has known this, even if the various theories of the atonement are intellectually unsatisfying.

Gospel: Luke 11:1-13

This pericope consists of two parts: the delivery of the Lord's Prayer, followed by a catena of sayings on petitionary prayer.

The Lucan text of the Lord's Prayer in the RSV is shorter than the Matthean version, consisting of only five petitions, compared to Matthew's seven. The RSV follows the earlier Greek texts. The later text was assimilated to the Matthean form, which became traditional in the liturgy. The additional petitions of Matthew ("Thy will be done" and "But deliver us from evil") are probably liturgical expansions, each of the extra clauses being elucidations of the petition immediately preceding it. The simple address "Father" (Abba) was characteristic of Jesus. "Our Father in heaven" (Matthew) is again a formalized liturgical expansion.

A Jew of Jesus' day would have shrunk from calling God "Abba," for this was the familiar address of the child to his or her father. God would have been addressed as "our Father" or "my Father." Here lies the unique filial consciousness of Jesus, which is the foundation of his own life of obedience and of the Church's later Christological interpretation of his person. "Hallowed be thy name" is usually called the first petition, but it is probably a glorifying of the name of God, which in Jewish prayer always precedes petition. Each of the succeeding petitions is susceptible of an eschatological interpretation. Obviously this is the case with "Thy kingdom come." But the "bread" of the third petition (literally, "tomorrow's bread") quite likely means the messianic banquet. These two petitions pray for a foretaste already here and now of the blessings of the end.

"Forgive us our sins" in the fourth petition refers to the last judgment but is likewise anticipated in our justification. Our forgiveness of others does not earn God's forgiveness for us but is the condition of our continuance in forgiveness (see the parable of the unforgiving servant in Matt 18:22-35). In the next petition, "temptation" (Greek: *peirasmos*) is a technical term for the messianic woes. It is a prayer, not that God would stop tempting us to sin (for God does not do this, as St. James correctly observes), but rather for our preservation during the messianic woes, the final great tribulation, anticipated in the trials of faith during the Christian's life.

Matthew's comment on the Our Father takes up the petition for forgiveness; Luke's takes up the whole idea of petitionary prayer. Some modern devotional writers are squeamish about petitionary prayer, but in Jesus' teaching petition is prayer *par excellence*. Prayer in the Bible is primarily not mystical experience but working with God in carrying out his purposes in salvation history. The supreme petition of Christian prayer is for the Holy Spirit (v. 13). It is interesting that some ancient texts of Luke read: "Let the Holy Spirit come upon us and cleanse us," instead of the petition for tomorrow's bread. This is unlikely to be the true reading, but it is a significant early interpretation that supports the eschatological interpretation of "tomorrow's bread."

The doxology to the Lord's Prayer that appears in late texts of Matthew is not part of the original text. But it was Jewish custom to add a doxology, and Jesus probably expected his disciples to follow this. Here the *Missale Romanum* was more faithful to the letter of Scripture, while Orthodoxy and Protestantism are truer to the probable implicit intention of it!

There are parallels in Jewish prayers to every petition of the Our Father. But this does not deprive it of its originality. The meaning of each of Jesus' petitions is formed by his proclamation of the kingdom of God, not as a purely future hope, but as a reality already proleptically present in his own person.

The Homily

The most obvious choice for the homilist today would be to take the Our Father as a model of Christian prayer. It might be pointed out how it begins with God, putting his purposes first, and then goes on to our needs, but only insofar as they fit in with God's purposes.

The text from Colossians is of the type that German scholars of the Bultmann school would find rather hard to preach about, for it seems to deny the element of "not yet" in our Christian existence—we are already raised in Christ. Yet the author is not content to have Christians rest upon their laurels. As he goes on to say in chapter 3, *if* (or *since*) we are raised with him, we must live up to our new state. That needs to be brought out if the homily is based on the second reading today. This means that it would be difficult to do justice to this week's reading without drawing upon the passage assigned for next Sunday.

EIGHTEENTH SUNDAY OF THE YEAR

Reading I: Ecclesiastes 1:2; 2:21-23

Ecclesiastes is not one of the most loved books of the Bible. In fact, we may sometimes wonder why it is in the canon at all. But with that taste for shocking paradox that was characteristic of him, Sir Edwyn Hoskyns used to say that Ecclesiastes is the most Christian book in the Old Testament! What he meant was that Ecclesiastes is a ruthless exposure of what human life is apart from God and, if taken really seriously, prepares the way for a hearing of the gospel of Christ. Ecclesiastes is not so much good news as it is the bad news that has to be heard before the good news becomes audible. "Vanity of vanities"—all of human life is ultimately futile and meaningless if viewed in itself, apart from God.

Responsorial Psalm: 95:1-2, 6-9

The *Venite* consists of two parts—the first a call to worship, the second a warning against neglect of the word of God. The first part is very popular among Anglicans as the invitatory canticle of Morning Prayer, but in most recent revisions the stern warnings of the second part have frequently been omitted. Yet it was this second part that the author of Hebrews (3:7–4:13) took up and expounded as especially relevant to his church. The situation of the people of this church was that they were growing stale instead of advancing in the Christian life, just as Israel grew tired in the wilderness.

Reading II: Colossians 3:1-5, 9-11

As we have seen earlier, Colossians goes further than Romans in recognizing the risen life as already a present reality in which the baptized share. But Colossians does not overlook the need for continual reiteration of the imperative ("seek the things . . .; put to death . . .; do not lie . . ."). Maintenance of the baptismal state of being raised with Christ depends upon constantly and actively seeking to live out the risen life.

    "Seek the things that are above," that is, a "transcendent quality of living. This transcendence is not to be understood spatially, as it were,

489

suggesting a neo-Platonic escape from this present world, but a qualitatively transcendent existence within the world. Our relation to God is not a 'religious' relationship to the highest, most beautiful, powerful and best Being imaginable—but our relation to God is a new life in 'existence for others,' through participation in the being of Jesus . . . the 'man for others,' and therefore the crucified, the man who lives out of the transcendent" (D. Bonhoeffer). Hence the apostolic writer concludes, not with the individualistic ascetic that we might have expected from his initial prohibitions of immorality, etc., but with an affirmation about the Christian community as a community in which there is not "Greek and Jew, circumcised and uncircumcised, barbarian, Scythian, slave, free man." Such distinctions belong to the penultimate, not to the ultimate. It is easy to translate these human divisions into contemporary terms.

Gospel: Luke 12:13-21

The gospel of this day draws together the thoughts of the first two readings and gives them precision. The rich fool is a man who lived his life without reference to God and was caught in the toils of futility and meaninglessness ("vanity of vanities!"). He organized his life without reference to the transcendent; he did not "seek the things that are above." So comes the crashing judgment: "This night your soul [that is, your life] is required of you." Because he viewed this present existence as autonomous, without any reference to God, because he organized it without reference to the transcendent upon which it depends (note how he thought his own existence was under his own control), it came as a shock to learn that it was God's to give and God's to take away again. The rich fool condemns himself to an existence that is, qualitatively speaking, a life in death.

The Homily

The homilist should have no difficulty today in relating the three readings and the psalm. They paint a realistic picture of much of modern life, in which God is not so much denied as regarded with indifference, and in which our real focus is on material concerns. The reading from Ecclesiastes points up what life without God is like already here and now, while the gospel reading brings home to us our plight when all these material things are stripped from us. It might be thought that such warnings apply more to the world outside, but much of our bourgeois Christianity is as materialistic as the outlook of our secularized neighbors.

NINETEENTH SUNDAY OF THE YEAR

Reading I: Wisdom 18:6-9

The Book of Wisdom, which, with its philosophical approach, appears to deal in timeless truths, nevertheless contains a long section that interprets the salvation history of Israel in terms of wisdom (11:2–19:22). It contains a lot of midrashic rewriting of the biblical accounts, much of it apparently emanating from the recital of the Passover haggadah in a wisdom milieu. That is what we seem to have here. "That night" is a reference to the night of the first Passover at the Exodus (see the Easter Proclamation: "This is *the night* when first you saved our fathers"). But between the Easter Proclamation and the midrashic haggadah of the Book of Wisdom there is a shift. "Our fathers" in the Wisdom passage means the patriarchs, who are credited with having received from God the promise (here "oaths," sworn by God) of the future Exodus. The author of Wisdom again reflects the paschal liturgy of his day by attributing to Israel's first Passover his own contemporary practice of "singing the praises of the fathers," that is, the Hallel psalms.

As the Christian Church reads this passage, it does so with further shifts. The Exodus contains within it the promise of the Christian Easter, just as the revelation to the patriarchs contained within it the promise of the first Exodus. The call of Israel foreshadows the call of the *ecclesia*. But just as the old Israel was a *communio sanctorum* of the Exodus generation and the patriarchs, so the Church is a communion of saints that embraces all generations.

Responsorial Psalm: 33:1, 12, 18-20, 22

This is a psalm of thanksgiving for the mighty acts of God in salvation history. Its accent on God's choosing of the people (the refrain, "Happy the people the Lord has chosen to be his own" and the verse "Blessed . . . the people whom he has chosen as his heritage") makes it a fitting response to the reading from the Book of Wisdom.

The doctrine of election has fallen into neglect in our day, largely because of a reaction against its distortion in Calvinistic theology. It is a thoroughly biblical doctrine. It does not (as Calvinism has often said) assert that God has picked out certain individuals for salvation and consigned the rest to damnation; rather, it states that God has chosen *a people,* first the old Israel, then Christ as the sole bearer of Israel's privileges and prerogatives, and, by incorporation into him, the Christian *ecclesia,* which is ultimately to embrace in its unity (at least in principle) the whole of humankind. "It is no formal election of a set of favorites of heaven, who were to earn rewards from which the rest of the world were excluded. It was the election of a people to know what are the rights of men, that they might be witnesses to all men of *their* rights" (F. D. Maurice). In this sense we may agree with article seventeen of the Thirty-nine Articles of Religion that "the godly consideration of our election in Christ is full of sweet, pleasant and unspeakable comfort."

Reading II: Hebrews 11:1-2, 8-19 (long form); 11:1-2, 8-12 (short form)

The eleventh chapter of the letter to the Hebrews is sometimes called "the roll call of the heroes of faith." Yet, strictly speaking, the Bible knows no heroes, for heroes are witnesses to their own achievements, whereas in Heb 11 the great figures of salvation history are brought forth, not for their heroism, but for their "faith," which, in the author's thought, is closely linked with hope. Faith is taking God at his word when he makes promises for the future. Thus, the Old Testament figures become examples for the new Israel, the new wandering people of God. The new people has also in each succeeding generation had to imitate Abraham, who "went out, not knowing where he was to go," and his family, who lived in tents because they had no abiding city here, but "looked forward to the city which has foundations."

Gospel: Luke 12:32-48 (long form); 12:35-40 (short form)

The core of this section of Luke is the parable of the waiting servants (vv. 35-38). There is a remarkable convergence between the first reading and this gospel, for in its Lucan form the original parable of the doorkeeper (see Mark 13) has been expanded with elements taken from the Christian paschal feast: "Let your loins be girded [see Exod 12:11] and your lamps burning, and be like men who are waiting for their master to come home." The early Christians literally believed that the return of their Lord would take place at the Passover, as the first Israel believed that the Messiah would come that night. When the Christ did not return literally at midnight, the Church celebrated the agape-Eucharist, in which he came in advance of his final coming. So the promise was fulfilled: "He will gird himself and have them sit at table and he will come and serve them." Every Eucharist, especially every Sunday Eucharist, is a reflection of the paschal Eucharist, and so the same promise is fulfilled here, too.

At the same time, the essential attitude enjoined upon the disciples— "Watch"— is a counterpart of the attitude inculcated in the second reading—the attitude of a faith that is prepared to go out, not knowing where it is to go. Both speak in different ways of that readiness to be on the move, not to get bogged down in false securities on the assumption that we have here an abiding city.

The Homily

In a remarkable way, here, in the middle of summer, the readings bring together themes that we associate with Easter and Advent. They might serve to remind us that in this apparently uninteresting season of ordinary time, the weekly Eucharist derives its meaning from those seasons when we look back and celebrate the mighty acts of God in the past and the saints and great figures of the past whom he has used to accomplish his purposes, and when we await the future consummation of history.

TWENTIETH SUNDAY OF THE YEAR

Reading I: Jeremiah 38:4-6, 8-10

This is the episode of Jeremiah in the muddy cistern. Jeremiah has been predicting the impending destruction of Jerusalem as a judgment from Yahweh. Quite naturally, the government regards this kind of talk as defeatist and treasonable, so it seeks to silence Jeremiah by lowering him into a muddy cistern. But on this occasion his life is spared through the good offices of Ebed-melech the Ethiopian.

The caption, "You bore me to be a man of strife for the whole world," which comes, not from this reading, but from Jeremiah's prayer (Jer 15:10, though the meaning there is probably "the whole land," that is, Judah, rather than "the whole world"), indicates that our interpretation of this reading today should concentrate, not upon Jeremiah's deliverance, but upon the fact that his proclamation of the word of Yahweh brought him rejection and suffering. Thus, the passion of Jeremiah foreshadows the passion of Jesus, adumbrated in the gospel reading.

Responsorial Psalm: 40:1-3, 17

A different selection of verses from this psalm is used on the second Sunday of the year in series A and is commented upon there. The reference to the "miry bog" in the second stanza links the psalm with the first reading. However, the main point today is the deliverance of the psalmist, whereas the main point of the Old Testament reading, as we saw from the caption and the gospel, lies in the rejection that results from being a bearer of the word of God.

Reading II: Hebrews 12:1-4

This is the exhortation concluding the roll call of Old Testament heroes of the faith. They were "witnesses" to the power of faith to endure against every temptation to apostasy. The author of Hebrews pictures the Old Testament worthies as a host ("cloud"—a good classical Greek term) of spectators standing by a racetrack and cheering on those who are now running the same race as they did in their day. The race we have to run is "set before us," that is, we have been entered for it (cf. the New English Bible) at our baptism. Like athletes stripping for the contest, we must strip ourselves of the constriction (this is the connotation of the adjective translated "which clings so closely") of sin.

But there is one who is even greater than the heroes of the Old Testament—Jesus, here described as the "pioneer and perfecter of our faith." In his earthly life he was the pioneer because he initiated the way of faith—the way through suffering to glory (v. 2b)—and its perfecter because he completed it, thus enabling believers to run the same race, through suffering to glory.

In the second paragraph of our reading, which begins a new section of Hebrews, the writer returns, as so often throughout his work, from Christological exposition to ethical exhortation bearing directly on the situation in the church to which he is writing. These believers were subject to hostility from their neighbors (pagan? Jewish?), but none of them have had to suffer martyrdom yet.

Gospel: Luke 12:49-53

The reading falls into two parts. The first (vv. 49-50) speaks of Christ's divine destiny to endure suffering. This first block of material is peculiar to Luke. The second part (vv. 51-53) speaks of the breakup of families caused by Christ and his message. This second block of material is paralleled in Matt 10:34-35. We will first consider the two parts separately and then discuss the implications for Luke's theology of his procedure in bringing them together.

The first part consists of two "I sayings," in which Jesus speaks of his mission as an accomplished fact. The first saying may well be authentic to Jesus, expressing his consciousness of prophetic mission, whereas the second saying, which refers to his martyrdom as a baptism (cf. Mark 10:38), looks like a *vaticinium ex eventu*, reflecting Christian baptismal theology (cf. Rom 6). This second saying is probably an amplification of the first authentic "I saying" by the early Church. The "fire" (a symbol of eschatological judgment) that Jesus came to cast upon the earth will be his call to decision in face of his eschatological message. The Church's additional "I saying," with its explicit reference to Jesus' death, will mean that after Easter Jesus' eschatological message was replaced by the Church's kerygma of the cross. This kerygma, too, calls for a decision.

The second (Q) saying, about the breakup of family ties, reflects an apocalyptic tradition going back to Mic 7:6. "Social disruption has always been associated in the oriental mind with the reign of terror which will precede the age of salvation, and it is not surprising that it figures in Jewish apocalyptic as one of the signs of the end" (J. Jeremias). It is difficult to be certain whether this saying goes back to Jesus himself or only to the post-Easter community. The situation, however, was found both in Jesus' ministry as a result of his call to decision and in the post-Easter community as a result of its kerygma of the cross.

By putting together these two traditions—the two "I sayings" and the saying about family divisions—Luke shows that the breakup of families is a consequence precisely of the kerygma of the cross. Luke has recently been criticized and downgraded for having no theology of the cross. It is true that he does not, like Paul and Mark, speak of the cross as an atoning death—but see Luke 22:19b-20 ["'. . . which is given for you. Do this in remembrance of me.' And likewise the cup after supper, saying, 'This cup which is poured out for you is the new covenant in my blood.'"], which is now generally regarded as authentically Lucan and not a textual addition, and which shows that Luke was familiar with the idea of atonement in liturgy.

Even though Luke does not appropriate the language of atonement for his own theology, he does have his own theology of the cross. It is that the cross is for Christ the divinely willed pathway to glory (see 24:26). Believers in turn are drawn into the same pathway of suffering (see the second part of our reading). This suffering may take various forms: rejection, ostracism from family and society, and, though this is not specified here, martyrdom.

The Homily

The message of today's readings may be summed up in the familiar saying "No cross, no crown." This was true of Jeremiah; of the cloud of witnesses; of Jesus, the pioneer and perfecter of our faith, who came to bring fire and to be baptized with a baptism of martyrdom; of the early Christians, who, as a consequence, experienced the breakup of families; and of many Christians today. It should not be difficult for the homilist to identify the precise form the cross takes in the lives of contemporary believers and to encourage them to run with endurance the race in which they have been entered.

TWENTY-FIRST SUNDAY OF THE YEAR

Reading I: Isaiah 66:18-21

The gathering together of all peoples of the world at Zion at the beginning of the messianic age is a frequent picture of the Isaianic and other Old Testament prophecies. Christian faith sees the fulfillment of these prophecies partly in the bringing of people from all nations into the catholic Church, and partly in the future coming of the Son of man to gather all the nations of the world into his kingdom.

John Mason Neale's translation of an early Eastern Orthodox hymn expresses this typology and this faith:

> Rise, Sion, rise, and looking forth
>   behold thy children round thee!
> From east and west, from south and north,
>   thy scattered sons have found thee:
> And in thy bosom Christ adore
> For ever and for ever more.

Responsorial Psalm: 117:1-2

This psalm, which calls upon all nations to praise the name of Yahweh, is cited by St. Paul (Rom 15:11) in a catena of Old Testament texts to illustrate the universal scope of God's redemptive purpose in Christ. It is, therefore, an appropriate response to the Old Testament reading, with its picture of the movement of all peoples to Zion.

Reading II: Hebrews 12:5-7, 11-13

At first sight this reading is divergent in theme from the other readings of this Sunday. Elsewhere the theme is the universality of the gospel; here it is the divine disciplining of the faithful.

Hebrews alternates between ethical exhortation and doctrinal-exegetical exposition. The exposition, which reaches it culmination in the long section on the high-priestly office of Christ (7:1–10:18), is intended to undergird the exhortation. This exhortation reflects the situation of the author's readers. They have been Christian for a long time and are yielding to discouragement and frustration. The "discipline" to which they are being subjected is probably not acute persecution but the petty pinpricks of their non-Christian neighbors.

Gospel: Luke 13:22-30

This passage, which culminates in the great proclamation that many will come from east and west and take their place in the kingdom of God, begins somewhat unpromisingly with the assertion (in response to the question whether many or only a few will be saved) that one can only enter that kingdom by a narrow door. The universalism of the Christian gospel is no easygoing thing. It is intended for all but is offered through Christ alone. The universality goes hand in hand with the "scandal of particularity." The messianic banquet is for those who are prepared to "eat the flesh" of the Messiah and to "drink his blood."

The Homily

The first reading, the psalm, and the gospel taken together suggest the common theme of the universality of the messianic banquet. The homilist could portray the anticipation of this in the life of the catholic Church, in which people of all nations are brought together before the throne of God. Does the Church in its life really transcend all differences of race, class, and sex? Where is there room for change in order that the Church may become more truly what it is?

The reading from Hebrews can be connected with the other readings about the universality of the Church in a way similar to the procedure of Hebrews itself. Christians today are not suffering acute persecution in most places, but they are troubled by the drift from the Churches and by the prevailing contempt for the gospel. This reading tells us that we have to face this "painful rather than pleasant" period because the Lord is disciplining his people. This discipline, however, is a sign of his love for his Church. Then the other readings undergird this exhortation with the reassurance that the gospel is indeed "catholic," for all people and for all times, and that all nations *are* destined to come into God's kingdom.

TWENTY-SECOND SUNDAY OF THE YEAR

Reading I: Sirach 3:17-18, 20, 28-29

This is a lesson on humility, chosen to fit the gospel of the day. Pride is the deadliest of the seven deadly sins, while humility is perhaps the most characteristic of Christian virtues. The humble person finds "favor in the sight of the Lord," not because that favor is a reward for humility, but because humility, like faith, means abandoning self-assertion, all trust in one's own righteousness, and allowing God to act where we can do nothing.

Responsorial Psalm: 68:3-4ac, 5-6b, 9-10

Psalm 68 is a confused melee of themes, thought by some scholars to be a series of headings to a number of different liturgical pieces rather than a unitary psalm. To read it is rather like reading the chapter headings of a book. Nevertheless, it contains passages of considerable beauty, and it is possible, as is done here, to combine excerpts from it into a meaningful hymn. This selection is a hymn of praise to God for granting his favor to the poor (the "humble" of the second reading).

Reading II: Hebrews 12:18-19, 22-24a

This reading from Hebrews would have fit last Sunday's theme far better—the movement to Zion. It presents a contrast between the law and the gospel, between Mount Sinai and Mount Zion. Coming to this mountain is the favor the Lord grants to the "humble."

Gospel: Luke 14:1, 7-14

The parables read here (vv. 7-11) and the ensuing exhortation are connected by their common context in a meal of Jesus. The parable looks like a piece of prudential advice on how to behave at a dinner party so as to avoid embarrassment. But since it is a parable, it must not be interpreted as a piece of worldly wisdom or even as a lesson in humility, as usually understood. It deals rather with an aspect of one's relationship with God. God, in the person of Jesus (see verse 8), is inviting all people to the messianic feast. The only way to respond to this invitation is to renounce any claim or merit of one's own. The Pharisees expected the best seats as a reward for keeping the Torah, but, like the outcast, they have to learn that salvation has to be accepted as an unmerited gift— exactly as we interpreted humility in the first reading.

The ensuing exhortation is likewise not a piece of worldly advice but a kind of parable, its point being that people's final acceptance at the messianic banquet depends on their acceptance of others now. In other words, forgive and God will forgive you. Thus, humility in the Christian sense is not purely a passive virtue; like faith, to which it is closely akin, it is highly active.

The Homily

The first reading and the gospel suggest a homily on the topic of Christian humility. This is a virtue that we can hardly attain by our own efforts, for then we become like Dickens' unattractive character Uriah Heep, who was always protesting, "What an 'umble man I am." Rather, humility is something that grows in us as the unconscious effect of being humbled on our knees before God in penitence. The lives of the saints give us plenty of examples with which to illustrate this. The homilist could also relate the coming to Mount Zion rather than to Mount Sinai with the theme of humility, as suggested in the commentary on the second reading.

TWENTY-THIRD SUNDAY OF THE YEAR

Today's three readings have very different themes: the discernment of God's will, possible only through the Spirit of God; the transformation of personal relations in Christ; and the renunciation of possessions as the prerequisite for true discipleship. It would tax our utmost ingenuity to discover a common theme in the three readings. The only discernible connection of thought is between the first reading and the responsorial psalm.

Reading I: Wisdom 9:13-18

This is part of the prayer that the Book of Wisdom puts on the lips of Solomon. The earliest version of Solomon's prayer is in 1 Kgs 3:6-9, where he prays for "understanding." Then comes 2 Chr 1:9-10, where he prays for "wisdom" to help him in performing the duties of kingship. The author of Wisdom expands on this point and enunciates the doctrine that the will of God can only be discerned by the help of wisdom and the Spirit of God—the parallelism suggesting that the two concepts are synonymous.

While verse 15 recalls Plato's *Phaedo*, the author does not teach a non-biblical dualism of body/soul. The body is a hindrance to the knowledge of God's will, not the seat of evil. It is its finite, not evil, character that is its drawback. Only God's Spirit, or wisdom, enables us to transcend that finitude.

Responsorial Psalm: 90:3-6, 12-14, 17

Verses 3-6, from the first part of the psalm, point up the contrast between God's eternity and human mortality. Compare this with the first part of the first reading. Verses 12-14, 17 come from the second half of the psalm, which is a prayer for God's favor as a compensation for human beings' fleeting life, so that despite their transitoriness their work may prosper. The prayer for wisdom in verse 12 recalls Solomon's prayer.

Reading II: Philemon 9b-10, 12-17

The letter to Philemon is the only personal letter of Paul that has survived. Onesimus, a slave who had run away from his master, Philemon, a Christian of Colossae, had joined Paul where the latter was in prison (Rome is the traditional view; Ephesus is popular today because of the distances involved: Colossae-Ephesus rather than Colossae-Rome). Under Paul's influence, Onesimus had become a Christian. In sending him back to his master, Paul commends him as "no longer a slave but a brother." Paul did not thereby abolish slavery (that would have been impossible for the ancient world) but transformed the relationship between master and slave. Not until the nineteenth century did the Christian conscience come to realize that slavery as an institution is wrong. Paul drew what consequences he could from his principle that in Christ there is neither slave nor free. Future generations will have to give their own implementation to that principle in the light of their concrete situation.

Gospel: Luke 14:25-33

This gospel consists of a string of sayings on the cost of discipleship, followed by two parables to illustrate the necessity of facing that cost (the tower-builder and the king going to war).

"Hate" (v. 26) is harsh. It has been suggested that the original Aramaic meant simply "love less than." But this in turn is probably too weak. The real meaning is that following Jesus means the surrender of the whole of one's life. Then, as we have already noted in an earlier passage, the disciple receives back from Christ those aspects of the old life that are now needed to provide the context in which the claims of discipleship have to be worked out.

The saying in verse 27 does not mean that all true disciples must be martyrs in the literal sense. Yet, martyrdom is discipleship carried to its ultimate conclusion. Hence the honor the Church has always paid to its martyrs.

The Homily

As we said above, there is a notable disparity of themes in today's readings. Accordingly, the homilist is advised to concentrate upon one of them and to disregard the others.

The reading from the Book of Wisdom deals with the question: How can I discern what is God's will for me? The homilist can point out the various ways in which we obtain the assistance of the Holy Spirit: through prayer and Bible reading; through the advice of other Christians, including our spiritual advisors; and imperceptibly through our participation in the regular liturgical life of the Church.

The letter to Philemon calls upon us to allow the Spirit of Christ to transform our relationships with others. It also poses the question (with which Paul does not deal): Do we have to change society before we can change personal relations, or does the change of personal relations lead

to changes in social structure? Should the Church support political liberation movements, or is its task to convert individuals and promote their
growth in holiness?

The gospel raises the uncomfortable question: How can a bourgeois
Church renounce all its possessions as a precondition for discipleship?

TWENTY-FOURTH SUNDAY OF THE YEAR

Reading I: Exodus 32:7-11, 13-14

The caption calls attention to Yahweh's abandonment of his intention to
punish Israel for making the golden calf and worshiping it. But the really
significant feature of the text is Moses' action as a mediator. He makes
intercession for the Israelites by pleading the promise of God to the
patriarchs. This picture caught the attention of the psalmist (Ps 106:23).
In this respect, as in others, Moses foreshadows the messianic work of
Christ.

There is no New Testament passage that directly recalls this incident,
but the same mediatorial function is ascribed to Jesus as is performed here
by Moses. On the cross Jesus prays: "Father, forgive them." He now lives
in heaven as the high priest to make intercession for his people (though
in Hebrews this is Aaronic rather than Mosaic typology); and he is given
the title "mediator" between God and his people (1 Tim 2:5, to be read
next Sunday) as Moses had been mediator between Yahweh and Israel.

Responsorial Psalm: 51:1-2, 10-11, 15, 17

It will help us to relate this psalm to the foregoing reading if we think
of it as uttered by Christ in his capacity as mediator. He takes our sin
upon himself, even to the extent of confessing our sin on our behalf. In
his work *Atonement and Personality* (1917), R. C. Moberly, an Anglican,
built up an impressive interpretation of the atonement as a perfect act of
repentance performed by Christ on our behalf.

Reading II: 1 Timothy 1:12-17

If, as many modern scholars think, the pastoral letters are the work of
a later author who was a member of the Pauline school, this passage is
nevertheless thoroughly impregnated with the mind of the Apostle. It
speaks of the understanding of the atonement that Paul acquired in the
miracle of his apostolic call. That was a sheer act of "overflowing grace"
to one who acknowledged himself to be the "foremost of sinners" because
he had persecuted the Church.

Gospel: Luke 15:1-32 (long form); 15:1-10 (short form)

The gospel consists of three parables: the twin parables of the lost sheep and the lost coin, and the parable of the prodigal son. (The short form gives only the twin parables.) The parable of the prodigal son already occurred by itself on the fourth Sunday of Lent in series C (q.v.). Prefaced   *413* by the twin parables, the story of the prodigal son acquires an accent it does not have when it stands alone. Taken alone, the emphasis is on the prodigal son's initiative in returning home. The twin parables emphasize the prevenient action of God in seeking and saving the lost, a thought that is then carried over into understanding the action of the father in the third parable: while the returning prodigal was still at a distance, his father "ran" and welcomed him home.

Thus understood, all three parables are linked with the atonement, which, as we have seen, runs like a thread through all the readings of the day. While the earlier readings employed the Christ-to-God aspect of the atonement, the gospel balances this aspect with the movement of God through Christ to humankind. The atonement is not the human act of the Son appeasing an angry Deity, but God's gift to his people, in which he undertakes to do for them what they could not do for themselves. Christ is the presence of God in human form for our sake, seeking and saving the lost.

The Homily

Do we need a mediator between ourselves and God? That question is suggested by the Old Testament reading. The gospel reading at first sight suggests that we do not. Did the prodigal son not go straight to his father? Eduard Schweizer has asked, Where is Jesus in this parable? The answer is that the parable is a commentary on what Jesus was doing—seeking out and saving the lost. He does that still in his word and sacrament, and it is there that we experience his mediation. The parable of the prodigal son puts in story form what the author of 1 Timothy puts in theological language: "Christ Jesus came into the world to save sinners."

TWENTY-FIFTH SUNDAY OF THE YEAR

Reading I: Amos 8:4-7

Amos, the prophet of social justice *par excellence,* denounces the rich who just cannot wait for the new moon festival or the sabbath day to be over so that they may engage in business and make profits, cheating and exploiting the poor in the process. He threatens them with divine judgment.

Responsorial Psalm: 113:1-2, 4-8

This is one of the first Hallel psalms (113–118), so called because they begin with "Alleluia" and celebrate the mighty acts of Yahweh. Verses 7-8 provide a striking contrast to verses 4-6, between the majesty of Yahweh and his condescension to the "poor." It is doubtless because of these final verses, with their reference to God's vindication of the poor, that this psalm was chosen as a response to the reading from Amos.

Reading II: 1 Timothy 2:1-8

Much of 1 Timothy consists of a Church order, setting out the duties of the Church's ministry and (so here) describing the liturgical activities of the Christian assembly. It represents an attempt on the part of the Pauline churches to consolidate their life after the pioneering missionary work of the Apostle.

Since the time of Cyrus, the Jewish community had prayed even for its pagan rulers, and the Church continues this practice. Such prayer recognizes the function of the state in relation to the gospel. If the state functions properly, it creates those outward conditions of tranquility under which the gospel may be preached and the life of the community may flourish. This positive view of the function of the state is found in most places in the New Testament (see especially Rom 13). But there is another side to the state—its potentially demonic side (Rev 13). Yet even the demonic state continues to fulfill some of its God-given functions of maintaining domestic peace and justice (there were police even in Nazi Germany, and they were not all brutal). To that extent it still merits the prayers and obedience of the Christian community, even if at other points some kind of resistance is the order of the day.

Gospel: Luke 16:1-13 (long form); 16:10-13 (short form)

The gospel consists of the parable of the unjust steward, followed by a string of sayings on the right use of wealth. These sayings probably did not originally belong to the parable, for the parable itself hardly intends to hold up the unjust steward as an example of the right use of wealth!

Taken by itself, the parable is a challenge of Jesus to his contemporaries to make a drastic decision for the coming kingdom of God before it is too late (cf. the parable of the wise and the foolish virgins). The string of sayings gives a new application to the parable: the disciples are to show as much intelligence in the use of wealth as the unjust steward did in his own interests.

The Homily

All the readings of this Sunday have some bearing on Christian responsibilities in relation to social justice, politics, and wealth, though, as we have seen, the proper interpretation of the gospel is problematical. The teaching about stewardship does not immediately arise from the parable, but, as has been suggested (F. C. Grant), the string of sayings following the parable represents some early preacher's sermon notes. Consequently, they had best be treated in separation from the parable. This would certainly have to be done by Episcopalians, who at this time of the year need to preach on Christian stewardship!

TWENTY-SIXTH SUNDAY OF THE YEAR

Reading I: Amos 6:1a, 4-7

Last Sunday's Old Testament reading dealt with the question of social injustice. Today's reading is a denunciation of private luxury. It forms a fitting companion reading for the parable of Dives and Lazarus, which is the gospel of the day.

Responsorial Psalm: 146:6c-10

This psalm initiates the last group of Alleluia psalms in the psalter, all of them hymns of praise to Yahweh for his mighty acts. Again, this psalm is highly fitting for this Sunday. Verses 9-10 echo the denunciation of the rich in the first reading and God's concern for the poor, the hungry, and the oppressed. It thus looks forward to the gospel.

Reading II: 1 Timothy 6:11-16

This passage from 1 Tim 6 has been interpreted as an ordination charge (E. Käsemann). In this charge the ordinand is reminded of the confession of faith made at baptism. The ordained minister has to teach this faith to others. This suggests an important relation between ordination and baptism. Ordination is the form that the fulfillment of their baptismal vocation takes for some. The "commandment" may be the actual ordination charge (see Moses' charge to Joshua at his ordination in Num 27:19), an Old Testament type that provided both the synagogue and the early Church (see Hippolytus' ordinal) with the model for their ordination practices.

Gospel: Luke 16:19-31

The first part of the parable of Dives and Lazarus is a well-known folk tale relating the reversal of fortunes in the next world. It is a conventional piece of moralizing. As so often with the Gospel parables, however, there is a surprise at the end—the dialogue between Dives and Abraham. This is where the real point of the parable lies. The rich man asks that Lazarus be allowed to convey a special warning to his five brothers, who are still alive. The answer is that they have the word of Scripture, and that is sufficient. Those who are unmoved by the message of Scripture will not be convinced by a miracle either, even by a resurrection. Such, presumably, was Jesus' point in telling the parable.

By placing the parable after the string of sayings on the right use of wealth, which follows the parable of the unjust steward, Luke (and evidently the compilers of the Lectionary) calls attention to the conventional part of the story—the reversal of the fortune of the rich and the poor in the next world.

Since the first part of the parable is conventional, it would be wrong to build up a doctrine of the next life on the reference to Abraham's bosom.

The Homily

In certain circumstances (for example, if an ordination is coming up in the diocese) it might be a suitable occasion to preach about ordination, as suggested by the second reading. The handing on of apostolic tradition faithfully from generation to generation is powerfully symbolized by the laying on of hands by a bishop in apostolic succession.

The Old Testament reading and the gospel provide a continuation of last Sunday's theme of the responsible use of wealth.

TWENTY-SEVENTH SUNDAY OF THE YEAR

Reading I: Habakkuk 1:2-3; 2:2-4

These verses give the gist of the three parts of Habakkuk. First the prophet cries out against the injustices that he and his people are suffering at the hand of foreign conquerors. How long will Yahweh let this go on and not intervene? Then comes the answer: Yahweh *will* intervene, but in his own good time. It may seem slow, but come it will. Meanwhile, the attitude required of Yahweh's servants is what the prophet calls "faith": "the righteous shall live by his faith." The meaning of the word translated as "faith" here (*'emunah*) is steadfast loyalty, holding on in obedience to Yahweh's law, even when it apparently pays no dividends. This word becomes very important both for the Qumran covenant and for the New Testament.

In the Qumran commentary on Habakkuk we read: "This [that is, our saying] refers to all in Jewry who carry out the law [that is, to the Qumraners]. On account of their labor and their faith in him who expounded the law aright [that is, the sect's founder, the Teacher of Righteousness] God will deliver them from the house of judgment." Here faith has already acquired its New Testament sense of personal trust. Compare Rom 1:17 and Gal 3:11, which develop the notion of personal trust adumbrated at Qumran to mean trust in the justifying act of God in Christ toward the ungodly. Hab 2:4 thus becomes the key text for Paul's doctrine of justification—a considerable development from the original meaning in Habakkuk. Heb 10:38 reverts closer to the original sense. For this author, faith recovers its meaning of holding on in the midst of adversity.

Responsorial Psalm: 95:1-2, 6-9

For commentary on this psalm, the reader is referred to the eighteenth Sunday of the year in series C. 492

Reading II: 2 Timothy 1:6-8, 13-14

Although belonging to the Pauline corpus, the Pastoral Epistles are widely regarded as deutero-Pauline, written within the Pauline school but reflecting the conditions of the generation after the Apostle himself and seeking to preserve his teaching in the new situation.

Two features of this passage may reflect the subapostolic situation: (1) the channeling of the ministerial *charismata* through the laying on of hands instead of by direct inspiration, as in 1 Corinthians ("the gift that is within you through the laying on of my hands"); (2) the consolidation of the apostolic message into a "pattern of sound words." Ernst Käsemann has characterized these developments as "early catholicism," which for him is a loaded term implying degeneration and corruption. But they can be recognized as legitimate and necessary adaptations in the changed situation, following the decease of the apostles and their consequent inability to exercise the kind of personal control over the *charismata* that Paul did in 1 Corinthians. For "Timothy"—and therefore all successors to the ministry of the apostles—must not merely preserve the tradition but give living testimony to it, that is, unpackage it and make it relevant to the contemporary world. Such testimony, the text warns, will involve a "share of suffering for the gospel." Newman, in his Anglican days, once startled the comfortable bishops of the established Church by saying, "We could not wish them a more blessed termination of their course than the spoiling of their goods and martyrdom" (Tract 1, 1833). Very unrealistic in the situation, no doubt, but soundly based on our text.

Gospel: Luke 17:5-10

The request "Increase our faith" comes immediately after a warning to beware of temptations to faith (*skandala*). The parable, which forms the second half of our gospel reading, is connected with the saying about faith, because it warns the disciples against supposing that faith, and the obedient service of the Lord in which faith is expressed, establishes a claim for reward. "When you have done all that is commanded you, say 'We are unworthy servants; we have only done what was our duty.'"

The Homily

The homilist could take up the first part of the gospel—the request for an increase of faith—and relate it to the Habakkuk saying taken in its original sense. Then the saying about the sycamore tree could be used as a vivid though deliberately absurd illustration of the power of faith.

If the homilist decides to concentrate upon the parable of the unprofitable servants, this could be linked with the Pauline doctrine of justification by faith and not by works, stated more concretely in Jesus' aphorism about the unprofitable servants.

As a third possibility, the homilist could develop the New Testament concept of apostolic succession as involving the guardianship of the apostolic faith, but also living testimony and preparedness for suffering. The elder Archbishop Temple inscribed over an archway at Lambeth Palace: "Apostolorum nobis vindicamus non honores sed labores."

TWENTY-EIGHTH SUNDAY OF THE YEAR

Reading I: 2 Kings 5:14-17

The most significant feature in the story about Naaman the Syrian occurs prior to our pericope. Naaman expected a spectacular cure and was annoyed when Elisha told him to go and wash in the Jordan—that puny little ditch, when there were far greater rivers back home! Reluctantly, Naaman was persuaded to try it. Jordan stands for the "scandal of particularity." There is no other name under heaven by which we must be saved. The gate is narrow, and the way is hard, that leads to life. Unless you eat the flesh of the Son of man and drink his blood, you have no life in you.

In antiquity, leprosy was regarded as the worst of diseases, and its cure an impossibility. Thus, the story became a parable of human beings' plight, from which they would only be delivered by the Messiah, that is, by a miracle at the end of time.

Another aspect of this story, which is taken up by the New Testament in Jesus' sermon in the synagogue at Nazareth (Luke 4:16-30), is the fact that Naaman was a Syrian and therefore excluded from the community of Israel. Thus, his healing foreshadows the universality of messianic salvation. Rejected by Israel, that salvation would be opened up to the Gentiles: "There were many lepers in Israel in the time of the prophet Elisha; none of them was cleansed, but only Naaman the Syrian" (Luke 4:27).

This theme of universality is also picked up in the gospel of the day, in which the nine lepers from the chosen people did not return to give thanks, but only the tenth, and he was a Samaritan.

Responsorial Psalm: 98:1-4

Psalm 98 is from a collection of magnificent enthronement psalms (Psalms 93, 96–100; see our comments on the responsorial psalm of Ascension Day). They are full of exuberant joy at the saving power of Yahweh, visibly expressed (according to scholarly theory) in the enthronement of the king at the new-year festival.

The refrain underlines the fact that the "nations" see God's saving power. If, as some think, the psalm originally celebrated Israel's return from exile in Babylon—it is certainly imbued with the theology of Second Isaiah, as the words "saving power," "victory," and "vindication" show— the nations are passive witnesses rather than active participants in the divine salvation. As spectators, they watch Israel return from exile and see in it an act of Yahweh's self-vindication. But in the Christian liturgical community, for which the saving power of God is manifested in the Christ-

89

event, this must be reinterpreted to mean that the nations actually participate in the salvation.

Reading II: 2 Timothy 2:8-13

Even if the modern critical view of the Pastorals as deutero-Pauline is correct (see last Sunday's comments), the first paragraph of this reading may well be part of Paul's genuine farewell letter to Timothy, onto which the passages directed against Gnosticism and toward setting up a Church order were grafted by the deutero-Pauline author. In any case, this passage fittingly reflects Paul's situation in prison at Rome just before his martyrdom. There is a poignant contrast between the Apostle's own condition—wearing fetters like a criminal—and his confident assertion that the word of God is not bound. (I heard this as a sermon text more than once in Germany during the Church struggle, when Pastor Niemöller and others were imprisoned by the Gestapo.)

Paul is also confident that his suffering will contribute to the forward movement of salvation history: "I endure everything for the sake of the elect, that they also may obtain the salvation . . . ." This notion is fairly common in the Pauline writings (see the catalogues of Paul's sufferings in 2 Corinthians and also Col 1:24). Here would be the basis for developing a scriptural understanding of the doctrine of the "merits" of the saints: suffering offered obediently to God is like prayer in that it contributes to the furthering of God's saving purpose.

The final part of the reading consists of an early Christian hymn, based on the Pauline conception of dying/rising with Christ (Rom 6), the dominical saying about confessing/denying Jesus now, and the Son of man confessing/denying the disciple accordingly at the parousia (Matt 10:33 and par.). Very striking is the twist given in the last two lines: even if we are faithless, God still remains faithful. This is quite contrary to the parallelisms of the three succeeding parts. The hymn is quoted here because its opening part illustrates the preceding verse, but then, like so many similar quotations, continues after it ceases to be relevant to its context, thereby proving that we do have a quotation here.

Gospel: Luke 17:11-19

We have already suggested how this reading may be linked with the first reading, and how cleansing from leprosy is a type of the messianic salvation. Also, we have called attention to another link between this gospel and the Old Testament reading—the universality of messianic salvation. But there is another theme in the gospel that could be developed, and that is the theme of gratitude. It is striking that all ten lepers were healed. The grateful one got no more than the others did, except the assurance from the Lord, "Your faith has made you well." Nor did the other lepers lose what they had. There was no punitive miracle returning them to their leprous state.

There is much to meditate upon here. The gifts of God are without repentance; gratitude has no ulterior motivation, for example to secure further blessings. Ingratitude is perhaps the most common of all human failings, as Shakespeare observed: "Blow, blow thou winter cold; thou art not so unkind as man's ingratitude."

The Homily

The homilist could develop either theme from the story of Naaman—the scandal of particularity or the universality of messianic salvation. Both themes can be related to the gospel; the second could also be related to the responsorial psalm.

If the homilist chooses the scandal of particularity as the theme, it gives an opportunity to answer the "blue domers," who ask, "Why go to church when I can worship God in the open air?" God has chosen *this* way for salvation—Christ alone, the word and sacrament alone—here on this Sunday morning. If the universality of messianic salvation is the theme, the homilist can counter the idea that salvation is the monopoly of wasps, including Catholic wasps!

There is a wealth of material for the preacher in the second reading. Paul's imprisonment and his confidence that his sufferings contribute to the advancement of God's purpose could be related to the imprisonment of Christians for their faith in various parts of the world today. Then, too, an authentically scriptural understanding of the doctrine of the merits of the saints could be provided. Or the homilist could take the hymn and expound the faithfulness of God, even when Christians deny him. What seems difficult, however, is to relate this reading to any of the other readings of the day, and it probably should not be attempted.

If the homilist wants to develop the theme of human ingratitude from the gospel reading, Albert Schweitzer's sermons on gratitude in *Reverence for Life* (New York: Harper and Row, 1969) would be recommended reading.

TWENTY-NINTH SUNDAY OF THE YEAR

Reading I: Exodus 17:8-13

It is puzzling to find this reading appointed for today. It has no apparent connection with any of the other readings except on one questionable interpretation (see below). It does not follow in sequence the first reading of the previous Sunday, nor does it appear to be particularly edifying. Despite the assurance in the second reading that "all scripture is inspired by God and profitable for teaching," the New Testament writers never make use of this incident. Their use of the Old Testament was definitely à la carte (see C. H. Dodd, *According to the Scriptures* [London: Nisbet, 1952] and B. Lindars, *New Testament Apologetic* [Philadelphia: Westminster, 1961]). The passage could be given a typological interpretation of Moses holding up his hands in intercessory prayer (so the *Jerome Biblical Commentary*), but this interpretation is uncertain. Moses' action is probably meant to be symbolic, like those of the prophets, which were thought to have potent influence on the course of events (so *Peake's Commentary*).

Responsorial Psalm: 121:1-8

This beautiful psalm of trust in divine protection needs little comment. If we have accepted the intercessory interpretation of the first reading, this psalm forms an excellent response to God's protection of his Church militant on earth. In any case, it suggests a reflection on the biblical truth behind the dogma of the "infallibility" of the Church, namely, that God will never finally forsake his Church, however severe his judgment upon it may be from time to time. His care and protection of the Church is exactly like that shown to the first Israel—never abandoning it, restoring it even after exile.

Reading II: 2 Timothy 3:14-4:2

This reading is taken from those parts of the Pastoral Epistles that register the concern of the subapostolic age to preserve apostolic truth (see above, twenty-seventh Sunday of the year). Of the whole body of the Church's tradition, Scripture is the most important part. "The New Testament canon appears not as separate from, or opposed to, the Christian tradition, but rather as an expression of it" (*Principles of Church Union*, 1966). One cannot be sure that the "Pastor" (that is, the author or redactor of these letters) meant by "sacred writings" or "scripture" our New Testament as well as the Old Testament. Most likely not, for there is no indication elsewhere in these letters that an embryonic canon of New Testament writings was already in formation. But certainly, as we read this passage today, it can be legitimately extended to cover both the Old Testament and the New Testament.

While the Pastoral Epistles are in some sense directed to the Church at large, their primary aim is to instruct the Church's ministers in apostolic succession. Hence one of the most important duties of the "man of God" (this is a term accorded to Moses in the Old Testament tradition, suggesting a possible link with the first reading) is the study of Scripture. This was nowhere put so well as by Cranmer in the ordinal of the Book of Common Prayer, in the bishop's exhortation to those about to be ordained to the priesthood:

"And seeing ye cannot by any other means compass the doing of so weighty a work, pertaining to the salvation of man, but with doctrine and exhortation taken out of the Holy Scriptures, and with a life agreeable to the same; consider how studious ye ought to be in reading and learning the same Scriptures . . . and for this self same cause, how ye ought to forsake and set aside, as much as ye may, all worldly cares and studies." And a little later in the same exhortation: ". . . that by daily reading and weighing the Scriptures, ye may wax riper and stronger in your ministry."

But, as we observed, the Pastorals are also in some sense directed to the Church at large, and this knowledge of the Scriptures, though especially the business of the clergy, is not exclusively confined to them. It is to be shared with the whole people of God. Exegesis is the special function of the priest, but it is meant to lead the people also to the exegesis of Scripture, an exegesis that is accomplished not merely in the understanding but in the living of the Christian life.

Gospel: Luke 18:1-8

The story of the unjust judge belongs to a class of parables that feature, not a typical everyday event with a surprising element in it, but a unique occurrence of a striking kind. Such parables are common to, though not confined to, the special Lucan material. As in the story of the unjust steward (Luke 16:1-9), to which it is akin, the central figure is an unsympathetic character. Not every aspect of his behavior is held up for emulation, but only one particular aspect of it. Having refused to listen to the woman's case, the judge eventually yields because of her continual pestering and agrees to hear it. Jesus' hearers are meant to infer from this aspect of the judge's behavior that God will indeed intervene and help his Church, even though he seems to forsake it.

By his editorial introduction (v. 1), Luke has shifted our attention away from the judge to the woman, and made her an example of persistent prayer. The Lord's question at the end, however, makes it clear that the judge is meant to be the central figure.

The Homily

If we take the intercessory interpretation of the first reading and the responsorial psalm, we can build up a picture of the Church in tribulation, and the assurance that God will not forsake it—again a question in the true biblical understanding of the Church's infallibility. God will never abandon his Church utterly and completely.

If the preacher's exegetical conscience permits acceptance of the interpretation in the *Jerome Biblical Commentary*, the Exodus text could be expounded typologically of Christ the heavenly priest interceding for his Church militant on earth. Otherwise, the text better be left alone.

The second reading provides an opportunity for the homilist to explain to the people his/her own particular responsibility for exegesis, and the need to enlist the whole *laos* in this enterprise. In one of his sermons preached nearly half a century ago in the chapel of Corpus Christi College, Cambridge, Sir Edwyn Hoskyns aptly said: "Whether the Church of England can present the truth of the Christian religion to our generation will depend very largely upon the extent to which well-disposed clergy and laity can cooperate in wrestling with the truth of the Church"—and for him that meant preeminently the truth of the Bible.

THIRTIETH SUNDAY OF THE YEAR

Reading I: Sirach 35:12c-14, 16-18b

This reading from Sirach (Ecclesiasticus) was obviously chosen to go with the parable of the Pharisee and the publican, as the caption indicates.

During the heyday of Biblical Theology, the wisdom literature was somewhat under a cloud. This was because it seemed hard to fit it in with the salvation-historical perspective that Biblical Theology had recovered. This wisdom literature appears to deal with general religious and ethical truths and problems, quite detached from the concrete heres and nows of salvation history. Typical of this attitude is the legend that Professor G. Ernest Wright constantly told his classes at McCormick and Harvard that he could not defend the place of Proverbs in the canon!

Now, however, there has been a reaction. The wisdom literature has a place in the canon that is as central as that of the salvation-historical and apocalyptic writings. And Jesus understood himself quite as much as the bearer of the heavenly wisdom (thus holding an implicit wisdom

Christology, which came to flower in the prologue of the Fourth Gospel) as he understood himself as the eschatological prophet, the announcer and bringer of the kingdom of God. He *does* deal in what we have recently somewhat despised as "general truths of religion and ethics," and this passage from Sirach is a worthy accompaniment to the illustrative story of the gospel reading, which also deals with a "general truth of religion and ethics."

Responsorial Psalm: 34:1-2, 16-18, 22

Very appropriately, this psalm is one of the wisdom psalms. Thus *Peake's Commentary:* "In [verses] 11-22 he [the psalmist] offers instruction very much in the style of the wisdom teachers, about the nature and rewards of the good life" (*ad loc.*). Similarly, the *Jerome Biblical Commentary* states: "A wisdom psalm, though it is widely classified as a psalm of thanksgiving" (*ad loc.*). The author of 1 Peter takes up this psalm as a commentary on the qualities of the good life as it should be lived by the newly baptized, thus giving his stamp to its Christian application.

Reading II: 2 Timothy 4:6-8, 16-18

This reading has no direct connection with the other readings of this day but is the conclusion of the reading in course of 2 Timothy. Like the reading for the twenty-eighth Sunday of the year, it is part of the (possibly genuine) *512* farewell letter of Paul to Timothy, into which the "Pastor" has inserted his Church order and defense against Gnosticism.

Paul has apparently been before the court once (the *prima actio*). It went favorably, but, as he poignantly laments, "All [that is, the Roman Christians] deserted me." Yet Paul anticipated only death for himself. Nothing here about the hope of release that marked his former imprisonments.

Why did the Roman Christians desert Paul? The letter to the Romans suggests that they may not have been very keen on his version of the gospel anyhow, and they would hardly want to expose themselves unnecessarily in Nero's court. Before very long a dire persecution was to break out over the whole community. (The present writer's chronology would place Paul's trial and execution about 60, and the Neronian persecution in which Peter fell in 64, though other chronologies are possible.)

Despite the gloomy prospects, however, Paul is full of ultimate confidence: "Henceforth there is laid up for me the crown of righteousness."

Gospel: Luke 18:9-14

This parable is of a type peculiar to Luke. There is no pictorial aspect that points to an eschatological interpretation, as in the normal parable. The story gives its example directly. The disciples are meant to pray, not like the Pharisee, but like the publican. Other illustrative stories are those of the Good Samaritan, the rich fool, and Dives and Lazarus. They inculcate religious and moral examples of a timeless kind and have no direct relation to Jesus' eschatological message. If, however, we allow that Jesus understood himself to be not only the announcer of the inbreaking of God's kingdom but also the embodiment and spokesman of the divine wisdom (see above), then such parables as these fall naturally into their place as part of his teaching. The Pharisee was quite right in performing his religious and moral duties. He was not like other people—extortioners, unjust, adulterers. Clearly, Jesus' hearers would say of the Pharisee that he was a righteous man.

The tax collector, on the other hand, had nothing to commend him. He was no better than the rest of his kind. There was no question but that he was the "bad guy." Yet Jesus pronounced him to be the "good guy." How could Jesus give a verdict that to his hearers would be nothing less than "outrageous" (E. Linnemann)? He did not mean that the Pharisee was wrong in his deeds of morality and piety, or that the tax collector was right in being a swindler and extortioner. What was wrong about the Pharisee was his approach to God: he prayed with himself; he set before God all his merits, compared himself with the publican, and said with Little Jack Horner, "What a good boy am I!"—thereby smashing his goodness with one blow. He came before God trusting in his own, really genuine righteousness. The tax collector, on the other hand, knew that he was a bad lot. He would not lift up his eyes to heaven but beat his breast and cried, *"Kyrie, eleison!"* He was accepted by God because he threw himself on God's mercy.

The Homily

If the reading from Sirach is chosen as the basis for the homily, the preacher need not shrink from dealing with such timeless truths as the statement that the prayer of the humble pierces the heavens.

If the second reading is chosen, the homilist will want to depict the circumstances of Paul's final trial and martyrdom, so far as these can be reconstructed from the text, and meditate upon the courage and faith of Christ's martyrs and the place of that martyrdom in salvation history. On this note, three points: Paul can speak of his martyrdom as a sacrifice (see Phil 2:17); he prays for the forgiveness of the deserters; and he can use the language of the passion psalm, Psalm 22: "rescued from the lion's mouth." The Apostle's martyrdom is a reproduction of the passion and sacrificial death of the Lord himself, not in the sense that the Apostle's martyrdom is in itself an atoning sacrifice, but in the sense that it will contribute to the accomplishment of God's purpose in salvation history by bringing the Gentiles into the messianic salvation. Paul, with his near perspective, thought that this was to be accomplished shortly. Things turned out differently—his martyrdom and that of Peter actually led to the firm establishment of the Church of Rome, which became the mother Church of the West. Thus indeed the Gentile world was brought into the redeemed community, and the blood of the martyrs became the seed of the Church.

The gospel reading offers a magnificent opportunity to proclaim the Pauline gospel of justification by faith apart from the works of the law in the concrete, untechnical, pictorial language of Jesus rather than in the complicated midrashic exposition of Paul.

THIRTY-FIRST SUNDAY OF THE YEAR

Reading I: Wisdom 11:22–12:2

This passage from the Book of Wisdom is a fine pre-Christian exposition of the universality of the divine mercy. It begins by asserting the utter insignificance of human beings in language reminiscent of Second Isaiah. Compare "speck that tips the scales" with "a drop from a bucket" in Isa 40:15. The thought of God's transcendence serves to magnify the condescension of his mercy. The mercy or love of God (the passage uses "love" as a verb but not as a noun, the latter being almost unique to the New Testament) manifests itself in two categories of action: in creation and preservation, and in the forgiveness of sin.

The striking and unique phrase "hast loathing for none of the things which thou hast made" was taken up in the Sarum form for the blessing of ashes on Ash Wednesday: "nihil odisti eorum quae fecisti." It so impressed Cranmer that he inserted it not only into his new collect for Ash Wednesday but also in the penitential office for that day and in the third of his Good Friday collects. The thought is that though human beings have made such an awful mess of God's creation, yet it still is God's creation. His immortal spirit still dwells in all things (12:1), and human beings can therefore plead with God not to allow his handiwork to be destroyed, just as a painter or sculptor could not bear to see the product of his or her genius devoured by fire or smashed to pieces.

It is not clear whether the author, a Hellenistic Jew, is thinking in Hebraic or Greek terms when he speaks of the indwelling of God's spirit in all things (see the Pentecost antiphon, "The Spirit of the Lord fills the whole world"). The "spirit" could be, as in Greek thought, *sophia*, the agent of divine immanence; or, more biblically, it could be *ruach*, the creative power of the transcendent God at work in created things. Probably the author thinks fundamentally in biblical terms but easily slips into Hellenistic language to express authentically biblical thoughts. The point is so incidental to his main concern (pleading to God that creation is his handiwork) that we should not use this passage to build up any particular cosmological or anthropological doctrine. In the New Testament, the dominant conception of the Spirit is not universal-immanentist but eschatological. The Spirit does not dwell in all things and all persons but is a gift to those who believe in Christ Jesus.

Responsorial Psalm: 145:1-2, 8-11, 13c-14

In the original Hebrew this fine psalm of praise is constructed in an acrostic pattern. Each verse begins with a letter of the Hebrew alphabet in order, from aleph through teth. It is a fitting response to the reading on the universal scope of the divine love and mercy. Note especially the last two lines of verse 9: "The Lord is good to *all*, and his compassion is over *all that he has made.*"

Reading II: 2 Thessalonians 1:11–2:2

In the latter part of the post-Pentecost season, the readings from the New Testament become progressively eschatological, thus leading up to the climax in the solemnity of Christ the King and the first Sunday of Advent. Like a musical composer, the Lectionary enunciates the theme that it will develop later on.

In German scholarship, 2 Thessalonians is often classed among the deutero-Pauline letters, but the basis for this is not very strong. Most English-speaking scholars assume that it was written by Paul himself after 1 Thessalonians in order to correct certain mistaken deductions that had been made either from the earlier letter or from the Apostle's teaching on his foundation visit. It appears that a false letter, purporting to be from Paul, had been circulated in the community at Thessalonica, asserting that the day of the Lord had already come. False prophets ("spirit" and "word") were making the same claim. Probably this points to some early gnosticizing tendencies similar to those that appeared a little later at Corinth (1 Corinthians) and Philippi (Phil 3).

In the Gnostic systems, people were divided into various categories in virtue of their creation. Some were pneumatics, who belonged to the upper realm of light, and some were psychics or "hylics," who belonged only to this world. The Christian gospel, as the false teachers understood it, revealed to a privileged elite their true nature. The gospel came, not to make people what they were not, but to restore the memory of their lost origin. Once they had recovered the knowledge of their true nature, there was no need for anything else, so the day of the Lord had really come. The elite already enjoyed immortality. For them the resurrection was already past (see 2 Tim 2:18).

This was, for Paul, a corruption of the gospel all along the line, and his letters, when not directed against Judaizers (like the first part of Galatians, and Romans), were directed against the early gnosticizers at one point or another of their teaching. Here in 2 Thessalonians his answer is that the day of the Lord has not yet come, and that there is much of a highly apocalyptic nature which must happen first (see 2:3-12).

Gospel: Luke 19:1-10

Luke has added this story to his Marcan source from his special material. It illustrates a theme common to the Synoptists—Jesus' eating with the outcasts of society. This type of behavior is attested in a remarkable number of different Gospel forms (parable, aphorism, pronouncement story [so here], and miracle story). This multiple attestation, as C. H. Dodd has argued, is strong proof of its historical character. Thus, one of the most certain facts we know about Jesus is that he ate with the outcasts.

Whether the story of Zacchaeus is based on a real occurrence or is a late composition we have no means of knowing. By his occupation Zacchaeus had excluded himself, in the popular estimation, from his people. He was a quisling who had thrown in his lot with the hated occupying power for the sake of pecuniary gain. But for Jesus this does not disqualify the tax collector from the messianic salvation; he also is a son of Abraham (and for Luke this implies—since now it is not the Law that ultimately determines a person's relation to God but a person's attitude toward Jesus—that so also are Gentiles, as Paul had argued). Zacchaeus' determination to see Jesus and his climbing up into the sycamore tree are taken as a sign of genuine faith, which could break through the barriers between God and human beings set up by the Law.

By entering Zacchaeus' house, Jesus dramatizes the coming of divine salvation. Zacchaeus' promise to restore what he had extorted from his fellow Jews is a measure of his repentance. It goes far beyond the legal requirements of restitution (see, for example, Lev 6:1-7). Now he hears the word: "Today salvation has come to this house," that is, to him and his whole household or family. As in Acts, the conversion of the head of the household carries with it all the other members of the family, a circumstance that led Joachim Jeremias to argue that the early Church practiced infant baptism in conversion situations. This suggests that the story, even if based on a genuine incident in Jesus' ministry, had been shaped for the Gentile mission. Now comes the pronouncement in which the whole story culminates: "The Son of man came to seek and to save the lost."

Critical scholars today are divided on whether Jesus actually used the term "Son of man." But they are generally agreed that even if he did, he did not directly identify himself with that figure, since the Son of man was to appear in heaven at the end as a transcendental figure, while Jesus was a lowly figure on earth. It was the post-Easter Church that identified Jesus first with the coming Son of man and later already in his ministry. But this identification was already implicit in Jesus' claim to be already dispensing eschatological salvation on earth. In this saying it is the Church speaking as it looks back on the whole earthly ministry of Jesus as an accomplished work ("he came"); it is the Church confessing that in that history the Son of man came to seek and save the lost. Such a claim was already implicit in the historical Jesus' conduct in eating with the outcast and in his interpreting that conduct by the parables of the lost sheep and the lost coin.

The Homily

The preacher will find plenty of material for a homily in the Old Testament reading: the paradox of God's transcendence, on the one hand, and his infinite mercy, on the other; or the truth that humanity and the world are still God's creation, despite human sin, and therefore basically salvable.

It is regrettable that the New Testament reading leaves us somewhat up in the air. We get a statement only of the false position, not Paul's reply (the Episcopal Lectionary has changed this reading to 2 Thess 1:1-5, 11-12 for this very reason). Perhaps the homilist is best advised, therefore, to concentrate on the first paragraph, the conclusion of the Apostle's thanksgiving and prayer, with which his letters normally begin. It presents the Christian life as growth in grace, a theme more characteristic of the earlier post-Pentecost season, prior to the development of the futurist-eschatological emphasis of the later Sundays.

In a homily on the gospel reading, the preacher would obviously turn to the punch line of the Zacchaeus story and expound the earthly life of Jesus as God's seeking and saving the lost—a seeking and saving that is a present reality in the Eucharist, when the Son of man (John 6:53!) comes under the forms of bread and wine to seek and save the lost.

THIRTY-SECOND SUNDAY OF THE YEAR

Reading I: 2 Maccabees 7:1-2, 9-14

This reading is part of the story of the martyrdom of the seven brothers and their mother during the persecution of the Jews who remained faithful to the law under Antiochus Epiphanes. The resistance was later organized into a successful revolt against the Syrian occupying power under the leadership of the Maccabees.

This passage provides evidence for the later development in Judaism of the hope for the resurrection from the dead: "The King of the universe will raise us up to an everlasting renewal of life . . . . One cannot but choose to die at the hands of men and to cherish the hope that God gives of being raised again by him" (cf. Dan 12:2). This later Jewish hope was not merely for the resuscitation of the earthly body and a prolongation of this present earthly existence, but of translation into an entirely new mode of existence (note particularly the words "renewal of life"). This existence so transcends this present life that it can only be spoken of by means of inadequate symbols (white robes, shining like stars, being like angels) or, in Paul, as existence in a "spiritual body."

Responsorial Psalm: 17:1, 5-6, 8, 15

This psalm, like so many in the psalter, is a personal lament. The psalmist is in distress; he cries out for vindication and ends on a note of confidence: "When I awake, I shall be satisfied." It is doubtful that this psalmist was thinking of the resurrection when he spoke of "awaking." He probably meant no more than the confidence that he would come through his present distress. But when juxtaposed with the first reading, the psalm acquires a greater depth of meaning. The earlier part becomes the prayer of the martyrs for vindication, and the confident ending an expression of resurrection hope.

Reading II: 2 Thessalonians 2:16–3:5

This selection straddles the two major parts of 2 Thessalonians. The first part, coming after the opening thanksgiving, wrestles with the doctrinal problem of the delay in the second coming, and concludes with a thanksgiving and exhortation. Verses 16-18, the first two verses of the reading, form a concluding benediction to this section. Chapter 3 then begins a second major section, consisting of ethical exhortations (see the following Sunday). This hortatory section is introduced with the Apostle's appeal for the prayers of the congregation (3:1-2) and an expression of confidence that God will enable the Thessalonians to grow in grace (3:3-5). These verses form the second part of the reading.

Gospel: Luke 20:27-38 (long form); 20:27-28a, 34-38 (short form)

This pericope is known as the "Sadducees' question." The long form of the gospel reading spells out the question in full. It is framed in terms of the Jewish law, and was an attempt by the Sadducees, who denied the resurrection. to reduce that hope to an absurdity by a fictitious and improbable case arising from the so-called levirate law (Deut 25:5; cf. Gen 38:8). Since that law is no longer relevant in the Christian Church, the option is given of omitting the question.

Jesus' answer makes two points about the resurrection. First (see our comments on the first reading), resurrection is not a prolongation of our present earthly life but an entirely new mode of existence, in which marriage and giving in marriage are unknown. Since in the new life there is no more death, there is no need for provision to perpetuate the human race (this explanation is peculiar to Luke).

The second point in Jesus' answer is that the Pentateuch, far from rendering the resurrection an absurdity, has an understanding of God that is fully consistent with such a hope. This conclusion is reached by an argument which would be convincing to Jesus' contemporaries but which seems artificial to us. The Bible goes on talking about God as the God of Abraham, Isaac, and Jacob even after their death—therefore they must still be alive.

The alert reader will note that the first answer deals with the problem of resurrection, a Palestinian-Jewish problem, whereas the second part really answers an entirely different question, namely, one about immortality, a more Hellenistic concept. One suspects that two different traditions have been combined somewhere along the line. The essential point— that of the second part of Jesus' answer—is that the Christian future hope depends, not upon wishful thinking, but upon the very nature of the God we believe in. God has revealed himself in biblical experience as essentially the God of the living. In biblical history, in both the Old and New Testaments, he enters into a personal relationship with human beings, and that relationship—God being the kind of God that he is, in fact being God and not anything else—cannot be destroyed, even by death. "Neither death nor life . . . will be able to separate us from the love of God in Christ Jesus our Lord" (Rom 8:39).

The Homily

There are two options for a homily based on the reading from 2 Maccabees. The homilist could use the seven brothers as examples of those who chose to "obey God rather than man," and relate this demand to the requirements of Christian life today in some quite concrete way. Or the homilist could develop the theme of resurrection hope, which for the Christian has been made a sure hope by the resurrection of Jesus Christ from the dead and by our union with him in baptism and the Eucharist. The latter theme suits the gospel reading and the theme of the year better.

The homilist who wishes to relate the reading from 2 Thessalonians to the eschatological note of the season should emphasize the Apostle's description of God as the giver of "eternal comfort and good hope." Insights can be gained from the recent theology of hope as expounded by J. Moltmann and J.-B. Metz.

An alternative, less attuned to the dominant note of the season, would be to speak of intercessory prayer. The Thessalonians are invited to cooperate with the labors of the Apostle. Through their prayers they have the privilege of contributing to the "speeding on" and "triumph" of the word of God. Our intercessions tend to be mostly for the health and safety of the people for whom we pray. Not that this is wrong, so long as it is included within the overall purpose and will of God. We pray that they may have health and safety to enable them to do the will of God more effectively. But the Apostle's overriding concern—and it should be the overriding concern of our intercession, too—is that the word may speed on and triumph. That is a model of what prayer in the Christian community should be concerned about even today.

Once again, this suggests to the preacher a certain agnosticism about the nature of the future life: one can think of it in Hebraic terms as resurrection, or in Hellenistic terms as immortality. What matters is the kind of God we believe in, and the faith that if God is God, the relationship into which he has entered with us in Christ is inalienable.

THIRTY-THIRD SUNDAY OF THE YEAR

Reading I: Malachi 4:1-2a

Nothing is known of the prophet Malachi. Even his name, which in Hebrew means "My messenger," may simply be a deduction from Mal 3:1. Nor is it known when he wrote, though he probably came after the Exile. It is therefore impossible to place his prophecies in a concrete historical situation, as they should be, like all Hebrew prophecy. But this does not matter much for the present reading, since it has a timeless quality about it—the warning that the day of the Lord is coming and that it will spell doom for all the arrogant and evildoers. But for those who fear the name of God, that day will mean vindication and salvation, beautifully described as the rising of the sun of righteousness with healing in its wings. In his well-known Christmas hymn, Charles Wesley applied these words to the birth of Christ:

> Risen with healing in his wings
> Light and life to all he brings,
> Hail, the Sun of Righteousness!
> Hail, the heaven-born Prince of Peace!

Thus interpreted, this reading strikes two notes. One is the last judgment, which will be dominant on the next two Sundays, and the other is the coming of Christ in his nativity, which will be developed on the latter Sundays of Advent. The end of the old Church year dovetails with the beginning of the new.

In the perspective of Malachi, however, the positive part (the rising of the sun with healing in its wings) refers to the last judgment just as much as does the negative part (the warning to the arrogant and evildoers). Karl Barth once protested that for many Christians the last judgment had become a dire expectation of doom (think of the *Dies irae!*), whereas the New Testament Christians looked forward to "that day" with joy, waiting for and earnestly desiring the coming of the day of the Lord (2 Pet 3:12, RSV margin).

Responsorial Psalm: 98:5-9

This is another of the enthronement psalms, which celebrate the kingship of Yahweh. It has already been used earlier in this Church year (see the twenty-eighth Sunday of the year).

511

Reading II: 2 Thessalonians 3:7-12

Here we are in the substantive exhortation of the second major part of 2 Thessalonians (see the previous Sunday). This idleness was apparently occasioned by a highly concrete situation. There were members in the church at Thessalonica who, perhaps misled by some early gnosticizing movement, believed that the day of the Lord had already come. Since they thought that they were in heaven already, the curse of having to work (Gen 3) had been removed. They could therefore eat, drink, and be merry.

Gospel: Luke 21:5-19

Once more we must remember that the literary style of apocalyptic is a peculiar one. The authors do not conceive themselves to be predicting, in an abstract, uninvolved way, the "last things" that are to happen centuries hence; rather, they are interpreting the present crisis in which they are involved as the last crisis of human history, to be followed very soon by its consummation. Also, apocalyptic literature tends to expand in transmission. Material is added as commentary to what is already there, and this is then adapted in the light of unfolding events. As history proceeds, the original crisis may get worse, or it may be temporarily lifted.

A good example of this process is the transmission of the so-called Apocalypse of Enoch, which suffered additions and alterations over a period of some 150 years. So, too, is it with our Lord's apocalyptic words. There can be no doubt that he predicted the destruction of the temple. In fact, that was one of the charges brought against him at his trial, although his accusers could not make it stick (Mark 14:58; 15:29; John 2:19; see Acts 6:14). With the series of crises in Judean history that mounted to a crescendo during the sixties of the first century A.D., this nuclear saying of Jesus was expanded into a "little apocalypse." Traditional apocalyptic material, with its predictions of cosmic disasters preceding the end, together with allusions to the events that were already unfolding, were combined with genuine sayings of Jesus. One cannot always be sure where the genuine sayings of Jesus end, and where the apocalyptic material and descriptions of actual events begin. But in this passage we may reasonably conclude that the predictions of historical disasters—wars, earthquakes, pestilence, famine—reflect the events of the sixties, although some of it is described in conventional apocalyptic language. The predictions of persecutions are genuine warnings of Jesus, addressed to his disciples (vv. 12a, 16-19) but elaborated in the light of what actually happened to Peter, Paul, James the Just, and others during that decade (v. 12b). The promise of divine assistance to the disciples in the time of trial reflects an original promise of Jesus of the gift of the Holy Spirit.

The Homily

Clearly the homilist would be attracted by the passage about the rising of the sun of righteousness in the first reading. There are two options: to expound it in reference to the first coming of Christ as a preparation for Advent and Christmas, or to speak of the joy that Christians should associate with the last judgment. The responsorial psalm could be brought in to support the latter point, with emphasis given to its eschatological aspect: the Lord *comes* to judge the earth; he *will judge* the world with righteousness.

The second reading prompts the observation that idleness today is hardly likely to be due to an overrealized eschatology. It is no longer true that those who do not work are not allowed to eat, as was the case in the subsistence-level economy of New Testament times. For that very reason this passage points up an interesting problem of what is called hermeneutics—the problem of getting the text to say the same thing in a completely altered situation. We can no longer get the same meaning if we just report the text verbatim; its expressions have to be changed in order to put across the same idea. In a society whose economic injustices condemn a large segment of the population to unemployment, it is no good just to lift the text about those who refuse to work not being allowed to eat, and to use it as an argument against welfare payments. That is what fundamentalist middle America may sometimes be tempted to do. Of course, there are shirkers in all societies, and they need the warning of this text. But they are just as likely to be found among the affluent as among the poor. After all, this text was directed precisely against the "strong," those who thought they were already "there," already in the kingdom of God. It was not directed against the weak, who were conscious that spiritually they were the have-nots of this world. The hermeneutical task is therefore a really delicate one, demanding of the preacher the utmost sensitivity. Remembering that in Christian behavior the paramount criterion is the law of love, the homilist will be able to avoid a false hermeneutic in seeking to translate the New Testament injunctions into an entirely changed situation.

The gospel reading confronts the homilist with two problems, one arising from its highly complex character, the other from the fact that it refers to a first-century crisis that no longer obtains today. The best thing to do with such literature is to treat it as an inspired insight into the meaning of history. History is a constant struggle between the forces of good and evil. The Christian has no right to expect that everything is going to get better and better, or that Christ's cause will progress without hindrance. All the Christian knows for sure is that God will eventually bring good out of evil, that the right will triumph in the end, and that the Christian's task in the present is to show patience and endurance: "By your endurance you will gain your lives" (Luke 21:19).

CHRIST THE KING

It was a happy inspiration when Pope Pius XI made the last Sunday of October the feast of Christ the King. Although in some ways it duplicated certain themes of Ascension Day, it provided for a distinctive emphasis on Catholic social action, the counterpart of the social gospel in American Protestantism. It also provided liturgical support for the social teachings of the great papal encyclicals from Leo XIII on.

Now the time has come for a review of Pius XI's action. Feasts governed by the secular calendar, like the "last Sunday in October," lack sound precedent in liturgical history. The feast of Christ the King, if it is to be observed at all ought to be integrated into the Church year. Moreover, there is a danger of isolating the kingship of Christ from its proper biblical context, which is eschatological. His enthronement at the ascension is the opening act of his final eschatological reign, and his continued heavenly rule between the ascension and his return marks the progressive defeat of the powers of evil. For he must reign until he has subjected all his enemies under his feet.

These needs were met by another happy inspiration, namely, the transference of the feast to the last Sunday of the Church year. This Sunday has always had a strong eschatological tone, even with the traditional readings. Johann Sebastian Bach composed a setting of *Wachet Auf* ("Sleepers, Awake") for this Sunday, which in German Lutheranism is known as *Ewigkeitssonntag* (Eternity Sunday).

Reading I: 2 Samuel 5:1-3

David was always regarded as the ideal king, and when the messianic hope developed, it was natural that the Messiah should be thought of as a Son of David. He would be not only a descendant of David but also the type of king that David was.

There are two attitudes toward kingship in the Old Testament. One, representing the royal ideology of the Davidic court, pictures the king as the sacramental expression of Yahweh's kingship. This passage from 2 Samuel is an expression of this line of thinking. It stresses the humane sides of kingship—the solidarity of the king with his people ("We are your bone and flesh") and the king as shepherd. These traits were taken up on a higher level in the Christology and ecclesiology of the New Testament. Christ is one with his body the Church, and he is the Good Shepherd, who lays down his life for the sheep. He knows his sheep by name.

But there is another attitude toward kingship in the Old Testament. All human kingship risks a denial of the ultimate sovereignty of Yahweh, who alone is king. This other ideology is conscious that kingship can easily degenerate into tyranny. Chapter 8 of 1 Samuel is the classical formulation of this view.

The first attitude is expressed in the English coronation service, the second in the American Constitution, with its elaborate system of checks and balances. The dialectical tension between these two views is maintained in the New Testament. In Rom 13 the state is the minister of God (the Greek word is *leitourgos,* a liturgical functionary: the English monarch is vested at his/her coronation in quasi-priestly vestments), whereas in Rev 13 the state is the beast from the abyss. This dialectic must be maintained in any doctrine of the state, and not even the American Constitution should be interpreted undialectically! Liturgical minister and great beast—all states can be either of these, and even both at the same time.

Responsorial Psalm: 122:1-5

The pilgrims sang this psalm as they went up to Jerusalem for the festivals. The first part expresses the pilgrims' excitement as they arrive within the sacred precincts. They rejoice in the unity that Jerusalem symbolizes as the crowds, representing all the tribes, flow together to the temple of Yahweh.

In some strands of post-exilic Judaism, it became part of the eschatological hope to envisage a day when the nations would flow together to Jerusalem (see Isa 25:6). The New Testament sees this hope partially fulfilled in the admission of the Gentiles into the Church, and completely realized in the final coming of Christ. See especially Rom 9–11, where Paul develops the thought that in bringing the collection from the Gentile churches to Jerusalem he is symbolizing the partial fulfillment of this hope, and propounds the conviction that his mission will contribute decisively to the final fulfillment, when the fullness of the Gentiles will be gathered in and all Israel will be saved (Rom 11:25-26).

Reading II: Colossians 1:12-20

Verses 15-20 form one of the great Christological hymns of the New Testament, comparable to Phil 2:6-11 and John 1:1-14. Some scholars regard it as a baptismal hymn. Verses 12-15, which precede it, certainly fit a baptismal context very well when they speak of "our" (that is, the Christian community's) being qualified to participate in the inheritance of the saints, and of our translation from darkness into the kingdom of the Son of God, for that is precisely what happens in baptism.

But the hymn itself is purely Christological and has a cosmic sweep. It speaks about two different works of the Son of God. His first work in his preexistent state is his agency in creation and preservation. It describes this preexistent state and work in terms derived from the wisdom concept as it had been developed especially in Hellenistic Judaism. In the second part of the hymn (from verse 18), it speaks about his redeeming work. This work is not stated in chronological order, but it does refer to the incarnation ("in him all the fullness of God was pleased to dwell"), to the cross[1] and its cosmic, reconciling effects, to his resurrection as the first-born from the dead, and to his establishment of the Church as his body.

It was a bold step when the Greek-speaking Christians identified Jesus of Nazareth as the incarnation of the heavenly wisdom and claimed for him all the theology of wisdom that had been worked out in Hellenistic Judaism. It seems at first sight a far cry from his simple message of the inbreaking of God's kingdom. Yet Jesus himself had claimed to be the mouthpiece of the divine wisdom (for example, Luke 11:49). It was a natural development of this that the Greek-speaking Christians identified him as the incarnation of the personified wisdom of later Jewish tradition. This enabled them to oppose the gnosticizers who denied the salvability of creation and interpreted redemption to mean redemption *from* creation, by asserting that the redemption effected by Christ was the redemption *of* creation. If the wisdom of God means God going forth out of being in himself in creative and redemptive activity, then this early Christian hymn proclaims that it is the same God who creates and redeems.

What has all this to do with the kingship of Christ? The preface of the hymn gives the answer. It is precisely the acts of God in Christ celebrated in the hymn that have transferred us into the kingdom of his beloved Son. The kingship of Christ means that the eternal Son of God who became incarnate in Jesus is the "cosmocrator"—the ruler of the universe. The Church, his body, is the sphere in which that kingship, though still hidden, is acknowledged and proclaimed. The world is the universe over which Christ's kingship is destined to prevail.

Gospel: Luke 23:35-43

It must be admitted that the story of the penitent thief comes as an anticlimax after the tremendous cosmic sweep of the hymn from Colossians. The kingship of Christ is certainly one of the themes of this gospel. First there is the taunt of the crowds and the inscription on the cross—the one

---

[1] This is probably a Pauline or Paulinist addition to the hymn.

ironical, the other intended as a false charge but true for the eyes of faith. Then there is the penitent thief's request that Jesus remember him when he comes to his kingly power, and the assurance that the thief would to-day be with him in paradise. The first two texts domesticate the idea of kingdom. Jesus is king of the Jews, not of the cosmos. The third text in-dividualizes it, and, one is almost tempted to say in the context of this Sunday, trivializes it. Of course, Christ's kingdom has its domestic and individualistic aspects. It *is* the kingdom of the Jews, of the religious, of the Church, as well as of the universe. And he is the king of the believer who is brought to penitence by the contemplation of the cross.

The Homily

In preaching on the Old Testament reading, it is possible to speak either of the Christian doctrine of the state and to bring out its dialectical character, or, to fit better with the theme of this Sunday, of King David as a type of Christ the King, who is at one with his people and is their shepherd.

The second reading offers the homilist an opportunity to be quite specific about the kingship of Christ. It is not just an abstract idea; in in-volves the doctrines of the creation, redemption, and reconciliation of the universe, and of the Church as the sphere in which his reign is already acknowledged and proclaimed.

The homilist could draw out the domestic and personal aspects of Christ's kingship from the gospel, but to do justice to the cosmic breadth of this Sunday's celebration of the kingship of Christ, more adequate material will be found in the first two readings.

SELECTED SOLEMNITIES, FEASTS AND NATIONAL HOLIDAYS

While some of the following observances do not replace a Sunday, they are days for which liturgical provision is made. It is therefore deemed useful to offer commentary on the readings provided for these occasions in the various Lectionaries.

NEW YEAR'S EVE
(Lutheran only)

New Year's Eve is not part of the Church year, so it is omitted from most Lectionaries. Nevertheless, it has an important place in human life, particularly in a society that is not so bound to the rhythms of nature as pagan ones were. (When human life was so bound in the English-speaking world, New Year's Day was observed on Lady Day, March 25, which coincides with the beginning of spring.)

Reading I: Jeremiah 24:1-7

This reading consists of the prophet Jeremiah's vision of two baskets of figs and its interpretation. Encouraged by false prophets, the inhabitants left behind in Jerusalem at the time of the first exile (597 B.C.) had grown complacent. They believed that they were specially privileged; they would survive and become the basis for a reconstructed nation. Not so. As the vision of the baskets of figs showed, it was the exiles who would be given a new heart and a renewed covenant. They were the good figs.

Reading II: 1 Peter 1:22-25

The first letter of Peter consists of liturgical and homiletical materials addressed to the newly baptized. In conversion and baptism we are consecrated to obedience to the truth, that is, to faith in the gospel, the faith that is professed in the baptismal creed. This, in turn, is to lead to love of our brothers and sisters, to our fellow Christians, the community into which baptism has admitted us.

The exhortation goes on to warn against selfishness. Like Paul, however, the author cannot stay with exhortation long, and in the next verse he reverts to the baptismal experience, to the indicative behind the imperative. In language similar to that of the Johannine school (cf. John 1:13; 3:3, 5), he speaks of baptism as a rebirth—not a natural birth but a supernatural one—effected by the word of the gospel, which is Jesus Christ, the utterance of God's self-expression (*rhēma*).

Responsorial Psalm: 102:24-28

This is one of the traditional seven penitential psalms. However, it does not contain any expression of penitence and is classified by modern scholars as an individual lament. Its chief preoccupation is with the sufferings of the individual, though in the middle it widens its scope to include the future of the whole nation (vv. 12-17).

The verses selected for today contain first the final lament (vv. 24-25), and then an acknowledgment of the transience of human life and of the whole creation as contrasted with the eternity of God (vv. 26-28). Compare Psalm 90, which, in its metrical version by Isaac Watts, "O God, our help in ages past," is also frequently used on New Year's Eve.

Gospel: Luke 13:6-9

Jesus here refers to two recent disasters, otherwise unknown to historians. One was the outrage of a tyrant, the other an accident involving construction workers. He draws from both events a warning for Israel. Unless the nation repents, it too will perish. Repentance means, for Jesus, accepting his message of the kingdom of God. The parable of the fig tree reinforces the challenge to repent.

On this occasion the thought is that every year is a "year of grace," given to us by God as an opportunity to seek to be purged of our sinfulness and to bring forth the fruit of obedience.

The Homily

The year begins with the month of January, a name derived from the Roman god Janus, whose statue was placed over doorways and faced both ways. So on New Year's Eve the homilist may encourage the congregation to look both ways—back to the past and forward to the future. The backward look calls to mind our past sins and God's mercies (the first reading and the psalm). The forward look prompts us to pray that we may grow in grace and bring forth fruit (the first reading and the gospel).

CONVERSION OF ST. PAUL, Apostle

Reading I: Acts 22:3-16 or Acts 9:1-22

There are actually *three* different accounts of the conversion of St. Paul in the Acts of the Apostles—the two alternative readings here and the third in chapter 26. If, however, we want a firsthand reference to this event, we have to go to what Paul himself writes about it. He does not describe his experience in detail, as the three accounts in Acts do, but only alludes to it briefly on four occasions (Gal 1:15-16; 1 Cor 15:8-9; 1 Cor 9:6; Phil 3:7-9).

From Paul's references we gather that he did not understand his experience on the road to Damascus as a conversion or as an ordinary vision, as the author of Acts understands it, but as a resurrection appearance in which he received his call to be an apostle. In fact, Paul never thought of himself as being "converted," in the sense that he abandoned one religion for another. He remained a Jew but found fulfillment of his Judaism when he became a believer in Jesus as the Messiah and was sent as his apostle to the Gentiles.

Acts gives a different presentation. Concrete details of the event are portrayed: the light, the voice from heaven, the effect on Paul's companions. More important, the purpose of the vision in Acts is not an apostolic call but a direction to seek our Ananias in Damascus. And it is Ananias who mediates to Paul, not an apostolic call (that can only come directly from the risen Lord), but a call to be a missionary.

The only points of agreement between Acts and Paul's own references are the location near Damascus and the outcome—Paul's universal mission. The differences are to be explained from the fact that Luke was writing in the subapostolic age, which looked back to the Twelve as the exclusive founders of the Church (Luke, in fact, is the first Christian writer to use the familiar phrase "the twelve apostles"; for him they are a *numerus clausus*). For the author of Acts, Paul cannot properly be an apostle because he did not directly witness the Christ-event (Acts 2:22). The vision merely resulted in his conversion, and he embarked on his mission as one who stood in a kind of succession to the apostles, not as a direct witness to the Christ-event. He thus served as a model for the Church of Luke's own day.

The historical truth of the matter is that Paul stood in a sort of intermediate position. While he claimed to be an apostle on the strength of his apostolic call (Gal 1; 1 Cor 15:8-9), he was also dependent on tradition derived from others who were apostles before him (1 Cor 11:23; 15:3).

Acts exaggerates one side of the truth (Paul's dependence) at the expense of the other, just as Paul himself exaggerates the other side (his independence) in Galatians. It is only in 1 Corinthians that he gives a properly balanced presentation, recognizing both his independence and his dependence.

Responsorial Psalm: 117:1-2

This psalm, which calls upon all nations to praise the name of Yahweh, is cited by Paul (Rom 15:11) in a catena of Old Testament texts to illustrate the universal scope of God's redemptive purpose in Christ. It is therefore an appropriate response to the first reading about Paul's universal mission.

Gospel: Mark 16:15-18

The problem of the so-called canonical ending of Mark's Gospel is discussed under Ascension Day in series B. There we note that the command to baptize is taken from a tradition that may well be earlier than the parallel in Matt 28:16-20. This is because it speaks of proclaiming the gospel rather than making disciples, which is typical of Matthew. At the same time we must note that both the language in which the command to preach is couched ("proclaim," "gospel," "believe," "world") and the scope of the mission (all the world) represent the language and outlook, not of Jesus or the earliest Palestinian Church, but those of the Hellenistic mission, including Paul. Since Paul claimed that his apostolic call (as he prefers to think of it, rather than as a conversion) was identical in meaning with the post-Easter appearances to the original apostles, this passage is eminently suited for today's feast.

Much is made in this text of the signs that accompany the apostolic preaching: exorcisms in the name of Christ; speaking in tongues; the more bizarre signs of taking up serpents and drinking poison unharmed; and the more normal sign of healing the sick by the laying on of hands. The taking up of serpents is paralleled in Luke 10:19, where in a slightly different form (treading on serpents) it appears in a similar context of a missionary charge. Drinking poison is not mentioned elsewhere in the New Testament, though Papias (second century) mentions one instance of this. Are the two bizarre signs meant as deliberately staged demonstrations, or do they promise protection in case of accident? Fundamentalist sectarians who have taken them to be staged demonstrations have sometimes done harm to themselves. We had better leave such signs to the second century, where they belong, and say that God always provides appropriate signs to accompany the preaching in each and every age.

271

The Homily

It has not been our policy to provide comment for apostles' feasts that cannot replace a Sunday. However, an exception has been made for this day because the Conversion of St. Paul marks the end of the week of prayer for Christian unity. Much could be said on this topic, but we must stick to the readings.

All the readings share a common theme: the universality of the apostolic mission. It is a historical fact that the ecumenical movement began (in Protestantism) in the mission field. The divisions of the Church were there first seen to hamper the mission (waste of resources; unseemly competition among the denominations; the importation of alien divisions from Europe and America among the converts, divisions that were not there before; and the consequent loss of credibility). Where the Church's mission is taken seriously, there the need for unity will be urgent.

February 2

PRESENTATION OF THE LORD

Reading I: Malachi 3:1-4

This passage is an excerpt from a section in which a series of questions is addressed to Yahweh. The statement "You have wearied the Lord" is given in response to the question "How have we wearied him?" (2:17). The answer is: by denying Yahweh's justice. Therefore Yahweh will visit his people with judgment. He will send a messenger (the name Malachi means "My messenger," which may be the reason for the attribution of the name to this book). The messenger will announce a covenant. Then Yahweh will come to his temple and will purify his ministers and priests so that they may offer pure sacrifices in the temple.

Christian tradition finds the fulfillment of this prophecy in (1) the sending of John the Baptist (the messenger); (2) the incarnation—Yahweh coming in the person of Christ to his temple; and (3) the Eucharist, identified by the early Fathers as the pure offering. The purpose of the incarnation was seen in the establishment of the eschatological worship of God by a new, eschatological people.

Responsorial Psalm: 24:7-10

In the Anglican liturgical tradition this psalm is associated with Ascension Day. It is equally suitable today, for it is one of the entrance psalms, composed for the processional entry of the king into the temple, thus fitting in with this feast and the first reading.

Reading II: Hebrews 2:14-18

In this passage we have one of the clearest statements of the doctrine of the incarnation in the New Testament. In itself it would not necessarily imply the Son's preexistence, for it simply says that he was human like us and shared our common humanity. But the word "shared" (*meteschen*) is in the aorist tense, which implies that he began to share our humanity at a particular moment, and that there was a time when he did not share it. Further, the hymn with which the letter to the Hebrews opens (1:1-4) shows clearly that the author accepted the preexistence Christology, and therefore his statements here about the humanity of Christ must be taken as an assertion of a real incarnation. This is stated in three terms: "shared," "partook of the same nature," and "made like his brethren in every respect." Note here that the term *homoiōma*, "likeness," has been introduced into Christological vocabulary already in the New Testament. Later on, the cognate *homoiousios* was found to be inadequate in a Christological context. The New Testament authors, had they known of the later heresies of Docetism and Arianism, would probably have avoided these terms. But when the author of Hebrews speaks of "likeness," he certainly intends full identification with our humanity. The phrase "in every respect" makes this clear.

Note also the purpose clause "that he might . . . ." This defines the soteriological purpose of the incarnation. The doctrine of the incarnation is not pure metaphysical speculation. It is concerned with the reality of our salvation, as Athanasius and, later, Anselm were to stress. Here that purpose is defined as twofold: (1) the destruction of death and the defeat of the devil (the *Christus victor* type of atonement language, championed a generation ago by the Swedish theologian Gustav Aulén); (2) Christ's ongoing work as high priest: because of his humanity and experience shared with us, he is able to be a sympathetic and merciful high priest. It is stated that he is a high priest "in the service of God," that is, his high priestly service is performed in a Godward direction. He offers his sacrifice to God the Father once for all when he passes through the veil at his ascension, and he continually pleads it before the Father (Heb 7:25; 9:24). This is the first occurrence of the term "high priest" in Hebrews. The author proceeds like a musician, giving a few prior adumbrations of his theme before developing it at length. Christ functionally "became" high priest at his ascension. We can see how the idea developed from Ps 110:1, one of the earliest *testimonia* to be used after Easter. From Ps 110:1 the author of Hebrews moved to verse 4 and so developed the doctrine.

Gospel: Luke 2:22-40 (long form); 2:22-32 (short form)

The long form of the gospel consists of the whole pericope of the presentation, in which Anna as well as Simeon respond to the appearance of the Christ child in the temple. The short form omits the part about Anna and the concluding summary about the subsequent growth of the child. Unfortunately, the short form loses some of the point: there is a one-upmanship in the comparison of Jesus and the Baptist that the short form misses. After his birth, John the Baptist is hailed by only one prophet (his father Zechariah, who sings the *Benedictus*), whereas the Christ child is hailed by two (Simeon with the *Nunc dimittis,* and Anna with her thanksgiving to God and her testimony to the bystanders). In addition to this one-upmanship, and perhaps as part of it, Simeon testifies to the universality of the mission of the Christ child: he is to be not only a glory of Israel but a light to illumine the Gentiles.

One curious feature of this account is that Simeon is given *two* oracles—the *Nunc dimittis* and the allocution to Mary, the mother of the child. It has been suggested that this duplication of oracles is the result of Luke's subsequent addition of the canticle to his infancy narrative.

The *Nunc dimittis* is probably an early Christian liturgical psalm. Originally this psalm praised God, not just for the birth of the Messiah, but for the Christ-event in its entirety. The second oracle is parallel to that pronounced by Elizabeth in Luke 1:42b-45, though it is rougher in style. The first oracle blesses God for the coming of the Christ and the prospect of salvation for the Gentiles, while the second predicts the future role of the child and his fate in Israel.

The Homily

The presentation of Christ in the temple is the last of the feasts belonging to the incarnation cycle. Although by itself the Lucan infancy narrative does not operate with an incarnation Christology, in combination with the reading from Hebrews it may be interpreted in incarnational terms. The saving purpose of the incarnation and the destiny of the Christ child should be the homilist's theme today.

March 25

ANNUNCIATION

Reading I: Isaiah 7:10-14

This text can be interpreted at two quite different levels, though there is a real connection between the two.

First, there is the meaning of the text in its original historical situation. This situation is described in 2 Kgs 16:5-9. Syria has entered into an alliance with the northern kingdom of Israel against the southern kingdom of Judah, of which Ahaz is king. Together they have laid siege to Jerusalem. Isaiah offers Ahaz a sign that everything will eventually turn out successfully, but Ahaz refuses such a sign, doubtless because he does not want Isaiah's advice. But Isaiah gives the sign anyway: "A young woman shall conceive and bear a son, and shall call his name Emmanuel." It is probable that the young woman in question is the wife of the king, and the son to be born, Hezekiah. The sign, then, will concern the continuation of the Davidic dynasty, a sign that God is with his people. This is the first level of meaning.

At the second level, the text is taken up by the evangelist Matthew and applied to the birth of Jesus. The Lucan infancy narrative also echoes it (see Luke 1:31), thus indicating that this application represents a tradition earlier than the two evangelists. In the Septuagint translation used by the evangelists, "young woman" is rendered *parthenos* ("virgin"). In a sense, the resultant application of Isa 7:14 is far removed from what the prophet originally intended—he was thinking only of the immediate political situation and of the certainty that God would shortly intervene on the side of Judah. But in linking this assurance with the continuance of the Davidic line, Isaiah had expressed a hope that continued in Israel and that, for the Christian Church, found its final fulfillment in the birth of Christ from the Virgin Mary. He is the true Emmanuel, God-with-us.

Responsorial Psalm: 40:6-10

This excerpt from Psalm 40 is used today in preparation for the citation of this passage in the next reading. Note, however, that it acquires its appropriateness for a feast of the incarnation from the Septuagint text, which reads "a body hast thou prepared for me" instead of "thou hast given me an open ear."

Reading II: Hebrews 10:4-10

This is one of the most important passages in Hebrews, for it defines Christ's sacrifice as the offering of his body (that is, the instrument of his will) in obedience to his Father. This, says the author of Hebrews, building upon Psalm 40, the responsorial psalm, is the whole *raison d'être* of the incarnation. Christ took a body so as to have an instrument by which to offer this perfect obedience to the will of God.

Gospel: Luke 1:26-38

Annunciation stories are a regular literary form of Scripture. There are a number of such stories in the Old Testament (for example, the births of Isaac, Samson, and Samuel), and of course Luke has already recorded the annunciation of John the Baptist.

We should make full allowance for this literary form in assessing this narrative. The purpose of annunciation stories is to acquaint the *readers* with the role that the person about to be born is to play in salvation history. It is thus a device to effect this end, not a historical narration. At the same time, there are elements in the story of Jesus' annunciation that surpass the other annunciation stories. The usual situation is that of a miraculous birth granted to a barren couple—in the case of Isaac, to parents who were even past the age of begetting children. In the case of Jesus, it is an annunciation to a young woman without a husband. The emphasis rests on the creative act of the Holy Spirit rather than on the virginal conception *per se,* which is its presupposition.

All that the historian can say with certainty is that the basic elements in this tradition are earlier than Matthew or Luke, for the name of Mary, her virginity, and the function of the Holy Spirit are common both to Matthew and Luke, who are otherwise entirely independent of one another at this point. Many would also argue that these traditions can be traced back to the earliest Palestinian stratum of Christianity. Beyond that point, however, the historian *qua* historian cannot go. The exegete must deal rather with the meaning. What is the kerygmatic thrust of the annunciation? It is that the history of Jesus does not emerge out of the stream of ongoing history. As Adolf Schlatter put it, it expresses the transcendental origin of the history of Jesus. Or, as Sir Edwyn Hoskyns put it, the incarnation is "a dagger thrust into the weft of human history."

Our response to the annunciation story should be not to accept it as an entertaining story or even to insist merely on its historicity and leave it at that. As such, it would still be "flesh," which profiteth nothing. Our response should rather be the affirmation of faith in the transcendental origin of Jesus' history.

The Homily

Although this feast has some Mariological undertones, its primary thrust is Christological. Since it always falls in Lent or is transferred to after Easter, the homilist has the opportunity to stress that the whole purpose of the incarnation is to lead to the cross and the resurrection (see the traditional postcommunion collect of the day), thus combating a purely "incarnational soteriology." By this is meant the view that our salvation derives simply from the Son of God's having taken to himself our human nature. As the reading from Hebrews makes clear, the whole purpose of the incarnation is that the eternal Son should assume a body in which he could offer himself as a sacrifice of perfect obedience on the cross. It is the destiny that the angel points up in the annunciation story.

June 24
BIRTH OF ST. JOHN THE BAPTIST
VIGIL

Reading I: Jeremiah 1:4-10

This is the story of the prophet Jeremiah's call. The first two verses are commented upon on the fourth Sunday of the year in series C. The added verses bring out the pattern of thought that reappears in the birth story of John the Baptist. This pattern has two parts: (1) the predestination and election of someone to fulfill a particular role in salvation history; this takes place at conception or in the womb or at birth; (2) the implementation of the call when the prophet has grown up. Like Moses and unlike Isaiah, Jeremiah shrinks from his call. Usually the New Testament draws a parallel between Jeremiah and Paul (Gal 1:15) rather than with John the Baptist. But the double vocation—to destroy and overthrow, to plant and build—corresponds fittingly to the two sides of the Baptist's message. On the one hand, he was to warn Israel to flee from the wrath to come, while on the other hand he was to promise the arrival of the Coming One who would bring salvation by gathering wheat into his barn.

Responsorial Psalm: 71:1-4a, 5-6b, 15ab, 17

This psalm is classified as an individual lament. It is a cento of verses from other psalms and serves as the prayer of a sick, aged person who in the past has experienced God's protection and now feels bereft. Verses 1-5 are from the first part, a plea for deliverance. Verse 15 is a concluding vow to praise the Lord, and verse 17 a vow to proclaim to others the righteous deeds of God.

Reading II: 1 Peter 1:8-12

Our comments on the second Sunday of Easter in series A cover the first 75
two verses of this reading. Commentators are divided as to whether verses
10-12 refer to Old Testament prophets or to Christian ones. On the one
hand, the description of their activity (searching out Scripture, that is,
the Old Testament, and applying it to the present-day life of the Christian community) suggests Christian prophets (so Selwyn). On the other
hand, the way in which the prophets are distinguished from the present
Christian community, standing against it instead of being part of it, suggests that the author is referring to Old Testament prophets (so Beare).

The answer to this dilemma is probably this: the writer is *really* thinking
of the Old Testament prophets but is describing their work in terms of
the Christian prophets. It was the basic conviction of the whole New Testament that the Old Testament was written exclusively for Christians. This
was a hermeneutic practiced already at Qumran and was probably taken
up by both John the Baptist and Jesus before the Christian prophets arrived on the scene. Thus we find John the Baptist applying to himself (as
Qumran had already done) the text of Second Isaiah, "Prepare ye the way
of the Lord." So later the Old Testament prophets, in New Testament
perspective, were speaking of the sufferings destined for Christ and of his
subsequent "triumphs" or "glories" (that is, Christ's resurrection, ascension, and sitting at God's right hand).

This passage was chosen for today not only because John the Baptist
indulged in the kind of midrashic activity attributed to prophets here, but
also because he, especially as presented by the Lucan birth narratives, was
one who summed up the entire message of the Old Testament prophets
just as this message was on the brink of fulfillment.

Gospel: Luke 1:5-17

This is the story of the annunciation of the Baptist's birth. It follows the
pattern of annunciations in both the Old and New Testaments. This story
has the following elements:

1. An angelophany (Luke 1:11)
2. Reaction of fear (1:12)
3. The message (1:13-17)
    a. Address of recipient by name (1:13)
    (b. Description of recipient is missing.)
    c. Command to fear not (1:13)
    (d. Prediction of conception is missing.)
    e. Prediction of birth (1:13)
    f. The future child's name (1:13)

    (g. Etymology of the name is missing, though we know that John [Jochanan, Johannes] means "grace of God.")

    h. The future role of the child in salvation history (1:15-17)

  4. An objection by recipient and/or request for a sign (1:18)

  5. The sign given as reassurance (1:19, 22).

It will be noted that 3h is longer than any other element and is an invariable feature of all the biblical annunciations. It therefore enshrines the whole purpose of the annunciation genre: to convey the role that the child is to play in salvation history. Thus, annunciations are not historical reporting but literary creations developed on the basis of the child's subsequent history, which is presupposed.

The Homily

Like Christmas, this day lends itself more readily to remembrance of the past than to proclamation for the present. Today's texts invite the homilist to speak of how John was destined for his role from the time before his conception, and to say what that role was. How is the Baptist's role fulfilled in the Church today? A collect in the old Book of Common Prayer drew a parallel between the Baptist and Christian ministers:

"O Lord Jesus Christ, who at thy first coming didst send the messenger to prepare thy way before thee: Grant that the ministers and stewards of thy mysteries may likewise so prepare and make ready thy way by turning the hearts of the disobedient to the wisdom of the just . . . ."

Compare the role of the Baptist as it is described in the annunciation story (v. 17) with the final clause just quoted.

MASS DURING THE DAY

Reading I: Isaiah 49:1-6

Part of this reading (49:3, 5-6) is covered on the second Sunday of the year in series A. Clearly, the second servant song is here being applied 109 to John the Baptist, whereas the servant of Isaiah is more often associated with our Lord. Evidently this is why this particular selection has been replaced in the Episcopalian and Lutheran versions of the Lectionary. The Episcopal reading is Isa 40:1-11 (see the second Sunday of Advent in series 205 B). The Lutherans use Mal 3:1-4, for which comment is provided on February 2, the Presentation of the Lord. 537

Responsorial Psalm: 139:1-3a, 13-15

This psalm expresses God's concern for the individual from the moment of conception in the womb. Its classification as a psalm is disputed. Is it a wisdom psalm? Or is it a psalm of lament? It has an intensely personal and individualistic character that puts it in a class by itself. It is probably of a mixed type, perhaps due to combination with verses from other sources.

The psalm is structured as follows: verses 1-6: God's knowledge of the individual; verses 7-12: God's inescapable presence; verses 13-18: God's creative work, especially in conception, pregnancy, and birth.

The selection of this psalm for today's feast was probably determined by the third of these sections. If it is true of all of us as individuals that God knows us from the womb, how much more the great figures of salvation history, especially John the Baptist, than whom there is none greater born of woman!

Reading II: Acts 13:22-26 (Episcopal: 13:14b-25)

This passage is from one of the greatest kerygmatic speeches in Acts. These speeches are neither tape recordings of what was said (in this case by Paul) on the particular occasion nor Thucydidean compositions, that is, composed by the author of Luke-Acts and put into the mouths of his *dramatis personae*. The truth lies somewhere in between. The speeches enshrine very primitive Christological formulas outlining the career of Jesus (it is from this part that our reading comes), but then expanded into a sermon of the type preached in the services of the Hellenistic and Hellenistic-Jewish communities, with adaptation by the author himself.

This particular speech features a recitation of Israel's salvation history, passing rapidly from the sojourn in Egypt to the reign of David, then skipping to the Christ-event. A unique feature of the Christological part is that it expands the beginning of Jesus' career by a rather lengthy mention of his forerunner, John the Baptist—hence its choice for this occasion. Note that the Jesus story here begins with John the Baptist, not with Jesus' birth. This is contrary to the way Luke designed his Gospel, a probable indication of the pre-Lucan character of this section.

John the Baptist is here portrayed as the precursor of the Christ-event, a Christian interpretation. As we pursue the "quest of the historical Baptist," we find that the historical John probably spoke more generally of the Coming One, who could have been an apocalyptic Son of man type of figure or Yahweh himself. In any event, John the Baptist's expectations were clearly apocalyptic in character, a framework of thought that he passed on to Jesus and his disciples, and to the early post-Easter community.

Gospel: Luke 1:57-66, 80

This reading consists of the birth, circumcision, naming, and public presentation of John the Baptist. The Lutheran and Episcopalian readings extend to the *Benedictus*, the Song of Zechariah, which is commented on separately below.

Luke is here resuming his Baptist source, having inserted the pre-birth part of his Jesus material (the annunciation to Mary and the visitation of Mary and Elizabeth). In the account of the birth of the Baptist, there are two causes for joy—one private, the other public. The first cause is the removal of the stigma of Elizabeth's barrenness. The public cause is the dawning of the messianic salvation. Here is a double manifestation of God's "mercy," his steadfast covenant-love.

The circumcision of the child signifies his incorporation into the Jewish covenant community. This is theologically important, for it enables Luke to show that the Christian movement emerges out of Judaism, and is indeed an authentic development of it. As a consequence, Luke can present Christianity to Theophilus and to his Greco-Roman audience in general as a *religio licita*, a religion entitled to come under the same umbrella of Roman toleration as the parent Judaism.

The naming of the child is also theologically important. In the abandonment of the priestly name Zechariah, the priestly succession is broken by the dawn of messianic salvation.

There are some puzzling features to the story. Naming was not normally associated with circumcision. The custom of patronymy (using the father's name for the son) was unusual, whereas paponymy (using the grandfather's name) was normal. Then, too, how did Elizabeth get to know that the child's name was to be John? How did Zechariah communicate with her, when he was suffering from temporary aphasia? Probably Luke does not mean us to ask these kinds of questions but wants us to concentrate on the theological message that the story is meant to express.

Verse 80, which tells us that John the Baptist spent his whole life in the desert until the beginning of his public ministry, offers plausible evidence that he was brought up at Qumran. The counterargument that the whole of verse 80, because of the first part, which is modeled on the story of Samuel, is clearly Lucan redactional composition is not conclusive, since the second part of the verse could come from Baptist tradition.

The Benedictus: Luke 1:68-79 (Lutheran and Episcopalian)

The Song of Zechariah has the style of the psalms. We know that at Qumran the practice of psalm composition and singing was continued, and passed thence to the early Christian community of *'anawim*, whence all the Lucan canticles appear to be derived. It was widely thought for a time that the *Benedictus* was taken over by Luke from his Baptist source, but more recently it has come to be regarded as more probable that it came from the same Christian source as the other Lucan canticles (R. Brown, J. Fitzmyer). This is mainly because of the Davidic character of the messianic salvation that it celebrates.

Like the other canticles, too, the Song of Zechariah is separable from its immediate context, and, like them, it looks as though it could have been inserted in a better place, namely, after verse 64, where we are told that Zechariah blessed God, but are not told the words he used. This is thought to be a sign that Luke added the *Benedictus*, as he did the other canticles, after composing the infancy narratives as a whole—another argument against his having derived them from a Baptist source.

The hymn is a cento of phrases from the Old Testament psalms. It falls into two parts: verses 68-73, which celebrate the messianic salvation, and verses 76-79, which speak of the role of John the Baptist in connection with that messianic salvation. The second part looks as though it has been added to an original *'anawim* hymn in order to adapt it to the context of the Baptist's birth.

It is further noteworthy that the verbs in the first part are all in the aorist tense. This means that they are celebrating a messianic salvation that has already come—in other words, it is a hymn of the post-Easter community. The verbs in the second part, however, are in the future tense. Could it after all be the case that the second part of the hymn comes from the Baptist community, which believed that John the Baptist had heralded the messianic salvation but that it had not yet occurred? At this stage this was their point of difference with the Christians; later they may have gnosticized John the Baptist as the revealer of gnosis.

Put together in this way, the canticle is admirable for use on this day, as well as during Advent and in the daily office of Morning Prayer.

The Homily

The vigil Mass celebrated the conception of John the Baptist; the Mass of the day celebrates his birth and naming, which mark the dawning of God's "great mercy," and are therefore a cause for "rejoicing." John the Baptist's birthday is kept on the summer solstice, whereas Jesus' birth is at the winter solstice: "He must increase but I must decrease." In Christian perspective John the Baptist has an important though limited role. If we connect that role with the role of the clergy, we can use the figure of John the Baptist to say that the clergy, too, must decrease while Jesus must increase. They, too, have an important though limited role. That role is to introduce people to the messianic salvation rather than to be that salvation themselves.

June 29

STS. PETER AND PAUL, Apostles

There are very few critical historians today who would deny that both Peter and Paul suffered martyrdom in Rome. However, June 29 is not the date of their martyrdom. In fact, it is unlikely that they were martyred on the same day. Some New Testament scholars would place the death of Paul at the conclusion of the two-year imprisonment with which Acts closes (about 62), and Peter's death during the Neronian persecution in 64, a view that this commentator favors. Why, then, June 29? To quote P. Battifol, "The festival of the two apostles will be celebrated on the same day, June 29, not because this date is the anniversary of their martyrdom, but because it is the anniversary of the institution of a joint observance in their honor." Oscar Cullmann, the Swiss Protestant scholar, agrees, adding that the choice of June 29 was due to the earlier association of this day with the founder of the city of Rome, Romulus. This Christian observance in Rome began in 258.

Historically, it is difficult to connect the foundation of the church in Rome with Peter or Paul. There must have been Jewish Christians in that city before Claudius expelled all the Jews from Rome in 48 (see Aquila and Priscilla, Acts 18:2). By the time Paul wrote Romans (ca. 56), there were both Gentile and Jewish groups in Rome (the strong and the weak of Rom 15). Apparently the former had arrived between the expulsion of the Jews in 48 and the death of Claudius in 54, while the Jewish Christians would have drifted back after Nero's succession. This is what created the tensions that are discussed in Rom 15. Galatians 2:7 states that Peter and Paul were recognized as the heads of the Jewish and Gentile missions respectively. In view of this, it may be claimed that Peter and Paul were indirectly responsible for the foundation of the Roman church.

VIGIL

Reading I: Acts 3:1-10

It has been a dominant view among scholars that the author of Acts had no traditions to refer to when he wrote his work. Dibelius argued that this was because the apostles preached Jesus, not themselves. But we know from Paul that his opponents did preach themselves, boasting of their own marvelous exploits, while the news of Paul's apostolic successes and achievements were spread from church to church. It is not surprising, therefore, that this story has all the traits of a miracle story—diagnosis, cure, and demonstration—and portrays the apostles rather in the image of the divine man. Like John's Gospel, however, the author of Luke-Acts uses this and similar stories as a springboard for a lengthy discourse. This discourse takes the form of a kerygmatic speech. Thus, the author corrects his source's view that the apostles were merely figures of the divine-man type.

Responsorial Psalm: 19:1-4b

It is interesting how this psalm has undergone development in Christian usage. The first part speaks of the revelation of God in creation. "Their message" is the message of the created order, the heavens, the firmament, day and night, that "the hand that made us is divine." But Paul identifies the "they" of verse 4 with the preachers of the gospel, specifically the Jewish Christian apostles, whose labors he considers, by about A.D. 56, to have failed (Rom 10:18). In Christian liturgical usage, Psalm 19 has accordingly been used on evangelists' and apostles' feasts. Paul thus gives full justification for its use today as a response to Acts 3.

Reading II: Galatians 1:11-20

This section from Galatians is an important piece of Pauline autobiography. The preacher to the Gentiles was notoriously reticent about his apostolic call. Only when misrepresented did he feel it incumbent upon him to set the record straight. The opponents in Galatia had accused him of being entirely dependent on the Jerusalem apostles for his call, and of falsifying the apostles' teaching by dropping the requirement of circumcision for Gentile converts. In answer to the first charge, Paul goes over what happened to him between the experience on the road to Damascus and his first visit to Jerusalem three years later (two by ancient inclusive reckoning). He had embarked immediately on his mission after his call (that, and not retreat, was the probable purpose of the visit to Arabia, according to contemporary scholars), and when he went up to Jerusalem, it was not to seek authorization from the apostles but to visit with equals.

This reading brings together the two apostles Paul and Cephas, while being primarily concerned with Paul.

Gospel: John 21:15-19

This scene comes from the so-called appendix to John's Gospel. Although apparently added later by a member of the Johannine school, it enshrines far earlier material than the other resurrection traditions in John 20. Indeed, John 21 has its roots in the first appearance to Peter, reported in the early list of 1 Cor 15:5, alluded to in Luke 24:34, and narrated in a variant tradition (as many modern scholars, including Catholics, now think) in Matt 16:17-19. In this call Peter was appointed the first of the apostles to witness the resurrection and given the pastoral task of feeding the sheep. It is obvious that this latter function has to continue in Christ's Church.

The last paragraph clearly reflects knowledge of Peter's martyrdom (by crucifixion?) and is, in fact, the earliest evidence we have of it.

The Homily

Today's double commemoration of Peter and Paul and its early history indicate that its real significance is the celebration of the foundation of the ancient Church of Rome, which became the mother of the Churches throughout the West. As such, this feast is of ecumenical importance for all Western Christians. It is perhaps even more significant that the Church of Rome had a double foundation—the Petrine and the Pauline missions, the mission to Israel and that to the Gentiles, the apostolate to the circumcised and the free gospel apart from the law for the Gentiles, the institutional and the charismatic-evangelical. Those streams in Christianity and Church life, which we normally take to be antithetical—Rome and the Reformation—are here held together in tension (see Rom 15!), but in what is hopefully a fruitful tension. Is that perhaps the mission of Rome today: to be both Petrine and Pauline, Catholic and evangelical? It would be exciting for the homilist to explore the contemporary ecumenical implications of this double foundation of the Church of Rome.

MASS DURING THE DAY

Reading I: Acts 12:1-11

Herod Agrippa reigned over the tetrarchy of Philip (see Luke 3:1) from 37 C.E. and over Galilee from 39 C.E. He died in 44 C.E. For reasons that are not clear, Agrippa reversed the hitherto prevailing policy of the Jewish authorities toward the Aramaic-speaking Christians and persecuted them. Presumably by now this was a move that was likely to make him popular. As a result, some of the leaders of the Aramaic-speaking Church were maltreated, James bar Zebedee was executed, and Peter was arrested (Acts 12:1-4).

All this serves as a preliminary to the story about Peter's miraculous escape from prison, the first part of which (vv. 5-11) forms the rest of today's reading. We have no other historical record of this imprisonment, and the circumstances of Peter's escape follow a conventional pattern familiar in Hellenistic literature (see the similar story about Paul and Silas in Philippi in Acts 16:25-29). The self-opening door is a conventional feature of these miraculous escapes. Anyhow, the picture that Luke portrays is that the Church prayed fervently for Peter during his incarceration, and the Lord delivered him by an angel. Peter remained completely passive throughout the escape—in a dream, as it were.

The main features of the story are pre-Lucan, but the picture of the Church at prayer, a favorite motif in Luke-Acts, and Peter's final acclamation (v. 11), which functions like the choric ending of the healing stories, will be redactional additions. Here we find the theological content of the story: the fervent prayer of the Church furthers its mission. God had much for Peter still to do, right up to the time of his martyrdom, which we celebrate today.

Responsorial Psalm: 34:1-8

This psalm occurs also on the fourth Sunday of Lent in series C and is commented upon there. Note that today the refrain, "The angel of the Lord will rescue those who fear him," picked up from the fourth stanza, follows aptly upon the story of Peter's miraculous escape in the first reading. A cynic might ask, Where was the angel of the Lord when Peter was martyred at Rome? We may reply that the angel of the Lord was there then, too, to take Peter to heaven. With the firm establishment of the community at Rome through the labors of Peter and Paul, their task on earth had been fulfilled. *412*

Reading II: 2 Timothy 4:6-8, 17-18

See the thirtieth Sunday of the year in series C for comment on this passage. The New Testament contains no account of Paul's martyrdom. His farewell letter (part of which may be preserved here in an otherwise deutero-Pauline writing) is the closest we can get to any reference to his death (but see also Acts 20:18-36). *517*

Gospel: Matthew 16:13-19

See the twenty-first Sunday of the year in series A for comment. This passage has been variously interpreted in the Church, so far as the continuance of the Petrine office is concerned. The usual Protestant interpretation, which also has some patristic support, is that the "rock" refers to *161*

Peter's faith, and that therefore this text lives on effectively in the Church's continuing to confess Jesus as Messiah. Eastern Orthodox and Anglicans have generally seen the continuity of the Petrine office in the collective episcopate. Of course, the traditional Roman Catholic position has always been, at least until Vatican II, that this text was intended from the start to be the Lord's institution of Peter in that office which is still perpetuated in the papacy. Since Vatican II, Roman Catholic scholars have put forward a more nuanced view that would see in this text the beginnings of a trajectory that was destined to lead eventually to the papacy, while Anglican and Lutheran scholars have been prepared to recognize under certain circumstances a role for the papacy in a reunited Church which would represent an acceptable implementation of this text.

The Homily
Given today's gospel, the homilist might like to open the eyes of the congregation to the carefully nuanced post-Vatican II interpretation of the text and to the ecumenical rapprochement that has come about since then. If the homilist chooses to do this, the relevant portions of the following publications would help in preparing the homily:

Peter in the New Testament, ed. Raymond E. Brown et al. Minneapolis: Augsburg Publishing House, and New York: Paulist Press, 1973.

Papal Primacy and the Universal Church: Lutherans and Catholics in Dialogue V, ed. Paul C. Empie and T. Austin Murphy. Minneapolis: Augsburg Publishing House, 1974.

Anglican-Roman Catholic International Commission: The Final Report. Cincinnati: Forward Movement, 1982.

Alternatively, the suggestions for the vigil homily might be followed in relation to the readings from Acts and 2 Timothy.

July 4
INDEPENDENCE DAY

Provision for this day as such is made only in the Book of Common Prayer (Episcopal). The Lutheran Book of Worship has a "National Holiday."

Reading I: Deuteronomy 10:17-21
This passage deals with the motives for obedience. These are to be found in Yahweh's majesty and awesome justice, to which expression is given in a series of titles. These motives bring out the contrast between the

teaching of the prophets on justice and the society in which they lived, where justice was often tardy.

The passage calls attention to the need for showing justice to the *ger*, the independent foreigner resident in Israel. These people were personally free but enjoyed no political status. Their position was often like that of migrant workers in the United States, and was vastly different from that of regular resident aliens, who enjoyed many of the privileges of citizenship. The people of Israel are reminded that they too were in a similar position when they were in Egypt. The fact that they had once been liberated should make them especially sensitive to the insecure position of the *ger*.

Reading II: Hebrews 11:8-16

For comment on this passage, see the nineteenth Sunday of the year in series C.

495

Gospel: Matthew 5:43-48

This is the climax of the antitheses of the Sermon on the Mount—the command to love one's enemies. It is widely thought that the antithetical form of these sayings is due to Matthean redaction (the parallels in Luke lack the antithetical form, and therefore the form as such can hardly go back to Q). However, the content of most of these sayings is coherent with Jesus' general radical stance, so they may be regarded as authentic in substance.

Jesus' command to love the enemy is so radical, even when compared with its Old Testament or Jewish parallels, as to be distinctive. There is no actual command in the Old Testament to hate one's enemies, and in fact there are occasional commands to love them (Isa 24:19; Exod 23:4-5; Prov 25:21-22). On the other hand, the psalms are full of cries of vengeance upon enemies. Qumran continued this line of teaching: "Hate all the sons of darkness" (1 QS 1:9-10). This, however, was not personal hatred but a hatred of those who opposed the Qumran community and all that it stood for. In Matthew the enemies in view are especially the enemies of Matthew's Christian community, those who are persecuting it. That would include both synagogue Jews and Roman political authorities. If only the Church had consistently carried out this injunction throughout its history!

NATIONAL HOLIDAY
(Lutheran)

Reading I: Jeremiah 29:4-14

The date of this passage must be placed between 597 and 586 B.C., that is, during the first Exile, when Zedekiah was puppet king. This pericope is taken from Jeremiah's letter to the exiles in Babylon. He urges them to build houses for themselves and to settle down to a real community life. The Exile is going to last quite a long time. Second, they must seek the welfare of the state, even though it is an alien state. Third, the exiles will eventually be restored to their homeland.

Reading II: Romans 13:1-10

Given the fact that this pericope has played such an important, and sometimes fateful, role in the history of both the Lutheran and Anglican Churches since the Reformation, it is remarkable that it has not been read in the ordinary course of Sundays. One is tempted to suppose that it has been deliberately omitted! It propounds a "conservative" doctrine of the state that is not too popular today. The state is here the servant of God, a minister of God's wrath against sin, and the promoter of God's righteousness. This is a line of teaching that goes back to the time of Jeremiah (see the first reading) and Second Isaiah (where Cyrus of Persia is called "God's anointed").

Modern Christians (especially in post-Nazi Europe) often regret that St. Paul says nothing about what is to be done when the state ceases to maintain justice and promote the good, and instead becomes itself an instrument of tyranny and injustice. What would Paul advocate— submission, passive resistance, or armed rebellion? One other scriptural passage deals with this problem, namely, Rev 13, where the state (Nero's Rome, which persecuted the Christians) is equated with the beast from the abyss. But even there the utmost that is recommended is passive resistance. Nowhere in the New Testament is armed rebellion justified.

The truth is that the New Testament does not offer a complete doctrine of the state. But we do have to take into account both Rom 13 and Rev 13. The state has a God-given function to hold evil in check and to promote the good. However, it is also always potentially demonic. To the extent that the state acts as the servant of God, it is entitled to our respect, our obedience to its laws, and our payment of taxes. Where the state is a democracy, the way to rectify it if it is unjust is by our votes. Where Christians cannot change the state's policy, the normal reaction must be that of passive resistance and readiness to suffer. Armed rebellion can only be an *ultima ratio* (see Dietrich Bonhoeffer), undertaken only after much heart-searching and prayer.

Gospel: Mark 12:13-17

Form-critically this is a pronouncement story, told for the sake of the punch line, "Render to Caesar . . . ." This passage has been involved in much the same controversy as Rom 13. It is a little more qualified in its recognition of the right of the state to command our obedience and our taxes, for it holds this right in the perspective of the paramount right of God. Caesar is entitled to his penny, but God requires the whole of life, including that part which we give, namely, the penny. The state, therefore, has only a limited right to our obedience, and where it conflicts with our allegiance to God, we must obey God rather than human authorities— and suffer the consequences if need be.

The Homily

These readings, especially the Lutheran ones, call for an examination of the place of the state within the Christian scheme of things. Any Christian estimate of the state must do justice to the dialectic between Rom 13 and Rev 13, even when our text is Rom 13 alone.

The Episcopalian readings, especially the gospel, also place the state within the context of the sovereignty of God. Law must always serve humanity, not some abstract theory; it must always be applied to the concrete situation. Law must always take human weakness into account. Law must be applied without discrimination against the alien or the weak. Law must never absolutize the status quo.

August 6

TRANSFIGURATION

Reading I: Daniel 7:9-10, 13-14

As we point out on the second Sunday of Lent in series A, the transfiguration appears there as a curtain-raiser to the passion. Today the accent is rather different. The transfiguration can now be considered for its own sake. It is related to Christology, to the understanding of the person of Jesus.

The keynote is struck by the first reading, the vision of the Son of man as he is presented before the "ancient of days." Note that the scene is not of a coming of the Son of man to earth, but of his being brought before the presence of God. The analogue is the ascension rather than the

43

second coming. The transfiguration as related in the gospel reading, in which Jesus' face shines like the sun and his garments are white as light, shows that it is he who is to be glorified like the Son of man. For although nothing is said in Daniel about the shining face or the white garments of the Son of man, similar features are combined with the picture of the ascended Christ as the Danielic Son of man in chapter 1 of the Apocalypse. The transfiguration reveals Jesus in his earthly existence as the one who is to be exalted as the Son of man after his suffering. It is an "anticipation of his eschatology" (G. Kittel).

Responsorial Psalm: 97:1-2, 5-6, 9

The psalm picks up the theme of kingship from the Danielic vision. Of course, it concerns the kingship of Yahweh, but there is no difficulty for Christian interpretation in shifting the term "Lord" from Yahweh-Kyrios to Christos-Kyrios.

Reading II: 2 Peter 1:16-19

This passage contains an account of the transfiguration that, according to some scholars, is independent of, and in some respects more primitive than, the accounts in the Gospels. As it stands, it serves two purposes: (1) it reinforces the pseudonymous claim of the letter to have been written by the apostle Peter. We have to remember that the second century, when this letter was probably written, had very different ideas about pseudonymity from ours. It was a device to enable an authority, now dead, to continue to speak in the changed circumstances of the Church subsequent to his death. By claiming to have been present at the transfiguration, the author reinforces his claim to be speaking in the name of the apostle Peter. (2) The transfiguration story is used to prove that the Christian gospel is not based upon a myth, but upon an event that actually happened, namely, the earthly life of Jesus. Of course, this historical event receives interpretation, albeit in mythological terms, for the Danielic Son of man is unquestionably mythological in origin. But a myth *per se* is an entirely unhistorical speculation. The gospel involves the use of mythological concepts, but it uses them to interpret history, which is a very different thing.

Gospel: Matthew 17:1-9

Commentary on this passage is provided on the second Sunday of Lent   43
in series A.

The Homily

It is quite clear that the homily should draw out the Christological significance of the transfiguration story. It unveils the glory of the ascended Christ in the midst of his incarnate life. We encounter the glory of Christ, not in a transcendent sphere apart from his incarnate existence—that would be to follow a "cleverly devised myth"—but precisely in his historical existence as that is extended to us in the word and sacrament. Nor, on the other hand, can we regard him merely as a figure of the past, making him an ideal for some cause we are keen on today, as in some contemporary theologies of revolution. Because of his ascended glory, unveiled in the transfiguration, he belongs not to the past as a mere human example, but to the present as the ever contemporary Lord. In this way we can seek to do justice to the traditional Chalcedonian definition of Christ as divine and human "without division or separation."

August 15

ASSUMPTION OF THE BLESSED VIRGIN MARY

The continued observance of the assumption on a Sunday when August 15 falls on that day would seem to contradict the new general principle that only dominical feasts should displace the regular Sunday propers. Perhaps the significance of this is that Mariology, rightly understood, is an aspect of Christology. The Blessed Virgin Mary is nothing in herself, but is of great importance in salvation history as the chosen instrument of the incarnation.

For an Anglican, who is not committed to the dogma proclaimed by Pope Pius XII in 1950, the assumption of Mary belongs to the poetry of the Christian religion, something we sing about in hymns but only a pictorial expression of the scriptural truth: "All generations will call me blessed." This is how the assumption is treated in a well-known Anglican hymn:

> O higher than the cherubim,
> More glorious than the seraphim,
>   Lead their praises,
>   Alleluia.
> Thou bearer of the eternal Word
> Most gracious, magnify the Lord,
>   Alleluia.
>   (Athelstan Riley)

It was in the same spirit that in the seventeenth century a statue of the crowned Madonna and Child was placed over the porch of St. Mary the Virgin, the university church at Oxford.

Reading I: Revelation 11:19a; 12:1-6a, 10ab

The meaning of this mysterious passage is obscure, and many interpretations have been suggested. The child who is born is clearly the Messiah. This is shown by the application of the messianic Ps 2:9 to the child in verse 5, and by the proclamation that follows his exaltation to the throne of God (v. 10). But who is the woman? There are three possibilities:

1. She is the old Israel, the nation from whom the Messiah came. Much in this passage suggests the old Israel waiting for the birth of the Messiah. The Old Testament background suggests this (see Isa 66:7). According to this view, the seer is taking up and partly Christianizing earlier pictures of Israel waiting for the coming of the Messiah.

2. The woman is the Church, the new Israel, the mother of the faithful. This is supported by 12:17, which speaks of other children belonging to the woman who "keep the commandments of God and bear testimony to Jesus."

3. An interpretation popular among medieval expositors and revived in a somewhat more sophisticated form in recent Catholic exegesis (and clearly accepted by the choice of this passage for this feast) equates the woman with the Blessed Virgin Mary.

Probably there is no need to choose between these three interpretations. For Mary is the daughter of Zion, the quintessential expression of the old Israel as the community of faith and obedience awaiting the coming of the Messiah, the community in which the Messiah is born. But she is also the quintessential expression of the new Israel, of those who "believe" and are justified on the grounds of their faith, of those who obey his word and who suffer for the testimony of Jesus.

Responsorial Psalm: 45:9b-11, 15

In its original intention, this psalm celebrates the marriage of an Israelite king to a foreign princess. In order to fit it to its liturgical use here, an allegorical interpretation has to be given. The king in the psalm has to be equated with the Messiah (there is New Testament precedence for this in Heb 1:8-9); the queen, with Israel, his bride. This provides an indirect connection with the Blessed Virgin Mary as the personification of Israel. But the allegory must not be pressed. Not only does it do violence to the original meaning, but it does not fit the desired application. For Mary is the mother rather than the bride of Christ, and she is his bride only insofar as she is the personification of the true Israel, one who believed in him (Acts 1:14).

Reading II: 1 Corinthians 15:20-27

This is the passage to which the Protestants appeal against the dogma of the bodily assumption of Mary. It asserts that all human beings are in bondage to death, and that they can only attain to immortality through the resurrection of the dead. Christ, however, has broken the bondage of death and has become the first fruits of the dead. Meanwhile, all in Christ await their resurrection until the parousia. There is, therefore, no place in the "order" for a prior resurrection of the Blessed Virgin Mary: Christ the first fruits, then at his coming those who belong to Christ.

It must be left to Catholic exegetes to square the dogma of the bodily assumption of Mary with this scripture. As an Anglican, the present writer would simply claim that the life which all believers have is inalienable by death, that therefore the Blessed Virgin Mary, like all the saints, has some kind of continuing existence in Christ (see Rev 6:9), and that we express the high honor due her by picturing her as exalted to the very throne of God.

Gospel: Luke 1:39-56

This gospel falls into two parts—the visitation narrative and the *Magnificat*. There is an interesting textual problem in verse 46. Some manuscripts read "Elizabeth said," a reading that would fit the typology: Hannah-Samuel/Elizabeth-John the Baptist. It is arguable, however, that in the structure of the Lucan infancy narratives, the purpose of which is to bring out the relation of John to Jesus as that of forerunner to the Messiah, of inferior to superior, the *Magnificat* must be assigned to Mary. Perhaps the pre-Lucan source, which quite likely came from the "Baptist" circles, had attributed the song (modeled on the song of Hannah) to Elizabeth, and Luke himself transferred it to Mary.

The *Magnificat* should be read, not as an individual utterance of Mary, but as the utterance of the representative of the true Israel. This is indicated by the switch from the first person singular to the third person plural in verse 50. It is the true Israel personfied by Mary who rejoices in the Lord at the coming of the Messiah, whose humiliation ("low estate") the Lord regards, and who henceforth will be called "blessed" as the people to whom the Messiah has come. This is not to downgrade Mary, but to exalt her role as the key-pin of salvation history.

The Homily

Today the subject matter of the homily is set by the title of the feast. It is the homilist's task to show what the glory of Mary in heaven has to say for our own lives: the assurance that where she is, we all expect to be. Thus, we may deal, not with what is distinctive about Mary (except for the timing of her ultimate salvation), but with what we have in common with her as fellow Christian believers.

First Monday in September
LABOR DAY

In the Roman Catholic Lectionary, today's liturgy is entitled "Blessing of Human Labor," which is included among the Masses for Various Occasions. Other Masses, such as that for Civic Observances, for the Progress of Peoples, for Peace and Justice, or for St. Joseph the Worker, may also be used on this day.

OLD TESTAMENT READINGS

Reading 1: Genesis 1:26–2:3

This passage receives comment as the first reading for the Easter Vigil (see *65* series A). In the present context this story is read for what it says about the created order. It is important to notice that labor is not treated in the Bible exclusively as a curse imposed after the fall (as the Nazis accused the Jews of teaching from the Old Testament), and therefore as an evil to be avoided as much as possible. Rather, labor has a dignity in that through it humanity is invited to share with God in his activity in creation. The curse of Gen 3 applies to the conditions under which we are forced to work after the fall. The Bible recognizes both sides of the dialectic: the dignity of labor and its wearing toil.

Reading 2: Genesis 2:4b-9, 15

For comment, see the first Sunday of Lent in series A. Note that both the *38* P (Priestly) and J (Yahwist) sources regard human work as part of the created order.

Episcopal Reading: Sirach 38:27-32

This interesting passage contrasts the labor of the working classes with that of the intellectuals, that of the craftspersons with that of the scribes. Written from the scribes' point of view, the pericope somewhat grudgingly concedes that the maker of seals, the smith, and the potter are as necessary for the well-being of society as is the intellectual.

NEW TESTAMENT READING

2 Thessalonians 3:6-12, 16

Commentary on 2 Thess 3:7-12 can be found on the thirty-third Sunday *526*
of the year in series C. We confine our comments here to verses 6 and 15.

Verse 6 marks the beginning of a new section. At this point Paul (or
the deutero-Pauline author of the letter) turns to parenesis, that is, ethical
exhortation. This teaching claims the authority not just of Paul but of
"our Lord Jesus Christ." It is directed against certain Christians who are
idle and refusing to work. The probable clue to their behavior is that they
are gnosticizing Christians who believe that through Christ they have
already been transferred to heavenly existence and therefore do not have
to concern themselves with mundane matters. Such people are probably
to be shunned, not because they are lazy, but because they hold to false
teaching. Verse 16 is a concluding epistolary blessing.

The teaching about work belongs to a particularly concrete situation
in first-century Christianity. It would be wrong to lift it out of its context
and apply it directly to our situation today. For instance, it would be a
misuse of this passage if we were to take it as a condemnation of the poor
who cannot find work and who have no alternative but to live on welfare.
Rather, it is a condemnation of any kind of antisocial behavior in the
sphere of human labor.

RESPONSORIAL PSALMS

Responsorial Psalm 1: 90:2-4, 12-14, 16

For comment on this psalm, see the twenty-third Sunday of the year in *502*
series C and the twenty-eighth Sunday of the year in series B. The refrain *357*
highlights the psalmist's prayer to God to grant success to his labors.

Responsorial Psalm 2: 127:1-2

This is a wisdom psalm. It was sung at the autumn festival as a prayer
for God's blessing on the ensuing year. Verse 1 asserts that human labor
cannot succeed without the help of Yahweh. The second stanza is particularly relevant to the hustle and bustle of city life today, though it suggests also that this is by no means a modern affliction!

GOSPELS

Gospel Reading 1: Matthew 6:31-34

For comment, see the eighth Sunday of the year in series A. *127*

Gospel Reading 2: Matthew 25:14-30

For comment, see the twenty-third Sunday of the year in series A. *194*

The Homily

Work belongs to the very structure of human life as created. In Gen 1 and 2 it precedes the fall and therefore is not a punishment for sin. It belongs to human creatureliness, not to human sinfulness. Thus it has an essential dignity. This applies to all kinds of work—that of the hands as well as that of the brain (see the Episcopalian reading from Sirach).

Yet, as Gen 3:17-19 (not one of the readings provided) reminds us, human labor, like everything else, is affected by the fall. Labor itself is not evil, but the conditions under which it is performed may be evil. It becomes an area in which the fallenness of humankind takes its toll in *hard* labor, an area in which the exploitation both of human beings and of natural resources is always a danger, and an area in which behavior is often antisocial (see the New Testament reading).

While recognizing the dignity of human labor, the Bible does not romanticize it, and neither should the homilist. The first gospel reading, with its condemnation of anxiety, highlights another expression of human sinfulness in the area of work, namely, making greed for profit the sole motive of work. The second gospel reading reinforces the social significance of labor: it is an area in which service to the community may be rendered.

September 14

TRIUMPH OF THE CROSS

In Lutheran and Episcopalian usage, this feast is known as Holy Cross Day.

Reading I: Numbers 21:4b-9

The literal meaning of the serpent story is fairly obvious. The Hebrew people, as they wandered through the desert after the Exodus, were afflicted by the bites of venomous serpents. Moses cured them by setting up a bronze serpent. When the people looked at this serpent, they were cured.

No doubt this story has primitive origins in a Canaanite snake cult that was fostered in Israel until Hezekiah's reformation (2 Kgs 18:4). But the story has been taken over into the religion of Yahweh and purified of its cultic associations. The bronze serpent becomes a sign of Yawheh's healing presence. In the Fourth Gospel this incident is seen as a type of the cross (see below).

Reading I (Episcopal and Lutheran): Isaiah 45:21-25

Second Isaiah more than once adopts this setting for his poem: a courtroom scene in which the nations are brought before Yahweh and made to witness that Israel's return from exile is his mighty act. The concluding part of this scene provided a quarry from which a pre-Pauline hymn to Christ celebrated the messianic salvation, which Paul redacted (Phil 2:6-11) in accordance with his *theologia crucis* and which forms the New Testament reading for today's feast. Hence the fittingness of this passage for Holy Cross Day.

Responsorial Psalm: 78:1-2, 34-38

This psalm, the longest in the psalter except for Psalm 119, is a didactic poem on Israel's salvation history. It is thought that it may have been used in the annual liturgy of the renewal of the covenant, an observance featured also in the Manual of Discipline of the Qumran community.

The present selection consists of four stanzas. The first stanza (vv. 1-2) is a wisdom introduction, emphasizing the didactic nature of the poem. The second stanza (vv. 34-35) selects that part of the Exodus story that corresponds to the episode of the fiery serpents (hence its suitability as a response to the reading of that story). God's discipline and chastisement produce repentance, however temporary. The third stanza (vv. 36-37) speaks of the people's later relapse into the sin of unfaithfulness. The fourth stanza (v. 38) speaks of God's unwearying compassion. Such compassion was exhibited in the episode of the fiery serpents and preeminently on the cross.

Reading II: Philippians 2:6-11

The Pauline adaptation of the early Christian hymn to Christ is also used each year on Palm Sunday and is commented upon there in series A. 54

Reading II (Episcopalian alternative): Galatians 6:14-18

Comment on this reading is given on the fourteenth Sunday of the year in series C. 483

Reading II (Lutheran alternative): 1 Corinthians 1:18-24

Confronted by specific concrete problems in his churches, Paul goes back to the central message: the kerygma of Christ crucified. Of course, this has further implications. It implies that God sent his Son into the world for his salvific mission. It implies that God has raised him from the dead, for without the resurrection the cross would not be perceived or proclaimed as saving event. It implies that Christ has been exalted to the right hand of God, for only so does he continue to be present in the kerygma. It implies that he will come again in glory, for only then will the triumph of the cross become effective on a cosmic scale.

The concrete situation envisaged in 1 Corinthians is spelled out in our comments for the third Sunday of the year in series A. To what is said 113 there we would add that the Corinthians were exhibiting gnosticizing tendencies. They viewed salvation as am impartation of knowledge mediated by the sacraments. This had the effect, not of changing them, but of uncovering what they already were. It is to this misinterpretation of the gospel that Paul applied the word of the cross. The Corinthians regarded the cross as "folly." They probably thought of it as an embarrassing event that was simply the gateway through which Christ had to pass in order to return to the true realm of the Spirit, which he had never really left. According to Paul, however, such an attitude, if taken seriously, would simply show that the Corinthians were "perishing." They were cut off from authentic existence. But to those who were on the way to salvation ("being saved"—note the present tense: salvation is not accomplished once for all but is the inauguration of a process) it was paradoxically the wisdom and power of God.

Gospel: John 3:13-17

Comment on this gospel can be found on the fourth Sunday of Lent in 241 series B.

Gospel (Lutheran): John 12:20-33; (Episcopalian): John 12:31-36a

The episode about the Greeks at the feast coming to see Jesus provides the setting for the last of the public discourses of Jesus in the Fourth Gospel. It forms a climax to chapters 11–12, and indeed to the whole public ministry. The hour of Jesus' glorification is something to which the Gospel has looked right from the beginning (see the first miracle at Cana of Galilee). This glorification is to be effected through the "lifting up" of the Son of man—a typically Johannine double entendre, meaning both his being lifted up on the cross and his exaltation to heaven. When that double event happens, and not before, the way will be open for the Gentiles to come in. Hence the Greeks cannot at present see Jesus and they disappear from the story.

We have here an incident that has been merged into a dialogue. Probably it was originally a pronouncement story or a setting for a (now submerged) parable, the parable of the grain of wheat that must die before it can bring forth fruit.

The Homily

The feast of the Holy Cross provides an opportunity for the homilist to handle the cross in a way different from that in which it has to be handled in Passion Week and on Good Friday. At that season we pass through the cross and passion with Christ, spiritually sharing his death in order that we may later participate in his resurrection. On Holy Cross Day we look back on the cross and contemplate its efficacy in drawing all people to faith and salvation, viewing it in the light of the resurrection as the triumph of God, hidden now but to be universally acknowledged at the consummation. Pictorially, we may say that in Passiontide we contemplate the suffering Christ hanging on the cross (the suffering crucifix), and on Holy Cross Day we contemplate the triumphant Christ (the triumphant crucifix, with Christ fully clothed and crowned).

The Swedish Lutheran bishop Gustav Aulén wrote a fine book entitled *Christus Victor*, in which he lays great, though one-sided, emphasis on the cross as triumph. There is a place for both the suffering and the triumphant crucifix, and the Church year provides opportunities for both. There is also a hint of the Abelardian view of the atonement in the image of the brazen serpent. Contemplation of the cross has itself a saving effect (as in the experience of Charles de Foucauld).

November 1

ALL SAINTS

All Saints' Day is one of the most loved feasts in the Church year. At least this is so for Anglicans, and I suspect the same is true for Roman Catholics. The feast marks the transition from the earlier part of the post-Pentecost season, with its emphasis on growth in grace, to the last Sundays of the Church year, when the emphasis shifts to the "last things," the final consummation of history.

It is not entirely clear whom we are to include in this celebration. Originally it was a commemoration of early martyrs whose names were unrecorded and who therefore were not, and could not be, included by name on the day of their martyrdom. They were not, in the language of the later West, officially "canonized," although they may have qualified if anything had been known about them. Yet, the New Testament calls all baptized Christians "saints," *hagioi,* holy ones. Even in writing to the Corinthians, whom he has to castigate for the worst possible moral offenses, Paul can call them "saints" (1 Cor 1:2; the Greek means "called as saints," not just "called to be saints," as the RSV translates it). Their sanctity was not a moral achievement, not even the complete triumph of grace in their lives, but rested upon their having been made objectively holy by baptism (see 1 Cor 6:11). Yet, it was a natural development that the term "saint" should have come to be reserved for those in whom grace had its most signal triumph, for those who had achieved the Pauline imperative "Become what you are."

In the light of this New Testament doctrine, All Saints' Day could be interpreted as a commemoration of all the faithful departed. But the Church has traditionally separated this wider commemoration from All Saints' Day and observed it on the day following. Thus she has drawn a distinction between those for whom she finds it natural to thank God for the victory they have achieved by his grace, and those for whom she finds it more fitting to pray that God have mercy on them in "that day" (see 2 Tim 1:18).

Reading I: Revelation 7:2-4, 9-12

The Book of Revelation is not meant to be a timeless description of what it is like in heaven. Like all apocalyptic literature, it was written to encourage the faithful in a time of great distress. Writing about A.D. 96, John the Seer expects a great persecution to break out against the Church in Asia Minor. Many Christians will die a martyr's death. He seeks to assure them that this outburst of hostility against the Christian community (by the emperor Domitian?) is the prelude of the End, when God will vindicate his martyrs. So the seer describes the triumphant state that awaits them in this symbolic language of white robes, palms, etc., and pictures them as singing the song of triumph that was probably sung in the Church on earth (perhaps a paschal hymn), "Salvation belongs to our God . . . . Amen! Blessing and glory . . . !"

If we take the seer's words literally, he was mistaken in thinking that his crisis was the last of the crises before the End. But that is the literary method of all apocalypses. Each succeeding crisis in the Church's history confronts us with the eternal issues of life and death. History is a struggle between good and evil in which, through the victory of Christ, the victory of the faithful is assured. Meanwhile, in the very midst of her tribulations on earth, the martyr Church already sings the songs of victory in her liturgy.

In another way, too, the Church is an anticipation of the kingdom of heaven. For she, too, is a pluralistic fellowship consisting of "people from every nation, race, tribe and language" (caption).

Responsorial Psalm: 24:1-4b, 5-6

This psalm is of a liturgical type, not an expression of personal piety like many of the psalms. It was probably used in early days to accompany a procession of the ark to the temple. Two choirs sing antiphonally. One asks, Who is worthy to ascend the hill of the Lord? The other replies, Those who have the necessary moral qualities. When Psalm 24 is used as a response to Rev 7 on All Saints' Day, the temple becomes a figure for the consummated kingdom of heaven. Those deemed worthy to enter are the Christian saints.

Reading II: 1 John 3:1-3

The first letter of John was written to condemn the false teachings that were afflicting the churches around A.D. 100. This heresy involved a denial of the true humanity of Christ and a wrong understanding of Christian existence. This passage is concerned with the second aspect. The false teachers represented some kind of gnosticizing movement. They based their system of beliefs on what they claimed to be a revealed "gnosis," or knowledge. They claimed that they were already perfected, and therefore had no need to make any moral effort.

Against such teaching our author insists on the element of the "not yet" in the Christian life. It does *not yet* appear what it shall be. To be a child of God already here and now is only an advance installment of our final salvation. The writer is making the same point that Paul was making when he called the gift of the Spirit a "down payment." The final consummated state is, for the Christian, still a matter of hope. Meanwhile, the present task should be to purify oneself from sin as Christ is pure.

Note also the element of healthy agnosticism in this author's description of the future state. He cannot describe it, except to say that "we shall be like him." That warns us to take the language of the Apocalypse, not as a literal description, but as valuable hints that suggest a truth to be grasped intuitively, though incapable of definition. It is enough to know that we, and all the saints, shall be "like him."

Are we to suppose that the saints are already "like him"? Or do they, too, have to wait until he appears? Holy Scripture gives no clear answer. We are told all that we need to know for our present existence. We have been made God's children; we have a hope of achieving the ultimate destiny for which we were created, and meanwhile our task is to strive for purity of life.

Gospel: Matthew 5:1-12a

The beatitudes form the opening of the Great Sermon. In Matthew it is the Sermon on the Mount, in Luke the Sermon on the Plain. Matthew's purpose in choosing this location is that he understands the teaching of the sermon as the new law, corresponding to the old law given on Mount Sinai, and for him Jesus is the second Moses, the giver of the new law.

Each of the beatitudes falls into two parts. The first part describes the humiliation of the present, the second the glory to come. The beatitudes are addressed, not to all people indiscriminately, but to the disciples, to those who have left all to follow Jesus. Note that in Luke the beatitudes are all in the second person plural. Here Luke is probably original, for the "you" style has survived in the last of Matthew's beatitudes. So Jesus is addressing those who have left all to follow him. *They* are the poor— in spirit, as Matthew correctly explains. They are the ones who realize that they are spiritually the have-nots, who have no righteousness of their own, and therefore they hunger and thirst for (God's) righteousness.

The second group of beatitudes is more activistic. It is the merciful, the pure in heart, and the peacemakers who are pronounced blessed. Faith, if it is genuine, works through love, as Paul put it. It is those who combine both the passive and active sides of a true relation to God who are pronounced, already here and now, to be blessed, and promised future participation in the kingdom of God.

It has often been observed that the beatitudes describe the life of Christ himself. He was all the things and did all the things the beatitudes enumerate. And that brought him to the cross, and beyond that to the resurrection. All Saints' Day suggests the further thought that the saints are those who most perfectly manifested the Christ-like character described in the first part of the beatitudes, and who therefore now partake of the promises in the second part: *Theirs* is the kingdom of heaven; *they* are now comforted; *they* have inherited the "land," *ha-aretz*, the promised land of the kingdom of God; *they* are filled with the delights of the messianic banquet; *they* have obtained mercy; *they* have achieved the full potentialities of divine filiation.

The Homily

There are several themes that could be developed in today's homily. In a situation of crisis the homilist could draw out the promise of ultimate victory for God's cause. The theme of the Church's liturgy on earth as an anticipation of the victory song of heaven could also be developed. Or one might speak of the Church catholic as transcending all nations, races, tribes, and languages, and perhaps relate this quite concretely to local tensions within the parish, with a plea that the Church should be a model community in which these differences, though not denied, are transcended.

Perhaps the most suitable theme for All Saints' Day would be a reflection on the purity of life manifested in the saints. In this way the second reading could be linked with the sixth beatitude read in the gospel: "Blessed are the pure in heart, for they shall see God." The homilist could take the beatitudes first as a description of the life of Christ, and then the lives of the saints as a reflection of that life. That could be followed by an exhortation to the congregation to strive to follow Christ's life as exemplified in the lives of the saints, so that we, too, may become partakers of the inheritance of the saints in light.

November 2
ALL SOULS

The readings for All Souls' Day are to be chosen from the thirty-five readings provided for Masses for the Dead in the Lectionary. Comment on all these readings can be found on pages 595–617.

November 9
DEDICATION OF ST. JOHN LATERAN

Reading I: Ezekiel 47:1-2, 8-9, 12
Ezekiel, who prophesied during the Babylonian Exile, had probably served as a priest before the Exile. The latter part of his book (chs. 40–48) consists of visions of the temple as it will be restored after the return from exile. In point of fact, the visions serve as a kind of idealized blueprint for the later rebuilding of the temple. Out of it will flow a river of water (the mythical river of God or sacred river), which will have miraculous effects on the land. From the east will issue a stream that will flow down into the Dead Sea, making its waters sweet and healthy like the Mediterranean. The Dead Sea will then swarm with fish, and trees yielding fruit all year round will grow on its banks. Their leaves will have healing properties (an image taken up later in the Book of Revelation).

Responsorial Psalm: 45:2-3, 5-6, 8-9
This is one of the royal psalms, celebrating the marriage of the king with a foreign princess. Usually it is thought to have been composed for an actual royal wedding, though the identity of the king in question is in dispute. Some, however, take it to be an ode used in the ritual of the sacred marriage that they think took place every year in early Israel.

In later times this psalm acquired a messianic connotation in Judaism. It was interpreted Christologically in the Christian Church, the bride being the people of God in each case.

The first two stanzas praise the king for his beauty, while the third stanza introduces the figure of the queen for the first time.

Reading II: 1 Corinthians 3:9c-11, 16-17

Paul uses the image of building for the Church—building a temple, a house, or both. He describes his apostolic labors in terms of building. As an apostle, he lays the foundation, which is the gospel of Jesus Christ. The superstructure is built by others, that is, by the local ministry.

Two points need to be made here. One is that the term "edify" is connected, not with "edification" in a pietistic sense, but with building up (*edificare*) the Church as a corporate entity. The other point is that the temple imagery in this context signifies primarily the place of the indwelling Spirit of God, not a place of worship. Richard Meux Benson, the nineteenth-century founder of the Society of St. John the Evangelist, an Anglican religious order, used to protest that an overemphasis on the presence of Christ in the reserved sacrament tended to obscure the more important scriptural truth of the presence of Christ through the Spirit in his body, the Church.

Here the foundation, laid by the Apostle, is Jesus Christ himself. The foundation marks out the shape of the building to be erected. It is the task of the successors of the apostles to see to it that the Church keeps the shape of its original foundation as the superstructure is erected upon it. Those whose work it is to build the superstructure will be under judgment at the last day and will have to give an account of how they have built.

Gospel: John 2:13-22

For comment, see the third Sunday of Lent in series B.   *238*

The Homily

The reading from 1 Corinthians serves as a bridge between the other readings. Here the image of the temple about which the first reading and the gospel speak is applied to the Church. This reminds us that the Church of Jesus Christ does not consist of buildings made of stone—or of any other material, for that matter—but of people. The church building as such has no special sanctity of its own but is holy because it is there that the people of God, the Church, the body of Christ, meets. I often recall a powerful illustration of this truth from World War II. On the Sunday morning after Coventry Cathedral had been blitzed by the *Luftwaffe*, the congregation met in the living room of the provost's home and celebrated the Eucharist. The medieval building was gone but the people of God remained!

The Old Testament reading suggests another possibility for the homily. The rivers flowing from the temple suggest how liturgy must change the world outside. The church is designed as a space for the performance of the liturgy, but from it the people of God must go out into the world to transform it. Note that this turns the response inside out: "world" instead of "city of God."

Fourth Thursday of November
THANKSGIVING

The following readings may be used in the United States and Canada on their respective Thanksgiving Days (Roman Catholic). The Episcopalian provisions are also included here.

OLD TESTAMENT READINGS

Reading 1: 1 Kings 8:55-61

Earlier portions of Solomon's prayer at the dedication of the first temple are used on the ninth Sunday of the year in series C. Today's reading is the closing benediction of the prayer. Its theology is obviously later than the time of Solomon, being clearly Deuteronomic. There are four petitions:

1. that Yahweh may be with Israel now as he was with the patriarchs;
2. that Israel may keep God's law;
3. that Yahweh may maintain the cause of his people;
4. that all the peoples of the earth may know that Yahweh is God.

The universalism of the four petitions is especially characteristic of the later Deuteronomic theology.

It is important to observe the role that the recital of God's mighty acts in the past plays in biblical thanksgiving, the purpose of this recital being that God may extend the same actions into the present—the biblical notion of anamnesis.

Reading 2: Sirach 50:22-24

This excerpt comes from the conclusion of Sirach's praise and thanksgiving for the heroes of Israel's past, concluding with Simeon ben Jochanan, the Maccabean high priest. It is interesting to note that the German Lutheran hymnodist Martin Rinckhart (1596–1649) based his well-known hymn *Nun danket alle Gott* on this excerpt. Perhaps it will help our Lutheran brothers and sisters to recover the judicious liturgical use of deuterocanonical selections to note that their forebears had less scruples!

470

Reading 3: Isaiah 63:7-9

This is part of a long intercessory psalm that explicates the prayer described in chapter 62. It begins with a historical prologue describing the Exodus deliverance and recalls how Yahweh was present with his people in all their afflictions (this shows that Yahweh was the kind of God who could eventually become incarnate).

This excerpt begins with an expression of thanksgiving and goes on to call for a continuous renewal of the redemptive act. The date is uncertain, but since Jerusalem was evidently in ruins, it must have been composed during or shortly after the Exile.

Reading 4: Zephaniah 3:14-15

These verses are part of the reading for the third Sunday of Advent in   *382*
series C and receive comment there. The return from exile that this text presupposes was an obvious occasion for national thanksgiving. In applying the text today, we must be careful not to suggest that the United States is the successor to Israel as God's people. That is the danger of civic religion. The history of our country is never a salvation history, though civil blessings create the context for salvation history, and as Christians we must give thanks for them accordingly.

Episcopal Reading: Deuteronomy 8:1-3, 6-10 (17-20)

For comment, see Corpus Christi in series A.   *105*

NEW TESTAMENT READINGS

Reading 1: 1 Corinthians 1:3-9

For comment, see the first Sunday of Advent in series B.   *202*

Reading 2: Ephesians 1:3-14

For comment, see the fifteenth Sunday of the year in series B.   *325*

Reading 3: Colossians 3:12-17

For comment, see the feast of the Holy Family in series A.   *24*

Episcopal Reading: James 1:17-18, 21-27

See the twenty-second Sunday of the year in series B for comment.   *343*

RESPONSORIAL PSALMS

Responsorial Psalm 1: 1 Chronicles 29:10-12

This is the Chronicler's version of David's prayer over the offerings for the building of the first temple, which was accomplished by his son Solomon. It has doubtless been adapted from the liturgy of the temple as the Chronicler knew it in his own day. The second and third stanzas were taken up into seventeenth-century Anglican liturgies as a presentation sentence at the placing of the alms and bread and wine on the holy table.

Responsorial Psalm 2: 113:1-8
For comment, see the twenty-fifth Sunday of the year in series C. *506*

Responsorial Psalm 3: 138:1-5
For comment, see the twenty-first Sunday of the year in series A and the *160* fifth Sunday of the year in series C. *459*

Responsorial Psalm 4: 145:2-11
For comment, see the fourteenth and twenty-fifth Sundays of the year in *142* series A and the thirty-first Sunday of the year in series C. *169*
520

Episcopal Responsorial Psalm: 65 or 65:9-14
For comment, see the fifteenth Sunday of the year in series A. *144*

GOSPELS

Gospel Reading 1: Mark 5:18-20
At some time during the pre-Gospel oral transmission of this exorcism story, it must have been expanded into a missionary story. A former demoniac who has been healed begs Jesus to be allowed to stay with him and become a disciple. Surprisingly, Jesus refuses this request and tells him to go back to his own home and family and to tell them what the Lord (that is, Yahweh) has done for him. The man goes home accordingly and tells what *Jesus* has done for him. This is not because he confuses Jesus with Yahweh; it means simply that he recognizes Jesus as Yahweh's agent. The point that is being made today is that gratitude must take the form of witness, whether as a disciple, as it was in some cases, or as a witness, as it was in the case of the Gerasene demoniac.

Gospel Reading 2: Luke 17:11-19
See the twenty-eighth Sunday of the year in series C for comment, and *512* note there the reference to Albert Schweitzer's sermon on gratitude.

Episcopal Gospel Reading: Matthew 6:25-33
This classic passage ("Be not anxious") comes from the Q material and

is placed by Matthew in the Sermon on the Mount. In Q it was probably not part of the Great Sermon, since Luke has it in a different place (Luke 12:22-31). It consists of a series of wisdom sayings, although they are related to Jesus' eschatological proclamation (see verse 33). The injunction not to be anxious is thus not a recipe for mental health but a challenge to put the kingdom of God first. The injunction employs the argument *a maiore ad minus,* from the greater to the lesser: If God created the body and life, how much more will he provide such lesser things as food and clothing.

As Professor Eduard Schweizer has observed in his commentary on Matthew, "We are not to worry, because worry drives out joy and makes action impossible, and God is encountered in acts. The choice therefore is not between action and passivity but between two different kinds of action." The true kind of action that is expected of us is to seek the kingdom of God and his righteousness, that is, the law of Moses, as expounded in Jesus.

The Homily

The homilist could contrast the nature celebrations of Israel's neighbors and of the other nations in the world today with the historical celebrations of ancient Israel and Thanksgiving Day in our own country. Most nations, whether developed or otherwise, celebrate harvest in one way or another. But such celebrations tend to be nature festivals. Only in ancient Israel and in the United States is the thanksgiving a celebration of historical events. In Old Testament Israel these events were related to salvation history; in the United States they are related to civic religion. When the Israelites gave thanks for the harvest, they gave thanks for the Exodus and for the occupation of the land of Israel, the great foundation events that made all subsequent harvests possible as bounty from God. Similarly, when Americans give thanks, they recall the first Thanksgiving held by the Puritan settlers in New England. The lateness of this festival, at the end of November (Canadians, for instance, celebrate Thanksgiving Day on the first Monday in October), is a reminder of this piece of American primal history.

December 8

IMMACULATE CONCEPTION

This is not a feast in the calendar of the Episcopal Church (although in the calendar of the Church of England, December 8 is marked as the Conception of the Blessed Virgin Mary, and in 1928 it was provided with a collect but no readings). To Anglicans it appears that this doctrine (a) is not in Scripture, (b) was unheard of until the Middle Ages, and (c) even then was not universally accepted (Aquinas, as is well known, did not hold it). They would feel that it is contrary to Paul's statement on the universality of human sin (Rom 3:9, 23) and to the statement of Article XV that Christ alone was without sin.

Nevertheless, we must try to understand how and in what sense Roman Catholics hold to it. The dogma of 1854 was careful to make the Immaculate Conception entirely dependent in advance on the redemptive act of God in Christ: "The Virgin Mary at the moment of conception was preserved in advance from all defilement of original sin by a unique privilege of grace in view of the merits of Jesus Christ." But why should such a claim be asserted? What biblical considerations led to a desire to affirm it? Perhaps we may understand it as *the way* in which Roman Catholics seek to affirm something that the Bible affirms and that other Christians also would want to affirm without the dogma, namely, that it was the total surrender of Mary to the divine will that, humanly speaking, made the incarnation possible.

The rest of us would, for biblical and historical reasons, want to dissociate ourselves from this particular way of affirming that total obedience of Mary, so crucial for the incarnation. Yet, we can respect the reasons for the Roman Catholic acceptance of the dogma and share with them that biblical truth which the dogma is a way of affirming, that is, the total surrender of Mary to the divine will, a surrender made possible by the prevenient grace of God.

Reading I: Genesis 3:9-15, 20

The story of the fall is generally regarded today as an etiological myth, that is, it expressed how faith understands the origin of evil. Eden cannot be located on a map, nor can the eating of the forbidden fruit be dated. The story of Adam and Eve is the expression of profound truths about humanity; for example, it asserts that the woes of human life are largely brought about by human beings' rejection of their divine destiny. Yet, that evil is something greater than human sin. It is a transsubjective reality, symbolized by the serpent. Verse 15 is traditionally known as the *protevangelium*, the earliest promise of humankind's final conquest of evil.

It should be noted, however, that the text actually speaks only of the perpetual antagonism between human beings and the serpent. It is clearly because of the *protevangelium* that this pericope was chosen for today. The seed of the woman who achieved the final triumph over evil was born through Mary. The early Church Fathers drew a contrast between Eve and Mary, similar to Paul's contrast between Adam and Christ. Eve, by her disobedience, let evil into the world; so Mary, by her obedience, made it possible for the victor over evil to enter the world.

Responsorial Psalm: 98:1-4

An almost identical selection of verses, but with a different refrain and a fourth stanza, is used at the third Mass of Christmas. If we take the *protevangelium* as the promise of human victory over evil, this psalm thanks God for that victory, achieved through the Christ-event, which Mary's obedience made possible.

21

Reading II: Ephesians 1:3-6, 11-12

Ephesians is probably a circular letter in which a faithful disciple sums up Paul's achievement and elucidates its significance for the Pauline churches after the Apostle's death. The opening thanksgiving sets the salvation effected by God in Christ in the context of the whole sweep of salvation history, beginning with God's purpose "before the foundation of the world." It is appropriate for today because the "us" who are chosen includes the Blessed Virgin Mary, the first of those who believed (Luke 1:45). This reading strongly affirms that Mary was what she was solely through the salvation effected by God in Christ (see the papal decree of 1854).

Gospel: Luke 1:26-38

This reading occurs on the fourth Sunday of Advent in series B and is commented upon fully there. Today we note that there is no gospel passage that relates or affirms the Immaculate Conception, but that this is the passage which most emphatically affirms the obedience of Mary that made the incarnation possible. Its use here supports our interpretation of the dogma of the Immaculate Conception as a way of affirming this fact about Mary that is so important for all of us.

213

The Homily

The readings chosen for this feast suggest that the emphasis of the homily should be twofold: (1) the dogma of the Immaculate Conception, properly understood, does not compromise the essential truth that all persons, the Blessed Virgin Mary included, belong to a fallen humanity (first reading), and that their salvation depends on Christ alone—again, the Blessed Virgin Mary included (second reading). (2) The affirmation of her Immaculate Conception is a *way* of affirming the biblical truth of Mary's total commitment in faith and obedience to God's will for her (gospel), a commitment made possible by the grace of God.

LECTIONARY FOR WEDDINGS

Holy Scripture and the Christian faith affirm that "the bond and covenant of marriage was established by God in creation," and that it "signifies to us the mystery of the union between Christ and his Church." It is not, therefore, a matter of human convention or convenience, however much the precise forms marriage takes are shaped by society. The purpose of readings and homilies in the marriage rite is to address the word of God for marriage to this specific marriage that is being solemnized on this particular occasion.

OLD TESTAMENT READINGS

Reading 1: Genesis 1:26-28, 31a

The creation of man and woman represents the climax of the P (Priestly) account of creation. It is generally acknowledged today that the creation stories in Gen 1 (P) and Gen 2-3 (J) are not a revelation of *how* or *when* the universe came into being (we have to go to people like Carl Sagan for a contemporary answer to those questions). Rather, they adapt contemporary creation myths to express the understanding of human beings and their place in the cosmos arising from Israel's Yahweh-experience. The climax of the cosmic process is the emergence of humanity, male and female, stamped with God's image. This is not something that can be deduced from scientific data, but an affirmation that arises from the experience of Israel's encounter with Yahweh.

Many interpretations have been offered for the concept of the divine image. "Image" and "likeness" are not quite the same thing in Hebrew. "Likeness" is a closer definition of the meaning of "image." Without the addition, image could be (and perhaps was, at an earlier stage of the tradition) interpreted in a merely physical sense. With the addition of "likeness," "image" acquires a spiritual dimension: man and woman, like God and unlike the animals, are personal beings; they have self-consciousness and a freedom for self-determination.

Creation in the divine image means, above all, that as persons, man and woman are created for relationship—relationship with God and with

578

other human beings. Marriage is a special form of that relationship. However, because human beings are fallen beings, that relationship with God for which they were created has become perverted, and the same holds good for their relationship with other human beings and indeed with the whole created order. Thus this word—that human beings are created in the divine image—cannot be spoken without a recognition of this perversion and also its restoration in Christ, who is himself the image of God. So the word spoken to a man and a woman who come to be married is that marriage is part of the created order, that it shares the consequences of the fall, and that in Christ a restoration of what marriage is meant to be is offered.

Another very significant feature of this reading is the command "Be fruitful and multiply, and fill the earth" (v. 28). The statement about the divine image highlights the unitive purpose of marriage—the mutual relationship of man and woman in wedlock. The command to be fruitful highlights the procreative purpose. There has been much debate in recent times about the relative importance of these two purposes. Which is the primary purpose? Genesis 1 takes them both together: the procreative is the *outcome* of the unitive. When the Priestly creation story first took shape, the command "fill the earth" had a real urgency. Natural disasters and the changes and chances of life meant that the survival of the human race was very problematic. Responsibility for its continuance meant being fruitful and multiplying.

Under modern conditions we have done an all too good job of it, and our problem is just the opposite—the continuance of the human race is threatened by the population explosion. Hence responsibility for the continuance of the human race, which is laid upon us by this text, requires a direction of behavior quite different from what was required in the past. The issue between *Humanae Vitae* and the Anglican bishops at Lambeth in 1958 (who favored the responsible use of artificial methods of contraception) is not whether parenthood should be responsible and births limited— both are agreed on that—but *how* that may best be done. Thus, we can agree basically at least on what obedience to this text means today.

Reading 2: Genesis 2:18-24

This is the creation of man and woman as given in the J (Yahwist) creation story (which is actually earlier than the P form). It is a much more naive myth: God places the man in the garden. But the man needs a "helper fit for him," that is, a companion both physical and intellectual (the common term "helpmeet" is a nonword arising from a misunderstanding of the King James translation: "a help meet [that is, fit] for him"). So God creates the animals and brings them to the man for him to name, that is, to see how he would regard them in relation to himself. The animals are all right as far as they go—they can be helpful and, to a limited degree, are companions. But they are not on the same level intellectually or emotionally. So God creates a woman out of Adam's rib.

This famous story expresses first the close affinity between man and woman—both are human. But does it also mean that woman is subordinate and inferior to man? That deduction was made from this story by a long line of exegetes, from St. Paul (1 Cor 11:8-9) through St. Thomas Aquinas and Richard Hooker to the very recent past. True, the word "helper" may suggest subordination and inferiority, as though the woman's whole function was to cook Adam's dinner and darn his socks. However, the Hebrew word *ezer* ("help") is used more often than not to speak of Yahweh as the help of Israel, and one might also argue that it suggests that the woman is superior! In any case, the word contains no inherent suggestion of either superiority or inferiority. We may best understand it today as denoting partnership.

Verse 24 serves as the narrator's comment. For him, the story of the rib stresses, not the man's superiority over the woman, but the unity of the marriage established by the marital relationship: they are to be one flesh. Until recently, it has been common to interpret "flesh," like the other anthropological terms in the Bible, as denoting the human person in its entirety, considered under the aspect of its createdness, frailty, and mortality. Hence "flesh" in Gen 2:24 has been taken to refer to the complete unity of two persons in marriage—not, of course, ignoring the physical side, which remains its basis. But this interpretation of biblical anthropology has been convincingly challenged by Robert H. Gundry in *Sōma in Biblical Theology* (Cambridge University Press, 1976). He concludes that "according to the unsophisticated meaning of 'flesh,' becoming 'one flesh' needs to refer quite simply to physical union through sexual intercourse, and to nothing more" (p. 62). No doubt this will seem to many to be an impoverishment of meaning. To that we would respond: (1) this is not all that the Bible has to say about the union between husband and wife; already verse 18 ("helper"!) recognizes that their relationship is more than purely physical; (2) we should welcome the statement that the union is basically physical. All too often the modern world accuses the Church and even the Bible of being Manichean in their attitude toward sex. However much that may have been true of the Church in some periods of its history, it is certainly not true of the Bible.

Reading 3: Genesis 24:48-51, 58-67

This passage, the story of Isaac's marriage with Rebekah, comes from the

J (Yahwist) narrative. It gives a delightfully idyllic picture of the love of man and woman in the ancient Near East. However, we must beware of overromanticizing it.

The story begins with Abraham's servant relating to Laban his prayer of thanksgiving. He has blessed Yahweh for leading him "by the right way." This means the providence of God, but the providence of God taking measures to implement his promise to Abraham and to carry out his purpose in salvation history, not making possible romantic love.

Nor should we romanticize the fact that Isaac is said to have been "meditating" in the field in the evening, for commentators tell us that the verb may actually mean "to dig a hole," a euphemism for "to relieve nature"—hardly a propitious situation for his first meeting with his bride-to-be.

The Church has traditionally upheld the conjugal felicity of the patriarchs as models for Christian marriage. Thus, in the Book of Common Prayer of 1552 there was a prayer that "as Isaac and Rebecca lived faithfully together, so these persons may perform and keep the vow and covenant betwixt them made," and later there was a prayer that the newly married woman might be "as wise as Rebecca." Such prayers have been removed from modern liturgies, but the underlying idea is still present in the Scripture readings.

Reading 4: Tobit 7:11b-15 (NAB: 7:9-10, 11-15)

Tobit is a deuterocanonical book, that is, a book not found in the Hebrew canon but in the Greek Bible. Fragments of this book have been discovered at Qumran, showing that it has a Semitic origin. It was written in the early third century B.C. to show the importance of family life in times of disaster. It belongs to the genre of pious fiction, like the (proto-)canonical books of Ruth and Jonah.

This passage comes from a long section dealing with the marriage of Tobias and Sarah (7:1–10:13). Sarah had been married seven times, but each time the groom had died before the marriage could be consummated. It required a great deal of courage on Tobias' part to risk marrying this unfortunate woman! In any case, it was not romantic love. The marriage had been arranged by God and approved by the parents. This book suggests that a happy marriage is based on the will of God rather than on the desire for sexual gratification. This, it seems to me, is what Pope John Paul II meant when he said that there is no place for "lust" in Christian marriage. Lust is using another person for self-gratification and results in the depersonalization of that other person. It treats the other as an "it" instead of a "thou."

It is interesting how influential the story of Tobias has been in the history of Christian marriage, for it survived the Reformation, which tended to downgrade the deuterocanonical or apocryphal writings. In Anglicanism, which has always regarded these writings as profitable "for example of life and instruction in manners," there is a reference to this story in one of the marriage prayers in the 1549 Prayer Book: "As thou didst send the angel Raphael to Thobie and Sarah, the daughter of Raguel, to their great comfort; so vouchsafe to send thy blessing upon these thy servants." More surprising is the continued use of the story among the Amish. Professor Bruce Metzger tells us in his book *An Introduction to the Apocrypha* (New York: Oxford University Press, 1957) that their *Minister's Manual* instructs the minister at a wedding to tell the story of Tobit, and offers this explanation: "Even though this is an Apocryphal book and is not counted among the books of Holy Scripture, still, it represents a beautiful lesson which strengthens the pious and god-fearing in the faith, especially as regards marriage, and in all trials and troubles it leads one in the hope that God will bring things to a joyful end" (p. 14).

Reading 5: Tobit 8:4-9a

The picture of Tobias getting up from his wedding bed and saying his prayer is rather amusing today. We would think him a rather pompous person and would find it more natural if he and his wife Sarah (now called Edna) had knelt down and prayed together *before* going to bed. I recall a retreat conference in England on the text "Pray without ceasing," in which it was suggested that constant prayer is a continuous attitude rather than a continual activity of vocal prayer. A healthy English schoolboy batting at cricket should not be praying just as the bowler delivers the ball but should be concentrating on hitting the ball. The same might apply to one's wedding night.

Anyway, the prayer expresses a beautiful understanding of marriage as partnership. It quotes the story of Adam and Eve, and specifically the words "It is not good that man should be alone; let us make a helper for him like himself." This shows us that these words apply not only to Adam and Eve but to every couple that gets married. God meant that *this* particular man should not be alone, and has made *this* particular woman and brought her to be his partner. And most moving is the petition that they may grow old together. Perhaps if more couples entered their marriage with this prayer and resolve, there would be fewer instances of middle-aged spouses trading in their aging partners for newer models!

Reading 6: Song 2:8-10, 14, 16a; 8:6-7b

The title of this work, "Song of Songs," means that it was regarded as the loveliest of all songs, just as the Holy of Holies was the holiest place in the temple. It is attributed to Solomon because it is classed among the sapiential books, and all sapiential literature was regarded as written under the patronage of Solomon. Also, Solomon happens to be mentioned six times in the Song, though in such a way that he could not possibly be its author.

The subject of the Song is the love of a youth and maiden in a country setting. The Song consists of startlingly uninhibited erotic poetry, conceived, however, in such a spirit that it is not really contradictory to the spirit of the Tobias story, for eros and lust are not, as Pope John Paul II tried to explain, necessarily the same thing. Sexual attraction is not sinful but is a part of the goodness of God's creation; it becomes sinful when it is exploitive of the other for one's own self-gratification.

This reading falls into two parts, which come from chapters 2 and 8 respectively. Both parts are spoken by the maiden. The first part might be entitled "the springtide of love," though in the second half of the first part the maiden reports her beloved's proposal for a love-tryst. The second part is the bride's hymn to love. It is a powerful description of the intensity of sexual passion: "love is strong as death . . . . Many waters cannot quench love, neither can floods drown it." Frankly, one has to admit that this is often not true of purely physical passion; a marriage based exclusively on that is unlikely to last. Perhaps part of the trouble is that Hebrew had no word for agape as distinct from eros. For the love that is strong as death can only be that of eros constantly transformed by agape. One commentator says that love here described "could only have meaning in a lifelong monogamous marriage." We can agree so long as it is eros redeemed by agape.

Reading 7: Sirach 26:1-4, 13-16

Again, Sirach is part of the wisdom literature of the Old Testament. Only this time the work is not anonymous. It was written originally in Hebrew by Jesus ben Sirach in 180 B.C. and translated into Greek fifty years later by his grandson. Much of it, including this passage, consists of advice from a father to his adolescent son. It naturally includes advice on sex and marriage. This reading is a description of a good wife, written very much from the husband's point of view and commenting on her contribution to her husband's happiness. Perhaps that is why this passage was not included in the Episcopalian marriage service!

Reading 8: Jeremiah 31:31-32a, 33-34a

Jeremiah's prophecy of the new covenant is commented upon on the fifth

Sunday of Lent in series B. This is, of course, a covenant promised to   *243*
Israel as the people of God and fulfilled, in Christian understanding, in
the Christ-event. Both the Old Testament (Hosea) and the New Testament (Eph 5; see below) provide ample justification for seeing in the marriage covenant an analogy to the covenant between God and his people.
At the same time, we must remember the difference. God's covenants with
his people are dispensations conferred upon an inferior party by a superior;
the marriage covenant is an agreement between two equal partners.

NEW TESTAMENT READINGS

Reading 1: Romans 8:31b-35, 37-39

Comments on this passage can be found on the second Sunday of Lent   *235*
in series B and on the eighteenth Sunday of the year in series A. As ap-   *153*
plied specifically to marriage, the point of this passage is that it is only
as human love between a man and a woman is transformed by the love
of God in Christ that it can become that agape which endures. Since
nothing can separate us from the love of God in Christ, Christian marriage has a strong promise of which the world can know nothing.

Reading 2: Romans 12:1-2, 9-18 (long form); 12:1-2, 9-13 (short form)

The opening part of this reading is provided comment on the twenty-
second Sunday of the year in series A. Verses 1-2 serve as a bridge be-   *163*
tween the theological argument of Rom 1–11 and the ethical exhortation
of the later chapters.

The hortatory material covered by this reading is divided into
paragraphs, of which the second is omitted in the short form. The first
of these paragraphs (vv. 9-13) is an explication of the love command in
relation to Christian community, while the second paragraph is an explication of the commandment of enemy love derived from the teaching
of the historical Jesus as preserved in the Great Sermon of the synoptic
tradition.

As applied to the married life, the passage suggests that a Christian
family should not be closed in upon itself but open to the world outside
the Church. Only so—and especially in the practice of hospitality—can
Christian family life be a witness to the world and so fulfill the prayer:
"May their life together be a sign of Christ's love to this sinful and broken
world, that unity may overcome estrangement, forgiveness heal guilt, joy
conquer despair. . . . Grant them such fulfillment in their mutual affec-
tion that they may reach out in love and concern for others" (Book of
Common Prayer 1979, 429).

Reading 3: 1 Corinthians 6:13c-15a, 17-20

Comment on this passage can be found on the second Sunday of the year   *289*
in series B. In the context of the marriage service, it says to us that marriage "is an honorable estate"—a state of life that is wholly consistent with
our bodies' being members of Christ, and a state of life in which it is entirely possible for God to be glorified in our bodies. And "body," like
"flesh" (see comment above on Gen 2:18-24), does not mean "person" but,
quite realistically, the human being in his or her physical constitution.

Reading 4: 1 Corinthians 12:31–13:8a

This is part of the famous Pauline hymn to charity, together with its introductory verse, 12:31. It receives comment on the fourth Sunday of the   *456*
year in series C. It is the supreme description of that agape which must
transform eros if a marriage is to become truly a Christian marriage and
to endure until death. The fourth paragraph ("Love is patient . . .") should
be a subject of constant meditation for married people.

Reading 5: Ephesians 5:2a, 21-33 (long form); 5:2a, 25-32 (short form)

Again, this reading is expounded in the Sunday readings, under the twenty-   *339*
first Sunday of the year in series B. In that part of the household code
that speaks of the duty of the husband to his wife, the author (Paul or
a close disciple, a member of the Pauline school) has expanded the code's
injunction with an exposition of the theme of the relation between Christ
and his Church. This suggests that the more a Christian couple share in
the life of the Christian community and experience in their own lives the
love of Christ for his Church, the more they will learn of their own relationship and be enabled to conform to that model.

Reading 6: Colossians 3:12-17

For comment, see the feast of the Holy Family in series A. In the context   *24*
of the wedding service, particular emphasis should be placed on the need
for constant and mutual forgiveness on the part of the couple, motivated
as it is by the fact that the Christian is one who has received the forgiveness
of the Lord. Nowhere more than in marriage is the Lord's teaching on
the need of forgiving seventy times seven necessary. Also important is
the statement that agape binds together everything in harmony, and that,
of course, includes the marriage relationship.

Reading 7: 1 Peter 3:1-9

This reading is from another household code (see the readings from Colossians and Ephesians). There are also similar codes in 1 Timothy and

Titus, although they do not include the duties of husbands. It is characteristic of these codes that the injunctions ("be submissive"—of that more anon—and "live considerately") are expressed by a Greek participle rather than an imperative. They are not so much commands as *descriptions* of the way things are done (D. Daube). The participle implies that this is the accepted way of doing things in first-century society, so it must be done for a Christian motive and in a Christian way. For that is the real emphasis of the household codes. They are derived from Hellenistic-Jewish usage, which in turn got them from Stoicism. They therefore describe the mores of contemporary society and seek to Christianize them.

This consideration suggests that in implementing the code today, we should not seek to repristinate the mores of a society that no longer exists, but should seek rather to Christianize the mores of *our* society. We live in a society in which women are not regarded as inferior but as equal to (though, of course, in certain ways different from) men. Our concept of the marriage relationship is therefore one of partnership.

The overall concern of this particular adaptation of the household code seems to be the relationship between a Christian wife and her pagan partner. Unlike 1 Corinthians, this writer does not recommend the Pauline privilege (1 Cor 7:15) but urges the wife to behave in a way that will win over the unbelieving husband to the Christian faith. This can be done "without a word," that is, not by preaching at him but by "reverent and chaste behavior." Then comes a puritanical onslaught on the use of cosmetics that is not likely to be heeded in contemporary life. But it still has relevance: outward use of cosmetics is no substitute for beauty of character, and much time and money are squandered on them. "Let nothing terrify you" (v. 6) probably refers to the intimidation attempted by husbands who disapprove of the wife's new faith.

The counsels for the husbands assume that both parties are Christians—it was far less likely that a Christian husband should have a pagan wife than vice versa. Reference to the wife as being of the "weaker sex" is not likely to be accepted today. It is probably a vestige of the ancient view that women were lower in moral stamina than men. Anyhow, the point is that despite this commonly accepted opinion, Christian husbands are to "bestow honor" on their wives, first, because as Christians they are joint heirs of grace, and second, because lack of respect for the wife would be an impediment to the prayers of the couple.

Verses 8-9 form a concluding general exhortation, applying not only to married couples but to all members of the community. Still, they do apply in a special way to married couples, especially the injunction not to return evil for evil or reviling for reviling.

Reading 8: 1 John 3:18-24

For comment, see the fifth Sunday of Easter in series B. This is another *266* exhortation to Christian agape, which in the marriage relationship must transform eros.

Reading 9: 1 John 4:7-12

These verses are covered on the sixth and seventh Sundays of Easter in *269* series B. They are yet another exhortation to agape. *275*

Reading 10: Revelation 19:1, 5-9a

This passage comes from the culminating vision of the fall of Babylon— that is, imperial Rome as the persecutor of the Christian Church. The author, like all apocalyptists, thinks of this crisis (the persecution under Domitian?) as the final crisis of world history, and sees as its outcome the final triumph of God's saving purpose for the world. Babylon the great harlot is judged, and a multitude in heaven join in the first of two Hallelujah choruses. The second Hallelujah chorus (the one Handel used) is one of triumph at the marriage of the Lamb (the Messiah) and his bride, the redeemed community. The bride is clothed in linen, the eschatological garment, which is contrasted with the ostentatious purple and scarlet of the great harlot. This eschatological garment is interpreted as the righteous deeds of the saints, that is, in later terminology, their merits. Note, however, that these righteous deeds or merits are not deeds or merits of the saints themselves, for it is *granted* to the bride to be clothed in them, that is, they are gifts of grace.

This reading closes with the fourth of the seven beatitudes in the Apocalypse: "Blessed are those who are invited to the marriage supper of the Lamb." Here the Church appears both as the bride of the Messiah and as his invited guests—a confusion of thought typical of the flexibility of apocalyptic imagery, showing that it must not be pressed.

Two images stand out when this reading is used at a marriage service. One is the bridal dress. This is not merely a matter of social custom or fashion. It calls attention to the eschatological symbolism of the marriage celebration. Not only is marriage a symbol of the mystical union now existing between Christ and his Church (as in Ephesians), but it is also a symbol of the future final union between the Messiah and the redeemed. The crowns placed on the heads of both the bride and the groom in the Orthodox rite have a similar eschatological significance. Second, when the marriage rite culminates in the nuptial Eucharist, this particular marriage is integrated into the eschatological marriage of the Messiah and his people. The guests at the wedding participate in this symbol of the final eschatological marriage feast.

RESPONSORIAL PSALMS

With one exception, all the responsorial psalms of the wedding liturgy have received comment in the appropriate places of the Sunday Lectionary, so the homilist should check the Index. Also, attention should be paid to the responsorial refrain, which highlights the connection between the psalm and the marriage service. The one psalm that has not been commented upon is:

Responsorial Psalm: 148:1-4, 9-13

This psalm is one of the festal hymns of the psalter, a hymn of praise to God the Creator sung by the whole created order. It is thus very similar to the Song of the Three Holy Children (*Benedicite omnia opera*). The creation of the world is here presented as a first stage in the creation of Israel, the people of God (vv. 20-21). Salvation history rests upon the foundation of world history. The verses given here omit the salvation-historical part and concentrate on creation and world history. The penultimate verse of the selection calls upon young men and maidens (including the couple to be married) to join in creation's paean of praise. The act of marrying is itself an act of creation's praise to its Creator, and the marriage service articulates that praise.

GOSPELS

Gospel Reading 1: Matthew 5:1-12a

For comment, see the fourth Sunday of the year in series A and the feast of All Saints (November 1). There has been much discussion as to whether the first four beatitudes are intended to indicate activities (like the next three) or dispositions. Georg Strecker has recently suggested that at the pre-Matthean level they were taken to denote dispositions, but at the level of the Matthean redaction they denote activities. It is helpful to take them as activities in the context of the marriage service. They indicate the kind of behavior required of all Christians, but now especially of a Christian husband and wife. 115 567

Gospel Reading 2: Matthew 5:13-16

See the fifth Sunday of the year in series A for comment. In the context of marriage, this excerpt suggests that the Christian home is to be a light to the world (see the prayers quoted from the Book of Common Prayer under New Testament Reading 2). 119 584

Gospel Reading 3: Matthew 7:21, 24-29 (long form); 7:21, 24-25 (short form)

The difference between the long and the short forms is that the short form omits the part about the house built on sand. For commentary, see the ninth Sunday of the year in series A. The couple about to be married are here challenged to build their house on rock. If it is to be Christian, their home must be a place where the words of Jesus are heard and kept.

Gospel Reading 4: Matthew 19:3-6

Matthew is following Mark 10:1-12 but adapting the pericope to his more Jewish environment, so that it takes the form of a rabbinic disputation on the marriage law. In Matthew the Pharisee sets out right at the beginning of the pericope to trap Jesus, whereas in the Marcan form this does not happen until the end of the story. The Pharisees in Matthew are trying to get Jesus to take sides with either Shammai or Hillel over a question of interpretation of the Torah. The Torah said that a man could divorce his wife for "some unseemly thing," and there was naturally some argument among the scribes over what an "unseemly thing" might be. According to Hillel, it meant any reason whatsoever, anything in a wife that gave her husband cause for displeasure. Hillel said, for example, that a man could divorce his wife for burning his dinner. For Shammai, however, it meant only one thing—adultery.

In answer to this question, Jesus sweeps away all considerations of the interpretation of the Torah and goes back to the original order of creation, combining Gen 1:27 with 2:24. Since Moses, divorce had been a concession to fallen humanity. Marriage is an ordinance of creation, not a result of the fall.

The modern world finds Jesus' teaching on the indissolubility of marriage impossibly hard, and perhaps it has always been. It is noteworthy that in various ways the Churches have felt compelled to make concessions as Moses did. In fact, this started to happen as soon as Jesus' eschatological commandment was converted into ecclesiastical law, as we see from the Matthean exception and the Pauline privilege. An eschatological commandment is of its very nature impossible without the eschatological message and the gift of eschatological salvation that it confers. Insofar as men and women are outside that salvation, to that extent are they still in that state of hardness of heart that compelled Moses to permit divorce.

Gospel Reading 5: Matthew 22:35-40

The double commandment of love—this passage is expounded on the thir-

tieth Sunday of the year in series A. Applied to marriage, it says that there   *185*
can be no agape between husband and wife which has not first been purged
of self-love by the agape of God (subjective genitive: their love for God).

Gospel Reading 6: Mark 10:6-9

This is the Marcan parallel (and according to the two-document
hypothesis, the source) of the fourth gospel reading above. The only difference, as we have seen, is that in Mark it lacks the context of a conflict
story between Jesus and a Pharisaic opponent. The consequence is that
Jesus' eschatological command about the permanence of marriage is not
placed here in the context of the Pharisaic debate about the proper grounds
for divorce. The primary emphasis is on marriage as a divine ordinance
in creation.

Gospel Reading 7: John 2:1-11

The story of the wedding at Cana of Galilee receives comment on the second Sunday of the year in series C. There the emphasis is on the miracle   *449*
of the wine as an epiphany of the divine glory in the incarnate Christ.
In the context of a marriage service, the emphasis will be on the setting
of the miracle—a wedding.

In the opening exhortation of the service for "the Celebration and Blessing of a Marriage" in the 1979 Book of Common Prayer, this episode is
alluded to in the following words: ". . . our Lord Jesus Christ adorned
this manner of life by his presence and first miracle at a wedding in Cana
of Galilee." In the nuptial Eucharist the Lord Jesus Christ comes as a wedding guest as assuredly as he did at Cana, but in his sacramental presence,
affirming *this* marriage as a divine ordinance in creation and offering his
transforming power to redeem that marriage from the effects of human
frailty and sin.

Gospel Reading 8: John 15:9-12

For comment, see the sixth Sunday of Easter in series B. This is part of   *270*
the allegory of the vine and the branches. As applied to marriage, this
passage of Scripture asserts that agape in marriage is only possible if the
couple abide in the agape of God (objective genitive: God's love for them).

Gospel Reading 9: John 15:12-16

This is a continuation of the preceding gospel reading. Here the emphasis
is on the fruit produced through abiding in Christ. That fruit is the keeping of Jesus' commandments and effective petition in his name. In the context of marriage, the commandment of Jesus to be kept is the command-

ment of maintaining the marriage union intact (or, as Dietrich Bonhoeffer would put it, allowing the marriage to uphold the couple) and the petition to be addressed to God is a prayer for one's marriage partner (a thought that can be illustrated from the story of Tobias in the fifth Old Testament reading above).

Gospel Reading 10: John 17:20-26 (long form); 17:20-23 (short form)

This is part of our Lord's high priestly prayer in the Johannine account of the Last Supper. Comment on it is provided on the seventh Sunday of Easter in series C.

Jesus is praying for the disciples' unity in love. The long form of the reading goes on to ground this unity explicitly in the eternal unity of the Father and the Son (in the Sarum rite the nuptial Mass was a Mass of the Holy Trinity) and in the revelation of that love in the incarnate life of Christ. But since Johannine thought repeats itself by revolving around and around a common theme, the same ideas will be discovered in the short form, too. The oneness of husband and wife in marriage is a microcosmic expression of the horizontal unity of believers with one another as well as of the vertical unity (which other readings have emphasized) between Christ and his Church.

The Homily

The homilist is confronted not only with a plethora of Scripture readings but also with a plethora of themes for the homily. We will mention just a few.

1. All marriage liturgies have related the particular marriage being solemnized to the story of Adam and Eve. The homilist can help the couple and all those present to hear this, not as the story of "our first parents," but as the story of *this* man and *this* woman. God has made this man and this woman for each other and has brought them together "for the help and comfort given one another in prosperity and adversity . . . for the procreation of children and their nurture in the knowledge and love of the Lord" (Book of Common Prayer 1979). Such a homily would draw upon the first, second, and fifth Old Testament readings, and upon the fourth or sixth gospel reading.

2. Many of the readings speak of love. The reading from the Song of Songs (the sixth Old Testament reading) is frankly erotic, and eros is therefore affirmed, though distinguished from mere lust in the second reading from Tobit (fifth Old Testament reading). See also the third Old Testament reading; the fourth, eighth, and ninth New Testament readings; and the first, fifth (or seventh), eighth, ninth, and tenth gospel readings.

440

All of these passages speak of agape, by which eros must be redeemed. Many of the New Testament readings, taken as they are from the parenetic sections of the letters, indicate what agape means concretely in human relationships, including those of husband and wife. A marriage sermon on Christian love as the rock on which marriage must be built (third and fourth gospel readings) would be appropriate.

3. The third New Testament reading (see also the covenant passage, the eighth Old Testament reading) expounds marriage as a sign of the unity between Christ and his Church, a theme that is picked up in the prayers and exhortations of the marriage rite in the various liturgies. This symbolism could be expounded in the homily, with the suggestion that the more deeply the couple participate in the life of the Church, the more their own relationship will be nourished. Alternatively, the tenth reading gives this symbolism a future-eschatological slant, which can be connected with the symbolism of the bridal dress.

4. Some of the readings call attention to the outward-looking aspect of married life and to the Christian home (second New Testament reading, especially the long form, and the second gospel reading). Both of these texts speak to the married state as one that is meant to be an example to others, both Christians and non-Christians.

LECTIONARY FOR FUNERALS

The Homily at the Burial of the Dead

In Protestant circles there is a widespread expectation that the address at a funeral service should take the form of a eulogy of the deceased. This is curious in view of the fact that the Reformation started as a result of Luther's rediscovery of the gospel of justification by faith apart from the works of the law! Equally curious are the eighteenth-century tombstones in Protestant churches, with their lengthy encomiums of the virtues of the deceased. In reaction against this, Anglicans have traditionally refrained from preaching at all at funeral services, and I suppose the same has been true, until the recent reforms, in the Roman Catholic Church.

Since the task is new to many of us, the question arises: What form should the homily at Masses for the Dead or at burial services take? It may be argued that it is legitimate to deliver a eulogy in certain circumstances: when the deceased was well known and belonged to a tight-knit community (for example, a small village) or to a particular society (for example, a business firm, an academic institution, and so on), or when the dead person was a well-known member of a larger society (for example, a public leader or a general). It should be realized, however, that this is not the priest's or minister's proper job but an *opus alienum*, a "strange work." The eulogist is acting as the mouthpiece of a this-worldly community, not as a *minister verbi Dei*, a "minister of the word of God."

If a eulogy is desired, it sometimes would be appropriate that it be delivered by a member of the community concerned rather than by the priest or minister. However, if the latter does deem it appropriate to deliver the eulogy, he or she should be aware of its theological perils. It is all too easy to represent a person's achievements as personal merits rather than as the fruit of grace, and to forget the apostolic injunction "Judge nothing before the time." And because of the charitable rule "De mortuis nil nisi bonum," any summary of the deceased's life will probably be partial and limited. On such occasions, therefore, when a memorial address seems appropriate, it would be best to confine one's remarks to a brief résumé of the dead person's career, such as might appear in an obituary notice, with a restrained evaluation of significant contributions to the community of which the person was a part.

Obviously the *opus proprium* of the homilist at a Christian funeral service is to address the realities of death and bereavement. But here we have to beware of offering secular comfort. For instance, it may be tempting to to posit for the dead person a pseudo-immortality, suggesting that the deceased lives on in his or her works and thoughts and lasting achievements, or in our memories, or in his or her descendants. No, the only Christian message in the face of these realities is the word of the gospel with its offer of judgment and salvation, of repentance and faith. Death is the "wages of sin" (Rom 6:23). As the myth of Gen 3 inculcates, death (not as a biological fact but as an existential reality) is an alien intruder, not God's original intention for humanity. Death came as the ultimate expression of humanity's separation from God, which is the consequence of its fallenness. Death, it has been said, is the sacrament of sin.

Since death holds us in bondage, we are in need of redemption, and this is what the gospel offers us in Jesus Christ. He, the new Adam, has broken through the gate of death and opened up the way to eternal life. It is important to remember that eternal life has to do not merely with duration but with our relation to God. Christian theology has varied in its attitude toward intrinsic immortality. Often today "immortality or resurrection from the dead" are offered as alternative possibilities—the former Platonist, the other alone biblical. More recent scholarship, however, seems to suggest that this alternative is an oversimplification (see R. H. Gundry, *Sōma in Biblical Theology* [Cambridge University Press, 1976]). It seems consistent with the biblical message as well as with the Church's tradition to hold that the "soul" (the core of human personality) survives physical death. However, the fact is that such survival in itself is neither here nor there. This survival is not what the New Testament means by "eternal life," which, as we have said, is a matter of right relationship with God. Wrong relationship with God is the real death that Christ, by his death and resurrection, has overcome, and this victory over the wrong relationship constitutes the offer of the gospel and the theme of Christian proclamation in the face of death and bereavement. Only in Christ, the second Adam, will all not merely survive but be "made alive."

One final point. Catholics believe that at death the faithful dead enter an intermediate state, usually called "purgatory" (Anglicans generally prefer to speak of "paradise"). Protestants tend to deny an intermediate state and to hold that a person goes to heaven or hell immediately upon death. Our presuppositions on this matter will affect the way we handle the funeral texts. It is my presupposition that the eschatology of the New Testament requires the notion of an intermediate state. The decisive event of the future is not our own individual deaths but the parousia of Christ.

The dead are therefore in the same situation in relation to that event as we are. Hence a corollary: the Paulinist author of the Pastorals can pray for Onesiphorus (who is evidently dead): "May the Lord have mercy upon him in that day." Those who accept this eschatological framework frequently assume that there is a particular judgment at death as well as a final judgment at the parousia. We shall come across suggestions of this in the readings for Christian burial.

OLD TESTAMENT READINGS

Reading 1: Job 19:1, 23-27b

For general introductory remarks on the Book of Job, see the fifth Sunday of the year in series B. Chapter 19 forms the climax of Job's lament. He has been completely abandoned by family, friends, and—he feels— even by God. In a way characteristic of the Israelite (and discernible in Teviot's Song in *Fiddler on the Roof*), Job argues with God and complains of the way God has treated him. He feels so strongly about it that he wants his words to be put on permanent record (vv. 23-24). Then, in words immortalized by Handel, he makes a magnificent leap of faith, also typical of the Israelite. God will indeed vindicate him at the last: "I know that my *go'el* lives." Unfortunately the text is highly uncertain, and we cannot tell whether the Book of Job was thinking of a vindication in this life or of one after death. Perhaps, however, we can allow canonical exegesis to decide the matter. We are not bound to Job's original meaning but can allow his partial insight to be amplified by the New Testament, and particularly by 1 Cor 15 (which may fittingly be read along with the passage from Job at a funeral service).

Reading 2: Wisdom 3:1-9c (long form); 3:1-6, 9abc (short form)

It is not true to say that the Old Testament nowhere exhibits a belief in the immortality of the soul. This is certainly not true if we include the deuterocanonical literature, of which the Book of Wisdom is a part. Here it is the immortality of the righteous that is being asserted rather than general immortality, but in any case it presupposes a body-soul duality that many have denied in recent times to be germane to biblical thought.

Be that as it may, we must once more, as we did with the reading from Job, set this passage in the context of the canon as a whole. When we do that, we must interpret the righteous to be those who are "rightwised" by the blood of Jesus, not by their own intrinsic merits. Only to them is true immortality offered as a gift, that is, an immortality in which not merely physical but existential death is overcome.

297

Reading 3: Wisdom 4:7-15

This passage wrestles with the problem of those who are cut down in the prime of life. The traditional view was that the wicked die young and the just live to an honorable old age, a belief obviously refuted by experience. By contrast, this passage teaches that true age is to be found in a virtuous life. Life is to be measured qualitatively rather than quantitatively. The language used to designate life after death employs a different imagery (showing how loosely we should stick to such imagery: it is suggestive rather than descriptive). Instead of speaking of immortality, it uses the "rapture model." The young person is caught up to heaven at the time of death. As usual, the question of whether this rapture occurs before or after death is left open.

Reading 4: Isaiah 25:6a, 7-9

See the twenty-eighth Sunday of the year in series A, where this pericope is paired with the parable of the great banquet. Here our attention is inevitably focused on verse 8, "He will swallow up death for ever," a verse that is cited in 1 Cor 15:26, 44 and alluded to in Rev 7:17 (cf. 21:4).

178

    This passage comes from the Apocalypse of Isaiah (chs. 24–27). It announces the coming time when the curse of Gen 3:19 will be canceled forever. At this stage of the Old Testament, this can hardly mean the resurrection of the dead, but only that the covenant people of Israel will not die any more. The New Testament quite legitimately reinterpreted it in the light of Jesus' Easter victory.

Reading 5: Lamentations 3:17-26

The Book of Lamentations consists of a series of laments over the fall of Jerusalem in 586 B.C. When a large percentage of the people of God were transported to Babylon and their identity was destroyed, only two alternative conclusions could seemingly be drawn: either Yahweh had himself suffered defeat or he had abandoned Israel. But there was a third possibility, a bitter one indeed, but one that nevertheless offered a ray of hope. It was that the prophets were right—the Exile was indeed God's judgment on his people's faithlessness to the Torah. This is the view expressed in these five laments, from the third of which this pericope is taken. Old Testament scholars regard it as the latest of the five laments, composed at a time when the horrors of exile had been mitigated but when there was as yet no hope of restoration, such as we find in Second Isaiah. It is a message of Yahweh's *chesed*, his steadfast covenant love, and it exhorts the exiles to hang on. Yahweh will intervene.

How is a passage that applied originally to the fate of a nation to be transposed to the death of an individual? Like the Exile, death is an expression of God's judgment on sin: the wages of sin is death. As we observed in the introduction, human mortality is the final expression of our fallenness, our separation from God. But as for the exiles who still lived under Yahweh's covenant, so for the believing Christian the sting of death has been removed by the *chesed* of God in the death and resurrection of Jesus.

Reading 6: Daniel 12:1-3

For commentary on this passage, see the thirty-third Sunday of the year in series B. It is the *locus classicus* for the biblical conception of resurrection as the eschatological transformation of the physical body rather than as the resuscitation or reanimation of a corpse. 368

Reading 7: 2 Maccabees 12:43-45

For a general introduction to this book and for specific comment on the Maccabean martyrdoms, see the thirty-second Sunday of the year in series C. This passage comes at the end of the section narrating a series of battles 523 with neighboring peoples (12:2-45). It is the clearest statement of the late-Jewish resurrection hope in the deuterocanonical literature of the earlier covenant. As a logical consequence of the resurrection hope, prayer for the dead is inculcated.

At the time of the Reformation, prayer for the dead was rejected completely by the more radical Reformers in what was an understandable but excessive reaction against the medieval obsession with purgatory. And it was probably this particular verse from our reading that led Protestants generally to reject what they came to call the "Apocrypha" (the deuterocanonical literature). The Lutheran and Anglican Churches did not go quite that far, for in the confessional writings of both traditions the Apocrypha are recognized as valuable for "instruction for life and manners," though not to establish doctrine. Today a more relaxed attitude is developing among many Protestants, with the realization that the Septuagint was the Bible of most of the New Testament authors.

On the specific subject of prayer for the dead, Luther countenanced it up to the point of burial, and the ancient "Requiem aeternam" prayer is found in German Lutheran hymnals for use at funerals to this day. In Anglicanism all such prayer was removed in the second Prayer Book of Edward VI, though some of the petitions in the Book of Common Prayer are susceptible of interpretation as oblique prayers for the dead, and indeed were so interpreted by Anglicans in the seventeenth and eighteenth centuries. For instance, there was a petition that "we with them [that is, the departed] may be partakers of thy heavenly kingdom." The Tractarians revived explicit prayer for the dead, and it has become generally accepted in the American Episcopal Church, though still opposed in the Church of England by conservative evangelicals on the grounds that it is unscriptural.

Quite properly, prayer for the dead is oriented toward the eschatological hope, as in this text from 2 Maccabees. It should be a prayer that God may prepare the dead for the final resurrection at the last day and have mercy on them at that day, that they may enter into the consummation and bliss of the resurrection life.

NEW TESTAMENT READINGS

Reading 1: Acts 10:34-43 (long form); 10:34-36, 42-43 (short form)

Commentary on these verses is provided on the Baptism of the Lord in   *33*
series A; on Easter Sunday in series A; and on the sixth Sunday of Easter   *72*
in series B. In the context of a funeral service, the text highlights the theme *268*
of the resurrected Christ as the judge of the living and the dead. The
Christology of this very primitive kerygmatic speech (Christ as the coming judge) is rooted in the earliest post-Easter community's identification of the risen One with the coming Son of man. Eventually the clause found its way into the Apostles' Creed ("He shall come to judge the living and the dead"). It is a salutary reminder of our own accountability for all of our lives before the throne of God.

Reading 2: Romans 5:5-11

Part of this reading receives comment on the third Sunday of Lent in series   *44*
A, and part on the eleventh Sunday of the year in series A. In the context   *134*
of a funeral service, the central statements are: "we shall be saved by him [Christ] from the wrath of God" and "we shall be saved by his life." The first is said to depend on the fact that we are already now justified, the second on the fact that we are now reconciled. In the undoubtedly authentic writings of Paul, the word "salvation" is used of our final consummation. Paul would never have asked the question "Are you saved?" It is justification (being put right with God) and reconciliation (being made one with God) that are present realities. Only because we are already here and now justified and reconciled—that is, brought out of our state of alienation from God—that we have a hope of future salvation. Only the justified sinner can face death with assured hope.

Reading 3: Romans 5:17-21

Romans 5:12-19 is discussed under the first Sunday of Lent in series A. *39*
We confine ourselves here to comment on the additional verses (20-21)
and on the relevance of the pericope as a whole to a funeral context.

Verse 20 (and also verses 13-14, omitted in the short form on the first
Sunday of Lent in series A) is a parenthesis about the role of the Law in
the history of humankind after the fall and before the Christ-event. The
role of the Law was to "increase the trespass." How does the Law do this?
In two ways: (1) by inciting to sin (see Rom 7:7). St. Augustine tells the
story of a youthful prank of stealing a neighbor's pears from his tree; the
paternal prohibition incited the desire to steal them; (2) by creating the
illusion that virtue is attainable by unaided effort, thereby resulting in
the sin of pride.

In verse 21 Paul returns to the theme of verse 17, that in the period
of salvation history before Christ, under Adam, sin reigned in death, but
that now, correspondingly ("as . . . so") as well as ("all the more") by
contrast (verse 17 spoke of a contrast rather than a correspondence), as
a result of Christ's saving act, grace rules through righteousness to eternal life.

A concordance will show that this passage offers a theology of death.
Death for humanity is more than just a natural, physical event, the cessa-
tion of biological life, though it is that, too. It has an existential
significance. It is coordinated with "trespass," "disobedience," "sin," and
"condemnation." The very fact of our dying says that we live under all
these things. Death is the finalization of fallen humanity's wrong relation
with God. It is the final expression of what was true all along through
life: cut off from God, under his wrath—in short, dead though living.
Death is the experience of God's final judgment on fallen life. That is the
presupposition of the Christian message. But then it goes on to proclaim
that through the saving act of God in Christ, especially in his death and
resurrection, death has been conquered. Sin is replaced by righteousness,
by eternal life as a gift solely from Christ.

Reading 4: Romans 6:3-9 (long form); 6:3-4, 8-9 (short form)

Commentary on Rom 6:3-11 can be found under the Easter Vigil in series *69*
A (Epistle). Our passage explicitly connects Christian burial with Christian baptism. In baptism the believer died and was buried. The Christian
life is a life of constant dying to sin and thereby implementing what baptism symbolized. Hence all the words about resurrection in this passage
are in conditional or purposive clauses or in future tenses: "that we might
walk," "we shall live," and so on.

The Christian life is a *partial* realization of the future resurrection life. This says several things that are relevant at the moment of death. If we believe that resurrection means only the new life in Christ that we live on this earth after baptism, and see no point in the hope of a life after death, we are ignoring the fact that the Christian life, however good it may be, falls far short of perfect life of resurrection. Our life, even the best of Christian lives, even the lives of the saints, are characterized by a "not yet" that cries out for completion. "Eye has not seen nor ear heard what God has prepared for those who love him." The strongest ground for believing in a future consummation is this "not-yetness" that characterizes our present life in Christ.

Reading 5: Romans 8:14-23

For comment on Rom 8:14-17, see Trinity Sunday in series B; for Rom 8:18-23, the fifteenth Sunday of the year in series A. Once again, the Christian hope for life after death depends on the quality of Christian experience in this life that begins at baptism. There we are given the Spirit, by which we are constituted children of God and so enter into Jesus' own primal "Abba experience" (Schillebeeckx). This relationship of being a child of God is of its nature inalienable, that is to say, our tie with God cannot be snapped by death. For Jesus, this "Abba experience" involved obedience and therefore suffering in this life as the prelude to glory hereafter. For us, the same pattern holds good: being a child of God means obedience and therefore suffering in this life as the essential prerequisite for sharing Christ's glory hereafter.

This glory is characterized in a number of ways: the revealing of the children of God; the glorious liberty of the children of God; adoption as children; the redemption of our bodies. The cosmic context in which Paul places the hope of the individual believer suggests that the moment this glory is attained is not to be identified with the moment of individual death but with the moment of the final cosmic consummation.

Reading 6: Romans 8:31b-35, 37-39

Romans 8:31b-34 is treated on the second Sunday of Lent in series B; Rom 8:35, 37-39 on the eighteenth Sunday of the year in series A. The caption here quite rightly highlights verse 38: "Nothing can really come between us and the love of Christ." I take the genitive in this phrase to be a subjective genitive—the love of Christ (or the love of God encapsulated in Christ [v. 39]) for us, concretely actualized in his death on the cross (see Gal 2:20). It is this redemptive act of God in Christ that has justified us and reconciled us with the Father, that is, has brought us into a right relation-

284
144

235
153

ship with God. This relationship cannot be destroyed by death. It is "inalienable" (Cullmann).

The language in which Christian hope for life beyond the grave is expressed is so highly mythological that it does not speak very clearly to contemporary men and women. That is why so many Victorian hymns about the afterlife, like

> There is a blessed home
> Beyond this life of woe

leave us cold. But this passage from St. Paul, couched as it is, not in the first-century language of apocalyptic imagery, but in the perennial language of personal relationships, speaks to us today as clearly and persuasively as it did when it was first written. It is in these words more than anything else that the modern Christian is likely to express the hope for a life beyond this one. And it is this passage, rather than the more traditional passages, with their highly apocalyptic imagery, that is likely to be chosen today, and therefore most likely to require the homilist's exposition at a liturgy for the dead.

Reading 7: Romans 14:7-9, 10b-12

Verses 7-9 of this passage are treated on the twenty-fourth Sunday of the year in series A. Read in a funeral context, they make much the same point as the previous passage, namely, that the right relationship into which God in Christ has brought us cannot be broken by death. Even in death we are still related to God, we "die to the Lord." Quite rightly the caption highlights this thought: "Alive or dead, we belong to the Lord." *167*

But the reading continues to include verses 10b-12, which introduce the further point about judgment: "We shall all stand before the judgment seat of God." The intervening half-verse (10a), omitted here, relates this thought specifically to the concrete situation Paul was addressing to the Roman community, with its tension between Jew and Gentile. By omitting verse 10a, the Lectionary generalizes the thought of judgment, thus making it particularly applicable for a funeral service. This is one of the texts that led later Christians to the doctrine of particular judgment. Paul could not have meant this, yet it would seem to be a reasonable inference. It is a salutary reminder to the living that we must all give an account of ourselves, that is, of our faith and of our lives, before the great Judge.

Reading 8: 1 Corinthians 15:20-24a, 25-28 (long form); 15:20-23 (short form)

This reading is covered on the feast of Christ the King in series A and, except for verse 28, on the Assumption of the Blessed Virgin Mary (August *196* *559*

15). The long form consists of two paragraphs, the second of which is omitted in the short form. The first paragraph is concerned with the human and subjective angle, with the stages in the process leading to the resurrection of all believers, while the second paragraph is concerned with the cosmic and objective angle, with the process leading up to the final defeat of death. The conclusion of the second paragraph is likely to puzzle the ordinary person in the pew, and perhaps the shorter reading is provided for that reason.

Two perplexing theological problems arise from these readings and their caption. The caption states quite categorically that "all" will be brought to Christ. The thought is taken from verse 22: ". . . in Christ shall *all* be made alive." Does that mean that all will finally accept Christ and so be brought to life in him? The dilemma is this: on the one hand, if God is love, he can work his will to salvation only with the free acceptance of human beings. His love is such that he respects our freedom even to reject his salvation. Therefore we must conclude that not all will be saved. On the other hand, if God is sovereign, he cannot allow his purpose—our salvation—to be finally defeated. Therefore all must eventually be saved. We cannot see any solution to this dilemma on this side of the End except by denying one side of the truth. We have to hold in tension the two truths of God's sovereignty and God's love, and leave the reconciliation of this tension to him. There may be circumstances in which this particular reading and this particular problem should be addressed at a funeral, but normally this question would be a rather abstract one for such an occasion.

The second problem is posed by the apparent subordinationism of verse 28: "When all things are subjected to him, then the Son himself will also be subjected to him who put all things under him, that God may be everything to every one." Perhaps the most helpful answer to this problem is to be found in the comment of Karl Fezer (at the Evangelisches Stift, Tübingen, when I studied there in 1938–39: "Christ is not a God alongside of God. He lives and reigns in order that God's name may be perfectly hallowed, God's kingdom come fully, and God's will may be done on earth as hitherto it has been done in heaven."

Reading 9: 1 Corinthians 15:51-57

This is the magnificent peroration of Paul's great chapter on the resurrection of believers. He announces this teaching as a "mystery," presumably an apocalyptic revelation given to himself or to some other early Christian prophet. What exactly is the mystery? Much of what follows is conventional apocalyptic imagery: the "eschatological trumpet" and the resurrection of the dead. Other material consists of traditional resurrection beliefs in apocalyptic circles: resurrection conceived as eschatological transformation into an entirely new and transcendent mode of existence; a formula citation from Isa 25:8 (vv. 54b-55); and then the typical Pauline teaching on sin, law, and death (v. 56). None of this requires a special revelation. Perhaps the clue to the precise content of the "mystery" is to be found in 1 Thess 4:15-18, where Paul speaks of a "word of the Lord" (by which he means a saying of the risen Lord conveyed to a Christian prophet) to the effect that the resurrection of the believers will occur in two separate stages: the resurrection of the dead in Christ and the rapture of the living.

Essentially the same teaching appears here, though the focus is different, in that here the eschatological transformation is applied equally to the living and the dead. The particular problem that occasioned the adjustment of salvation history that the "word" or "mystery" effected, namely, the problem created by the death of some of the believers before the anticipated imminent parousia, is no longer one that concerns us today. We accept the fact that all of us, so far as we can tell, will die before the parousia (whereas Paul's "mystery" was correcting the opposite opinion, namely, that all the believers would *live* until the parousia).

The important truth that this text teaches us today is that the resurrection life involves a complete transformation of our present existence, not its prolongation or restoration. This transformation is described in a series of contrasts: perishable/imperishable, mortal/immortal. Thus, resurrection has to be sharply distinguished, for the believers as well as for our Lord, from resuscitation or reanimation. Paul, of course, expected this transformation to take place at the parousia, not at the point of individual death. Therefore he must have accepted some form of intermediate state, which he elsewhere characterizes as "being asleep" (1 Thess 4:14). We cannot infer anything about its precise nature.

Reading 10: 2 Corinthians 5:1, 6-10

This is the most difficult and controverted of all the Pauline texts relating to the Christian hope beyond death. Some commentators hold that between writing 1 and 2 Corinthians, Paul changed his mind about the future hope. When he wrote 1 Corinthians, he was still expecting an imminent parousia, leading to the resurrection of the dead and the rapture of the living. Now in 2 Corinthians, it is alleged, he has shifted his ground. With the delay of the parousia, this no longer provides the framework of his future hope; instead, that hope has become individualized. Paul is not thinking of the resurrection of all the faithful at the parousia but of the individual believer at death. It is at individual death rather than at the parousia that the believer will acquire the resurrection body, here pictured as awaiting us in heaven, like a coat on a peg, ready to be put on, or a house ready to be occupied.

It is doubtful whether Paul has so radically changed the framework of his future hope. The letter to the Philippians, which he wrote either around the same time as 2 Corinthians (if we place it in the Ephesian period) or several years later (if we place it in the Roman imprisonment), shows quite clearly that Paul never abandoned the parousia as the framework of his eschatological hope for the individual believer (Phil 3:21). Accordingly, we must interpret the present passage within that framework. There are two key words that will help us to do this. The first is "we have." Although this is in the present tense, it should be taken in a future sense: "we shall acquire at the (general) resurrection." Taken in this sense, it does not support the notion of an individual resurrection. It follows from this that the resurrection body is not a sort of Platonic reality, existing eternally in the heavens, but a new divine creation that will come into being at the commencement of the eschatological age.

The second key word occurs in the omitted part of the reading. This is the word "naked" in verse 3. Paul shudders at the thought of being in a state of "nakedness," by which he means a disembodied state. This would happen if Paul were to die before the parousia. When he wrote 1 Corinthians, he was apparently assured that he would be among the living at the parousia (1 Cor 15:15). Now he is not quite so sure, and therefore thinks it is quite possible that he would have to go through an intermediate stage of "nakedness," or disembodiment. What has changed is not the framework of Paul's future eschatology but the timing. For us today, that timing is essentially the same. We, too, have to expect an intermediate state before the final consummation.

Reading 11: Philippians 3:20-21

Comment on these verses can be found under the second Sunday of Lent in series C. To what is said there we would add that it is now evident that Paul is quoting here, as he so often does (cf. Phil 2:6-11), from pre-Pauline hymnic material. This hymn apparently antedates the *mysterion* or word of the Lord (see above) of 1 Thessalonians and 1 Cor 15, which distinguished between the fate of the dead and that of the living at the parousia. It assumes the rapture model for all. It is unfortunate that the caption speaks of our "wretched" bodies. This conveys the wrong idea. Paul speaks of our *humiliation* (RSV: "lowly body"). The contrast is with the glory of the resurrection body. It is not a degrading of the body at the expense of the soul.

408

Reading 12: 1 Thessalonians 4:13-18

For comment on this passage, see the thirty-second Sunday of the year *190* in series A. Note that the caption highlights what the commentary there took to be the permanent message of this pericope (v. 17b), ignoring the highly colored apocalyptic imagery. But Paul does not comfort the Thessalonians by telling them that dead believers are now "with the Lord" in bliss forever. Rather, he assures his readers that those already dead have not missed out on the parousia; they are at present "asleep," though they are still "in Christ. " Only at the parousia will they be "with the Lord." In other words, this passage, like the others, assumes an intermediate state.

Reading 13: 2 Timothy 2:8-13

For comment on this passage, see the twenty-eighth Sunday of the year *512* in series C. For our present purposes it is important to note that the death referred to in the hymn quoted in verses 11-13 is not physical death but baptismal death, for only that death is death "with him" (see Rom 6:3-11). It is our baptism that provides the ground of our hope for life after physical death.

Reading 14: 1 John 3:1-2

For comment on these verses, see the fourth Sunday of Easter in series *263* B. Here we would only add that it is at the final consummation ("when he appears," v. 2) that we shall see him as he is and be like him. The Johannine theology, like the Pauline, assumes an intermediate state and operates within the framework of the parousia.

Reading 15: 1 John 3:14-16

The context of this passage is the later Johannine polemic against the gnosticizing Docetists. The Docetists thought that they were saved because of their religious experience. The Johannine writer insists *per contra* on the ethical criterion. It is not the excitement of religious experience that assures that we have passed from death to life, but whether or not we love our brothers and sisters. Not to love is to be spiritually dead. Hatred is equivalent to murder, for it is a denial of life, and those who hate are cut off from authentic existence ("eternal life"). Yet, although he applies the ethical criterion so rigorously, the Johannine author is not a mere moralist preaching "workery." For love of others depends upon the prior fact of the love with which Christ "laid down his life for us," not merely as an example but as the enablement of our loving others.

One may perhaps wonder what precise relevance this pericope has for a funeral service. We may suggest that it shifts our concern away from physical death to the death to self that love involves. Life out of death is true relationship with both God and our fellow believers. A life of this quality cannot be destroyed by physical death, for those who love have already "passed out of death into life."

Reading 16: Revelation 14:13

This reading is just a single verse, which is unfortunate, since it does not seem to relate to what precedes or follows, and it looks like a floating saying that has been inserted arbitrarily into the text. Although John the Seer comes from a milieu very different from that of Paul, he has the same eschatological belief about the life of believers after death. They die "in the Lord" (cf. 1 Thess 4:16 and 1 Cor 15:18). And they "rest" (a different word from Paul's "sleep," but the meaning is the same).

In the seer's community these words are applied quite specifically to the martyrs (as "labors" suggests), and this is the clue to the meaning of the phrase "their deeds follow them." Their sufferings for Christ will be remembered in the day of judgment.

There is a long tradition, however, for taking this saying out of its original context of martyrdom and applying it to the death of believers in general. For these words have always been pronounced at the graveside in the Anglican burial office. In that case the deeds that follow them will be their good works, which God will remember in the day of judgment.

Reading 17: Revelation 20:11–21:2

The first paragraph of this passage depicts the universal judgment of the dead ("great and small"). The judge ("him who sat upon the throne") is God rather than Christ, for the picture is taken from the Book of Daniel, where the judge is the Ancient of Days. The "books" are God's record of all human deeds. There is also another book, the "book of life," a register that includes the names of all those who were destined for eternal life, as we infer from the fact that those whose names are not entered were condemned to the "lake of fire." All this language is, of course, symbolic. The eschatology varies somewhat from other apocalyptic traditions, where it is only the righteous who are resurrected.

The second paragraph depicts the final consummation under two images: "a new heaven and a new earth" and the "new Jerusalem." The language is traditional. (For the "new heaven and a new earth," see Isa 65:17; 66:22). "New" here means completely, eschatologically new, not another of the same kind. Compare "new Jerusalem" with "heavenly Jerusalem" in Gal 4:26 and Heb 12:22.

Modern scientists are divided about the form the end of the world will take. Some think in terms of a gradual slowdown, others in terms of another "big bang." Later apocalyptic tends to support the second view. But for apocalyptic this does not betoken the end of the human race. There will be resurrection, judgment, and final bliss or damnation. Such passages are not to be taken as a *vade mecum* of Christian doctrine, for they are largely mythological. However, the truth they express is that we are accountable for our lives, and that their quality will determine our ultimate destiny.

Reading 18: Revelation 21:5a, 6b-7

This reading overlaps with the previous one, extending its second paragraph to cover the description of the ultimate salvation. Once again, we remind ourselves that the language is mythological, and so is suggestive rather than descriptive. Yet, as Martin Kiddle has written, "John's attempt to depict the new order is extremely successful. He does not, on the one hand, present us with a mere list of abstractions; his symbols give us something to grasp and treasure. And on the other hand, the abstraction embodied in the symbols is conveyed in striking clarity."

Negatively, the new order involves the destruction of all that is wrong with our present life: pain, sorrow, death. Positively, it involves intimate communion between God and humanity. The latter is expressed in the language of Ezekiel (cf. verse 3 with Ezek 37:37)—enjoyment of the "water of life" and divine filiation.

RESPONSORIAL PSALMS

Since it is less likely that the homily will be based upon the psalter, and since, with the exception of no. 10 (Psalm 143), all of these psalms are commented upon elsewhere in this volume (for references see the Index), we will confine ourselves to relating each psalm specifically to the funeral context.

Psalm 23:1-6

This is undoubtedly the favorite psalm at funerals, at least among Anglicans, partly because it is the best known of all the psalms and partly because it speaks pointedly to the situation of death, especially in verse 4.

Psalm 25:6, 7bc, 17-18, 20-21

At the moment of death, the penitent thief on the cross prayed that he might be "remembered." This psalm contains a similar prayer: "According to thy steadfast love [*chesed*, covenant love] remember me." When God remembers, he acts—in this case by applying the benefits of his merciful act on the cross to the needs of the dying sinner.

Psalm 27:1, 4, 7, 8b-9a, 13-14

This psalm of lament expresses confidence in God's deliverance, and while the original meaning of the "land of the living" was this earth as opposed to sheol, at a Christian funeral it may legitimately be extended to mean the consummated kingdom of God at the resurrection life.

Psalms 42:1-2, 4bc; 43:3-5

Psalms 42 and 43 are really a single psalm. Its original sense was the expression of the longing of the worshiper to be restored to the presence of God through participation in the worship of the temple. In this context, to "see God face to face" (see the refrain) may be fittingly identified with the beatific vision for which Christians hope after the parousia.

Psalm 63:1-5, 7-8

Here again the thirst may be identified with the desire for beatific vision, as in the preceding psalm.

Psalm 103:8, 10, 13-18

That God is kind and merciful and that he is the source of our salvation is something that can be uttered over the grave only in the light of Christ's death and resurrection. Apart from that, the ultimate truth about human life is that our days are like grass, that we flourish like a flower of the field, and that when we are gone we are known no more.

Psalm 116:5-6, 10-11, 15-16ac

In this thanksgiving psalm, as in Psalm 27 above, the original sense was deliverance from earthly distress, and, as there, the "land of the living" means life on this planet. Once again, however, we may take it in a Christian sense to refer to deliverance out of death into the resurrection life.

Psalm 122:1-9

In our previous comments on this psalm, we noted that the pilgrimage to Zion, of which its original sense spoke, already had eschatological implications. Now the "house of the Lord," or temple, will be the new Jerusalem realized at the End (see the New Testament readings 17 and 18, with which this psalm might suitably be paired).

Psalm 130:1-8

Out of the depths of death we cry to the Lord for deliverance. We join in prayer with the dead as they, like us, await the final resurrection.

Psalm 143:1-2, 5-7b, 8ab, 10

As noted above, this is the only psalm not previously commented upon. It is the last of the seven traditional penitential psalms, all of which were used at burial services in medieval times. It is an individual lament, arranged here in four stanzas.

Stanza 1: a cry for mercy. For the psalmist, as for Luther, the basic problem of human life was: How can I find a gracious God who, despite my lack of any righteousness of my own, will set me in a right relationship with him?

Stanza 2: a recalling (*anamnesis*) of the past mighty acts of God before him (see above, second reading). For us these mighty acts would include preeminently God's saving act in Christ, particularly his death and resurrection. It is the making present of these mighty acts of the past that will solve the psalmist's present problem and bring him into a right relationship with God.

Stanza 3: as in other psalms, it is particularly in the "morning" that God acts redemptively. In the funeral context, this "morning" may be identified with the resurrection morning.

Stanza 4: a prayer for the future. Now that the psalmist has been delivered from his distress, he wants to learn to do God's will and live under his guidance.

This psalm would be especially suitable for use as a response to the readings from Romans (especially Rom 5:5-11), which relate the death of the believer to his or her justification and reconciliation.

GOSPELS

Gospel Reading 1: Matthew 5:1-12a

The beatitudes serve as the gospel reading for the feast of All Saints and for the fourth Sunday of the year in series A and are commented upon there. Here, in the context of a funeral, we may note that for Christians there is still poverty, mourning, oppression, hunger, thirst, and so on, but that in the midst of these, believers are already "blessed" (*makarioi*), that is, partakers in advance of the complete reversal that is promised with the kingdom of God. Thus, there *is* sorrow at Christian funerals, yet joy breaks through.

567
115

Gospel Reading 2: Matthew 11:25-30

Comment on this passage is given on the fourteenth Sunday of the year *142*
in series A. Since that commentary was written, there has been further
research on the two sayings combined in this Matthean pericope. As a
result, we may now say that we have here *two* wisdom sayings, that is,
sayings developed from the wisdom tradition and put on the lips of Jesus:
the cry of jubilation (vv. 25-27) and the Savior's invitation (vv. 26-30).
Jesus was portrayed as wisdom's eschatological envoy and spokesman,
and then finally, by the time of Matthew, as the personal embodiment
of wisdom.

The first saying is, as we noted before, from Q. The second saying,
while peculiar to Matthew, may nevertheless have been present in the version of Q used by Matthew (Q-Mt). The cry of jubilation was liturgical,
as I suggested. The Savior's appeal was originally uttered by the wisdom
of God; now it is ascribed to Jesus himself as the embodiment of wisdom,
issued to those "who labor and are heavy laden." This appeal has to be
sounded at a funeral Mass and is obviously the reason why the pericope
was chosen for this occasion.

Gospel Reading 3: Matthew 25:1-13

The parable of of the wise and the foolish maidens receives comment under
the thirty-second Sunday of the year in series A. In the context of a funeral *190*
liturgy, our attention had best be given to the meaning of the parable at
the redactional level, where the bridegroom is allegorically identified with
the Son of man returning at the parousia. If we may take the death of
the individual as a partial anticipation of the parousia (see what was said
earlier about particular as contrasted with general judgment), then the
parable may be read in this context as a warning to the survivors: "Watch
therefore, for you know neither the day nor the hour" (not only of the
return of the Son of man but also of your individual death).

Gospel Reading 4: Matthew 25:31-46

The exegesis we give to this pericope for the feast of Christ the King in
series A has proved somewhat controversial and has been called into ques- *191*
tion. There we maintain that it is not a humanitarian lesson, as it is
generally understood to be, but "an assertion of the 'shaliach' principle,
according to which the acceptance or rejection of an accredited agent involves the acceptance or rejection of the sender, and the further assertion
that acceptance or rejection of the accredited agent, like acceptance or
rejection of the sender, will be validated at the last judgment." We are
still convinced that this was the meaning of these sayings *at the Jesus level.*

But we think it more likely that at the redactional level the evangelist understands it as an allegory of the last judgment of the "nations" (that is, those who have become disciples as a result of the mission inaugurated at Matt 28:16-20). As elsewhere in Matthew, they are to be judged according to whether they have kept the *nova lex*, the love commandment. What was originally figurative language in Jesus' sayings about the acceptance or rejection of his emissaries is now taken literally as illustrations of the love commandment.

Gospel Reading 5: Mark 15:33-39; 16:1-6 (long form); 15:33-39 (short form)

On the Marcan passion narrative, see Passion Sunday in series B, and on the Marcan resurrection pericope, see the Easter Vigil in series B. 247 254

The unique feature about the long reading here is that it combines Christ's death, burial, and resurrection (in the angelic proclamation) all together in a single reading. It portrays Jesus as the one who has shared what this person whose funeral is now being celebrated is now passing through—death and burial. But it goes on to speak of something that this person has not yet experienced, namely, resurrection. Therefore, this dead person has the prospect, after the eschatological interval ("three days"), of sharing that experience, too.

The short form deals only with the death of Jesus, so a homily based upon it would have a quite different focus. It should be focused on the loud cry "My God, my God, why hast thou forsaken me?" Christianity does not romanticize death as though it were a friend, translating it automatically into bliss. Rather, death is the "last enemy," the sign of our alienation from God. But Jesus, by entering completely into that alienation, as exhibited by his last cry, has overcome it. Therefore the enemy has been robbed of its power. Henceforth death, not in itself but because of what Jesus has done to it, becomes the gate to life eternal.

Gospel Reading 6: Luke 7:11-17

This reading occurs on the tenth Sunday of the year in series C and is commented upon there. That Jesus actually did raise the dead seems attested by his own words in the answer to John (Matt 11:5: "the dead are raised up," unless that is meant symbolically, as Bultmann, who nevertheless accepted the saying as authentic, maintained). Important in the form of that saying is the use of the passive, "the dead are raised," which indicates that raising of the dead is an act of God, not of a human wonderworker. 475

At the level of the pre-Gospel tradition, we note first that the form critics held that stories of raising from the dead were Hellenistic in origin and express a view of Jesus as "divine man," *theios aner*. Against that we note the markedly Semitic character of the language of this story—such turns of phrase as "God has *visited* (*paqad*) his people." Then there is the Christology: Jesus acts, not as a divine man, but as prophet, of the Elijah/Elisha type. All of this seemingly points to a Palestinian origin for the narrative, based perhaps on a general memory that raisings of the dead were believed to have been performed by Jesus, and written up after the model of the Elijah/Elisha raisings.

In the Lucan redaction Jesus is presented as *the* eschatological prophet. He is not just *a* prophet, but the one in whom God has definitively "visited" his people, that is, has come in his own presence to them. We should not dismiss "eschatological prophet" as a "low Christology," for no Christology could be higher than the view that God is uniquely and eschatologically present in Jesus—nothing, that is, until the rise of ontological Christology in the Hellenistic churches, in which Jesus was identified as the incarnation of the preexistent Logos or Son of God. For Luke, Jesus expresses his eschatological activity chiefly in compassion, especially toward the outcasts of society, including women, as here. Note the typical Lucan pathos of "the only son of his mother, and she was a widow."

This suggests that this is an especially appropriate passage to read and preach on when it is desired to speak of God's consolation to the mourners. Remember that the miracles of Jesus' earthly ministry are "prefigurations" of the supreme miracle of his death and resurrection, whose saving effects are in turn made present in the sacraments of the Church and finalized at the parousia.

Gospel Reading 7: Luke 12:35-40

Comment on these verses is given on the nineteenth Sunday of the year *495* in series C. We concentrated there on the parable of the waiting servants (vv. 35-38). In the funeral context, we should notice the saying about the coming of the Son of man (v. 40). This saying was probably added as an application of the parable at some earlier stage in the history of the tradition (it is already present in Matthew and therefore in Q), though it does not go back to Jesus himself. For him this would have been a straightforward crisis parable; now, however, at the pre-Gospel and redactional levels, the focus is upon the suddenness and unexpectedness of the coming of the Son of man.

The story of Stephen's martyrdom (Acts 7:52) seems to warrant our regarding the death of an individual as involving an anticipation of the parousia encounter with the Son of man. That being the case, we are entitled to apply the parable not only to the parousia but also to its anticipation in individual death. It is a warning to those who are left behind: Be prepared, for death may come upon you suddenly, and woe to the unprepared. So the Litany of the Book of Common Prayer prays: "From dying suddenly and unprepared, Good Lord deliver us." These reflections suggest that this reading would be especially appropriate when death has been sudden and unexpected.

Gospel Reading 8: Luke 23:33, 39-43

Most of this reading is commented upon for the feast of Christ the King *531* in series C. Today's selection sets the context in the crucifixion and relates the story of the penitent thief. The story is hardly historical. According to the earlier passion narrative (Mark), both thieves railed against Jesus. The Lucan version is pretty certainly an edifying homiletical addition. We therefore cannot naively take the promise "Today you will be with me in Paradise" as authentic dominical teaching about the life after death delivered from the cross. But we can take it as being in accord with the general trend of the New Testament, and it is on this that the Church bases its teaching about the intermediate state.

Gospel Reading 9: Luke 23:44-49; 24:1-5 (long form); 23:44-49 (short form)

The Lucan passion narrative is commented upon in its entirety on Pas- *416* sion Sunday in year C. This excerpt, in both its longer and shorter forms, parallels the longer and shorter forms respectively of the fifth Gospel reading above. Both forms here highlight the words from the cross: "Father, into thy hands I commit my spirit" (see the caption). According to Mark, Jesus' last word from the cross was from Ps 22:1, while according to John it was "*Tetelestai*—It is accomplished." Tradition has harmonized these two words by placing them in succession. Actually, however, they are not tape recordings but alternative theological interpretations of Jesus' death.

Luke's word, from Ps 31:5, is the night prayer of the pious Jew (the same psalm was later taken into Christian use for Compline), combined with the historically authentic address "Abba." It indicates that for Jesus death was not the end of his Abba relationship to God. It is the assurance that death will lead to his resurrection.

In the context of the funeral service, the text contains an assurance for the Christian in the face of death: just as we lie down each night in the hope that we shall wake up to a new day, so the Christian dies in the hope through Christ of the new morrow of the resurrection. The homilist could here connect death and burial to the daily routine of going to bed, as Paul Gerhard did in his evening hymn, where he pictures our taking off our clothes and shoes as a daily reminder of our mortality.

Gospel Reading 10: Luke 24:13-35 (long form); 24:13-16, 28-35 (short form)

For comment on the Emmaus story, see the third Sunday of Easter in series *78* A. The caption points up the pattern of suffering-glory that characterizes the kerygmatic Christology expressed in the Lucan resurrection narratives. It suggests that the same pattern, through suffering to glory, is applicable to Christian death because Christ has trodden the path before.

Gospel Reading 11: John 6:37-40

These verses come from the bread discourse of John 6, but except for the echo in the phrase "came down from" and the reiteration of the promise "I will raise him up at the last day," there is no direct connection with the theme of the bread from heaven. We have here the characteristically Johannine juxtaposition of realized and future eschatology. On the one hand, the believers are already given to the Son and come to him and see him and are not cast out but already have eternal life. On the other hand, they will be raised up at the last day and then will not be cast out but will see the Son and have eternal life. To understand John, we have to hold in tension the "already" and the "not yet," and not eliminate the tension (as Bultmann did) by attributing the refrain "I will raise him up at the last day" to a later hand. A Christian believer has the assurance that the experience of Christ in this life is not something that will be cast away at death but will be consummated beyond death.

Gospel Reading 12: John 6:51-58

This pericope is commented upon twice: for Corpus Christi in series A *106* and for the twentieth Sunday of the year in series B. It is the section of *337* the bread discourse that relates most explicitly to the Eucharist. It therefore suggests that the homilist should draw a connection between holy communion and Christian death. Ignatius called the Eucharist "the medicine of immortality." The traditional Anglican words of administration included the prayer that the body and blood of Christ might "preserve thy body and soul to everlasting life." Reception of holy communion nourishes the new life begun in baptism, a life of "abiding in Christ," a life that cannot be extinguished by physical death but will continue to eternity.

Gospel Reading 13: John 11:17-27 (long form); 11:21-27 (short form)

The story of Lazarus is read in full on the fifth Sunday of Lent in series *51*

A and is discussed there. Both the long and the short forms here contain the central pronouncement of the story: "I am the resurrection and the life." The whole of this verse through "shall never die" has been the opening sentence in the Anglican burial office ever since the Reformation. It is sometimes thought that the resurrection or Easter emphasis at funerals is a new idea (at least in Western Christendom), but that is not really so; the lugubrious associations of funerals are due mostly to the trappings that have grown up around the service, partly in the Middle Ages and partly in Victorian times. While one should never make light of the negative side of death, either theologically (death *is* the last enemy, the wages of sin, and so on) or psychologically (people need to work out their grief, and the funeral rite should give it full expression), the message of the resurrection should cut clearly across all these negative considerations. Otherwise the funeral Mass is not authentically a service of Christian burial.

Gospel Reading 14: John 11:32-45

Again, see the fifth Sunday of Lent in series A for comment. The actual *51* raising of Lazarus, as we have noted, is a dramatization of the great declaration "I am the resurrection and the life." When used as one of the Lenten readings, it points forward to baptismal resurrection. I remember Sir Edwyn Hoskyns suggesting in class one day that the command "Unbind him, and let him go" was parabolic of the baptismal release from sin. The Greek word for "let go" (*aphete*) is the same word used for the forgiveness or remission of sin and denotes liberation. Baptismal release from sin and death is finalized in the resurrection of the dead at the End, and to that too the raising of Lazarus points.

Gospel Reading 15: John 12:23-28 (long form); 12:23-26 (short form)

John 12:20-33 is commented upon under the fifth Sunday of Lent in series *244* B. The parable of the grain of wheat, which may originally have been a parable of the kingdom of God, has been reinterpreted by the Johannine school as a prediction of Jesus' death and its consequences. By selecting the same parable for reading at a Christian funeral, its application undergoes yet another shift. The grain of wheat that has to die in order to bear fruit says something also about the death and burial of believers. They too must die in order to bear fruit. First, from the time of their baptism they must die daily in order to bring forth the fruit of the Spirit. Then, finally, they must die in order to shine forth in glory. Paul would have added that those who live until the parousia will likewise undergo a change that is equivalent to death (see Paul's use of the same image of the grain of wheat in 1 Cor 15:37-38, which suggests that the Apostle himself already applied this parable of Jesus to the death of believers).

Gospel Reading 16: John 14:1-6

For comment on John 14:1-12, see the fifth Sunday of Easter in series A. *84* The caption focuses our attention on the statement of the Johannine Christ that there are many rooms in his Father's house, a statement that perhaps simply satisfies our curiosity but does not concern us existentially unless we take it with the ensuing assurance: "I go to prepare a place for you" and with Jesus' promise to come again and take us to himself. The "house" of the Father seems to be a recognized Jewish expression for heaven. The "rooms" (Greek: *monai*, places to stay in, cognate with the verb *menein*, the Johannine word for "to dwell or abide in") are likewise part of the stock of apocalyptic imagery.

There can be no question about the apocalyptic origin of the whole saying, and therefore the "I will come again" must have originally referred exclusively to the parousia. The question is, however, is that the way the evangelist would have understood it, or has he demythologized the eschatology so that it is realized in the coming of the Paraclete to dwell with the believers? The connection of rooms (*monai, menein*) with the indwelling of Christ suggests this possibility. But, as so often in the Fourth Gospel, we probably should not restrict this saying to one meaning. The coming again will include the coming of Christ through the Spirit at baptism, the anticipation of the parousia in the death of the individual believer, and the parousia as a cosmic event. The homilist would probably want to focus on the second of these levels of meaning. Christ has prepared a "room" for the believer in the intermediate state that follows death, just as he found "room" to dwell in the believer through the Paraclete while that person lived on earth, and will find a room for him or her in his consummated kingdom.

Gospel Reading 17: John 17:24-26

For comment on John 17:20-26, see the seventh Sunday of Easter in series *440* C. Here we may zero in on the phrase "be with me where I am" and connect it with the three meanings of *monai* ("rooms") that we uncovered in the preceding gospel reading. In his high priestly prayer Jesus prayed for all who will come to faith as a result of the apostolic mission, and therefore also for this person who has just died, that he or she may be with him where he is. That prayer will be answered partially at the death of the individual and in the intermediate state, and fully after the parousia.

The Homily

The homilist is confronted with a bewildering variety of passages and themes for a funeral liturgy—no less than fifty-two readings (and I leave it to the mathematicians to calculate the number of permutations and combinations of readings that would be possible!). This makes it difficult, if not impossible, to make specific homiletical suggestions. It may perhaps be of some help if we arrange the passages under certain thematic headings and suggest several possible aspects of death and what aspects of the Christian message they express.

1. Death as an alien intruder into human life, the last enemy to be destroyed (Old Testament reading 4; New Testament readings 8, 9, 17, 18; gospel reading 6).

2. The wages of sin (New Testament reading 3; responsorial psalms 9, 10).

3. Resurrection life begins at baptism and justification (Old Testament readings 2, 3; New Testament readings 2, 4, 5, 13, 14, 15; responsorial psalm 8; gospel readings 1, 11, 12, 13, 14, 15).

4. This resurrection life is inalienable, and death cannot destroy our new relationship with God through Christ (Old Testament readings 2, 3; New Testament readings 5, 6, 7, 13, 14, 15; responsorial psalms 2, 3; gospel readings 1, 11, 12, 13, 17).

5. Particular judgment (Old Testament readings 2, 3; New Testament readings 1, 7, 16; responsorial psalms 6, 7, 9; gospel reading 4 might also be so applied).

6. The intermediate state, waiting for consummation (Old Testament readings 1, 4, 5; New Testament readings 8, 10, 12, 16; responsorial psalms 2, 3, 4, 5, 7, 9, 10; gospel readings 3, 7, 15, 16, 17).

7. Parousia—general resurrection and judgment (Old Testament readings 1, 6; New Testament readings 1, 8, 9, 11, 12, 14, 17; gospel readings 2, 3, 5, 7, 11, 12, 15, 16, 17).

8. Life in the consummated kingdom of heaven (Old Testament readings 1, 2, 3, 4, 6; New Testament readings 4, 8, 11, 12, 14, 18; responsorial psalm 8; gospel reading 17).

Index of Biblical Readings
and Responsorial Psalms

	SUNDAYS			SFH	WF
	A	B	C		
GENESIS					
1:1–2:2	65				
1:26-28, 31a					578
1:26–2:3				560	
2:4b-9, 15				560	
2:7-9; 3:1-7	38				
2:18-24		353			579
3:9-15		311			
3:9-15, 20				575	
9:8-15		230			
11:1-9	95	276			
12:1-4a	41				
14:18-20				444	
15:1-6; 21:1-3		222			
15:5-12, 17-18			407		
18:1-10a			487		
18:20-32			489		
22:1-18	65				
22:1-2, 9, 10-13, 15-18		234			
24:48-51, 58-67					580
EXODUS					
3:1-8a, 13-15			410		
12:1-8, 11-14	58				
14:15–15:1	66				
15:1-18	66				
16:2-4, 12-15		332			
17:3-7	44				
17:8-13			514		
19:2-6a	134				
19:3-8a, 16-20b	95	276			
20:1-17		237			
22:21-27	184				
24:3-8				285	
32:7-11, 13-14			504		

SFH = Solemnities, Feasts, Holidays   WF = Weddings, Funerals

	SUNDAYS			SFH	WF
	A	B	C		
34:4b-6, 8-9	101				
LEVITICUS					
13:1-2, 45-46		300			
19:1-2, 17-18	123				
NUMBERS					
6:22-27				26, 224, 396	
11:25-29		352			
21:4b-9				562	
DEUTERONOMY					
4:1-2, 6-8		342			
4:32-34, 39-40		283			
5:12-15		308			
6:2-6		364			
8:1-3, 6-10 (17-20)				572	
8:2-3, 14b-16a				105	
10:17-21				552	
11:18, 26-28	128				
18:15-20		294			
26:4-10			405		
30:10-14			485		
JOSHUA					
5:9, 10-12			412		
24:1-2a, 15-17, 18b		339			
1 SAMUEL					
1:20-22, 24-28			394		
3:3b-10, 19		289			
16:1b, 6-7, 10-13a	47				
26:2, 7-9, 12-13, 22-23			464		
2 SAMUEL					
5:1-3			529		
7:1-5, 8b-12, 14a, 16		211			
12:7-10, 13			476		
1 KINGS					
3:5, 7-12	150				
8:41-43			470		
8:55-61				571	
17:10-16		366			

SFH = Solemnities, Feasts, Holidays   WF = Weddings, Funerals

SFH = Solemnities, Feasts, Holidays   WF = Weddings, Funerals

	SUNDAYS			SFH	WF
	A	B	C		
22:7-23b	53	247			
22:25b-31		266			
23:1-6	47, 80, 178, 196	328			607
24:1-6	12			566	
24:7-10				537	
25:4-9	172	231, 292			
25:4-14			377		
25:6-21					607
27:1-8a	93				
27:1-14	112		407		608
29:1-10	32		402		
30:1-12b	67	320	428, 473		
31:1-24	62	252	420		
32:1-11		300	476		
33:1-19	82				
33:1-22			494		
33:4-22	42, 65	284, 359			
34:1-6			412		
34:1-8		335		551	
34:1-14		337			
34:1-22		339	517		
40:1-9	109	289			
40:1-17			496		
40:6-10				540	
41:1-13		303			
42:2–43:5	69				608
45:2-9				569	
45:9b-15				558	
47:1-8				89	
50:1-15	131				
51:1-13		243			
51:1-15	35, 39				
51:1-17			504		
51:10-17	69				
54:1-6		350			
62:1-8b	126				
63:1-7	190				
63:1-8	162		479		608
65:9-13	144				
65:9-14				573	
66:1-20	86		482		

SFH = Solemnities, Feasts, Holidays   WF = Weddings, Funerals

	SUNDAYS			SFH	WF
	A	B	C		
67:1-7	158		434	27, 224, 397	
68:3-10			500		
69:7-34	137				
69:13-36			485		
71:1-17			456	542	
72:1-13	29	226	399		
72:1-17	5				
78:1-38				563	
78:3-55b		332			
80:1a-18		202	384		
80:8-19	176				
81:2-10b		308			
83:2-10			394		
85:8-13	156	206, 325			
86:5-16a	148				
89:1-18	140				
89:1-28		212			
90:2-16				561	
90:3-17			502		
90:12-17		357			
91:1-15			405		
92:1-15		315	467		
93:1-5		373			
95:1-9	44, 165	295	492, 509		
96:1-10c	182		447		
96:1-13				16, 216, 387	
97:1-9			439	556	
97:1-12				18, 217, 389	
98:1-4		269	511	576	
98:1-6				21, 218, 390	
98:5-9			526		
100:1-5	134		430		
102:24-28				534	
103:1-11			410		
103:1-12	167				
103:1-13	123	305	464		
103:1-20b		275			
103:8-18					608
104:1-9		223			

SFH = Solemnities, Feasts, Holidays   WF = Weddings, Funerals

	SUNDAYS			SFH	WF
	A	B	C		
104:1-30	96	277			
104:1a-34	99	279			
104:1-35c	65				
107:23-31		317			
110:1-4				445	
112:4-9	118				
113:1-8			506	573	
116:1-9		347			
116:5-16c					608
116:10-19		234			
116:12-18	59			286	
117:1-2			470, 499	536	
118:1-23	70, 72	257			
118:1-29		263			
118:2-24	75	258			
118:2-27b			426		
119:1-34	120				
119:57-130	150				
121:1-8			514		
122:1-5			530		
122:1-9	2				608
123:1-4		322			
126:1-6		362	379, 414		
127:1-2				561	
128:1-5	24, 193	221	392		
128:1-6		354			
130:1-8	49	311			609
131:1-3	186				
137:1-6		240			
138:1-5				573	
138:1-8	160		459, 489		
139:1-15				545	
143:1-10					609
145:1-14	142		520		
145:2-11				573	
145:2-18	169				
145:8-13b			432		
145:8-18	153				
145:10-18		330			
146:6c-10	8, 114	345, 366	507		
147:1-6		297			
147:12-20				105	
148:1-13					588

SFH = Solemnities, Feasts, Holidays   WF = Weddings, Funerals

	SUNDAYS			SFH	WF
	A	B	C		
PROVERBS					
8:22-31			442		
9:1-6		336			
31:10-13, 19-20, 30-31	192				
ECCLESIASTES					
1:2; 2:21-23			492		
WISDOM					
1:13-15; 2:23-24		319			
2:12, 17-20		350			
3:1-9c					595
4:7-15					596
6:12-16	189				
7:7-11		357			
9:13-18			502		
11:22–12:2			519		
12:13, 16-19	148				
18:6-9			494		
SONG					
2:8-10, 14, 16a; 8:6-7b					582
SIRACH					
3:2-6, 12-14	23	220	392		
3:17-18, 20, 28-29			500		
15:15-20	120				
26:1-4, 13-16					583
27:4-7			467		
35:12c-14, 16-18b			516		
38:27-32				560	
50:22-24				571	
ISAIAH					
2:1-5	1				
5:1-7	175				
6:1-2a, 3-8			459		
7:10-14	11			540	
9:1-4	112				
9:2-7				15, 215, 387	
11:1-10	5				
12:2-6	67				
12:2-3, 4b-6			382		

SFH = Solemnities, Feasts, Holidays   WF = Weddings, Funerals

SFH = Solemnities, Feasts, Holidays   WF = Weddings, Funerals

	SUNDAYS			SFH	WF
	A	B	C		
23:1-6		327			
24:1-7				533	
29:4-14				554	
31:7-9		361			
31:31-34		243			
31:31-32a, 33-34a					583
33:14-16			377		
38:4-6, 8-10			496		
LAMENTATIONS					
3:17-26					596
BARUCH					
3:9-15, 32–4:4	68				
5:1-9			379		
EZEKIEL					
2:2-5		322			
17:22-24		314			
18:25-28	171				
33:7-9	164				
34:11-12, 15-17	195				
36:16-17a, 18-28	69				
37:1-14	95	276			
37:12-14	49				
47:1-2, 8-9, 12				569	
DANIEL					
3:29-34	102				
7:9-10, 13-14				555	
7:13-14		372			
12:1-3		368			597
HOSEA					
2:14b, 15b, 19-20		305			
6:3-6	131				
JOEL					
2:12-18	35				
2:28-32	95	276			
AMOS					
6:1a, 4-7			507		
7:12-15		325			
8:4-7			506		

SFH = Solemnities, Feasts, Holidays   WF = Weddings, Funerals

SFH = Solemnities, Feasts, Holidays   WF = Weddings, Funerals

	SUNDAYS			SFH	WF
	A	B	C		
9:36–10:8	135				
10:26-33	138				
10:37-42	140				
11:2-11	9				
11:25-30	142				610
13:1-23	145				
13:24-43	148				
13:44-52	151				
14:13-21	154				
14:22-33	157				
15:21-28	159				
16:13-19				551	
16:13-20	161				
16:21-27	163				
17:1-9	43			556	
18:15-20	166				
18:21-35	167				
19:3-6					589
20:1-16	170				
21:1-11	52				
21:28-32	174				
21:33-43	177				
22:1-14	179				
22:15-21	182				
22:34-40	185				
22:35-40					589
23:1-12	187				
24:37-44	3				
25:1-13	190				610
25:14-30	194			561	
25:31-46	197				610
26:14–27:66	55				
28:1-10	70				
28:16-20		284		90	
MARK					
1:1-8		207			
1:7-11		228			
1:12-15		233			
1:14-20		293			
1:21-28		296			
1:29-39		299			
1:40-45		301			

SFH = Solemnities, Feasts, Holidays   WF = Weddings, Funerals

	SUNDAYS			SFH	WF
	A	B	C		
1:57-66, 80				546	
1:68-79				546	
2:1-14				17, 216, 388	
2:15-20				19, 217, 389	
2:16-21				28, 224, 397	
2:22-40		221		539	
2:41-52			393		
3:1-6			380		
3:10-18			383		
3:15-16, 21-22			402		
4:1-13			406		
4:21-30			457		
5:1-11			460		
6:17, 20-26			462		
6:27-38			465		
6:39-45			468		
7:1-10			471		
7:11-17			475		611
7:36–8:3			477		
9:11b-17				445	
9:18-24			479		
9:28-36			408		
9:51-62			481		
10:1-12, 17-20			483		
10:25-37			486		
10:38-42			488		
11:1-13			490		
12:13-21			493		
12:32-48			495		
12:35-40					612
12:49-53			497		
13:1-9			411		
13:6-9				534	
13:22-30			499		
13:31-35			409		
14:1, 7-14			501		
14:25-33			503		
15:1-32			505		
15:1-3, 11-32			413		
16:1-13			506		

SFH = Solemnities, Feasts, Holidays   WF = Weddings, Funerals

SFH = Solemnities, Feasts, Holidays   WF = Weddings, Funerals

	SUNDAYS			SFH	WF
	A	B	C		
10:11-18		264			
10:27-30			430		
11:1-45	51				
11:17-27					614
11:32-45					615
12:12-16		245			
12:20-33		244		564	
12:23-28					615
12:31-36a				564	
13:1-15	59				
13:31-33a, 34-35			432		
14:1-6					616
14:1-12	84				
14:15-21	87				
14:15-16, 23b-26			442		
14:23-29			435		
15:1-8		267			
15:9-12					590
15:9-17		270			
15:12-16					590
15:26-27; 16:12-15		281			
16:12-15			443		
17:1-11a	93				
17:11b-19		275			
17:20-26			440		591
17:24-26					616
18:1–19:42	63	252	421		
18:33b-37		373			
20:1-9	73	257			
20:19-23	99	279			
20:19-31	76	259	427		
21:1-19			428		
21:15-19				549	
ACTS					
1:1-11				89	
1:12-14	92				
1:15-17, 20a, 20c-26		274			
2:1-11	98	279			
2:14, 22-28	76				
2:14a, 36-41	79				
2:42-47	74				
3:1-10				548	

SFH = Solemnities, Feasts, Holidays   WF = Weddings, Funerals

	SUNDAYS			SFH	WF
	A	B	C		
3:13-15, 17-19		260			
4:8-12		262			
4:32-35		258			
5:12-16			426		
5:27b-32, 40b-41			428		
6:1-7	82				
7:55-60			439		
8:5-8, 14-17	85				
9:1-22				535	
9:26-31		265			
10:25-26, 34-35, 44-48		268			
10:34-38	33		402		
10:34-43					598
10:34a, 37-43	72	256			
12:1-11				550	
13:14, 43-52			429		
13:14b-25				545	
13:22-26				545	
14:21-27			432		
15:1-2, 22-29			434		
22:3-16				535	
ROMANS					
1:1-7	12				
3:21-25a, 28	128				
4:18-25	132				
5:1-5			443		
5:1-2, 5-8	44				
5:5-11					598
5:6-11	134				
5:12-15	137				
5:12-19	39				
5:17-21					599
6:3-9					599
6:3-11	69				
6:3-4, 8-11	140				
8:8-11	50				
8:8-17			441		
8:9, 11-13	142				
8:14-17		284			
8:14-23					600
8:18-23	144				
8:22-27	96	277			

SFH = Solemnities, Feasts, Holidays   WF = Weddings, Funerals

	SUNDAYS			SFH	WF
	A	B	C		
8:26-27	148				
8:28-30	151				
8:31b-34		235			
8:31b-35, 37-39					584, 600
8:35, 37-39	153				
9:1-5	156				
10:8-13			405		
11:13-15, 29-32	158				
11:33-36	160				
12:1-2	163				
12:1-2, 9-18					584
13:1-10				554	
13:8-10	165				
13:11-14	2				
14:7-9	167				
14:7-9, 10b-12					601
15:4-9	5				
16:25-27		212			
1 CORINTHIANS					
1:1-3	110				
1:3-9		202		572	
1:10-13, 17	113				
1:18-24				563	
1:22-25		238			
1:26-31	115				
2:1-5	118				
2:6-10	120				
3:9c-11, 16-17				570	
3:16-23	124				
4:1-5	126				
5:6b-8	73	257			
6:13c-15a, 17-20		289			585
7:29-31		292			
7:32-35		295			
9:16-19, 22-23		298			
10:1-6, 10-12			411		
10:16-17				105	
10:31–11:1		300			
11:23-26	59			445	
12:3b-7, 12-13	99	279			
12:4-11			448		

SFH = Solemnities, Feasts, Holidays   WF = Weddings, Funerals

SFH = Solemnities, Feasts, Holidays   WF = Weddings, Funerals

SFH = Solemnities, Feasts, Holidays   WF = Weddings, Funerals

	SUNDAYS			SFH	WF
	A	B	C		
11:8, 11-12, 17-19		223			
12:1-4			496		
12:5-7, 11-13			499		
12:18-19, 22-24a			501		
JAMES					
1:17-18, 21-27				572	
1:17-18, 21b-22, 27		343			
2:1-5		345			
2:14-18		348			
3:16–4:3		350			
5:1-6		352			
5:7-10	8				
1 PETER					
1:3-9	75				
1:8-12				543	
1:17-21	77				
1:22-25				533	
2:4-9	83				
2:20b-25	80				
3:1-9					585
3:15-18	86				
3:18-22		231			
4:13-16	93				
2 PETER					
1:16-19				556	
3:8-14		206			
1 JOHN					
2:1-5a		261			
3:1-2		263			605
3:1-3				567	
3:1-2, 21-24			394		
3:14-16					605
3:18-24		266			587
4:7-10		269			
4:7-12					587
4:11-16		275			
5:1-6		258			
REVELATION					
1:5-8		373			

SFH = Solemnities, Feasts, Holidays   WF = Weddings, Funerals

SFH = Solemnities, Feasts, Holidays   WF = Weddings, Funerals